ST. MARY'S COLLEGE OF MARYLAND LIBRARY
ST. MA
W9-ADF-679

THE EARLY EMPIRES OF CENTRAL ASIA

The Early Empires OF CENTRAL ASIA

A Study of the Scythians and the Huns and the part they played in world history

WITH SPECIAL REFERENCE TO THE CHINESE SOURCES

By WILLIAM MONTGOMERY McGOVERN

D. PHIL. (*Oxon*)

Professor of Political Science Northwestern University
One Time Lecturer on Chinese and Japanese, School of Oriental Studies, University of London

Chapel Hill

THE UNIVERSITY *of North Carolina* PRESS

1939

COPYRIGHT, 1939, BY
THE UNIVERSITY OF NORTH CAROLINA PRESS

MANUFACTURED IN THE UNITED STATES OF AMERICA
Van Rees Press · New York

REPRINTED AND BOUND BY
NORTH CAROLINA STATE UNIVERSITY PRINT SHOP
RALEIGH, N. C., JULY, 1965–LITHO. USA

The University of North Carolina Press, Chapel Hill, N. C.; The Baker and Taylor Company, New York; Oxford University Press, London; Maruzen-Kabushiki-Kaisha, Tokyo; Edward Evans & Sons, Ltd., Shanghai; Dekker en Nordemann's Wetenschappelijke Boekhandel, Amsterdam.

9050

DEDICATED

TO

KENNETH WALLACE COLEGROVE

PROFESSOR OF POLITICAL SCIENCE

NORTHWESTERN UNIVERSITY

Dear Kenneth:

I am dedicating this little work to you as a slight token of my appreciation for your many acts of kindness, and for your constant encouragement and assistance.

As you are thus forced to stand as god-father to this volume I feel that I owe you an explanation of how it came to be written.

Several years ago while collecting material for my course on *Nationality and Nationalism,* I became especially interested in the countries of Eastern Europe and the Near East, especially Finland, Hungary, and Turkey.

As time went on I became deeply impressed with the role played in these countries by historical tradition. In trying to understand and evaluate present day political movements, I was constantly faced with the necessity of dealing with their historical background. I was soon convinced that I could never comprehend the present day attitude of the peoples inhabiting these countries unless I delved into the racial, linguistic, and cultural heritage.

All three of these peoples came, or claim to have come, from Central Asia. It was, therefore, necessary to try and find out something about the history of Central Asia. I was soon struck by the astonishing lack of authentic information regarding this subject. Out of this region has come wave after wave of peoples, conquering peoples for the most part who have profoundly affected the whole course of world history, yet regarding these waves of migration we have amazingly little information. There are to be sure a large number of articles and monographs, mostly of a highly technical nature dealing with some obscure phase or other of the subject, but there was not a single book to which I could turn to secure a "bird's eye" view of the whole field.

In a passing mood I determined to prepare, largely for my own benefit, a short monograph covering the more important phases of Central Asiatic history. I hoped to cover the whole field in about a hundred pages, but alas and alackaday, I soon found myself involved, in fact submerged, in a huge undertaking. There was such a striking difference of opinion among the various scholars who had touched upon this field that I felt bound to go rather thoroughly into all aspects of the subject in order to be able to distinguish fact from fiction.

First of all I tried to collect all the modern western or secondary sources which dealt with the field, or at least those which were written in English, French, and German. Most of these will be found cited in my bibliography. Unfortunately I know no Russian. My good friend and former student, Mr. Andrew Haensel, a native Russian, was kind enough to go through a great deal of the Russian material on my behalf and provide me with very excellent summaries. But though I was able to secure many interesting and valuable suggestions in this way, I have cited none of the Russian sources as I was unable to use them at first hand. Incidentally I might add that interesting though they were, none of these Russian sources materially modified any of the information I secured from the scholars of Western Europe.

I soon found, however, that all of the secondary sources, valuable though they were, were inadequate for my purpose. In order to understand the true course of events, it became necessary to delve into the primary sources. Unfortunately these primary sources were written in a wide variety of languages, of which the most important were Latin, Greek, Chinese, Persian and Arabic. Incidental information had to be secured from Armenian and Turkish sources.

Life is short and languages are many. Several months of roaming through the countries of the Near East gave me a fair smattering of Turkish and Persian and a ground work in Arabic, but this smattering was far from enabling me to cope with the scholarly and highly technical historical treatises written in these languages. Hence for all this material (and also for everything written in Armenian, of which I know nothing) I have had to rely upon translation into one or other of the European languages. Fortunately most of the material written in these languages dealing with Central Asia has already been translated.

The remnants of a classical education permitted me to deal with the Latin and Greek sources with greater ease. In consequence all citations from such sources are to the original texts. Even so I make no pretenses to being a classical scholar (Greek, especially, is very wearying to the flesh) and wherever adequate translations were available, I joyfully used them, as can be seen by reference to the bibliography.

It so happens that way and above the most important sources for the history of Central Asia were written in Chinese and incorporated in one or other of the Chinese dynastic histories. In fact, in accuracy and in comprehensiveness the Chinese sources far outweigh all the other sources put together. By good fortune I grew up as a boy in the Far East and hence learned to read and write Chinese along with English. Professional duties in later years forced me to retain and add to my knowledge of the Chinese literary language.

As a result I found the study of the Chinese texts dealing with Central Asia less difficult than many of the other tasks confronting me. Nevertheless no man, certainly no foreigner, can claim to have a perfect knowledge of classical Chinese. In consequence, I have been careful to consult all the available translations of the Chinese material and to compare my own translations with those of my much esteemed predecessors. In many cases references to these translations has saved me from egregious errors. In some cases a careful study of the original texts has convinced me that not only Homer but such great masters of Chinese as Chavannes, de Groot, Parker, Hirth, and Weiger have occasionally nodded, and have been bold enough to differ from their interpretations. Wherever (especially in Books III and IV) translations were not available, I have launched forth on my own account.

Generation follows generation, and in most cases the scholars of tomorrow will be able to improve upon the would-be scholarship of today. I am sure that I have made not a few mistakes. But I have been careful to cite, in the notes, all the sources from which my information was secured in the hope that later workers in the field may be able more easily to point out my errors.

I should perhaps add that the main body of the book was written for the average educated layman who might be interested in a curious and little known phase of Oriental history. For this reason I have endeavored to keep the text simple, straightforward, and comprehensible. All citation of authorities, all obscure and technical points, the discussion of all problems still in dispute among scholars have been relegated to the end of the book, and can well be ignored by the average reader. I would only ask that if any scholar do me the honor of reading this work that he will be good enough to go through this supplementary material before passing judgment on the book as a whole.

* * *

As the weeks, the months, and now the years have rolled by I have accumulated an enormous amount of information regarding the history of Central Asia from the earliest times down to the present day.

At your encouragement, in fact at your demand, I have put together most of the material dealing with the earlier periods of this history for publication in the present volume.

Should the present work meet with a favorable response—and if you again hound me into activity—I hope to empty my crowded desk drawers of the remaining material and prepare a book dealing with the later Empires of Central Asia and with the situation at present prevailing in that region.

Ever your sincere friend,

William Montgomery McGovern

ACKNOWLEDGMENTS

I AM under very deep obligation to several persons for aid in preparing the present work. Especial mention must be made of the following persons:

Mrs. William H. Moore for her generosity in sending me to Hungary, Turkey, and Persia in order to collect additional material; Prof. Addison Hibbard, Dean of the College of Liberal Arts for his aid in securing the publication of this work; to my good friends Prof. A. R. Hatton, Chairman of the Political Science Department, Northwestern University, and Prof. W. Y. Elliott, Chairman of the Government Department, Harvard University, for granting me the necessary leisure to carry on research work.

I am greatly indebted to the advice and assistance given me by Prof. Fay Cooper Cole, of the Anthropology Department, University of Chicago; and to Prof. A. T. Olmstead and to Dr. J. C. Debevoise, of the History Department, University of Chicago. I had the great pleasure of being able to thresh out at great length many of the problems affecting the relations between Central Asia and the Near East with Messrs. Olmstead and Debevoise, and as a result was saved from committing many egregious blunders.

I am equally indebted to Dr. C. S. Coon, of the Anthropology Department, Harvard University; to Prof. Walter Clark, of the Sanskrit Department, Harvard University; to Dr. B. Rowland of the Fine Arts Department, Harvard University; to Mr. L. Ward of the Peabody Museum; to Mr. L. Warner of the Fogg Museum; and to Dr. F. R. Wulsin. All of these gentlemen were kind enough to read the manuscript with great care and suggest important changes.

I am also obligated to Dr. G. Sarton, Lecturer on the History of Science, Harvard University; to Dr. A. Coomeraswamy, of the Boston Fine Arts Museum; to Profs. M. Rostovtseff and G. Vernadsky of the History Department, Yale University, for several suggestions.

I am deeply grateful to Dr. J. C. Ferguson, for many years adviser to the Chinese Government, and one of our leading Sinologists; and to Dr. J. Pettus, President of the College of Chinese Studies, Peking, China, for their aid and advice in dealing with the Chinese sources, and for their introductions to many notable Chinese scholars with whom I was able to discuss some of the problems which arose in revising this manuscript. I am also indebted to Prof. K. Shiratori of the Tokyo Imperial University for several interesting suggestions.

I was able to collect a great deal of information owing to the kindness of some of Hungary's leading scholars. My especial thanks are due to Dr. S. de Takacs, of the Hopp Museum, to Prof. Gombocs of the Budapest University; to Dr. Homan and to Dr. Fettich of the Hungarian National Museum.

Last but not least I must express my gratitude for the invaluable aid given me by three of my graduate students: Mr. R. W. E. Reid, now at the University of Hawaii; Mr. Stanley Boggs, now at Harvard University; and Mr. S. Jacobson, now at University of Chicago. Mr. Reid labored like a slave preparing the final draft of this manuscript while I was in China, cut off because of the unfortunate hostilities from all postal communications with the outside world. Mr. Boggs prepared the maps from which the maps included in this volume were drawn. All three have aided me by reading through the proof.

W.M.M.

CONTENTS

Book Four

THE LATER HUNNISH KINGDOMS

ILLUSTRATIONS

MAPS

THE EARLY EMPIRES OF CENTRAL ASIA

CENTRAL ASIA IN WORLD HISTORY

The Expansion of the Term "World History"—Central Asia and the Domestication of the Horse—The Origin of Trousers—Central Asiatic Art—Central Asia and the Passage of Culture Stimuli from East to West, and West to East—Glass, Silk, Printing, Gunpowder—Political History: The Scythians—The Huns—Central Asia and Chinese History—Central Asia and Persian and Indian History—The Asiatic Invasions of Europe—The Huns, Avars, Bulgars, and Hungarians—The Seljuk and Ottoman Turks—Central Asia and Present Day Politics—The Asiatic Inhabitants of Europe Today.

During the last century there has been a great change in the scope of what is called "world history." In the eighteenth century, "world history" meant the story of Greece and of Western Europe, prefaced by an account of the Jews taken from the Old Testament. Then came the tremendous advance made by historical research, especially in the field of Near Eastern archaeology, with the result that into the view of world history was brought an account of the development of civilization in Egypt, Babylonia, and Assyria.

Still more recently, the boundaries of world history have been extended to the East. For many decades, isolated scholars have delved into the records of India and China, but it is only since the beginning of the present century that historians as a whole have come to recognize that the developments of these Eastern countries are of world importance, and cannot be excluded from a picture of the evolution of humanity.

But there still remains a vast and truly important area which has been too frequently ignored save by a handful of specialists. This area is Central Asia—a region of significance to all problems affecting the general history of mankind.

I

The cultural, political, and economic life of Europe and even of America owes much to the impact of Central Asia. We shall consider in turn each of these contributions to world civilization. Let us begin with the manners and customs (called "culture traits" by the anthropologists) that had their origin inside of this area.

Man's subjection of wild animals to his own use has been one of the important factors in human civilization. We now know that the wild horse was first domesticated on the steppes of Central Asia, and that it was from this region that the "horse-culture"—the use of the horse for driving and later for riding—gradually spread to other parts of the world. Thus, it is not surprising to find that many objects associated with horses—the saddle, and in later times, the stirrup—likewise had their origin in Central Asia.

Even more interesting is the effect that Central Asia has had upon clothing, especially upon masculine costume. By reason of their domestication of the horse, and their adoption of horseback riding, the early inhabitants of Central Asia were forced to discard the loose skirt-like costume which had been well-nigh universal among early peoples, and to develop that ingenious piece of clothing that we call trousers. For centuries, the wearing of trousers was confined exclusively to the inhabitants of Central Asia, but in time, as horseback riding became more common so did the custom of wearing trousers spread from Central Asia to all parts of the globe.

Closely associated with horseback riding is another product of Central Asia, namely boots, which gradually took the place of the slippers and sandals that had formerly been almost universally worn. These early boots were made either of leather or of felt, a fact which indicates that in all probability the art of felt-making was another culture trait which gradually made its way from Central Asia to all the other parts of the world. At a somewhat later time, it was the Central Asiatics who initiated the custom of putting heels on boots and shoes.

We are in the habit of thinking of the inhabitants of Central Asia, in both ancient and modern times, as being essentially barbaric. For this reason it is of interest to find that recent archaeological work has brought to light the fact that the ancient inhabitants of Central Asia developed a high artistic tradition. More important still, scholars have now been able to demonstrate that this early Central Asiatic art exerted a measurable influence upon the artistic development of Europe on one side, and upon China and the Far East on the other.

Central Asia's original contribution to culture history has thus been far-reaching. Still more important has been the role that this region has played in the transmission of culture traits from one part of the Old World to the other.

For many years it has been recognized that much of our own "European" culture goes back, through Rome and Greece, to "the conquest of civilization" made by the ancient inhabitants of Egypt and the Near East; but until recently it was generally supposed that the great classic civilizations of India and of the Far East were the products of a completely separate and independent cultural evolution. Historical research and archaeological discoveries made in the last few years have shown the error of this assumption. Long before the beginnings of recorded history there was transmission and diffusion of cultural stimuli between the Near East, where "civilization" had its origin, and all other parts of Europe and Asia.

In later times, the direction of culture diffusion was often reversed. New inventions, new ideas, new manners and customs continued to spread from Europe or the Near East to the East, India, and China, but quite as frequently it was India or especially China which was ahead of the western lands and was thereby able to contribute culture traits that had a profound influence upon the whole history of the Western World. It was the constant exchange of these stimuli between East and West which makes it possible to speak of world history as opposed to the history of any one particular region.

The point of special importance in this connection is that most of these exchanges of culture traits took place by way of Central Asia. It was the Central Asiatics who took European inventions and gave them, for example, to the Chinese, and in return brought many Chinese inventions back to Europe. Because of this fact it is obvious that if India and China are to be admitted within the portals of world history it is imperative that Central Asia be treated in the same way.

We need cite only two or three outstanding examples of the manner in which Central Asia by acting as the intermediary between the West and the East has greatly affected the cultural development of all mankind. This exchange of culture traits started long before the commencement of written history. The fact that at the dawn of history the peoples of both the Near East and Northern China made use of the wheel and the plow, and that inhabitants of both regions cultivated wheat, millet, and barley has long made it seem probable that there was some cultural connection between the two peoples. This theory has been strengthened by excavations at Anau in Central Asia which point to the fact that the civilization which once flourished at this spot was indeed a sort of missing link between the early Near Eastern and Far Eastern civilizations. This theory has now been definitely proved by the discovery in Northern China of certain prehistoric pottery remains that show strong traces of western influence.

Coming down to historic time, we find that in the period immediately following the campaigns of Alexander the Great, the West was again able to give a great cultural stimulus to the Far East through the agency of the peoples inhabiting Central Asia. A Greek school of art established in the northern part of what is now Afghanistan exerted widespread influence in different parts of Turkistan and through Turkistan eventually reached China, causing a complete revolution in Chinese painting and sculpture. It is also probable that the great change which took place in Chinese music at this time was also due to the effect of Greek influence.

The importation of Graeco-Roman glass through Central Asia into the Celestial Empire had a profound effect upon Chinese craftsmanship and led indirectly to the invention of Chinese porcelain. Later still, in the seventh and eighth centuries A.D., domestic life in China was greatly modified by the introduction through the Turkish tribes inhabiting Central Asia of European articles of furniture such as beds, tables, and chairs. Curiously enough, until very modern times, the Chinese were the only Oriental people to adopt these household conveniences. Finally, we should add that Nestorian Christianity at one time secured a large number of converts among the peoples of Central Asia. From Central Asia, Nestorianism made its way into China, and, in the seventh century A.D., there was already a flourishing Christian community in the Chinese capital.

Closely associated with the contact between China and Europe was the intercourse that the Celestial Empire enjoyed with Persia. Persian influence was especially noticeable in the field of agriculture. In the second century B.C., China, because of her contacts with Central Asia, was able to import from the Iranian world alfalfa and the grapevine. In the centuries which followed many other cultivated plants made their way across Central Asia from Persia to China and gave rise to a great change in the Chinese domestic economy. Iranian influence was also of importance in the development of Chinese armor and in Chinese military strategy. Again, not without significance is the fact that Manicheanism, a third-century form of Persian religion, was long a rival of Christianity in Central Asia, and, along with Christianity, also found a foothold in the Celestial Empire.

Curiously enough, most of the communication between India and China took place not directly, but through the mediation of Central Asia and of the Central Asiatics. Though India and China are in close geographical proximity, the intervening country is so rugged and broken as to make direct intercourse extremely difficult. For this reason communication between the two countries has nearly always been carried on either by sea or else through the roundabout route across Central Asia.

It was through Central Asia that Buddhism spread from its original home in India to China and to other countries in the Far East. Indeed, many of the early missionaries who converted China to Buddhism were not Indians at all but natives of Central Asia, a fact which helps to account for some of the marked differences between the Indian and Chinese forms of the Buddhist religion. This question of Buddhist origins is important, because, as is well-known, the coming of Buddhism to China completely revolutionized the cultural life of nearly all peoples in the Far East.

So far we have emphasized the transmission of culture traits from Europe and the Near and Middle East across Central Asia to China. But it should not be forgotten that all the time that China was receiving stimuli from the West she was also transmitting back to the West along the same channel many features of her own civilization.

From ancient days, certain Chinese cultivated plants such as the peach and apricot were carried westward through Central Asia and Persia to the European world. In later times other Chinese plants such as rhubarb, ginger, and tea became favorite articles of export to the West.

As early as the time of Emperor Augustus, China became specifically known to the Roman world because of her production of silk. In the centuries that followed, the importation of silk from the Celestials became a very important factor in the commercial life of the Roman Empire. The Great Silk Road from China to Rome passed through Central Asia, and more than once struggle for the control of this section of the road led to important political changes. In later times, the trade in Chinese porcelain almost reached the proportions of the silk trade.

In the realm of invention, the connection between China and the West (through the mediation of Central Asia) is equally pertinent. The Chinese on occasion managed to perfect their own inventions. An instance of this sort is paper. The art of paper-making was discovered by the Chinese in the second century A.D. The manufacture spread to Central Asia in the eighth century, and was soon acquired by the Arabs who in turn transmitted the secret to the Europeans. On all essential points, the European method of paper-making is merely a copy of the old Chinese craftsmanship. Closely associated with the manufacture of paper was the custom of issuing paper money. This practice which was well-known in China from an early period spread to Persia (and thence westward) during the thirteenth century through the agency of the Mongols, a Central Asiatic people, who for the moment ruled both China and Persia.

In some cases, the Europeans were able to make improvements on the Chinese inventions which came to them across the desert sands of Central Asia. The development of the art of printing is illustrative of instances of this sort. The printing of books was common in China as early as the beginning of the tenth century but, for the most part, the Celestials stuck to the primitive method of block printing. The use of movable type was not entirely unknown in the Far East, but this technique was never fully developed until the fundamental idea behind printing had passed from the Far East into Europe.

In some cases the Chinese half-invented something without fully realizing the possibilities of their invention. A classic example is to be found in the field of chemistry. The Chinese through their alchemical speculations became interested at a very early period in certain chemical experiments. In some cases the results of these experiments passed from the Chinese to the Arabs and thence to Europe. Among the chemical gleanings which thus passed westward was a knowledge of pure saltpeter, a substance known to the Arabs as "Chinese snow." In China, the acquaintance with saltpeter led only to fireworks (the Arabs called sky rockets "Chinese arrows") but once this knowledge reached Europe it led to the invention of gunpowder.

A similar instance is provided by the "south pointing chariot" used only for the finding of "lucky sites" in China, but which led to that remarkable instrument which the Western World called the compass. It is not surprising that the compass, unlike most other Chinese inventions, came to Europe, not by way of Central Asia, but southward by way of the maritime route.

II

We have seen that Central Asia has long played a prominent part in the culture history of mankind, both as a center where many customs and arts have developed and as the mediator between all the major culture centers of the ancient world.

Equally significant is the part which Central Asia has played in the political history of the world. This, for the most part, has been the result of a long series of migrations and invasions carried out by peoples who regarded Central Asia as their motherland.

In this connection we can ignore such hotly disputed points as whether the original home of all the "Aryan" or Indo-European peoples was, or was not, in Central Asia. Suffice it here to say that, after being discarded for a while, the belief that the Indo-Europeans did originally hail from Central Asia has again come into prominence and commands the support of many competent authorities.

However hotly this point may be disputed, there can be no doubt as to the historic importance of the invasions carried out by various Central Asiatic peoples, who, no matter whence they originated, found themselves at some time residing in the heart of Asia. From a very early day, Central Asia was inhabited by at least two separate and distinct racial and linguistic groups, which for want of better names are referred to as the Scythians and the Huns. "Scythian" is the most suitable term to apply to all the peoples inhabiting Central Asia who belonged to the "Great White Race" (to use Professor Breasted's expression) and who spoke an Aryan or Indo-European language. By "Hun" is meant that group of peoples who dwelt originally further to the east and hence absorbed a great deal of Mongoloid blood, for which reason they are often, though somewhat erroneously, referred to as members of the "Great Yellow Race." More important still, the Huns spoke a language that was completely alien to the Aryan world and which is usually termed Turanian, though it might better be called Ural-Altaic.

Many centuries ago the Scythian or Indo-European element in the population of Central Asia almost entirely disappeared, but this historic tragedy must not blind us to the fact that the group was once the dominant element in the region now known as Turkistan, and that from Turkistan its members spread outwards in all directions with momentous effect upon all surrounding countries. To the west, Scythian bands overran all of Southern Russia and penetrated even to the center of Europe. To the east, other Scythian bands wandered far into Eastern Asia and for centuries had possession of what is now Northwestern China, thus giving the Chinese their first known contacts with peoples of "European" race and language.

Most important of all was the effect which the Scythian migrations had upon the regions to the south of Turkistan. It was the Scythians, in the broadest sense of the word (perhaps we should say, the ancestors of the historic Scythians) who, at the very dawn of history, swept over the Persian Plateau and into Northwestern India, thereby permanently bequeathing to both of these regions a population which was predominantly white in race and Indo-European in language.

In later times, the Indo-European inhabitants of Persia and India abandoned their early nomadic habits and settled down into agriculturalists. This made them the mortal enemies of their distant cousins, the Scythians proper, who continued to dwell in Turkistan, and who retained their nomadic habits accompanied by a passion for raiding and looting. Again and again these later Scythians invaded and plundered their distant kinsmen to the south, who were deemed to have grown too soft and too fond of luxury. On several occasions, these plundering expeditions led to permanent conquest and occupation.

The Parthians who ruled over Persia for nearly five centuries (from 247 B.C. to 226 A.D.) are classic examples of a Scythian group who moved southwards from Turkistan and established political control over the agricultural peoples inhabiting the Persian Plateau.

During a large portion of the time that Persia lay in the hands of the Parthians, most of Northern India fell a prey to several other Scythian groups who are generally lumped together under the general head of Indo-Scythians. Many of these Indo-Scythian rulers in addition to being notable empire builders were magnificent patrons of the arts. Under their patronage, an entirely new type of art and literature arose which was destined to have a permanent influence upon later Asiatic civilization.

Turning now from the Scythian to the Hunnish group (the other major group in the population of Central Asia), we find that during the period that Turkistan was ruled by the Scythians, Mongolia was dominated by various Hunnish tribes generally spoken of as Hiungnu, a term given them by the Chinese who for many centuries lived in almost constant fear of Hunnish attacks. The Great Wall of China was built in 214 B.C., for the purpose of keeping the Hunnish nomads out of the fertile plains of the Yellow River. Shortly afterwards the Hunnish inhabitants of Mongolia, who had previously been broken up into a large number of separate tribes, united to form a single empire, which in one form or another lasted for over three hundred and fifty years (209 B.C. to A.D. 160). During a good portion of this time, the Hunnish Empire was a serious rival to China for political leadership and supremacy in the Far East.

After many bitterly waged wars, the Chinese managed to prevent the Huns from securing a permanent lodgement in China until the close of the third century A.D. Then, internal disorders weakened the Celestial Empire with the result that the Huns (at first the Huns proper, and later, various other Turanian peoples) made themselves masters of all Northern China. Turanian domination of this region lasted for over two centuries (or until A.D. 581).

Towards the close of the sixth century, the Chinese succeeded in sweeping out these Turanian overlords, and in the period which followed, especially during the rulership of the glorious Tang dynasty (618-908) were able to secure control not only over their own destinies but also over most of Central Asia as well. With the fall of the Tang dynasty, however, China again suffered from internal troubles with the result that the empire once more fell a victim to hordes of Turanians who poured in from Central Asia.

In the thousand years which elapsed between the fall of the Tang dynasty, in the year 908, and the establishment of the Chinese republic, in 1912, native dynasties continued to rule over isolated parts of the empire, chiefly Southern China, but the country as a whole was under native Chinese rulership for less than three hundred years (1366-1644). During the rest of this millennium, the Celestial Empire was either partly or wholly ruled by various Hunnish or Turanian peoples.

From 1120 to 1278, Northern China was governed by the "Iron Barbarians," then by the "Gold Barbarians," and finally by the renowned Mongols of Chingis Khan. In 1278, Southern China, which had hitherto been able to maintain its independence, crumbled before the onslaughts of Kubilai Khan, the grandson of the great Chingis, and for the first time in its history the whole of the Celestial Empire was subjected to Turanian overlordship.

Mongol rulership in China endured for only ninety years. The dynasty of Chingis Khan fell largely because of its inflationary policy resulting in the over-issue of paper money. Ju Yuan-jang, a Buddhist priest, impressed with the misery of his countrymen led the rebellion; and, after the expulsion of the Mongol troops, in 1368, founded the Ming or "Bright" dynasty. But China was not yet free of foreign masters. In 1644, another group of Turanians, this time the Manchus who lived to the northeast (in Manchuria) swept over the Celestial Empire and ruled it with an iron hand until 1912.

The historic importance of the Huns and other Turanian peoples was not confined to the Far East. Towards the close of the second century A.D., the Scythian or Indo-European people who had hitherto been the dominant element in Turkistan underwent a rapid degeneration. Eventually they were pushed out or absorbed by the Huns who slowly moved westwards. By the fifth century A.D. the Huns had complete control of all parts of Turkistan, and thereby became the immediate neighbors of the Sasanid Empire which ruled the Persian plateau. Conflicts between the Persians and the Huns (in this case the so-called White Huns) soon followed, in the course of which one of the most powerful of the Sasanid monarchs was killed (A.D. 484), and for many years the Persians were forced to pay a heavy tribute to the Hunnish tribesmen to save their lands from being ravaged.

In the sixth century, the Huns proper were succeeded as overlords of Turkistan by the Turks, a people closely affiliated with the Huns as regards both race and language. The fact that Huns gave way to Turks brought no relief to Persia. Indeed, the Turks soon proved that they were more dangerous neighbors than their predecessors. For some centuries, to be sure, the Turks contented themselves with occasional inroads into Persian territory, but in 1040, the powerful Seljuk Turks overran the whole of Persia, and shortly thereafter made themselves masters of all the countries in the Near East.

Two centuries later (1218), when the power of the Seljuk Turks had decayed, their place as overlords of Persia was taken by the Mongols, and for over a century Persia was an integral part of the vast Mongol Empire. No sooner had the Mongol Empire broken up than the Mongol-Turkish hordes led by Timur the Great (more poetically called Tamerlane) reëstablished Turanian ascendancy over the Persian Plateau. A short period of native rulership followed, but from 1750 to 1932 Persia was again ruled over by Turanians, this time represented by the Kajar Turks. Even today, though Persia is again governed by a Persian, more than one-fifth of all the inhabitants still speak Turkish, a living memorial to the centuries of Turanian domination.

India has a similar tale to relate. In the fifth and sixth centuries A.D., one branch of the White Huns, the people who had created such havoc in Persia, poured through the mountain passes into India and destroyed the Gupta Empire, one of the greatest native kingdoms ever to arise on Indian soil. The state created by the Huns soon broke up, but the Hunnish invasion had a permanent effect upon the personnel of India's ruling class. The old royal families disappeared one by one, and the proud Rajput and other native (Hindu) families who constitute the aristocracy of India today are considered by most scholars to be the descendants, not of the old indigenous aristocracy, but of the foremost Hunnish warriors.

The story of the Turanian invasions of India was not yet finished. The subsequent Turanian waves spread still further and had even more far-reaching and permanent effects. As long as the spread of Muhammadanism rested in Arabic or Persian hands, India suffered but little from Muhammadan inroads, but once the Turanian Turks were converted to the Islamic faith the fate of India was sealed. Beginning about the year 1000, groups of Turkish and Afghan soldiers raided India, at first for booty and later for conquest and settlement. By A.D. 1200, the invaders had consolidated their conquest, and from this time until the rise of the English power in the eighteenth century, India as a whole was governed by various alien Muhammadan dynasties. Most of these foreign rulers were of Turkish (Turanian) origin, and were supported by Turkish soldiers. Conspicuous among these Turanian dynasties was that of the Moguls or Mughals (a name derived from Mongol, though the Mughals were in reality more Turkish than Mongol) which lasted from the year 1526 until well into the nineteenth century. After 1700, their real power weakened, but until 1835 the British continued to coin money in the name of the Mughals, their nominal overlords in India, and the Mughals did not cease to rule in name until the year 1858. The effect of the Turanian invasion of India has never been effaced. For instance, Muhammadanism, which was introduced by the invaders, still claims the allegiance of seventy million of India's 320 million inhabitants, with the result that today the controversies of Muhammadans and Hindus are one of the most disturbing factors in the government of the largest commonwealth in the British Empire.

III

So far we have dealt only with the effect of the Hunnish or Turanian invasions upon the historical development of the other peoples of Asia. The effects of these invasions are so patent that they have long been recognized by all students of history, and thus it is unnecessary for us here to emphasize their importance.

When we turn from Asia to Europe, we find that the effects of the Turanian invasions, being largely indirect, are less obvious and hence have frequently been ignored. Nevertheless, it may with truth be said that the political geography of Europe has been in part the result of the waves of Turanian people who in the fourth century began to pour over the European continent. Indeed, it may even be claimed that the very structure of modern Europe has been profoundly moulded by the impact of the Turanian invasions.

Among the most important factors in the shaping of the European world as we know it today are the fall of the Roman Empire, the pushing of the Germanic peoples into the west of Europe, the introduction of the Slavic peoples into Central and Southern Europe, the Renaissance and the revival of the ancient classics in Western Europe, and finally the voyages which led to the discovery of the New World. In the background of all these stupendous events lurk the hordes of Central Asia.

It is of course impossible with the complicated events of world history to speak of absolute causes. Every movement listed above was the result of a vast concatenation of causes, but in each case it can be shown that one of the most, if not the most, important of the immediate conditioning causes was the invasion and conquest of some portion of Europe by peoples of Central Asiatic origin.

From Central Asia came the forces that overthrew the Roman Empire. To be sure, the invasions which the Asiatics themselves led from the plains of Hungary into Western Europe did not turn this trick. The invading horde of Asiatic barbarians streaming into Gaul and into Italy, though they inspired consternation and terror, led to no permanent settlements, and the political upheaval which they caused was of transitory duration. It was the settlement of the Germanic peoples in the Roman Empire that caused the break-up of the old system. The Goths made the first serious inroads into Italy and Southern France, and into part of Spain. The Suevi and the Vandals occupied the remaining portions of Spain and Africa. The Burgundi moved into central France, and the Angles and the Saxons took over the portion of Britain which had once been a Roman colony.

So much, of course, is known to every schoolboy, but what the schoolboy forgets, or is never told, is that the German tribes who appeared to the Roman world as conquering invaders seemed to themselves and to the Huns of the epoch just before Attila to be hordes of dispirited refugees. The respect that these Gothic tribes had for the Roman legions was great, but far greater was the terror with which they viewed the wild fantastic horsemen from the distant plains of Central Asia who had suddenly appeared in their midst. It was this heart-piercing fear that forced them to break through the Roman outposts and sweep over the Roman provinces.

The connection of the Huns with some of these migrations is something which we can deduce only from indirect evidence. The German tribes had no chroniclers to record the causes of their invasions, and the internal developments of the barbarian tribes drew the attention of few Roman writers. In some cases, all that we can say is that the migration of the German tribes to the West coincided both in time and in place with the coming of the Huns from the East.

Where, however, evidence of any sort is available, where we have any contemporary chronicles of this eventful period, all of them lead us to associate this westward movement of the Germanic tribes with the preceding impact of the Hunnish invaders. We know that the East Goths were settled in South Russia and were slowly spreading eastward until they were subjected by the Huns, and forced to accompany their Asiatic masters as auxiliaries to the borders of the Roman Empire. We know that the West Goths, who, as dreaded conquerors, were the first to sack imperial Rome, entered the Empire as refugees, after having been overwhelmingly defeated by the Hunnish hordes.

If it was the Huns who constituted the driving force that hurled the German tribes over the borders of the Roman Empire, it was the Asiatic successors of the Huns, the Avars, who appeared upon the scene a hundred years later and brought about a settlement of the Slavs within the limits of the now sadly dismembered remnants of the Roman Empire. The Slavs, a people almost, if not entirely, unknown to earlier history, were slowly migrating westward, taking over the territory left vacant by the Germans. But it was the Avars, cousins of the Huns, and themselves refugees before the still more powerful Turks, who accelerated the pace of the slow-moving Slavs and who definitely drove them across the Roman boundaries.

It was the Slavic auxiliaries of the Avars who were forcibly settled in Pannonia and Noricum, and who thereby became the ancestors of the Slovenes of today. The Croats and the Serbs had a somewhat similar origin. As the West Goths were allowed by the Roman officials to come within the Roman Empire after their defeat by the Huns, so also were the defeated Croats and Serbs encouraged by Emperor Heraclius at Constantinople to settle within the limits of the East Roman Empire, to serve both as colonists in a desolated region and as buffer peoples in case of further Avar attacks.

It was the Bulgarians, another Asiatic people, who caused the Slavizing of another portion of the East Roman Empire, for it was the old Asiatic Bulgarians who first forcibly wrenched the northeastern provinces from the Byzantine emperor. Before the imperial soldiers could reconquer the region, it had been so thoroughly settled by the Slavs whom the Asiatic Bulgarians had brought with them and with whom they amalgamated that it was added permanently to the domain of Slavic culture.

The fate of the Slavic peoples already so strongly influenced by the advent of the Asiatics was to receive one further indelible impress from an Asiatic source. Various Slavic kingdoms and principalities stretched in a long unbroken line to the east of the German tribes. There were Slavic states all the way from Greece to the shores of the Baltic. For a time it appeared that these Slavic states might weld themselves into one great Slavic empire, with a uniform religion and a uniform literature. The coming of the Magyars or Hungarians into the heart of the Danube valley at the end of the ninth century destroyed all chances of this homogeneous Slavic development. The Magyars formed an alien wedge between the northern and the southern Slavs, and from this time onward the two great branches of the Slavic peoples were driven into widely divergent lines of development.

The southern Slavs were drawn into the circle of Byzantine influence; they acquired a version of the Greek alphabet and adopted the Greek form of Christianity. Meanwhile the northern Slavs, i.e. the Poles, the Czechs, and the Slovaks, adopted the Latin letters in use among their German neighbors and the Roman form of Christianity.

This break-up of the Slavs into the northern and southern branches completed the series of great events in European history brought about by the invasions of those Asiatics who came into Europe by the route north of the Black Sea. But just as the last of these invaders were settling down as the inhabitants of the kingdom of Hungary, another great group of Asiatics was forcing an entrance into the Western World by another route, that which lay to the south of the Black Sea into Asia Minor, and thence over the Straits of Marmora into the Balkans.

A great wave of Arabic-Muhammadan conquest had separated Africa (including Egypt), Palestine, Syria and Mesopotamia, both politically and culturally from Europe, and made them a part of the Eastern World. For four hundred years, Asia Minor had stood fast against the Muhammadans, remaining as a province of the Roman Empire, and as part of the European heritage. But in 1070, the Seljuk Turks, who had already swept from the steppes of Central Asia over the once mighty kingdom of Persia, attacked the Byzantine Empire, and in the battle of Manzikart did what the Arabs at the height of their glory had never been able to do, and, by seizing the greater part of Asia Minor, reduced cultural Europe to the limits of geographical Europe.

For some three hundred years it appeared as if this would be the worst of their ravages. It seemed that Europe proper would be immune to their attacks; but when the Seljuks began to weaken in the struggle with Europe, their place was taken by their cousins the Ottoman Turks, fresh from the steppes of Asia, and shortly afterwards the whole of Balkan Europe, including Constantinople itself, the old culture center of Europe, fell into their hands. The result was that, whereas in the southeast, cultural Europe had once extended into geographical Asia, now cultural Asia stretched far into geographical Europe.

The capture of Constantinople by the Turks in 1453, has long, and with reason, been looked upon as one of the turning points in European history. From the fall of Rome to the fall of Constantinople, the center of gravity in European culture was in the East and not the West. The ancient arts and letters, not only of Greece but also of Rome, had been neglected in the old imperial city and in the barbaric states which had once been provinces in the West Roman Empire, but these arts and letters were still appreciated and still studied in Constantinople, and in the provinces which continued under Byzantine sway. Unfortunately, there was little cultural communication between the East and the West. Ironical it is that the inhabitants of western Europe relearned much concerning the ancient glories of their own provinces through the Arabs who, before invading Spain, had come into contact with the Greek scholars in the Near East. Cultural forces could not come directly across Europe from Constantinople to Rome. They reached western Europe by way of Asia Minor, North Africa and Spain, where they were imposed upon the Christian inhabitants of that kingdom and thence passed to their fellow Christians across the Pyrenees.

The decay of Arabic culture had put an end to much of this cultural communication, and for a time it appeared that when Constantinople and the surrounding provinces fell into the hands of the barbaric Turks the whole body of classical learning would disappear forever. But, fortunately, the very shock of the fall of Constantinople brought about a change for the better. Many of the scholars who had dwelt in Byzantium until the coming of the barbarian Turk now fled for their lives, and after various vicissitudes many of these fugitives settled down in the countries of Western Europe, more particularly in Italy, the Christian country which was nearest them and with which they were most familiar.

The coming of the Byzantine scholars, the direct result of the Turkish conquests, was a powerful contribution to the reawakening of learning in the West. No doubt the West was, by this time, ready for the great change by reason of other internal developments. No doubt the Renaissance was a movement far more important and more comprehensive than the mere reawakening of interest in classical learning. But it is certain that the revival of learning brought about by the immigration of the fugitive Byzantines set its indelible stamp upon the humanist movement which had just started. The fact that for four centuries afterwards the word "scholarship" meant primarily a knowledge of the Greek and Latin authors, and that Greek is still considered an essential feature of a liberal education is due in no small measure to the forced migration of the Byzantine pedagogues to the West just when the West was awakening from its long intellectual slumber.

Classical learning, brought about by the Renaissance, is now, with the advent of a wider scope of the sciences, beginning to lose its hold. On the other hand, every day adds to the importance of the second event, one result of the Turkish conquest of the East, namely, the discovery of America.

It must not be forgotten that prior to the fall of Constantinople, there was an active trade between Europe on the one side and China and India on the other, and that the fluctuations in this Oriental trade had much to do with the rise and fall of several of the great European cities. The good people of Europe demanded that whatever else might happen, they still be able to secure fine silks from China, spices from the East Indies, and cotton prints and precious stones from India.

In the old days, the Greeks, among the Europeans, had held a virtual monopoly of the Oriental trade, and much of the wealth and population (around two million) of Constantinople was supported by this trade. With the gradual decay of the Greek or East Roman Empire, the Italian cities, especially Venice and Genoa, secured a large share of this eastern commerce, and maintained trade routes by which the commerce was placed on a regular basis.

In the thirteenth century, two centuries prior to any direct sea connection between Europe and the East, Italian merchants (among them the celebrated Marco Polo) had made their way all over China and India, and had acquainted Europe with the great wealth of these countries. There was an Italian bishop and numerous Italian missionaries who resided in the Celestial Empire. As a result of these contacts the ancient luxuries of the East came to be regarded as necessities by the people of Europe.

It was just at this time that the Turkish conquest of Constantinople took place and nipped the bud of growing Eurasiatic commerce. With the consolidation of their position, the Turks, who had formerly allowed the European caravans to pass through their territories, now put an end to any direct overland communication between Europe and the more distant East. At first, the Europeans were allowed to carry on trade through Turkish intermediaries, but soon the overwhelming difficulties of this method became apparent, and the westward movement of Asiatic merchandise, once a mighty stream, became a feeble and irregular trickle.

It was this sudden stoppage of the Oriental trade that spurred adventurous spirits among the Europeans to seek some new method of securing direct contact between Europe, India, and China. Since the Turks, seemingly invincible, controlled all the available land routes to the East, it was necessary that the new lines should be by sea. Here there were two obvious routes, as well as the third, less obvious, and seemingly fantastical one hit upon by Christopher Columbus.

As the Europeans were well aware that both China and India were washed by the sea it appeared to them highly probable that they could reach the lands of their dreams either by sailing to the north of Europe or to the south of Africa. These were the two obvious routes.

It was the English who were largely responsible for the attempts to secure a passage to China by means of the northern route, by sailing through the Arctic Sea. Their attempts ended in failure, owing to the climatic obstacles which lay in their path. It was in carrying out these attempts that the English came into direct contact with the rising Russian Empire, and thus the chief result of the attempt to secure a northern passage was that Queen Elizabeth sent a special embassy to the Court of Ivan the Terrible, and for a while it seemed that there might arise a definite alliance between the two nations.

It was the Portuguese who were responsible for the development of the direct sea route between Europe and the East, by sailing to the south of Africa. Vasco da Gama rounded the Cape of Good Hope just forty-five years after the fall of Constantinople; and thereafter, for nearly a hundred years, the Portuguese held a preponderating influence in the Eastern seas. The coasts of Persia and of India, the Straits of Malacca, and the southern coast of China were all subject to European influence to a far greater extent than was possible in the days when communication between East and West was limited to the land routes, so that the cutting off of land routes in the end enormously increased rather than decreased the commerce between Europe and Asia. When Portugal's trade with the East began to slump, Dutch enterprise entered the Orient and augmented the commercial and political relations between East and West. And when Holland in turn fell off in her trading, France and England were ready to step into the breach.

It was of course this southern route that led to European hegemony in Asia, but even more interesting is the way in which the attempt to find a short passage to Asia led to the discovery of America. It must not be forgotten that Columbus did not set out upon a mere journey of exploration. His purpose was not to seek new and unknown lands, or to chart new and unknown seas. His purpose was merely to see if he could not by sailing westward reach the East. He bore with him letters, not to whatever sovereigns of whatever lands he might find, but to the Grand Khan of Cathay, and he died happy, not in the thought that he had discovered a new continent, but in the belief that he had come to the islands which lay off India.

The part in the discovery and opening up of America played by the East and the attempt to open up westward routes to take the place of those closed by the Turks did not cease with Columbus. John Cabot, an Italian in English service, in 1497 sailed from England on the westward voyage in search of Zipango or Japan. Captain John Smith, under authority of the London Company of Merchant Adventurers, paddled up the Chikohominy River in an attempt to discover the South Sea. Some years later, Sir Martin Frobisher, commissioned by the Cathay Company of London, sought the Northwest Passage between Greenland and the mainland. And Hendrik Hudson, on behalf of the Dutch East Indies Company, in his good ship, the "Half Moon," ran on the shoals of Albany seeking to nose his vessel into the China Sea by the way of the Palisades.

IV

So far, we have spoken only of the place of Central Asia in the past. But it is not to be implied that these plateaus and mountain valleys and the peoples who still occupy them do not remain worthy of the serious consideration of all students of international affairs.

To be sure, the role of the Central Asiatics has been greatly transformed by the events of the last few centuries. The Scythian or Indo-European group which once formed such an important element in the population of Central Asia is now almost entirely extinct, apart from the small and obscure group of Ossetes, on the northern slopes of the Caucasus Mountains, and one or two of the petty tribes living on the Pamirs.

Even the Hunnish or Turanian peoples who at one time caused all of the nations of Europe and Asia to tremble at their name have fallen far from their high estate. Today, most of the Turanian inhabitants of Central Asia are controlled by aliens, either by the Russians or by the Japanese. Many of them are scarcely conscious of their ancient heritage. With these groups, the feeling of "national" existence, long dormant, has only been rearoused within the past few years.

In Siberia, the Turanians, though scattered over a wide area, are so disintegrated and dispersed that there remain but two comparatively small areas which can still be called truly Turanian. In all of the rest of Siberia, the Russian pioneers have an unfettered hand.

In Manchuria, whence have come, time after time, peoples who have dominated large sections of Eastern Asia we find a peculiar situation. Nominally, Manchuria is again an independent empire ruled over by a native Manchu. Actually, Manchuria (now styled Manjouguo or Manchoukuo) is but a puppet state in the hands of Japan. More to the point, of the thirty-odd million inhabitants of Manchuria there are scarcely a hundred thousand persons of Turanian speech. Most of the inhabitants speak Chinese, and apart from the imperial family and a few aristocratic clans, the hundred thousand Turanians are the least powerful, in fact the most despised, members of the population.

In Mongolia, the home of the world-conquering peoples led by Chingis Khan, there remains scarcely a trace of ancient glory. For over two centuries prior to 1912 the Mongols were controlled by the Chinese Empire over which they themselves had once ruled. Since 1912, though once more free from Chinese rule, these Mongols, at least the Mongols of Outer Mongolia, have been little more than puppets in the hands of Russian intriguers. In Kashgaria, or Eastern Turkistan, the Turks are still subject to the Chinese, while the Turkish inhabitants of Western Turkistan, or Turkistan proper, are now subjects of the Russians. Even the little Khanates or kingdoms of Khiva and Bukhara which retained a shadowy independence until 1920 are now incorporated in the Union of Socialist Soviet Republics, which means of course that they are completely dominated by Russia.

There are, however, many signs that the Turanian inhabitants of Central Asia are entering upon a new era. The same nationalist movement which had such a profound influence upon Europe during the nineteenth century has already begun to find its way among the native inhabitants of Central Asia. It would appear that the greater part of Siberia is definitely and forever lost to the Turanians were it not for the fact that two peoples inhabiting Siberia (the Buriats and the Yakuts) have been organized into "autonomous republics" and it may well be that these two units will play a significant role in the future development of this entire region.

In Manchuria, recent events have shown that the Manchu national tradition, though extremely decadent, is not entirely dead. The existence of this tradition undoubtedly aided the Japanese in bringing about the separation of Manchuria from China. It is certain the Japanese will carefully nourish this tradition to the end that it will serve as a powerful aid in keeping Manchuria permanently separated from the "Eighteen Provinces" or China proper.

In Outer Mongolia, though the Russians retain effective control, the Mongols have been organized in the Socialist Soviet Republic of Outer Mongolia, which is nominally completely independent, and in which all the high offices are in the hands of native Mongols. The officials for the most part are young "intellectuals" strongly imbued with the nationalist tradition, and under their auspices the native population is becoming thoroughly conscious of its glorious heritage, and is anxious to play once more a dominant part in Asiatic politics.

A similar state of affairs exists among the Turkish inhabitants of Turkistan. In place of the old imperialist bureaucracy maintained by Czarist Russia, the Bolsheviks have reorganized the whole of Turkistan in such a way that all of the native Turkish population is grouped into a number of "autonomous republics." Some of these republics are members of the Russian federal republic (the Russian Socialist Federal Republic); others are granted even greater powers of self-control by being given the status of "independent" members of the Union of Socialist Soviet Republics, from which union they may in theory resign any time they choose.

In point of fact, the Russians still maintain absolute control over Turkistan, but the organization of these Turkish "republics" has enormously fostered the growth of nationalist feeling among all the Turanian peoples of Central Asia. It is not impossible that some of these republics may again become the seats of powerful and really independent Turanian states. And for this reason a study of the peoples of Central Asia possesses political as well as historical interest.

At the same time, the Central Asia of the twentieth century is of importance to the political scientists not only because of its potential future strength but also because of its actual weakness. It is this weakness which has caused several of the Great Powers to attempt to dominate various portions of Central Asia. This in turn has led to intense rivalry between the Powers, a rivalry which more than once has led to international crises.

In the nineteenth century, the peace of the world was more than once imperilled by the conflicting interests of England and Russia. Anglo-Russian conflicts were usually occasioned by Russia's aggressiveness in Central Asia. In 1907, many of these difficulties were smoothed out, and since this date there has been less talk of Central Asiatic rivalries leading to immediate hostilities between the British and Russian empires. But many of the fundamental difficulties were merely thrust into the background rather than permanently solved, and should Russia at any moment revert to a policy of aggressiveness and attempt to annex Tibet or even Kashgaria (Eastern Turkistan), it is probable that anti-Russian feeling would again dominate British public sentiment.

In the last few years, rivalry between Russia and England has been overshadowed by a similar competition between Russia and Japan. As soon as Nippon seized control of Southern Manchuria (in 1905), she became a factor in the settlement of Central Asiatic affairs. Since that time, Japanese influence in Central Asia has constantly augmented until today, she is mistress of all of Manchuria and of a large portion of Inner or Southern Mongolia.

The Tokyo government has already shown a lively concern in Outer or Northern Mongolia, which territory is at present dominated by Russian interests. Should the Japanese ambitions in this region develop into an attempt to secure political domination or, on the other hand, should the Russians seek to reëstablish some of their former rights over Manchuria, there is no doubt but that hostilities would ensue, jeopardizing the peace of the whole world.

Before closing our survey of Central Asiatic problems in modern times, a word should be said regarding the present status of some of the peoples who are known to have migrated from Central Asia to other portions of the world. In this connection, we are faced with a curious paradox. We know that the Scythians, who spoke an Indo-European language and hence are ultimately linked with the peoples of Europe, spread from their home in Turkistan both into Eastern Europe and into Southern Asia. Today, all traces of the Scythians and their language have disappeared from Europe; but, in Asia, the descendants of the Scythians still occupy a prominent position, for if we use the term Scythian in the broad sense of the word, we may say that all the inhabitants of Persia and of Northern India are descendants of the ancient Scythians, and still speak languages that are closely affiliated with the Scythian tongue. The Persians and the Hindus are now making a bid for world sympathy and recognition on the basis of their Indo-European origin, and the consciousness of this racial and linguistic relationship is a matter of pride to them.

The Huns and the other Turanian groups, on the other hand, were unquestionably a people of Asiatic origin. These Turanians, as we have seen, not only invaded but also settled down in many different regions, both in Asia and in Europe. Today, however, all these Turanian groups that dwelt in China proper and in India have completely lost their ethnic and linguistic identity, and it is only in the Near East and in Europe that Turanian migrants from Central Asia still maintain a consciousness of their Turanian origin and pride in their racial ancestry.

A large number of recent books and articles upon Persia and India have focused the attention of the West upon the revival of nationalist sentiment in these two countries, and have shown the part that the consciousness of their Indo-European origin has played in stimulating the development of these nationalist movements. Far less acquainted, however, is the modern world with the strength and importance of the nationalist movements among the Turanian inhabitants of the Near East and Europe. And thus a few words should be devoted in this place to them.

Undoubtedly, the best known of these Turanian groups are the inhabitants of the new Turkish republic. No longer is Turkey the "sick old man" of Europe. Turkey is now the strong, vigorous young man of Asia Minor—a power which has defeated the Greeks in war and worsted the English in diplomacy. Before the World War, the Ottoman Empire was a decaying state, ashamed of its Asiatic background. Now it is a growing nation, a nation intensely proud of the belief that its inhabitants migrated from the vast steppes of Central Asia.

Let us not forget the fact that though Asia Minor, the present stronghold of the Turks, belongs geographically to Asia, historically it belongs to Europe. Prior even to the birth of Christ, the majority of the inhabitants of Asia Minor had adopted the Greek language and Greek culture, while spiritually the whole territory was almost a suburb of Greece. Its adoption into the Roman Empire only tightened the bonds which connected it with Europe. Many of the letters supposed to have been written by the apostle Paul were addressed to the young but rising churches of Asia Minor—a fact which reminds us that, even in the sphere of religion, Asia Minor belonged to the world of Rome and the West. Although its origin was Asiatic, Christianity became one of the cultural bonds between the various provinces of the Roman Empire.

Even when Palestine, Syria and Mesopotamia were lost to Christianity and to the Eastern Roman Empire, Asia Minor remained a bulwark of European philosophy, tradition and language and it was not until four centuries later that this fertile region, which almost unassisted had valiantly defended itself from the Persian and the Arab, at last fell before the new and terrible scourge from Central Asia, the Seljuk Turks. For this reason it may be said that when Europe lost Asia Minor to the Turks she was shorn of one of her most valuable possessions and, by the same token, that the Turks, in retaining their hold upon this region, deserve to be considered as Asiatics who continued to dwell upon European soil. As a buffer state between the true Europe and the true Asia, the new Turkey, in spite of its moderate size, will continue to be an important factor in the course of world politics.

Turning now from Asia Minor to Central Europe, we find in Hungary an island of Asiatic people strenuously maintaining their Asiatic language and traditions though surrounded on all sides by peoples speaking European languages and following European traditions. Originally, Hungary was but an outpost of a solid Asiatic wedge which stretched in a continuous line westward from the plateau of Central Asia through the steppes of Southern Russia to the Hungarian basin. This line has long since been broken by the southward expansion of the Russian Empire, so that the Magyars or Hungarians are now cut off from all contact with their Asiatic kinsfolk. But the Hungarians, prior to the World War, seem not to have lost by this isolation. Until recent times, their cousins, the Finns, were peasants dominated by European masters, whereas, in Central Europe, until the dismemberment of Hungary in 1919, it was the Asiatics who were the masters of a vast body of peasantry European in speech and in origin. Even now, Hungary, though shorn of much of her territory, or because of the very fact that she has been shorn of too much, is one of the most dangerous of the sore spots in Central Europe. Hungary remains a strong compact nation of "Asiatics" with a fierce sense of patriotism and of nationalism, highly incensed over the fact that in the break-up of their kingdom large numbers of their fellow Magyars were forced to become subjects of various European states. And it is not unlikely that her desires to reconquer at least a portion of the territory which has been lost to her may lead to serious complications in central European politics.

The Bulgarians are another people of Asiatic origin residing in Europe. For centuries, there were two Bulgarias, or Volgarias—one in the Balkans, the White Volgary, the other on the Volga River, the Great or Black Volgary. Unlike the other Asiatic peoples of whom we have spoken, the Bulgarians (the Balkan Bulgarians) have lost their

Asiatic language, while most of their ancient Asiatic traditions and customs have been absorbed into those of the vast mass of Slavic peoples whom they conquered. Nevertheless, the historic tradition of their Asiatic origin is still keenly felt by most of the Bulgarians of today. It is in no small measure due to this tradition that they refuse to coalesce with their neighbors, the Serbs, who are of true Slavic origin, and it was also one of the reasons why the Bulgarians refused to act as the puppets of Czarist Russia at the time when the Romanovs employed the doctrine of Pan-Slavism as an excuse for seeking the domination of Balkan politics.

A final word should be said regarding the Lapps, the Finns, and the Esthonians who dwell in Northeastern Europe on or near the shores of the Baltic Sea. In the past, these peoples have had small influence on world history, inasmuch as the field of their activity lay too far away from the early political and cultural centers. However, within the last few years, the Finns and the Esthonians have won for themselves a relatively more important place in the sphere of international politics.

All three of these peoples speak Finno-Ugrian languages, and hence must be grouped with the Turanians. All three peoples represent remnants of a great wave of migration which once covered the whole of Northern Russia with Asiatic settlers. In modern times, the northern expansion of the Slavs has driven a wedge between the Asiatic dwellers on the shores of the Baltic and their cousins in Asiatic Russia. For a time it seemed as if the pressure of European domination would drive the Asiatic peoples of the Baltic out of existence, or at least force them to give up their Asiatic languages and their Asiatic traditions. But they managed to keep their identity, and in the nineteenth century, when the Romantic movement and consequent revival of the spirit of nationalism gave them a fresh spirit of energy, we find them rising more and more triumphantly from their low estate. Consequently, upon the break-up of the Russian Empire, the Finns were able to reappear upon the stage of world affairs as the independent republic of Finland, and the Esths as the independent republic of Esthonia.

The old land-owning European aristocracies in Finland and Esthonia have been forced to relinquish their estates to the Asiatic peasants. The hold which European languages secured in these two countries has been forcibly loosened, and the old Asiatic tongues have been raised to the status of official languages. Even more remarkable, both the Finnish and the Esthonian tongues have been made the media of a virile literary activity.

V

From what has been said it follows that, throughout the historic period, Central Asia has played an important role in the development of world events. Thus it is clear that a study of the history of Central Asia itself, though much neglected in the past, has a significance and a value.

The present treatise upon the rise and fall of the early Scythian and Hunnish empires is offered as an introduction to the study of the later empires that dominated Central Asia and carried their sway to all parts of Asia and to half of Europe.

Book One

THE ARYAN BACKGROUND

CHAPTER ONE

THE EARLY INHABITANTS OF TURKISTAN

The Claim that Turkistan was the Cradle of the Human Race—The Early Vase-Painters in Central Asia—The Excavations at Anau—The Tripolye Culture in Southwest Russia—The Early Cultures of Northwestern China—Possible Affiliations of these Cultures—The Rise of the Northern Nomads—Their Racial, Linguistic, and Cultural Affiliations—The Expansion of the Northern Nomads from Central Asia—Their Conquest of Northern India and Persia.

THE REALLY early history of Central Asia is still unknown to us. Some scholars have maintained that this region was the cradle of the whole human race, but we have as yet no proofs. Wherever mankind may have originated, it is certain that at a very early period Central Asia was not only inhabited, but inhabited by a people with a high degree of culture.[1]

In view of the later history of Turkistan, the heart of Central Asia, and its intimate associations with nomadic peoples, it is rather surprising to find that a study of the archaeological material which has been discovered in the last few years leads us to the conclusion that a large portion of Turkistan was at one time occupied by a people or rather a group of peoples (no doubt several different races and languages were represented) whom we may refer to collectively as "Vase-Painters," a group of peoples who were more or less sedentary, and who were primarily interested in agriculture.

The archaeology of Central Asia is still in its infancy, so that we have no exact information regarding the extent and duration of the Vase-Painters' civilization. But the excavations carried out under the direction of Pumpelly near the little village of Anau in Southern Turkistan have thrown much light upon what the manners and customs of one group of early inhabitants of Central Asia must have been.

From the excavations made in this area it is obvious that the early inhabitants of Anau, far from roaming about from place to place, were settled in towns and villages, and dwelt in houses made of sun-dried brick. The economic life of the Anau people centered around agriculture, the principal crops being wheat and barley. For meat they depended entirely upon the chase, slaughtering various wild animals which roamed in the neighborhood. How they secured these animals is something of a mystery, since no spearheads or arrowheads have been found.

What is most remarkable is that for a long period these early inhabitants of Southern Turkistan made no use of domesticated animals, not even the dog. It was not until several centuries after the establishment of the settlement at Anau that the inhabitants became acquainted with domestic animals such as dogs, horses, cattle, sheep, and pigs.

The earliest settlement at Anau goes back to the time when mankind relied principally upon flint and stone instruments, but was already acquainted with the use of copper. The most remarkable feature of this civilization was its pottery, for though this primitive people had no knowledge of the potter's wheel, their pottery was very graceful in shape, and was painted with geometrical designs showing great artistic skill.

Pumpelly himeself believed that the beginnings of the Anau civilization should be placed as far back as 8000 B.C. This claim for antiquity is undoubtedly exaggerated, but most authorities are willing to admit that the Anau settlements were in existence in 4000 B.C., and were thus contemporary with the beginnings of cultural life in Egypt and in Mesopotamia.[2]

We have, of course, no knowledge of the linguistic affinities of these early inhabitants of Southern Turkistan, and only scanty indications as to their race. But considering the fact that we have long been accustomed to regard Central Asia as the homeland of the Mongolian or Mongoloid peoples, it is interesting to observe that the skeletal material found at Anau shows that the peoples of this area definitely belonged to the Caucasoid or "White" group of races. In fact, it would appear that the majority of them were closely akin to the so-called Mediterranean Race —the race which still preponderates in Southern Europe.[3]

Very interesting are the comparisons which have been drawn between the Anau civilization and the culture which arose in Southwest Russia and Northern Rumania, a culture usually given the name of "Tripolye." The inhabitants of this region, like those of Anau, had their life centered around agriculture. They too produced a beautiful and very characteristic type of painted pottery. These are but two of several features which lead us to the belief that the origin of the Tripolye culture is to be associated with the East in general with Turkistan in particular.[4]

Equally important is the fact that in the last few years a number of very early specimens of painted pottery have come to light in Northern and Northwestern China. The analogies between this pottery and that of Anau and Tripolye, more especially the latter, have led many scholars to the conclusion that this early Chinese pottery was made as a result of stimuli from the West.[5]

This theory, plus the fact that early China developed an agricultural

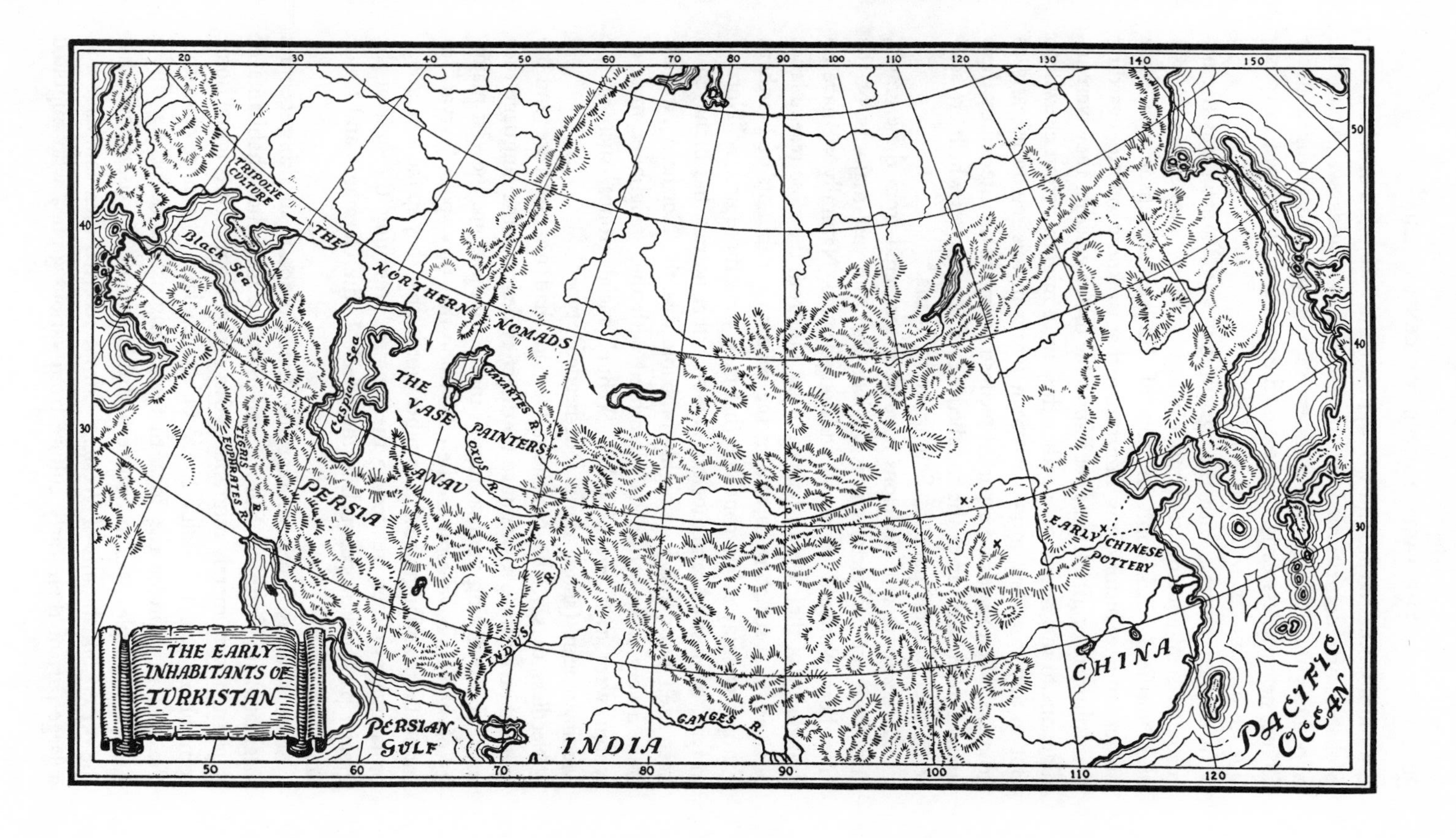
THE EARLY INHABITANTS OF TURKISTAN
TRIPOLYE CULTURE
THE NORTHERN NOMADS
Black Sea
Caspian Sea
THE VASE PAINTERS
JAXARTES R.
OXUS R.
ANAU
PERSIA
TIGRIS R.
EUPHRATES R.
INDUS R.
PERSIAN GULF
INDIA
GANGES R.
EARLY CHINESE POTTERY
CHINA
PACIFIC OCEAN

community centered around wheat, millet and barley (all of which were probably first domesticated in the Near East), adds weight to the hypothesis that though the Chinese race is probably indigenous to China, nevertheless early Chinese civilization first developed in consequence of contacts with Central Asia.[6]

In marked contrast with the agricultural Vase-Painters was the nomadic or semi-nomadic civilization which arose in Southeastern Russia and Northern Turkistan.[7] In view of the great significance of these nomads in later history, it is unfortunate that we know so little regarding their ultimate origin. It is as yet impossible to say whether they were indigenous to this region or whether they were migrants from elsewhere. But in any case they must have been living in this region as early as 3000 B.C.[8] We can secure a partial reconstruction of the life led by these nomads from a study of the so-called Red Ochre graves which are scattered over various parts of Southeastern Russia.[9]

A large number of skeletons have been recovered from these graves, and from these skeletons it is obvious that the vast majority of the "Northern Nomads" were tall and long-headed. Naturally we have no knowledge of their eye or hair coloring, but from the close resemblance of their bony structure to that of the modern inhabitants of Northern Europe, we may safely conclude that they were more or less "Nordic" in type. It must be remembered, however, that no race has managed to keep itself pure, and it is highly probable that the Northern Nomads from a very early period had interbred with their neighbors, most of whom were members of other "White" racial groups, such as the Mediterranean (short, dark, long-headed) type.[10]

Needless to say, the Northern Nomads had no literature and no method of writing, so we have no direct evidence of the language they spoke. But working upon a mass of indirect indications, the vast majority of scholars have come to the conclusion that they spoke "Aryan" or Indo-European languages or, in other words, that they spoke a language or languages closely related to the tongues prevailing throughout the greater part of Europe, such as the Greek, Latin, Germanic and Celtic languages.[11]

Some scholars [12] believe that the Indo-European speaking peoples originated in Northern Europe and that the nomadic inhabitants of Turkistan were merely migrants to this region from their original home somewhere near the Baltic Sea.[13] Other scholars, who now constitute the majority, prefer the idea that the original home of the Indo-European peoples was in Southern Russia and in Turkistan, and that the present inhabitants of Western Europe received their language and a large part of their early culture from various groups who migrated westwards from Central Asia. It is as yet impossible to settle this important problem, but at least we can say that at the moment the weight of opinion and evidence lies on the side of those who support the theory of the Central Asiatic origin of the Indo-European linguistic group.[14]

When we attempt to study the manners and customs of these Northern Nomads, we are faced with many difficulties. Historical data are entirely absent, so that we are forced to rely on the scanty archaeological evidence which is available, and upon the facts which a study of comparative philology has brought to light.[15]

Judging from this material we find that on certain points these Nomads did not differ radically from the earlier Vase Painters. Like the latter, the Nomads were acquainted with agriculture. And like the latter, the Nomads when we first become aware of their existence still made use of various stone implements but already knew the value of copper and bronze. The use of iron came considerably later. The Nomads were also in the habit of making pottery, though their pots differed radically in design from those of the more artistic Vase-Painters. But unlike the Vase-Painters, who were sedentary, the Northern Nomads, as their name implies, tended to move from place to place, and as a result were forced to rely in large measure upon the breeding of animals for their food supply, and for transport.

Of especial interest to us is the close association which sprang up between these Northern Nomads and the horse. Horses are known to have existed sporadically at a very early time in different parts of the old world. They were certainly known to the Vase-Painters of Anau, of Tripolye, and of Northwestern China, but among these peoples horses remained relatively unimportant adjuncts. With the Northern Nomads, on the other hand, the horse played an all important role, and the spread of these Nomads into other regions is nearly always associated with the spread of horses and horsemanship.[16]

We must now face the problem of just how and when the spread of these Nomads took place. The data for drawing conclusions is very scanty, but there is a general consensus of opinion that there was a great shifting of populations shortly before 2000 B.C., possibly because of some change in climate, and that it was about this time that the Aryan inhabitants of Central Asia began to exert pressure upon all surrounding regions. In any event, this expansion must have gone on comparatively slowly, for it was not until 1000 B.C., a millennium later, that this period of migration reached its culmination.

It is highly probable that this slow but steady expansion from Central Asia took place in several directions. The region least affected by this migration was the North, probably because of the heavy forestation of

Siberia and Northern Russia. The presence at a later time of Aryan peoples in Kashgaria or Eastern Turkistan reaching to the borders of China shows that a certain amount of migration must have been directed towards the East. It is, moreover, certain that many of these early Aryan inhabitants of Turkistan also made their way westward along the steppes of Southern Russia, which, geographically speaking, are but annexes to the steppes of Central Asia. But for the expansion to the East and the West, we have only scanty and scrappy information.[17]

Far different is it with the migrations which took place to the South, for though many phases of this southern migration are unknown to us, we are at least able to reconstruct in broad outline the story of the principal features of the expansion which took place in this direction. It appears clear that shortly before 2000 B.C. certain Aryan tribes moved southward from Northern Turkistan and succeeded in dominating practically all of Southern Turkistan. The earlier inhabitants of this region were for the most part either annihilated or absorbed by these invaders, though it is probable that small groups of them survived for a lengthy period, but only by becoming tributaries or vassals to the dominant Aryan tribesmen. All the known facts lead to the conclusion that the center of Aryan power at this period was in that portion of Southern Turkistan known as Bactria, a region which occupies the northern slopes of the Hindu Kush Mountains.[18]

As time went on this conquering Aryan people or group of peoples, finding that Southern Turkistan was insufficient for their needs, continued their expansion still further to the South. Pushing over the Hindu Kush Mountains they mounted the northeastern portions of the Iranian Plateau and made themselves masters of this region.

It is probable that these early Aryans did not possess even the semblance of a centralized political organization. In fact it would appear that these invaders were broken up into numerous tribes and subtribes each one of which possessed full liberty of action. Some of the smaller groups, more adventurous than the rest, moved rapidly westward and, either as a small conquering aristocracy or as mercenaries in the pay of non-Aryan rulers, succeeded in establishing several important kingdoms in different portions of the Near East.

It was to these small adventurous groups that we owe the first mention of Aryan proper names in the ancient cuneiform records of the Mesopotamian Empires. In the period between 1900 and 1500 B.C. we note the sudden appearance of a number of "barbarian" peoples who overthrew most of the then existing Empires and carved out for themselves kingdoms, many of which existed for several centuries.

Among the barbarians who are known to have ruled in various parts of the Near East during this period are the Kassites who conquered Babylonia, the people of Mitanni who ruled in the upper Euphrates Basin, and various smaller dynasties in Syria. Research has shown that these barbarians as a whole spoke languages which are in no way associated with that of the Aryan stock, but in each case we find in the records concerning them a large number of proper names that are markedly Aryan in character. The existence of these names has led the scholastic world to conclude that all of these people were organized into political entities and ruled over by a small group of Aryan leaders. It is further agreed that these leaders must have come from the East, an indication that the Aryan occupation of the Iranian Plateau was already well under way.[19]

It must, nevertheless, be borne in mind that these early Aryan adventurers in the Near East marked only a passing phase. They did not succeed in imposing their racial type or their language upon the Mesopotamian and Syrian kingdoms in which they momentarily played so important a role. In fact, these Aryan adventurers were completely absorbed in the surrounding population. The permanent Aryanization of the middle East was accomplished not by these military adventurers but by the main body of the Aryan tribes which at first remained behind in Eastern Iran but which slowly pushed their way into the surrounding territories.[20]

One division of these tribes following in the path of the military adventurers progressed slowly to the west and the southwest and eventually dominated all of the Iranian Plateau. Ousting all of the intervening peoples who formerly lived in this region, they eventually became the immediate neighbors of the Semites who constituted the great bulk of the inhabitants of Mesopotamia and the adjacent territory. Most of the Semites at this period were subject to the Assyrian Empire, and it is from the records of this Empire that we get our first definite mention of the Madai or Medes and the Parsuash, presumably the Persians, the two Aryan peoples who were destined in later times to establish great empires in the East. The first allusion to these peoples dates from 836 B.C., and from this fact we may infer that the greater part of the Iranian Plateau had been occupied by the Aryans at least as early as this time.[21]

Another division of the Aryans instead of moving westward progressed gradually to the east and southeast and eventually succeeded in dominating all of Northern India, pushing out or absorbing the darker-skinned Dravidians who had previously occupied this region. At first the Aryan invaders were confined to the basin of the Indus River (originally the Sindhus or Hindus, hence the word Hindu) in

Northwestern India, but ultimately they were able to secure control over the Ganges basin further to the east, and also over a considerable portion of the peninsula portion of India, known as the Dekkan. We have no definite information regarding the date of the Aryan invasion of India, but this event is generally supposed to have taken place some time prior to 1000 B.C.[22]

CHAPTER TWO

SCYTHIANS AND SARMATIANS IN THE NORTH

The Beginning of Documentary History—The Cimmerians—The Migrations and Early Conquests of the Scythians—Later History of the Scythians—Decay of the Scythians and Rise of the Sarmatians—The Massagetae, Aorsi, Alani—The Sakas and Kanggü—The Racial Position of the Scythians—Their Language—Scythian Culture—Domesticated Animals and the Importance of the Horse—The History of Horseback Riding—Scythian Clothing and the History of Trousers—Arms and Armor—Tents—Political Organizations—Customs in Warfare—Marriage—Funeral Customs—Religion—Scythian Art.

So FAR we have spoken of peoples who appear at the very dawn of history, regarding whom our information is far from exact. But beginning with the seventh century B.C., archaeological evidence begins to be supported by documentary evidence. At first this evidence is rather scanty, but as time goes on the records become more complete, and we are able to gain a fairly adequate idea of the manners and customs of the various peoples who rose and fell in Turkistan.

Throughout this historic period there was a sharp distinction between Northern Turkistan and Southern Turkistan. Though the peoples inhabiting these two regions belonged to the same general stock and had many cultural traits in common, they no longer regarded themselves as kinsmen and allies but rather as bitter rivals and enemies. Northern Turkistan was associated historically and culturally with the steppes of Southern Russia, and it is from the Greek colonists who settled along the northern shores of the Black Sea that we gain most of our information regarding the inhabitants of Northern Turkistan. Southern Turkistan, on the other hand, came to be associated ever more closely with the adjacent Iranian Pleateau. When the Persians at last succeeded in establishing control over the Iranian Plateau, Southern Turkistan was also included in the Persian Empire with the result that our information regarding the inhabitants of Southern Turkistan during this period is derived largely from the ancient Persian inscriptions and from those Greeks who interested themselves in Persian history.

Let us examine what the Greek records and the findings of modern archaeology have to tell us regarding the peoples of Northern Turkistan and their colleagues, the inhabitants of Southern Russia. The early Greek chroniclers have bequeathed us the names of many separate tribes who dwelt at various times in different parts of this vast area.

It is not necessary for us to list all of these names since the Greeks themselves recognized the close affinity which existed between most of these groups and classified them into two main divisions—the Scythians and the Sarmatians. Even between the Scythians and Sarmatians there were a great many points of affinity, for which reason the name Scythian was frequently used to include all of the inhabitants of the steppe region during this period. Following the Greek custom, we may call all the peoples who inhabited Northern Turkistan at this period Scythians; but, even while doing so, we must remember that there was a sharp difference in many respects between the Scythians proper, who lay to the west, and the Sarmatians who lay farther to the east.

According to Greek tradition, the earliest known inhabitants of Southern Russia were a mysterious people known as the Cimmerians, who also appear in Assyrian records under the name of Gimirrai. Concerning them little is really known. It is quite possible that the Cimmerians were distantly related to the Scythians and were originally emigrants from Central Asia, but for the moment we must be content to leave this matter undecided, for the Cimmerians disappeared from history at an early date, transmitting to posterity little more than their name.[1]

The Cimmerians were succeeded in the annals of history by the Scythians proper. It is clear from the Greek chroniclers that these Scythians originally dwelt in Northern Turkistan and set upon their migrations only because of pressure exerted by some of their neighbors. Their entrance upon the threshold of recorded history takes place when they moved out of Turkistan and, in turn, drove out the Cimmerians, making themselves the masters of the steppe-lands of Southern Russia. We are in doubt as to the exact time when this conquest took place. It is certain that in the seventh century B.C. the Scythians were already masters of the Russian steppe-lands, but it is quite possible that their migration into this region had taken place at least a century or two earlier.[2]

Not content with their vast empire in Southern Russia, the Scythians made frequent forays in other regions. Archaeological records show us that at a very early period one branch of the Scythians settled far to the west in what is now Rumania and Hungary. From historical evidence, we also know that in the seventh century another group of Scythians moved southward through the Caucasus and appeared in Armenia and Media just as the Assyrians and the Medes were battling for the mastership of the Near East.[3]

The Scythians were induced to act as allies of the Assyrians, with the result that the Medes were temporarily humbled and the final triumph

Portrait of Scythians

(From an early Greek vase). Cf. Chap. II.
(*After Minns*)

Portrait of Scythians

(From an early Greek vase). Cf. Chap. II.
(*After Minns*)

Fragments of Early Pottery from Central Asia (Anau) and from N. China (Honan). Cf. Chap. I. (*After Andersson*)

of the Median Empire was postponed for nearly three decades. Herodotus tells us that the Scythians who battled with the Medes were eventually forced to return to their homes in Southern Russia. This may well be true of the bulk of the invading tribes, but judging from other sources a goodly number of Scythians settled in various portions of Asia Minor and there managed to maintain a separate existence for several centuries.[4] In spite of these incursions to the west and the southeast, the vast majority of the Scythians remained in Southern Russia, their newly acquired homeland. From the seventh to the fifth centuries B.C., the center of the Scythian Empire continued in the eastern portion of Southern Russia not far from the banks of the Don River. Eventually, however, pressure from the east forced the Scythians to move westwards. Archaeological finds show that during the fourth and third centuries the Scythian kings held their courts in the steppe-lands north and northwest of the Krimea.[5]

All during this period, the internal development of the Scythians is very little known to us, and history makes specific mention of the Scythian Kingdom only when it came into contact with one or another of the great world empires. Thus, for example, we know that Darius, the great ruler of the Persians, became involved in a minor and indecisive war with the Scythians shortly after he landed in Europe and just before he made his ill-fated attempt to conquer Greece.

Over a century later, Philip of Macedon, the father of the illustrious Alexander, became involved in a conflict with the ruler of the Scythians. This hostility between Macedonia and the Scythian Empire was renewed a short time afterwards as we hear that during the time when Alexander was engaged in his conquest of Asia, one of Alexander's generals undertook another campaign against the Scythians, a campaign which ended in complete disaster.[6]

In addition to these conflicts with the "Great Powers," the Scythians also came into contact—very intimate contact—with the Greek colonies scattered along the northern coast of the Black Sea. The Scythians were never a maritime people and seldom showed any desire to conquer and suppress these Greek colonies, all of which owed their existence to the need for a sea trade between Southern Russia and the Greek motherland. But though the Scythians were willing to see the Greek colonies continue in existence, they not infrequently imposed a fairly heavy tributary tax upon these colonial governments as a price for being left undisturbed. The contacts thus established between the Greeks and the Scythians proved of the greatest importance. The Greeks were able to secure the raw materials necessary for the support of the homeland, while the Scythians, either as tribute or by way of trade, secured many priceless art objects made by Greek artisans. Many of these objects were especially made for the Scythian trade and betray a curious blending of Greek and Scythian art motives.

Recent archaeological discoveries have shown us that many of these articles of Greek manufacture, secured in the first instance by the Scythians, gradually made their way eastwards into the heart of Central Asia. Some of them have even been excavated in distant Mongolia. This fact is of primary importance when we come to consider the origin of many of the artistic designs which later developed among the peoples of Turkistan.

The Scythian Empire was long able to remain overlord of many of the Greek colonies scattered along the coast of the Black Sea. The Scythians were, moreover, as we have seen, able to fight on fairly equal terms with the great Persian and Macedonian Empires; but before long they received a death blow from the east. Sometime in the second or first century B.C., their power was completely broken, though scattered Scythian tribes, by taking refuge in various isolated regions, managed to maintain a separate existence for several centuries longer. Among these isolated regions which are specifically known to us are the Krimean Peninsula and also Dobruja, that curious little section of modern Rumania which lies just to the south of the mouth of the Danube River.

The decay and eventual downfall of the Scythians was due almost entirely to invasion by their distant kinsmen, the Sarmatians. All during the many centuries the Scythian Empire was at its height, Sarmatians and numerous similar peoples continued to occupy Northern Turkistan; but, owing to the great isolation of this region, we know very little of the internal developments which took place during this period.[7]

When we come to consider what few facts are known to us, we find that the name Sarmatian, though originally confined to a single tribe, was soon used as a general term for a great number of different, though no doubt similar, tribes scattered throughout different portions of Central Asia. Among these numerous tribes, there are only three or four that are of sufficient importance to warrant their separate mention.

In early times (the sixth century B.C.) a large part of Northern Turkistan, and especially Northwestern Turkistan, was dominated by a tribal group called Massagetae by the Greek historians. These Massagetae caused the early rulers of the Persian Empire a great deal of trouble. Herodotus tells us that Cyrus, the founder of the Persian Empire, met his death while fighting against this people.[8] The power of the Massagetae lasted for several centuries, but in the second century B.C., predominance in Northwestern Turkistan passed into the hands of another

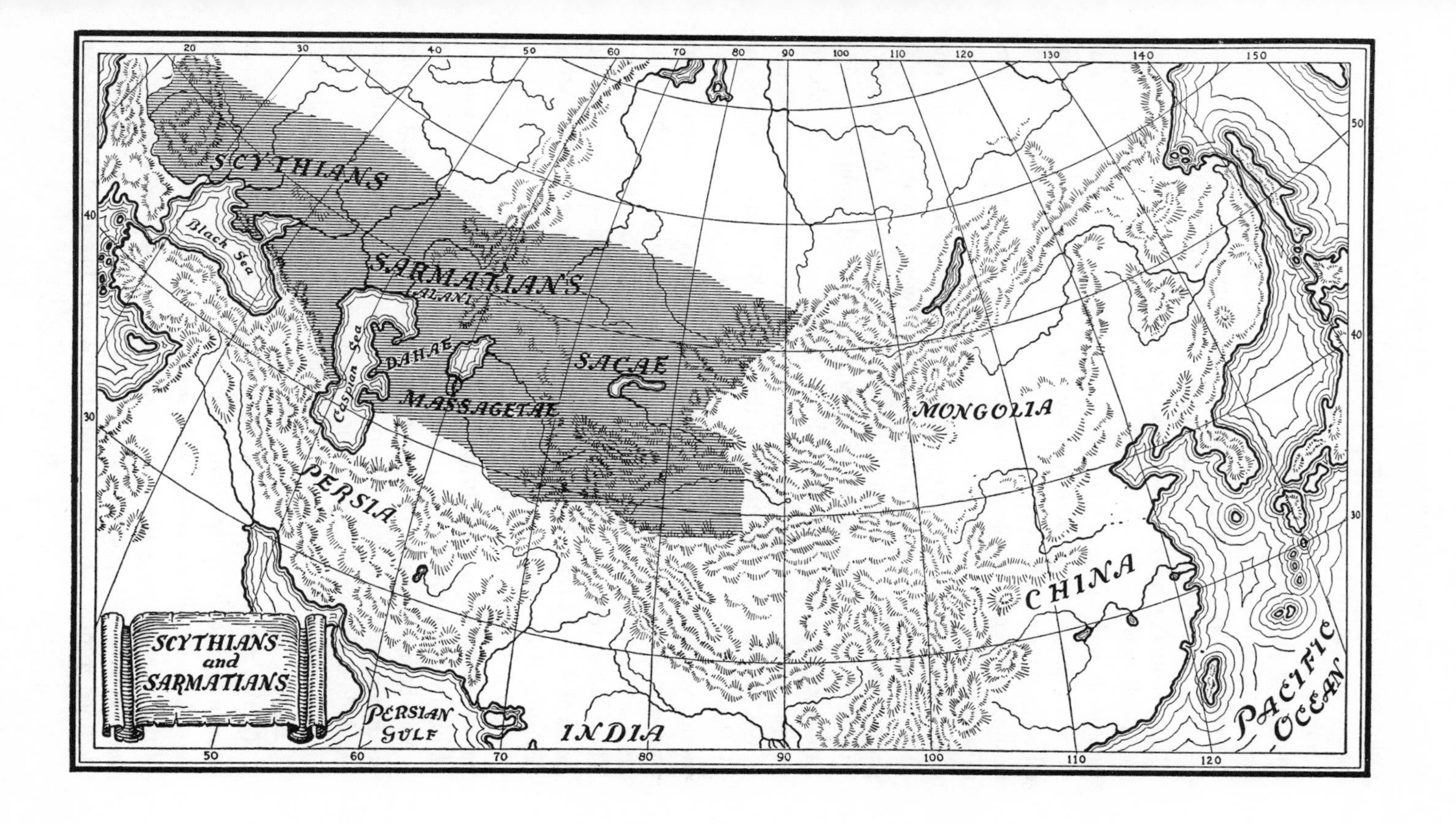
SCYTHIANS and SARMATIANS
SCYTHIANS
SARMATIANS
ALANI
DAHAE
SACAE
MASSAGETAE
Black Sea
Caspian Sea
PERSIA
PERSIAN GULF
INDIA
MONGOLIA
CHINA
PACIFIC OCEAN

group called the Aorsi. Three centuries later (the first century A.D.) the Aorsi were, in turn, succeeded by the Alani.[9]

Among the various peoples inhabiting northern Turkistan in early times, it is perhaps the Alani who are the most interesting and most important, because of the part that they were later destined to play in world history. Starting in Central Asia, they later, as we shall see hereafter, spread to many different parts of the world. One branch of the Alani eventually migrated to Spain and Northern Africa; and their blood still flows in the veins of the peoples dwelling in those regions. Another branch of the Alani made their way to the northern slopes of the Caucasus, and this branch, under the name of Ossetes, still maintains its ancient language and has preserved its ethnic identity all through the centuries, the only one of the numerous Sarmatian groups to survive the ravages of time.

Whereas it was the Massagetae, the Aorsi, and the Alani who, one after another, dominated the plains of Northwestern Turkistan in the period just before and just after the birth of Christ, Northeastern Turkistan was in the hands of several other tribal groups, speaking languages identical or at least closely related to those of the abovementioned groups and with a similar culture, but bearing different names. In the region just north of the Jaxartes River and including the Ili River Basin and the northern slopes of the Celestial Mountains dwelt the Sakas. At times these Sakas, by ravaging the frontiers, were able to cause the Persian Empire a great deal of trouble. At other times large numbers of Sakas entered the service of the Persian Empire. These Sakan regiments were among the most famed of all the fighting forces of Asia. In later times, when Alexander the Great invaded Central Asia, the Sakas again came to the forefront, and the youthful world conqueror was forced to engage in several bloody combats with the Sakan tribesmen in order to secure stability and order on the outposts of his far-flung empire.[10]

The Sakas, like their neighbors, the Alani, were destined to play an important part in later history. But whereas the Alani spread westwards into Europe, the Sakas chose the lands to the south of them for the seat of their later actions; and at one time they were lords of much of Eastern Iran and Northern India.

To the north of the Sakas dwelt another important tribal group, known to us only by the name Kang-gü, a name given to them by the early Chinese historians—the only persons to record even the existence of this group in early times. But though this group was ignored by the early Persian inscriptions and the Greek historians, the Kang-gü were destined to play a significant role in the later history of Central Asia, and so it is necessary to record their existence in Northeastern Turkistan at this early time.[11]

To the east of the Sakas and the Kang-gü were several tribes which we must include under the general term, Sarmatian. It is possible that some of these Sarmatian tribes at one time occupied the western part of the Mongolian Plateau. It is certain that peoples closely linked both racially and linguistically to the Sarmatians occupied the greater part of Kashgaria or Chinese Turkistan. But all of these eastern tribes are best known to us from the Chinese sources and were, moreover, associated historically with the non-Sarmatian tribes of Mongolia, so we may best deal with these easterners when we come to a discussion of the rise of the Hunnish Empire in Eastern Asia.

We know very little of internal events or developments in Northern Turkistan during this period, for the contemporary chroniclers seldom considered the Sarmatian tribes worthy of special treatment and mentioned them only when one or another of them invaded the frontiers of, or otherwise caused damages to, one of the great historic monarchies. Our knowledge of the Sarmatians is therefore confined largely to the pressure which they exerted upon the inhabitants of adjacent regions.

As in earlier days, the great Siberian forests prevented any wholesale migration to the north. We know, from historic documents, that the Sarmatian tribes frequently attempted to make inroads into Southern Turkistan and, no doubt, had an acquisitive eye upon the fertile districts of the Iranian Plateau; but, as long as the powerful and well-organized Persian Empire was in existence, it was almost impossible for the Sarmatians to make any permanent advance in this direction.

The presence of Sarmatian or semi-Sarmatian tribes in Kashgaria and the extreme western part of China shows that the Sarmatians must have exerted considerable pressure to the East, but we know from recorded history that the most usual and most successful direction of expansion was to the West across the steppe-lands of Southern Russia. As we have already seen, the Scythian conquerors of Southern Russia originally came from Northern Turkistan; and, as we have also seen, these Scythians were in turn displaced by the various Sarmatian tribes which slowly but relentlessly pushed westwards.[12]

After this brief historic survey, we may now turn to a discussion of the racial, linguistic, and cultural affiliations of the various Scythian and Sarmatian tribes. In the first place, we must note that though the Scythians and Sarmatians in later times were bitter political enemies, the authors of antiquity are practically unanimous in making the two groups into sister nations; and we have every reason to suppose that the two groups are ultimately derived from the same common stock.[13]

The descriptions given us by the classical Greek authors of the physical appearance of the ancient Scythians and Sarmatians are somewhat ambiguous and contradictory, with the result that many wild speculations have arisen regarding the possible racial affinities of these peoples. The few skeletal remains which have been excavated from Scythian and Sarmatian graves, however, combined with the extremely realistic portraits of Scythians and Sarmatian tribesmen found on Persian rock inscriptions and especially on Greek vases excavated in Southern Russia, make it abundantly clear that the overwhelming majority of both groups were members of one of the Caucasoid or White Races.

It is of especial importance to note the high aquiline noses, the deep-set eyes, and the long beards and mustaches worn by the Scythians and Sarmatians pictured on the Greek vases. These features in themselves are clear proof that the Mongoloid element which we later find all over Central Asia, if it existed at all in Turkistan at this early period, must have been extremely insignificant.

Unfortunately, neither the skeletal material nor the portrait vases give us any indication as to the natural coloring of the peoples we are considering. But the fact that the majority of the skeletons of this period which have been dug up correspond with the Nordic skeletons of Western Europe, combined with the express statement of one of the classical authors that the Alani, the greatest of all the Sarmatian peoples, were tall, fair, and well built, makes it certain that the Nordic race must have constituted an important element in Central Asia during the Scythian and Sarmatian period.

At the same time, it should be noted that *some* of the skeletal remains dating from this period show decided traces of round-headedness. These round-headed skulls are, however, in no way Mongoloid and merely confirm us in our belief that the round-headed Alpine race was also well represented among the early inhabitants of Central Asia. These Asiatic Alpines, like their distant cousins, the present-day inhabitants of Central Europe, though of course "White," must have been decided brunettes.[14]

Turning now from race to language, we find ourselves faced with an initial difficulty. Neither the Scythians nor the Sarmatians ever felt it necessary to adopt a system of writing; this means that not a single connected passage of the Scytho-Sarmatian language or literature has been preserved to us. None of the Greek authors ever took the trouble to prepare a Scytho-Sarmatian word list; and this means that we must abandon all hope of recovering the Scytho-Sarmatian language in its entirety.

We are, however, fortunate enough to possess a number of important hints that aid us in ascertaining at least to which language group the Scytho-Sarmatian language was related. Many of the authors of antiquity tell us definitely that this language was very similar to the tongues spoken by the Medes, the Persians, and the Parthians; or, in other words, that the Scythians and Sarmatians spoke what we would now call an Iranian language.

This statement is rendered very credible by a study of the Scytho-Sarmatian proper names—names of persons, Gods, and places, which have been preserved to us by the Greek and Roman authors. The classical writers were extremely slipshod in their transcription of these proper names with the result that many were so transformed as to be unintelligible, but in a large number of cases these names have very clear Iranian affiliations.

In addition to these proper names, we have other indirect evidence in support of the statements that the Scytho-Sarmatians of ancient times spoke languages that we closely relate to Persian. One fact of importance, in this connection, is that the Ossetes, the direct descendants of the Alani, still speak a very archaic form of Iraniam quite different from, but obviously closely related to, early Persian. Equally significant is the fact that numerous manuscript remains, dug up in Kashgaria and dating from the early middle ages, show that the inhabitants of this region, who were for the most part distant cousins of the Sarmatians, spoke Iranian languages until at least the ninth century A.D.

In view of this vast mass of evidence, we may take it as definitely established that the Scythians and Sarmatians spoke languages which were not only definitely Indo-European, but which more specifically belonged to the "Aryan" or Indo-Iranian group. Even more to the point, these languages spoken in Northern Turkistan and the surrounding regions were far closer to the Iranian than to the Indian branch of the Indo-European group.[15]

Turning now from the linguistic to the cultural affiliations of the Scythians and Sarmatians, we have first of all to notice one or two remarkable features that sharply distinguished this group from most other Indo-Europeans. We have already seen that from very early times all Indo-Europeans must have been acquainted with the horse, as well as with several other domesticated animals. But with most of these Indo-European groups the use of the horse remained a secondary feature and did not prevent the cultural development of the people along lines completely disconnected with horses and horsemanship. Thus, for example, the use of domesticated animals, including the horse, did not prevent most of these peoples from developing their primitive agriculture to a very high stage, with the result that they soon abandoned their semi-nomadic mode of existence and settled down to fixed habitations.

In marked contrast to this line of evolution, we find that the Scythians and Sarmatians, who dwelt in a land which was pre-eminently suited to pasturage, tended to lose the little knowledge of agriculture they once possessed and to concentrate their attention upon the cultivation of their huge herds of domesticated animals, among which the horse played an ever more important part. We know from the classical authors that all of the Scytho-Sarmatian tribes went in for hunting wild animals, and that some at least were expert fishers. Although the knowledge of agriculture was never completely lost by these peoples, and fishing, hunting, and agriculture tended more and more to become lesser accomplishments, it is certain that Scythians and Sarmatians relied to an ever greater extent upon flocks of domesticated animals for their economic existence.[16]

Among the domesticated animals, horses, cattle, and sheep played the major role. We are expressly told that no pigs were domesticated, a fact which is of great interest when we remember that among many of the Indo-European groups dwelling in Europe pigs were already kept in large numbers. We are certain that the Scythians made use of dogs, but it was around the horse that their whole life was centered.[17]

These domesticated animals served, of course, to provide a constant food supply for their masters. In this connection, it is of interest to note that in addition to eating beef and mutton the Scythians and Sarmatians also ate horseflesh and seem to have considered it a great delicacy.[18] Far more important than any meat, however, was milk and its various products.

It would seem that milk was occasionally used for food by a number of the early Indo-European peoples, though usually it was only an incidental and relatively unimportant item in the daily diet. With the Scythians and Sarmatians, on the other hand, it formed the principal food supply. It is probable that they, like other peoples, sometimes made use of cow's milk; but it is certain that with them it was mare's milk which played the all-important part in domestic economy.

We are led to believe, moreover, that the use of raw milk among the Scythians and Sarmatians, as among the later inhabitants of Central Asia, was comparatively rare, and that it was doubtless drunk, as in later times, principally by children and by invalids. Far more important than raw milk was fermented mare's milk which was consumed in enormous quantities and constituted the most important single item in the daily diet. This fermented mare's milk, called by the

Greek authors *oxygala,* was, of course, exactly the same thing which is now known under the Turkish name of *kumis* and which is still widely used all over Central Asia. Another food very popular among the ancient Scythians which is still in common use in Central Asia was a sort of sour cheese made from this fermented mare's milk.

We know that in addition to drinking their *oxygala* or *kumis* the Scythians and Sarmatians were also very fond of grape wine. The grape does not grow in the steppe-lands of Turkistan or Southern Russia, but grapes and wine-making were known to the Greeks and also to the inhabitants of Southern Turkistan, so the Scytho-Sarmatians had no difficulty in securing their wine by way of barter.[19]

Kumis was prepared and kept in wooden receptacles. For certain kinds of cooking, skin cooking pots were also in use; but, for most of the cooking which had to be done, round, single-footed copper cauldrons were employed. Several of these ancient cauldrons have been dug up in recent years. The Scytho-Sarmatians were not entirely unacquainted with pottery, but because of their nomadic life they paid scant attention to pots and pottery making and, as far as possible, preferred to make use of more substantial utensils. Drinking cups, for example, were usually made of horn, but we know that on ceremonial occasions use was made of a drinking bowl made out of the skull of a fallen enemy. The classical authors make no mention of leather receptacles but it is probable that the Scythians, like the modern nomads of Central Asia, made frequent use of such objects.

But though the Scytho-Sarmatians were able to secure enough wood to make bowls, they had great difficulty in getting enough to use for fuel, living as they did on the open steppe country ill-supplied with trees and bushes. Herodotus tells us that the Scythians made use of dry bones as fuel, but this information is undoubtedly false since bones, no matter how dry, will not burn. It is probable that the ancient Scythians and Sarmatians, like the modern inhabitants of Central Asia, made extensive use of dried dung cakes as fuel for warmth and for cooking.[20]

One of the most important features of the Scytho-Sarmatian cultural life was the fact that all of these tribes used their horses for riding rather than for driving. At first sight there seems nothing remarkable in this fact, until one remembers that, paradoxically enough, in nearly every part of the old world we have definite evidence that horses were driven long before they were ridden. When we study the early history of China, of India, of Mesopotamia, and of Egypt, we find that for many centuries after the introduction of the horse, horseback riding was either unknown or else played a very subordinate role; the principal use to which the horse was put was to draw heavy war chariots. Even among the Indo-Europeans, the founders of the horse culture, horsemanship was usually associated with chariot driving and not with horseback riding. The Greeks in Homeric times were well-acquainted with the horse, but seem to have used this animal almost exclusively for drawing war chariots. In the seventh century B.C., we hear of races between mounted riders at the Olympic games, but for many centuries thereafter chariot racing remained far more popular. At about the same time (seventh century B.C.) we first hear of mounted soldiers, but for a very lengthy period cavalry remained a minor and relatively insignificant branch of the Greek armies. It was not until the time of Alexander that cavalry became an important element in Hellenic warfare.

In Rome horseback riding seems to have been known at a very early period; the order of "equites" or "Knights" is evidence of this fact. And from the classical authors we know what cavalry constituted a well-known branch of the Roman army. But it is significant to remember that in point of numbers and importance the cavalry was always much inferior to the infantry. Beginning with the period of the Civil Wars most of the cavalry consisted of foreign auxiliaries, and even then cavalrymen were strictly limited in number, the typical legion consisting of about three hundred cavalrymen to six thousand infantrymen. As with the Greeks, the Romans preferred chariot racing to horseracing.

The early Germanic and Slavic tribes made but little use of the horse; it was chiefly the Celts who were sufficiently adept at horsemanship to make use of cavalry as a regular feature in warfare. Even among the Celtic tribes there was a marked difference between the groups inhabiting the islands of Great Britain and those inhabiting continental Europe. The former, like most of the other Indo-Europeans, depended largely upon war chariots in fighting, and it was only the Celts of Central Europe who were noted as mounted warriors. We know that the Celts were in contact with the Scythians at a very early time, and we have every reason to suppose that the eastern Celts adopted much of their horsemanship from the Scythians.

Even in Central Asia itself horseback riding must have been practiced some time after the use of the horse to draw wagons and chariots. The early Hindus, the first cousins of the Iranians, and who at one time dwelt in Northern Turkistan, were chariot drivers rather than riders. From this fact we may deduce that the art of riding developed subsequent to the departure of the Indian branch of the Aryan peoples from this region.

When we attempt to retrace the early history of civilization, it appears that at a very early period the peoples of Mesopotamia invented the wheel, and shortly thereafter the chariot. Having as yet very scanty if any acquaintance with the horse, they made use of either the cattle or of asses to draw these chariots. The fact that the cattle are far more fitted for driving than for riding was probably the real reason that driving everywhere preceded riding.

From Mesopotamia the use of wagons slowly made its way to Central Asia where it was eventually adopted by the early Indo-Europeans. At first these Indo-Europeans used cattle to draw their wagons (we know that even in Scythian times cattle were still employed to draw the native tent wagons); but, after these Indo-Europeans had succeeded in taming and domesticating the horses which roamed wild over the Asiatic steppes, it occurred to them at first, not to ride these animals, but to substitute the horse for the slower moving cattle in pulling their wagons. Once this change had been effected, the evolution of the wagon to the war chariot was an easy and natural development and was adopted by most Indo-European peoples and by many non-European groups as well.

It was not, however, until many centuries later, when the Indo-Europeans had dispersed to many different parts of the world that those Indo-Europeans who continued to reside in Central Asia, namely the Scythians and Sarmatians, hit upon the brilliant and original notion of mounting the animal they had long been accustomed to driving. In view of this important change and of the many results that led from it, we must consider the Scytho-Sarmatians, though otherwise good Indo-Europeans, as the creators of a new and important subculture.[21]

With the adoption of riding, a number of important developments were bound to follow, especially as regards horse trappings; and it is not surprising to find that these horse trappings, some useful, such as bits, others purely ornamental, such as metal decorations for the harness, play a major part in all Scythian and Sarmatian tombs. The use of bridles dates from very early times, when horses were still driven rather than ridden; but, with the development of riding, it was necessary to invent a saddle. It is of some interest to note that whereas some sort of saddle was presumably known both to the Scythians and the Sarmatians, we have reason to believe that stirrups were known only to the Sarmatians. This shows that in Northern Turkistan, the true home of the horse and of horsemanship, there was a continuous development of horse trappings, even after the Scythians had departed for their new home in Southern Russia.[22]

Even more important than the invention of horse trappings was the effect which the custom of riding horseback had upon clothing. The most interesting of the changes in costume brought about in this way was the invention of trousers, the only costume which permitted free use of the legs while on horseback.

It is significant that trousers were completely unknown in the New World and in Australia prior to the coming of the White Man. They were equally unknown to the primitive cultures of Africa south of the Sahara. Of even greater interest is the fact that they were absent from all the great culture centers of antiquity.

Even in China, which is now so famous for its trouser culture, because of the fact that even women wear trousers, we find that in early times the clothing consisted of loose robes. It was not until the beginning of the third century B.C. that the Chinese first became acquainted with the use of trousers, and it was not until the seventh century A.D. that the use of trousers became at all common among them. We know from direct historical evidence that the adoption of trousers in China was directly due to culture influences radiating from Central Asia.

In India we find a similar development. Because of the fact that the early Indo-Iranian invaders of India were interested in driving rather than in riding, the Hindus in ancient times never adopted trousers; and even today trousers form no part of the true Hindu culture. It is only the Muhammadans of India, the inheritors of Iranian and Central Asian tradition, who make use of trousers to a considerable extent. Still farther to the West, we find that trousers were unknown to the ancient Sumerians, Babylonians, and Assyrians in Mesopotamia. They are still unknown to the true Bedouin Arabs of today. In view of what has been said, it is not surprising to find that trousers were unknown to the Egyptians and to the other early inhabitants of Northern Africa, but it is a little remarkable that they were never worn by either the Greeks or the Romans. The ancient Germans and, as far as we know, the ancient Slavs also used skirts or skin robes in place of trousers. In fact the only Europeans to use trousers in any form were the Celts.

Here again it is necessary to distinguish between the Celts of the British Isles and the continental Celts. The former continued to make use of the kilt, itself a continuation of the old prehistoric and pre-Indo-Germanic costume of Europe, while the latter were noted for their trousers, called by them *bracca,* from which we get, incidentally, our modern name of breeches. The Roman term *Galla Braccata,* the trouser-wearing Gauls, is an indication of the widespread use of trousers among the continental Celts. It was undoubtedly from the Celts that the Germans eventually learned the use of trousers.

In view of this ancient association of the Celts with trousers, it is very interesting that it is chiefly among the Celtic speaking persons of the British Isles that we find men who wear skirts. In view of this geographic distribution of costume among the early Celts, there can be no doubt but that the continental Celts adopted trousers only after and because of their long contact with the Scythians.[23]

Now that we have mentioned trousers it would be well to deal with one or two other features of the Scythian costume. We know, for example, that both the Scythians and Sarmatians made use of leather boots in contrast to the sandals worn in most of the older centers of civilization, and it is highly probable that the use of leather shoes and boots, like trousers, originated in Central Asia and slowly spread to the other parts of the world. The upper part of the body was covered by a coat or robe held together not by buttons but by a belt around the waist. This coat was worn very loose but had close fitting sleeves. Not infrequently the coat had sewn on it gold or bronze plaques by way of ornament. The head was covered by a cap. Among many of the tribes this cap was peaked or pointed at the top.[24]

An interesting point arises when we try to determine the materials out of which all these articles of clothing were made. In various ancient graves in Central Asia, a number of woven articles of clothing, made of wool, have been found; but the classical authors assure us positively that the Scythians were unacquainted with weaving, so that the woven material found in the graves was probably of Greek origin. The true Scytho-Sarmatian costume was made of skins and furs, cut and sewn together to give them the proper shape. For ordinary occasions the skins for these costumes were provided by the various rodents which swarmed all over the steppe country.[25]

In addition to ordinary clothing, the Scythians and Sarmatians were very fond of adorning themselves with jewelry, such as finger rings, bracelets, and neck-rings or torques. Earrings were also worn, though it seems that among the ancient Scythians as among many of the modern inhabitants of Central Asia, it was customary for the men to wear an earring only in one ear. For the most part these ornaments were made of gold and were of native workmanship. Those who could not afford gold ornaments made use of beads, either home-made of clay or stone, or of glass imported from the Mediterranean area.

To admire themselves in all this finery the Scythians (or was it only the Scythian women?) made use of very artistically designed bronze mirrors, many of them surprisingly like the metal mirrors found in early Chinese graves.[26]

In connection with clothing, a word should be said concerning the defensive armor worn by the Scythians and Sarmatians in time of war. This armor consisted chiefly of shields and breast plates. Frequent use was also made of helmets. In early times all of these articles were made of leather, but in later times this leather armoring was strengthened by having sewn on it scales of other material so as to form what is known as scale armor. The classical authors tell us that these scales were of horn or horses' hoofs, but archaeological research has shown that much of this scaled armor was made of bone, of bronze, and of iron. The scales were arranged like feathers and were sewn on to a leather or stuff backing. In later times, the horses as well as the men were provided with the scale armor.

It is worthy of note that the Sarmatians were far better equipped with scale armor than were the Scythians. This fact fits in very well with the theory that scale armor originated either in Southern Turkistan or on the Iranian Plateau and spread into Northern Turkistan only after the Scythians had left this region and taken up their residence in Southern Russia.[27]

Turning now from defensive to offensive weapons, we find that both the Scythians and Sarmatian were well-equipped with all of the then known implements of warfare. We know, for example, that they used battle axes, spears, and swords. The Scythian sword was short, little more than a dagger, while the typical Sarmatian sword was much longer. Otherwise, however, there was little difference between the weapons of the two peoples. Occasional use was made of the lasso and also of the sling, but neither of these two weapons ever played an important part in actual warfare.[28]

Far different was it with the bow and arrow. In fact, the bow and arrow may be regarded as the most important of all the weapons in use among the early inhabitants of Northern Turkistan and Southern Russia. Some of the Sarmatians seem to have made less use of the bow than the Scythians, but even among the Sarmatians the bow remained an integral and all-important part of military equipment.

These bows, though short, were very strong, being for the most part composite rather than single bows. The arrowheads were either of bone, of stone, of bronze, or of iron. Some of the Sarmatian tribes seem to have poisoned their arrowheads, but this custom was far from universal. In order to facilitate their transportation, they made use of a combined quiver and bow-case, called by the Greeks a *gorytus*. Many of these, beautifully ornamented, have been dug up in various Scythian graves. It was customary for the Scythians and Sarmatians to shoot their arrows from horseback, an art which awakened considerable astonishment among the neighboring peoples, who frequently referred to the Scythians not by name but as "the horse-bowmen." [29]

It was the Scythians who were chiefly responsible for the reintroduction of the bow and arrow as a popular weapon of offense among the various peoples of Europe and Asia. The bow is, of course, a very ancient weapon and one which, until modern times, was found in many different portions of the world. Considering this fact, it is rather remarkable that so many of the great military powers in early times made but scanty use of it. Most of the savage tribes of both North and South America were experts with bow and arrow, but the great empires that grew up in Peru and Mexico employed entirely different types of weapons.

The same thing is true of the Old World. Many of the barbarous peoples of Europe and Asia made use of the bow, but the vast mass of the soldiers of ancient China made use of other weapons. The bow was, of course, well-known to the Greeks and Romans. There were, in fact, special archers among the soldiers of both peoples, but the chief weapons remained the pike or javelin and the sword. Among the Germanic peoples, the bow was little used. In ancient times it was only in Egypt, Babylonia, and Assyria that the bow was at all common.

In contrast with this situation in early times, we find that in medieval China and in medieval Europe the bow again was of every great significance in military operations, and there is good ground for supposing that the revival of the popularity of the bow and arrow was due in no small part to influences radiating from Central Asia—if not from the Scythians proper, at least from the later inhabitants of this region who had inherited most of the Scythian traditions. There is one curious difference between the methods of warfare employed by the ancient Scythians and the medieval Europeans. The Scythians were both horsemen and archers, while the Europeans were either horsemen or archers. In Europe, as we know, the use of the bow and arrow was largely confined to the yeomen peasantry who fought on foot, while the mounted knights preferred to make use of the lance or sword. On this point, the European knights were in agreement with those Sarmatian tribes which, though well-acquainted with the bow, tended to make especial use of the lance and sword.

Speaking of some of these Sarmatian tribes, Tacitus, the great Roman historian, tells us "In the onset of cavalry they are . . . irresistable. Their weapons are long spears or swords of an enormous size which they wield with both hands. The chiefs wear coats of mail, formed with plates of iron or the tough hides of animals, impenetrable to the enemy but to themselves an incumbrance so unwieldy that he who falls in battle is never able to rise again." This description of the Sarmatians of the first century A.D. seems almost like a portrait of the European knights of the Middle Ages.[30]

Turning now to the domestic architecture of the Scytho-Sarmatians, we find that this represented one of the characteristic features of their culture. Being essentially nomads with no liking for cities and towns, or even for fixed habitations, the Scytho-Sarmatians were able to use neither the brick nor sun-dried brick architecture of Persia and China nor the wooden architecture characteristic of northern and western Europe; rather they used tents made of felt. Unfortunately none of the classical authors have given us adequate descriptions of the Scythian or Sarmatian tents so that we are left in some doubt as to their exact shape, but it is highly probable that the Scytho-Sarmatian tent dwelling was the direct ancestor of the type of tent now known under the name of *yurt* or *kibitka,* which is still the standard form of house architecture among the nomadic inhabitants of Central Asia.

This yurt is quite different from the conical "wigwam" tent found in Siberia and among many of the North American Indians. It is also very different from the square saddle back tents in use among the Tibetans and the Arabs. The yurt is cylindrical in shape and can best be compared in appearance with a small gas tank. "Its framework consists of a wooden lattice in six to ten separate divisions which can be widened out or pushed together for packing. Above this is the roof frame of light rafters which come together in a ring above."

In the modern yurt and in its prototype, the ancient Scythian tent, the lattice-work which serves as a frame is covered with felt. As Laufer has pointed out, the art of felt making is in all probability another culture trait diffused from Central Asia. It was unknown in pre-Columbian America. It has always been absent from Africa. Even in Egypt where sheep were reared and their wool woven into cloth, felt was never manufactured. Felt was known both to the Greeks and Romans on the one side of Central Asia and to the Chinese on the other, but neither in the West nor in the East did felt making assume important proportions. Among the Chinese, in fact, though the use of sheep was well-known, wool was almost never used for clothing. In Central Asia, on the other hand, from the days of the Scythians down to the present time felt making has always played an important part in native culture. For this reason, we may conclude that the art of felt making was first developed by the Scythians and Sarmatians.

It was, of course, essential to the Scythians and Sarmatians as steppe dwellers that their habitations be easily transportable. Among the modern inhabitants of Central Asia, this aim is achieved by having the yurts so constructed that they are easy to pull apart again. The wooden lattice-work and the felt covering fold into a very small space and hence can be carried on horseback with no great inconvenience.

In ancient times, among the Scythians and Sarmatians, portability was secured by mounting the tents on carts which, as we have said before, were usually drawn not by horses but by cattle. In many cases, the tents and the wagons were inseparable, so that a Scythian village was portable in a very strict sense of the word. It is probable, however, that in some cases the tents were so constructed that they could be transferred from the wagons to the ground.[31]

The furniture inside the Scytho-Sarmatian tents must have been simplicity itself, consisting for the most part only of felt mats or carpets. In some cases woven carpets took the place of the felt type. In fact, it seems likely that all woven carpets are merely a development of the felt variety, and that for the woven carpet we are indebted to the peoples of Central Asia, either to the Scythians and Sarmatians in the North or more likely the peoples with a somewhat higher degree of civilization inhabiting Southern Turkistan and the Iranian plateau.[32]

Before closing our discussion of the manners and customs of the ancient Scythians, a word must be said regarding their social organization. The Scythians and Sarmatians, like most of the other peoples of their times, excepting of course the inhabitants of some of the Greek states, were thoroughgoing monarchists and lived under the leadership of their rulers, some of whom, no doubt, were little more than petty tribal chieftains, while others were kings in every sense of the word. Unlike the early Germanic tribes, among whom the "chiefs" or "princes" frequently possessed very little real authority, these Scytho-Sarmatian rulers possessed a great deal of power over their fellow tribesmen. It was these rulers who divided the loot between the warriors after a successful battle. It was they who acted as judges in all cases of dispute. Some of them even objected to being considered ordinary mortals and claimed to be descended from some deity or other.[33]

Many of the Scytho-Sarmatian tribes lived in complete independence of all the other groups; but among the Scythians, at least, we know that a large, well-organized state existed for several centuries. This state included within its domains a large number of different tribes of Scythian origin in addition to holding in subjection a great many different groups of subject peoples. We know that this Scythian state was divided into four major provinces, and that each of these provinces was subdivided into a number of "nomes" or districts, each one of which was governed by a "nomarch" or governor. These nomarchs, in spite of their name, were in all probability not the appointed rulers of territorial districts but were rather hereditary chiefs of the various tribes or sub-tribes into which the Scythian "nation" was divided. This means that throughout its existence the Scythian Empire remained essentially feudal in composition.[34]

Succession to the national throne and to the leadership of each tribe was definitely on an hereditary basis, but we find no mention of the law of primogeniture. Any one of the sons could succeed his father; and, in view of what is known of the later peoples of Central Asia, it is probable that the succession in many cases passed not from father to son but from brother to brother. Not infrequently a ruler would divide his domain between his various sons, and in such cases it was not unusual for the youngest son to secure the lion's share of the legacy.[35]

It was the principal duty of these kings and tribal chieftains to lead their people in war, and Herodotus has several interesting things to tell us concerning the methods of warfare employed by the Scythians. The Scythians and Sarmatians were always essentially irregular cavalrymen and adopted the tactics best suited to cavalry. They avoided formal, pitched battles, retired willingly before the regular troops of any invader (since they had no towns or fields to defend), but were ever ready to harass the enemy on his flank or rear, to cut communications, and to prepare ambushes after enticing pursuit by means of pretended flights.

According to Herodotus, when a Scythian had slain an enemy, he immediately drank some of the blood of his fallen opponent. After this he cut off the head of his victim to use as a voucher in the allotment of booty. After this booty had been received, it was customary to scalp the severed head and preserve this scalp as a permanent memorial of martial enterprise. Not infrequently a good Scythian warrior collected such a large number of these scalps that he was able to make of them a whole cloak which he wore with a great deal of pride. Some warriors used the skin taken from the hands of their victims to cover their quivers and bow-cases; others preferred to stretch whole skins upon wooden frames and carry them about.

In addition to the use of these scalps and skins, it was a common Scythian custom, as we have seen, to make the skull of an enemy into a drinking cup. It was, moreover, the custom for the governor of each district to prepare once a year a ceremonial bowl of wine. A sip of this wine was given to each tribesman who had slain a man during the previous year. Those who had not killed an enemy were not allowed to drink, and were disgraced accordingly.[36]

A word should now be said regarding marriage and family life among the Scythians and Sarmatians. In contrast with several of the other primitive peoples of Europe and Asia who adopted a "mother-right" system, the Scytho-Sarmatian peoples from the time they are first known to us had a strongly entrenched patrilineal system whereby family descent was counted exclusively on the father's side; and in addition the paterfamilias had almost patriarchal control over the lives and property of all the members of his family.

Both the Scythians and Sarmatians permitted polygamy, and we know that many of the rulers and nobles had several wives, though it is probable that the stress of poverty kept the majority of the tribesmen monogamous. The polyandry of the Tibetans and some of the other later peoples of Central Asia (e.g. the Ephthalites) never seems to have affected the Scytho-Sarmatian culture, though we are told that some of the Sarmatian tribes inhabiting Northern Turkistan were extremely lax in their code governing sexual relations.

In the course of one of his stories, Herodotus tells us, incidentally, that one of the Scythian kings, after his father's death, married one of his step-mothers. This anecdote is of importance inasmuch as it shows that the Scytho-Sarmatians probably followed the custom, well known to have existed among the neighboring Huns in Mongolia, whereby a son was always privileged to take over as wives all the ladies of his father's harem, always excepting his own natural mother.[37]

Like many other primitive peoples, the Scythians believed that illness came not from natural causes but from "black magic" or a spell cast by some malicious person. Thus, for example, if a king became sick, it was believed that some person had sworn falsely by the royal hearth, thus calling down the ill will of the gods. In such a case, three medicine men or priest-wizards were called in, and by divination they attempted to discover the person who had cast the spell over the king. In most cases, the man thus accused by the wizards was found guilty and beheaded, his goods being distributed among the wizards, irrespective of whether or not the king recovered from his illness. Occasionally, by appealing to other wizards, the accused was able to demonstrate his innocence, in which case it was the custom to put the accusing wizards to death.

The execution of the wizards on such occasions was carried out in a rather peculiar fashion. A wagon drawn by oxen was loaded with brushwood. The wizards, tightly bound and with their mouths gagged, were thrust into this brushwood which was then set alight. The oxen, startled by this fire, rushed off into the surrounding plains. Sometimes both the wizards and the oxen were burned together, but other times the oxen managed to break away from the blazing wagon and escaped with only a scorching. When for any reason one of these wizards was put to death, it was customary not to let any of his sons survive; all the male offspring were slain with the father; only the females were allowed to live.

When an ordinary tribesman died, his nearest of kin laid the deceased upon a wagon and took him around to all of his friends in succession. Each friend received the funeral cortege with great ceremony and prepared a banquet for the occasion. At these feasts, the corpse was always served with a portion of all that was set before the others. This feasting went on for forty days, after which the burial took place. Shortly after the burial, all persons who had had any contact with the corpse were forced to undergo a ceremonial purification.

A small felt tent was erected on the ground. Inside this tent a dish containing red-hot stones was placed. One by one the Scythians went inside this tent, holding in their hands some hemp seeds. These seeds were thrown on the hot stones, thereby causing a thick vapor to arise, a vapor such as no Greek (or Turkish) bath could exceed. Incidentally, this ceremonial purification was the only type of ablution known to the Scythians, as they never, under any circumstances, washed their bodies with water.

The funeral of a royal personage was a much more elaborate affair. First of all the corpse was embalmed and then placed on a special wagon to be taken on a ceremonial tour through many of the Scythian tribes. When the funeral cortege reached the geographical limits of any tribe, the tribesmen, to express their grief, were expected to lacerate themselves in various ways. The hair was shorn off, and in addition it was customary to cut off a piece of the ear, to scratch the forehead and nose, and to thrust an arrow through the left hand.

After this ceremonial tour, the corpse was at last brought to the special district where it was customary to bury all persons of royal blood. Here a grave was dug, square in shape and of enormous size. The body was placed in the grave, stretched upon a carpet. Spears were placed in the ground on either side of the corpse and beams stretched across the tops so as to form a roof which was covered by a thatching of twigs.

In the open space around the corpse, if the corpse happened to be a king, it was customary to bury one of the royal concubines who was specially strangled on this occasion. It was also customary to kill and bury in or near the royal tomb several other persons who had served the deceased king, such as his cupbearer, his cook, his groom, and his body servant. Some of the royal horses were also slaughtered and placed near the entrance of the tomb. After this had been done, the Scythian tribesmen set to work and raised a vast mound over the grave, all of them vying with one another and seeking to make it as tall as possible. Even these elaborate rites did not quite complete the funeral ceremonies. They were concluded a year after the death of the king, when fifty slaves and fifty horses were slaughtered and placed around the royal tomb.

The funerals described by Herodotus in such great detail refer only to the Scythians, but it is probable that many if not all of the Sarmatian peoples went in for similar practices. It should, however, be noted that, according to Herodotus, some of the Sarmatian peoples, who in his time still inhabited Northern Turkistan, sometimes ate instead of burying the bodies of the dead. Among the Massagetae, he asserts, it was customary not to wait for aged persons to die a natural death but to aid their demise in a very efficient manner. When a man grew old, all of his kinsfolk gathered together and offered him up in sacrifice, offering also some cattle at the same time. After the sacrifice, they boiled the flesh, both human and animal, and feasted upon it. Those who thus met their end were reckoned the happiest. If a man died of disease, they did not eat him, but buried him in the ground, bewailing not their, but his ill-fortune. This is a very interesting story, but it must not be forgotten that Herodotus had much more intimate knowledge concerning the Scythians than he had regarding the Sarmatian Massagetae, and it may well be that his stories regarding the latter were based upon unfounded rumors.[38]

The story of the Scythian burial customs leads us to a description of the religious beliefs and customs prevalent among the Scytho-Sarmatian peoples, though it must be admitted that we have little accurate information on this subject. We know from Herodotus that the Scythians were polytheists, worshipping a number of different gods and goddesses, and it is probable that the same thing was true of the different Sarmatian peoples, though the Massagetae, undoubtedly due to Persian influence, worshipped only the sun god. It is rather curious to find that, among the Scythians, the highest honors were paid not to a male but to a female deity, the supreme mother goddess, Tabiti. It is, however, probable that this deity had no place in the original Scythian pantheon, and that her worship was due to influences emanating from Asia Minor where the mother goddess, at an early period, was all-important.

Next in importance to the mother goddess was a father god, corresponding to the Roman Jupiter or the Greek Zeus and called by the Scythians, Papoeus, probably only a variation of the native word for father. The only other deity to play an important part in the Scythian pantheon was the god of war, corresponding to the Roman Mars or the Greek Ares.

In the early days, at least, the Scythians made no use of images in their worship of the gods, though animal sacrifices were frequently made to their divinities. The animal was invariably strangled so as to prevent the shedding of blood. In spite of the frequency of these sacrifices, there was a complete absence of altars and temples except for the peculiar altars erected in honor of the god of war. One of these altars was placed in the center of each district. It consisted merely of a great pile of brushwood with a square platform on top. Three sides of the huge altar were perpendicular, while the fourth was sloping so that persons might walk up it. An iron sword was planted on the top of these altars and served as the representation of the god of war.

Each year numerous sacrifices of cattle and of horses were made at these altars. But in addition to animals, it was also customary to make human sacrifices; libations of wine were first poured over the heads of the victims, after which they were slaughtered over a bowl so that none of the blood might be wasted. This bowl was then taken to the top of the altar and the blood poured over the sacred sword. The right hands and arms of the victims were then cut off and tossed high into the air.

It is obvious that the oaths taken by the Scythians had some peculiar religious significance. When a solemn oath had to be taken, a large earthen bowl was filled with wine; then the parties to the oath, wounding themselves slightly, let some of their blood drop into the wine. They then plunged into the mixture a sword, some arrows, a battle-axe, and a spear, all the while repeating prayers. Finally each of the contracting parties drank a draught from the bowl, and the oath was thereby sealed.

It is probable that control over religious matters rested in the hands of the wizards or soothsayers, whom we have already had occasion to mention. It seems, however, that among the Scythians there were two sorts of wizards. One, which we may call the normal type, in addition to their other activities, foretold the future by manipulating a bundle of willow wands. The other type of wizard included a special class of persons, called Enareans or Women-men by Herodotus, who were probably homosexuals. The members of this group dedicated themselves to the service of the goddess of love. They too went in for fortune telling; but, in place of the willow wands, they made use of the inner bark of the linden tree. Taking a piece of this bark, they split it into three strips; and, while turning and unturning these strips around their fingers, they made their prophecies concerning future events.[39]

We cannot conclude our discussion of the Scythians and Sarmatians without a brief word concerning their art. Though a people essentially barbaric in many respects, archaeology has shown us that they possessed a very high artistic sense, and some of the most beautiful objects from the antique world have been dug up from Scythian and Sarmatian graves. Some of these objects were of Greek workmanship, or at least of Greek inspiration, but many others differ radically from all Greek models and were undoubtedly produced by native artisans, inspired by their own native traditions. Some of these traditions may prove to have had their ultimate origin in Iran and Mesopotamia, but at least the Scythians and Sarmatians so modified these original stimuli as to produce for themselves an entirely new type of art.

Most of these Scythian art objects consist of gold ornaments which were attached either to clothing or to horse trappings. These ornaments are characterized by a very peculiar type of animal design. Sometimes the designs are highly naturalistic, and the animals portrayed are easily identified. Among the animals most commonly portrayed are the lion, the reindeer, the elk, the wolf, and the horse. Sometimes the animals are imaginary, as the griffin, and not infrequently the real animals are so conventionalized as to be little more than heraldic designs. Not uncommon is the use of two or more animals in mortal combat. From the mass of evidence now before us, it seems highly probable that this Scytho-Sarmatian animal style spread to all parts of the ancient world and had an important effect not only upon European art but upon the art of ancient China.

The later Scythian and especially the Sarmatian art was characterized by another important feature, which is usually called the polychrome style, by which is meant the use of a plain gold background in which were inset a number of different colored stones in such a way as to form a definite design. This polychrome style never appealed to the Chinese, but it was of the greatest importance in the later art of Persia and India. At present it is impossible to determine whether this style spread from Iran to Central Asia or from Central Asia to Iran, but there was undoubtedly a close affiliation between the art motifs of the two regions. Of even greater interest is the fact that this polychrome style spread from the Sarmatians westward to Europe and greatly affected the European art designs throughout the early Middle Ages.[40]

CHAPTER THREE

BACTRIANS AND SOGDIANS IN THE SOUTH

The Bactrians and other Inhabitants of Southern Turkistan—Their Relation to the Scythians and Persians—The Early History of Bactria—The Rise of the Achaemenid Empire and its Conquest of Bactria—The Conquest of Bactria by Alexander the Great—Bactria under the Selucid Empire—The Rise of the Bactrian and Parthian Kingdoms—The Later History of Bactria and Parthia—Bactria and Zoroastrianism—Iranian Culture as Portrayed in the Avesta.

DURING THE long period that Southern Russia and Northern Turkistan were inhabited by the Scythians and Sarmatians, Southern Turkistan continued to be occupied by a number of quite different peoples, the most important of whom were the Khwarazmians, the Sogdians, and the Bactrians. It was the Bactrians who played the major role during this early period of history, for which reason the whole of Southern Turkistan during this era is frequently, though rather erroneously, referred to as Bactria or Bactriana.

Throughout the greater part of early history there was almost constant enmity between the inhabitants of Northern Turkistan and of Southern Turkistan (comparable to the enmity which long exists between the Lowland Scotch and the English), but this conflict must not blind us to the fact that the inhabitants of both regions originally belonged to the same stock and remained closely affiliated as regards race and language. The Bactrians and Sogdians, like the Scythians and Sarmatians, consisted essentially of a mixture of the various White Races. Like the Scythians and Sarmatians, they also spoke Iranian dialects closely allied to the language which we know as classical Persian, although it is probable that the Bactrians and their immediate neighbors, having less contact with non-Iranian peoples, kept their language more pure than the adventurous Scythians and Sarmatians who were constantly conquering and intermingling with peoples speaking a different tongue.[1]

Even as regards their cultural life, there were many important features common to the peoples inhabiting Northern Turkistan and Southern Turkistan. This community of culture extended also to the various peoples inhabiting the Iranian Plateau, such as the Medes and the Persians. Among the culture traits common to these regions are many of the features that constituted such an important and distinctive element in the life of the Scythians and Sarmatians—the riding rather than the driving of horses, the habit of shooting arrows from horseback, and the wearing of trousers. When one remembers that all these features are lacking in the early civilization of India, it becomes obvious that they are features resulting from special developments among the Iranian peoples and shared in by practically all persons speaking Iranian languages.[2]

But though there were a great many points of similarity and even of identity between what we may call the Northern Iranians and Southern Iranians, there were also many important points of divergence; and, on most of the points whereon the Bactrians and their neighbors differed from the Scythians and Sarmatians, we find that they were in essential agreement with the inhabitants of the Iranian Plateau. It is probable that this similarity was in existence at an early date and was due to a close correspondence in the economic life of the inhabitants of Southern Turkistan and the Iranian Plateau, but it is certain that this similarity was strengthened by the fact that for a lengthy period Southern Turkistan was closely related politically with the Persian Empire and its successors.

The Northern Iranians, that is the Scythians and Sarmatians, though subjected to many alien influences, yet succeeded in maintaining their political independence until long after the beginning of the Christian era, and once conquered they completely disappeared from history. The Eastern Iranians, however, that is the Bactrians and Sogdians in Southern Turkistan, together with several closely related groups in the eastern portion of the Iranian Plateau, were destined to have a very different political history inasmuch as they were soon incorporated in the great centralized empire which arose in the western part of the Iranian Plateau. Though Bactria was early a great culture center,[3] it was never more than a petty kingdom from the political point of view; and it was the Western Iranians, the Medes and the Persians, who first succeeded in creating political units large enough and important enough to merit mention in world history.

This fact need cause no surprise. Both the Medes and the Persians had long lived in close proximity to the great culture centers of Mesopotamia, such as the Elamite Kingdom, and the Babylonian and Assyrian empires. The Medes were for a time directly subject to the Assyrians, while the Persians (i.e., the inhabitants of Pers, the modern province of Fars) were equally exposed to western civilization. As a result both the Median and the Persian Empires were modeled in large measure upon the earlier Mesopotamian prototypes.

Among all the various Iranian peoples, it was the Medes who first succeeded in forming a really important empire. After 612 B.C., when Assyria was conquered, Media with its capital at Ecbatana (the modern

Hamadan), was a political unit of great historic significance and of vast extent, but we have no reason to believe that this Median Empire ever succeeded in dominating Eastern Iran or Southern Turkistan.[4]

When, however, after a very brief existence Media fell, and Cyrus (who reigned 558-529 B.C.), the king of the Persians, succeeded in establishing the great Achemenid Empire, the political jurisdiction of the Western Iranians became enormously extended. After Cyrus had conquered Asia Minor and before he invaded Babylonia, he turned his attention to the east and northeast. Not content with conquering the eastern portion of the Iranian Plateau, he invaded Southern Turkistan and brought the Bactrians, Sogdians, and Khwarazmians within the limits of his empire. On the banks of the distant Jaxartes River (the Sir Darya of modern times) he established a city, called by the Greeks Cyropolis, as a bulwark against the wild Sarmatian tribes of the north.

Tradition has it that Cyrus eventually met his death while fighting against the Massagetae, one of these Sarmatian peoples, and as a result of this tragedy, all attempts to conquer the nomadic Sarmatians were abandoned. But Cambyses, the son and heir of Cyrus, seems to have had no difficulty in retaining control over Bactria and the other agricultural regions in Southern Turkistan. However, in the troubles following the death of Cambyses, it seemed for the moment as if the newly established Achemenid or Persian Empire had come to an untimely end. Province after province revolted and secured its independence, and we have good grounds for supposing that the Eastern Iranians also succeeded in breaking away from Persian control.[5]

Before long, however, under the brilliant reign of Darius the Great (521-485 B.C.), the Achemenid Empire was reëstablished in all of this pristine glory. All of the provinces which had once acknowledged the overlordship of Cyrus and Cambyses were again brought under Persian control, and in addition several new regions were added to the Persian Empire.[6] In the old Persian rock inscriptions, erected by Darius, we find a list of the satrapies or provinces into which the Persian Empire was divided at this period. Among these provinces are the names Bactria, Sogdia, and Khwarazmia, clear proof that during the reign of Darius all of Southern Turkistan was again incorporated with the Persian Empire.[7]

The Persian supremacy over this region was now so well established that it did not again disappear until the Achemenid Empire itself came to an end, though there are indications of occasional revolts, and it is possible that in later times Persian control over the outlying regions was more nominal than real. We know that in the army assembled by Xerxes, the successor of Darius, the Bactrians, the Sogdians, and the

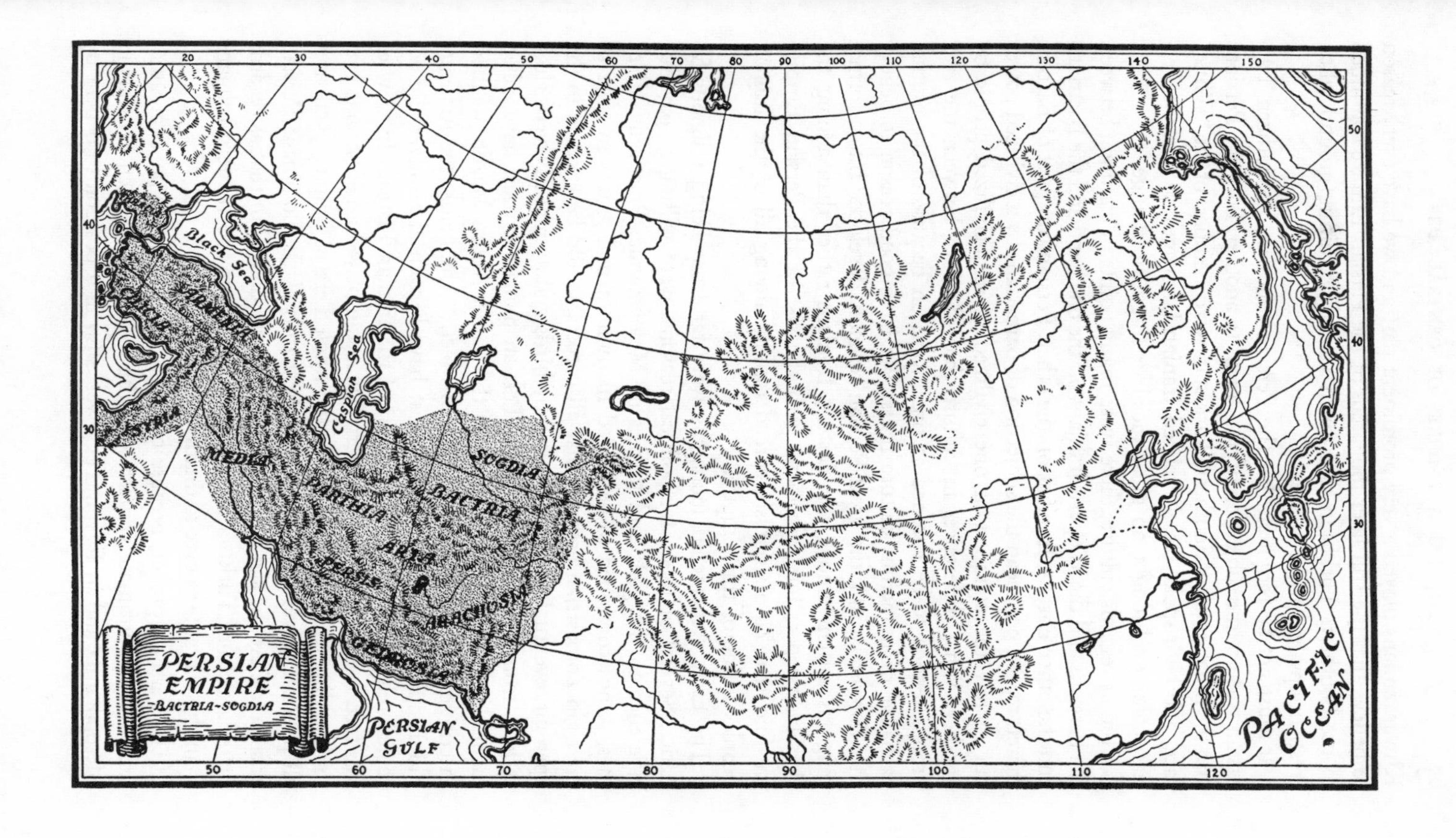
PERSIAN
EMPIRE
BACTRIA-SOGDIA
Black Sea
Caspian Sea
ARMENIA
CILICIA
SYRIA
MEDIA
PARTHIA
SOGDIA
BACTRIA
ARIA
PERSIS
ARACHOSIA
GEDROSIA
PERSIAN
GULF
PACIFIC
OCEAN

Khwarazmians played a very prominent part and we have every reason to believe that the still later monarchs of the Persian Empire continued to use Southern Turkistan as a much valued recruiting ground when fresh troops had to be secured.[8]

It must not be forgotten that the Persian conquest of Southern Turkistan was not the subjection of one "race" to another. Both the Persians and the inhabitants of Southern Turkistan were members of the "White" race, and both spoke closely related Iranian languages, so that the Persian conquest brought no great racial or linguistic change.

Even as regards culture, there were many points in common between the Persians and the Western Iranians on the one hand and the Bactrians and the other Eastern Iranians on the other. Persian conquest of Bactria, therefore, did not mean the subjection of barbarians by a civilized power but merely the conquest of one civilized or semi-civilized people by another. What differences in culture that did exist between the two groups tended to be lessened as time went on because of the mutual exchange of numerous culture traits. We have good reason to believe that Zoroastrianism, the great Persian religion, developed into a formal religious system among the Eastern Iranians rather than among the Persians proper; but coincident with the rise of the Persian Empire we find that Zoroastrianism spread rapidly among all of the Iranian peoples inside of this Empire.[9]

The early Achemenid monarchs were far from being religious fanatics. Several of them, for political reasons, were willing to pay due reverence to the gods and images of Mesopotamia. Practically all of these kings continued to be buried in monumental graves in spite of the rigid Zoroastrian precepts that all corpses should be exposed to the open air, eventually to be devoured by birds and animals. Nevertheless, at least from Darius onwards, the Persian monarchs must have called themselves Zoroastrians; the use of the name, Ahura Mazda, in their inscriptions is sufficient evidence of this fact.[10] And before the Achemenid Empire fell Zoroastrianism must have become the universally accepted religion of all the inhabitants of the Iranian Plateau. In view of this fact, it is obvious that Southern Turkistan played an enormous part in moulding the general culture of the whole Persian Empire, even after all political power had passed into the hands of the dominant Persian aristocracy. At the same time, there can be no doubt but that as regards material culture Turkistan received far more from the Western Iranians than she was able to give to them.

The Persians proper, because of their geographic and political situation, were in intimate contact with the high cultures then existing in Mesopotamia and in Egypt. They were also in a position to benefit by cultural exchanges with Greece, which was already developing a high civilization. The result of all these culture influences is clearly seen in the ruins of Persepolis, the favorite residence of the Achemenid monarchs. Here we find the extensive use of stone and of fluted columns, borrowed from Egypt, side by side with many architectural motives, such as the use of steps, and glazed brickware, borrowed directly from Assyria. The Persian system of writing was also of Mesopotamian origin.

Herodotus tells us that the Persians were noted for their willingness to borrow and use all manner of things from their neighbors so that we need not be surprised at the highly composite nature of Persian civilization. We must certainly believe that many of the culture traits which the Persians borrowed from their civilized neighbors made their way to the inhabitants of Eastern Iran and Southern Turkistan, though unfortunately we have as yet very little evidence upon which to base this belief, because of the fact that up to the present archaeologists have given scant attention to this problem. In any event, it cannot be denied that the Persian occupation of Southern Turkistan forms a most important epoch in the historical development of this region.[11]

Scarcely less significant were the results of the Alexandrian conquest. Alexander the Great not only destroyed the Persian Empire by capturing its capitals and forcing its king, Darius III, the last of the Achemenids, to flee; but he also personally directed a lengthy expedition into Southern Turkistan. After the fall of Darius, a man called Bessus who was Satrap or Governor of Bactria declared himself king and set out to create for himself a new empire in which he hoped to include all of the Eastern Iranians. This action excited the wrath of Alexander, and he determined to crush the new kingdom before it had time to consolidate its position. Alexander was already in Eastern Iran, in what is now Afghanistan, and early in 329 B.C. he marched rapidly northward. Crossing the Paropanisus or Hindukush Mountains, he descended into Bactria and before long made himself master of Balkh, its capital and principal city.

Terrified by the approach of Alexander, Bessus, the would-be founder of the new kingdom of the Eastern Iranians, fled northward and, crossing the Oxus River (the modern Amu Darya), took refuge in the province of Sogdia; but even here he was not safe from Alexander's all powerful armies. Although Bessus had burned all available boats, the youthful conqueror by means of skins filled with reeds succeeded in getting his army safely across the Oxus and advanced rapidly into Sogdia. So impressed were the Sogdian nobility by Alexander's prowess that they attempted to forestall further trouble by seizing Bessus and dragging him into the Macedonian camp.

Bessus, of course, was duly executed, but even this event did not satisfy Alexander's ambition. Continuing his march into Sogdia, he soon captured Maracanda, the modern Samarkand, then the capital of this province. He next advanced to the banks of the Jaxartes River, the old frontier of the Persian Empire, and there established a new city near the modern city of Khujand. Like so many other cities founded by the Macedonian conqueror, this new settlement was called Alexandria. Crossing over the Jaxartes River, he routed the nomadic Saka tribesmen and forced their chiefs to tender their submission. But even Alexander, like his Persian predecessors in this region, found that it was impossible to establish a stable government in the heart of the nomad country, and he soon returned to the settled provinces of Sogdia and Bactria.

The course of events forced Alexander to remain in Southern Turkistan the whole of the following year (328 B.C.). Serious rebellion broke out in Sogdia, and it was necessary to crush these before he could proceed elsewhere. It was also necessary to reduce, one by one, a number of isolated mountain strongholds which had hitherto stood out against Macedonian domination. It was in connection with the capture of one of these strongholds that Alexander met and later married a young Bactrian noblewoman named Roxane. It was this Roxane who was the mother of Alexander's only legitimate child.

It is clear from Alexander's actions in Southern Turkistan that his aim was not mere casual conquest but rather thoroughgoing and permanent annexation. In accordance with his usual plan, the young conqueror established in the principal cities of this region numerous colonists, especially brought from Europe. Some of these colonists were Macedonians, but the vast majority were Greeks from the old centers of Hellenic civilization. When in 327 B.C. Alexander marched southward and embarked upon the conquest of India, he took care to leave behind him not only these civilian colonists but also ten thousand foot soldiers and three thousand cavalrymen to serve as a permanent garrison.[12]

Alexander's conquest of Southern Turkistan was destined to have far-reaching results, for, although the Macedonian World-Empire broke up immediately after Alexander's death, Greek influence was to remain the most important factor in Turkistan for over two hundred years and indirectly was able to affect the cultural life of all Central Asia for several additional centuries.

Following Alexander's death in 323 B.C., there was a wild scramble for power between the principal generals in the Macedonian army.[13]

After several years of fighting (in 312 B.C. to be exact), one of these generals, Seleucus, managed to make himself master of by far the greater part of the Macedonian possessions in Asia. Starting with control over Syria and Mesopotamia, he rapidly extended his control over the Iranian Plateau, and before long the Satraps of Bactria and Sogdia were forced to submit themselves to his jurisdiction. As a result of these conquests all of Southern Turkistan was definitely incorporated in the Seleucid Empire, and the fortune of this region came to depend upon the orders issued from the two Seleucid capitals, one of which was at Seleucia in Mesopotamia, and the other at the even more distant city of Antioch in Syria. The bonds uniting Turkistan with the Greek world thus became stronger than ever.[14]

The empire carved out by Seleucus remained intact for several decades, but during the reign of Antiochus II (261-246 B.C.), the grandson of Seleucus, there was a great weakening of the Seleucid Empire. Though Antiochus gave himself the title of Theos, or "The Divine," he was notable only for his love of luxury and debauchery. He neglected all matters of state, and his favorites, both male and female, had almost complete control over the conduct of public affairs. It is not surprising, therefore, that during his reign several of the outlying provinces of the Seleucid Empire broke out in rebellion and managed to secure their independence.[15]

The most notable of these rebellions was that started in 256 B.C. by Diodotus or Theodotus, the satrap of Bactria or, as he is usually called, Governor of the Thousand Cities of Bactria. As a result of this rebellion, Diodotus succeeded in making himself an independent monarch. The Bactrian kingdom which he established included not only Bactria proper but also the province of Sogdia and much of what is now Afghanistan. Diodotus himself was a Greek, and practically all of the governing class in the Bactrian monarchy were of Greek descent so that the establishment of this new kingdom, though of great political importance, did not involve any cultural change. Southeastern Turkistan remained as much as ever subjected to Greek tradition.

Only a few years later, however (247 B.C.), Southwestern Turkistan and the adjoining regions of the Iranian Plateau underwent a revolution which was of the greatest significance both from the political and cultural point of view. It was at this time that a group of nomadic warriors from the steppes of Central Asia, called the Parnae, led by a chifetain called Arsak, overran Southwestern Turkistan and then, mounting the Iranian Plateau, overthrew the Seleucid governor of the province of Parthia, the modern Persian province of Khurasan, and established an independent principality of their own.

These nomadic warriors took the name of Parthians after the name of the province they conquered and which they made the center of their administration, but it must not be forgotten that they originated far to the north, on the plains of Northern Turkistan. The classical authors, in fact, tell us that the Parnae were merely a branch of the Dahae who were in turn a branch of the Massagetae. This, of course, means that the Parnae belonged to the group of peoples that we have called Sarmatians, the Iranian nomads of the north.[16]

The revolt of the Bactrians and the Parthians meant that all of Southern Turkistan and most of Eastern Iran was definitely detached from the Seleucid Empire. The loss of so vast a region must have been a bitter blow to the Seleucid monarchs, but for several years they were so troubled by affairs in the western portion of their empire that they could not undertake a systematic campaign against either the Parthians or the Bactrians, both of whom, being left to themselves, managed to strengthen and consolidate their position in preparation for any attempt at reconquest which the Seleucid monarchs might later make.

In 237 B.C. one such attempt at reconquest was actually made. But on this occasion the Seleucid ruler, Seleucus II, was decisively beaten by a Parthian army and, before he could call up fresh forces and arrange for a new campaign, further troubles developed in the western portion of his empire. As a result of these disturbances, he was forced to abandon all hope of reëstablishing Seleucid supremacy over the Parthian and Bactrian domains.[17]

Three decades later (209-206 B.C.) the Seleucids renewed their attempt to regain their lost provinces in the east and this time with somewhat greater success. Led by Antiochus III, usually called "The Great," the Seleucids managed to invade Parthia and capture the Parthian capital at Hecatompylos. When the Parthian king fled northward and took refuge in Southwestern Turkistan, Antiochus immediately marched into this region and secured a number of fresh victories. Nevertheless, the Seleucid monarch must have felt that it was impossible entirely to suppress the Parthian state, and at the end of his campaign we find him acknowledging Parthian autonomy under its native monarch, though the latter was forced to render rich tribute and admit Seleucid overlordship.

A similar result attended the campaign against Bactria, which Antiochus proceeded to invade after settling Parthian affairs. In Bactria the dynasty founded by Diodotus had been replaced by a ruler named Euthydemus, another person of Greek descent. Euthydemus made a valiant attempt to protect his kingdom from invasion, but he was defeated in several battles and at last was forced to stand a lengthy seige in his capital at Balkh.

It is probable that Antiochus, had he persisted, could have starved the defenders of Balkh into submission; but, becoming wearied with the campaign, he eventually offered Euthydemus favorable terms and they were at once accepted. Antiochus permitted the Bactrian monarch to retain his government with the title of King, but the latter was to acknowledge Seleucid supremacy and to agree to an offensive and defensive alliance with the Seleucid Empire. The Bactrians were further forced to provide Antiochus with ample provisions for his army and for all their battle elephants. To cement the treaty a marriage was arranged between the son of the Bactrian King and a daughter of the Seleucid Emperor. The favorable terms granted to the Bactrian monarch were largely the result of the latter's representations that a strong Bactria was needed to keep in check the Sakas and other northern nomads who were a perpetual threat to all civilization in this region.[18]

As a result of Antiochus' successful campaigns in Southern Turkistan and Eastern Iran, it seemed as if all this region was to remain for an indefinite period under Seleucid control. Both Parthia and Bactria, to be sure, remained autonomous, but both definitely acknowledged Seleucid supremacy, and both were forced to offer heavy tribute to the Seleucid court. It was not long, however, before all of the results achieved by Antiochus' campaigns in the east were rendered null and void. Antiochus himself was decisively defeated by the Romans in 190 B.C., and with this defeat the prestige and glory of the Seleucid Empire departed forever.[19] The successors of Antiochus upon the Seleucid throne were all comparatively weak men, and what energies they possessed were devoted to contending with the Romans and Jews in the west. It was impossible to devote any serious attention to the east with the result that both Bactria and Parthia were soon able to reëstablish their complete independence. Not content with this regained independence, both countries embarked upon a career of conquest, and in the course of a few decades had developed from small and relatively insignificant kingdoms into large and powerful empires.

The fate of Bactria during this period is of especial interest to us.[20] It is certain that at no time did the Greeks constitute more than a comparatively small minority in the kingdom of Bactria, for the vast majority of the population of this region were Iranian in origin and continued to speak Persian or rather the Bactrian and Sogdian dialects of Persian. The Greeks did, however, manage to give a Hellenic veneer to the whole country, but only because they occupied all of the higher administrative and military posts, and because most of the cities were modeled on the Greek plan.

The shepherds and farmers, the inhabitants of the countryside and the villages, were Iranians; but most of the cities were dominated by the Greek colonists who brought with them their language, their religion, their institutions, their drama, and their art. There were about a dozen such cities in Bactria, founded either by Alexander or the early Seleucids, and each one of them was a center radiating Greek civilization in all directions. It was undoubtedly these cities that gave a Greek tone to the whole kingdom.

The Bactrian army was largely recruited from the Greek population, but this very fact was ominous for the continuance of Greek control over Central Asia. Every battle fought meant the death of hundreds of men, and this in turn meant that the Greek element in the population, never every large, rapidly diminished. If it had been possible to secure fresh colonists or military recruits from the Greek motherland, all would have been well, but this course of action was rendered impossible by various factors, the most important of which was the fact that the non-Greek kingdom of the Parthians formed a geographic wedge between Bactria and the Greek motherland to the west.

In spite of all these handicaps, the Greek rulers of Bactria became wedded to a policy of political aggrandizement, and in a remarkably short time they were able to double the size of their kingdom. The rising strength of the Parthian kingdom made it impossible for the Bactrians to do much in the west, so that most of their campaigns were directed to the east. It is very possible that they secured some sort of control over the city states which then existed in Kashgaria or Chinese Turkistan, but concerning this matter we have no exact information. It is, however, certain that between 190 and 180 B.C. the Bactrians invaded and conquered a large portion of Northwestern India. The leader of the Bactrian armies on this occasion was Demetrius, the eldest son and heir of Euthydemus. As a result of these conquests, the Bactrian kingdom included all of Southeastern Turkistan, all of Afghanistan, and a large portion of Northern India.[21]

Had they been able to retain unified control over all of this area, Demetrius and his successors would have been among the most powerful rulers of the ancient world, but unfortunately the Bactrian Greeks, like the European Greeks, were much given to political intrigue, and in 175 B.C., only a few years after the conquest of India, a general named Eucratides who had remained behind in Bactria rose in revolt and managed to secure for himself a large portion of the Bactrian domain.

Thereafter, there were two rival and bitterly hostile Bactrian dynasties. One of them, consisting of the descendants of Demetrius, continued to rule over a good portion of India; while the other dynasty, consisting of Eucratides and his heirs, continued to rule over Bactria proper and the surrounding regions. This tendency to dissolution, once started, was difficult to stop. Before long both branches of the Bactrian Empire broke up into a number of sub-kingdoms, each of them independent and each of them bitterly hostile to the others. This disintegration was a death blow to all hopes of maintaining Greek political supremacy in the east, but it did not prevent the Graeco-Bactrians from making a deep and lasting impression upon the cultural life of all the regions they occupied. This was true not only of Bactria and Eastern Iran but also of Northern India.

We have definite archaeological evidence of the enormous influence which Greek art exercised upon the art, especially the religious art, of Northern India. A special school of art, the Gandhara school, grew up on the borders of Bactria and India, a school reflecting all the technique of the Greeks but devoted to the service of the Buddhist religion. This school continued to hold sway over Buddhist painting and sculpture for many centuries; and, when Buddhism eventually spread over the whole of Central Asia and into China, it carried with it this Gandhara school of art. Even in the paintings of the fifth and sixth centuries A.D. in Kashgaria or Eastern Turkistan, Greek influence is still clearly traceable.[22]

While the Bactrian monarchs were extending their sway over India and other regions in the east, the Parthians devoted most of their attention to expansion in the west. The real founder of the Parthian Empire as contrasted with the Parthian Kingdom was Mithradates I who reigned from 173-138 B.C. Up to this time, the Parthians had ruled over a relatively small domain, consisting principally of Southwestern Turkistan and the province of Parthia proper in Northeastern Iran. Even in this region Parthian supremacy had always been extremely insecure. But when Mithradates came to the throne, he immediately began a long series of wars as a result of which Parthia became a serious contendant for world supremacy. Early in his career he became embroiled with the Graeco-Bactrian rulers who lived to the east of him and managed to wrest from them several important cities, such as Margiana, the modern Merv, and Aria, the modern Herat.

Far more important, however, were the campaigns which Mithradates undertook against the Seleucids in the west. At this time the Seleucids still had control over all of Western Iran, including the province of Media in the north and Pers in the south. Mithradates not only conquered all this region but in addition invaded and secured possession of Mesopotamia, driving the Seleucids west of the Euphrates. Thereafter the Seleucid Empire consisted of little more than Syria.[23]

The Seleucids made one great effort to reconquer the eastern portion of their empire. Their monarch, Demetrius II, raised a huge army and succeeded in winning several victories over the Parthians, but before long (in 140 B.C.) the wily Mithradates succeeded in catching his opponent off his guard, with the result that Demetrius was not only defeated but was taken prisoner. A few years later (129 B.C.), the Seleucids made a final attempt to recover their power on the Iranian Plateau, but once again they met with disaster, the Seleucid monarch, Antiochus VII, being killed and his army scattered. With this event, all hope of reëstablishing Greek supremacy over the Iranian east was forever shattered.[24]

The later history of the Parthians is of no especial interest to us.[25] Altogether the Parthian Empire endured for over five centuries (247 B.C.-A.D. 226), but for the most part our knowledge of Parthian history is amazingly scanty. The line of their kings is long and confused. Many of them are known to us only because of their coins. The chief interest centers in the conflicts between the Parthians and the Romans who had taken over the heritage of the Seleucids and their policy of Hellenization. Many of the greatest of the Romans—Pompey, Crassus, Mark Antony, Trajan, and Marcus Aurelius—were involved in the repeated attempts of the Romans to break the power of the Parthians. In spite of constant internal discord among the Parthians, Rome was never able to inflict a decisive defeat upon its eastern rival. Crassus and Mark Antony, in fact, were themselves defeated; Crassus was killed, and his head was brought before the Parthian king.

Trajan did succeed in pushing the Parthians out of Mesopotamia and for a brief moment established Roman supremacy all along the Tigris and Euphrates, but the Romans found that they had bitten off more than they could chew, and within a year the frontiers of the Roman Empire were once more brought back to Syria. Even in A.D. 217, only ten years before the downfall of the Parthian dynasty, Artabanus, the last of the Parthian kings, signally defeated a Roman army that had been sent against him.[26]

And yet the Parthian kingdom which mustered almost incredible strength to resist the mightiest empire in the world was, internally, weak and amorphous. The kingdom always retained a feudal character, and only a small portion of the vast territory nominally incorporated in its boundaries was directly governed by Parthian kings and their satraps. The remainder consisted of small vassal kingdoms which acknowledged Parthian supremacy, but which retained a large measure of autonomy.[27]

Throughout the long course of their history the Parthians remained under the bondage of their nomad tradition. True to this nomadic background the Parthian army consisted almost entirely of cavalry. It should be noted, however, that the Parthians made use of two different types of mounted soldiers. Noblemen wore heavy armor and fought chiefly with swords and spears, like many of the Sarmatian warriors. The common people were light armed horse-archers like the ancient Scythians.[28]

It was the chiefs of the nomadic bands who were the early pillars of the Parthian Empire, and it was these chiefs who later became great magnates with huge estates and with armies of slaves. Even in later times the connection between the Parthians and the Iranian nomads of Central Asia was not entirely lost. Whenever a Parthian monarch lost his throne, he almost always took refuge with the nomadic Dahae or Sakas, and not infrequently was restored to power by them.

Thus, though the Parthian conquest of Persia was the conquest of Iranians by Iranians, the Parthians tended for several centuries to keep true to the nomadic traditions they had brought with them from Central Asia. At the same time, these Parthians were inevitably influenced by the two great culture complexes with which they came into intimate contact, namely, the Greek and the Persian complexes, which not only dominated Iran and Mesopotamia but which had long exerted a strong influence throughout Central Asia.

Though it was the Parthians who had expelled Greek political control over Iran, they could not free themselves from Greek traditions. This is evident from the Parthian coins, for the Parthians continued to use the Attic standard of currency. Coins were struck with Greek inscriptions, and, on these coins, the kings were given typical Greek titles, such as *Dikaeos,* "The Just," *Epiphanes,* "The Revealed God," *Basileon,* "King of Kings." More astonishing still, many of the Parthian monarchs proudly called themselves *Philhellene,* "Protector of Hellenism." [29]

It is probable that the Parthians retained the general structure of the Greek administration. It is certain that Greek long remained one of the official languages of the state and that the Parthian rulers posed as patrons of Greek literature. We know, for example, that when the head of Crassus was brought to the Parthian court, the king was witnessing a performance of a play by Euripides. This persistence of the Greek tradition is no doubt due in large measure to the fact that the Parthians were never good city-dwellers, and that many of the principal cities of the Parthian kingdom continued to be inhabited largely by Greek merchants.[30]

The Greek tradition, however, became weaker decade by decade, and gave place gradually to a revival of the old Persian tradition. This is all the more intelligible to us since we know that the Parthians were themselves an Iranian people distantly related to the Persians. The Greek language fell more and more into desuetude and an Iranian dialect became the official tongue. The early coins of Mithradates I, the oldest of the Parthian coins which have come down to us, picture the monarchs as beardless, following the Greek mode, but all of the later monarchs are depicted with their hair and beards long after the old Persian fashion. The Parthian rulers all bore Persian names, such as Mithradates, Tiridates, Artaban, and Chosroes (Cyrus).[31]

Most important of all, the Parthians were instrumental in the revival of the Zoroastrian religion. Not only did they acknowledge the old Persian gods and build fire altars, but they did something which even the Achemenids had failed to do, namely, they exposed even the royal dead to the vultures and the dogs as strict Zoroastrian doctrine demanded. It was under the Parthians that the attempt was first made to collect once more the ancient sayings of Zoroaster and his followers—which with the commentaries were to form the Avesta, the Zoroastrian Bible.[32]

This work of collecting and editing the sacred sayings of the earlier period was not completed in Parthian times. It is probable that the bulk of the Avesta as we know it today was not compiled until the members of the Sasanid dynasty (226-A.D. 642) had succeeded the Parthians as masters of the Iranian Plateau. But from the contents of the Avesta and from the archaic nature of the language employed therein, it is clear that a goodly proportion of the book was composed many centuries before it was first written down. During the many centuries in which the contents of the Avesta were retained only in the memory of the Zoroastrian priests, it is probable that a good deal of editing and interpolation took place. During disturbed times, important passages were forgotten and hence were forever lost. At other times new passages were inserted or old passages altered so as to make them refer to peoples and events long subsequent to the original composition of the Avesta. But in spite of these calamities it is generally agreed that this collection, even in its present form, gives us a fairly accurate account of the material and social life of the early Iranians.[33] Of especial importance for the purposes of the present work is the fact that much of the Avesta is closely associated with Eastern Iran and Southern Turkistan.

The Avesta professes to give us a picture of the life and teachings of the great prophet, Zoroaster or Zarathustra. It is generally believed that Zoroaster was born in Media, the northwestern portion of the

Iranian Plateau, but it seems fairly certain that he left this region at an early age and that the scene of his activity was laid in Eastern Iran. The language of the Avesta differs in many respects from "old Persian," and we have good reason to suppose that it represents the dialect spoken by the inhabitants of Eastern Iran. Some scholars go even further and speak of the Avesta language as old Bactrian. This is at best an unproved assumption, but at least we can feel sure that the Avesta, and with it official Zoroastrianism, originated somewhere in Eastern Iran. The west of Iran is scarcely ever spoken of in the Avesta, while the rivers and districts in the east are often mentioned. Bearing these facts in mind, it is clear that the Avesta is of especial importance for the light that it throws on the manners, customs, and beliefs common in Eastern Iran and Southern Turkistan in early times and this is all the more significant since most of the existing historical documents are silent on these important matters.

It is greatly to be regretted that as yet there are many grave doubts as to the age of the different portions of the Avesta. These doubts extend even to the period in which Zoroaster lived. Though no one doubts that Zoroaster was an historic person, and though many salient features of his life are also beyond dispute, there are grave differences of opinion among scholars as to the date of Zoroaster's mission and the founding of the Zoroastrian religion. Some authorities are firmly of the opinion that Zoroaster must have lived in at least 1000 B.C. or even earlier. Others assume that he lived in the period 900-700 B.C. Still other authorities vigorously defend the position that the Iranian prophet lived in the sixth century B.C. and was a contemporary of Cyrus Cambyses and Darius.

In view of this surprising lack of unanimity among the specialists in this field it is impossible for us to draw any definite conclusions at the present time. Suffice it to say that most scholars agree that the *Gatha* or metrical portions of the Avesta go back to Zoroaster himself and hence at least to early Achemenid times (if not earlier). There is greater doubt regarding the prose portions of the Avesta, but we probably shall not err greatly if we assign them to the late Achemenid and early Parthian periods. Such being the case we may conclude that the Avesta paints a picture of the material and social culture of the Iranians (and especially the Eastern Iranians) during the period which we have covered in our brief historical survey.[34]

From the Avesta it is clear that the early inhabitants of Bactria and the surrounding regions were long torn between devotion to their flocks and devotion to their fields. From very early times the people gained their living from both cattle-breeding and agriculture. Even in the earliest portions of the Avesta, in the *Gathas,* or songs supposed to have been composed by Zoroaster himself, we hear the common people spoken of both as cattle-breeders and as husbandmen, and the words "field" and "herds" are frequently employed together. From all that is known to us it would appear that at first the breeding of cattle was equal to, or even more important than, agriculture, but as time went on especial emphasis was laid upon the raising of crops. It was this dependence upon agriculture that served to form the great cultural barrier between the Northern Iranians and the Southern Iranians, between the inhabitants of Northern Turkistan on the one hand and the inhabitants of Southern Turkistan and the Iranian Plateau on the other.[35]

Among the animals specifically mentioned in the Avesta are sheep, goats, the horse, the cow, the camel, the dog, and the cock. It would seem that the pig was unknown, possibly as the result of a religious or social tabu, though no such tabu is specifically mentioned. The ass is mentioned only once and this animal played a very minor role in the economic life of the people at this period. This is in great contrast to the Semitic peoples farther to the west where the ass was long the most important of the domesticated animals.

In modern historical times the peoples of Northeastern Iran have gone in much more for the raising of sheep and of goats than for the breeding of cattle, and the cattle which do exist in these regions are by no means superior in beauty or in other good qualities. It was far different in ancient times. Sheep and goats are mentioned only occasionally in the Avesta, while the cow assumes a very important and prominent place, both in the economic and in the religious life of the Avestan people. Hence we must conclude that in early days the raising of cattle was far more general than the raising of either sheep or goats.

Cow's milk was a favorite article of food, as were butter and various forms of cheese. Beef, which is now almost unknown in Persia and which is tabu among the orthodox Hindus of India, seems to have been universally eaten. Cowhide was also used for the making of leather, but the most important and interesting uses of the cow were for the supply of cow (or bull) urine. This cow urine was employed almost daily for the ceremonial washing and cleansing of polluted persons and objects. This use of cow urine is still universal among the modern Zoroastrians of Persia and India. Oxen were employed for plowing the fields, for carrying loads, and for drawing wagons.

As important as cattle was the horse, even among the settled peoples of Eastern Iran. This is shown by the frequent use of the word for horse (*aspa* in the Avestan dialect) in the formation of proper names of kings and heroes. Among these proper names was Arvataspa—"Master of

War-like Horses"—and Huaspa—"Having Good Horses." Another person whose name was connected with the word for horse was Vishtaspa, the princely patron of Zoroaster, through whose support Zoroastrianism first secured official recognition among the Iranian peoples.

The peoples of Iran, like the Scythians and Sarmatians of the north, were well acquainted with kumis or fermented mare's milk, but the principal use of the horse was for transportation, especially in times of war. The Avesta makes frequent mention of chariots, especially of war chariots, and of chariot-racing. From this it is evident that driving, the earlier form of horse-transportation, was still known to the eastern Iranians; but it is equally evident from the texts that horseback riding was already very common and in later times became almost universal.[36]

A word must be said regarding the camel. It is certain that the camel, at least the so-called Bactrian or two-humped camel, is indigenous to Central Asia and was probably first domesticated in that region. For this reason it is rather remarkable that we find no specific reference to the camel among the Scythians and Sarmatians, although among the latter peoples at least its existence and usefulness must have been known. In marked contrast to this silence concerning the use of the camel among the Northern Iranians, we find that the Avestan peoples made frequent mention of this animal and valued him highly. In fact, the ancient Iranian word for camel (*ushtra*) forms part of the word Zarathustra, the native name for Zoroaster. In the Avesta whenever domestic animals are regularly enumerated, we find that the camel ranks below the horse but above the cow.

Frequent references in the Avestan texts show that the dog was well known and highly valued among the Eastern Iranians in ancient times. This is in marked contrast to modern times where, largely as the result of Muhammadan influences, the dog is regarded as an impure animal and is neglected and abused. In the Avesta the dog is sacred and inviolable. Whoever, by neglect, caused the death of a dog had to undergo a very severe punishment. So sacred was the dog that he formed a necessary part of certain religious ceremonies. Thus, for example, when a person died, it was required that a dog be brought in to view the corpse before any other funeral arrangements could be made.[37]

The mention of the cock and the hen in the Avesta is of especial interest. The household fowl was first domesticated somewhere in Indo-China and from this region slowly made its way westwards. The mention of this animal in the Avesta shows that it had made its way to the Iranian Plateau at an early period, but we have good reason to suppose that it was unknown in Europe until the rise of the Persian

Empire. It was, indeed, the Persians who were directly responsible for the introduction of the chicken into the west, as is evidenced by the fact that the Greeks frequently referred to this creature as the "Persian" or "Median Bird." [38]

But though the Avesta and the people mentioned therein were much concerned with domesticated animals, they laid equal emphasis upon agriculture and the planting of fruit trees. Cultivation of the fields was regarded almost as a religious duty, and the winning of the soil from the desert was looked upon as being especially meritorious in the eyes of Ahura Mazda, the Supreme Deity. The Eastern Iranians in Avestan times had long since passed beyond the hoe stage of agriculture and were well acquainted with the use of the plow. We find no mention of manuring, but several passages in the Avesta speak of well digging and of irrigation, and it is probable that elaborate irrigation systems were already well-known even at this early period.

We are in some doubt as to just what plants were cultivated by the Eastern Iranians, but it is certain that wheat, millet, and barley were well-known and that wheat constituted the chief crop. Though not specifically mentioned in the Avesta, we know from other sources that alfalfa and the grape were grown from a very early period in Eastern Iran and the surrounding regions. We do find frequent mention of wine in the Avestan texts, and it is probable that this wine was grape wine for the most part, though we know that at times of great religious ceremonies frequent use was made of an intoxicating beverage made from the mysterious haoma plant.

Special sacrificial cakes were made from wheat flour. At ordinary times wheat, barley, and millet were either cooked in water or were ground to flour and made into flat loaves baked in an earthern oven. It goes without saying that the ancient Iranians, like their descendants, the modern Persians, were unacquainted with such things as knives and forks and ate their food with their fingers.[39]

Among these Eastern Iranians, the use of tents had not been forgotten; but the vast majority of the population had already learned to dwell in fixed habitations. The Avesta gives us no description of the shape or construction of these early houses, but we may take it for granted that they already conformed to the standard Near Eastern type of habitation, flat-roofed and built of sun-dried brick.[40] This type of dwelling is serviceable but highly impermanent, and this accounts for the fact that archaeology has not yet brought to light a single edifice built at this early period. Some of these dwellings may have been isolated farmhouses, but from very early times the Iranians have been accustomed to dwell together in villages. The Avesta makes occasional mention of roads, but it is probable that these roads were little more than trails beaten out naturally by the footsteps of men and animals.

Household furniture consisted almost entirely of pots and pans and of rugs and carpets. In contrast with the Scythians and Sarmatians, it is probable that woolen carpets were more plentiful than felt rugs.[41]

We know comparatively little regarding the clothing of the early Eastern Iranians. Some of their clothing was undoubtedly woven, wool being the principal material; but even in Avestan times the Eastern Iranians, like the Scythians and Sarmatians, made frequent use of garments prepared from the skins of animals.

By religious law every devout Zoroastrian was required to wear a special white shirt next to his skin and also a sacred girdle (corresponding to the sacred thread of the Brahmans) around his waist. Children of both sexes were required to don these garments at the age of puberty. The Avesta makes no mention of that all important garment, trousers; but we know from other sources (Herodotus and the Persian inscriptions) that practically all the Iranian people made constant use of this article of clothing.

The dress of the priests differed considerably from that of the laity. The most important of the priestly robes consisted of a long white tunic reaching to the ankle. The priests also made use of a white turban, while the laity for the most part contented themselves with sheepskin caps. A skull cap was worn even inside the house, as going bareheaded had early come to be regarded as impious.

Similarly, from early times people were enjoined not to go unshod. Sandals and shoes were universally worn both by men and by women. The custom of wearing sandals was probably of Mesopotamian origin, while the wearing of shoes was a cultural feature linking the Eastern Iranians with their distant cousins, the Scythians and Sarmatians.

We know that the Eastern Iranians made frequent use of golden ornaments, such as finger rings, earrings, and necklaces; but these ornaments call for no special comment.[42]

The weapons used by the Eastern Iranians in warfare differed in no essential respects from those common among the Scythians and Sarmatians. In the Avesta we find frequent mention of swords, spears, battle-axes, maces, slings, and bows and arrows. From Herodotus we know that the bow and arrow was the favorite weapon among most of the Iranian peoples. The defensive weapons of the Eastern Iranians also differed in no essential respects from those employed by the Scythians in the north and consisted of shields, helmets, and corselets or breastplates. As in the north, this armor was originally made of leather, later of metal scales on a leather background, and finally of metal sheet armor. This similarity in armor is undoubtedly due to the fact that in defensive weapons the Scythians and Sarmatians were strongly influenced by their southern neighbors.[43]

Turning now from the material to the political and social culture of the Eastern Iranians, we notice first of all that they, like the Scythians and Sarmatians, were thoroughgoing monarchists. It is rather interesting that the Avestan word for king was *ḳhshatra* from which term is derived the modern word shah, the title still applied to the rulers of the Iranian Plateau.

But though the Iranian monarchs were absolute autocrats in the sense that their actions were unchecked either by a council of elders or by a popular assembly, they were nevertheless bound in many respects by custom and by law. The fact that many of these laws had religious sanction made it extremely difficult for the kings openly to break with legal practice or tradition. In the original Avesta no less than seven sections, a third of the total work, were devoted to legal matters. In view of the close association with religion, it is not surprising to find that the Zoroastrian priests managed to retain all the higher judicial positions in their own hands, with the result that all important lawsuits came before them for decision.

It is unnecessary for us to examine any of the details of the system of law in vogue among the early Eastern Iranians, but we should know that the Zoroastrian law code made ample use of trial by ordeals. When the guilt or innocence of a person was in doubt, he was forced to submit himself to one or another of thirty-three different ordeals. He might be required to walk through fire, pour molten metal on his body, eat excessive quantities of food, or cut certain portions of his body with a knife. The idea behind all these ordeals, of course, was that by divine assistance an innocent man could go through the ordeals unscathed. It would be of great interest if some scholar would trace the connection between these Iranian ordeals and those in vogue among the Germanic peoples of Northern Europe.[44]

The Avestan texts throw a good deal of light upon the social organization among the Eastern Iranians. The earliest texts mention only a three-fold division of society, namely the priests (called *Athravan*), the warriors, and the husbandmen or peasants. The later texts add to these three classes a fourth consisting of artisans.[45] The very fact that the artisan class is a later addition is not without significance. In later times, the Iranians became noted throughout the whole of Asia as excellent artisans and merchants. In earlier times, however, the vast bulk of the Iranians were simple peasants acquainted with only the rudiments of manufacture and trade. The pottery, weaving, and metallurgy which existed were household and family industries.

The four classes of Iranian society correspond in a general way to the four castes which arose among the Hindus, but there was one great difference between the social hierarchies of the two peoples. In India each of the four classes developed into rigid hereditary castes. Among the Iranians, this development took place only as regards the priestly class, the other three classes remaining social and economic divisions with no bar against a man passing from one class to the other.

The priestly class did, however, succeed in making their position hereditary; and no man could aspire to a sacerdotal position unless he were born into a priestly family. There was, however, one distinction between Iran and India, even as regards the priestly class. In India a priest was required to be of Brahman extraction on both his father's and his mother's side. In Iran a woman belonging to a priestly family was not permitted to marry a man from one of the other three classes, but a priest might marry a woman of any class without in any way affecting the legitimacy or priestly standing of his descendants.[46]

Speaking of marriage of the priests leads us to discuss one or two other rather curious features of the marital relationship as laid down in the Avestan texts. In the first place, the Avesta strongly recommends marriage for everyone irrespective of class or occupation. Celibacy was regarded as something abnormal and more or less evil. Zoroastrianism, therefore, had no sympathy with the feeling which developed in many religions, that priests and saints should abstain from matrimony.

The Avesta enters into no discussion of the relative merits of monogomy and polygamy; but we know that Zoroastrianism never sought to prohibit polygamy, and tradition tells us that Zoroaster himself was possessed of no less than three wives. Divorce was also permitted. In addition to being polygamous, the Eastern Iranians were strict adherents of the patrilinear system, whereby descent was counted only on the father's side. To insure perpetuity of the family, the Avesta also permitted legal adoption, and an adopted son had all the rights and privileges of a natural son. The fact that the Avesta prescribed stringent punishment against prostitution and homosexuality shows that both of these institutions must have been well-known to the Eastern Iranians.

By far the most interesting feature of the Avestan marital system was the permission and encouragement given to incest. This is a point on which the Iranians differed radically from their cousins, the Hindus, among whom marriage between blood relations was regarded with horror. Among the Iranians the marriage of brother and sister, of uncle and niece, and even of mother and son was permitted. In fact the marriage of blood relations was regarded as an institution of divine origin. Even in the later Zoroastrian texts, we find incestuous marriages extolled, and we are informed that such marriages are capable of wiping out mortal sins and serve as a powerful weapon against the machinations of the Evil Spirit. Even among the present day Zoroastrians, kindred marriages are by no means unknown, and, in contrast to popular belief, these incestuous unions are not attended by disastrous results to the children.[47]

Turning now to the Avestan references to illness and the cure of illness, we find that the Eastern Iranians still maintained very primitive ideas on the subject, inasmuch as they believed that many diseases were due to demoniac possession, to black magic, or to the effects of an evil eye cast upon an enemy. For this reason, it is not surprising to find the Avesta recommending the recital of spells and incantations as a cure for sickness. As a natural consequence of this attitude, from a very early time the practice of medicine was confined to the priesthood; and we find that Zoroaster himself was regarded as a great physician.

In addition to the use of prayers and charms, the Avesta also permitted physicians to employ plants and herbs and even surgery in the treatment of certain diseases. It is rather amusing to find that the Avesta prescribes a sort of preliminary examination for all budding surgeons. Before a doctor could operate upon any godly Zoroastrian, it was necessary for him to have tried his surgical art upon at least three unbelievers. If these unbelievers died, the loss was not considered great; but, if on the other hand he attempted to operate on a true believer before he had proved his skill on unbelievers, he was guilty of a mortal sin.[48]

In spite of the divine efficacy of the Zoroastrian priest-physician, the Eastern Iranians proved mortal and retained the habit of dying off from illness or old age. When death did take place, the Avesta was very rigid in its regulations as to the disposal of the corpse. Most important of all was the law that the corpse could be neither burned nor buried but had to be exposed on a lonely place where it could be eaten by wild birds or beasts. A person who buried a corpse or who permitted it to be buried was guilty of a heinous offense.

This curious method of disposing of the dead is of especial interest because of the fact that it was known neither to the Hindus nor even to many of the peoples speaking Iranian languages. Thus, for example, we find that the Scythians and the ancient Persians of Persia proper (i.e., Southwestern Iran) were in the habit of burying their dead. The fact that certain other peoples in Central Asia, such as the Tibetans, also go in for exposing the dead makes us believe that this was a custom of non-Iranian origin but which at one time was widespread through certain portions of Asia, and that this custom was later adopted by the Bactrians and other Eastern Iranians, by accident becoming incorporated as an integral part of the Zoroastrian religious system.[49]

We have so frequently referred to Zoroaster and Zoroastrianism and their effect upon the early Eastern Iranians that it would be well for us to give a brief glance at one or two of the purely theological features which underlay the whole Zoroastrian system. In many ways we can best understand Zoroaster if we regard him not as the founder of a completely new religious system but as a reformer of existing religious beliefs and practices. It will be remembered that the early Iranians and early Hindus had a common religious background. In this background there figured various types of supernatural beings, including two special groups, called *Devas* and *Asuras* by the Hindus and *Daevas* and *Ahuras* by the Iranians.

As time went on and the Hindus developed their religious system, their *devas* developed into the gods on high, the object of universal adoration; while the *asuras* came to be regarded as little more than goblins, greatly inferior to the *devas* and more to be feared than worshiped. Among the Iranians, possibly as the result of the reforming zeal of Zoroaster, there was a complete reversal of this line of development. The *daevas* came to be regarded as the wicked demons, the source of all evil and trouble, while the *ahuras* were the true gods, the source of virtue and salvation.

More important still, in Iran under the guidance of Zoroastrian polytheism, the worship of numerous *ahuras* soon gave way to monotheism, to the adoration of the one supreme *ahura,* called Ahura Mazda, the lord and master of the whole universe. Beneath Ahura Mazda was a whole hierarchy of celestial beings, among them Mithra, later destined to play an important part in the religious life of Rome; but these inferior deities were little more important than the cherubim and seraphim of the Hebrew theology. In marked contrast to Ahura Mazda, the supreme god, was Angra Mainyu, the Lord of Evil, the leader of all the *daevas* or demons. The good and evil in the whole universe was due to the conflict between Ahura Mazda and Angra Mainyu. To this extent Zoroastrianism was essentially dualistic, but the faithful were assured that eventually Ahura Mazda and his hosts would be triumphant, and that the Lord of Evil would sooner or later be annihilated.[50]

Zoroastrianism has frequently been said to inculcate sun worship, but strictly speaking this is not true. In the Avestan texts we find expressions such as "the Sun is the Eye of Ahura Mazda" or "the Sun is the body of Ahura Mazda"; but from the context it is obvious that these expressions were merely poetic and symbolic. Light is indeed the essence of Ahura Mazda; hence the sun, the chief source of perceptible light, was chosen as the best symbol of the supreme being.

Scarcely inferior to the sun was fire, which diffuses light and hence was regarded as the holiest and purest element. In one passage fire is actually referred to as the son of Ahura Mazda. All fire, from the fire on the household hearth to the fire on the great sacrificial altars, was regarded as sacred; and great care was taken to see that this fire was not polluted or defiled. Incidentally, early Zoroastrianism knew nothing of churches or temples in the ordinary sense of the word. The nearest approach to such edifices in Iran were small but very sacred fire altars, erected for the most part on mountain tops, some distance away from all human habitations.[51]

In addition to its god and its devil, Zoroastrianism taught belief in the doctrines of immortality, the Last Judgment, the reward and punishment of mankind by consigning them either to heaven or to hell, but, as all of these doctrines are merely prototypes of similar doctrines in Christianity and Muhammadanism, they call for no special discussion.[52]

Although in its early days Zoroastrianism appears to have been a missionary religion, as soon as it became a rigid and rather complicated theological system with its hierarchy of hereditary and intensely conservative priests, it ceased to be a religion which could readily be adopted wholesale by alien peoples. As a result, we find that all through its history orthodox Zoroastrianism was confined to persons speaking an Iranian language and united by blood and tradition to one or another of the historic Iranian peoples.

But though orthodox Zoroastrianism by its very nature could not be propagated abroad, many of the Zoroastrian doctrines were destined to have a wide influence upon peoples of many different times and places. This was especially true of the various groups inhabiting Central Asia; and, when we find travelers among the modern Mongol groups speaking of the Mongol tendency to expose their dead, of the special consideration shown to the dog, and of the great reverence for fire, we know that these customs and these tendencies are merely the result of Iranian influences spreading through the centuries to all parts of Central Asia.[53]

Book Two

THE FIRST HUNNISH EMPIRE

CHAPTER FOUR

THE EARLY INHABITANTS OF MONGOLIA

Chinese References to the Northern Barbarians—First References to the Huns—The Jou Dynasty of China and its Relations with the Northern Barbarians—The Northern Barbarians and the Downfall of the Early Jou Dynasty—The Chinese Feudal Kingdoms and their Relations with the Northern Barbarians—The Racial and Linguistic Affiliations of the Northern Barbarians—Their Early Culture, and their Later Adoption of the Scythian Culture—Political and Social Organization.

FROM THE beginning of recorded history, Mongolia and the adjacent regions have been the motherland of fierce tribesmen who have carved their way to plunder and overlordship if not to everlasting fame. From the Mongolian Plateau has poured forth wave after wave of invading hordes who at times have reduced to subjection every one of the Asiatic Empires and more than once have made themselves dictators of half of Europe.

Considering the importance of this region and of the peoples who have come from it, it is remarkable that the early history of Mongolia is almost completely unknown to us. The first inhabitants of this vast area possessed no system of writing and hence have left to us no literary monuments. Scientific excavation would, no doubt, throw much light upon the racial and cultural affinities of the early "Mongolians"; but as yet the serious archaeological investigation of this territory has barely scratched the surface, and has provided us with very scanty material for study.

The only people possessed of a literary tradition who had any early contact with the Mongolians were the Chinese, and hence it is to the Chinese records that we are forced to go when we seek information regarding the primitive inhabitants of this area. Even these Chinese records, however, are far from giving us an adequate picture of the people dwelling in Mongolia until they come to the events of two centuries before Christ.

Some of the Chinese chronicles, such for example as the celebrated *Book of History,* claim to tell us of events which occurred in 2500 B.C. or even earlier;[1] but practically all modern scholars are agreed that these early chronicles are semi-legendary in character. For this reason, we cannot take too seriously many of the remarks these chroniclers make regarding China's "barbarian" neighbors.

Beginning with the ninth century B.C., the Chinese historical records become far more accurate and trustworthy; but at this time, and for several centuries thereafter, the Chinese historians had very little interest in any people who were outside of the Celestial Empire. In fact these alien tribes were only deemed worthy of mention when one or another of them carried out some successful raid upon Chinese territory. Scanty and incomplete as they are, however, these early Chinese notices regarding their neighbors are not entirely lacking in interest or value; and it is well worth our while to consider briefly those references which concern themselves with China's northern acquaintances.

Among the "barbarians" who lived to the north of China and invaded the Celestial Empire from time to time were a group called the Rung, another called the Di, and still a third group which is sometimes called Hün-yu and sometimes Hien-yün. Both of these names are obviously attempts to transliterate the native name of that group of peoples who are known to us in the West as Huns.[2]

When we examine more closely the various Chinese references to these barbarian peoples, it becomes evident that the term Rung was one of very general application and was a common designation for a great number of different peoples of widely divergent ethnic character. Among these various Rung tribes, however, there were undoubtedly many that belonged to the same ethnic group as the Di and the Hien-yün (who are supposed to have been very closely interrelated). This group in turn is generally believed to have been the ancestors of the people later known as Hiung-nu, who were the founders of the first great Hunnish Empire.

We have no means of ascertaining when these "barbarians"—whether called Rung, Di, or Hün-yu—first came to inhabit Mongolia and the northern frontiers of China. But from the Chinese legends regarding the earliest rulers of their own land, it would appear that even these gentry were forced to contend with the ancestors of the same tribes who are so well-known to us from their place in the later and more accurate records.

Thus, for example, the fabulous Huang-di or Yellow Emperor, who is supposed to have ruled over the Celestial Empire about 2600 B.C., is said to have waged a successful war against the Hün-yu. Though many of the events recorded concerning the Yellow Emperor's reign are mythical in character, it is usually supposed that such a person really did exist and that the story of his conflict with the Hün-yu or early Huns did have some basis in fact.[3]

The Chinese have another legend to the effect that sometime after the downfall of the Hia dynasty, the first of the great Chinese imperial dynasties, which took place in 1818 B.C., a descendant of the last ruler of this line fled to the north and took refuge with the Huns. The legend further relates that the Huns not only gave a cordial welcome to this runaway prince, but in addition elected him to be their ruler. In fact, it is claimed that the rulers of the later great Hiung-nu or Hunnish Empire were all descended from this Chinese exile.[4] Very little credence can be given to this legend, and it is worthy of mention only because of the fact that belief in this story had some effect in later times upon the attitude assumed by the Chinese towards the Huns and by the Huns towards the Chinese.

But though we may well doubt the legend that a Chinese prince became the recognized ruler over all the Hunnish tribes in the north, it may well be that the story has a slight foundation in fact. We know, beyond contention, that in later times numerous Chinese renegades, who found it impossible to remain longer in the Celestial Empire, made their way northward and were hospitably received by the rulers of the Hunnish tribes. It is quite possible, therefore, that a similar state of affairs existed in these early semi-historic times; and that not one but several Chinese, of noble and even of princely rank, who got into trouble at home, found an asylum among the primitive inhabitants of Mongolia. These Celestial exiles undoubtedly intermarried with the people with whom they took refuge, a matter of great significance when we come to deal with the problem of the racial composition of these early "Northern Barbarians."

Of far greater interest than either of the two above mentioned legends are the stories told concerning the intimate relationships existing between the "Northern Barbarians" and the ancestors of the Chinese Emperors of the House of Jou. The Jou dynasty is generally regarded as the most glorious of all the Chinese ruling houses. Not only did the monarchs of this house rule over China for a far longer period than the members of any other dynasty, but it was during the Jou period that China developed her great classical civilization. It was during this period that the Five Classics were compiled. It was during this period that the great sages, such as Confucius, Mencius, and Laodse (Lao-tse) lived and wrote their works.

Considering this fact, it is rather surprising to find that the House of Jou owed its early fame to its connection with the wild barbarians of the north and west. When the ancestors of the Jou dynasty first definitely emerge upon the horizon of history, we find them to be feudal lords of a small community in the extreme northwest portion of China. In this region they were surrounded on all sides by various tribes of Northern Barbarians (who are called on this occasion Rung and Di).

In fact it seems highly probable that these feudal lords were themselves of barbarian origin and were originally tribal leaders of small barbarian groups, who had come under the influence of Chinese civilization and won for themselves a minor place in the Chinese feudal hierarchy.[5]

The barbarian origin of these early ancestors of the House of Jou did not, however, prevent them from being the object of frequent attack on the part of their fellow tribesmen who had not come within the orbit of Chinese civilization. The very fact that these feudal lordlings had adopted something of the Chinese mode of life made it all the more difficult for them to withstand the attacks made by their barbarian neighbors and kinsmen. At any rate, in the middle of the fourteenth century B.C. we find that the then reigning feudal lord (called Tan Fu) was forced to retire from his fief on the Chinese frontier and create for himself a new settlement a little further to the southeast. This new settlement was called Jou—hence the name given to the dynasty in later times.

But though Tan Fu and his followers were forced to abandon their early home because of their inability to cope with barbarian attacks, once these refugees settled in their new domain they were soon able to rise to a position of power and eminence such as they had never known before. Less than a hundred years after this ignominious flight, the "Dukes of Jou," as these feudal lords were now called, were the objects of universal respect and admiration, both because of their military power and because of their personal integrity.[6]

The real founder of the greatness of the House of Jou was Tan Fu's grandson, who is usually known in the Chinese annals as Wên Wang, the "Literary" or "Civilized" King. Throughout all subsequent periods, every schoolboy in China has been brought up on tales of this ruler's wisdom and virtue. Wên Wang is credited with the composition of a large part of the famous *Book of Changes,* a mass of inchoate nonsense, which is regarded by the Celestials as their most awesome and sacred book.

Even in military affairs Wên Wang betrayed remarkably humanitarian principles, especially when one remembers his "barbarian" background. When embarking on a military campaign, he gave strict orders to his soldiers that they should harm no non-combatant, that they were to destroy no dwelling or any wells or woods, and finally that they were to pilfer no domestic animals from the innocent peasants. Those who disobeyed his orders were shown no mercy.

In spite of this humanitarianism, Wên Wang was eminently successful. Partly by force and partly by diplomacy he was able to bring under his influence a large number of his fellow feudal lords, and on his death he was far more powerful than the nominal ruler of the Celestial Empire, the last representative of the Shang Dynasty, the second of China's great historic dynasties.

This Celestial Emperor, alarmed by the perpetual inroads of the barbarians from the north and west, appointed Wên Wang to be Lord Protector of the Western Marches, with orders to repel these bold invaders. Unmindful of the fact that his own grandfather had been forced to flee before the same barbarians, Wên Wang proceeded to carry out these instructions; and in this border warfare he was nearly always successful. We are specifically told that among the barbarian tribes thus castigated were the dreaded Hien-yün in the north.[7]

Fourteen years after Wên Wang's death, or to be exact, in 1122 B.C., the latter's son, usually called Wu Wang or the Martial Ruler, deposed the last degenerate scion of the House of Shang and established himself as the Supreme Ruler of the Celestial Empire, becoming thus the first *de jure* monarch of the Jou dynasty. In spite of this accession of dignity, Chinese sentiment has always regarded him as of less importance than his father; for which reason we may omit any discussion of his reign, apart from the fact that he, too, undertook several campaigns against the Northern Barbarians and even succeeded in bringing several of these tribes into direct submission to his empire. The Chinese thus found that the best way to remove the danger of barbarian invasion was to place a reformed barbarian upon the imperial throne.[8]

For well over a century we hear of no further incursions upon the northern frontiers of China; but, as time went on and emperor succeeded emperor upon the throne, the power and prestige of the Jou dynasty gradually weakened. The Northern Barbarians were not slow to take advantage of this fact. Those who had submitted to Chinese jurisdiction revolted and succeeded in reëstablishing their independence. Those who had always remained independent became much more bold in their raids upon the Chinese frontier.[9]

Some of these raids must have caused an enormous amount of damage. This we know not merely from dry accounts in the historical chronicles but also from the deep feeling shown in some of the popular poems and songs of the period which have been preserved for us in the *Book of Odes*. From time to time some of the later degenerate Jou Emperors managed to lead or rather send a successful punitive expedition against these Northern Barbarians. Here again popular sentiment regarding these wars is reflected in the *Book of Odes,* and on more than one occasion we find the populace rejoicing over the fact that the hated Hien-yün had been hurled beyond the frontier.[10]

But though even the later rulers of the House of Jou were able to wage successful campaigns against the Northern Barbarians, in the end their foes were again able to gain the upper hand largely because of treachery on the part of one of the great feudal lords within the Celestial Empire. This memorable event took place in the early part of the eighth century B.C. (781-771 B.C.) when the Emperor Yu sat upon the imperial throne. This Son of Heaven was a weak and dissolute man. Though possessed of a legitimate consort and, through her, of a legitimate heir apparent, the Emperor fell madly in love with a beautiful concubine, called Bao-Se, who was presented to him shortly after the commencement of his reign.

His Imperial Majesty wasted all the resources of the empire trying to please his new favorite, but it seems that it was difficult to satisfy all the lady's whims. We are told that it was especially hard to make her smile. In the hope of amusing the beautiful but stolid lady, the Emperor decided to play a practical joke upon some of his feudal lords.

It had long been a custom in the empire for beacon fires to be lighted on the hills surrounding the capital as a signal that the imperial residence was being attacked. Upon seeing this signal, the feudal lords in the nearby regions immediately armed their retainers and rushed to the aid of their monarch. On one occasion the Emperor Yu, by way of causing a little excitement, lighted these signal beacons without any danger being imminent. The feudal lords, true to their bond, immediately poured into the capital only to find that they had been fooled. All this needless commotion greatly amused the beautiful Lady Bao-Se, and she burst into gales of laughter. Charmed with the fact that he had at last found a way to amuse his favorite, the Emperor repeated this performance several times with the result that the feudal lords were disgusted at being made the objects of ridicule and refused to respond to the signals any longer.

It was just at this time that the Emperor got into serious trouble with one of his more distant feudal lords, the Marquis of Shên. This nobleman was the father of the Emperor's legitimate consort and the grandfather of the heir apparent. For this reason, he was not at all pleased by recent events at the imperial court. When the Emperor at last formally deposed the legitimate Empress and her son from their high rank and substituted for them the Lady Bao-Se and her son, the noble Marquis of Shên completely lost his temper and prepared to seek vengeance. Things became still worse when it became apparent that the Emperor wished not merely to depose but also to assassinate the rightful crown prince. It was at this stage that the Lord of Shên decided upon open rebellion.

Fearful lest he be unsuccessful should he attack the imperial capital

Buddhist Image of the Kushan Period

The face of this Bodhisattva is usually supposed to be modelled after a Kushan chieftain and therefore illustrates the appearance of the Yuejï. Cf. Chaps. IV and X. (*After Grousset*)

A Buddhist Image from Kashgaria

Illustrating the spread of Greek influence in Central Asia. (*After Fischer*)

(*Left*)

An Early Image of the Buddha

A product of the Gandhara school, illustrating Graeco-Bactrian influence upon Eastern art. Cf. Chap. III. (*After Fischer*)

Coins of Eucratides, one of the Greek Kings of Bactria in Central Asia. Cf. Chap. III. (*After Rawlinson*)

The Great Wall of China

The original wall was constructed in 214 B.C. as a protection against the Hiungnu or Huns. Cf. Chap. V.
(*After Geil*)

without assistance, his lordship entered into treasonable negotiations with some of the barbarian tribes in the northwest—not the Hien-yün on this occasion, let it be noted, but their kinsmen and neighbors, called the Küan or Dog barbarians. These barbarians were delighted at the prospect of securing a little easy loot and immediately entered into the proposed arrangement.

When it became evident that these hordes were marching upon the capital, the signal beacons calling for assistance were immediately set ablaze; but the feudal lords of the surrounding districts, though not actively disloyal, felt that another trick was being played upon them and refused to take any action. As a result the barbarian tribesmen were able to seize and kill the Emperor with no great difficulty. The empire was thrown into consternation. Taking advantage of the general bewilderment, the barbarians ransacked the capital and secured an enormous amount of booty, including many of the historic state jewels. More important still, though these barbarians were soon forced to retire from the capital, they managed to retain for a much longer period several strategic posts well within the limits of the Celestial Empire; and from these posts they continued to terrorize many of the surrounding districts.[11]

For some time, the Chinese nobility remained in a state of hopeless confusion. But at last the great feudal lords took matters into their own hands and reëstablished a semblance of order. By agreement between these great lords, the legitimate crown prince was placed upon the imperial throne (this was the Emperor Ping) with the result that the Jou dynasty was seemingly reëstablished as masters of the Celestial Empire. As a matter of fact, however, this reëstablishment of the Jou dynasty was largely nominal. Neither the new monarch nor his descendants were ever in a position where they could really control the vast territory which was nominally subject to their jurisdiction.

One of the first acts of the new Emperor was to transfer his capital from the city of Hao in Western China to the city of Loyang in Eastern China. By reason of this change, the later monarchs of this house are usually spoken of as members of the Eastern Jou dynasty in contrast with the much more glorious rulers of the earlier, or Western Jou dynasty. Incidentally, this change of capital was in itself a manifest sign of weakness, for we are distinctly told that the migration to the east was due to fear of further attack by the barbarians of the north and west.[12]

All during the Eastern Jou dynasty (770-250 B.C.), real power rested with the great feudal lords, each one of whom was a practically independent sovereign inside of his own domain. Several of these petty states lay just to the south of Mongolia; and, with the complete decay of the central administration, the ruler of each one of these principalities was called upon to repel the inroads of the northern Barbarians. The records tell us that the feudal lords were for the most part eminently successful in their conflicts with these barbarians. Many of the barbarous tribes were brought into direct subjection to one or another of the frontier principalities, while others were driven back far to the north and forced to confine their activities to the plains of Mongolia. The Chinese chronicles make frequent mention of the conflicts between the frontier principalities and the northern and western Barbarians, but fortunately we are spared the necessity of dealing in detail with any of these petty border wars. To us these references are of importance only because they occasionally make allusion to the manners and customs of their barbarian opponents.[13]

At this point, it may be well to pause for a moment and consider briefly just what these references do tell concerning the racial, the linguistic, and the cultural affinities of these early inhabitants of Mongolia.

The most perplexing of these problems is that relating to the racial affinities of these early inhabitants of Mongolia. Owing to the extreme scarcity of really accurate data on this matter, the field has been left open to wild speculation. It has usually been taken for granted that the early inhabitants of Mongolia were "Mongolian" or Mongoloid in appearance—i.e. typical representatives of the Yellow Race. It has even been suggested that these earlier inhabitants of Mongolia ran truer to the pure Mongoloid type than their neighbors, the Chinese; and that the Chinese, especially the Chinese of the north, who are usually considered more Mongoloid in type than the southern Chinese, may well have received some of their more striking physical characteristics by reason of intermarriage with some of the early hordes of invaders who swept down from the Mongolian Plateau.

In this connection, however, it should be noted that the results of the little archaeological work done just to the north of the Mongolian Plateau are completely incompatible with this hypothesis. Thus, for example, in southern Siberia, in the region now inhabited by the Buriat Mongols, all of whom are now typically Mongoloid in appearance, archaeological work has brought to light a number of skeletons dating from an early period. All of these skeletons were markedly long-headed, in striking contrast with the modern Mongol skulls, the great majority of which are round-headed. It is, therefore, definitely established that in the very heart of the Mongolian domain the characteristically round-headed race of the present day was preceded by a race of a very different type.

So far archaeology has thrown little light on the problem of the coloration of this early long-headed race; but the Chinese records would lead us to believe that this early population had "red hair, green eyes, and white faces," and we have every reason to believe that this description was not greatly inaccurate. In this connection, however, it must be borne in mind that this long-headed and presumably blond type is known to have inhabited not Mongolia proper, but southern Siberia immediately to the north of Mongolia. It is quite possible, in fact probable, that this early, blond, long-headed type spread into northern Mongolia; and it is not at all impossible that in very early prehistoric times this type was predominant all over the Mongolian Plateau.[14]

In contrast with this blond, long-headed type, which maintained its existence in the north until historic times, were the tribes in direct contact with the Chinese, such, for example, as the Hien-yün and the other direct ancestors of the later Huns. Though explicit evidence is lacking, we have every reason to believe that the various barbarian groups which carried out periodic raids upon the Chinese frontier were both brunette and round-headed.

But when we admit that these Northern Barbarians were both brunette and round-headed, this is far from saying that they were Mongoloid in appearance. In this connection, great stress should be laid on the difference between the Turk and Mongol racial types. To quote Professor Smith: "In many books on anthropology the Mongol is confused with the Turkish race. The profound difference between these two peoples can not be too strongly stressed; it would be difficult to find two peoples more clearly differentiated one from another. The features of the Turkish people are prominent in contradistinction to the extremely flat face of the Mongol race. Their hair is wavy and oval in section as opposed to the Mongol which is straight and round in section. The Turks have full flowing beards and are, in fact, among the hairiest peoples of the earth, while the Mongol is characterized by a lack of hair. The Turks are really a highly specialized branch of the Alpine race."

When one remembers that the Turks and the other members of the Alpine race are affiliated with the "White" races of Europe, while the Mongols are affiliated with the "Yellow" races of eastern and southeastern Asia, it is obviously of the greatest importance for us to determine whether the early inhabitants of Mongolia were of the Turk or of the Mongol type. In this connection a passage in one of the Chinese dynastic histories is of very great significance. This passage tells us that the Huns were easily distinguished from the Chinese by the fact that the former had large prominent noses and were extremely hairy.[15]

In view of this specific evidence, it can scarcely be doubted for an instant that the Huns who constituted the bulk of the early population of Mongolia belonged definitely to the "Turki" rather than to the "Mongol" type. This in turn means, surprising though it may seem, that the Huns were ultimately of "White" origin rather than an offshoot of the great "Yellow" group of races.

But though the early Huns were thus associated with the races of the West rather than with the races of the East, we know from the Chinese records that there was a great deal of intermarriage, or at least of interbreeding, going on between the Northern Barbarians and the inhabitants of Northern China. This interbreeding had a good deal of effect upon the racial appearance of the northern Chinese (it is possible that the broad-headedness of the northern Chinese may be due, at least in part, to this cause); but it is no less certain that this same interbreeding had a marked effect upon the Hunnish tribes in the north. As time went on, and this interbreeding continued, an ever greater number of the Hunnish tribesmen began to show the Mongoloid characteristics.[16]

Had the Huns, the earliest of the historically known inhabitants of Mongolia, continued to inhabit the Mongolian Plateau, it is probable that the Turki type would have been completely swamped by the infiltration of Mongoloid racial characteristics; but we may confidently assume that their great migration to the West took place when the Turki type was still the predominant element in their racial composition. The complete "Mongolization" of Mongolia did not take place until some time after the great bulk of the Huns had removed themselves from direct Chinese influence by settling in Turkistan.

Turning now from the problem of race to the problem of language, we find that practically all scholars are agreed that the early inhabitants of Mongolia spoke one or another of the languages which are usually called either Turanian or Ural-Altaic. The niceties of philology are entirely outside the scope of our present work. We have neither the space nor the time to deal with the grammar or the vocabulary either of the Turanian languages as a whole or any of the Turanian languages individually, but it may be well to indicate some of the marked peculiarities of these languages, particularly those which distinguish the Turanian languages from all other linguistic groups. In this connection it is of especial importance to bring out the sharp differences between the Turanian languages, on the one hand, and the Indo-European languages, and the Tibeto-Chinese group of languages on the other.[17]

The most important feature of all Turanian languages is that they are agglutinative, which means that, unlike the Tibeto-Chinese tongues, the Turanians have a complicated grammar and go to great lengths to express subtle differences in case and tense. On this point the Turanians agree with the speakers of Indo-European and Semitic languages, but there is still a profound difference between these various linguistic groups. Whereas the Indo-Europeans and Semites frequently express inflection by changing the root word (e.g. man-men; come-came), the Turanians on the other hand have unchanged and unalterable root words and express grammatical change by adding certain suffixes to these root words (e.g. in Turkish: *khatun*—a woman, *khatun-lar*—women; *gel-mek*—to come, *gel-iyorum*—I come, *gel-dim*—I came).

In like manner the Tibeto-Chinese languages have, properly speaking, neither prefixes nor suffixes, neither prepositions nor postpositions. The Indo-European languages have all of these grammatical oddities (though there are far more prepositions than postpositions), while the Turanian languages have suffixes but no prefixes, have postpositions, but no prepositions; that is, they say "you-to" and not "to you," "here-from" and not "from here."

The Turanian languages are further distinguished from the Tibeto-Chinese languages in that the latter are essentially monosyllabic and make frequent use of tones. On these matters, the Turanian languages agree with the Indo-European and Semitic languages. But to make up for this the Turanian languages differ from the two latter groups by the fact that they make no use of grammatical gender, and by the fact that they have no relative pronouns. Another minor point, but one of some interest, is the fact that the Turanians have an aversion to placing two consonants together at either the beginning or the end of a word (e.g. *st*retch, compa*ct*).

It may further be noted that many, though not all, of the Turanian languages are characterized by vowel harmony or the rule that all the vowels in any word must belong to the same vowel group (e.g. *khatun-lar,* women; but *el-ler,* hands).

From what has been said it is obvious that the Turanian languages form an independent and strongly differentiated linguistic group. It is worthy of remark, however (and is especially significant in view of what has been said regarding racial affinities) that whereas all attempts to link in any way the Turanian and the Tibeto-Chinese language group have ended in failure, several scholars believe that the Turanian and Indo-European languages may ultimately prove to have a common origin.[18]

As we have seen, it is universally agreed that the early inhabitants of Mongolia all spoke a language, or rather languages, belonging to this Turanian or Ural-Altaic linguistic group. It is now our duty to inquire whether it is possible to go still further and determine which of the various Turanian languages was the dominant tongue during this early period of Mongolian history.

In this connection it should be remembered that it is usual to divide the Turanians into five separate and distinct linguistic stocks. The first of these is the Finno-Ugrian group, spoken in modern times by the Hungarians, the Finns of Finland, and by various Finnish tribes in the eastern part of European Russia. The second is the Samoyed group, now spoken by a number of primitive tribes scattered throughout Western Siberia and the adjoining regions. The third is the Turkish group, spoken by vast numbers of persons now living not only in Turkey but also in Central Asia and elsewhere. The fourth is the Mongol group, spoken by practically all the persons now inhabiting Mongolia and by the Kalmucks in Southeastern Russia. The fifth, and last, is the Tungus group, spoken by the Manchus and also by the various primitive tribes scattered throughout Northern Manchuria and Eastern Siberia.

As far as I know, no one has as yet attempted to link the poor bedraggled Samoyeds with the early masters of the Mongolian Plateau, but for each of the other four groups we find that, at one time or another, doughty protagonists have arisen, claiming that their group alone is entitled to the distinction of being the lineal and linguistic descendants of the ancient Hunnish lords of Mongolia. In this connection, it should be borne in mind that we have no evidence for the belief that in early times linguistic unity prevailed all over the Mongolian Plateau. It is quite possible and even probable that several of the tribes, grouped together by the early Chinese records as Northern Barbarians, spoke several different languages, even though all or nearly all of these barbarians spoke languages belonging to the Turanian group as a whole. In fact, even at the height of its power, the Hunnish Empire was a confederation of widely divergent tribes and never succeeded in becoming a single homogeneous state.

In later times, when the Huns managed to secure control over Turkistan and Southern Siberia, it is certain that many Finno-Ugrian and Samoyed tribes were included in the Hunnish confederation and hence became entitled to the name of Huns. At the same time, it is extremely doubtful if any of these Finno-Ugrian or Samoyed tribes ever secured a foothold upon Mongolia proper; and hence they must be omitted from our discussion of the early inhabitants of the Mongolian Plateau.

In like manner, it is certain that, at the height of the later Hunnish Empire, a large number of Tungusic tribes in Manchuria and Eastern Siberia became subject to its jurisdiction. It is even possible that some of these Tungusic tribes, at one time or another, secured a foothold upon the northeastern part of the Mongolian Plateau. But it is impossible for us to believe that these Tungusic tribes ever constituted any really important element in the ethnic composition of Mongolia during the period we have under survey.

Now that the Finno-Ugrians, the Samoyeds, and the Tunguses have been eliminated, there remain only the Mongols and the Turks to be discussed. As the result of the work of many generations of scholars, it may now be taken for granted that during this early period Mongolia was inhabited both by Mongol and by Turkish tribes, so that the only question still to be solved is whether it was the Mongols or the Turks who constituted the bulk of the population and whether it was the Mongols or the Turks who made up the basic nucleus of the later Hunnish Empire.

Several decades of acrimonious dispute by scholars of all nationalities have thrown a great deal of light upon this subject, and at present we find the vast majority of the specialists in this field accepting the dictum of the Chinese dynastic histories that the Huns spoke a Turkish language. In fact it is now generally believed that it was not until many centuries after the fall of the Hunnish Empire that the Mongolian speaking group constituted more than a small minority in the "Mongolian population." Incidentally, this conclusion, which is arrived at by purely linguistic reasoning, fits in very well with what we know regarding the racial affinities of the early Huns, inasmuch as it enabled us to believe that these Huns were both "Turks" in race and "Turkish" in language.[19]

We are now in a position to turn our attention to the discussion of the cultural life of the early inhabitants of Mongolia. We have every reason to assume that the racial and linguistic position of the Huns and the other Northern Barbarians remained relatively unchanged during the many centuries under consideration. But this is not true of the cultural life of these peoples, and it is necessary for us to distinguish sharply between two very different modes of life, one earlier and the other later.

First, a word regarding the earlier mode of life. For many years it was customary to regard the early Huns as typical followers of the steppe type of culture, i.e., as militant horse nomads, similar in their mode of life to the Scythians and Sarmatians of Turkistan. Many persons, in fact, regarded the Huns and the other Turanian peoples as the originators of this steppe type of culture, and assumed that the Indo-European nomads of the West must have borrowed their horse culture from the early inhabitants of Mongolia.

A careful study of the early Chinese records shows that this supposition is entirely erroneous. Thus, for example, one of the early Chinese writers, when enumerating some of the barbarian tribes bordering on the Celestial Empire, says of the Northern Barbarians (who are here called Di) that they lived in caves, that they wore clothes made of wool, and that some did, while others did not, eat (i.e., cultivate) grain. No part of this description tallies with what we know of the true horse nomads of the steppes.[20]

Even more important in this connection is the tale of a great battle fought in 714 B.C. between the Northern Barbarians, this time called Rung, and the Chinese, in which the Chinese, following their usual custom, made use of war chariots; while the barbarians, following *their* custom, fought on foot. A hundred and seventy years later, 541 B.C., there was another such encounter, this time further to the west, in what is now Shansi Province, between the Chinese and the barbarians, who on this occasion are again called Di. In a council of war, the leader of the Chinese forces spoke as follows: "The enemy fight on foot, while we have chariots. The battle will be fought in a narrow pass, where the chariots can not be maneuvered. If we substitute ten men on foot for each chariot we shall be certain of victory. I therefore command all warriors, myself included, to fight on foot."

When one of the officers refused to carry out these orders, on the ground that his dignity did not allow him to fight on foot, he was immediately decapitated, and his head was carried around as a warning to all other possible objectors. Incidentally, as a result of these tactics, the barbarians suffered an overwhelming defeat.[21]

From these references it is clear that as late as the sixth century B.C. the early inhabitants of Mongolia were far from being the superb cavalrymen of later days. They were nomads, but foot nomads, and in all probability were hunters and food gatherers like the early Finns, though it is not unlikely that they practiced a rude system of agriculture.[22] In any case, it is certain that the horse culture had not as yet revolutionized their lives.

When one remembers that long before this period the Scythians and Sarmatians of Turkistan were noted because of their horsemanship and their cavalry tactics, it is clear that it was the Turanians who borrowed their horse culture from the Iranian nomads of the West, rather than the other way around. Furthermore, we shall find, even in much later times (the first century B.C.) when the Huns had become noted cavalrymen, horses from the Iranian West were still considered far superior to any possessed by the Turanians.[23]

All during this time, however, there was a constant infiltration of cultural influences from the West to the East. We have definite archaeological evidence of this sweep of civilization in the discoveries made by Kozlov in Northern Mongolia. In some tombs in this region, which undoubtedly belonged to early Hunnish chieftains, various art objects have been found with decorations which are identical with designs common among the Iranian nomads in Turkistan and Southern Russia. Of equal interest is the fact that other objects found in these graves betray unmistakeable Greek influences and were probably brought across Central Asia from the Greek colonies established along the northern coast of the Black Sea.[24]

Far more important than the artistic influences which the Iranian nomads of the West had upon the Turanian nomads of the East was the fact that the Turanian inhabitants of Mongolia adopted, almost in their entirety, the manners and customs of their Iranian neighbors to the West. The single most important borrowing was, of course, the use of the horse for riding; but with the adoption of the horse there followed a wholesale revolution in manners and customs so that the whole material culture of the Turanian peoples was completely transformed. It is as yet impossible for us to state just when this great transformation took place, but it must have been approximately 400 B.C., or roughly halfway between 541 B.C., when we are told that the Turanians were still fighting on foot, and 300 B.C. when these same Turanian peoples had already become expert cavalrymen. The evidence for this change, though conclusive, is, like most other things in the Chinese records, vague and indirect.

After the fall of the Western Jou dynasty (771 B.C.), China was broken up into a number of feudal states, all of them nominally subject to the Emperor of the Eastern Jou dynasty, but all of them completely autonomous in actuality. One of these feudal states was the Kingdom of Jao which occupied much of what is now the province of Shansi, and hence lay close to the Mongolian frontier. One of the rulers of this little kingdom (Wu Ling by name, who ruled from 325 to 298 B.C.) made a great name for himself by his successful wars with the Northern Barbarians. But we are told that his success was only achieved when he made his soldiers adopt the barbarian costume and fight in barbarian fashion.[25]

As we have already seen, it was the old custom of the Chinese to fight from war chariots. Up to this period, however, the principal weapon of the Celestial soldiers had been the short sword; and the Chinese costume, both civil and military, had consisted of loose robes and of slippers or sandals. Under the new orders issued by the King of Jao, the Chinese troops were to follow the Hunnish custom and shoot with bows and arrows and fight with long, in place of short, swords. Furthermore, the soldiers were to learn to shoot and fight on horseback in accordance with Hunnish customs. The orders to adopt the Hunnish mode of dress probably meant that, in place of slippers and loose robes, the Jao soldiers were to wear boots and trousers, the costume best suited to cavalrymen.

In many ways the King of Jao proved to be a great pioneer. After his time, war chariots gradually came into disuse throughout the whole of China, and in the course of the following centuries the Chinese people as a whole, and not merely the troops on the Mongolian frontier, learned to wear shoes and trousers.

In the present instance, however, we are concerned not with the Chinese but with the Turanians, and for us the great importance of the story about the King of Jao is that we learn thereby what a great transformation had taken place among China's northern neighbors. Two centuries earlier, we have seen, they had lived and fought on foot. We are led to infer that at this earlier period the Northern Barbarians had used the sword rather than the bow and arrow as their principal weapon of attack. Though details are lacking, it is highly doubtful if the Huns at this earlier period had used either boots or trousers.

After the death of the King of Jao, there is nothing of especial interest in the Chinese records concerning the inhabitants of Mongolia until the close of the third century B.C. About this time, however, the Celestial historians suddenly began to manifest a great interest in the manners and customs of their northern neighbors so that we may secure a fairly adequate picture of the contemporary Hunnish cultural life.

At this time, practically all of the various tribes inhabiting Mongolia were absorbed in a newly established confederation, headed by a tribe known as Hiung-nu. The Hiung-nu were undoubtedly the descendants of the people who in earlier times were known as the Hun-yü or Hien-yün; and, as it is now universally admitted that the Hiung-nu were, in part at least, the ancestors of the people known to the European chroniclers under the name of Huns, we shall refer to them as Huns throughout the remainder of the present work. It is also certain, as we have seen, that these Huns were closely related to the barbarians known as Di and to many of the tribes called Rung. But at this period all these lesser tribes were absorbed in the Hiung-nu confederation and completely disappear from history.

From the Chinese accounts, it is obvious that all of the peoples incorporated in the newly established Hunnish union had a fairly homogeneous culture and that this culture corresponded very closely to that which had evolved among the Iranian nomads of the West. In fact, it is evident that at this time practically all the peoples of Central Asia, from the steppes of Southern Russia to the plains of Western Manchuria, had come to have the same general mode of life, irrespective of the race to which they belonged or the language which they spoke. In this connection, it is interesting to note that the great Hunnish ruler who created the Hunnish "Empire," an empire which included peoples of many different races and languages, speaks of himself as the Lord of all those who shoot bows from horseback, thus marking a characteristic feature in this widespread steppe culture.[26]

As illustrations of the mode of life of their northern neighbors, the Chinese tell us that the Huns possessed no walled cities nor even fixed residences but were constantly moving about from place to place in order to secure fresh pasturage for their herds. In spite of this nomadic existence, however, each household and each tribe had a certain area of land reserved for its own exclusive use; and in this area no other group might pasture its flocks.

We are told that the Huns lived in tents, the walls of which were made of felt, and from the way in which the Chinese refer to these tents it would appear that these shelters had already assumed the form of the yurt or dome-shaped tent so characteristic of the Turkish and Mongolian peoples of later time.

The clothing of the Huns, like their furniture, consisted of skins and of felt. These skins were sewed together by means of threads made of hemp or leather. It would seem that the Huns were ignorant of, or at least made no use of, the art of weaving.[27]

The contemporary chroniclers give us no further details regarding these Hunnish clothes, but later Chinese tradition has it that they included the following items: First of all, a pair of full trousers, strapped tightly around the ankles. The feet were covered by leather boots which were sometimes provided with felt soles. The upper part of the costume consisted of a loose robe which reached to the knee or even below; but, though loose, the sleeves fitted closely around the wrists. This robe was kept fastened not by buttons but by a long leather belt, the ends of which hung down in front. In times of war, one of these leather robes served as a sort of armor. Over this robe a short cape made of fur was sometimes worn.

The lobes of the ear were pierced to allow the wearing of earrings. The head was usually covered by a fur cap or hat. Much of the hair was shaved off, but it was customary to leave a tuft of hair on the top of the head and two short braided tresses, one behind each ear.[28] The two tresses worn by the Huns may be regarded as the forerunner of the Chinese pigtail. As is well known, the wearing of a single pigtail was a custom of recent origin in China, this mode of hairdress being imposed upon the Chinese by the Turanian Manchus when they conquered the Celestial Empire in the seventeenth century.

We are expressly told by the ancient Chinese chroniclers that the

Huns engaged in no agricultural pursuits, and this statement was, no doubt, broadly speaking, true, certainly as regards the dominant tribes inside of the Hunnish confederacy. At the same time it is certain that several of the peoples incorporated in this confederacy, among them the Kirghiz in Southwestern Siberia and the Dunghu in Southeastern Mongolia, are known to have engaged to some extent in agricultural pursuits. Furthermore, one or two casual remarks in the Chinese chronicles show that even in the heart of the Hunnish domain some form of agriculture was not entirely unknown. In this connection, it is interesting to note that the Turkish language, the tongue supposedly spoken by the Huns proper and the majority of their subjects, is surprisingly rich in root words concerned with agricultural plants and instruments.[29]

These facts strongly substantiate the theory that the early Turanians were not originally members of the true nomadic horse culture, and that in many places they had already evolved from wild plant gatherers to settled agriculturalists when their development in this direction was suddenly arrested by their contacts with and their conversion to the steppe culture practised by the Iranian nomads of the West.

The rise of the Hunnish Empire undoubtedly tended to suppress the development of agriculture among the Turanian peoples of Eastern Asia. It was easier to follow the mode of life adopted by the dominant Hunnish clan and live most exclusively from flesh and milk. This flesh the Huns secured partly by shooting wild beasts and birds (fishing played a very small part in the life of the steppe peoples), but the great bulk of the animal food came from huge flocks of domesticated animals. The most common of these were horses, sheep, and cattle. Camels, donkeys, and mules were also reared, but in smaller numbers. Surprisingly enough, swine, which played such an important role in the life of the Tungusic tribes of eastern Manchuria and among the inhabitants of China proper, were almost unknown to the steppe nomads.

Among the three major domestic animals (horses, sheep, and cattle), the horse undoubtedly ranked as the most important, with sheep coming next. Horses were valued not only for riding purposes, but also for their skins, for their flesh and, in the case of mares, for their milk. From casual references in the Chinese chronicles, it is evident that even at this early date the copious use of *kumis,* or fermented mare's milk, was already customary among all the Hunnish peoples.[30]

The ancient Chinese histories make no mention of pottery making or of metallurgy among the Huns, and as a result it has been argued that they were ignorant of both these arts. The complete absence of pottery among the modern Kalmuks (or western Mongols) and other modern Turanian peoples has encouraged the belief that pottery making, at least, was almost unknown to the early nomads of Mongolia. It is, therefore, fortunate that archaeology has come to our rescue in this matter and has shown that a crude unglazed pottery (but ornamented, for the most part, with geometrical designs) was being made in different parts of Mongolia at the time when the Hunnish Empire was at its height.

Archaeology has also helped us in solving the problem as to the working of metals among the inhabitants of the Hunnish Empire. Excavations around Minnusinsk in Southwestern Siberia have shown that the peoples in this area had reached a high development in the making of copper, bronze, and iron objects at a time when they must have been subjected to Hunnish invasion and conquest. It is, however, highly doubtful if this Siberian metal culture ever exerted much influence over the inhabitants of Mongolia proper, for which reason the excavations of the Japanese archaeologists in Eastern Mongolia are of especial value. Torii's work has shown that the casting of copper and bronze objects was an art unknown to the ancient inhabitants of Mongolia (all such objects found in this area being obviously of Chinese origin), but the knowledge of iron working must have been widespread among most, if not all, of these Turanian peoples. In consequence we are led to the conclusion that the arrowheads, swords, and other weapons used by the Huns must have been of indigenous workmanship.[31]

Apart from looking after their flocks, the principal occupation of the Hunnish tribesmen was war. The training of the youths in martial exercises started at a very early age. While still babies, they were taught to ride on the backs of sheep, and to shoot with miniature bows and arrows at birds and at rats. When older, they were taught to secure food by shooting at foxes and hares. As soon as they were able to span a full sized bow, the boys were admitted into the ranks of the warriors.

We are further told that the Huns were accustomed to undertake their raids when the moon was waxing, and to lie quiet when it was waning. Like the later Turks and Mongols, the Huns were not ashamed to retreat before superior numbers, since they could always come back when the enemy army had demobilized. The principal weapon was, of course, the bow and arrow which was shot from horseback, but the Huns also made use of swords and spears for hand to hand fighting. When a Hunnish warrior had captured some loot or a prisoner, he was congratulated by being given a bumper of wine (*kumis*) to drink; and in addition the loot or the prisoner became his private possession. These prisoners of war were either killed or became the slaves of their Hunnish master.

The Chinese chronicles solemnly inform us that the Huns were ignorant of *Li,* or etiquette, and *I,* the principles of morality, which means, of course, that the Hunnish standards of etiquette and morality differed widely from those in vogue in the Celestial Empire. What especially shocked the Chinese was the fact that especial attention was paid to the young and strong (it was they who received the tidbits in the way of food), while the old and feeble were treated with scant reverence.

Equally shocking from the Chinese point of view was not the system of polygamy which prevailed among the Huns, for this was as common among the Chinese as among the "Barbarians," but the fact that among the Huns when a man died, his son married all of his father's wives except his own mother. In the absence of a son the younger brother would take over the wives of an older brother. This custom, which was very widespread among practically all the early Turanian peoples, was undoubtedly the result of a desire to look after the husbandless women who would otherwise have been unprotected.

The Huns possessed, of course, personal names, but, unlike the Chinese, they made no use of family names. This absence of family names, however, did not prevent the Huns from keeping elaborate genealogical trees or from being very proud of their descent from illustrious chiefs. Incidentally, in counting their descent the Huns seem to have reckoned almost exclusively on the father's side, being in this respect, unlike the Dunghu or "Eastern Barbarians" and other primitive peoples to the north and east of Mongolia, among whom there were strong traces of a system of counting descent through the mother.

But though the Huns reckoned ancestry from father to son, there was no trace of the law of primogeniture. Not infrequently, moreover, it was the younger brother rather than the son who would succeed to the chieftainship of the tribe or confederacy, especially if the late chief's sons were minors or for other reasons were incapable of leading the warriors in battle. This was true not only of the Huns but of all the later Turanian peoples. And this absence of a clearly defined law of inheritance was destined to prove disastrous to the various Turanian empires from the days of the Huns down to modern times, for the death of a ruler was usually followed by a wild scramble for power among all the surviving brothers and sons and hence gave rise to perpetual civil wars.

Though there were frequent diplomatic negotiations going on between the Huns and Chinese, we are expressly told that the Huns never learned from the Chinese the art of writing. This is a sad blow to archaeologists, to whom this means that they must abandon all hope of finding any Hunnish historical records or even simple inscriptions.

At the same time, it is not surprising to find that the Huns were unable to master the Chinese ideographs, because the latter are very ill-suited to the writing of any Turanian languages. It was not until many centuries later that any of the Turanians became literate (the Turks in the eighth century A.D.); and, when they did so, they utilized not the Chinese ideographs but a phonetic script derived from one of the Near Eastern alphabets.

Considering the long historical contacts which existed between the Huns and the Chinese, it is rather remarkable how little the two peoples borrowed from one another. It was only in their political organization that the Huns had certain features that were derived from Chinese sources. Thus the Huns, like the Chinese, applied to their rulers the title of Exalted Son of Heaven. Moreover, the Hunnish hierarchy of officials was arranged in pairs, such as left and right princes, left and right marshals. And in this hierarchy, the Huns, like the Chinese, gave precedence to the "left" officials over their "right" colleagues. It should be noticed, however, that, whereas the Chinese officials were supposed to receive their posts on the basis of merit, among the Huns practically all of the higher offices were hereditary.[32]

We are told that every morning the Shanyu or the Supreme Ruler of the Huns made formal obeisance to the sun, and every everning to the moon. There were three major festivals during the year. In the first month of each year, the Shanyu, surrounded by all the principal tribal chiefs, made a solemn sacrifice. In the fifth month, there was another such conclave at which offerings were made to ancestors, to heaven, to earth, and to various supernatural beings. In the ninth month of each year, there was still another general assembly of a more secular nature at which a general census was taken both of the tribesmen and of their animals. This is all we know regarding the religious beliefs and practices among the Hunnish peoples except that the Huns had a number of "Shamans," wizards, or witch doctors, and that these Shamans exercised a great deal of influence over their fellow tribesmen.

Vaguely associated with religious ideas were some of the special ceremonies practised by the Huns. Thus we are told that when making solemn oaths and covenants, the Huns sacrificed a white horse and had the various members of the covenant drink the blood of this animal mixed with wine. The fact that the Huns sometimes made ceremonial drinking bowls out of the skulls of their slaughtered enemies was also probably due to some hidden religious motive. This custom was taken over by the Huns from their western neighbors, the Scythians and Sarmatians.[33]

Though Hunnish custom ran directly counter to Chinese ideas of ceremony and etiquette, it is certain that the former were very strict in the observance of some of their own ceremonies. Among the more curious of the Hunnish principles of etiquette was the rule that before any foreign envoy could be received in audience by their Shanyu, it was necessary for the envoy to blacken his face.[34]

We are told that the laws of the Huns were very simple. It was very rare that a criminal was imprisoned. Jails were too expensive. For a minor offense he had his ankles crushed. For major offenses death was the penalty. Justice was very speedy; the disposal of a case never took longer than ten days.

The dead were buried with much ceremony. The corpse was dressed in finery, and gold and silver objects were placed in the grave. Not infrequently the Huns, like the Scythians, followed the barbaric custom of killing off some of the concubines and retainers of a great chief when the latter died in order that they might follow him in the spirit world. In this connection, it may be added that the Chinese were shocked by the fact that the Huns placed no mound tablets or trees over the grave, and that they did not wear mourning for the dead.[35]

CHAPTER FIVE

THE RISE OF THE HUNNISH EMPIRE, 209–141 B.C.

The Ethnogeography of the Far East in the Third Century B.C.*—The Dunghu, Dingling, Wusun, and Yueji—The Rise of the Tsin Dynasty in China—Shï Huangdi's Campaign against the Huns and the Building of the Great Wall—The Rise of the Han Dynasty—Touman and the Rise of the Huns—Maodun and the Establishment of the Hunnish Empire—Conquest of the Dunghu—Defeat of the Dingling—Conquests in Kashgaria—War with China—Reign of Giyu—Establishment of Balance of Power with China —Migration of the Yueji and Wusun to the West.*

THE PRECEDING chapter described the manners and customs of the Huns. Our attention will now be engaged by the history of the rise of the Hunnish Empire, the first Turanian Empire of which we have any historical record. This, as we have already said, took place in the third century before Christ.

At the time of which we speak, most of Mongolia was already in the hands of the Huns or their immediate allies. To the north of Mongolia lay the vast forested region now known as Siberia. It is probable that various Turkish, Mongolian, and Tungusic tribes were already living in the southern portion of Siberia, and that beyond them, farther to the north, there dwelt the different branches of the primitive Paleo-Asiatic group of peoples. Of these peoples our knowledge is scanty. The dense forests of Siberia were so unsuited for cavalry warfare that the Huns seldom or never made an attack in this direction.

To the east of the Huns, in the eastern part of Mongolia and the western part of Manchuria, were a powerful group of people known as the Dunghu or Eastern Barbarians. Like the Huns, these Dunghu were horse-nomads. In fact, in most essential respects, the "Eastern Barbarians" had manners and customs so much like the Huns that a study of one group throws much light upon the other. Formerly it was usual to regard these Dunghu as Tunguses (largely because of the purely accidental similarity of names), and hence, as the ancestors of such peoples as the Manchus. We now know that the Dunghu were either Mongols or Turks, with the weight of opinion in favor of the former. Though they were destined to be conquered by the Huns, some of the Dunghu tribes survived as separate units; and later, after the fall of the Hunnish Empire, they were able to play an important part in Far Eastern history.

Still further to the east, we find Northeastern Manchuria occupied by various Tungusic tribes which were given the collective title of Sushen. Many centuries later these Tungusic peoples were able to make history, but during the period of the Hunnish Empire they remained primitive hunters and fishers, ignorant even of the horse culture and with little or no political organization. Southeastern Manchuria at this period was peopled largely by Koreans, who were already strongly influenced by China and Chinese civilization and were completely alien to the nomadic Huns and Dunghus. Like Siberia, Northeastern and Southeastern Manchuria was heavily forested, and hence both these regions remained comparatively free from Hunnish invasion.

To the west of Mongolia and of the Hunnish Empire lay the vast steppe region of Turkistan, occupied at this time, as we have seen, not by Turks but by peoples speaking Iranian languages. Northern Turkistan was dominated by the nomadic Sarmatian tribes, while Southern Turkistan was in the hands of such peoples as Bactrians and Sogdians, who had already taken up agricultural pursuits. These facts are already known to us. But an additional word should be said regarding the peoples who occupied the border lands which lay between Turkistan and Mongolia.

Immediately to the east of Southern Turkistan was the region watered by the Tarim River, and usually known as Chinese Turkistan. The name, Chinese, however, is singularly inappropriate for this area has formed part of the Chinese Empire for only a short time during its long history. Nor is the name, Turkistan, any more suitable, since the region was not inhabited to any large extent by the Turks or any other Turanians until the ninth century A.D. For this reason (following the example of M. Grousset) we prefer to call the region Kashgaria, after Kashgar, its principal city.

In the third century B.C. practically the whole of the area which we have agreed to call Kashgaria was in the hands of peoples speaking Indo-European languages. Most of these peoples spoke an Iranian language, and hence a language related to that spoken by the peoples inhabiting both Northern and Southern Turkistan. But in the northeastern portion of this region (Kucha and Turfan) a language was spoken which is usually called Tokharian. Tokharian has a unique linguistic position. Though undoubtedly a member of the Indo-European language family, it belongs not to the eastern (or Satem) group inside of this family, as do Sanskrit and the Iranian and Slavic languages, but rather to the western (or Centum) group, the only other members of which live in Western Europe. It is still a mystery how the Tokharians with their western language managed to find their way to this extreme eastern outpost of the Indo-European world.

There was also one other important distinction between the various peoples inhabiting Kashgaria. Most of the inhabitants in this region, like the peoples of Southern Turkistan, had abandoned their nomadic mode of living and had accustomed themselves to an agricultural and urban life. They were never able to group themselves into a single large political unit but, like the early Greeks, were divided into a large number of city states. The Chinese records speak of more than twenty-six of these metropolitan principalities, of which the most important were those centered in or near the places which are now called Khutan, Yarkand, and Kashgar in the south and west, and Kucha, Karashahr and Turfan in the north and northeast.

In the extreme eastern and northeastern part of Kashgaria or, in other words, in the region adjoining the Hunnish dominions in Mongolia, were a number of tribes which were still horse-nomads with a steppe culture similar in all essential respects to that of their Turanian neighbors, the Huns. The two tribes most frequently mentioned were the Wusun and the Yuejï, both of whom were destined to play an important part in later history. There have been many attempts to fix the linguistic affiliation of these two tribes. At present practically all scholars are agreed that both the Wusun and the Yuejï spoke Indo-European languages, but there is some dispute as to whether these languages belonged more specifically to the Iranian or the Tokharian group. In view of all the known evidence it is more reasonable to suppose that they must be classified with the Iranians.

The exact status of the peoples who inhabited the region to the north of Kashgaria—a region which included Zungaria, Southwestern Siberia, and the extreme northeastern portion of Northern Turkistan—is still open to doubt. The Chinese records tell us that among the inhabitants of this region were three peoples known as the Gienkun, the Dingling, and the Hugie. Scholars are agreed that the Gienkun were none other than the Kirghis, and that the Dingling and the Hugie were probably the ancestors of the people later known as Uigurs.

The Kirghis, of course, are well-known to us as a people who have frequently played a role in history and who still exist today. Though the Uigurs have now died out, they were for many centuries even more important than the Kirghis to whom they were probably distantly related. In modern times both the Kirghis and the Uigurs are known to have spoken Turkish as their mother language, from which fact it would appear that even in the third century B.C. this region was occupied by Turanian speaking peoples.

It so happens, however, that the Chinese have a tradition that the ancient Kirghis were decidedly blond in appearance, or, as the Chinese say, were tall with white skin, red hair, and green eyes. From this fact several scholars have argued that the Kirghis are really Indo-European in origin and have become Mongoloid in appearance and Turkish in speech only because of their long contact with the Turanians in the East. It is quite possible that the same thing was true of the other two tribes. In any case, we may assume that even though these three tribes were Indo-European in origin, the process of their "Turanization" had begun by the time the Hunnish Empire had reached its height, and hence we may include them with the Turanians rather than with the Indo-Europeans.[1]

The Huns were destined to have many conflicts with the peoples to the east and to the west of themselves, but their most arduous and historic campaigns were directed against the Chinese in the south. It is, therefore, especially necessary that we survey the condition of things in the Celestial Kingdom at the time of the rise of the Hunnish Empire. The Chinese are so fond of talking of the antiquity of their empire that we are likely to forget that prior to the third century B.C. China was a very small state. Neither Manchuria, Mongolia, Kashgaria, nor Tibet were in any way subject to Chinese rule. In what is now China proper the domain of the Chinese "empire" extended only as far south as the Yangtze River. For all practical purposes, therefore, the China of this period consisted only of the middle and lower sections of the Yellow River basin.

Even inside of this relatively small domain, the power of the central government was very limited. As we have already seen, though the emperors of the Eastern Jou dynasty (770-256 B.C.) claimed to be the lords of the whole of China, in point of fact the country was broken up into a number of feudal kingdoms or principalities, the rulers of which paid very little attention to the wishes of their nominal overlord.

Owing to the fighting which was constantly going on between the "Barbarian" inhabitants of Mongolia—the ancestors of the Huns—and the feudal states in the northern part of China, the northern states came to have a distinct advantage over their neighbors to the south; for not only did these Northerners become inured to fighting under difficult conditions, but they were also able to take advantage of the many lessons in tactics and equipment taught them by their conflicts with the militant nomads of the north. It was the Prince of Jao, one of these northern states, it will be remembered, who first introduced into his army the use of mounted archers, and was thereby enabled to win many a signal victory.

It was, however, not Jao but its neighbor to the west, the principality of Tsin, which was able to take full advantage of the new tactics and was thereby put in a position to crush all the other feudal states and secure control over the whole of China. The heavily armed and slow moving armies of the central and southern states were no match for the lightly armed horse regiments which poured from the mountain crannies of Tsin.

The establishment of Tsin's powers as the predominant state in China goes back to the prince, Jao-siang, who ruled over the principality from 306 B.C. to 251 B.C. It was at this time that most of the other feudal states were subdued, and the last suzerain of the Imperial Dynasty of Jou driven from the throne (256 B.C.). Even so, this enterprising prince did not as yet dare to assume the title of Supreme Ruler for himself.

This final step was taken by Jao-siang's grandson, the great Jeng, better known as Tsin Shï Huangdi or "the First Emperor of the House of Tsin" who ruled from 246 B.C. to 210 B.C. It is this man who must be regarded as the founder of China's military and political greatness. China under the Jou dynasty had been a feudal and patriarchal kingdom. Shï Huangdi made of it a centralized, well-organized and powerful empire. Wishing to wipe away all the evils of the old regime, he ordered the burning of all books except those dealing with science or agriculture.

Not content with having conquered all of historic China, he deliberately embarked upon a policy of military expansion, one result of which was the incorporation of South China (Canton, etc.) for the first time within the limits of the Celestial Empire. He also extended the frontiers of China on the northeast and northwest. Last but not least he sent out numerous expeditions directly to the north, most of which were directed against the Huns. As a result of these campaigns, most of the "Barbarians" were pushed back into the Gobi desert and Inner or Southern Mongolia thus came for the first time within the sphere of influence of the Chinese Empire.

The hold of the Chinese over Inner Mongolia, however, was very insecure. The great Emperor feared that at any moment the Northern Barbarians would not only return to their old domain but also begin again their favorite task of ravaging Northern China. Consequently he gave orders for the construction of what we now know as one of the wonders of the world—the Great Wall of China (214 B.C.)—which was designed to secure his empire from invasion by the warlike tribes inhabiting Mongolia.

We know that several of the earlier feudal princes had erected similar barriers on a smaller scale in the northern part of their realms, so that the task set by Shï Huangdi was largely to link together the previously existing walls in such a way as to make the Great Wall a unified line of defense. We also know from the later Chinese chronicles that many changes and additions were made to the Great Wall in subsequent times, so that the Wall as we find it today is far from being the work of one generation. Nevertheless, the idea of a single barrier stretching from east to west across the northern frontier of China and measuring more than fifteen hundred miles in length is undoubtedly due to the initiative of the man who has well been called "The Napoleon of the Far East," and due credit should be given him. In spite of the Wall the Turanian inhabitants of the north have frequently succeeded in invading and conquering all or parts of China. But this great monument of engineering enterprise is far from having been a failure, for it has undoubtedly aided the Chinese in keeping out at least some of her troublesome neighbors to the north. It would certainly seem that it was of value in repelling the original Huns. As we know, the Huns, defeated in their attempts to conquer China, eventually turned west and, driving the Goths before them, caused the premature downfall of the Roman Empire. For this reason some scholars have suggested that the building of the Great Wall of China was one of the important contributing factors in Rome's downfall.

It is of some interest to note that Meng Tien, the Chinese general who defeated the Huns and who was charged with the actual construction of the Wall, is popularly (though probably erroneously) credited with the invention or at least the improvement of the writing brush, one of the most important features of Chinese culture. In any case Meng Tien was one of China's greatest generals, and it is rather tragic to read of his untimely end. Shortly after the death of his master, the great Emperor, he was ordered to commit suicide. This order was given for purely political reasons, of course, but ostensibly it was because his construction of the Great Wall had cut some of the pulses of good Mother Earth and thus disturbed some of the terrestrial spirits. The Chinese superstition against disturbing the surface of the ground, a nation which has seriously impeded the building of railways in modern times, is thus seen to have a lengthy historical background.

The great Emperor had changed the title of the rulers of China from *Wang* (King) to *Huangdi* (Emperor); and, instead of choosing a dynastic name as was customary in the Celestial Empire, he had called himself, as we have seen, merely Shï Huangdi or First Emperor with the intention that his son should be the Second, his grandson the Third Emperor, and so on for all eternity. But alas for human plans and ambitions. Shï Huangdi died in 210 B.C. His son and successor proved to be a weakling, and four years later the Tsin dynasty came to an end.[2]

For four years the Celestial Empire was in a state of anarchy, but in 202 B.C. Liu Bang, a soldier of fortune from Central China, managed to secure control over the whole country and established a new dynasty which was given the name of Han. The Han dynasty in one form or another lasted for over four hundred years (or from 202 B.C. to A.D. 220). It proved one of the greatest ruling houses with which China was ever to be blessed. During the period of its rule, art, literature and science flourished to an unprecedented degree. It was in this period that China first came into close and direct contact with the outside world; under the patronage of this house Buddhism was intoduced, and along with Buddhism came cultural influences from India, from Persia, and even from the Greek world.

From a political and military standpoint also the Han dynasty was of the greatest importance. Under the Tsin dynasty China proper became unified and centralized, but it was not until the Han period that the Chinese Empire secured mastery over the whole of the Far East. The rise of the Han dynasty to power was naturally of the greatest importance to the Huns and other Turanians in the north. The Hunnish Empire and the House of Han were established at almost the same time. By a curious coincidence they both weakened and were destroyed within the same generation. For many decades they were bitter and evenly balanced rivals, and on at least one occasion it seemed as if the Huns rather than the Hans were to become masters of Eastern Asia. If this eventuality had taken place the history not only of Asia but of the whole civilized world would have been radically different.

Before dealing with the lengthy wars between China and the Huns, let us turn back and see how the Hunnish Empire came to be formed. About the year 215 B.C., when we first begin to get detailed descriptions of events which occurred among the Northern Barbarians, we find that the seat of the Hunnish tribal confederation was not in what is now known as Outer Mongolia, to the north of the Gobi desert (the seat of the later Mongolian Empire), but in Inner Mongolia, to the south of the desert and immediately adjacent to Chinese territory. At this time the leader of the Huns was a man called Touman. Touman must have had a strong and forceful personality, but even so he was no match for Shï Huangdi, the founder of the Tsin dynasty, with his great general, Meng Tien; and as a result of the latter's campaigns in the north (214 B.C.), Touman and his Hunnish hordes were forced to retreat to the north, or into outer Mongolia, in which position they were for the moment free from all further fear of attack.

Only five years later the Tsin Emperor and his general, Meng Tien, were both dead; and, in the confusion and anarchy which followed, the

Chinese were no longer able to guard their northern frontier. Taking advantage of this opportunity, Touman led his hordes back to the south and in a short time was able to reconquer practically the whole of Inner Mongolia (209 B.C.). His headquarters were near the present city of Kukukhoto, to the northeast of the great bend in the Yellow River.

The Huns were now quite as powerful as they were before the Chinese campaign in the north. In fact they were probably stronger, because prior to this even the Hunnish tribal organization was exceedingly weak and ineffectual; the pressure from the Chinese invading army seems to have been the driving force which caused the Northern Barbarians to forget their tribal differences and form a powerful political organization under the leadership of a single chieftain. But though the Hunnish nation was now a power to be reckoned with, it was still far from being a great empire. China proper was still free from Hunnish invasion; and in Central Asia the Dunghu in the east and the Yuejï and Wusun in the west, to say nothing of the various other peoples in the north, were still independent and unconquered powers. Touman had to be content with having welded the Huns into a nation. It was reserved for his son, the great conqueror Maodun, to transform this nation into a vast empire.[3]

It was the tragic fate of Touman to meet his end at the hands of this great son of his. Maodun was the eldest son and the natural heir of Touman, but in his declining years the latter fell under the influence of a young and beautiful concubine who strove to have her own son made the heir of the Hunnish Kingrom. At the suggestion of this woman Touman attempted to get his eldest son out of the way in a very artful fashion. It was the custom of the Huns to exchange hostages with the Yuejï, the powerful Indo-European people who then dwelt in the region immediately to the southwest of the Hunnish domain. Taking advantage of this custom, Touman sent Maodun to reside among the Yuejï; and, while he was still there, Touman suddenly declared war upon his neighbors, thinking, of course, that the Yuejï would kill off his unwanted son by way of retaliation.

Maodun, however, got wind of what was up. Stealing a swift horse, he managed to make good his escape and returned to his father's encampment. Touman was so proud of his son's exploit that a nominal reconciliation was effected, and Maodun was placed in command of a special brigade of ten thousand warriors. For Maodun, however, it was not so easy to forgive or forget, and shortly afterwards (209 B.C.) he succeeded in murdering his father, his father's concubine, all his brothers and half-brothers and, in addition, all the Hunnish chieftains who would not render him implicit obedience.

It is a characteristic feature of most of the Turanian empires that they were not the result of gradual expansion or development but rapidly became enormous empires under the leadership of a single great man and under the reign of his successors slowly but surely declined. The fortunes of the Hunnish Empire were an excellent example of this characteristic. During the long rule of Maodun, which extended for over thirty-five years or from 209 to 174 B.C., the Huns reached the zenith of their power. After his death the new empire remained stable for two or three generations and thereafter rapidly disintegrated.

In modern times Maodun has become a great hero among all of the Turanians and even such peoples as the Hungarians and the Turks class him along with, or above, Attila, Chingis Khan, Osman, or Timur as one of the great glories of the "Turanian race." It may seem strange that a gentleman who killed off his father, his brothers, and other kith and kin should be made into a "glory of his race," but it must be admitted that Maodun had a certain justification for his bloodthirsty actions, and he certainly lived in a bloodthirsty time and place.

In any case, it would seem as if the rise of the Hunnish Empire was really due to his own individual genius, and especially to his ability to teach his people the merit of concerted action. Up to this time the Huns had been accustomed to fight in open order and individually. Maodun made use of whistling arrows and with them trained his followers to unified action. "An order was issued by him to the effect that when he shot one of his arrows at a definite goal his soldiers were to fire at the same goal under fear of decapitation. To break the former deep-rooted habit of irregular fighting on the part of these wild hordes and to train them to the word of one chief commander required a master mind and an iron will power."

This change in tactics was so radical that it may be supposed that Maodun could only have learned of the new tactics from some completely alien source. Some scholars think that Maodun's strategy was borrowed from the Iranian Yueji with whom he had formerly been a hostage. If so, it is another instance of the great debt owed by the Huns to their Indo-European neighbors to the west.

Maodun's desire for concerted action, moreover, was not confined to the sphere of military tactics but extended to that of political organization. As far as we can gather, the Huns, up to this period, had only the simplest tribal organization—in fact, almost no organization at all. Maodun introduced an elaborate and complicated hierarchy of officials, headed by twenty-four nobles, each of whom ruled over at least ten thousand warriors. At the top of this hierarchy were the Left and Right "Worthy Princes." The Left Worthy Prince was a sort of viceroy of the Eastern portion of the Hunnish Empire, while the Right Worthy Prince was viceroy over the western part; the Supreme Ruler, in this case Maodun himself, kept direct control over the central portion. As we have already seen, the Left Worthy Prince had precedence over his colleague and was usually regarded as the heir apparent to the Supreme Ruler of the Empire.

Unlike the more closely knit Chinese Empire organized by the rulers of the Han dynasty, the Hunnish Empire always preserved a certain element of "feudalism," for, though all of the twenty-four members of the hierarchy were subject to the Shanyu, each one of them was lord and master of a specific area. Even more important, each of these high officials had the right to appoint his subordinate officers and officials, the lords of ten, of a hundred, and of a thousand soldiers. In spite of their decentralization, as long as Maodun and his more active successors were in power the Hunnish Empire remained a unified state, subject to the orders of one man. We are told, moreover, that two of the hierarchy of twenty-four (the Gudu or Felicitous Lords) were specifically charged with assisting in the administrative business of the state as a whole.[4]

Shortly after his accession to power Maodun began a series of military exploits which resulted in his petty state becoming a vast empire. Unfortunately many of these exploits are known to us only in a most sketchy fashion, since we hear of them only through the Chinese sources, and the Chinese authors were little interested in describing the wars which the Northern Barbarians chose to carry on among themselves.

We do know, however, that Maodun's first war was in the east, where he invaded the territory of the Dunghu or Eastern Barbarians who then lived in and ruled over Eastern Mongolia and Western Manchuria. When Maodun first came to the throne, Dunghu tribesmen were quite as powerful as the Huns, and, from the records we have, it is obvious that Maodun for some time stood in great fear of them. When the Dunghu demanded tribute in the form of horses and women, these were meekly handed over. It was only when the Dunghu, despising the weakness of their rivals, began to annex a goodly portion of the Hunnish territory that Maodun, in desperation, led his army to the east. The Dunghu tribesmen were caught completely unawares and were overwhelmingly defeated. Their territory became part of Maodun's domain, and most of the Dunghu themselves were incorporated bodily into the Hunnish tribal organization. Only a few scattered tribes, such as the Wuhuan and the Sienbis (concerning whom we shall later have much to say), were able to retain an independent or semi-independent organization. This campaign brought the boundaries of the Hunnish Empire either to or almost to the Pacific Ocean.

Not long afterwards Maodun and his cohorts turned their attention

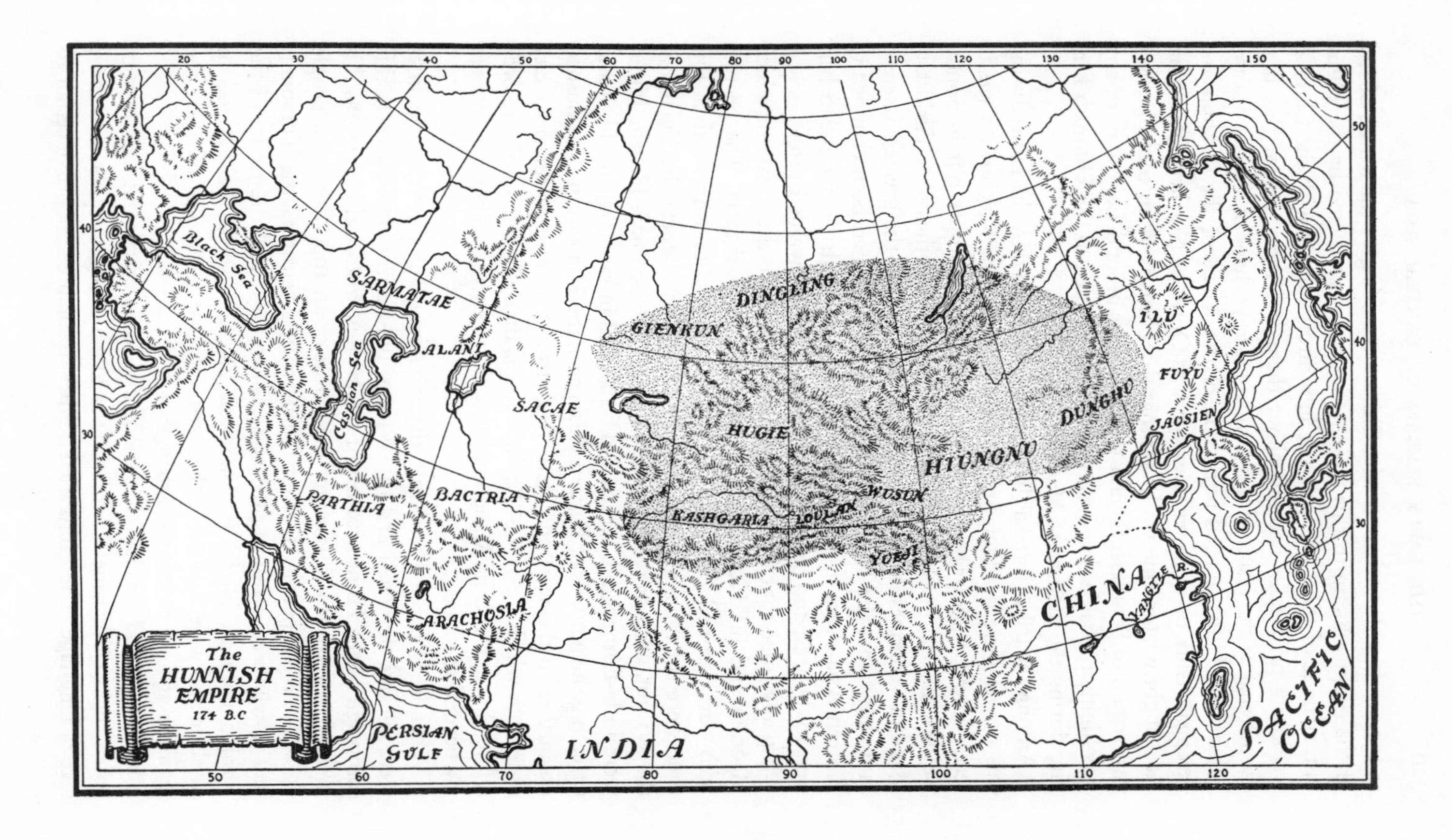
The HUNNISH EMPIRE 174 B.C
Black Sea
SARMATAE
Caspian Sea
ALANI
SACAE
PARTHIA
BACTRIA
ARACHOSIA
PERSIAN GULF
INDIA
GIENKUN
DINGLING
HUGIE
KASHGARIA
LOULAN
WUSUN
YUEJI
HIUNGNU
DUNGHU
ILU
FUYU
JAOSIEN
CHINA
YANGTZE R.
PACIFIC OCEAN

to the north and northwest. The Chinese records give the names of five of the peoples living in this region who were conquered by the Huns, but, as none of these groups came into direct contact with the Chinese, we know practically nothing about them but their names. But it is certain that as the result of this campaign, or perhaps of a series of campaigns, the Huns secured possession of the whole of the Orkhon and Selenga basins, or what we now know as Outer or Northern Mongolia. At a slightly later time we know that the Huns were in control of the vast region of Southern Siberia which centers around Lake Baikal, and it is highly probable that even this area was added to the Hunnish Empire during the lifetime of Maodun.

Among the tribes listed as having been conquered by the Huns during this period were the Dingling and the Gienkun or Kirghis. As we already know, these tribes lived not in Mongolia proper but in Southwestern Siberia, in Northern Zungaria, and in Northeastern Turkistan. Maodun's conquest of these peoples is therefore of the greatest interest, as it shows that the Huns, who for centuries past had been confined to Eastern Asia, were at length able to break through the mountain barriers to the west and begin their fateful progress towards Europe.

Equally important from our point of view were the invasions which Maodun and his Hunnish hordes effected in Kashgaria. The peoples who were destined to feel the full weight of the Hunnish inroads at this time were the inhabitants of Eastern Kashgaria, namely the Yuejï and the Wusun, who, as we have seen, though horse-nomads like the Huns, were Indo-European in speech and Caucasoid in race. But in addition to defeating the nomads of Eastern Kashgaria, the Huns must have pushed on farther to the west and secured control over most of the petty city states into which the rest of Kashgaria was then divided, for the records tell us that at this time Maodun conquered twenty-six other states which lay beyond the Yuejï.

When it is remembered that the inhabitants of these principalities were all, like the Yuejï and the Wusun, Indo-European in speech, this campaign of the Huns becomes of the greatest historical interest, as this is the first recorded instance of the defeat of an Indo-European people by a Turanian people. During the preceding centuries the Turanians had slowly been acquiring the arms, the culture, and the tactics of the Iranian nomads. Now the Turanians had completed their period of tutelage and were able to use their arms and the tactics learned from the Iranians against the teachers themselves.

But while the Huns had thus conquered Kashgaria, it must not be supposed that at this time Kashgaria was much changed either as regards race or language. The Huns tried neither to colonize the province nor to impose their language upon the subject people. For several decades the native inhabitants continued the even tenor of their lives, unaffected by the Hunnish conquests except for the fact that they were forced to send tribute to the Hunnish court. We know that the Huns even allowed the rulers of these petty kingdoms to retain their thrones as long as these monarchs were willing to acknowledge the overlordship of the Hunnish Shanyu.[5]

In view of the later history of the Huns and of the other peoples of Central Asia, we are especially interested in these early Hunnish campaigns against the west and southwest, but unfortunately the Chinese records tell us only that such campaigns took place and give us no details. To make up for this, these records give us rather too much detail regarding the endless conflicts between the Huns and the Chinese. These conflicts are less interesting and less important for the simple reason that for nearly three-quarters of a century neither party was able to win any decisive victory, and during this time there was practically a stalemate in the struggle for supremacy between the two powers. For this reason we may content ourselves with citing only two or three of the outstanding events in this quarter of the world.

The first and in many ways the most exciting of the conflicts between the Huns and Chinese at this period took place shortly after Maodun had established his empire in the north, and Liu Bang or Gao-di, to give him his dynastic name, the founder of the Han dynasty, had firmly fixed his empire in the south. It will be remembered that from 206 B.C. to 202 B.C. China was in a state of anarchy which was only ended in the latter year, by which time Gao-di had defeated practically all of his rivals for the throne and had secured a firm hold over the whole of China proper.[6]

Proud of his victories in his native land, Gao-di decided to try and follow in the footsteps of Shï Huangdi and General Meng Tien by undertaking a campaign against the Northern Barbarians. Trusting none of his generals, the Emperor in 200 B.C. (shortly after ascending the throne) placed himself at the head of a huge army and marched north. But on this occasion the Celestial Emperor was completely out-generalled by the wily ruler of the Huns.

During this campaign the bulk of the Chinese army consisted of infantry, while Maodun, of course, relied upon his mounted archers, and thus insured for his army greater mobility of action. After a few skirmishes the Hunnish army simulated defeat and pretended to flee to the north. Gao-di fell into the trap; and, leaving a large portion of his army behind because of the slowness of their movements, he himself with a small body of men pushed on rapidly in pursuit of what he believed to be his fleeing enemy. When the Chinese Emperor reached a point close to the modern city of Da-Tung in Shansi province, Maodun with all of his Hunnish hordes suddenly turned and surrounded the Chinese camp, cutting it off from all supplies and reinforcements.[7]

For over a week Gao-di remained caught in this trap with seemingly no prospect of escape. Curiously enough relief came in the end by treachery within the household of the Hunnish ruler. The Chinese Emperor managed to establish secret communication with the chief wife of Maodun and by means of rich presents won her over to his side. By working upon his superstitious fears, the Hunnish Empress persuaded her husband to allow the Celestial Emperor and his followers to escape from their trap and return to China.

This escape of Gao-di from the ambush set for him by the Huns must be regarded as one of the most significant events in world history. If this ruler who had just reëstablished order in China had been killed, it is probable that China would have relapsed into anarchy for another century, and the important development of culture which took place during the Han dynasty would have been indefinitely postponed. Even more important was the effect of this escape upon the Huns. Had they overwhelmingly defeated the new Han dynasty, it is highly probable that they would have invaded and conquered China itself. Had this taken place, the Huns would have remained forever linked with the Far East. As it was, the escape of Gao-di meant that China retained its independence. After three hundred years of fighting, the Huns and their Turanian allies were driven off into the west with the eventual result that the Huns and their successors were destined to destroy not the Chinese but the Roman Empire.

But though in the end the Chinese were to overthrow the Hunnish Empire rather than the Huns the Chinese Empire, this development did not take place until long after Maodun and Gao-di had been laid away in their graves; for the moment the advantage lay distinctly with the Huns. After his narrow escape from the ambush the Celestial Emperor had no stomach for further campaigns against the Northern Barbarians.

The Huns were allowed to remain in undisputed possession of the whole of Mongolia; and in addition every year the Chinese sent "presents" in the form of silk, wine, and choice eatables to Maodun's court in order to keep the Huns in good humor. Last but not least Gao-di strove to placate the great Hunnish ruler by sending to the latter's harem one of the most beautiful ladies of his court. The Chinese Emperor, in fact, was so much in fear of his northern rival that he originally planned to send his own daughter to be the bride of the Hunnish ruler. Gao-di's consort, later the notorious Empress Lü, however, was indignant at the prospect of having her child handed over to a barbarian, and she forced her husband to abandon the proposition, sending instead one of the young ladies-in-waiting at his court. Maodun does not seem to have noticed the deception.[8]

It seems rather sardonic, remembering that Gao-di had been saved from defeat and death by the intercession of Maodun's wife, that he should have requited this favor by sending a Chinese princess to be her rival in the harem of the Hunnish Shanyu. Nevertheless this diplomatic move seems to have met with great success; for, seemingly as a result of the influence of this Chinese lady, China remained free for some years from serious attack on the part of the Huns, though there were indeed frequent small-scale raids and incursions. The Han dynasty and with it China was thus preserved by the influence of two women, one a jewel-loving Hunnish empress and the other an artful Chinese lady-in-waiting.

Not long after this, it looked for a moment as if another marriage might weld the Chinese and Hunnish empires into one huge state. Gao-di, the founder of the Han dynasty, died in 195 B.C., only five years after his defeat at the hands of the Huns. On his death all powers passed into the control of his widow, the Empress Lü, who either as regent or in her own right ruled over the empire for nearly fifteen years (194 to 180 B.C.) and thus became the first of China's famous, or rather infamous, female despots.

Wishing to take advantage of the situation, Maodun, the Hunnish ruler, sent a letter to the Chinese Empress, telling her that he was lonely and hinted that he would not be averse to becoming the husband of the good lady, by which step the two empires would become one, to the benefit of everyone concerned. China's Iron Lady was strongly opposed to accepting this proposal, but for diplomatic reasons she did not dare send back a positive refusal. In fact, she composed an epistle to Maodun, thanking him for his interest but stating that her age and physical condition made her unequal to the task of receiving his affections. "I have become short of breath, my hair and teeth are falling out, my gait has become halting—but I possess two imperial carriages and two four-horse teams, and these I send to you that you may always ride therein."

This soft answer seems to have flattered the Hunnish ruler, for instead of becoming angry at the rejection of his suit, he apologized for his ignorance of etiquette and sent several presents to the Chinese court in return for the imperial chariots. As long as the Empress Lü remained on the throne, relations between the Northern and Southern Empires remained reasonably friendly.[9]

Maodun, the creator of the Hunnish Empire, died in 174 B.C., and was succeeded by his son Giyu, also known as Lao-shang, "Old-High," or Venerable Shanyu. It is not unusual for Turanian empires to disintegrate immediately after the death of their founders, but Giyu, who ruled over the Huns for sixteen years (174-160 B.C.), managed to keep the Hunnish Empire intact and, at least in some of his campaigns, fully matched any of his father's military exploits.[10]

Shortly after Giyu's accession, Wên-di, who had succeeded the Empress Lü as master of the Celestial Empire and who still thought it necessary to stand in well with the Hunnish court, sent another Chinese noblewoman to be the bride of the new Lord of the Northern Barbarians. This bride was provided with a rich dowry in the form of brocaded silks and many other precious ornaments. It is rather remarkable that the long continued contacts between the Chinese and the Huns, in the course of which the Huns became familiar with the art and industry of the Chinese, did not result in the Northern Barbarians giving up their old Altaian culture and adopting wholesale the civilization of the Chinese. But though the Huns were perfectly willing to accept Chinese wives and concubines and were only too anxious to acquire Chinese articles of luxury, they rigidly maintained their ancient manners and customs in all essential respects.

Curiously enough they were encouraged in this attitude by some of the renegade Chinese who made their way to the Hunnish court. We have preserved for us a remarkable address which a Chinese eunuch made to Giyu. This man had been forced very much against his will to accompany the Chinese lady sent to become Giyu's bride. Once arrived at the Hunnish court, he soon accustomed himself to his new mode of life and became one of the most loyal counsellors of the Hunnish Emperor. In fact he became one of the leaders of the conservative party, and was constantly urging the Huns to accept no snub from the Chinese envoys. He vigorously attacked the notion that the Hunnish culture was inferior to that of the Chinese.

The Chinese chronicle relates that when the Shanyu showed a great fondness for Chinese dress and food, the eunuch adviser spoke as follows: "The population of the whole Hunnish empire is scarcely as great as that of a single Chinese district, yet the Huns form an allpowerful nation largely because they have their own dress and food and are not forced to depend upon Chinese products. Should, however, the Shanyu cause the hearts of his people to change so that they will require Chinese luxuries, they will fall entirely under Chinese influence. If they clothe themselves in silk, their clothes are torn by the thorns and bushes as they ride along, a proof that silk garments are inferior to the skin and felt garments of the Huns. The Huns show no great liking for Chinese articles of food, a proof that the Chinese diet is in no way superior to the milk products of the Huns."[11]

It would seem that Giyu followed the eunuch's sage advice because we know that for many decades thereafter the Huns remained politically and economically independent of the Chinese.

The renegade eunuch, however, was not content with urging the Huns to lead their own life, but was constantly advising them to renew their raids upon China, his own native land. As a result of his influence the peace which had lasted for several years was at length broken. In 166 B.C. Giyu, at the head of an army of one hundred and forty thousand cavalry men, broke through the Great Wall and invaded Northwestern China. He killed the local governor and captured vast numbers of men and animals. Pushing still further to the south, the Huns came within a few miles of Chang-an, the Chinese capital (near the modern city of Si-an), and even succeeded in burning one of the imperial palaces.

To repel this invasion the Emperor Wên-di placed in the field an army of a thousand war chariots (with about a hundred thousand infantry) and an additional hundred thousand cavalrymen. Being desirous of securing military glory for himself, Wên-di at first thought of commanding this huge army in person; but, being persuaded by the Empress to abandon this project, he placed his most trusted generals in command of the expedition and ordered them to repel the Huns at all costs. Giyu, the Lord of the Huns, followed the usual Hunnish tactics and retreated north of the Great Wall on the approach of the Chinese army but without losing any of his booty or any of his prisoners.

The result of this campaign showed very clearly that for the moment there was an almost complete balance of power between the Chinese and Hunnish empires. The Huns might undertake extensive raids into China, but they were unable to effect any permanent conquests in the Celestial Empire. The Chinese, on the other hand, though they were able to expel the Huns, were unable to invade the Hunnish dominions or to inflict any serious defeat upon the Hunnish army. The rulers of both empires recognized that for the time being neither side could gain a decisive advantage over the other, with the result that both sides abandoned hostilities and negotiated a treaty of peace.

In this treaty it was stated that "all the territory north of the Great Wall is the country of the bowmen and is subject to the Hunnish Shanyu, and all the territory south of the Great Wall is the country of hats and girdles and is subject to the Chinese emperor." In other words the Huns were to remain lords of what is now Manchuria, Mongolia, Zungaria, and Kashgaria, while the Chinese were to remain in possession of China proper. It should be noted, however, that much of what is now Southern

China still consisted of completely independent kingdoms, and that Tibet was still free from both Chinese and Hunnish control. This meant that as regards size the Hunnish Empire was between four and five times as large as the Chinese Empire, although, of course, China was far more populous and far more wealthy.

In the negotiations between the Chinese and Hunnish rulers it was further provided that to prevent border disputes in the future, no Hun was to pass south of the Great Wall and no Chinese north of it. Even more interesting is an item where the Chinese Emperor states that, as the Huns live in the north with its devastating cold, he (Wên-di) has ordered that each year his ministers shall provide the Huns with suitable amounts of brocades, silk, and rice, these things being unobtainable in their native land. This, of course, was merely a delicate way of bribing the Huns to desist from their raids into Chinese territory. As the result of these negotiations the Chinese and Huns remained on comparatively friendly terms as long as Giyu stayed on the Hunnish throne.[12] This meant, however, only that as the Huns had given up their attacks on China they were able to turn their attentions elsewhere.

It is typical of the Chinese historians that in the main account of the life of Giyu they wrote only of the relations which this Hunnish chief had with the Celestial Empire. However, in casual references in other portions of these ancient works we find mention of the events of Giyu's life for which he is chiefly entitled to a permanent place in world history, namely, his attack upon the Yuejï which caused the latter to move westward and change the whole course of history in India and the Near East.

It will be remembered that the Yuejï were nomads speaking an Indo-European language and living in Northwestern China (the present province of Gansu) and Northeastern Kashgaria. They were more or less hereditary enemies of the Huns, for we know of at least one attack made on them by Touman, the first of the Shanyus of whom we have record, and of at least two campaigns carried out by his son, Maodun, the real founder of the Hunnish Empire. Maodun was successful in defeating the Yuejï and in reducing them to a state of vassalage, but the latter were still far from being crushed.

Some time during Giyu's reign (approximately 165 B.C., but the Chinese records give no exact date) the Yuejï must have made an attempt to reassert their independence, for we hear of a final great campaign of the Huns against the Yuejï in which Giyu succeeded in completely crushing his enemy. Having captured and killed the king of the Yuejï, he made of the latter's skull a ceremonial drinking vessel which was used by Giyu and his successors for many generations thereafter.

This overwhelming defeat caused the complete collapse of the Yuejï kingdom as it was then constituted. A small portion of the Yueji fled to the south and took refuge among the Tibetan (Kiang) tribes of the Nanshan Mountains. This group was known as the Little Yueji. The greater portion of the Yueji, however, determined to place an even greater distance between themselves and their Hunnish persecutors. They could not flee to the East for here lay the Chinese Empire which was already strong enough to repel any invader, nor to the North for here lay the empire of the Huns. Immediately to the West of the Yueji lay the numerous city states of Kashgaria, but this land of deserts and settled oases was little suited to the Yueji because of their nomadic habits. In addition, it was still too close to the Huns, for this people now claimed jurisdiction over all of Kashgaria. The fierce and warlike Kiang might allow a small section of the Yueji to seek refuge among themselves, but they would certainly object to the occupation of their territory by any large group of strangers. In desperation, therefore, the bulk of the Yueji fled far to the Northwest to the Zungarian basin and there settled along the banks of the Ili River and near the shores of Lake Issik-Kul. Before locating in this region, however, the Yueji were forced to drive out the Sakas, the previous occupants of this area.

The expulsion of the Sakas from Zungaria was fraught with far-reaching consequences. We are told expressly in the Chinese annals that some of these Sakas fled to the South and founded the kingdom of Gipin in Northwestern India. An even greater number of these Sakas must have fled to the West and Southwest, for the classical authors tell us that just about this time the Greek domain in Sogdia or Transoxiana was overrun by various branches of the Saka people.[13]

The Yueji were not, however, to be left long in the possession of their new home, for only a few years later they were subjected to a new attack on the part of the Wusun. It will be remembered that the Wusun were formerly neighbors of the Yueji in Eastern Kashgaria. Both peoples had been attacked and defeated by the great Hunnish Shanyu, Maodun. Shortly after this the Yueji and the Wusun fell to fighting among themselves. The Yueji gave the Wusun a sound thrashing and slew the Wusun ruler. The Wusun then fled to the North and took refuge with the Huns. The heir to the Wusun throne, concerning whom many marvelous stories are told, grew up as a page in the Hunnish court. There he so won the affections of the Shanyu, who can have been no other than Giyu, that the latter not only placed the young man on his father's throne as Lord of the Wusun, but also aided him in his desire to avenge his father's death.

To avenge his father's death meant, of course, to attack the Yueji. In the meantime the Yueji, as we know, had abandoned their old home and settled in Zungaria. Undeterred by this fact, the young man led his forces to the West. Here he succeeded in inflicting such a defeat upon the Yueji that the latter were again forced to migrate still farther to the West. This event must have taken place about 160 B.C. After achieving this victory the Wusun themselves settled down in Zungaria, in which region they continued to dwell for several centuries, in fact until they disappear from history.

The Chinese chronicles go on to say that after the Yueji were pushed out of Zungaria by the Wusun, they moved on and over-ran and occupied Sogdia and what they called Dahia or Bactria.[14] As we have already seen, the Greek kingdom of Bactria, which included Bactria proper south of the Oxus and Sogdia or Transoxiana north of the Oxus, had already suffered a great deal from the molestations of the Sakas when the Yueji had first moved into Zungaria. In fact, Sogdia had been given over to the Sakas, and the Greek monarchs had been content with maintaining themselves south of the Oxus.

The arrival of the Yueji only a few years after the Sakas brought still further and even more far-reaching changes in the political geography of that section. As the Yueji moved in, the Sakas were forced to move out. Taking the line of least resistance, most of these Sakas migrated still farther to the Southwest and climbed up onto the Iranian Plateau. Invading the Parthian kingdom, which then occupied most of Iran, they settled in the old province of Drangiana which soon became known as Sakastan, the country of the Sakas, the modern province of Sistan.[15]

Both the Yueji and the Sakas were destined, in later years, to play an important part in the history not only of Iran but also of India. For this reason it is apparent that the Hunnish leader, Giyu's, greatest achievement was not his frequent bickerings with, or invasions of, China, important as they seemed to his contemporaries, but rather his relentless campaign against the Yueji, which directly or indirectly was the cause of a sweeping change in the whole ethnic map of Central Asia. Giyu himself did not live long enough to witness the full effect of the events for which he was responsible, for he died in 160 B.C. shortly after the Wusun had driven the Yueji out of Zungaria. He was succeeded by his son, Günchên, who was destined to rule over the Huns for thirty years, or until 126 B.C.[16]

China also experienced a change in rulers at about the same time, for in 157 B.C. the philosophic Wên-di died and was succeeded by his son Ging-di. Ging-di was not an ideal ruler. He was capricious, narrow-minded, and niggardly. As a result, he was far from popular with his subjects. It is not surprising, therefore, that there were several rebellions during his reign, led for the most part by junior members of the imperial family who wished to secure the throne for themselves. One of the most important of these rebels, the prince of Jao, even sent secret messengers to Günchên, the Lord of the Huns, in an attempt to secure Hunnish co-operation for his project.

To the Huns this must have seemed a magnificent opportunity to invade the Celestial Empire. Günchên, however, seems to have been of a very peaceful disposition, for he made no attempt to aid his would-be ally, nor in any other way did he disturb China during this troubled period, with the result that all the rebellions were put down and Ging-di was able to establish himself firmly on the throne. The Chinese Emperor greatly appreciated this act of forebearance on the part of his barbarian neighbor, and we find him renewing the ancient treaty of amity, sending another Chinese princess to be the bride of the Shanyu, and keeping up the payment of a heavy tribute to the Hunnish court. In addition, he did much to further friendly commercial intercourse between the two countries. As the result of this policy, China and the Hunnish Empire remained at peace for many years, the old balance of power being retained between them.[17]

We have little information as to what was taking place in other parts of the Hunnish Empire during the long reign of the Shanyu Günchên. The only item which the Chinese chroniclers have seen fit to record, and that in a most incidental and casual way, is that during this period the Hunnish control over the Wusun was greatly weakened. The Wusun had been able to expel the Yuejï and settle in Zungaria largely because of the support given them by the Huns. But by this time the Wusun had become sufficiently powerful to feel that they could stand on their own feet, and the Lord of the Wusun refused to appear at the Hunnish court, a sign that he ceased to regard himself a vassal any more. Günchên sent a body of picked troops against him, but the Hunnish army was defeated, after which event the jurisdiction of the Huns over the Wusun became largely nominal.[18]

The fact that the Wusun had been able to break away from the Hunnish Empire was in itself a sign that this empire was beginning to suffer from internal decay, but to contemporaries this decay was scarcely noticeable, and until 140 B.C. the Huns still formed the largest and most powerful single unit in the Far East, or for that matter anywhere in Asia.

CHAPTER SIX

THE HUNS AND CHINESE STRUGGLE FOR SUPREMACY, 140–101 B.C.

The Chinese Empire under Wu-di—Jang Kien's Embassy to the West—Renewed Hostilities with the Huns—The Trap at Mayi—Alternate Victories and Defeats—Transfer of the Hunnish Capital—Campaigns of Wei Tsing and Ho-Kü-bing—Capture of the Hunnish Images—Chinese Secure Control of the Gateway to the West—Battle of the Sand Storm in the North—Later Campaigns—The Chinese Capture Jaosien—Negotiations with the Wusun—Alliance between the Chinese and the Wusun—Establishment of Chinese Hegemony in Kashgaria—Chinese Campaigns against Dayuan.

An important event in the history of Eastern Asia was the death of the Chinese emperor, Ging-di, and the accession to the throne of his son, the great emperor Wu-di. Wu-di, literally the Martial Emperor, was in some ways the most remarkable man ever to sit upon the dragon throne. In most oriental countries the founder of a dynasty is its greatest and most glorious representative. Wu-di, however, was a marked exception to this rule. When he came into power, the Han dynasty had ruled for over sixty years and had boasted of several able rulers, but all of them were eclipsed by the exploits of the new sovereign. It was Wu-di who made of China a strong unified kingdom, and then expanded this kingdom into a huge empire.

In 140 B.C., the so-called Chinese Empire consisted only of China proper; and even this region retained many feudal characteristics, inasmuch as the country was broken up into a number of vassal states each ruled over by its own liege lord. The Central government, moreover, was largely dominated by members of an hereditary aristocracy. Wu-di changed all this. Practically all the vassal states were abolished, and every province was put under the supervision of the central government. Wu-di, moreover, like Louis XIV of France, felt that as long as his chief ministers and officials were recruited from the members of the higher nobility, who assumed that they had an hereditary right to office, he could not count upon their complete subjection to himself. We find, therefore, during this reign that the most important military and civil officers were appointed more and more from the members of the petty bourgeoisie, or even from the lowest strata of social life. As the result of this policy China became, for the first time since the establishment of the Han dynasty, an absolute monarchy in fact as well as in name.[1]

Wu-di spent as much time in expanding his dominion as in consolidating his power at home. In consequence, the Chinese Empire more than trebled in size during this one reign, though it should be remembered that it was an unusually long one, lasting for fifty-three years (140 to 87 B.C.). Much of this expansion was in the south, but with this phase of his activity we have no concern here. Of especial interest to us are the military and diplomatic campaigns in the north, as a result of which China secured control over most of Korea in the northeast, and Kashgaria in the northwest. More important still, Wu-di succeeded, at long last, in defeating and humiliating the Huns and in driving them north of the Gobi desert.

Wu-di's interest in northern expansion started at the very beginning of his reign. In 138 B.C., only three years after he ascended the throne, we find that he was already planning an attack upon the Huns. As yet, however, he did not dare engage with these dreaded opponents unaided. Remembering the humiliating defeat which the Huns had inflicted upon the Yueji a generation previously and believing that the Yueji would be anxious to secure revenge, the emperor thought of sending an embassy to this people, proposing a joint attack upon their common enemy.

The envoy selected for this purpose was a man named Jang Kien, who was thereby destined to become one of China's most famous explorers and diplomats, the first Chinaman of whom we have record to enter into personal contact with the peoples and kingdoms of Western Asia. Up to this time Western Asia (including Persia and India) and Eastern Asia had constituted two separate worlds with no known historical contact between them. It was Jang Kien who broke through this barrier and thereby paved the way for Indian, Persian, and even Greek and Latin influences to enter into the previously isolated Celestial Empire.

The account of Jang Kien's embassy to the West has come down to us and constitutes one of the most interesting sections of the ancient Chinese historical records.[2] Jang Kien was forced to undergo many hardships. At the start he was accompanied by more than a hundred persons, but of this group only two survived. Moreover, thirteen years elapsed between Jang Kien's departure from, and his return to, China. Much of this lapse of time was due to the fact that on their way to Yueji the adventurous envoys were captured by the Huns and remained virtually prisoners among them for more than ten years. Jang Kien consoled himself during this period by taking a Hunnish maiden to wife and raising a brood of children.

Eventually he managed to escape from the Huns, but instead of returning to China he determined to carry out his original mission and went on with his journey to the West. After several further adventures he arrived at last at the court of the Yuejï ruler. The Yuejï at this time had settled down in Southern Sogdia, i.e. just north of the Oxus River, but had already begun their invasion and conquest of Bactria to the south of this stream. Jang Kien did his best to enlist the Yuejï in the project of a joint Chinese-Yuejï attack upon the Huns. The Yuejï, however, having conquered for themselves a new territory which was far richer and more fertile than they had ever possessed before, were in no mood to return to the East and renew the conflict with their ancient adversaries.

Jang Kien remained for more than a year among the Yuejï; and then, being still unable to persuade the latter to accept a Chinese alliance, he determined to return to his own country. On his return journey he took a southerly route, going along the northern flanks of the Kun-lun or Nan-shan Mountains in the hope of keeping out of the clutches of the Huns. In spite of these precautions, he was again captured and imprisoned by the Huns. This time, however, his imprisonment lasted only a year; for in 126 B.C. the Hunnish Shanyu, Günchên, died, and in the confusion following his death Jang Kien managed to escape once more. This time he succeeded in reaching China, where he was welcomed by the Emperor Wu-di who rewarded him with the title of Marquis and the post of Imperial Chamberlain.

Considering that Jang Kien was completely unsuccessful in carrying out the original purpose of his mission, the securing of an alliance with the Yuejï, it may seem somewhat surprising that he was so handsomely rewarded on his return to his native land. Wu-di, however, was sensible enough to realize the enormous value of the services which his envoy had given to the Celestial Empire.

In the first place, Jang Kien brought back with him knowledge of the grape and alfalfa. These two valuable plants had previously been unknown in China, but as the result of this mission to the West both plants were quickly transplanted to Chinese soil and soon formed an important part of Far Eastern domestic economy. These were only the first of a long series of agricultural loans which the Chinese were to receive from the Near East as the result of Jang Kien's opening of the passage between East and West.

Equally important was the fact that Jang Kien first gave to China her knowledge of the existence and position of India. Though he was never there himself, he had heard many accounts of it and realized what important results would accrue if direct communication between China and India could be opened up. As a result of his urging, several attempts were made to send an embassy directly southwest from China to India, thus avoiding the dangers of travel through Kashgaria, which was still dominated by the Huns. For the moment all of these attempts ended in failure, but at least they resulted in China's getting acquainted with Yunnan and the surrounding regions, and this indirectly led to their subsequent incorporation within the Chinese Empire. Most important of all, however, was the fact that Jang Kien brought back with him news of all the peoples then inhabiting Kashgaria, Zungaria, and Turkistan. Largely as a result of this knowledge, the Chinese during the next century were able to expand to the West and bring much of this region within their own domain.

Let us pause for a moment and see just what was the condition of affairs in the West at the time of Jang Kien's embassy. Immediately to the west of China, and reaching as far as Lake Lopnor, was the region formerly occupied by the Wusun and Yuejï; but, when both of these peoples had been driven to the West, it had been taken over by the Huns who had founded there two or three petty Hunnish principalities. Directly to the south were the nomadic and warlike Kiang people, the ancestors of the later Tibetans.

To the west of Lake Lopnor was the "country of the 36 principalities," or of the numerous city states. As we know already, the inhabitants of this region were practically all Indo-European in speech; but they differed from their fellow Indo-Europeans, the Wusun and the Yuejï, and from the Turanian Huns in that they practised agriculture and lived in walled towns and villages. Though each of these city states was allowed to retain its own ruler, they were all in vassalage to the Huns. The Huns, moreover, maintained military governors in Karashahr and one or two places in order to collect tribute from all of these vassal states.

To the north of Kashgaria lay the Tien Shan or Celestial mountains and beyond this Zungaria or the Ili Basin, still occupied by the Wusun. To the west of Kashgaria lay the Tsung Ling Mountains or the Pamirs; and beyond these lay the kingdom, called by the Chinese Da-yüan, and known to us in later times either as Farghana or Khukand (Kokand), which occupied the upper valley of the Jaxartes River.

The inhabitants of Da-yüan, like those of Kashgaria, were an agricultural people dwelling in walled cities of which there were said to be more than seventy in all. But though the population was not nomadic, this region was famous for its excellent horses; according to the Chinese, these horses were the best in all the world. The warriors of this country, like the nomadic Yuejï and Huns, fought from horseback, their principal weapons being the bow and arrow. At the time of Jang Kien's embassy, this region still constituted a completely independent country ruled over by its own king.

To the west of Da-yüan lay the two kingdoms of Yuejï and Kang-gü. The Yuejï, of course, are by this time old friends of ours, as we have traced their migration from Northwest China through Zungaria to their present position in Southern Sogdia or Transoxiana. Jang Kien tells us that in his time the court of the Yuejï king was still north of the Oxus, but he adds that they had already attacked and conquered Dahia or Bactria which lay to the south of the Oxus.

It would appear that all traces of Greek rulership over Bactria had disappeared at this time for Jang Kien had nothing to tell us about the Greeks and informs us merely that the native (Iranian) population were agriculturalists, lived in walled cities, and that they were also shrewd traders. Each of these cities had its own chief or prince. This lack of unity, coupled with the fact that the population was far from martial in its inclinations, meant that the Yuejï had little difficulty in overrunning the country.

The Yuejï themselves still retained their nomadic habits, though no doubt they were already beginning to settle down as a landed aristocracy. In Jang Kien's time the Yuejï were still united under a single monarch; but we find that a few years later they broke up into five principalities, of which the most important was that known to the Chinese as Guei-Shuang, the rulers of which later conquered all of Eastern Iran and Northern India, founding the dynasty known to the Indians as the Kushan.

The Kang-gü occupied the region directly north of the Yuejï, or in other words most of Sogdia, the land between the Oxus and Jaxartes River, where we later find the cities of Bukhara and Samarkand. At this time the Kang-gü also dwelt on both sides of the middle Jaxartes River basin, because we find them in the region where the city of Tashkand was later to arise. Jang Kien tells us that the Kang-gü were nomads with manners and customs identical in the main with those of the Yuejï. Jang Kien has nothing to tell us about the earlier history of the Kang-gü, but we have every reason to believe that they had long lived in Northeastern Turkistan, and had moved southward into Sogdia in the wake of the Yuejï when the latter people made their spectacular conquests of the lands which had once belonged to the Greek kings of Bactria.

At a later period the Kang-gü were destined to play an important role in history, but in Jang Kien's time they cannot have been very powerful for he tells us that they were under the political influence both of the Yuejï and of the Huns. At this time they still comprised a single state, but a little later they, like the Yueji, broke up into five separate principalities.

Jang Kien himself went only as far as the domain of the Yueji and Kang-gü, but he gives us some hearsay information regarding the countries still further to the West. He tells us that to the northwest of the Kang-gü (i.e. in Northwestern Turkistan) there dwelt the nomadic Yentsai, and that to the west of the Yueji (i.e. in Southwestern Turkistan and in the western portion of the Iranian Plateau) there dwelt the settled Ansi. The Yentsai of the Chinese traveler are undoubtedly the same as the Aorsi of the classical writers, the descendants of the Massagetae or at least their successors as the masters of Northwestern Turkistan. It is certain that the Ansi of Jang Kien and the other Chinese historians is the same as our Parthia. The word Ansi, the older pronunciation of which was Ansak, was as near as the Chinese could come to transcribing the name Arsak, the founder of the Parthian Empire.

We have already seen that there is very reason to believe that all the important peoples inhabiting Turkistan at this period belong to the "white" or Caucasoid race and spoke languages belonging to the Indo-European, or more specifically the Iranian, famliy. This belief is strengthened by a passage in the early Chinese chronicles which states that "all the inhabitants [of Turkistan] have deep set eyes and are very hairy.... They speak many different dialects, but all of these dialects belong to one general family and the different peoples are able to understand one another."

Jang Kien tells us nothing about the inhabitants of Northeastern Turkistan, but we know from other sources that it was still occupied by the Gienkun or Kirghiz and the mysterious Dingling, who were still directly subject to the Huns.[3]

After this lengthy digression upon the peoples and countries which lay to the west of China and the Hunnish Empire, we may now return to a discussion of the further fortunes of the Huns themselves.

In 138 B.C. when the Emperor Wu-di first sent Jang Kien to the West, he hoped to be able to fight the Huns with the aid of the Yueji. Pending the arrival of this aid, he thought it necessary to remain on seemingly friendly terms with the Northern Barbarians. The treaty of peace and amity was renewed; another Chinese princess was sent to the Shanyu's harem, accompanied by the usual presents of silk and brocades.

Five years elapsed, however; and in 133 B.C., having received no word from Jang Kien, who was still a prisoner in a Hunnish camp, the Emperor thought that he must abandon all thoughts of aid from the West. If the Huns were to be defeated, it must be by the Chinese acting alone. Even so, the Chinese did not as yet dare risk an open campaign against their northern neighbors, and they planned to secure a signal victory by an act of out and out treachery.

A plan was conceived whereby the Shanyu and his court were to be lured to the little town of Ma-yi, or Horse-town, on the northern frontier and there attacked and either killed or captured. There was sent to the Hunnish court a petty trader, a native of Ma-yi, who pretended to throw in his lot with the Huns and who, after speaking of the rich wealth of goods stored in his native city, offered to guide his new masters there so that they could capture both the city and the goods with the greatest ease.

For the moment the Shanyu Günchên fell into the trap. Placing himself at the head of an army of a hundred thousand riders, he burst through the Great Wall and proceeded to march on Ma-yi. In the meantime a Chinese army of three hundred thousand was hidden in various parts of the surrounding country and there lay quietly, waiting for the Huns to reach their goal. For a time it looked as if the Chinese strategy would be successful and the Hunnish army completely surrounded. When only a few miles from Ma-yi, however, the Hunnish Shanyu suddenly noticed that though there were herds of animals all over the plains there were no shepherds to look after them. His suspicions aroused, he stopped his march forward and attacked a small military outpost, capturing there an official who under threat of death revealed to the Huns the plot which the Chinese had so carefully concocted. On learning of this, the Shanyu and his army immediately turned around and retreated to the north; and, though the Chinese forces followed in hot pursuit as far as the Great Wall, they were able to accomplish nothing.[4]

After the Ma-yi incident, it was obvious that all thoughts of peace and good will between the Chinese and Hunnish empires were impossible, and thereafter for many years there was almost constant warfare between the two nations. For the first ten years of this conflict the fortunes of war were fairly evenly divided between the two parties. Both sides suffered enormous losses without being able to wrest a decisive victory from the other.

In a general way it may be said that the Chinese were victorious in the West while the Huns had the advantage in the East. In the West the Chinese succeeded, in 127 B.C., in capturing the Ordus country, that region south of the Yellow River where this stream makes its long detour into Southern Mongolia. This victory, however, meant only that the Chinese had recaptured the territory which once formed part of Shï Huangdi's domain (after 214 B.C.) but which had fallen back into Hunnish hands after the death of the great conqueror. To make up for this victory, however, the Chinese in the same year were forced to allow the Huns to occupy several districts farther to the East, in the northern part of the present provinces of Shansi and Hobe.[5]

An important change took place in 123 B.C. when the Huns moved their capital, or shall we say military headquarters, north of the desert to some place in the Orkhon or Selenga basin, probably somewhere near the modern city of Urga, and certainly in the region where the Mongol empire later was to arise. Up to this time, it will be remembered, the center of the Hunnish power had been in Inner Mongolia, south of the desert and quite close to the Chinese frontier, so that the transfer of the court to the north must be taken as a sign of weakness.

To be sure the northern migration took place after the Huns had won a notable victory wherein they annihilated one Chinese army and captured another. The move, moreover, was prompted by the principles of military strategy; or, as the Chinese records say, the Huns hoped by migrating to the north to lure the Chinese army into pursuing them across the Gobi Desert, in the belief that the Chinese troops would be exhausted by their long march and would then prove an easy prey to the Hunnish horsemen.[6]

Notwithstanding all this, the transfer of the capital showed that the Huns had abandoned the offensive and were now on the defensive, which in turn meant that the old even balance of power between the Chinese and Hunnish empires had been definitely broken in favor of the Chinese. We may say that after this northern migration the Huns were never again to regain their old predominant position.

Up to this time all power in the Hunnish Empire had been in the hands of their Shanyus, and each of these Shanyus had been remarkably competent, able to overcome all tendencies toward disintegration and decay. In 126 B.C., however, in the midst of the conflict with China, Günchên, the last of the great Shanyus, died. His son should have succeeded to the throne, but as the result of a coup d'etat a younger brother of Günchên was raised to the host of Shanyu. These events seem to have caused much trouble and confusion in the Hunnish lands.

More important still, the usurper and his successors proved to be men of very indifferent caliber. Each of them ruled for only a short time and was unable to carry through a steady policy either in regard to internal administration or external warfare. During the period 140-87 B.C., throughout which time China was ruled over by a single emperor, no less than seven men occupied the Shanyu's throne, none of whom, apart from Günchên, is worthy of special mention.

While the Huns were thus being led by men of secondary quality, the Chinese were fortunate enough to find themselves in possession of a number of generals of unusual ability. Of these it is necessary to mention only two, Wei Tsing, the commander-in-chief of the Chinese forces after 124 B.C., and his even more brilliant nephew, Ho Kü-bing.

The Generalissimo, Wei Tsing, was a classic example of the Emperor Wu-di's ability to choose outstanding leaders from the lowest strata of society. Wei Tsing was the illegitimate son of a slave girl. As a boy he was shepherd and later a groom in the employ of a feudal lord before securing a commission in the army. His entrance into the army and his early promotion, incidentally, were due not so much to his own merit as to the influence of his half-sister, who entered the imperial harem as a concubine and later rose to the position of Empress Consort. But though Wei Tsing owed his early opportunities to his sister, he soon proved his own worth; and his later advancement was due almost entirely to his own energy and ability. We are not surprised to hear that he was a good archer; but it is noteworthy, considering his low origin, that he was punctilious in the treatment of his officers and affable in his dealing with the soldiers, an attitude which resulted in the loyalty that was the cause of many of his victories.

Even more brilliant than Wei Tsing, however, was the latter's nephew, Ho Kü-bing, who distinguished himself as the leader of the Chinese light cavalry. Ho Kü-bing received his first command at the early age of eighteen. This appointment was no doubt due to the influence of his powerful uncle, but in a remarkably short time the youthful commander proved himself to be one of the most gifted military leaders of the age, and rode from victory to victory. His premature death at the age of only twenty-four proved to be one of the greatest disasters which befell China during the Han dynasty.

In the words of the old Chinese chronicle, "None of the troops of the other generals could compare with those of Ho Kü-bing. Commanding only specially chosen soldiers (the elite of the army), Ho Kü-bing was able to penetrate far into the enemy territory. With his company of the ablest riders, he was always to be found in the van of the main army. . . . The other generals were constantly getting into trouble because they were unable to keep up with him or join forces with him at the appointed time. For this reason Ho Kü-bing's prestige waxed greater day by day until in the end it equalled that of the commander-in-chief."

Reading between the lines of the ancient records, we can see that much of Ho Kü-bing's success was due to the fact that the youthful commander completely abandoned the traditional Chinese military tactics and introduced the use of lightly armed and rapidly moving cavalry as the chief weapon of offense.

A Hunnish Shanyu or Emperor
According to Chinese Tradition. Cf. Chap. VI.
(*After Laufer*)

An Ancient Chinese Tomb
Reputed to be that of Ho Kü-bing, the general who broke the power of the first Hunnish Empire. Cf. Chap. VI.

We have already seen that much of the success which the Tsin dynasty had had with its foes, including the Huns, was due to the fact that the Tsin armies had relied so largely upon cavalry charges. With the fall of the Tsin dynasty and the rise of the House of Han, which at first was far less subject to Turanian and Iranian cultural influences than were the Tsin rulers, the Chinese had neglected their cavalry and had relied once more upon the cumbersome war chariots and heavily armed infantrymen. It was largely for this reason that the early Han emperors had suffered so severely from the Hunnish armies of bow-shooting horsemen.

Ho Kü-bing, therefore, in organizing his brigade of light cavalrymen, had forged a weapon which forever after placed the Hunnish armies on the defensive. The Chinese, with their developed arts and crafts, had always been able to manufacture better arms than the Huns. Now, while retaining their superior arms, the Chinese were able to match the Huns in the one point on which the Huns had long been superior, namely, their ability to move rapidly from place to place.

The first great defeat which Ho Kü-bing with his new tactics was able to inflict upon the Huns was in 121 B.C. The scene of this campaign lay to what was then the northwest of China proper, in the eastern part of Kashgaria, and in the western part of the modern province of Gansu. This was the region formerly occupied by the Wusun and Yuejï, which the Huns had subsequently conquered and occupied, establishing there a number of petty vassal Hunnish states, only two of which, however, seem to have been of any special importance.

In his earlier campaigns (127-124 B.C.) Wei Tsing, the commander-in-chief, had already encroached upon this region; but it was reserved for Ho Kü-bing to strike the smashing blow which forever destroyed Hunnish supremacy in the area. In 121 B.C. the brilliant young commander led two expeditions into this region, in the course of which he killed or captured nearly forty thousand Huns including a number of petty kinglets and tribal chiefs. We have the interesting statement added that among the booty which he collected was a golden image with which the king of one of the vassal kingdoms was accustomed to worship Heaven (God). This is the first time that we hear of any images among the Huns, and many scholars believe that this was probably a Buddhist image which had reached the western Huns from Kashgaria or Turkistan, where Buddhism was already spreading with great rapidity. If so, this is the first contact which China was to have with Buddhism. It should be noted, however, that the first Buddhist temple was not erected in the Celestial Empire until nearly two centuries later.[7]

Ho Kü-bing's startling victories in the West had important consequences. Later in the same year (121 B.C.) two of the most important Hunnish vassal states broke away from the Hunnish Empire and voluntarily subjected themselves to Chinese rule. The way in which this came about is rather interesting. We are told that the Lord of the Hunnish Empire was furious with his vassal princes in the West for the way in which they had allowed themselves to be defeated by Ho Kü-bing's army. He ordered these vassal kings to come to the court and explain their conduct. The vassal princes, however, were so frightened by this order, that they thought it would be better to throw themselves on the mercy of the Chinese rather than face the fury of their own overlord. While negotiations were still going on, one of these princes, the "king" of Hiujiu, repented of his intended treachery and wished to draw back. His colleague, the "king" of Kunsie was disgusted with this vacillating conduct and promptly slew his co-conspirator, adding the latter's subjects to his own. At the head of his whole people, who are said to have numbered about forty thousand, he then marched to the Chinese frontier and demanded to be taken under the protection of the Celestial Empire.

The Emperor Wu-di treated his new subjects with marked consideration. The vassal king and several of his subsidiary tribal chiefs were granted not only rank and titles but also money and estates. The son of the murdered king of Hiujiu was made a page at the Imperial Palace, and later rose to the highest offices in the land. The bulk of the subjected Hunnish population, though nominally incorporated within the Empire, were allowed to retain their own manners and customs and were finally settled in various parts of the frontier.[8]

This displacement of the population left the lands formerly occupied by the vassal kingdoms greatly underpopulated, a fact of considerable importance in later history. But in any case the Chinese Empire had secured a considerable accession of territory and this in a very strategically important place. In the first place a wedge had been driven between the Huns to the North and the Kiang or Tibetans to the South; and the Chinese had always been fearful lest the Huns be able to secure the support of the Kiang in some of their military campaigns.

Even more important was the fact that the Chinese Empire was brought into direct contact with Kashgaria and the other peoples and countries which lay to the West. To be sure, the city states of Kashgaria were still subject in a general way to the Huns; but the Chinese by this time were well aware that most of these principalities had no especial love for their Hunnish masters, from whom they differed in language and in manners and customs, and that they would be only too willing if a favorable opportunity presented itself to break their tie with the Hunnish Empire. In later times the Chinese were to make full use of their opportunity to establish direct contact with the West, but for the moment they had to confine themselves to the bitter conflict with the Huns who still lay scattered all along the northern frontier.

In 119 B.C. the Emperor Wu-di determined to make a supreme effort to crush the Huns once and for all. Two huge armies were raised. One of them was entrusted to the dashing Ho Kü-bing with orders to attack the eastern part of the Hunnish Empire. The other army, led by Wei Tsing, the commander-in-chief, in person, was ordered to march straight north from the Chinese frontier and attack the Shanyu's forces in the very heart of the Hunnish domain.

Galloping at the head of his army, Ho Kü-bing soon entered what is now Eastern Mongolia. Pushing several hundred miles to the North, he met and attacked the Hunnish Viceroy of the East. This official, who had previously defeated all the Chinese armies sent against him and who had wrought untold havoc in the northeastern frontier of China, now met his match. After a short conflict he turned and fled. During this campaign, Ho Kü-bing killed or captured more than seventy thousand of the Hunnish forces.

Equally noteworthy was the campaign directed by Wei Tsing against the center of the Hunnish Empire, a campaign which was to lead him into conflict with the flower of the Hunnish army, commanded by the Shanyu in person. In accordance with his prearranged plan, the Shanyu and his army lay in waiting just to the north of the Gobi Desert in the hope that the Chinese forces would be exhausted by their long march through this barren region and would be ill-prepared to withstand a serious attack.

As soon as the Chinese army came within sight of the Hunnish forces, it was hastily arranged in battle array. Wei Tsing had with him a number of war chariots; but, instead of using them in a useless charge against the Huns, he ordered them to be arranged in a circle so that they formed a sort of fortress which could be used as a base of operations. The main fighting was entrusted to the cavalry.

All day long the Chinese and the Huns fought their desperate battle with no advantage gained by either side. In the early evening a strong wind arose. It must have been one of those terrible sandstorms for which the Mongolian plains are so noted, for we are told that it blew sand and gravel into the faces of the combatants so that they could no longer see one another. Wei Tsing took advantage of this invisibility and moved his right and left flanks forward in such a way as to completely encircle the Shanyu and the few picked warriors the latter had around him. The Shanyu, seeing that he was surrounded by superior numbers, felt that the fight was hopeless and thought only of escape. Bursting through the encircling Chinese, he mounted his chariot, drawn by six mules, and fled rapidly to the far Northwest. Though hotly pursued by the Chinese, he succeeded in outdistancing his opponents.[9]

This Battle of the Sandstorm really concluded the long series of campaigns directed by the Emperor Wu-di against his northern enemies. The power and prestige of the Huns had been broken. Thereafter, for many a year, they were forced to confine their activities to northern or Outer Mongolia, and during this period the northern frontiers of China were comparatively free from serious attack.

But, though the power of the Huns had been broken, it had not been destroyed. The Huns were still masters of a large kingdom, and their administrative and military organization remained intact. To be sure the Chinese had captured or slaughtered between eighty and ninety thousand Huns, but their own losses had been almost as great. The Chinese had been especially unfortunate with their horses, for out of the hundred and forty thousand animals which were sent out on these campaigns less than thirty thousand returned.

The Chinese felt the loss of these horses very deeply, for China was not yet a horse-breeding country, and the total supply of these animals was very small. In fact we are expressly told by the Chinese historians that one of the principal reasons why the Empire did not attempt to complete the task of destroying the Hunnish kingdom was that there were not sufficient horses to embark upon another extensive campaign.

We are told that another important reason for the Chinese being content with leaving things as they were was the fact that in 117 B.C., only two years after these campaigns, Ho Kü-bing died. Ho Kü-bing was the one Chinese general who had invariably been successful in his conflict with the Huns, and the court felt that without his leadership or assistance further warfare would be inadvisable. Incidentally, the Chinese erected over the tomb of the brilliant young general a statue of a horse stamping on a Hunnish warrior. Lost from sight for many centuries, it was recently discovered by some French archaeologists, and now constitutes the earliest known Chinese attempt to sculpture a horse.[10]

In the light of what has been said, it is not surprising that the next few years brought very few drastic changes in the relationship between the Chinese Empire and the Huns. A short time after the Battle of the Sandstorm we find the Chinese sending an envoy to the Shanyu, demanding that he declare himself a vassal of the Emperor Wu-di. The Shanyu, in spite of his defeat and flight, was so furious at this proposal that he kept the Chinese envoy a prisoner, and there was nothing the Chinese could do to effect his release. A few years later (111 B.C.) the Chinese again sent two armies into Southern Mongolia in the hope of freeing this and other envoys retained by the Huns; but, though the two armies scurried hither and yon in the region south of the great desert, they did not succeed in securing a single contact with any of the Hunnish forces; and they did not dare march into the homeland of the Huns which was now north of the desert.

In the following year (110 B.C.) we find a similar situation arising, only in this case the Emperor Wu-di himself essayed to play the part of a martial hero. This was shortly after the imperial troops had conquered and killed the king of Yue, the ruler of what is now Southern China, and incorporated this territory within the Celestial Empire. The Emperor thought that this would be a favorable opportunity to make a triumphal tour to all the outlying regions in his domain.

He included the northern frontier in this tour; and, while he was in this area, he bethought himself of making a great military demonstration in the hope of impressing the barbarians in the North. Assembling an army of a hundred and eighty thousand men, he marched for some distance into Southern Mongolia, and then sent an envoy to the Hunnish Shanyu who made to that monarch the following remarkable declaration: "The head of the king of Yue now hangs on the gates of the Imperial Palace. The Son of Heaven has now arrived on the northern frontier at the head of the Imperial army. Why should the Hunnish Shanyu remain skulking in the cold and inhospitable north? Let the Shanyu come to the south and either meet the emperor in open battle or else become a subject and pay reverence to the Imperial throne."

Seemingly the Shanyu preferred to remain in his cold and inhospitable north, for he paid no heed to the message and contented himself with adding the new envoy to his group of Chinese prisoners. To be a Chinese ambassador in those days entailed being subjected to a whole series of thrills, suspenses, and adventures.

Again the emperor felt himself powerless to remedy the situation and shortly afterwards disbanded his army and returned to China.

Six years after this bit of bravado (104 B.C.) the Chinese again attempted to interfere in Hunnish affairs. At this time a new Shanyu had recently ascended the throne, called because of his youth the "Child Shanyu." The Child Shanyu soon showed himself to be of a cruel and bloodthirsty disposition with the direct result that there was much uneasiness and discontent within his realm. One of his subordinates, who must have been a fairly close relative, conceived the idea of rebelling and placing himself upon the Hunnish throne.

Not feeling himself strong enough to stand alone, this official entered into treasonable correspondence with the Chinese court, in the course of which he promised to become an acknowledged vassal of the Han dynasty if the latter would aid him in carrying out his proposed coup d'état. The Emperor Wu-di was only too delighted to join in so interesting a plot; and, in the following year (103 B.C.), one of the ablest of the Chinese generals, Chao Bu-nu, was sent into Mongolia at the head of an army of twenty thousand persons to render whatever aid might be necessary.

Unfortunately for the Chinese plans, however, just as the pretender was about to gather his forces about him and break out into open rebellion, the plot was discovered. The pretender himself was put to death, and the Chinese who had already penetrated some distance into Mongolia were forced to beat a hasty retreat. Not content with having crushed the revolt, the Shanyu was determined to wreak vengeance upon the Chinese for their underhanded activities. Putting himself at the head of an army four times as large as that of the Chinese, he succeeded in overtaking and completely surrounding the latter when they were only a few miles from their own frontier. Seeing that further conflict was useless, the Chinese general and his whole army surrendered to the Huns. From this it can be seen that nearly two decades after the Battle of the Sandstorm the Huns were still far from being crushed or their power completely destroyed.[11]

But though the Chinese during this time had been able to do little more than maintain the status quo in their relations with the Huns, they had been far more fortunate in their dealings with other neighboring peoples. Historically one of the most significant of the Chinese conquests of this era was that which led to the permanent annexation of the southern part of what is now China proper. Ever since the beginning of his reign the Emperor Wu-di had been much interested in this region and had gradually drawn larger and larger parts of it within the orbit of the Chinese Empire. Things came to a head in 111 B.C. when open warfare broke out between China and the kingdom of Nan (southern) Yüe. As we have already seen, the monarch of this realm was soon killed; and the kingdom itself, which corresponds to the modern provinces of Guangdung and Guangsi, became an integral part of China. Shortly thereafter (110-109 B.C.) the rulers of the kingdoms of Tien, in the southwest and embracing much of the modern province of Yunnan, and of Dung (eastern) Yüe, in the southeast—the modern province of Fugien—declared themselves to be vassals of the Emperor Wu-di and thereafter were forced to follow in most matters the advice of specially appointed Chinese ministers and residents.

Of more interest, from the point of view of the present work, is the fact that in 108 B.C. the Chinese completed the conquest of the kingdom of

Jaosien (Chosen) which occupied a region corresponding to modern Northwestern Korea and Southeastern Manchuria. Although this region broke away from the Celestial Empire less than two centuries later, the Chinese influence on this area was destined to have a lasting effect. Unlike the nomadic Huns, the inhabitants of Jaosien were for the most part a settled people and were willing and even anxious to adopt most of the essential elements of Chinese civilization. For this reason the whole region tended to remain, spiritually at least, a Chinese sphere of influence, even after all political and military bonds had been broken.

Of special significance to us is the fact that the Chinese conquest of Jaosien, which carried with it domination over many of the tribes inhabiting the country immediately north of this kingdom, greatly strengthened the strategic position of the Chinese Empire with relation to the Huns. China now touched upon the eastern as well as the southern frontier of the Hunnish domain, and her generals could undertake a flank attack in the event of renewed Hunnish aggression. By the time that China had lost control of Jaosien, the Huns had long ceased to be a serious menace.[12]

Most important of all, it was during this period that China was able to increase her power and prestige enormously in the region west of the Hunnish Kingdom, namely in Zungaria, in Kashgaria, and in Turkistan. These developments are of such direct interest to us that we must consider them somewhat more in detail.

Curiously enough China's first endeavors to extend her sphere of influence in this direction were made, not in Kashgaria immediately adjacent to her, but at the expense of the Wusun, who inhabited Southern Zungaria. In dealing with this people, however, diplomacy rather than military force was utilized.

The Chinese records tell us that it was our old friend, Jang Kien, who was at the bottom of the attempt to bring the Wusun under Chinese influence. Jang Kien's motives on this occasion were undoubtedly selfish. Returning from his first embassy to the West, he had been given a title and a high official rank. Subsequently, he had become engaged in some of the campaigns against the Huns. As a general he had proved himself so incompetent that a judicial tribunal had sentenced him to death; but, in accordance with a good old Chinese custom, by spending a large sum of money the death sentence had been commuted to one which merely deprived him of his ranks and titles. Jang Kien, being anxious to reestablish his position, petitioned that he might be sent on a mission to the Wusun, with the purpose of inviting the latter to return to their old home in Kashgaria, east of Lake Lopnor.

It will be remembered that it was this region which had been captured from the Huns in the campaign of 121 B.C. and which was now under Chinese jurisdiction but was still almost uninhabited. It was felt that if the Wusun would only resettle in this district, the Huns would be deterred from any attempt to recapture it.

The Emperor Wu-di acceded to the proposal of Jang Kien and in 115 B.C. the latter again set out for the West. He took with him a large escort and many rich presents. In addition, he was allowed to promise the Wusun ruler the hand of a Chinese princess in marriage if he should be willing to fall in with the Chinese plans.

On arriving at his destination, Jang Kien tried his best to win the Wusun court over to his ideas, but he found himself faced with a hopeless situation. The Wusun tribesmen were unimpressed by the tales of China's greatness and remained in healthy awe of their immediate neighbors, the Huns. They felt that by returning to Eastern Kashgaria they would evoke the wrath of the Huns and be once more subject to Hunnish invasion.

Moreover at this time there was much internal dissension among the Wusun. Their Kunmi or king was old and could no longer exercise despotic power over his subjects. Though he was still nominally lord of all the Wusun people, one of his sons and one of his grandsons had broken away and formed semi-independent principalities. The Kunmi, therefore, did not dare take it upon himself to conclude a treaty on a matter which would involve the destinies of all of his nominal subjects.

Because of this situation Jang Kien found his proposals rejected. He decided to make the best of a bad job; and, taking advantage of his position far to the West, he sent out various members of his staff as envoys to India, Bactria, Parthia, the Yuejï, and other outlying countries in the hope their missions might lead to more intimate contacts. Without even waiting for the return of these subsidiary envoys (all of whom came back to China in due course of time) Jang Kien set out on his journey back to his native land. He succeeded in taking back with him for a visit a number of Wusun tribesmen, nominally to act as guides and interpreters, but really in order that China might keep in some sort of touch with the Wusun, and in the hope that these western nomads might be impressed with the size and greatness of the Celestial Empire.

In spite of Jang Kien's failure to secure a definite alliance, the Emperor seemed quite pleased with his envoy's conduct and again appointed him to high office. Jang Kien was not destined to enjoy the return of prosperity for long, however, as he died within a year of his return from this last memorable journey.

The real fruit of Jang Kien's diplomacy did not become evident until several years after the great envoy's death. The Wusun tribesmen who had been brought to China returned eventually to their native country and reported that China was a very rich and populous country, which report greatly increased the estimation in which she was held there.

The Huns, moreover, were very angry when they heard that the Wusun had been willing to accord Jang Kien a friendly reception and even made threats of war in retaliation for what they considered an act of treachery—for was not the Wusun territory, nominally at least, a part of the Hunnish Empire? In view of this situation the Wusun court sent envoys to China. These envoys ignored the old proposal that the Wusun return to Kashgaria but stated that their ruler wished to enter into more intimate relations with the Celestial Empire and begged that a Chinese princess be sent to him in marriage. After considerable negotiation the Chinese agreed to this proposal; and in 105 B.C. one of the ladies-in-waiting, accompanied by a rich dowry, set out for the long journey to Zungaria where she was duly married to the Wusun ruler.

The good Chinese lady seems to have had a miserable time. She found herself married to an old man with whom she was not even able to carry on a conversation, since the couple were unable to speak one another's languages. In fact, the marriage remained largely a nominal one, for the royal couple met only once or twice a year, and then only on the occasion of some great feast.

Overcome with homesickness and loneliness, the princess took refuge in poetry. She composed an ode which at length came to the august ears of the Emperor in her native China and filled him with compassion. In fact this poem has become a household favorite in the Celestial Empire and has been incorporated in nearly all native poetic anthologies. In rough translation it reads as follows:

"My family has married me off, alas, somewhere under Heaven's broad dome.
I live in an alien and distant land, alas, with the King of the Wusun.
My dwelling is a tent, alas, with its walls of felt.
For food I have only meat, alas, and for drink only milk,
While here, I do nothing but dream of my own country, alas, and my heart is sore.
I wish only that I were a wild goose, alas, and could fly back to my native land."

A short time after this poem was written, her lord and master, realizing that he was old and feeble, decided to hand the good lady over to his grandson and heir. The princess was horrified at the prospect of marrying the grandson after being married to the grandfather and sent a messenger back to the Chinese Emperor, asking for his advice in the matter. His Imperial Majesty, however, sent back a note ordering her to overcome any moral scruples she might feel and become the bride of the heir apparent, adding that he had need of her services in keeping the Wusun in alliance with China in her wars against the Huns.

The princess meekly did as she was ordered but died shortly after giving birth to her first child. Whereupon the Emperor sent out another Chinese lady-in-waiting to take her place. The new princess was stronger and less fastidious than her predecessor, for she lived to a ripe old age and married not only the reigning lord of the Wusun but also several of his successors, by whom she had a large brood of children, many of whom played a prominent part in the latter history of Central Asia. As a result of these matrimonial alliances, China came to exercise an ever larger influence over the Wusun tribesmen, although their dominion was never actually incorporated within the Chinese Empire.[13]

Further to the South, in Kashgaria, China was to secure even greater and more direct control, though not until she had fought many bloody battles. The base of operations in this area was, of course, the region east of Lake Lopnor, which had been captured from the Huns. After the vassal Hunnish states in this locality had surrendered to the Chinese, and their inhabitants had been settled in various other parts of the Celestial Empire, this whole land was left almost devoid of people. Such a state of affairs obviously could not last. At first, as we have seen, the Chinese were desirous of inviting some friendly nomadic people, such as the Wusun, to move in and settle down. But since this project failed, the Chinese began to incorporate the region within the administrative limits of the Chinese Empire and gradually to fill it with settlers sent out from China proper.[14]

This plan of action must have started in 111 B.C.; for in that year we find the vacant lands broken up into four administrative districts, in each of which a town or settlement was established to serve as a political and economic center. Of these four districts, the only one we need mention was the district and town of Dunhuang, the farthest west of the four. Dunhuang long constituted the western outpost of the Chinese Empire, and it was through this settlement that the Chinese envoys passed on their way to negotiate treaties with the distant kingdoms of the West.

In recent years important archaeological work has been carried on in and around Dunhuang, and this has given us many intimate glimpses of the life led by the Chinese colonists in the early period of Chinese expansion to the West, though most of the remains date from a period somewhat later than the one with which we are now dealing.

The settlement and organization of Dunhuang and the surrounding districts instead of ending China's frontier problems only led to further difficulties and responsibilities. The Chinese, using Dunhuang as a base, proceeded to send out a large number of diplomatic missions to the West, sometimes as many as ten in one year. All of these embassies had to pass through either the kingdom of Loulan or that of Güshï (Turfan), two states of no great size or importance but which completely blocked the way between the Chinese territory and the other states of Kashgaria.

The rulers of these two states were still strongly under Hunnish influence. Not only did they report to the Huns all of China's activities in the West, but in addition, spurred on by Hunnish emissaries, they proceeded to attack and rob a number of the Chinese envoys who passed through their dominions. Obviously this state of things could not be allowed to continue if China was to retain her prestige in Central Asia. Accordingly, in 108 B.C. a Chinese general was dispatched at the head of an army to secure retribution.

Galloping at the head of only seven hundred cavalrymen, the general in question defeated and captured the king of Loulan whose dominion lay on or near Lake Lopnor. Then, pushing to the north, the Chinese army won a signal victory over the forces of the kingdom of Güshï (Turfan) which lay along the southern slopes of the Tien Shan or Celestial Mountains. Güshï, though defeated, was far from being crushed and for many decades continued to be a thorn in China's side, but at least for the time being it was forced to desist from further attacks upon the Chinese embassies.

Loulan, with its king captured, was forced to be more subservient. In fact this principality was compelled to declare itself a vassal state and send tribute to the Chinese courts. Even here, however, relations with the Huns were not entirely broken off, for we find Loulan sending a hostage not only to China but also one to reside among the Huns. Though China did not succeed in annexing either Güshï or Loulan, her victories over these states resounded through the length and breadth of Kashgaria and even among the countries still further to the West.[15]

The next military campaign which China waged in the West was directed, strangely enough, not against some of the other petty states of Kashgaria but rather against the distant kingdom of Da-yüan, which lay to the West of the Tsungling (Pamir) Mountains. The trouble with Da-yüan started in 104 B.C. because of the treatment accorded a Chinese embassy. Da-yüan enjoyed the reputation of having the best horses anywhere in the world, and the Chinese always speak of the horses from the region as the "blood-sweating Celestial steeds." The Emperor sent an envoy to Da-yüan to secure a number of these famed horses for himself and his court. Not only did the envoy fail to secure the horses;

but, entering into a violent dispute with the natives, he was killed by the governor of one of the subsidiary districts in Eastern Da-yüan while on his way back to China.

The Celestial Emperor was furious at the murder of his ambassador and even more furious at the prospect of not being able to secure the horses on which he had set his heart. Accordingly he organized a huge army to punish the refractory kingdom of the West. We are told that though a portion of this army consisted of trained cavalrymen, the bulk of the force was made up of "bad young men" from various parts of the Empire, or in other words, of the criminals and riffraff of the provinces, the loss of whom would cause little sorrow to any one. All told this motley army numbered several tens of thousands. At its head was placed General Li Guang-li, who owed his post to the fact that he was the elder brother of the Lady Li, the Emperor's favorite concubine.

In 103 B.C. General Li Guang-li marched his army to the West, taking the route which led through the northern part of Kashgaria. The inhabitants of many of the city states through which he had to pass locked themselves up in their walled towns and refused to furnish the Chinese army with provender. The Chinese had no time to take these places by storm, with the result that a large proportion of the invading army died of starvation en route. When the army at last crossed the Tsungling Mountains and arrived in Da-yüan, only a few thousand soldiers remained; and most of these were in pitiable condition. It is small wonder, therefore, that they were overwhelmingly defeated by the forces of Da-yüan a short time afterwards.

Gathering together the remnants of his forces, General Li Guang-li retreated, without further ado, and at last reached Dunhuang, the western outpost of China. From there he sent in a petition to the Emperor, asking permission to disband what army there remained to him. The Emperor was beside himself with fury and sent out an order to the effect that if the general or any of his troops came another step nearer home, they were to be beheaded—with the result that General Li wisely decided to stay where he was.

Most of the ministers were in favor of abandoning all plans of punishing Da-yüan for her insolence. The Emperor, however, would hear nothing of this sage advice. He argued that if China should submit to defeat by a small nation like Da-yüan, she would offer herself as a laughing stock among all of the nations of the West; and, in addition, the Empire could never secure a supply of the Celestial horses.

A new campaign was, therefore, decided upon. All the prisons in the Empire were emptied of their inhabitants by offering the prisoners a pardon on condition that they volunteer for military service. Even larger numbers of "bad young men" were conscripted into the army; and the frontier people, many of them subjugated Huns, were forced to raise a large body of cavalry. This time, moreover, the army was provided with an immense number of transport animals, carrying provisions, so as to obviate all thoughts of famine.

Instead of picking out a fresh commander, however, the Emperor again appointed Li Guang-li to conduct the campaign, so that he might have a chance to wipe out his previous disgrace. At the head of this choice army of adventurers, criminals, and ne'er-do-wells, General Li retraced his steps and in 101 B.C. at last succeeded in entering Da-yüan and there proceeded to lay siege to its capital, in which the king and most of his troops had taken refuge.

After the siege had lasted over a month, the nobles in the city rose in revolt, slew their king, and sent his head to the besieging general with the following remarkable message: "We beg of you not to attack us any longer, for we are prepared to furnish you with the Celestial horses which you so ardently desire and, in addition provide your army with provisions. If, on the other hand, you insist upon unconditional surrender, we will kill off all our Celestial horses so you cannot secure them anyhow and will fight on until our western allies, the Kang-gü, can have time to come and relieve us."

General Li Guang-li felt it advisable to accept these terms. The natives were far from crushed. They retained possession of their army, their arms, and their city. But in addition to provisioning his army at a critical time, the Chinese commander had avenged his honor and that of his country. He was able, moreover, to secure possession of a large number of the coveted steeds which he took back with him to China. Finally the king who had insulted the Celestial Empire was dead and in his stead was elected a man who had always been friendly to China and who could be relied upon to pursue a pro-Chinese policy, so that on the whole the campaign may be said to have been crowned with success.

With charming and characteristic naïveté, the Chinese records tell us that on this campaign many of the officers engaged in a good deal of graft, liberally filling their pockets at the expense of their soldiers, as a result of which thousands of these soldiers lost their lives. This fact became perfectly well-known to the Emperor, but in consideration of the success of the expedition the Son of Heaven overlooked these offenses and all of the high officers who had taken part in the campaign were rewarded with ranks and titles.[16]

Because of her victory over Da-yüan, China found that she had acquired enormous prestige among all the petty states of Kashgaria. The rulers of practically all of these states immediately sent a son or a younger brother to present tribute to the Imperial throne and to remain there as hostages.

Not content with this, the Chinese proceeded to safeguard their position by erecting a series of military stations all the way from Dunhuang to Lake Lopnor, so that they could, without trouble, send out another expedition to the West in case such was found necessary. More important still, they established several hundreds of military colonies in the heart of Northern Kashgaria between the petty kingdoms of Karashahr and Kucha.[17] These colonies were placed under a military commander, whose task it was not only to administer the district immediately subject to him but also to be the "eyes and ears" for the Chinese government concerning all events in Kashgaria, and to protect and look after the needs of the numerous special envoys which China continued to send to various countries in the West.[18]

CHAPTER SEVEN

THE SLOW DECLINE OF THE HUNNISH EMPIRE, 100–51 B.C.

Stagnation among the Huns—Embassy of Su Wu and Its Disastrous Consequences—Renewal of Hostilities between the Huns and Chinese—A Series of Chinese Defeats—Li Ling and Li Guang-li—Subsequent Internal Decay of the Hunnish Empire—Westward Movement of the Huns—The Chinese Renew Their Attacks—Defeat of the Huns by the Wusun—Revolt of the Hunnish Vassal States—Civil War among the Huns—Submission of Huhansie to China—Establishment of Chinese Colonies in Kashgaria—Chinese Conquest of Loulan—Submission of Kucha to the Chinese—Unsuccessful Rebellion of Yarkand—Conquest of Güshi—Establishment of the Office of the Protector General of the West—Chinese Relations with the Wusun and the Tibetans.

IN THE year 100 B.C., the Chinese Emperor, Wu-di, was at the height of his glory. Absolute master of his subjects at home, he had conquered and either annexed or overawed his neighbors to the South, to the Northeast (Jaosien), and to the Northwest (Kashgaria). All that remained for him to do was to strike a decisive blow at his old enemies, the Huns. Twenty years earlier they had been defeated. It did not, therefore, appear impossible that they could be destroyed.[1]

For a moment, indeed, it seemed as if the expense of a major campaign could be spared and that the Huns would voluntarily submit to Chinese suzerainty. To be sure, they were still far from being crushed and only recently had won several notable victories over the Chinese; but the victory of the Chinese in distant Da-yüan had deeply impressed the Huns and made them willing to make peaceful overtures toward the Celestial Empire.

Moreover, the Hunnish Empire continued to suffer from internal decay. Shanyu followed Shanyu on the Hunnish throne, and none of them reigned for long, or proved to be men of really strong or forceful personalities. In fact for many years during this period much of the power in the Hunnish court was centered not in the hands of the nominal ruler, but rested rather with an able commoner named Wei-lu. Wei-lu was a person of Hunnish origin but he had been educated in China and was thoroughly familiar with the good and bad points of Chinese civilization. He had, in fact, first returned to the Hunnish court on a diplomatic mission from the Chinese. Shortly after his arrival in the Hunnish domain, however, he renounced his allegiance to China and, entering the service of the Shanyu, soon rose to high office, serving as an intimate adviser and unofficial prime minister not only to this ruler but to a number of his successors.

It was no doubt the result of his advice that the then reigning Hunnish ruler sent (in 101 B.C.) a special embassy to the court of the Chinese Emperor to negotiate a new treaty of peace and amity. The Shanyu went so far as to send a most humble message, calling himself a child who did not dare claim equality with his "Father-in-law," the Chinese Son of Heaven. All this was very pleasant, and in the following year (100 B.C.) the Emperor dispatched one of his court chamberlains, General Su Wu, to convey liberal presents to the Shanyu and to continue diplomatic negotiations, leading to a permanent peace.

Su Wu, though an able and thoroughly upright man, was not a good diplomat and was unable to bring the Shanyu to a position of real vassalage to the Celestial Empire. Discouraged by his failure, he was just about to return to China when an event took place which completely altered the relation between the Huns and the Chinese and ushered in another long period of warfare.

Some of the lesser members of Su Wu's embassy, furious at the failure of their mission to accomplish anything definite, decided to take desperate steps and entered into a conspiracy with some of the dissatisfied members of the Hunnish court with the avowed purpose of assassinating Wei-lu, the powerful court favorite, and of kidnapping the energetic Dowager Yenjï or Empress, of the Huns. The conspirators believed that if this coup succeeded, the Hunnish court would be dealt a staggering blow and would soon submit to Chinese jurisdiction. It was seemingly not thought necessary to secure the person of the nominal Shanyu. The ethics of a diplomatic mission attempting so bold a coup d'état does not seem to have been considered by these ancient worthies.

Unfortunately for themselves, the conspirators were caught just as they were about to strike. Naturally enough, the discovery of this plot caused a great sensation. The actual authors of the conspiracy were immediately put to death. Worse still, it was generally believed that all the members of the embassy, including Su Wu himself, were involved in the conspiracy; and though they protested their innocence, they were the objects of much suspicion and ill-will. At first the Shanyu wished to behead all of them but in the end consented to spare their lives if they would renounce their allegiance to China and become loyal Hunnish subjects.

Several of the leading members of the mission took advantage of this offer and were duly "naturalized"; but Su Wu himself, who felt that he had lost a great deal of "face" by the whole matter, decided that death was better than disgraceful surrender and, seizing his dagger, attempted to commit suicide. He was stopped in the attempt and, though desperately ill for many days, he eventually recovered.

As soon as he was well, the Shanyu and the all-powerful Wei-lu again tried to win Su Wu over to the Huns. At first they tried forceful means. Holding a naked sword in his hand, Wei-lu advanced toward the envoy, threatening to kill him unless the latter renounced his allegiance to China; but Su Wu remained immovable. Admiring this exhibition of loyalty and courage, the Hunnish leaders next offered Su Wu rank, titles, and riches if he would only become a Hunnish subject; but the envoy remained immune to all temptation.

Furious at this insolence, the Huns then threw Su Wu into a deep pit and there kept him for a long time without food or drink. But while he lay there, snow fell, and Su Wu drank the melted snow. For food he chewed the hair off his fur mantle. When the Huns, after a lapse of many days, found that the loyal envoy was still alive, they decided that he must be under the special protection of Heaven and so spared his life but banished him to a distant and uninhabited region near the North Sea or Lake Baikal. With a sly touch of humor they forced him to act as the shepherd of he-goats, saying that they would release him when these he-goats produced milk. For nineteen years Su Wu remained a lowly shepherd in the far North, but never for a moment did he renounce his loyalty to his master, the Son of Heaven; nor would he ever part with the staff of office given him by the Emperor as a symbol of authority, but used this staff as a shepherd's crook until it was almost worn away.[2]

Chinese history is so full of envoys and generals who were treacherous and disloyal that Su Wu by contrast has served for poets and painters as a shining example of unflinching devotion. Two thousand years later he is still a household name in his native land.

As the result of the failure of Su Wu's mission, the Chinese and Hunnish empires, instead of drawing closer together as had been hoped, immediately broke off all friendly intercourse. In fact, a period of active warfare commenced again, and hostilities did not cease until the Emperor, Wu-di, was laid away in his grave fourteen years later.

From the Chinese point of view these new campaigns led to very disappointing results. In view of his earlier victories over the Huns, the Emperor, Wu-di, no doubt hoped that by exerting every effort and using his best generals the Huns would be crushingly defeated and their empire broken up. Subsequent events showed that this hope was doomed to disappointment.

To be sure, most of the fighting took place north of the Great Wall, and hence more or less on Hunnish territory. Several Chinese armies, moreover, penetrated for hundreds of miles into the Hunnish domain and killed and captured thousands of the Hunnish tribesmen. But these expeditions led to no permanent results, and the victories achieved were more than counterbalanced by the fact that several of the Chinese expeditionary armies were surrounded and captured by the Huns. In fact, during this period China lost two of her most brilliant generals. These generals were not only defeated and captured but gave their allegiance to the Shanyu and rose to high office in the Hunnish court. One of these generals was Li Ling, the other Li Guang-li. A word must be said regarding both of these men.

Li Ling was the grandson of a man who had been a famous general in his time, and the young officer undoubtedly owed his first command to the fact that he came of a famous military family. He was, we are told, a superb bowman and horseman. More important still, he soon proved that he was a born leader of men.

For several years he served on the northern frontier, and thereby came into intimate contact with the Huns. In 99 B.C., when the great general Li Guang-li, the conqueror of Da-yüan, was preparing to head an expedition into the Hunnish territory, Li Ling was ordered to join the staff of the great commander and serve under him as transport officer. Li Ling, however, was loath to lose his independent command and sent in a petition to the Imperial Throne which read, "All the men under my command are from the south of China; and though they are all valiant, equally expert with swords and with bow and arrows and strong enough to wrestle with tigers, still it would not be well to mix them with other troops. I therefore humbly request permission to lead a separate expedition into the Hunnish domain, which would distract the attention of the Huns and prevent them from throwing all their forces against the army of General Li Guang-li."

To this the Emperor responded that if Li Ling wished to march independently into the Hunnish land he would have need of cavalry, and that so many cavalrymen had already been given to the Commander-in-chief that he had none to hand over to Li Ling. Upon hearing this Li Ling immediately replied, "I have no need of cavalry. I am already in command of five thousand infantrymen, and I ask only for permission to undertake the proposed campaign."

Unfortunately, however, Li Ling was not given a chance to make careful preparations before setting out on his new expedition. He, or rather one of his subordinate officers, wrote to the Emperor, saying that in the autumn the horses of the Huns were fat and well fed, and hence

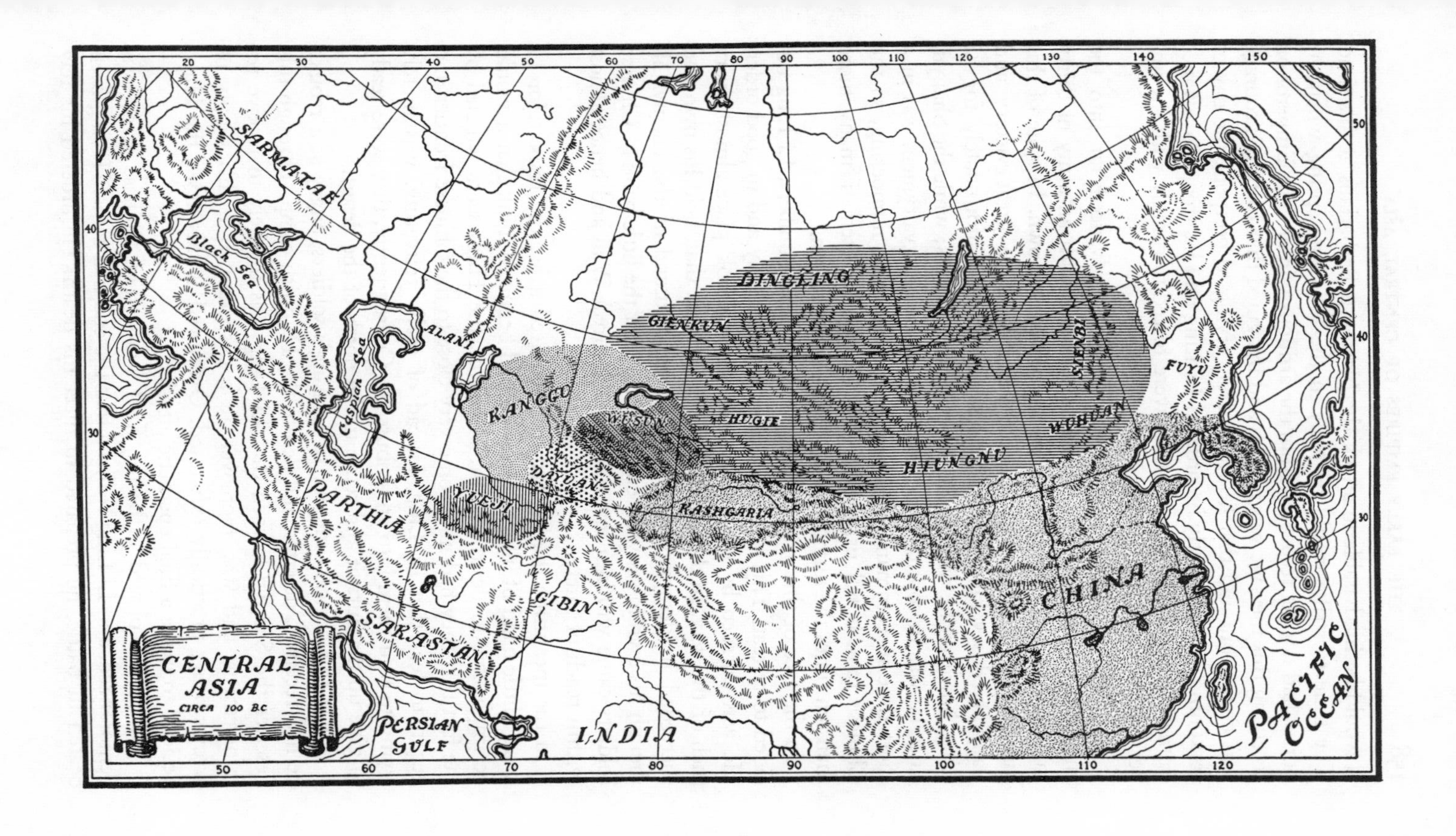
CENTRAL ASIA
CIRCA 100 B.C
SARMATAE
Black Sea
Caspian Sea
ALANI
KANGGU
WUSUN
DAYUAN
YUEJI
PARTHIA
GIBIN
SARAKASTAN
PERSIAN GULF
INDIA
DINGLING
GIENKUN
HUGIE
HIUNGNU
KASHGARIA
SIENBI
WUHUAN
FUYU
CHINA
PACIFIC OCEAN

it would be inadvisable to attack the Northern Barbarians at this time. The time to strike would be early in the following spring when the horses had not yet recovered from the arduous winter. The Emperor on receiving this message was furious and imagined that Li Ling's courage was oozing out and that he was merely trying to postpone the day of reckoning. Consequently he ordered Li Ling and his troops to advance immediately. The latter willy-nilly were forced to comply with the imperial command.

Marching straight to the North, Li Ling advanced far into the enemy's territory and there came face to face with an army of thirty thousand Huns, a force six times larger than his own. In spite of this disparity of numbers the Chinese general won a great victory and slaughtered several thousand of his opponents. Unfortunately for Li Ling, however, he was unable to get reinforcements; while the Shanyu, since he was in control of unlimited numbers of cavalrymen, was in a short time in command of a new army, this time numbering, so the Chinese records tell us, over eighty thousand horsemen, many more than ten times the number of Li Ling's infantrymen.

In the face of this overwhelming difference in numbers, Li Ling decided to retreat. This retreat was carried out slowly and in good order. He was pursued by the Huns, and fighting took place almost every inch of the way. In this fighting Li Ling more than held his own and succeeded in decapitating another three thousand of the enemy, although his own losses were enormous. At last the little band of Chinese soldiers came within a few miles of the Great Wall and hence almost within reach of safety.

In the meantime the Shanyu had acquired a healthy respect for Li Ling's little band of infantrymen and had begun to think that it would be impossible to destroy them. Moreover, the Huns were worried by the fact that they had now come very close to the Chinese frontier and began to fear that Li Ling, instead of really retreating, was merely trying to lead them into an ambuscade. Consequently, they were ready to give up the pursuit and retire to the north of the desert.

Just at this critical time one of Li Ling's soldiers, angry at a rebuke he had received, deserted and fled to the Hunnish camp. Through this deserter the Shanyu learned that Li Ling was unlikely to receive reinforcements and was, moreover, in a desperate strait, his supply of arrows being practically exhausted. Overjoyed at this news, the Huns decided to make a final energetic attack.

This attack proved to be the final straw. The Chinese army was demoralized, and Li Ling realized that the end had come. Having been beaten in battle, he prepared to meet his death. He ordered his few remaining men to disperse in small groups, each one taking a separate route to the frontier in the hope that some at least might come through safely. In the end four hundred out of the five thousand with which he started found their way back within the lines, but the general, Li Ling, was not among them.

Li Ling, in fact, seems to have made little effort to escape. "How can I," he said, "dare to face my master and report to him the disaster which has overtaken me?" Consequently, when he was overtaken and surrounded by a body of Huns, he quietly surrendered to them. The Shanyu, however, instead of killing or imprisoning his fallen adversary, treated him with the greatest consideration. When, a short time later, Li Ling consented to renounce his allegiance to China and enter the service of the Huns, he was given high rank, command over a section of the Hunnish army, and in addition was married off to one of the Shanyu's daughters. The fact that the good general already possessed a wife and family in China did not, of course, prevent him from enjoying his new connubial bliss.

In reading over the Chinese records, one is surprised at the large number of Chinese generals, who, after suffering a severe defeat, entered the service of the Huns and thereby again rose to rank and fortune. We have already had occasion to mention one or two of such cases, but there were many others which we have not thought it necessary to chronicle. To us it seems rather strange that a man who for years led Chinese troops against the Huns should all of a sudden be found leading Hunnish troops against the Chinese. But the real reason is not far to seek.

In China a general, if successful, was sure to acquire rank and riches. But if for any reason (and not always because of his own fault) he met with a severe military reverse, he knew that the least that he would suffer would be the loss of this rank and riches; he could, in fact, consider himself lucky if he did not lose his head as well. Consequently, after suffering such a defeat, a wise Chinese general would prefer to enter the service of the Huns rather than run the risk of returning to the Celestial Empire and being placed in the hands of a military tribunal.

The fate which subsequently befell Li Ling's friends and relatives in China proved that he was probably very wise in refusing to return to his native land. On hearing of Li Ling's defeat, the Emperor went into a towering rage. To suit His Majesty's mood most of the members of his court proceeded to pour abuse upon the fallen commander. It was only the Grand Astrologer, Se-ma Tsien, usually called the Herodotus of China because of his great book, *Shï-Gi* or *Historical Memoirs* (from which we have had occasion to quote so frequently), who dared to put forward the view that Li Ling had been unfortunate rather than incompetent. For this moral courage the great historian was rewarded by being summarily castrated.

A little later when it was rumored (and falsely rumored as it turned out) that the subsequent defeats of Chinese armies was due to Li Ling's training of the Hunnish troops, the Emperor, to secure revenge, ordered that all of Li Ling's near relatives, including his mother, his younger brothers, his wife, and his children be put to the sword.[3]

The defeat and capture of Li Ling in 99 B.C. was a bitter blow to China's pride, but this was nothing compared to the reverses suffered by Li Guang-li, who was considered to be China's greatest general. It was Li Guang-li who had conquered the distant state of Da-yüan and thereby brought the whole of Kashgaria within the sphere of Chinese influence. His prestige was immense; and, when he was sent out to do battle with the Huns, the Emperor confidently looked forward to a series of overwhelming victories.

Li Guang-li conducted three major campaigns against the Northern Barbarians. One was in 99 B.C. (the year in which Li Ling was defeated and captured by the Huns); the second took place two years later in 97 B.C., after which there was an interval of several years until 90 B.C. at which time he led his last and greatest expedition to the North.

In 99 B.C. Li Guang-li started out from Northwestern China and marched towards the Tien Shan or Celestial Mountains, his aim obviously being to strike a wedge between the Huns and the various city states in Kashgaria. At first the Chinese army was universally successful. Marching deep into the Hunnish territory, Li Guang-li met and defeated various detachments of the Hunnish forces, killing or capturing more than ten thousand of the enemy. But while he was withdrawing his troops back to China, he was overtaken and surrounded by a new Hunnish army. For several days the Chinese lay cooped up by the Huns, in the course of which time their food supply was practically exhausted. In the end a brilliant sortie, led by one of Li Guang-li's subordinate officers, broke through the Hunnish lines and allowed the main army to escape, but on arriving back in China it was found that two-thirds of the Chinese soldiers had perished during the campaign.

China felt that the loss of prestige, caused by Li Guang-li's narrow escape from capture, could not be allowed to stand; and two years later (97 B.C.) she sent out three new armies to do battle with the Huns, the main army, again commanded by Li Guang-li, numbering more than a hundred and forty thousand men. This time the generalissimo marched straight north from China and struck for the heart of the

Hunnish Empire which must have been more or less where the modern city of Urga now stands.

The Shanyu, on hearing of the approach of the Chinese army, sent all the Hunnish women and children far to the north while he himself, at the head of the main Hunnish host, lay waiting for the Chinese troops to arrive. At last the latter hove in sight, and the two armies joined battle. The result of this battle was indecisive, neither side being able to strike a conclusive blow; but the Huns won at least a moral victory as shortly afterwards the Chinese felt obliged to withdraw and begin the journey home. Li Guang-li's army was again pursued and attacked by the Huns, but this timë the pursuit led to no serious consequences.

The results of this campaign were so disappointing that several years elapsed before the Emperor could bring himself to order another northern expedition. Encouraged by this fact, the Huns again began their old pastime of raiding the northern frontiers of China. This obviously could not go on unchecked, and in 90 B.C. Li Guang-li was once more placed at the head of an army to attack the Huns and show them that the Celestial Empire could not be raided with impunity.

This time the generalissimo again succeeded in penetrating far to the north and defeated detachment after detachment of the Hunnish troops who had been sent out to stop him and force him to retire. It would appear that this campaign was merely to punish the Huns for their raiding and was not intended as a major attack directed towards destroying the Hunnish state. For this reason Li Guang-li should have been well content with the series of victories which he had won and should have retired to China without further risking the success of the expedition or the lives of his troops.

It so happened, however, that the political situation in his native land forced Li Guang-li to continue with his campaign in the vain hope that he might be able to strike a really crushing blow to the Huns. By this time the Emperor Wu-di was getting old, and there was already much speculation and much intrigue as to which of his sons was to inherit his throne. The sister of Li Guang-li, it will be remembered, was one of the Emperor's concubines and was the mother of a boy known as the Prince of Jang-I.

Li Guang-li was naturally anxious to have his nephew proclaimed the heir apparent at the expense of another more legitimate claimant (the son of the Empress Consort) and for this purpose had commenced an intrigue with the Prime Minister who was related to him by marriage.

While Li Guang-li was in the North busy fighting the Huns, news came to him that the plot to establish the Prince of Jang-I as heir apparent had been discovered, that the Prime Minister (Li Guang-li's co-plotter) had been publicly executed, and that, as Li Guang-li himself was out of reach, the Emperor had seized and imprisoned his wife and children. In the absence of a bold stroke it seemed highly probable that the generalissimo himself, in spite of his recent victories, would be cast into prison as soon as he returned south of the Great Wall. He thought that by achieving still further and even greater victories over the Huns, he might secure a pardon from the Emperor; and so instead of returning to China immediately he led his soldiers far to the North where he succeeded in overtaking and defeating a large Hunnish army. After this he was content to turn southwards and retire in the direction of China.

This last phase of the campaign, however, had completely exhausted his troops. Moreover, these troops, realizing that they had been sacrificed on the altar of their general's ambition, were mutinous and dissatisfied. These facts became known to the Hunnish Shanyu, so the latter immediately collected a large body of cavalrymen and set off in pursuit of the retreating Chinese soldiers. On catching up with them, he carried out a neat piece of military strategy.

Well aware of the fact that the Chinese were encumbered with a huge baggage train, he dug deep trenches in front of the Chinese line of march. When the Celestials arrived at this point, the trenches caused their lines to fall into confusion. This was the signal for the Huns to launch their attack. The Chinese army was soon completely routed and Li Guang-li himself fell into the hands of the Huns.

As in the case of Li Ling and other Chinese generals, however, the Huns instead of beheading or imprisoning the fallen Li Guang-li, treated him with the greatest honor and respect. Realizing that the future held nothing for him in China, the captured generalissimo was quite willing to enter the service of his captors. A short time later we find him married to a Hunnish princess and so high in favor at the Hunnish court that he even overshadowed the wily Wei-lu who had hitherto been the leading personage in the Hunnish Empire.

Needless to say, the Emperor Wu-di was furious at the news of the defeat of his army and the capture of his generalissimo, but there was nothing that he could do. He immediately ordered the execution of all of Li Guang-li's family to show his spite; but, during the three years of life which remained to him, he was unable to raise a new army to march against the Huns and had to content himself with sending envoys with insulting messages to the Hunnish courts. The Huns merely imprisoned the insolent envoys and went on their way undisturbed.[4]

At the time of the Emperor Wu-di's death in 87 B.C., it seemed as if the Hunnish Empire had entered upon a new lease of life and that it was once more almost as strong as it had been over fifty years earlier when Wu-di first came to the throne. To be sure China still retained control over Southern Manchuria (in the East) and over large portions of Kashgaria (in the West), but to most contemporaries it must have seemed as if these acquisitions were dangerously imperilled by the repeated defeats which the Chinese armies had received at the hands of the Huns.

In the remaining portion of Central Asia the Huns recovered much of their ancient power and prestige. We are expressly told that among the various peoples inhabiting Turkistan envoys from the Huns were at this period given far better treatment than envoys from China. When a Hunnish envoy, equipped with a letter from his Shanyu, arrived at the capital of any of the various kingdoms into which Turkistan was divided, the local ruler would provide him with provisions and means of transportation free of cost, but when a Chinese agent appeared on the scene he was expected to pay, and pay liberally, for any provisions or transport animals he required.[5]

It so happened, however, that the real decline of the Hunnish Empire actually began just about the time the old Chinese Emperor sank into his grave, a worn out and bitterly disappointed man.[6] Superstitious contemporaries believed that the decay of the Huns started with the curse laid upon them by Li Guang-li in his dying moments.

It will be remembered that Li Guang-li on being captured had entered the service of the Huns and had risen high in official favor, even displacing to some extent Wei-lu, the former court favorite. Wei-lu naturally resented being displaced by the newcomer and plotted revenge. His opportunity came a short time later when the Dowager Empress or Yenjï of the Huns fell desperately ill.

In accordance with Hunnish custom, she was treated by a "Shaman" or witch-doctor. Wei-lu used his influence with the witch doctor with the result that the latter announced that the illness of the Empress was caused by the anger of the ghost of the former Shanyu. In fact, the ghost of this departed worthy, speaking through the witch-doctor, was made to say "It has long been the custom of the Huns to make sacrifices to the spirits of the departed. Time and again the Hunnish warriors have sworn to offer up Li Guang-li as a sacrifice as soon as they laid hands upon him. Why has not this been done?"

The credulous Huns, on hearing these words from the dear departed, immediately seized upon poor Li Guang-li and killed him as an offering to the angry spirit. As he lay dying, the renegade general uttered loud imprecations and announced "My death will surely cause the downfall of the Huns."

Sure enough, no sooner had Li Guang-li been put to death than there followed many months of unusually heavy rain and snow fall. This caused a heavy death rate among the Hunnish flocks, and even among the Hunnish tribesmen there was much sickness. Frightened by these events, the Shanyu ordered that a special shrine be erected in honor of Li Guang-li's spirit in order that it might be appeased, but still the Huns continued to decline in power and in prestige. We sceptical moderns can smile at the tales of the effect of Li Guang-li's curse and can easily deduce other reasons to account for the slow disintegration of the Hunnish power during the decades which followed. In the first place, the fifty years of warfare with China had left their mark upon the Huns. Though the Huns in recent years had repulsed every Chinese army sent against them, it was only at the cost of untold thousands of killed and wounded; and the Hunnish population, never very large, could ill afford the loss of man power. Moreover, the herds of horses and cattle, the mainspring of Hunnish economic life, had suffered enormously from being harried hither and yon. In consequence the whole population, instead of wishing to carry on the war with the Celestial Empire, was only too anxious to secure a breathing spell in which to recover from their losses.

To make matters worse, the Huns just at this period began to suffer once more from internal dissatisfaction and disturbances which at times almost amounted to civil war. The capable Wei-lu died shortly after he had succeeded in putting his rival, Li Guang-li, out of the way; and with his death the responsibilities of state once more rested with the native Shanyus and hereditary Hunnish nobles, none of whom showed any great initiative or organizing ability. There was also a bitterly contested succession to the throne (in 85 B.C.—only two years after the death of Wu-di), as the result of which several of the powerful nobles refused to attend the new Shanyu's court or share in his councils.

In view of these facts it is not surprising to find that during this period the Huns, far from pursuing a positive and aggressive policy against China, constantly vacillated between attempts to come to a friendly understanding with the Celestial Empire on the one hand and a policy of keeping up their raids on the northern frontiers of China on the other. Thus, for example, in 81 B.C. the Hunnish court voluntarily sent back to China the famous envoy, Su Wu, who had been kept a prisoner among them for over nineteen years. At the same time several other Chinese prisoners were freed and escorted back to the frontier.[7]

This act having failed to produce any marked change in the policy of China, in the very next year the Huns again sent out a number of raiding parties in order to harass the northern provinces of the Celestial Empire. On this occasion they were easily driven off, many hundreds of the Hunnish tribesmen being killed and one of the important Hunnish leaders captured. It now seemed as if the Huns and Chinese had come to an impasse in their relations. The Chinese were unable to invade or crush the Hunnish Empire, while the Huns were unable to invade or inflict any serious injury upon the Chinese.

It is about this time that we notice a tendency of the Huns to move slowly to the West, a forerunner of the later movement which was to take them into the Plains of Turkistan and even to bring them to the borders of Eastern Europe. The reason for this slow drifting to the West is not far to seek. North of the Huns were the dense forests of Siberia, ill-suited to the Hunnish mode of life. To the South was China, and the Huns had found by bitter experience that there was no hope of expansion in that direction as long as China retained her political and military organization. Therefore, any attempt at expansion—to regain the size of the old Hunnish Empire of the preceding century—had to be directed either towards the East (Manchuria) or against the West (Kashgaria and Turkistan); and the Huns decided to concentrate their attentions upon the West.

This decision to move westward rather than eastward may be partly accounted for by the gradual growth in strength and power of the Wuhuan and Sienbi, the remnants of the Dunghu who had once been so decisively beaten by the Huns. As the Hunnish Empire decayed under the attacks of the Chinese armies, not only did the Wuhuan and Sienbi escape from the Hunnish yoke and resecure their independence, but they even began to crowd out the Huns in the eastern part of the latter's domain. In 78 B.C., in fact, the news came to China that the Wuhuan had raided the Hunnish territories and had broken up and desecrated the graves of some of the earlier Hunnish Shanyus. The Huns were so incensed at this action that they immediately raised a large army and inflicted a stinging blow upon the Wuhuan for their presumptuous conduct. But though the Wuhuan were thus temporarily held in check, the Huns realized, it would seem, that the Wuhuan and Sienbi would sooner or later recover their strength, and hence that it would be wise to concentrate their attentions on the West.

One of the most important results of the Hunnish movement to the West was the renewal of hostilities between the Huns and the Wusun. Several portions of the Wusun territory in Zungaria were occupied by the Huns. A little later the Hunnish Shanyu sent to the Wusun an envoy, demanding that the latter surrender the Chinese princess who was wedded to their ruler as a token that they were willing to break their alliance with the Chinese and resume their old status as vassals of the Hunnish Empire.

At this moment the Chinese princess, doubtless at the instigation of her husband, the Lord of the Wusun, sent in a piteous appeal to the Emperor of China, asking for armed assistance. At this time China was still ruled by the Emperor Jao-di, the great Wu-di's grandson and successor. Jao-di was still a mere boy, and a boy with little initiative or aggressiveness. Instead of deciding a course of action for himself, he turned the matter over to the council for discussion. While the council was still discussing the affair, the boy Emperor died (74 B.C.).[8]

His death was the cause of much internal confusion in the Celestial Empire so that for the time being nothing could be done to render aid to the Wusun. But no sooner had his successor, Emperor Süan-di (73-49 B.C.) mounted the throne than the Chinese princess, who still had refused to surrender herself to the Huns, again wrote to the Chinese court, imploring immediate assistance and stating that it was the obvious intention of the Huns to cut off all communication between the Wusun and China. This time the appeal was not in vain. In fact, the Chinese court decided to make the cry for help from Zungaria the basis of another huge attempt to crush the Huns once and for all. This campaign, conducted in 72 B.C., was the first major offensive campaign undertaken by the Chinese against the Huns since Li Guang-li's last disastrous escapade in 90 B.C., eighteen years previously.

On this occasion China raised no less than five separate armies, each one under the command of a well-known and supposedly capable general. Each of these armies was to attack simultaneously at different places in the Hunnish domain so that the Huns would be unable to concentrate their forces at any one point. The combined armies numbered more than a hundred and fifty thousand in all. In addition to this, Chang Huei, a very adroit Chinese officer, who had long been a prisoner among the Huns and who, in consequence, was well acquainted with the ways of the nomads, was sent to the Wusun as a liaison officer to aid in organizing native troops to make a flank attack upon the Hunnish domain.

All of the five Chinese armies succeeded in marching into the Hunnish Empire and inflicting a certain amount of material damage. More important still, they also succeeded in withdrawing their troops inside of the Great Wall without being pursued and defeated by the Hunnish forces, as had been the case with the campaigns conducted by Li Guang-li and so many other Chinese generals. This in itself was a great achievement. Nevertheless, the Chinese court felt distinctly disappointed with the campaign as a whole because no really crushing blow had been dealt.

Two out of the five commanding officers were, in fact, court-martialed on their return to China. One of these commanders, who bore the grand title of "Tiger-tooth General," was accused of not having marched far enough into Hunnish territory and also of having over-estimated the number of killed and captured Huns in his dispatches home. The other court-martialed officer was accused of even more serious crimes. It was said that he raped or at least seduced the widow of a subordinate officer when the latter's corpse was scarcely cold in its grave, a very serious offense from the Chinese point of view. More important still, it was claimed that he had shown too little eagerness in attempting to meet and attack the opposing army.

It seems that this general in marching northward had found the country practically deserted, so that he was able to kill or capture only nineteen of the Hunnish tribesmen. Just at this time he met a Chinese envoy who was returning from the North and who told him that a Hunnish army lay encamped a few miles further on. It was obviously the general's duty to proceed and attack the Huns, but the good officer was tired of his long march through the desert and wished to return to the fleshpots of China, so he ordered the envoy to make no public mention of the presence of the enemy and commanded his troops to start the march homeward. Unfortunately for himself, the whole affair leaked out shortly after his return home—hence the court-martial. While the case of the two generals was still in the hands of the judicial tribunal, both officers put a stop to all further inquiry by committing suicide.

The three other generals succeeded in avoiding any judicial inquiry into their actions. It was generally admitted that they had not gained any great glory or prestige, but officially it was stated that the reason the three officers had been able to kill or capture only such a relatively small number of Huns was not due to incompetence, but to the fact that the Huns had retreated before them, taking with them not only the weak and aged but also all of their flocks. After all, it would never do to court-martial at one time all five of China's leading generals.

Compared with the five divisional generals in direct command of the Chinese armies, Chang Huei, who was sent to coöperate with the Wusun, was eminently successful. With Chang Huei's assistance, the King of the Wusun raised an army of fifty thousand horsemen who marched eastward from Zungaria, and fell upon the western flank of the Huns, inflicting an immense amount of damage. The Wusun captured an uncle, a brother-in-law, and a daughter of the Shanyu, and forty thousand Hunnish tribesmen, and in addition secured an enormous amount of loot.

Though Chang Huei had been, or at least claimed to have been, of great assistance to the Wusun in organizing their army, the Wusun insisted upon retaining all of the Hunnish prisoners and booty for themselves. When Chang Huei protested about the unfair division of spoils, the Wusun promptly robbed him of his diploma and seal of office and sent him back to China. Having lost so much face by this humiliation, Chang Huei felt certain that he would be court-martialed and executed. To his astonishment, however, the Emperor, who felt that Chang had done much better than the five divisional commanders, raised the shamefaced liaison officer to the rank of marquis and even sent him back on another mission to the Wusun to distribute further presents to these somewhat obstreperous allies.

The campaign of 72-71 B.C., though bringing little military glory to the Chinese Empire, was really the beginning of the end as far as the Huns were concerned. Late in 71 B.C., the Hunnish Shanyu made a last desperate effort to retrieve the waning fortunes of his Empire. It is worthy of note that he directed his campaign not against China but against the Wusun, the chief cause of his recent misfortunes. Leading his troops over the Altai Mountains into Zungaria, the Shanyu made a surprise attack upon the Wusuns. Since the attack took place in winter, when hostilities were least expected, he succeeded in capturing a large number of the older and weaker Wusun tribesmen who were unable to flee. For the moment the Huns had to be content with this coup; and, without waiting to battle with the main Wusun army, the Hunnish forces prepared to return to Mongolia.

Just at this time, probably as they were recrossing the Altai Mountains, the Huns met with an overwhelming disaster in the form of an unusually heavy snowstorm. Thousands upon thousands of the Hunnish tribesmen and their horses died of cold and exposure, and it is said that only 10 per cent of the original army succeeded in returning to their homes.

The news of this disaster spread like lightning over the broad plains of Central Asia; and the surrounding peoples, most of whom had formerly been vassals of the Huns, hastened to seize this opportunity of revenging themselves upon a people who had long been their hated lords and masters. Almost simultaneously the Wusun in the West, the Dingling in the North, and the Wuhuan in the East renounced all semblance of vassalage and dispatched armies to make raids upon Hunnish territory. Not to be outdone when it came to taking advantage of a fallen enemy, the Chinese sent three armies from the South, and on this occasion the Celestial officers were able to slay and capture many thousands of the Northern Barbarians without fear of retribution.

To make matters worse, a great famine broke out over all portions of the Hunnish domain, and it is claimed that over one-third of the total population and over one-half of the flocks and herds perished as a result. The mighty Hunnish Empire of former days, once the serious rival of the Chinese Empire, was indeed laid low and could only hope for a few years of peace and quiet in which to recuperate its strength.[9]

Considering the terrific reverses they had suffered, combined with internal misfortunes such as famine, the Huns showed a great deal of reserve strength in not being entirely annihilated. The records show us that in the years that followed their resiliency under attacks from all sides was so great that they were once more able to put armies in the field and once more commence sporadic attacks upon the northern frontiers of China.

All hope of the resurrection of the Hunnish power, however, was completely wrecked by the internal revolutions which broke out in the Hunnish Kingdom just at this time. The Shanyu who ruled from 60-58 B.C., himself a usurper though belonging to the imperial family, proved so brutal and so unpopular a ruler that civil war broke out on all sides.

Even after this particular ruler had been forced to commit suicide and the legitimate claimant (whose name, Huhansie, it is necessary for us to remember since he was later to play a very important part in history) was placed on the throne in 58 B.C., order was very far from being restored. By this time the Huns had become so accustomed to bloody battles between rival pretenders that it was difficult for them to settle down once more under a unified rule. In fact, during the period 58-55 B.C., we find no less than five of the Hunnish princes setting themselves up as Shanyus and conducting bloody campaigns against one another.

By 55 B.C. Huhansie had succeeded in eliminating his four rivals; but no sooner had this been done than his own brother, Jïjï by name, rose in revolt and succeeded in causing Huhansie untold embarrassment. Neither of the two brothers could win a really crushing victory over the other. Consequently, for the next two decades Mongolia was divided into two separate kingdoms, which are usually known as the Northern and Southern Kingdoms. Jïjï's main strength was in the north, in what is now Outer Mongolia, while Huhansie was able to maintain control in the south or what is now known as Inner Mongolia.

The great cleavage of the Huns into northern and southern divisions reacted enormously to the advantage of China. As was to be expected, the Huns were kept so busy fighting among themselves that they had no chance to attack the Celestial Empire. Far more important was the fact that in 53 B.C. Huhansie, the lord of the Southern Huns, felt so hard pressed by his brother's hordes that he convened a grand council of his nobles to discuss with them the question of seeking safety and protection by formally submitting to Chinese jurisdiction.

Needless to say this project was made the center of a stormy discussion. Most of the Hunnish nobles violently opposed the idea. "It has always been the custom of the Huns," they said, "to admire spirited action and to despise servility. Mounted on their horses, they have always been ready to rush into battle without fear of death. For this reason their name and fame has been spread far and wide.

"At present, to be sure, there is a battle between older brother and younger brother for control of the Kingdom, but what matter is it if one or the other perishes as long as the imperial house goes on and provides rulers for our Empire? Though China is strong, she has never been able to crush the Huns. For what reason, therefore, should we submit to Chinese rulership? To do so would mean a break with all our traditions, would be insulting the spirits of our former rulers, and we would become an object of ridicule among all nations."

One or two of the most intimate advisers of the Shanyu, however, spoke warmly in favor of offering homage to the Celestial Empire, approaching the matter from a realistic point of view. "Each country has a period of prosperity and a period of decline. At present we see that Chinese influence is everywhere predominant, reaching even to the Wusun and the city states of Kashgaria. For many decades the Huns have been on the decline, and at present there is no chance of restoring their fallen fortunes. In spite of all our exertions, we have experienced scarcely a single day of tranquillity. If we now bow to the inevitable and subject ourself to China, we shall have peace and quiet; if not, we shall continue in a state of danger and uncertainty."

Although the notables in favor of the project were definitely in the minority, Huhansie himself was quite won over by their arguments and forced the others to agree to the plan. Moving southward at the head of his horde, he eventually came near to the Great Wall. From this point an envoy was sent to the Chinese court to announce the formal submission of the Huns and to ask that a time be appointed when the Shanyu might appear in person at the court to do obeisance.

When this envoy reached the Chinese court, there was much fuss and excitement. There was universal jubilation but also much controversy as to the treatment to be accorded the Shanyu when the time came for him to make his personal appearance. Should the Shanyu be forced to prostrate himself or be allowed merely to bow? Should the Shanyu be ranked above or below the rulers of the various principalities into which

China proper was still divided? These and a hundred similar questions caused the ritual-loving Celestials great mental perturbation. At length the Emperor decided the matter to his own satisfaction. The Shanyu was to be treated as a friendly vassal, enjoying the privilege of a guest, and not as a conquered enemy. He was to be accorded precedence over all the other vassal princes; but, in addressing the Emperor, he had to speak of himself as "Your Servant." He was not, however, to speak of himself by name. With reference to the last stipulation it should be remarked that in Chinese etiquette the use of one's personal name in place of a personal pronoun is considered a sign of complete submission to the interlocutor.

As soon as all these weighty matters had been settled, it was possible for Huhansie to make his ceremonial visit to China. This visit took place during the New Year's festivities in 51 B.C. and occasioned the display of much pomp and power on the part of the Chinese. The Shanyu was treated with every consideration in order to induce him to remain in vassalage to China. In addition he and his followers were given a large number of valuable presents. After all, the Huns had to be shown that it was well worth their while to submit to the Son of Heaven.[10]

* * * * * * *

Let us now leave the Huns to themselves for a moment and turn our attention to the events which had been taking place in Kashgaria and Zungaria during the period 100 B.C. to 51 B.C.[11]

In brief it may be said that the Chinese spent most of their time in extending and consolidating their power in this region. Li Guang-li's conquest of Da-yüan, or Farghana, in 101 B.C. marked the beginning of China's domination of the numerous petty states into which Kashgaria was divided; but for many decades the Chinese court was unable to assume direct and effective control over the whole region. In point of fact, China's control over Kashgaria was largely a matter of bluff or, to put it more politely, of military prestige.

As long as China was able to win victories over the Huns and other noted enemies, the princes of the petty Kashgarian states were perfectly willing to keep hostages at the Celestial Court and follow Chinese advice on all important political matters. But every time the Huns achieved a victory over the Chinese, these same princelings became exceedingly restive, and for the moment Chinese control became little more than nominal.

During this period, China had two bases of operation, both of which were under her immediate and effective control. One of these was the region east of Lake Lopnor which in 121 B.C. had been captured from the Huns and divided up into four administrative districts, of which Dunhuang was the most important. This was and still is an integral part of China. As it was immediately adjacent to Chinese territory and by this time had a preponderantly Chinese population, its control and defense were relatively easy matters.

The other base of operations was far away in Northern Kashgaria, midway between the city states of Kucha and Karashahr. In this region China planted two colonies, one at Luntai, the other at Küli. The inhabitants, most of whom were emigrants from China proper, were forced to render military service in case of need; but for the most part they were allowed to lead the life of settlers engaged primarily in agricultural pursuits, and the food grown by these people was of great value in maintaining the Chinese embassies which passed through Kashgaria from time to time. Each of these colonies was under the control of its own magistrate, but the Governor of Küli gradually came to assume control over all the Chinese activities in the Tarim basin.[12]

These two colonies constituted a Chinese island in the midst of a rather hostile sea. Surrounded as they were by peoples wholly alien to the Chinese in language and background, it was above all things necessary, if the colonists were to survive, that uninterrupted communication be maintained with the Chinese homeland through the outpost of Dunhuang. This meant that during this early period the Chinese had to pay especial attention to affairs in the native Kingdom of Loulan, since this native state, which lay near Lake Lopnor, almost completely blocked the path between China proper and the Chinese colonies in Northern Kashgaria. It is not surprising to find, therefore, that for the period 100 to 77 B.C. (when Loulan was finally and definitely subdued), the Chinese records which deal with the early history of Kashgaria devote most of their space to Loulan to the exclusion of most of the other native kingdoms.

It will be remembered that one of China's first exploits in Kashgaria had been the capture of the King of Loulan (108 B.C.). In 100 B.C. it was again necessary to lay hands on the ruler of this kingdom and force him to enter even more closely into subservience to Chinese interest. Even so, this monarch kept one hostage in the Chinese court and one at the court of the Hunnish Shanyu.

In 92 B.C. this potentate died, and on his death a curious situation arose. His eldest son and heir had been serving in China as a hostage, but the Chinese found themselves unable to send this person back to mount his father's throne. The reason for this was that this Loulan prince, while residing in the Chinese court, had been caught in a harem intrigue and by way of punishment had been castrated. As the Chinese did not wish the inhabitants of Loulan to know of this little episode, they sent out an envoy to announce that the Son of Heaven was so charmed with the presence of the heir that the latter could not be spared from attendance upon his Majesty. It was, therefore, advisable that the heir's younger brother be permitted to mount the throne.

This was done, but the new ruler died shortly after and was succeeded by a son who had spent some time as a hostage in the Hunnish court and who was distinctly pro-Hunnish in his sympathies. The Chinese did their best to persuade the new monarch to come on a visit to China, but the latter had great suspicions of what might happen to him on this visit and declined the invitation with thanks.

As time went on this ruler became more and more anti-Chinese in his political leanings. The Chinese records are honest enough to admit that he and his subjects had ample reason to dislike the Chinese, for the Celestial officers and officials who passed through Loulan frequently plundered and ill-treated the inhabitants and forced them to furnish food and supplies at ridiculously low prices. Even so, the Chinese could not afford to let the little question of justice stand in the way of safeguarding imperial ways of communication; and, after several Chinese officials had been murdered as they passed through Loulan, the government of the Celestial Empire knew that it was time to take definite action.

It so happened, however, that for the moment it was inconvenient to dispatch a large punitive expedition to Kashgaria, and so it was decided to try a little treachery. In 77 B.C. an eminent Chinese general was dispatched to the West to see what he could do. This officer took with him only a small body of picked men, but he was careful to carry along a goodly amount of silk, brocades, gold ornaments, and other costly articles. As he went along, he broadcast the information that he had been sent to pay friendly visits and make presents to the various rulers of the western kingdoms.

On arriving in Loulan, the monarch of this state was at length enticed into visiting the camp of the Chinese general, though he was careful to bring with him a strong guard. The Celestial officer treated his royal guest with the utmost friendliness and, after loading him with presents, ordered that a banquet be served. In the course of this feast, the King was copiously served with wine; and, when he became sufficiently intoxicated to have his suspicions lulled, the Chinese general whispered to him, "The Son of Heaven, my master, has ordered me to make a secret report to you—come into my tent that we may talk undisturbed."

The monarch rose and staggered into the nearby tent. As the two men were engaged in friendly conversation, two soldiers crept in from the rear and stabbed the King through the heart. The inhabitants of Loulan were so stunned by this action that they were unable to revenge this act of treachery. In fact, they meekly followed the Chinese general's advice and placed on the throne a younger brother of the murdered King who was known to be very pro-Chinese in his sympathies. It is interesting to note that the Chinese general was rewarded by the Emperor for his action by being made a marquis and given a feudal estate. The actual assassins were also suitably rewarded.

The Chinese were careful to see that everything was done to make the new King of Loulan completely subservient to their interests. He was showered with presents and was given a Chinese bride as a consort. Evidently he knew what was expected of him, for a short time after he ascended the throne, he addressed a memorial to the Celestial Emperor in which he stated "My predecessor (the murdered King) left several sons behind who wish to assassinate me. I, myself, having just returned after a long residence in China, find myself weak and alone. I should, therefore, appreciate it if China could afford me military protection. It so happens that in the middle of my domain there is a place called Isün where the land is very fertile. I should like to suggest that China send out a troop of soldiers to establish at Isün a military-agricultural colony as such a colony would serve to protect me against my enemies."

The Chinese were delighted to accept this invitation, and before long the new colony was in full blossom. The establishment of this colony marked the end of Loulan as a really independent kingdom. Though native kings were allowed to remain on their thrones, they were little more than puppets in the hands of the Chinese officials. To emphasize this change of status, the very name of Loulan was dropped, and the state thereafter was called Shanshan.[13]

Once Loulan had been completely subjugated, China was able to take a more active interest in the internal affairs of the other Kashgarian kingdoms. One of the first states to feel the full weight of Chinese military and diplomatic pressure was the state of Kucha, then one of the most powerful kingdoms in Northern Kashgaria and of especial interest to the Chinese since its boundaries lay just to the west of their colonies.

Even before the Chinese had completed their conquest of Loulan, they had come into active conflict with the King of Kucha, and on one occasion the Kuchanese had seized and killed the Civil Magistrate in charge of the Chinese colonies. For the moment the Chinese did not dare try to avenge this injury and pretended to ignore the matter, claiming that it was an accident. A few years later, however, or, to be more

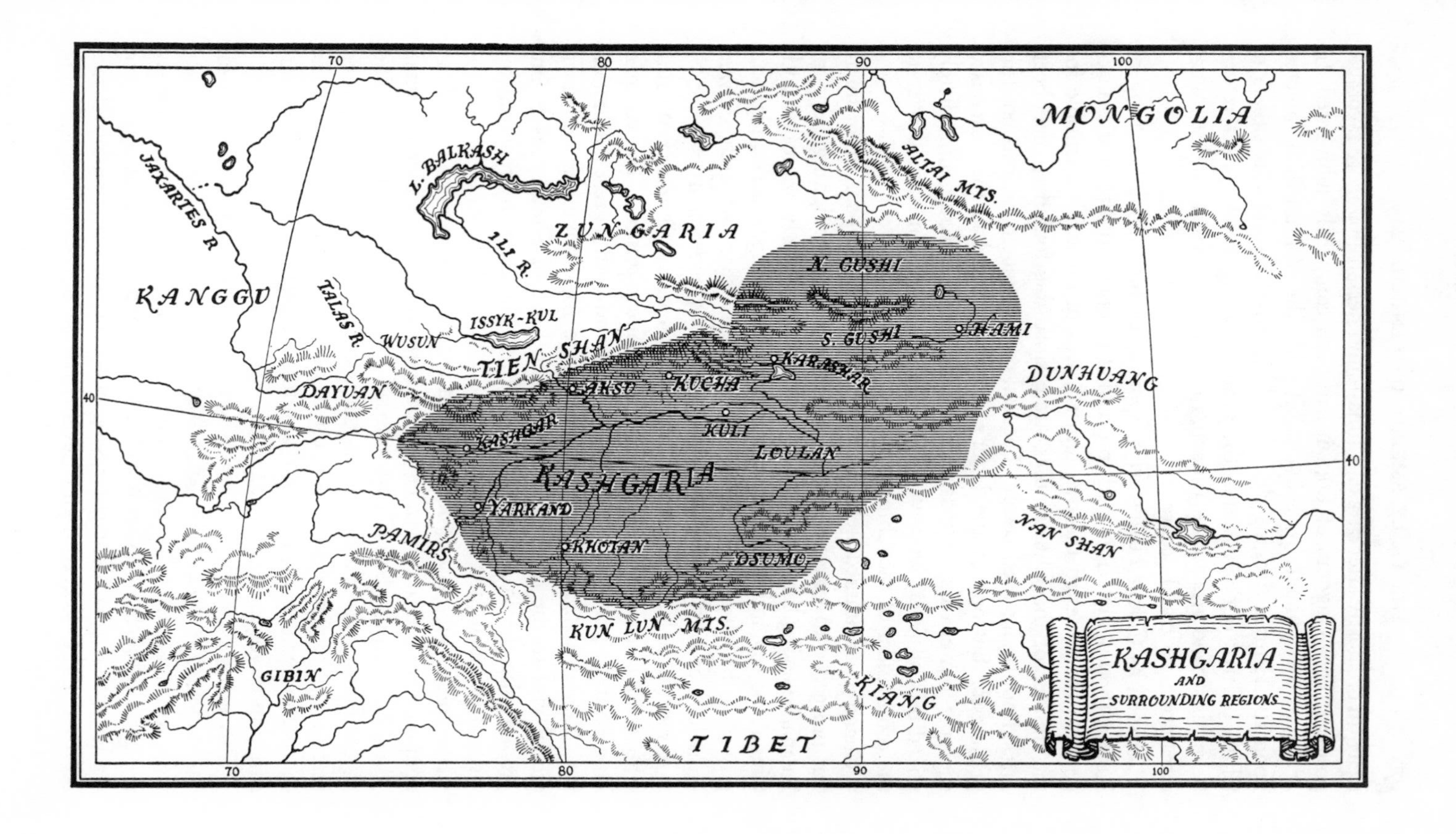

KASHGARIA
AND
SURROUNDING REGIONS
MONGOLIA
ALTAI MTS.
L. BALKASH
JAXARTES R
ZUNGARIA
ILI R.
KANGGU
TALAS R.
WUSUN
ISSYK-KUL
TIEN SHAN
N. GUSHI
S. GUSHI
HAMI
KARASHAR
DUNHUANG
DAYUAN
AKSU
KUCHA
KASHGAR
KULI
LOULAN
KASHGARIA
YARKAND
PAMIRS
KHOTAN
DSUMO
NAN SHAN
KUN LUN MTS.
GIBIN
KIANG
TIBET
40
70
80
90
100

exact, in or shortly after 71 B.C., China found herself in a more favorable position. The Kingdom of Loulan had been completely subjugated. In addition, the Chinese, in coöperation with the Wusun, had inflicted upon the Huns a stinging defeat. Taking advantage of this situation, China ordered our old friend, the general Chang Huei, on his return from his second visit to the Wusun, to march past Kucha and see what retribution he could secure.

As soon as Chang Huei's army approached his capital, the King of Kucha, thoroughly frightened, proceeded to open up diplomatic negotiations. He protested that he, himself, was in no way responsible for the murder of the Chinese magistrate since this foul deed had been carried out by his predecessor. The real culprit, moreover, was not this predecessor but one of the latter's ministers who had then exercised supreme power. To emphasize his innocence the King immediately seized this minister, who was still alive, and had him handed over to the commander of the Chinese army.

Chang Huei immediately cut off the head of this poor unfortunate but proceeded to take no further action against the reigning King of Kucha, believing that this monarch had been sufficiently impressed with China's power and prestige. In this instance Chang Huei's judgment proved to be very sound for thereafter the Kuchan monarch showed himself to be very pro-Chinese in his sympathy and actions.

A short time later he married the daughter of the Queen of Wusun, who it will be remembered was herself a Chinese princess. The Kuchan king's consort proceeded to imbue her husband with a great admiration for Chinese civilization, and in 65 B.C. the royal couple came on an official visit to the Celestial Empire. The Lord of Kucha was so impressed with the treatment he received that thereafter he renewed his visits at frequent intervals.

Still more to the point, he attempted to introduce into his own kingdom many of the culture traits he had witnessed in the Chinese capital. Thus, for example, he built for himself a new capital with streets and an encircling wall laid out in the Chinese fashion. Going still further, he forced the members of his court to don Chinese costumes, and the court ceremonial was revised so that it followed very closely the pompous ritualism in vogue at the court of the Son of Heaven.

This policy of Sinification seems to have invoked a good deal of ridicule among the other rulers of Kashgarian states. It is said that they were wont to remark "A donkey and yet not a donkey, a horse and yet not a horse—such an object is called a mule and reminds us forcibly of the King of Kucha." The good King of Kucha was immune to ridicule, however, and proceeded to draw ever closer the ties which bound him to the Celestial Empire; and on his death his son and heir continued the same policy.[14]

The only other native Kashgarian state with which China came into active conflict during this period was Yarkand, which at this time seems to have been the leading kingdom in Southern Kashgaria. The trouble in this region started when a certain King of Yarkand died childless. He had, to be sure, a number of brothers; but, instead of leaving the throne to any of these blood relatives, he chose for his heir a youth named Wannien who was the son of the King of Wusun and his Chinese consort. Why this youth from the nomadic Wusun far to the North, who, as far as we know, was in no way related to the reigning family of Yarkand, should be chosen to rule over this kingdom is something of a mystery.

The Chinese records merely state that the late King of Yarkand dearly loved this young man, and that the inhabitants of the state acquiesced in his selection as heir in the belief that the establishment of this person, who was half Wusun and half Chinese, would be pleasing both to the Wusun Kingdom and the Chinese Empire. Wannien was, therefore, duly installed as King of Yarkand, but he proved an unfortunate choice and turned out to be a cruel and irresponsible ruler. Taking advantage of his growing unpopularity, a younger brother of the late monarch rose in rebellion, slew Wannien, and placed himself on the throne. This event took place in 65 B.C.

Not content with this successful coup d'état, the new King of Yarkand proceeded to raise the standard of revolt against China. He killed off the Chinese envoy, who happened to be in the neighborhood; and then, fearing Chinese retribution, he set out to unite all the states of Southern Kashgaria into an alliance which aimed at overthrowing all of China's claims of suzerainty in this region.

He spread the rumor that the Huns had succeeded in recapturing Güshï (Turfan) and that all the states of Northern Kashgaria had risen in revolt against Chinese domination. Though these rumors were largely baseless, they were very successful in bringing the rulers of all the petty states of Southern Kashgaria to rally around the standard of the King of Yarkand, and for some time China lost all control of the whole of this region.

China was indeed in a very perilous position, certainly, as regards her Western Empire; and the territorial extension of the last fifty years might easily have been lost had it not been for the quickness and decision of a Chinese official, named Fêng Fêng-shï, who by chance was in the kingdom of Loulan or Shanshan. This official happened to be journeying to Kashgaria on a diplomatic and not a military mission;

but, without waiting for authorization by the home government, he immediately raised an army on his own responsibility and, marching to the Southwest, succeeding in storming the city of Yarkand. The revolting King of Yarkand committed suicide, and he was succeeded by a nephew who promised to be entirely subservient to Chinese interests.[15]

Curiously enough, Fêng Fêng-shï's brilliant military exploit was the cause of much heated debate in the ministerial council in China. Many persons, including the Emperor himself, wished to reward the intrepid official by raising him to the nobility and granting him a feudal estate. Other high councilors, however, argued that the worthy Fêng should be punished rather than rewarded for having dared carry on an important campaign on his own responsibility. In the end a compromise was effected, and Fêng was rewarded by being made a chamberlain at the Palace but without being elevated to the nobility. But though the estimable Fêng was deprived of his just reward, the blow which he struck at Southern Kashgaria, coupled with Chang Huei's work in Northern Kashgaria meant that China's hold over the western regions was made secure for several decades.

Now that Loulan, all of Southern Kashgaria, and most of Northern Kashgaria were under their control, the Chinese needed to take but one further step to render their Western Empire really secure. This was to strike a really smashing blow at the strategically all-important state of Güshï or Turfan.

The Turfan depression is really a northeastern annex of the Tarim basin or (Kashgaria) rather than an integral part of this region. At the same time, as long as this depression remained in alien and hostile hands, the Chinese had always to fear that a single campaign might result in a wedge being thrust between Kashgaria and China proper. The strategic position of the Kingdom of Güshï was further enhanced by the fact that this state covered a very large area and not only included within its domain the whole of the Turfan depression but also had control over a large section of territory north of the Tien-shan Mountains.

Güshï was, in fact, the only important Kashgarian state to have territory on both sides of this great mountain range. The importance of this fact is obvious; it meant that in the region north of the Tien-shan, Güshï was in immediate contact with the Huns, and in the region south of the Tien-shan this state could at any moment pour forth troops to attack the neighboring Kashgarian states without having to wait for favorable weather to bring an army over the mountain passes.

It is not surprising, therefore, that during the whole of this period under our immediate consideration (100-51 B.C.) both the Chinese and

Huns spent much of their effort in securing effective control of this strategically all-important buffer state. So strenuous were the exertions of both the Chinese and the Huns, and so fickle were the fortunes of war that control over Güshï passed constantly from one power to the other. No less than four times did the Chinese by extensive military campaigns succeed in bringing the kings of Güshï within their sphere of influence; but each time the Huns by redoubling their efforts managed to drive the Celestials from their coveted position of domination, and the latter were forced to start their task all over again.[16]

Fortunately, it is not necessary for us to examine the wearisome details of the way in which Güshï passed perpetually from hand to hand. For us it is sufficient to note that it was in 60 B.C. that the Chinese were able to strike the final blow which definitely and decisively brought the whole of the Turfan region and the surrounding territory within the orbit of the Celestial Empire.

It should be noted, however, that this blow could only be struck after the Huns were paralyzed by civil war and treachery. Soon after the establishment of the Hunnish Empire, it became the custom to depute the Hunnish control over the Kashgarian states to an official known as the Rïju King. As time went on the Chinese, as we have seen, displaced the Huns as overlords of many of these Kashgarian states; but those states, such as Güshï, which still remained under Hunnish domination continued to have their relations with the Huns through whomever held the office of Rïju King.

In 60 B.C. a new Shanyu, as we know, came to the Hunnish throne, a man who was exceedingly unpopular with many of his leading nobles. Among the men who detested the new ruler was the then officiating Rïju King. So fierce was his dislike that he decided that submission to the Chinese was preferable to remaining any longer under the domination of his hated overlord. Instead of coming directly to China, however, this disgruntled aristocrat came to Kashgaria and gave himself and his followers up to General Jeng Gi who, in addition to being in charge of the Chinese colony at Küli, was also the leading representative of the Chinese Empire in Kashgaria.

This General Jeng Gi was a person of rare sagacity and force of character. He at once saw that the Rïju King's submission to China gave the Chinese a golden opportunity to strike a final blow at Güshï without fear of Hunnish interference, and this he did. On this occasion he not only succeeded in conquering the whole region occupied by this state, but, wishing to obviate all further danger from this source, he proceeded to divide the Kingdom of Güshï into several smaller states.

We have already seen that Güshï alone among the Kashgarian kingdoms had territory both north and south of the Tien-shan or Celestial Mountains. Taking advantage of this natural or geographic division of the realm, Jeng Gi's first step was to establish a Northern Güshï and a Southern Güshï, so-called as the first lay north and the second south of the great mountain barrier. But this was not enough. Since the region north of the Tien-shan was in close proximity to the Huns and difficult of access for a Chinese army, Jeng Gi did not think it wise to allow Northern Güshï to occupy all of the territory which had formerly belonged to the undivided kingdom and so further divided this transmontane region into six small and more or less insignificant states.

For once in Chinese history the daring exploits of a man of genius did not remain unrewarded. In the year following these events not only was Jeng Gi raised to the nobility and given a splendid feudal estate, but he was also given a new and interesting appointment in Kashgaria.

Up to this time, as we know, each of the Chinese colonies in Northern Kashgaria had possessed one or more commanding officers. As time went on, the senior commanding officer at Küli had come to assume more and more plenipotentiary power in dealing with the surrounding native states, but so far this had been a matter of custom and convenience rather than of legal status or official authorization. Now, however, that the whole of Kashgaria had been safely brought into submission to the Celestial Empire, it was thought advisable to create an office, the holder of which would have full power to look after China's interests in the western regions. The title of this office was Protector General. In a general way it may be said that the holder of this post acted as Governor General of Kashgaria, having authority over the commanding officers of the Chinese garrisons and colonies and also supervision over the affairs of the various native kingdoms and principalities. In addition to all this, he was expected to keep in touch with all the outlying estates beyond Kashgaria, such as the kingdoms of the Wusun and Kang-gü, and keep the Chinese court informed of what was going on in this area.

In recognition of his services, Jeng Gi was the first person to be appointed to this new post of Protector General, and he served his term of office with credit and distinction. Incidentally, one of his first acts was to create a new capital for himself in the fortified town of Wulei in Northern Kashgaria, halfway between the old colonies of Luntai and Küli. This capital became, of course, the site of a garrison and the headquarters for many administrative officials, but the old colonies were allowed to go on undisturbed under their own local magistrates.[17]

The creation of the post of Protector General brought to an end one great period in the relationship between China and the western regions and marks the beginning of a new era. Heretofore most of the petty

Kashgarian states had paid homage to China but had done so individually. Now they found themselves incorporated within the Chinese Empire.

During this period, China made no special effort to include within her empire any of the countries in the West which lay outside of Kashgaria. Nevertheless, she continued to have fairly active intercourse with Farghana (Da-yüan), the Kang-gü and Yueji domains and the other kingdoms in distant Turkistan. Embassies, loaded with merchandise, were frequently exchanged between China and these outlying states. The Chinese were careful to call all the merchandise which the Chinese envoys distributed in the West "presents," while all the merchandise which the envoys from the western states brought to China was called "tribute."

By the use of this and other verbal subterfuges, China could claim that she enjoyed "sovereignty" over these Turkistan kingdoms; but the Chinese authorities were careful never to exercise most of the rights which go along with sovereignty and certainly never attempted to interfere in the internal affairs of these outlying domains. In the case of the Wusun, however, who lived just to the North of Kashgaria and hence were much closer to China, the case was somewhat different. Here China burned her fingers several times in an attempt to exercise real and not merely nominal sovereignty.

During most of this period, the Wusun were ruled over by a gentleman who was usually called the Fat King. This monarch was possessed of a Hunnish wife and also, it will be remembered, of a Chinese wife whom he had inherited from his cousin and predecessor in the kingship. The latter lady, who played a prominent part in history, presented her spouse with several children.

The influence of this Chinese princess with her husband, the Fat King, was quite strong. Consequently, for several years China and the Wusun enjoyed very friendly relations. It was during this time (71 B.C.) that the Chinese and the Wusun conducted their joint campaign against the Huns which did so much to weaken the Hunnish Empire. The Wusun, to be sure, seized all the loot acquired in this campaign and in addition treated the Chinese liaison officer in a very high-handed fashion; but the Chinese could not afford to take umbrage at this action and even sent their envoy to give the Wusun nobility additional presents. This is an indication that, though the Wusun definitely belonged within the Chinese sphere of influence, the Celestial officials were able to exercise very little effective control over their nominal vassals.

A few years later (65 B.C.) a plan was evolved which, it was hoped, would still further tighten the bonds of friendship and alliance between

China and the Wusun. The Fat King was persuaded to appoint the eldest son of the Chinese wife as the Crown Prince and Heir Apparent of the Wusun throne, and it was further agreed that this Crown Prince should be provided with another Chinese princess for a wife.

All this was very well, but diplomatic negotiations over such important matters as the dowry took such an inordinate length of time that five years elapsed before the bride-elect was dispatched from China on her long journey to the Northwest. This delay was fatal to the Chinese cause, for when the bridal party arrived at Dunhuang, the western outpost of China, it was learned that the Fat King was dead and that the Wusun people, instead of allowing the Crown Prince to ascend the throne, had chosen as their monarch an entirely different person. The new ruler, who became known to his contemporaries as the Mad King, was the son of the Fat King's predecessor and was the latter's cousin. Of great importance was the fact that he was the son not of the Chinese princess but of a Hunnish mother and hence was supposedly anti-Chinese in his political sympathies.

The Chinese, of course, were much upset by this change in the condition of affairs. They would much have preferred to see the legitimate Crown Prince ascend the throne, since he being the son of one Chinese princess and the bridegroom of another, would have been much more subservient to Chinese influence. But they felt that they were too weak to intervene in behalf of their candidate. The poor little bride-to-be was brought back to China, and the Mad King was allowed to retain the throne.

A short time later the Chinese were given cause to think they had secured a great diplomatic victory when the new ruler agreed to wed his predecessor's widow, the Chinese wife of the lately demised Fat King. It is worthy of note that this buxom lady, in addition to being the widow of the Fat King, was also the widow of the Fat King's predecessor and hence was the stepmother of the new ruler. To the Chinese mind, the marriage of stepson and stepmother was revolting, but the Chinese princess had quite overcome most of her traditional moral scruples and entered into this new marriage with a good deal of gusto, thinking, no doubt, that she would be able to dominate her new husband in the same way as she had dominated her two former spouses.

Though the good lady was now a grandmother and was well over fifty years of age, the Chinese records assure us that she duly presented her new lord and master with a son. In spite of this rather miraculous feat, the royal couple soon found that their temperaments were not very harmonious, and before long their matrimonial existence became excessively stormy.

The Queen no doubt felt that she was misunderstood. In any case she decided that it would be well for her to become a widow again, and that right speedily. At her instigation a great banquet was arranged, during the course of which the Mad King was liberally supplied with wine. When the monarch was half comatose from drink, a hired assassin rushed forward and attempted to hack the King's head off. The job was bungled, however; and the Mad King, though severely wounded, managed to leap on horseback and escape.

Thereafter there was open warfare between the King and the Queen and their respective followers. The Queen and her party managed to retain control of the capital—called Red Valley Citadel—but they were closely besieged for several months by troops attached to the cause of the King. Though the attackers were eventually forced to retire, civil war continued to rage in other parts of the kingdom.

All this was very embarrassing to the Chinese government, which could not make up its mind which cause to support. The Queen, being herself a native Chinese, was naturally more devoted to the Chinese interests; but openly to support her would mean that if the King were eventually successful, as he well might be, the Wusun alliance with the Chinese Empire would be entirely at an end. Owing to the uncertainty of policy on the part of the central Government, a number of individual Chinese officials who were foolish enough to back one side or the other suffered disastrous consequences. Thus, for example, certain officials who were accused of favoring the Queen too openly were brought back to China and executed. But not long afterwards another such official who publicly reviled the poor Queen for her unwifely conduct met with the same fate.

In the end, the Chinese authorities decided to await further developments before taking any definite action. Meanwhile steps were taken to protect the person of the Queen, but at the same time eminent doctors were sent to attend and nurse the King—and try and convince him that it was still the best policy to stand by the Chinese alliance. It was upon this sorry state of affairs that the epoch came to an end.[18]

But though the Chinese suffered a severe setback in their dealings with the Wusun who lay to the north of Kashgaria, they were fortunate enough to win a good deal of prestige and glory in their conflicts with the Kiang or Tibetans who lay to the south of Kashgaria.

By this time Chinese envoys had penetrated in the West to the furthest corners of Turkistan and had even established direct contacts with Parthia or Persia, but the interior or central portion of Tibet was still a closed book and was destined to remain so for several centuries. From early times, however, China had had intercourse with the various Tibetan peoples who lived in what is now the borderland between Eastern Tibet and Western China. These people were broken up into numerous small tribes, each of which was called by a special name, but it was the habit in Han times to refer to most of these tribes under the generic name of Kiang.

For many centuries the Chinese had engaged in petty border warfare with these Kiang tribes, but it was not until 63 B.C. that the Kiang began to be considered a serious menace to the Celestial Empire. Up to this time, the various Kiang tribes had shown so little cohesion and so little organizing ability that their border raids had been repulsed with little difficulty. In 62 B.C., however, news reached China that a great many of these Kiang tribes had given up fighting with one another and had formed a large inter-tribal confederation, with the result that these barbarians were assuming a much more insolent attitude toward the Chinese and were even beginning to encroach upon Chinese territory.

The Chinese officials were astonished by this display of unity on the part of the Tibetans and argued that this unity could never have been evolved spontaneously and was probably the work of Hunnish emissaries. The officials further believed that if this Tibetan confederation were allowed to maintain itself, there was grave danger that the Huns and Tibetans would form a close military alliance, with the result that the corridor leading from China to Kashgaria would be cut off and the latter region would thereby be permanently lost to the Celestial Empire.

It was decided, therefore, that it was necessary to strike a crushing blow at the Kiang confederation in order to remove all danger from this source. There was, however, some difficulty in choosing a general to lead the military expedition, as the man who by his experience was most suited to the post was over seventy years old. In spite of his great age, this officer pleaded to be entrusted with this campaign, and in the end his plea was granted.

In 61 B.C. he set out for the West. There, by a brilliant display of military strategy, based on Fabian tactics, coupled with an adroit use of diplomacy, the aged general soon succeeded in breaking up the Tibetan confederation. The particular tribe which served as the nucleus of the confederation was crushed, and the other tribes were lured into rendering their submission. In the following year, as the result of this dazzling success, the Chinese were able to establish military-agricultural colonies around Lake Kokonor, then considered a part of the Kiang or Tibetan territory, and in addition the defeated tribes were incorporated within a specially created vassal state.[19]

CHAPTER EIGHT

THE HUNS AS VASSALS OF THE CHINESE, 50 B.C.–A.D. 8

The Northern and Southern Hunnish Kingdoms—The Southern Huns as Vassals of the Chinese—Jïjï's Movement to the West and the Establishment of the Hunnish Kingdom in Turkistan—The Chinese Attack and Destroy Jïjï's Kingdom—The Huns are Reunited but Remain in Vassalage to the Chinese—Subsequent Relations between the Huns and Chinese—The Chinese Stabilize Their Control over Kashgaria—Chinese Relations with the Wusun—Events Among the Kang-gü—Chinese Relations with the Gibin—Rebellion of the Tibetans, and Its Suppression.

It will be remembered that when we last dealt directly with the Huns (51 B.C.), we found them divided into two separate and rival kingdoms. The Northern Kingdom was ruled over by a Shanyu named Jïjï; while his brother, Huhansie, held sway over the Southern Kingdom. It will also be recalled that Huhansie, the southern Shanyu, fearing lest he be overwhelmed by his rival, had formally declared himself a vassal of China and had placed himself under Chinese protection. Moreover, not content with this, he had paid a ceremonial visit to China and had sworn personal allegiance to the Celestial Emperor.

After staying in China for over a month, Huhansie was escorted back to the frontier. At his own request he and his followers remained stationed a short distance from the Great Wall, nominally in order to protect the Chinese outposts in case of attack by Jïjï or some other unrepentant and intransigent Huns. Orders were also given to provide the now submissive Huns with rice and other cereals which these barbarians could not grow for themselves. Finally it was arranged that a high Chinese military officer should reside at the court of Huhansie, ostensibly to aid the Shanyu in maintaining disciplne, but no doubt really in order to keep check upon China's new "submissive allies."

The friendly relation between Huhansie and the Chinese court, which started with this ceremonial visit, was destined to last for many years. Seemingly the fact that these southern Huns were under Chinese protection prevented their being attacked by Jïjï and his hordes, with the result that Huhansie's followers waxed prosperous and greatly increased in numbers—so much so in fact, that the supply of wild game in the region they inhabited became exhausted, and the tribesmen had some difficulty in securing adequate provisions.

The next development took place shortly after the Emperor Süan had departed this life and his successor, the Emperor Yüan, had mounted the Dragon Throne (48 B.C.). The new emperor sent two special envoys to the court of Huhansie just north of the Great Wall to see how his Hunnish allies were faring. The envoys, on arriving at their destination, found that the southern Huns were still suffering from an inadequate food supply, but otherwise were in a very flourishing condition. Not only had they overcome their fear of Jïjï, the rival Shanyu, and his followers, but in addition they were anxious to move northwards again and resume their old headquarters north of the Gobi Desert.

Huhansie, in fact, asked the Chinese envoys what would be the attitude of the Celestial Empire towards this northern migration. As these envoys could not undertake to supply Huhansie's hordes with food supplies for an indefinite period, they were unable to forbid the Huns to shift their headquarters. At the same time they were frightened lest these Huns, on settling once more in the distant region of Outer Mongolia, would forget their recent submission to the Chinese Empire with its consequent obligations and might resume the old Hunnish pastime of raiding and plundering.

In view of this situation, the envoys, without waiting to receive instructions from their home government, gave the Huns permission to move northward, but only on condition that the latter first enter into new and even more binding and sacred treaty obligations with the Celestial Empire. By the terms of this new treaty, which was drawn up on the spot, it was agreed that: "China and the Huns shall for all time constitute a single family. They agree that neither party shall ever deceive or attack the other. In case any raiding or plundering should take place, it is agreed that the guilty parties shall be duly punished, and that compensation be paid for all damages. It is further agreed that, in the event of attack, each party shall supply the other with military assistance. May all the calamities of heaven fall upon the persons guilty of violating this agreement."

To render this treaty still more sacred and inviolate, the Chinese envoys together with Huhansie and the latter's chief ministers, solemnly mounted a nearby mountain. There they sacrificed a white stallion. Its blood was poured into the Hunnish ceremonial drinking cup, fashioned from the skull of the King of the Yuejï, killed by the Huns over a century previously. This blood, after being stirred by a Hunnish ceremonial knife and spoon, was then reverently drunk by the Huns and Chinese. Who would dare violate a treaty so impressively and ceremoniously made!

After the ceremony was over, the Chinese envoys returned to their native country well pleased with themselves. To their astonishment, however, they found that many of the great ministers of state were violently opposed to the course of action they had pursued. These ministers argued that even if Huhansie returned to the North, he would never be in a position to be a serious menace to China, and that the envoys, by entering into "an entangling alliance" with the barbarians, had committed the Chinese of this and future generations to a course of action (such as sending military assistance) which might prove of the greatest inconvenience. Furthermore, these superstitious ministers added that the Shanyu was now in a position to call down the curse of heaven upon the Chinese in case the latter for any reason did not wish to live up to their obligations. These counsellors, therefore, advised the Emperor to punish the envoys for their presumptuous conduct and to send new envoys to the Huns with instructions to break the oath of alliance with as much pomp and ceremony as had been used in the making of it in the first place.

The Emperor was obviously affected by this advice, for we find him sentencing the two envoys to pay a heavy fine; but mature deliberation convinced him that any attempt to break the solemn covenant would do far more harm than good, so he decided to let the relations with the Huns stand as they were. Hence in 43 B.C., Huhansie, and his subjects carried out their projected migration back to Northern Mongolia without any opposition from the Chinese officials; and even after migrating, this section of the Hunnish Kingdom continued to regard themselves as being in close alliance with the Celestial Empire.[1]

The question now naturally arises—what, in the meantime, had become of the rival Shanyu, Jïjï, who had so long lorded it over Northern or Outer Mongolia? The answer to this query is an interesting one and throws much light on contemporary events in many different parts of Central Asia. Ever since his brother and rival, Huhansie, had thrown himself upon the mercy of China (53 B.C.), Jïjï had been in a quandary as to the best course of action to pursue. As long as Huhansie received Chinese support and protection, Jïjï felt that his rival could not be really crushed in a military campaign. At first he hoped, by diplomatic means, to be able to loosen the tie between Huhansie and the Chinese. With this end in view, Jïjï also entered into friendly relations with the Chinese court; and, though he would not formally declare himself a vassal nor come in person to the Chinese capital to do obeisance to the Dragon Throne, he sent his son to serve half as hostage and half as page in the Chinese court. Moreover, for several years thereafter he continued to send, at intervals, tributary presents to the Celestial Emperor.

But though Jïjï's son and other envoys from the Northern Huns were received in a friendly manner by the Chinese, the latter showed quite plainly that Huhansie and the Southern Huns, as avowed vassals, were their favorites. By 49 B.C. Jïjï had begun to realize that he would have to rely upon something other than diplomacy if he were to create for himself a really great empire. He determined to be a great conqueror even if he could not be a great diplomat.

Although Jïjï's original domain had been Northeastern Mongolia, it would seem as if he made no attempt to extend the boundary of his kingdom eastward. Common sense prevented him from marching southward and attacking the combined armies of China and his rival, Huhansie. Following an old ancestral urge, he determined to march westward and establish his headquarters in Zungaria and Turkistan.

First of all, he met and slew some of the minor Hunnish princes who had continued to lead a semi-independent life in Western Mongolia. Then, crossing over into Zungaria, he approached the territory of the Wusun. From this point he sent an envoy to the Kunmi, or King, of the Wusun, ordering him to join his empire. By this time the Wusun were very much under Chinese influence, so that instead of acceding to Jïjï's demand, the Lord of the Wusun slew the latter's envoy and then marched at the head of an army to attack Jïjï himself.

In the battle which ensued, Jïjï and his Hunnish tribesmen won a signal victory. But in spite of this fact, Jïjï did not think it wise for the moment to continue his war with the Wusun, but preferred to turn his attention northward and attack the smaller and weaker state of Hugie. It will be remembered that this people had originally been conquered by the great Maodun, the founder of the Hunnish Empire, so that, when Jïjï attacked and finally annexed this territory, he was only following in the footsteps of this illustrious ancestor.

After subjugating the Hugie, Jïjï continued his triumphal march to the North and West, invading and conquering the territory inhabited by the Gienkun and the Dingling. The Gienkun, it will be recalled, were the ancestors of the Kirghis and occupied a large portion of Northeastern Turkistan; while the Dingling, whoever they may have been, were settled partly in Northeastern Turkistan and partly in Southwestern Siberia.

Both of these peoples had been attacked and defeated by the illustrious Maodun a century and a quarter previously; but, whereas Maodun had been content to impose a vague sort of vassalage upon these adversaries and had then returned to his native Mongolia, Jïjï pursued a quite different policy. He made the Hugie, Gienkun, and Dingling territories the real nucleus of his empire; and, abandoning his headquarters in Northern Mongolia, he created for himself a new capital in the land of the Gienkun, or in other words, in Northeastern Turkistan. From his new headquarters, he again directed several campaigns against the Wusun; but, though he was generally successful in these military encounters, he was still unable to incorporate the Wusun territory within his newly reconstructed empire.

It was this western migration of Jïjï's which enabled his rival, Huhansie, to move northward in 43 B.C. and reoccupy the old Hunnish headquarters north of the Gobi Desert. It would seem, in fact, that Jïjï, at this time, had lost all interest in Mongolia, for apparently he took no steps to prevent the northern movement of his rival. As far as we can make out, he was so busy creating his western empire that he was quite content to let his brother secure control over the whole of his erstwhile domain in Northern Mongolia.

The westward migration of Jïjï and the northern migration of Huhansie brought about a curious situation. For several years, the Huns had been divided into two kingdoms which we have called the Northern and Southern Kingdoms. After all this shifting of population, the two rival Hunnish Kingdoms continued to exist; but they can no longer be called the Northern and Southern Kingdoms but must now be referred to as the Western and Eastern Kingdoms, the one in Zungaria and Turkistan, the other in Mongolia.

This shift in geographic position is of the highest significance in view of later developments in world history. Up to this time Turkistan had been predominantly, if not exclusively, Iranian—the Turanians being confined to Mongolia and Manchuria. With the construction of Jïjï's new kingdom, the Turanians had definitely won a real foothold in Turkistan. This was the beginning of that movement which was to drive all of the Iranians out of Northern Turkistan and make of this region the homeland of the most important of all the Turanian peoples, namely the Turks. More important still, the Turanians were brought much closer to the boundary of what we now call Russia, and the way thereby paved for the great series of Asiatic (or rather Turanian) invasions of Europe.

Jïjï's repeated attacks upon the Wusun, the friends and allies of the Chinese, had certainly done nothing to improve the relations between this Hunnish chieftain and the Celestial Empire. For some time, however, there was no open and definite break between the two powers. Nevertheless, in 44 B.C. (the year before Huhansie's return to the North) an event took place which proved to be of the greatest importance in shaping the destinies of the new Hunnish Kingdom of Turkistan.

It was in this year that Jïjï, furious over the fact that his son, still a page at the Chinese court, had not been treated with proper respect and consideration, sent a messenger to China demanding that this son be allowed to return to his father's kingdom. For some reason China not only acceded to this request, but sent the boy home under the escort of a high diplomatic officer. Months elapsed, and this official did not return. Eventually China discovered that Jïjï, to vent his spite against the Celestial Empire, had murdered the envoy and taken possession of all his belongings. This naturally caused a great deal of resentment and eventually led to open hostilities between Jïjï and the Chinese.[2]

Long before the Chinese took any steps to revenge the murder, however, Jïjï, who doubtless was suffering from a bad conscience, looked forward with dread to the time when a Chinese army would march against him, and began to cast about for new friends and allies. Just at this time he was approached with the offer of an alliance by the King of the Kang-gü. The Kang-gü, it will be remembered, were the Iranian nomads who occupied most of the Transoxiana region, including much of the region watered by the lower reaches of the Jaxartes River. This meant that to the East the Kang-gü had for immediate neighbors the Wusun, with whom they were usually on very unfriendly terms. To the Northeast of the Kang-gü was the territory of the Gienkun, which was now the center of Jïjï's kingdom.

Since the King of the Kang-gü and Jïjï were both perpetually involved in the conflict with the Wusun, it is not surprising to find the Kang-gü ruler sending an envoy to Jïjï, seeking an approchement. Jïjï entered into this alliance with much enthusiasm, as a step not only to settle old scores with the Wusun but also to put him in a better strategic position if and when China sought revenge for the murder of her envoy. The two rulers made a solemn treaty with one another; and, to make this treaty more binding, Jïjï married (as an additional wife) the daughter of the King of Kang-gü, while at the same time the Kang-gü ruler married a daughter of the other, surely a very interesting though somewhat unusual marital arrangement.

Jïjï also set out to make a personal visit to the court of the King of the Kang-gü. This must have taken place in the dead of winter, for we are told that, because of the intense cold, a great many of Jïjï's followers died on the way, and that by the time he reached his destination, he was attended by only three thousand warriors.

In spite of this setback caused by the climate, the Kang-gü gave the Hunnish chieftain a magnificent reception; and shortly thereafter the Huns and the Kang-gü armies, led in nearly all cases by Jïjï, made a number of attacks upon the Wusun. Most of these attacks were very successful, and on one occasion Jïjï succeeded in penetrating to the capital of the Wusun, a place called Red Valley Castle, probably in the

Narin (Upper Jaxartes) Valley, and there slaughtered most of the inhabitants and captured an immense number of cattle.

Even after this campaign, the Wusun were not completely crushed, but they no longer dared make any attack upon Jïjï and his allies. In fact these Wusun did not dare reoccupy the western and northwestern portion of their territory, which lay nearest to Jïjï's domain, with the result that vast stretches of land lay bare and deserted.

Jïjï was now at the height of his power and began to think of himself as a potential world conqueror. About this time he began to build for himself a huge walled city to serve as his capital. This in itself was an important event, for it is the first time that we hear of any Hunnish ruler deliberately erecting a settled habitation. We are told that in the building of this city five hundred workmen were employed for two years. The Chinese records are very vague as to where this new capital city was located, but certain indications lead us to believe that it was somewhere on or near the Talas River in Southeastern Turkistan.[3]

From this new capital, Jïjï sent out envoys to the surrounding countries, such as Da-yüan (Farghana) to the South and to the Yentsai who then occupied most of Northwestern Turkistan, demanding from their rulers that they pay him yearly tribute, and these rulers dared not refuse his demands, so great was Jïjï's power and prestige. According to the Chinese historians, Jïjï was not content with these vast new accessions of territory tributary to himself but began making active plans for the invasion and conquest to the Kingdom of the Yuejï (Bactria) and of the Ansi or Parthians.[4]

So great did Jïjï grow in self-importance that about this time he broke with his new friend and ally, the King of the Kang-gü, because the latter did not show himself reverent and respectful. What happened to the ruler of the Kang-gü himself we do not know; but the chronicles tell us that to revenge himself for this disrespect, real or imaginary, Jïjï slaughtered his new bride, the daughter of the King of the Kang-gü, together with several hundred other important Kang-gü subjects who happened to be within reach. Not content with killing these persons, he cut up their bodies into small pieces and then threw these bits into the nearby river. The bulk of the Kang-gü nation must have felt a deep resentment at this action, but for the moment, they felt powerless to show their anger. At any rate, the Kingdom of Kang-gü remained within Jïjï's newly created empire, and when a short time later the Chinese sent a diplomatic mission to Kang-gü to see how things were going in this region, Jïjï's influence with the Kang-gü nobility was sufficiently powerful to cause the Celestial envoys to be treated with the greatest disrespect.

These interesting events bring us down to the year 36 B.C. and the beginning of Chinese intervention. The Chinese, of course, had never forgiven Jïjï for his murder of their envoy seven years previously, nor had their ill will been abated by the disrespectful treatment accorded to their subsequent mission to Kang-gü. Nevertheless, the Celestial Empire was so busy attending to internal problems during this period that it had been impossible to come into open conflict with the presumptuous leader of the Western Huns. In fact, it is probable that China would have postponed decisive action for several years longer had it not been that she was fortunate enough to have an unusually bold and aggressive military officer in Kashgaria by the name of Chên Tang.

Chên Tang was a remarkably forceful personality, and the tale of his somewhat unorthodox actions makes interesting reading even today. Born of a poor family, he early showed an interest in books, and by his literary ability rather than by military exploits he soon secured for himself official employment. Some time afterwards, for a minor offense, he fell into disgrace and was put in jail. On being released, he petitioned to be sent on actvie service to Kashgaria, hoping that it would prove easier to find fame and fortune in this distant region. His request was granted, and he was appointed commander of the Chinese troops stationed in Kashgaria. In this position he was a mere subordinate and subject to the orders of the Protector General of Kashgaria, but as soon as Chên Tang arrived at his new post (36 B.C.) he did his best to persuade his superior that it was necessary to organize a campaign against the Lord of the Western Huns.

"It is the nature of the barbarians," he said, "to be governed by fear. Jïjï has already created for himself a huge Empire, and the fame of his exploits has spread far and wide. If we leave him alone, he will continue to grow in strength and prestige, and, unless we look out, even the petty states of Kashgaria will be so impressed with his strength that they will renounce their allegiance to China and be incorporated within his Empire. On the other hand, if we strike now before Jïjï has had an opportunity to weld firmly together his newly conquered possessions, we have a very good chance to inflict a crushing defeat which would forever render him incapable of causing further harm."

The Protector General was much impressed by these arguments, but, being a cautious person, he wished to refer the project to the home government before taking any definite action. Chên Tang was furious at this suggestion because, as he said, the counsellors of State, all having small minds, were certain to veto any far-reaching proposition. From this remark it is obvious that in spite of Chên Tang's literary upbringing he had a strong desire for direct action and little respect for the learned politicians at home.

After listening to Chên Tang's tirade, the Protector General immediately took refuge in a diplomatic illness, hoping that the news of his indisposition would postpone further action at least for the time being. But the intrepid military officer was not to be deterred by any such excuse as this. While his superior was lying comfortably in bed, he organized a large army from both the Chinese colonists and the native population of Kashgaria.

When he at last heard of these preparations, the Protector General immediately recovered from his illness and ordered that the troops be disbanded. This sent Chên Tang in a towering rage. Rushing into the presence of the Protector General, he drew his sword and shouted, "Now that the army has been raised, will you, stupid fellow, try to put a stop to its being used?" This powerful rhetoric made a great impression on the worthy Protector General who, forgetting all about his illness and his duty to the court, agreed to go on with the campaign and even placed himself at the head of the new army, though, needless to say, the more energetic Chên Tang accompanied the expedition and was, no doubt, the effective commanding officer.

Shortly after this, the new army got under way. Crossing over the Celestial Mountains, it proceeded to pass through the territory of the Wusun on the way to Jïjï's new capital. The first enemy to be sighted, however, were not the Hunnish hordes led by Jïjï but a detachment of the Kang-gü cavalrymen who succeeded in cutting up the baggage train of the Chinese army. But shortly thereafter Chên Tang rallied his troops, recovered everything the enemy had captured, and, in addition, inflicted upon them a stinging defeat.

In spite of this initial skirmish, the Chinese were very cautious in dealing with the Kang-gü tribesmen. They realized that the recent high-handed actions of the Hunnish monarch had alienated the affection of many of the Kang-gü, and they hoped by diplomatic means to lure the latter from their allegiance to Jïjï. For this reason, when, a short time later, the Chinese army entered Kang-gü territory, strict orders were given that there was to be no plundering or looting.

In addition, the Chinese officials managed to get into touch with some of the most dissatisfied Kang-gü leaders, and by expert cajolery these leaders were induced to coöperate with the invading army. This bit of diplomacy did not, of course, entirely obviate any further fear of attack on the part of the bulk of the Kang-gü tribesmen, but at least it enormously strengthened the position of the Chinese and enabled them to proceed with much less anxiety in their march to Jïjï's fortified capital.

When only a few miles from their goal, the commanders called a halt and, after building an entrenched camp, proceeded to find out what diplomatic negotiations would bring them before even attempting an armed attack. They were hoping no doubt that this further delay might furnish a chance for some of the dissatisfied elements in Jïjï's court to foment a revolution. Jïjï himself opened the negotiations by sending an envoy to ask the reason for the arrival of the Chinese.

For sheer effrontery the answer of the Chinese envoys was superb. "Sometime ago," they said, "you wrote to his majesty, the Emperor, expressing a desire to pay your respects to him in person. In the meantime you have fallen on evil days, have been forced to leave your native country, and are now forced to live in exile among the Kang-gü. Our Emperor, taking pity upon you, has sent us to escort you back to China." It was certainly very nice of the Emperor to feel pity upon a man who had carved out for himself one of the largest empires in existence!

Needless to say, the pressing invitation to return under escort to China was refused by Jïjï, and after further fruitless negotiations the Chinese army moved up to Jïjï's walled capital and began the assault. The details of the siege, though chronicled at great length, are not of especial interest to us and may be ignored, though one or two points are worthy of brief mention.

In the first place, we find it stated that the Chinese soldiery marched to the attack to the sound of crashing cymbals and drums. This fact is of interest in that it shows the great part which military music played in Far Eastern warfare from a very early time—a far larger part than with the contemporary armies in the West. In fact, it would appear as if the whole idea of military bands as a special unit spread from China through Central Asia to Europe. Thus, for example, the modern military bands of Europe would appear to have been adopted from the Ottoman Turks, and the Ottoman Turks in turn received their inspiration from the East. Certainly the Turanian peoples by their conflicts with the Chinese became acquainted with the use of military music at a very early time.

It is further of interest to note that Jïjï had flying over his capital a five-colored flag, from which it would appear that one of Jïjï's first steps after the establishment of his empire was the creation of a new "national" flag. Most of Jïjï's soldiers, of course, consisted of cavalrymen; but the records tell us that he also commanded a number of infantrymen. This is certainly very curious as it was the first time in centuries that a Hunnish leader had made use of unmounted soldiers.

Jïjï's capital must have been quite an imposing place, surrounded as it was by a huge earthern wall. Along this wall at various places were a number of towers, from which soldiers poured down a rain of arrows upon the besiegers. In addition to earth, however (or sun-dried bricks), wood played an important part in the building of the city and possibly of the towers. It was this wooden element in the structure which was to prove of the greatest misfortune to Jïjï and his followers, for the Chinese succeeded in pushing blazing bundles of faggots up to the city walls, and, in consequence, almost immediately the whole city was in flames.

It was at this moment that the Chinese delivered their main assault. The defenders were handicapped not only by the raging fire but also by the fact that the Kang-gü element in the garrison showed little zeal in continuing the fight. Worse still, the ambitious and energetic Jïjï had been wounded in the face by a chance arrow and was no longer able to direct operations. As a result of these calamities, the Chinese succeeded in making their way into the city and then broke into the women's quarters of the palace in which Jïjï had taken refuge. Before long a Chinese officer had cut off Jïjï's head and the battle was at an end, though the Chinese continued their slaughter and decapitated the chief wife of Jïjï, his oldest son, and numerous other leading lights in the Hunnish aristocracy.

As soon as the work of slaughter was over, the Chinese commanders, the Protector General and his energetic subordinate, Chên Tang, immediately sent a special messenger back to the Chinese court to carry back the decapitated head of Jïjï and to apologize to the Emperor for having carried on their campaign against the western Hunnish kingdom without having first secured permission from the Central Government. The arrival of this messenger at the Chinese capital caused an immense hubbub among the ministers of state. A great many of these worthy statesmen thought that Chên Tang and his colleague, far from being rewarded for their successful conduct of the campaign, should be severely punished for their effrontery in conducting an unauthorized expedition. In the end, however, after much petitioning and counter-petitioning had taken place, wiser counsels prevailed and both commanders were not only forgiven but elevated to the rank of marquis and granted feudal estates.

It is a matter greatly to be regretted that the Chinese chronicles are so busy describing the controversy over the reward or punishment of their commanders that they had no time to relate what happened to the western Hunnish kingdom after Jïjï's death. There can be no doubt that as a large and powerful political unit, this west Hunnish state ceased to exist at this time. It is also probable that much of the territory formerly under its control was incorporated, at least in name, within the domain of the east Hunnish kingdom, still ruled over by Huhansie, China's vassal and puppet. Still the fact remains that neither Huhansie nor

China secured, or even attempted to secure, direct control over Northeastern Turkistan, the center of the kingdom over which Jïjï had once ruled, and it is highly probable that the remnants of Jïjï's Hunnish cohorts continued to roam over the vast plains of this region, waiting for a favorable opportunity to reform themselves into a new political unit.

It is, morever, not improbable that some of these scattered groups continued to be ruled over by Jïjï's descendants. We know, to be sure, that Jïjï had a large number of wives (the Chinese records mention at least ten) and presumably a large number of children, some of whom, at least, may not have been present at the capital at the time of its destruction by the Chinese or may have otherwise escaped. Some scholars, such, for example, as the noted Sinologue, Hirth, consider that the great Attila, the ruler of the European Huns, was directly descended from some scion of Jïjï; and, though this is a hypothesis which is far from being proved, it is at least well within the limits of possibility.[5]

But though the Chinese records tell us nothing concerning the subsequent fortunes of the scattered fragments of the Western Huns, they do have a good deal to say regarding the destiny of Huhansie and the Eastern Huns.

The death of Jïjï and the destruction of his kingdom as an important political unit meant that nominal unity was restored to the Huns. Thereafter the only Hunnish state considered worthy of mention was that ruled over by Huhansie and his successors. Huhansie, however, was already a vassal of the Chinese; and his resumption of jurisdiction over all the Huns, subsequent to Jïjï's downfall and death, did not mean that his status with reference to China was in any way improved. Huhansie, in fact, received the news of his brother Jïjï's defeat and death with very mixed feelings. Though delighted to be rid of a very serious rival, he felt that this event had enormously strengthened the power of China and that, whereas China had formerly treated him, Huhansie, with great favor, this treatment might cease once the Celestial Empire no longer need fear any of Jïjï's machinations. In the circumstances there was nothing to do but to fawn upon the Chinese and renew his protestations of loyalty.

Huhansie, therefore, dispatched an envoy to China with a message that the Lord of the Huns had long wished to visit the Celestial Empire once more, and had only desisted from doing so as long as Jïjï was alive by the fear that the latter might at any time have struck a blow at the East Hunnish Kingdom. Now that this fear had been eliminated Huhansie begged permission to present himself once again at the Imperial Court.

This permission was readily granted, but it was not until 33 B.C. (thre years later) that Huhansie actually found his way from his northern home to the Chinese capital. Contrary to any fears which he might have entertained, the Hunnish leader was given a very cordial reception and was loaded down with valuable gifts. The old scheme of a matrimonial alliance, which had fallen into desuetude in recent years, was revived, and Huhansie, who already possessed a number of Hunnish wives, was given as an additional bride a very beautiful lady from the Emperor's own harem.

Encouraged by this very friendly treatment, Huhansie, shortly after his return to his native Mongolia, sent another messenger to the Chinese court with a very startling proposal. This was no less than that the Huns, being now friends and vassals of the Chinese, should be entrusted with all matters relating to the defense and protection of the Great Wall, in fact the whole northern frontier of the Celestial Empire. If this suggestion were adopted, Huhansie pleaded, the Chinese could dismiss all the frontier garrisons, both officers and men, at a great saving both of personnel and money.

Strange to relate, this proposition was for a time quite seriously considered by the Emperor's intimate advisers, but in the end one of the Chamberlains, who was well acquainted with the ways of the Northern Barbarians, strongly advised against it. In a lengthy memorial to the throne, he argued that to entrust the protection of the northern frontier to the Huns would be to put China completely at the mercy of her erstwhile enemies. "At present," he said, "the Huns claim to be our staunch friends; but these barbarians are notoriously fickle, and what would happen if they should suddenly change their attitude and become hostile again?"

As a result of these arguments, the Celestial Emperor decided to reject the Hunnish proposal but to do so in a very friendly and diplomatic fashion. A high officer was dispatched to the Shanyu to inform him that China felt compelled to maintain fortresses and garrisons on all her frontiers, not merely that she might be protected from foreign invasion, but also to see that the rascally element in the Chinese population did not break out of bounds and molest China's neighbors, such as her charming friends, the Huns! It was only for this reason that the Emperor did not feel that he was able to fall in with the Hunnish suggestion and abandon her posts along the Great Wall. Huhansie professed to be completely satisfied with this message and let the whole mater drop. Two years later (31 B.C.) he departed this life, thus closing a very important epoch in the development of the Hunnish nation.[6]

Huhansie left behind him a huge brood of children; and, for seventy-six years after his death (31 B.C.-A.D. 45), the Hunnish Kingdom continued to be ruled over by one or another of his numerous sons. In other words, during this long period succession to the Hunnish throne did not pass from father to son but from brother to brother. Altogether there were six Shanyus who sprang directly from Huhansie's loins. Such a succession is probably without parallel in world history.

For the first forty years after Huhansie's death, there was very little change in the relations between the Huns and the Chinese Empire. During this period the Huns continued as friendly vassals of the Chinese Emperor. In return the Chinese were careful to see that the Huns were treated with a good deal of consideration, lest the barbarians relapse into a hostile attitude; for all throughout this time China was slowly weakening owing to internal decay and could ill afford to renew active warfare on her northern frontier.

It is scarcely necessary to give more than two or three isolated examples of the diplomatic negotiations which took place between China and the Huns during these four decades. As instances of the great consideration which the Chinese showed to Hunnish susceptibilities may be cited China's refusal to receive a Hunnish renegade minister, and later China's willingness to receive and entertain the Shanyus on state visits, even when these visits were the cause of much trouble and expense.

The episode of the renegade Hunnish nobleman took place in 28 B.C. shortly after Huhansie's death. This person, who occupied a high rank, had been sent on an embassy to the Chinese court. After he had completed his mission and was on his way back to Mongolia, accompanied by a Chinese escort, the envoy suddenly stopped and told the commander of the escort that he wished to abandon his Hunnish nationality and asked to be received as a direct subject of the Celestial Emperor. "If you do not receive me," the envoy added, "I shall immediately commit suicide as I dare not return to my native country."

The matter was immediately referred back to the capital, and the council of state was asked for its advice. Several of the ministers reported in favor of granting the envoy's request to be solemnly enrolled as a Chinese subject, but two of the Emperor's trusted counsellors were strongly opposed to this course of action.

"In former times," they said, "when the Han dynasty was first established, and the Huns were perpetually plaguing our northern frontiers, it was quite properly the custom to offer money and titles to Hunnish notables who were willing to abandon their Shanyu and become subjects of our Emperor.

"Now, however, everything is different. The Shanyu is a friendly vassal of the Empire and has loyally observed all his obligations. How can we in good faith continue to receive tribute from the Shanyu and at the same time enroll amongst our subjects a disloyal minister who wishes to escape from the Shanyu's jurisdiction?

"Moreover, quite apart from ethical considerations, there is another thing to be borne in mind. The whole episode may be merely a Hunnish trick to test our good faith. It is quite likely that the Shanyu himself is at the base of the whole affair and made the envoy act as he has done in order to see what China would do in the circumstances. If we enroll the envoy among our subjects, it will merely give the Shanyu a good excuse to break off friendly relations with us and start once more a series of depredations upon our northern frontier."

The Son of Heaven followed this sage advice and refused the envoy's request. The Hunnish nobleman on hearing of this refusal, instead of committing suicide, as he had threatened, merely remarked, "I was out of my mind when I made my request anyhow," and promptly returned to the Shanyu's court in Mongolia. The fact that he received no punishment from the Huns for his attempted disloyalty and continued to hold his high office no doubt tended to confirm the Chinese suspicion that the whole thing was a trick.[7]

The episode of the Chinese being forced, for diplomatic reasons, to entertain a Shanyu very much against their will did not take place until several years later in 3 B.C. To be sure, in 25 B.C. the then reigning Shanyu had paid a state visit to China without arousing any opposition; but from that time onward, for the next two decades, the pressure of internal business had prevented the Hunnish rulers from presenting their respects in person. Consequently, when in 3 B.C. the Shanyu wrote asking permission to appear at the Chinese capital, the matter caused a good deal of commotion.

In the first place, no sooner did the message from the envoy arrive than the Emperor (an insignificant puppet by the name of Ai-di) fell desperately ill. This awakened the superstitious fears of the Chinese, and they recalled that on two former occasions, the visit of a Hunnish Shanyu had been closely followed by the sickness and death of the Emperor. From this it appeared obvious that the Huns usually brought bad luck with them when they came from their cold and distant home in the North.

The Emperor, an easily swayed individual, was much influenced by these superstitious fears. In addition, the ministers of state reported that the imperial treasury could, at the moment, ill afford the luxury of entertaining the Shanyu in the manner to which he was accustomed. Though the Shanyu always brought with him "tribute" to the Imperial Court, it was the custom, as we know, to lavish hospitality and expensive presents upon the Hunnish ruler and his followers, so that a state visit from the Shanyu always cast a heavy burden upon the state exchequer.

In view of these considerations, it was decided to ask the Shanyu to postpone, indefinitely, his proposed visit to the Chinese court. But before the envoy, charged with this message, could depart from the capital, one of the court chamberlains sent in a petition asking that the whole matter be reconsidered. In this petition the chamberlain painted a vivid picture of the troubles the Huns had caused China in the past and which they would undoubtedly cause again if, having been insulted, they once more took up arms against the Celestial Empire. "Even in legendary times, in the reigns of the Divine Emperors, Yao, Shun, and Yü, China was unable to subdue the Northern Barbarians. To speak of more recent events, let it not be forgotten that even the great conqueror, Tsin Shï Huangdi, was unable to penetrate far into the Hunnish domain and was forced to build the Great Wall to defend his Empire against their ravages.

"The early monarchs of our own Han dynasty were constantly occupied in fighting the Huns, yet they were able to accomplish very little. During the glorious reign of the Emperor Wu-di, the Huns were indeed driven far to the north; but even so, in spite of numerous campaigns costing fabulous sums and causing the deaths of myriads of our soldiers, the Huns were not really crushed nor would they consent to call themselves vassals.

"Our supremacy over these Northern Barbarians only began when the Huns became involved in civil war, and their ruler, Huhansie, to protect himself against his rivals, voluntarily came to China and proclaimed himself a friendly vassal. But even this was only nominal subjection and not absolute submission. Since this period, we have had to treat the Hunnish Shanyus with the greatest caution. When they wished to come to court, we could not refuse them; when they did not wish to come, we could not force them to do so. When they came, we have felt it necessary to treat them in a conciliatory manner and have tried to retain their good will by means of sumptuous presents.

"At the present time, the Shanyu in respectful submissiveness wishes to present himself before the imperial throne. To have a Shanyu come to court is exactly what generation after generation of our earlier Emperors strove in vain to bring about. Why throw away this glorious opportunity and talk of 'evil influences' or the deficit in the treasury? To reject the Shanyu's proposal is to cause the Huns to be hostile to us once more, and this will mean many more years of calamitous warfare and necessitate the expenditure of vast sums of money."

The arguments advanced in this petition so impressed the Emperor that he ordered the messenger who had been dispatched to the Shanyu with a refusal to be recalled, and a new dispatch was penned, graciously giving the Hunnish ruler permission to come to court. Owing to the Shanyu's illness, he did not arrive in China until two years later (1 B.C.); but, when he did come, he brought with him not the usual two hundred followers but a suite of five hundred retainers, hoping to receive an even greater number of presents. Though this must have been very galling to the ministers of state, the Emperor, bearing in mind the argument that the Huns must be kept in good humor at all costs, said nothing about the unwarranted increase in the number of retainers and treated his Hunnish visitors with the greatest consideration.[8]

A further instance of the fact that the Chinese felt it necessary to do nothing which would cause the Huns to rise in revolt was the way in which they were careful to respect the territorial integrity of the Hunnish domain. Only once did the Chinese make any attempt to detach any territory from the Shanyu's kingdom, and this ended in disaster and consequently with much loss of "face."

The details of this attempt are somewhat amusing. The Huns possessed a small strip of land which ran like a wedge into the northwestern part of China. The Chinese were naturally anxious to secure this territory both for economic and strategic reasons, but they did not dare openly demand that it be ceded to them. Consequently, the Chinese sent a special envoy to the Hunnish court. In the course of an interview with the Shanyu, this envoy casually brought the conversation around to the territory in question. The envoy stated that it would be very nice if the Shanyu could see his way to giving this region over to the Chinese, adding that the Emperor would be sure to reward the Huns very handsomely in case they were willing to take this action.

The Shanyu took this matter under advisement but in the end he refused to give up this region or any portion of the territory which he had inherited from his father. In addition the Huns sent a special messenger to the Chinese court to expostulate with the Celestial authorities for their action in seeking to diminish the size of the Hunnish domain.

The wily Chinese thereupon swore to the Hunnish representatives that their ambassador, in asking for the cession of the Hunnish territory, had acted completely without the consent or even the knowledge of the central government. In fact, the ambassador for his presumptuous action in this matter was undoubtedly guilty of a major crime and should be put to death. In the meantime, however, the Emperor had twice declared a general amnesty so that it was impossible to inflict the death penalty; but by way of punishment the ambassador was demoted from his high rank and sent as the governor of a petty district, and the Huns were further assured that never again would this official be allowed to meddle in Hunnish affairs.[9]

But though the Chinese Emperor felt forced to treat his Hunnish vassals with every consideration and to shower the latter with presents, he nevertheless insisted that the Huns keep within their own domain and not attempt to renew their domination over the other nomadic peoples of the North.

This problem came to a head when in 5 B.C. a petty princeling, one of the tribal leaders of the Wusun in the West, strove to gain a little glory for himself by making a sudden attack upon the Hunnish territory. For the moment he was successful, because he slaughtered a number of men and carried off a goodly amount of booty. Shortly afterwards, however, the Shanyu raised a Hunnish army and more than revenged himself upon the Wusuw chieftain by inflicting upon the latter a blistering defeat. The Wusun prince was so frightened by this reverse that he sent his son to serve as a hostage at the Hunnish court, thereby furnishing security that no further raids would be undertaken. All this was very fine until the Chinese court heard about the matter, and then there was the devil to pay, for the Chinese insisted that since both the Huns and the Wusun were immediate vassals of the Celestial Empire, it was highly improper that the Wusun should have a hostage among the Huns. In the end, the Huns gave way and the Wusun hostage was sent back to his native home.

Only a few years later, however, a somewhat similar incident caused even greater fuss and commotion. On this occasion two petty princelings who lived in Güshï or the Turfan area had a serious quarrel with the Chinese Protector General of Kashgaria. Frightened at the measures which the Governor might take against them, these two princes fled to the Northwest and took refuge with the Huns. The Hunnish Shanyu gave the runaways a cordial reception and allowed them to settle in the eastern part of his domain. As soon as the Chinese court heard of this event, there was much commotion and dissatisfaction. Two envoys were dispatched to the Shanyu's court with orders to demand that the refugees be expelled.

To this demand the Shanyu replied: "In the treaty which my father, Huhansie, made with China, it was agreed that everything south of the Great Wall was to be immediately subject to the Emperor of China and that everything north of the Great Wall was within the jurisdiction of the Lord of the Huns. It was further agreed that the frontiers of the two realms should remain inviolate, and that neither party should receive runaways from the other states. In accordance with this principle we have consistently refused to harbor refugees from China and have returned such persons to the Chinese authorities.

"In the present instance, however, the refugees come not from China proper but from an outlying country, and I see no reason why I should not afford them protection."

In spite of these arguments, the Chinese envoys insisted that the runaways be sent back to Kashgaria, and in the end the Shanyu meekly gave way. The two fugitive princes were escorted back from the Hunnish domain and were handed over to a Chinese General who was waiting at the Kashgarian border to receive them. The Shanyu did, indeed, make a last desperate effort to save his erstwhile guests by sending a special messenger to the Chinese capital with a petition that the lives of the two prisoners be spared. The Emperor turned a deaf ear to this petition. By his orders a general assembly of the leading rulers of the various petty states in Kashgaria was convoked, and in the presence of these worthies the heads of the two rebellious princes were struck off as a solemn warning of what would happen to all others who might take it into their heads to conspire against the Celestial Empire.

Not content with this drastic action, the Emperor sent a fourfold ultimatum to the Hunnish Shanyu, to the effect that, in the future, serious trouble could come to the Huns if they harbored a) anyone coming from China proper, b) anyone coming from the Wusun Kingdom in Zungaria, c) anyone coming from any of the vassal states in the "Western Region" or Kashgaria, and finally d) anyone coming from the Wuhuan in the East. For the moment the Huns agreed to abide by the terms of this ultimatum.[10]

Encouraged by the seeming success of this imperialistic policy, the Chinese then proceeded to go a step further. By this time the Wuhuan, in Southeastern Mongolia, who had formerly been incorporated within the Hunnish Kingdom, had recovered a large measure of independence. Nevertheless, they still felt it necessary to pay a small yearly tribute to their former masters in the form of presents of furs and woven stuffs.

In pursuit of their policy of trying to isolate the Huns from all contacts with the surrounding peoples, the Chinese sent messengers to the various scattered Wuhuan tribes, stating that it was no longer necessary for them to pay their tribute to the Huns. The Wuhuan were only too willing to accept this advice, and when, in the following year, the Huns dispatched the usual envoys to receive the tribute, they found that this tribute was nowhere forthcoming. This action led to the Huns sending a punitive expedition against the Wuhuan with the result that the latter were given a sound thrashing. Many hundreds of the Wuhuan tribesmen were killed, and their wives and children were carried away by the Huns as prisoners.

No doubt the Wuhuan looked to China for assistance in this crisis, but in the meantime China had fallen victim to a great internal disturbance. The last monarch of the early Han dynasty had been deposed, and a usurper named Wang Mang had mounted the Dragon Throne. For the moment he was too busy reorganizing the internal administration to send a military expedition to the North; and the Hunnish insolence in attacking the Wuhuan, avowed vassals and protégés of the Celestial Empire, was allowed to go unpunished.[11]

. . . .

Before dealing any further with the fate of the Huns, it is necessary for us to pause for a moment and consider one or two of the events which had taken place in Kashgaria and other portions of the "Western Regions" during the time in which the Huns were avowed vassals of the Chinese Empire—or in other words during the period 50 B.C.-A.D. 9.

In Kashgaria proper there is little to record during this period. China managed to retain her dominating position. The office of Protector General was filled by a series of very able men, so that the post itself came to be regarded with much awe by the Kashgarian native states. To facilitate the task of controlling the various companies of Chinese soldiers, scattered throughout this whole region, the post of Central Commanding Officer was created, but even this official was entirely subject to the orders of the Protector General.

The Chinese also went on with their policy of establishing military-agricultural colonies at various strategic points. One of these was in or near Yarkand in Southwestern Kashgaria; another was at Turfan or Southern Güshï in Northeastern Kashgaria near to the Hunnish borders. In view of the trouble which the Chinese had experienced in retaining control over this latter region, it is not surprising that elaborate precautions were taken that it did not again pass into enemy hands.[12]

In addition to keeping a garrison and a military-agricultural colony at Güshï, the Chinese also attempted to use this region as the outer end of a new road, running between China proper and the various native states of Kashgaria. Up to this time, both merchants and soldiers had used the route straight west from Dunhuang to Loulan on the shores of Lake Lopnor. From Loulan the road bifurcated. One branch, called the Northern Road, ran to the northwest to Kashgar and beyond.

The main road from Dunhuang to Loulan, however, was beset with many great geographic difficulties. Travelers who took this route were forced to carry with them a large supply of food and water as the road ran through salt marshes and completely desolate country. There was, to be sure, no other way of approaching Southern Kashgaria, so this route remained in use all during that period.

With Turfan under effective Chinese control, however, it was possible to approach Northern Kashgaria by opening up a route directly from Northwestern China to Turfan and then extending this route westward to Karashahr, Kucha, and Kashgar. This new route avoided many of the difficulties offered by the salt marshes and salt desert around Lake Lopnor, and, as time went on, this new highway came to be considered the northern route par excellence. It was along this road that most of the travelers between China and the "Western Regions" made their way.

The exact details of the Chinese administration at this period have not come down to us. All we know is that, not content with recognizing and negotiating with the kings or princes of the various native states into which Kashgaria was divided, the Chinese authorities also granted diplomas and seals to many of the subordinate officials in each of these native states, the total number of diplomas granted being 376 in all. This system of conferring diplomas directly upon the ministers of the native states undoubtedly served to strengthen China's hold upon the entire region.

The records tell us that at the beginning of this period the native states numbered thirty-six in all, but that in the course of the next few years a process of subdivision went on, with the result that by the end of the period the number of these native states had risen to over fifty. Unfortunately we are left completely in the dark as to exactly how, when, and why this subdivision took place. We do not even know what states were divided, nor whether this subdivision took place spontaneously or as the result of Chinese pressure; but, since the Chinese were always great believers in the old adage of divide and rule, we may assume that they at least looked with composure at the process of disintegration.[13]

But if, during the period under consideration, the Chinese were able to keep the Huns in vassalage and to dominate the Kashgarian native kingdoms even more completely, they were not always so lucky in their dealings with other portions of Central Asia. In the first place, it should be noted that it was during this period that China lost control over her territories in Southern Manchuria and Northern Korea. This territory, formerly occupied by the Kingdom of Jaosien, had been annexed by the Chinese in 108 B.C., so that it had formed part of the Celestial Empire for just over seven decades. Its loss to the Chinese was occasioned by the rise of the independent kingdom of Gaogüli, from which we get our name of Korea. Incidentally, it may be added that this new kingdom lasted until A.D. 688, and that until the latter date it was never again really subjected to Chinese domination.

Strangely enough, the loss of this territory caused the Chinese authorities very little distress. In fact, this important event is scarcely mentioned in the contemporary Chinese annals, largely no doubt because the rulers of Gaogüli continued to call themselves vassals of the Celestial Empire. In any case, this region had been originally conquered by the Chinese in order to encircle the Huns, and now that the Huns were no longer dangerous the direct administration of this region ceased to be of primary strategic importance.

Far more significant from the Chinese point of view were the constant disturbances which took place far to the West, among the Wusun in Zungaria, for the Chinese felt that at any moment these disturbances might lead to the loss of Kashgaria, which lay immediately to the south of the Wusun domain. It will be remembered that when we last dealt with the state of affairs among the Wusun, a highly awkward situation had arisen. The native ruler, the "Mad King," was at open war with his wife, and the Chinese authorities could not make up their minds which side to support.

Fortunately, this embarrassing position was ended a short time later when a Wusun princeling, a son of the former king and a stepson of the Chinese queen, murdered the Mad King and proceeded to seize the reins of authority for himself. Unfortunately, however, this action did not do much to allay the suspicions and fears of the Chinese authorities. This prince was the son of a Hunnish mother and was supposed to be pro-Hunnish and anti-Chinese in his sentiments. For some time, in fact, it looked as if China would use armed force to prevent the new ruler from retaining his throne, but in the end diplomatic negotiations prevented the outbreak of hostilities. A certain Chinese woman who was married to a Wusun nobleman undertook, on her own initiative, the part of a go-between, and as a result of her activities a compromise was agreed to.

The Wusun Kingdom was to be made into two separate divisions to be ruled over by two monarchs, entitled the Great Kunmi and the Little Kunmi respectively. The old capital, Red Valley Castle, and sixty thousand families were to be ruled over by the Great Kunmi, while the country to the northeast together with the remaining forty thousand families of the Wusun was to be ruled over by the Little Kunmi.

The new *de facto* ruler, the Hunnish stepson, in return for Chinese recognition and support agreed to take the subordinate position of Little Kunmi and to allow his half-brother, the son of the Chinese-born queen, to assume the rank and privileges of Great Kunmi. After some initial difficulties, this arrangement was duly carried out; and the Chinese settled back with a sigh of relief, thinking that they had disposed permanently of the Wusun problem.

A short time later, the Chinese princess, who had been the cause of most of the trouble but who seemingly was quite content with the new arrangement, began to feel the weight of her age; and, there being no more husbands in sight, she applied for permission to return to China. This was granted and the good lady, after a long and strenuous life among the Northern Barbarians, was able to die on and be buried in her native soil.

For some years, the division of the Wusun domain into the Greater and Lesser Kingdoms seemed to work very well. Naturally enough, the Chinese were able to exercise much greater authority over the Great Kunmi than over the Little Kunmi, since the former on his mother's side was of Chinese origin and was quite willing to be guided by Chinese advisers. But even the Little Kunmi, in spite of his Hunnish origin, remained faithful to his Chinese obligations as is witnessed by the fact that he refused to join in with the Hunnish hordes led by Jïjï (cf. *supra,* p. 188) and, in fact, slew the Hunnish envoys in order to please the Chinese authorities.

This state of things was too good to last, however; and when both the Great and Little Kunmis died and were succeeded, first by their sons and then by their grandsons, the two divisions of the Wusun nation began fighting with one another. As a result the Chinese were forced to send in a number of expeditions to restore peace and reëstablish the balance of power. These expeditions were the cause of much trouble and expense and led to no permanent gain. Before long the Chinese were heartily sick of the whole business, but, in view of the strategic importance of the Wusun territory, they felt that they were unable to shirk their responsibility.[14]

Still further to the West, the Kingdom of the Kang-gü, which occupied much of what is now Transoxiana, was the cause of even greater vexation to the Chinese. To be sure, the defeat which the Chinese inflicted upon Jïjï, who had dominated the Kang-gü territory for several years, was a great feather in the Chinese cap; and the Kang-gü were so impressed by this display of military prowess that thereafter they were quite willing to pay a nominal tribute to the Chinese authorities and even to maintain a hostage at the Chinese court. But even so, the Kang-gü were far from being model vassals, largely because they felt that their great distance from China rendered it unlikely that a military expedition would be sent against them. The Kang-gü hostage in China went about with a very lordly and arrogant manner, much to the disgust of the Celestial officials who felt that he set a very bad example to the other hostages at the Imperial court.

Still more scandalous was the treatment accorded to the Chinese envoys who journeyed to the court of the King of the Kang-gü. In spite of all Chinese efforts, the Wusun and the Kang-gü continued to exchange diplomatic missions with one another, and the Celestials were horrified to see that on several occasions the Wusun envoys were treated with more respect than their own. Worse still, at all official banquets the King and all his principal nobles insisted on being served before the Chinese ambassadors, thereby causing these latter gentlemen to "lose face."

In view of this awkward situation, the Protector General of Kashgaria, who had charge of all diplomatic negotiations with the Kang-gü, more than once suggested to his home government that it would be advisable to break off all intercourse with these arrogant barbarians and refuse any longer to receive either their tribute or their hostages. The Chinese court, however, was so pleased with the thought of exercising even nominal dominion over this distant kingdom that it rejected the Protector General's advice and allowed things to go on as they were.

The Chinese records tell us little or nothing concerning what was happening to the Yüeji during this period, but in the light of later events we know that the Yüeji were already losing their nomadic habits and were settling down as a governing aristocracy in Bactria and the adjacent regions. They were gradually growing in strength and numbers, preparing themselves for the great role which they were soon to play in world history. The Chinese, for once, were willing to let well enough alone and contented themselves with sending occasional embassies to this distant people who had once been their immediate neighbors and receiving Yüeji envoys in return.

At one moment, it looked as if this period might witness the opening up of intimate relations with the country called by the Chinese Gibin which then occupied much of Northwestern India. This region had been known to the Chinese for several decades past. In fact, at the time of the great Emperor Wu-di (140-87 B.C.), a Chinese envoy had not only succeeded in reaching this country but had played a part in a revolution which led to a change of monarchs. No doubt as the result of the reports brought back by this envoy, the Chinese had a fair knowledge of the geography and recent history of this interesting kingdom. They were aware that the royal house and the aristocracy of Gibin consisted of Sakas who had once occupied Zungaria, and who, on being expelled from the region by the Yüeji, had fled to the South and carved out for themselves a new domain in India. These Sakas had long since been absorbed by the native population of India and had given up their nomadic life, for we hear that inhabitants of Gibin were famous for their agriculture, commerce, and industry.

But, though intercourse between China and India was established soon after China first secured a dominating position in Kashgaria, this intercourse soon came to an untimely end when the government of Gibin proceeded to slaughter the later Chinese envoys who arrived in that country. Since China was not in a position to secure revenge for this action, her ministers decided to make no further attempt to communicate with the people inhabiting the hot plains of India.

Sometime about 25 B.C., however, the court of Gibin of its own accord dispatched an embassy to China, bearing tribute. These envoys apologized for the slaughter of the Chinese diplomats in times past and asked that regular communication between Gibin and China once more be established. At first the Imperial court was much pleased with the arrival of this embassy and planned to send a return embassy to escort the Gibin envoys back to their own country in order to pave the way for regular diplomatic intercourse. Just at this time, however, an influential minister sent in a memorial, suggesting that it would be wiser to continue the policy of nonintercourse with Gibin. "Friendly intercourse with foreign nations," he observed, "is advisable only in cases where we can thereby ward off attacks. Gibin is too far off for it to be dangerous even to our western domains. To dispatch a return embassy would merely be exposing our envoys to renewed danger and to incredible hardships.

"In order to pass from Kashgaria to Gibin, our envoys would have to traverse four or five countries, in each of which they would be subject to attack. The danger from natural obstacles is even greater. They would have to cross over great mountains, called the Headache Mountains as they cause headaches, fever and vomiting (obviously an allusion to mountain sickness). Then follows a path through the gorges thirty miles long and less than two feet wide. A single slip means being hurled into a bottomless chasm. Travelers along this road must go in single file and tie themselves together with ropes.

"In view of these difficulties, let us abandon all thoughts of sending an embassy to Gibin."

As a result of this memorial, the Chinese court gave up its plan of re-establishing regular diplomatic intercourse with India, although occasional trading missions continued to arrive from south of the Himalayan Mountains. The advice of this minister was no doubt very sage, but its acceptance showed that the old glorious policy of indefinite expansion was slowly being abandoned.[15]

The only place in which China showed any spark of its old militaristic and imperial spirit was in dealing with the Kiang tribes of Northeastern Tibet. These tribes had been put down in 62 B.C., but only twenty years later they again rose in rebellion and thereby caused the Imperial court much anxiety, all the more so as famine had raged in China proper for several years, and the Chinese populace were scarcely in the mood to welcome being conscripted for extensive military operations.

General Fêng Fêng-shï, the man who had put down the insurrection in Yarkand in 65 B.C., was appointed to be the leader of the expedition against the Tibetans, but when he demanded forty thousand troops for the campaign the politicians told him that he must be content with ten thousand. When Fêng protested that this small force would merely court disaster, he was grudgingly given an additional two thousand men. Very unwillingly the good general set out for the Southwest at the head of this army; and, though he exerted every effort, his gloomy forebodings were justified when he soon met with a very serious reverse. Whereupon Fêng sent back a messenger to the court, pleading for an additional thirty-six thousand soldiers, and presented the Emperor with a map of the Tibetan country, showing how large was the area which he was expected to subdue.

This time the Emperor and his ministers were really alarmed about the situation; and, in place of the thirty-six thousand troops asked for, they dispatched sixty thousand men. With these reinforcements, the Tibetans were soon defeated. Thousands of the rebels had their heads cut off, and those Kiang tribes who refused to submit after this defeat were driven far away into the interior of Tibet. The Chinese then established a number of new military-agricultural colonies in the Kiang territory to protect the borders from renewed attack.

General Fêng, who had been robbed by politicians of his just rewards in 65 B.C., at last received due recognition for his services by being elevated to the nobility and given a feudal estate. But, as is so frequently the case, this reward came too late in life for him long to enjoy it, for the old warrior died very shortly thereafter.[16]

Book Three

THE SECOND HUNNISH EMPIRE

CHAPTER NINE

THE REËSTABLISHMENT OF THE HUNNISH EMPIRE, A.D. 19–46

Wang Mang Usurps the Chinese Throne—His Arrogant Treatment of the Huns—Rebellion of the Huns—Mobilization of the Chinese Army—The Huns and Chinese Effect a Compromise—The Compromise Breaks Down—Renewed Hostilities and the Death of Wang Mang—Loss of Chinese Control over Kashgaria—Chinese Anarchy and the Reëstablishment of the Hunnish Empire—Hunnish Aid to Chinese Pretenders—Yarkand Secures Hegemony in Kashgaria.

THE WHOLE course of events in Central Asia, both in Mongolia and in Kashgaria, was much affected by the accession to the Chinese throne of the usurper Wang Mang in A.D. 9. Wang Mang is in many ways one of the most interesting figures in Far Eastern history. The later Chinese chroniclers have so vilified his character that his real greatness has been somewhat obscured, but in recent years we have been able to secure from the earlier accounts a more adequate appreciation of the great usurper's actions and aspirations.

During the last few decades of the first century B.C. the Imperial House of Han steadily degenerated. As time went on effective control over the affairs of state passed more and more into the hands of the Wang family. One of the empresses (the wife of the Emperor Yüan) had been a scion of the Wang clan, and through her influence various members of her family secured many of the high offices of state.[1]

Eventually Wang Mang, the most energetic and brilliant member of the Wang family, secured an almost complete monopoly of power. The Emperor Ping (or Peace) of the Imperial House of Han, who ruled from A.D. 1 to 6, was but a child puppet in the hands of the autocratic Wang Mang, and when the boy ruler attempted to rule in fact as well as in name he was promptly poisoned off by the ambitious minister, and an infant from the imperial family was placed on the throne, founding what was called the Sin or New Dynasty.

Chinese tradition makes of Wang Mang an iniquitous monster, but this is largely because he met with disaster in the end, and the Chinese historians have never been able to forgive a failure. Certainly Wang Mang was merciless to anyone who stood in his way. Not only did he poison off the Emperor Ping, but he even caused one of his own sons and also one of his own grandsons to commit suicide when the latter stood in the way of some of the great usurper's projects.

In spite of this phase of his character, however, Wang Mang must be considered as an idealist—a passionate, and in fact a somewhat fanatical, idealist. A slave to duty, he devoted all of his time to state affairs, allowing himself no time for recreation and very little for sleep. Unlike the other great officials of his time he avoided all dissipation and extravagance. His food and dress were simple in the extreme, and he distributed most of his huge private fortune for the promotion of worthy causes.

In marked contrast to Gao-di, the founder of the Hun Dynasty, who was an ignoramus and a boor, Wang Mang was himself a scholar of no mean parts, and in addition was a magnificent patron of learning and literature. He was especially devoted to the study of the ancient literary classics of China, and tried to remodel all of the institutions of the Empire so as to make them conform to the conditions which had existed more than a thousand years previously. Though he called his dynasty the Sin or "New" dynasty, much of Wang Mang's time was spent in reviving old and obsolete offices, in giving to existing offices the names and perquisites which they had had in the "Golden Age" of long ago, and in reëstablishing religious rites and ceremonies that had been completely forgotten for many hundreds of years.

By a curious and rather amusing paradox, Wang Mang's efforts to revive the government and customs of ancient times really resulted in many radical and startling innovations, which enable us to regard him as the forerunner of "planned economy," of the "corporative state," and even of socialism.

During the preceding two or three centuries many changes had taken place in the economic life of China. Proprietorship of land by small peasants had gradually given way to a system of agricultural capitalism. Most of the available land had become the property of great landed proprietors, and tenants were charged exorbitant rentals. Large numbers of the peasantry were reduced to such straits that they were forced to sell themselves into slavery.

Wang Mang sought to remedy this evil at one stroke by issuing an edict declaring that all land and all slaves were nationalized. Both land and slaves being the property of the Emperor they could neither be bought nor sold. Moreover, the land confiscated by the state was to be restricted among the people so that each family should have the use of an adequate amount of it. Wang Mang also attempted to have the government fix the prices of farm products, thus protecting the farmer against the merchant. In order to secure this uniformity Wang Mang made arrangements for the government to buy up all surplus crops in times of plenty so that the price would not go down, and to sell this surplus in years of bad harvest so that the price would not go up.

Previous to this time most of the state revenues had been derived from taxes on land. In order to equalize the financial burden Wang Mang ordered that in future merchants and members of the various professions should pay an income tax of 10 per cent. He continued the state monopolies of salt and iron, and in addition ordered that the manufacture and sale of wine and other alcoholic beverages become a state monopoly.

In these and in numerous other ways Wang Mang showed himself a forerunner of many of the prophets of the "New Deal." Unfortunately for himself and his plans, Wang Mang carried out his reforms too rapidly, and with little regard to the exigencies of practical politics. He believed that other persons would prove to be as idealistic as he was himself, and was astonished when dissatisfaction and finally rebellion became rampant. To us, however, it is not surprising that many of the upper and upper middle classes felt that their vested interests were at stake and did all that they could to undermine the new régime. Eventually the civil war broke out, and in A.D. 23 the rebels took the capital by storm and poor Wang Mang was murdered.[2]

What most concerns us about the fourteen troubled years of Wang Mang's reign is the fact that it was during this time that China lost most of her possessions in Central Asia. When Wang Mang came to the throne, the Wuhuan in the Northeast, the Huns in the North, and the Wusun in the Northwest were all acknowledged vassals of the Celestial Empire, and the Chinese Protector General in Kashgaria had almost complete control over the petty kingdoms in this region. By the time that Wang Mang was killed China had lost her jurisdiction over practically all of these outlying peoples and territories.

This short span of fourteen years can best be considered in three distinct periods. The first of these periods extended from A.D. 9 to 13, the second from A.D. 13 to 18, and the third from A.D. 18 to 23.

During the first period we witness the first breach in the friendly relations between the Chinese and the Huns. In A.D. 9, very shortly after his accession to the throne, Wang Mang sent an embassy to the Hunnish court to demand back from the Shanyu the seal of authority granted him by the rulers of the Han dynasty and to present to the Shanyu a new seal. This matter in itself was little more than a demand that the Huns recognize the legitimacy of the new order of things in the Celestial Empire, and since it offered no great difficulty the exchange of seals was duly effected. It so happened, however, that Wang Mang, wishing to emphasize the overlordship of the Chinese over the Huns, had slightly changed the wording of the seal. In its new form the seal was like one given to a lesser noble, one immediately subject to the Empire, rather than to a ruling, even though vassal, monarch.

This action put the Hunnish court in a very bad mood, and their irritation was increased by an act of the same Chinese embassy on its way back to China. On this journey the Celestial envoys came across several of the Wuhuan tribesmen who had been imprisoned and enslaved by the Huns a year or two earlier (cf. p. 204). The envoys insisted that as these Wuhuan were direct vassals of China, they must be freed and sent back to their own country immediately.

For the moment the Huns temporized and returned an evasive answer, but a few months later instead of complying with the Chinese demands regarding this matter, they decided to risk the perils of open warfare rather than submit any longer to China's insults and attempts at domination. Once again Hunnish hordes swept southward across the desert and began making numerous attacks upon the Chinese outposts.[3]

This was bad enough, but to make matters worse, the Huns soon began to receive assistance from the other peoples of the North who had formerly thrown in their lot with China. Strangely enough among the first peoples to rally to the Hunnish standards were the Wuhuan tribes, in spite of the fact that it was the Chinese attempt to protect the Wuhuan from the Huns that had led to the opening of hostilities. This change of front was in part due to China's lack of tact in dealing with some Wuhuan chieftains, and in part to the fact that the Wuhuan tribesmen found that the Chinese were unable to protect them and thought it better to throw in their lot with the Huns, whose star once more seemed on the ascendant.[4]

Even more serious from the Chinese point of view than the defection of the Wuhuan, was the fact that the countries in the West, the kingdoms of Kashgaria, began to show signs of unrest and disaffection. In A.D. 10 it was discovered that the King of Northern Güshï (Urumtsi) was carrying on negotiations with the Huns. In an attempt to nip the rebellion in the bud, the Chinese Protector-General of Kashgaria seized the rebellious King and executed him.

This, however, was the beginning rather than the end of the trouble in this region. Almost immediately afterwards the younger brother of the slain king led twenty thousand of his countrymen to the northeast and took refuge with the Huns. The Huns not only gave them a cordial welcome, but aided them in making a surprise attack upon the Chinese garrison which occupied their native country. This attack was eminently successful and many of the Chinese officers and soldiers were killed, though it would seem as if the Chinese for the moment were able to keep control over the occupied territory.[5]

A short time later the Chinese suffered an even greater blow to their prestige. So far signs of rebellion had been confined to alien people who had been bound to China merely by the threat of conquest or by hopes of favors. Now, however, disaffection was beginning to spread even among some of the Chinese officers and officials quartered in Kashgaria. Four fairly important members of the Chinese bureaucracy in this region entered into a plot to desert to the side of the Huns. After persuading several hundred of the local Chinese garrison to join them they murdered the Central Commandant, the chief military officer in Kashgaria, and after this little exploit the whole body of rebels fled to Hunnish territory where they, too, were warmly received by the Shanyu.[6]

When the news of all these untoward events reached the capital of China it caused an uproar. Wang Mang, who liked to issue edicts irrespective of whether or not they could be carried out, immediately proclaimed the dissolution of the Hunnish Empire as a unit and ordered that in its place there should be established no less than fifteen separate principalities, all of which of course were to be immediately subject to Chinese jurisdiction.

His proclamation was a very charming affair, but unfortunately it proved very difficult to carry out the projected division of the Hunnish domain, since the Huns simply ignored the imperial proclamation and continued to form a single empire. In order to give some actuality to his edict Wang Mang then dispatched a special embassy, escorted by ten thousand soldiers, to the borders of the Hunnish domain. This embassy was loaded down with valuable presents and had orders to get in touch with, and distribute these presents among, the numerous surviving sons of the great Shanyu Huhansie. It was Wang Mang's hope that the presents would induce at least fifteen of these Hunnish princes to revolt against the reigning Shanyu and accept the chieftainship of one or other of the fifteen principalities into which the Hunnish Empire was to be divided.[7]

This embassy met with an indifferent success. As its members did not dare penetrate far into Hunnish territory they were able to get in touch with only one of the Huhansie's sons. This prince bore the name of Hien and happened to have his headquarters quite near the Chinese frontier. Hien was induced to visit the camp of the Chinese embassy, was there loaded with presents, and was then solemnly proclaimed Shanyu. After this Hien was sent back to the Hunnish domain with orders to raise the standard of revolt against his brother, the reigning Shanyu in the North. To assure themselves of Hien's loyalty to the

Chinese Empire, the embassy was careful to take back with them to China one of Hien's sons, who was thus forced to serve as hostage in the imperial capital.

The envoys no doubt felt that their negotiations with Hien constituted a great diplomatic victory, but they were soon to realize that they were greatly mistaken. For Hien, on returning to Hunnish territory, instead of starting a revolt, as had been expected of him, immediately galloped to the legitimate Shanyu's court to assure his sovereign of his loyalty and to explain that his seeming dalliance with the Chinese was the result of his having been under duress.

The Chinese on hearing of this double-dealing on Hien's part were naturally exceedingly wroth and a short time later, in order to exact revenge, they executed Hien's son who had been taken back to China as a hostage. Later on the execution of this youth was to prove disastrous to Chinese diplomacy, but for the moment Wang Mang and his court were much more alarmed by the fact that the Chinese attempt to split up the Shanyu's Kingdom had put an end to all hopes of a peaceful solution of the difficulties between the Chinese and the Huns, and that the Hunnish ruler had doubled his military activities and was leading raid after raid into the northern portions of the Chinese Empire.[8]

Since diplomacy had failed Wang Mang was now forced to turn to the army in order to protect his domain from attack. And arms having been resorted to, Wang Mang was not content to remain on the defensive. He proclaimed that he was going to annihilate the Huns, and ordered the collection of three hundred thousand soldiers, together with a supply of provisions sufficient to last the troops for over a hundred days, so that they would be able to make an extended campaign in the desert. But the collection of these troops and of the necessary provisions and baggage train proved a much longer and more arduous task than had been anticipated, and as a result of this delay the first batches of troops to reach the northern frontier became demoralized by inaction long before the whole army could be assembled, and the prospects of carrying out a successful campaign became more and more dubious.

Just at this time (A.D. 13) the relations between the Chinese and the Huns entered upon an entirely new phase owing to the sudden death of the Hunnish Shanyu.

For the while the death of the Hunnish ruler worked out very well for Wang Mang and the Chinese Empire. There was some dispute as to who should succeed to the Hunnish throne, and among the various candidates there were some who were more and some who were less favorable to the policy of making peace with China. The fact that the Chinese already had an army of more than a quarter of a million soldiers on the frontier no doubt had something to do with the decision of the Huns to chose a ruler who could patch up a peace with China. Equally important was the fact that the most powerful minister in the Hunnish court at the time, a man called Dang, was very much under the influence of his wife, who was half Chinese by blood, being the daughter of a Chinese princess.

The wife worked upon the husband and the husband worked upon the other Hunnish nobles with the result that the man chosen to ascend the Hunnish throne was no other than Prince Hien, who had once carried on negotiations with the Chinese and upon whom the Chinese had tried to force the title of Shanyu two or three years earlier. It was believed, of course, that this prince was still *persona grata* to the Chinese Court and that his selection as Shanyu would smooth the way to the resumption of friendly intercourse with the Chinese Empire. The Huns were not aware that the Celestials had lost all faith in this prince and had publicly executed the hostage son the latter had sent to the Chinese capital.

Shortly after his accession Hien (who took the title of Wulei Shanyu), dispatched an embassy to China to open up peace negotiations. The news that Hien had mounted the Hunnish throne caused a good deal of embarrassment to the Chinese, and Wang Mang wished very devoutly that he had not executed the new Shanyu's son. He could only hope that this little matter would remain hidden as long as possible.

In the meantime Wang Mang hastily dispatched a return embassy to the Huns. This embassy blandly assured the new Shanyu that his son was alive and well. In addition the envoys congratulated the ruler on his accession to the throne, assured him of Wang Mang's friendship and favor, and gave to him and the principal members of his court a large number of valuable presents. Last but not least, by means of huge bribes the envoys managed to persuade the Shanyu to deliver to their custody the four ringleaders of the recent Chinese rebellion in Kashgaria who after murdering their superior officer had taken refuge with the Huns. These unfortunate conspirators, together with their wives and children, were hauled back to the Chinese capital and were there slowly roasted to death before a large and admiring public, as it was thought that this painful end would tend to prevent other similar rebellions in the future.

For the moment Wang Mang was filled with delight. The principal rebels had been executed. The Huns had decided upon a policy of peace, and the new Shanyu had admitted his at least nominal vassalage to the Chinese Empire. Taking advantage of this situation the usurper immediately disbanded the greater part of the huge army he had assembled in the North, and retained only a few swift squadrons at various strategic points along the frontier.

Before long, however, conditions again changed and this time for the worse. The news of the execution of his hostage son eventually reached the ears of the Shanyu and caused a distinct chilling of his friendly attitude towards China. He no longer made any great effort to repress raiding parties, with the result that small bands of Huns again and again broke through the Great Wall and harassed the various Chinese villages which lay near this barrier.

When the Chinese sent envoys to the Hunnish court to protest about these raids, the Shanyu merely said that the Huns and their allies were a rough and turbulent people, very difficult to control. He reminded the envoys that he was at the beginning of his reign and had not yet secured complete control over all the outlying tribes, but he assured the Chinese diplomats that as soon as he had established his position and had secured absolute power he would see that these irresponsible brigands were punished. The Chinese were forced to be content with this answer, for though the raiding continued, it was nearly always on a small scale. Hien, having been placed on the throne by the pro-Chinese party, was not in a position to unite the Huns in a massed attack on the Chinese Empire, and as long as he was alive the Chinese and Hunnish courts maintained at least nominally friendly relationships.[9]

But if during this period China managed to keep the Huns more or less in check, she was destined to suffer a severe loss to her prestige in Kashgaria. Just about this time the little Kingdom of Karashahr broke out in rebellion and murdered the Chinese Protector General of Kashgaria. In A.D. 16 Wang Mang sent an army into Kashgaria to put down this rebellion and to overawe all of the other surrounding kingdoms. For the moment all went well. Most of the petty kings and princes hastened to assure the invading general of their loyalty to China and even Karashahr professed repentance for her deeds and promised obedience in the future.

Shortly thereafter, however, the people of Karashahr caught the Chinese general off his guard and in a carefully laid ambush they managed to kill not only the general and his staff but also a large number of his troops. One of the lesser military commanders who had not been involved in this ambush managed to push on to Karashahr, during the absence of the latter country's main army, and there inflicted a terrific massacre of the civilian population, so that China's "honor" was partially avenged. But, even so, this commander was unable to retain control of the region and shortly thereafter prudently retired to China.

Fortunately Yarkand, the chief state of Southern Kashgaria, remained loyal to China, and owing to the example set by this kingdom, China retained her hold over the southern portion of her Western Empire. In addition, isolated Chinese garrisons were able to maintain themselves in various portions of Northern Kashgaria. One Chinese commander even managed to safeguard for some time Chinese control over far distant Kucha. Karashahr and the surrounding regions, however, were definitely lost to the Chinese Empire, and with the loss of these states it was obvious to all that China's star of Empire was rapidly waning.[10]

In 18 A.D. the relations between China and the Huns were again transformed by the death of Hien, the Hunnish Shanyu, after a reign of only five years. Hien's avowed policy of peace and friendship with the Chinese Empire had not proved very popular with the bulk of the Hunnish tribesmen, and consequently when his half brother Yu ascended the throne (with the jaw-breaking title of Hu-du-er-shi-dao-gao Shanyu) there was a distinct change in the foreign policy of the Hunnish Kingdom. This new Shanyu, to be sure, dispatched an embassy to the Chinese court with flattering messages, but this was solely in the hopes of receiving the usual gifts of gold, foodstuffs and brocades, and in spite of this embassy there was a marked stiffening in the attitude of the Huns towards the Chinese Empire.

In view of this altered situation, Wang Mang decided that there was nothing to do but strive to depose the new Shanyu and place a more subservient person upon the Hunnish throne. With this purpose in mind he induced the powerful Hunnish minister Dang together with his half-Chinese wife to visit the Imperial Court in China. Once Dang arrived in the Chinese capital he was solemnly proclaimed by the usurper to be the legitimate King of the Huns.

All this was very well, but both Wang Mang and his puppet Dang were well aware that before the latter could really exercise any jurisdiction over the Hunnish hordes it would be necessary for Chinese troops to invade the Hunnish territory and back up Dang's pretensions to the throne by force of arms. Wang Mang was nothing if not courageous and proceeded to raise another huge army to take the place of the one which he had disbanded five or six years previously.

Once again Wang Mang proved to be dogged by misfortune. Long before the new army could be recruited and drilled, Dang, the puppet Shanyu, sickened and died. This delayed preparations for several months but eventually Wang Mang decided to recognize Dang's son, who was already resident in China, as the rightful ruler of the Huns and to use the projected army to place the latter on the throne which had once been destined for his father. Orders were therefore sent out that the recruiting of troops should once more go on at full speed and that henceforward nothing should stand in the way of the often planned and as often abandoned project of a gigantic expedition against the Huns which would forever force these marauders into absolute subjection to the Celestial Empire.

Once again, however, the project of this huge punitive expedition came to naught, for while the troops for the new army were slowly being brought to the northern frontier, revolution broke out in various parts of China proper. Once started the rebellion spread like wildfire and in A.D. 23 the rebels entered the capital and hacked poor Wang Mang to pieces. In the subsequent sack of the city the pretender to the Hunnish throne also met his death, so that the legitimate Shanyu was henceforward able to rule without serious opposition or rivalry.[11]

During this same period (A.D. 18 to 23) there is nothing of importance to record regarding the situation in Kashgaria, except for the fact that it was during this period that the Huns were once more able to reëstablish their supremacy over large portions of this area. Bit by bit the various kingdoms and principalities in Northern Kashgaria broke down the last traces of Chinese rulership but since these petty states were not strong enough to stand alone they soon drifted back to a recognition of Hunnish overlordship, which in turn meant that they were forced to pay a heavy tribute to the Hunnish court.

The King of Yarkand alone was able to resist all of the Hunnish threats and cajoleries. The king of this state remained absolute in his loyalty to the Chinese cause. Most of the Chinese colonists and officials who still remained in Kashgaria fled to Yarkand for refuge, and through the efforts of the vigorous ruler of this state most of these refugees were able to make their way back to their native land. More important still, the example set by Yarkand inspired several of the other petty states in Southern Kashgaria to resist Hunnish aggression so that it was only in Northern Kashgaria that the Huns were able to reëstablish undisputed domination.[12]

The death of Wang Mang marked the end of all of China's imperialistic pretensions and aspirations for several decades to come. It also definitely marked the reëstablishment of the Hunnish nation as a separate and completely independent empire. During much of Wang Mang's reign, to be sure, the Huns and the inhabitants of the petty Kashgarian states had openly rebelled against Chinese domination, but never for a moment did Wang Mang renounce any of China's claims to absolute suzerainty over these peoples. Had he been allowed to rule a few years longer, it is probable that all of these peoples would once more have been incorporated within the Chinese Empire and this time not merely as autonomous vassals (which had been their previous position) but as completely subservient subjects of the Celestial Empire.

Wang Mang's tragic end completely altered the whole situation, for after he had been put out of the way it was several years before peace and order were reëstablished even within the borders of China proper. Numerous claimants for the throne, most of them descendants of the old imperial House of Han, arose on all sides, and for some time none of them was able to secure general recognition.[13] In view of this internal anarchy it is small wonder that the Huns and other "barbarian" peoples put aside all pretense, and resolutely refused to admit even the shadow of Chinese supremacy. In A.D. 24 one of these claimants to the imperial throne who for the moment had triumphed over his rivals sent an embassy to the Hunnish court in the hope of persuading the Shanyu to admit at least nominal vassalage to the new régime. The members of this embassy met with a polite but firm rebuff.

"In former times," the Shanyu said, "when the Huns were rent by internal conflict, the then Emperor of China rendered aid to my father, Huhansie. It was as the result of this aid that my father was able to unify and reign over the Hunnish Kingdom. It was quite proper, therefore, for him and his immediate successors my brothers to call themselves vassals and render allegiance to the House of Han.

"Now, however, the situation has completely changed. It is now China that is in a state of internal conflict. Moreover it should be remembered that the downfall of the usurper Wang Mang and the reëstablishment of the House of Han is largely due to the fact that Wang Mang met with steady opposition on the part of my subjects the Huns. The House of Han therefore really owes its present renewed prosperity to me and my people. Instead therefore of asking me to render homage to the new Emperor of China, the proper thing would be for this ruler to render homage to me."

The Chinese envoys were greatly upset by these bold words, but after some futile efforts at argument had failed to alter the situation they returned to their native land to announce the complete failure of their mission. Subsequent events proved that the Shanyu had been very wise in refusing to admit the supremacy of the particular prince—and self-styled Emperor—who had sent him this embassy, for before long this claimant to the imperial throne lost both his position and his life and China once more relapsed into anarchy.

In A.D. 25 another princeling of the House of Han proclaimed himself Emperor of China, taking for his title the name Guang-wu or Enlightened Warrior. This prince was a very able and active leader, and being, in addition, much favored by fortune it is not surprising to learn that slowly but surely he was able to bring all of China within his jurisdiction, thus establishing what is known as the Later (or as it is sometimes called, the Eastern) Han dynasty which ruled for nearly two hundred years or until A.D. 220. But though Guang-wu was thus eminently successful in the end, his climb to absolute power, even within the limits of China proper, was a long and rather slow process, and it was not until many years after his nominal accession to the throne in A.D. 25 that he was able to exercise real jurisdiction over any large area.

At first Guang-wu refused to become involved in matters pertaining to the outer barbarians, but in A.D. 30 he followed his predecessor's example and dispatched an embassy to the Hunnish court. This embassy was loaded down with rich presents and the envoys hoped by means of bribes to induce the Shanyu to return to his old position as nominal vassal of the Chinese Empire. The Shanyu was perfectly willing to receive any and all presents offered to him, but he resolutely refused to acknowledge vassalage in any shape or form. He knew that the Emperor was still far from being absolute master in his own house, and would be unable to conduct any extensive military campaign abroad. For this reason it is not surprising that the Lord of the Huns saw no reason to compromise on the all important question of independence.

The Emperor Guang-wu took this rebuff with good grace. He had no intention of crying because he could not grasp the moon, and he soon abandoned all plans of trying to reëxpand the limits of the Chinese Empire to its former huge extent, and contented himself with trying to lay the foundations for peace and orderly government within the limits of China proper.[14]

But though the Emperor of China was quite willing to abandon all ideas of aggression against the Huns, the Huns showed that they were not willing to abandon all ideas of aggression against China. Again and again the Huns harassed the northern frontiers of China. More important still, they decided to enter into the old game of king-making, and caused the Emperor Guang-wu untold trouble and embarrassment by actively supporting one of his rival claimants to the imperial throne. The rival in question was a man called Lu Fang, a native of the northwestern part of China who had become the leader of a small military band, half soldiers, half bandits, during the troublous times following Wang Mang's overthrow.

As the anarchy increased Lu Fang was able to set up a sort of military jurisdiction over a fairly wide area, and as a result began to harbor even more extensive ambitions. Realizing that public opinion was strongly in favor of reëstablishing the Han dynasty, the members of whose house bore the family name of Liu, Lu Fang changed his name to Liu Fang and claimed to be descended from the great Emperor Wu-di by a Hunnish princess. This story gained wide credence, with the result that Lu Fang's following greatly increased.

The territory over which Lu Fang had control was immediately adjacent to the Hunnish Kingdom, and the pretender felt that it was advisable for him to get into friendly touch with these powerful neighbors. In fact Lu Fang promised to render homage to the Hunnish Shanyu if the latter would support him in his efforts to become the ruler of the whole of China. It was no doubt this offer which caused the Huns to render Lu Fang such valuable assistance in the years that followed.

The period of Lu Fang's greatest prosperity was from A.D. 30 to 36. During this period he and his Hunnish allies had possession of a considerable portion of Northern China. The Emperor Guang-wu was forced to send expedition after expedition against his northern rival, and though these expeditions were led by his best generals they were able to little more than hold their own and prevent Lu Fang's influence from spreading to the South.

Lu Fang, however, was unable to prevent his subordinate leaders from disputing among themselves. As a result of these internal conflicts Lu Fang's army gradually broke up. In A.D. 37 he was forced to abandon his kingdom, and fleeing to the North, he took refuge with his patron, the ruler of the Huns. For the next three years the pretender continued to live quietly at the Hunnish court waiting for another opportunity to strike a blow for the throne. By this time the Huns felt that they had backed the wrong horse and made little or no effort to aid their puppet to reëstablish his kingdom although they continued to raid on their own account at various places in Northern China.

By A.D. 40 the Huns had grown tired of the continued presence of Lu Fang, since they felt that the latter was of no service to them. Moreover, Guang-wu, the Emperor of China, had offered a large reward for the capture of his rival. The Huns thought they could rid themselves of an unwanted guest and collect a goodly sum of money at the same time by handing over the unfortunate Lu Fang to the Chinese authorities. Lu Fang got wind of this "double cross" that was being played on him and rescued himself by a bold stroke. Instead of waiting for the Huns to seize and hand him over to the Chinese, he fled of his own accord to the Chinese frontier, and told the authorities there that he regretted his past rebellious actions and wished to submit himself to the will of the Celestial Emperor.

The Emperor, who was ignorant of the plan of the Huns to hand over the rebel, was overjoyed at receiving the submission of so important a person, and instead of executing Lu Fang heaped presents upon him. In fact, he was made the governor of one of the northern provinces and granted the title of King. The Huns naturally were furious at all this, but a sense of shame prevented them from attempting to collect any of the blood money.

In spite of his renewed prosperity, Lu Fang still possessed a very uneasy conscience. Only two years later (A.D. 42) when the Emperor Guang-wu seemed to be a little chilly in his treatment of the ex-rebel, Lu Fang began to fear for his life, and abandoning his new kingdom he again fled to the North and took refuge in Hunnish territory. This time, for some reason or other, the Huns made no attempt to hand him back to the Chinese authorities, and the refugee was allowed to live in obscurity in the Hunnish domain until his death a few years later.[15]

But though after A.D. 42 Lu Fang ceased to be a disturbing factor on the northern frontier, the relations between the Chinese and the Huns showed no visible improvement. In A.D. 44 and again in 45 the Huns swept down into Northern China and inflicted an enormous amount of damage, although they made no attempt permanently to annex or govern the territory which they devastated. In several of these raids we find it recorded that the Wuhuan and the Sienbi acted in conjunction with the Huns, from which we may gather that all during this period (A.D. 23-46) the Huns were able to exercise at least some sort of jurisdiction over their eastern neighbors.[16]

But if the revived Hunnish Empire was thus able to maintain absolute control over all of Mongolia and, in addition, dominate the peoples inhabiting Western Manchuria, it failed in its attempt to maintain its overlordship over the petty kingdoms in Kashgaria and other regions in the West. This in itself was a sign that this second Hunnish Empire, great as it was, could never equal the size and glory of the first Hunnish Empire established over two centuries previously.

It will be remembered that when the usurper Wang Mang died (A.D. 23) most of the Kashgarian states had broken away from Chinese jurisdiction and had reverted to dependence upon the Huns. Here and there a few small Chinese garrisons and outposts remained, but in the years of anarchy following Wang Mang's death, the Huns found no difficulty in destroying these last traces of Chinese occupation, and for several years it seemed as though Kashgaria or at least Northern Kashgaria was once more an integral part of the Hunnish Empire. There was only one fly in the ointment, as we have said, namely the fact that the little kingdom of Yarkand in Southern Kashgaria succeeded in maintaining its independence. This independence was entirely due to its own efforts, and not at all to Chinese support, but in spite of this fact the people of Yarkand remained pro-Chinese in their sympathies and continued to call themselves vassals of the Celestial Empire.

The inability of the Huns to conquer Yarkand might not have been so important had the Hunnish ruler and his ministers been diplomatic in their treatment of the other Kashgarian states, most of which had quite willingly renewed their vows of allegiance to the Shanyu. Unfortunately for themselves, however, the Hunnish officials in charge of Kashgarian affairs proved insatiable in their demands for taxes and tribute, and before long many of the petty kingdoms which only recently had regarded the Huns as their liberators from Chinese oppression began to feel that in changing masters they had jumped from the frying pan into the fire. Several of these kingdoms, in fact, were so disappointed with their new situation that they again began to look to China for assistance. China herself was still in such a state of anarchy that she was unable to offer any direct military support, but at least China's friend and nominal vassal Kang, the King of Yarkand, stood ready to offer assistance to any state which was ready to rebel against Hunnish oppression.

The activities of this energetic ruler of Yarkand were greatly aided by the moral support lent him by an enterprising Chinese general who for several years had acted as self-appointed Governor of Dunhuang and other portions of Western China. This gentleman (Dou Rung by name) was unable for some time to make up his mind to which one of the various pretenders to the imperial throne of China he should offer his allegiance, but in the meantime he managed to preserve peace and order in the region under his own jurisdiction and in addition was keenly interested in preserving Chinese prestige in Kashgaria in the hope that sooner or later this region might be reincorporated within the Celestial Empire. With this end in view the worthy general thought he saw a favorable opportunity arise in A.D. 29 and in that year, on his own responsibility, he dispatched a messenger to King Kang of Yarkand with a diploma granting the latter the title of "Great General of the Western regions," and officially recognizing him as the chief representative in Kashgaria of His Imperial Majesty the Emperor of China, even though there was still some doubt as to which of the rival claimants really was the Emperor of China.

The Chinese general's diploma was far from being a legally valid document, but it seems to have inspired the King of Yarkand to even greater activity, and as the result of this activity the Hunnish yoke over most of the Kashgarian states was shaken off. As far as we can make out, King Kang made no effort to dispose or change any of the existing rulers of the various Kashgarian kingdoms, contenting himself merely with aiding the existing rulers to expel the Hunnish envoys and officials who tried to lord it over them. It would therefore be incorrect to say that Kang conquered the whole of Kashgaria, but at least in consequence of his exploits he came to be regarded as the leading figure in Kashgarian politics and diplomacy. It goes without saying that Kang's success also did much to restore China's waning prestige in Central Asia, although it must not be forgotten that China was still not in a position to send either soldiers or officials to Kashgaria and thereby reestablish her former jurisdiction.

In A.D. 33 King Kang died and was succeeded on the throne of Yarkand by his brother Hien who was destined to become one of the most vivid and interesting personalities in the whole history of Kashgaria. Hien soon proved that he was even more energetic and ambitious than his predecessor. This predecessor had interfered very little in the internal affairs of the surrounding kingdoms, contenting himself with exercising vague general supervision over them. Hien however was filled with the zest for power, and soon after his accession he invaded two nearby states, deposed their kings, and placed on the vacant thrones two of his own nephews.

This was merely an early indication of the aggressive action which Hien was later to take with many of the other Kashgarian kingdoms. Even in these early years, however, Hien seems to have had complete domination over all the states in the southwestern portion of the Tarim basin.

In spite of these early successes Hien continued to assume a very humble tone in his dealings with the Chinese Empire. In A.D. 37 we find him sending in tribute to the court of the Emperor Guang-wu who by this time was fairly well established on the Dragon Throne. Four years later (A.D. 41) he again sent an embassy to China laden with tribute, but this time, in addition to offering up their presents, the envoys of Hien were instructed to petition the Emperor of China to reëstablish the old office of Chinese Protector General of the Western Region which had fallen into abeyance during the usurpation of Wang Mang.

This proposition caused quite a stir in the Chinese capital. The Emperor himself had not the slightest intention of wasting men or money in an attempt to reëstablish effective military and political domination over Kashgaria, as he had not yet succeeded in bringing about complete order within China proper. His Imperial Majesty therefore looked somewhat askance at the project of appointing anyone to the post of Protector General.

The old General Dou Rung, however, who had formerly granted King Kang the honorary title of "General in Command of the West," and who was now living in the capital on terms of intimacy with the Emperor, put forward a plan which he said would allow the Chinese the prestige of maintaining a Protector General in Kashgaria and yet would not entail any new expense or responsibility. This plan was nothing other than granting to Hien, already the dominant figure in Kashgaria, the courtesy title of Chinese Protector General of this region. The granting of this title would not only be a reward to the kings of Yarkand for their loyalty in the past, but would also cause them to be even more subservient to China in the future. Though somewhat dubious, the Emperor decided to adopt this plan, and an official seal granting Hien the title of Protector General was duly made out and handed to the envoys from Yarkand with instructions to hand it over to their master.

Shortly after this, and long before the envoys had been able to reach their native land, another official handed in a memorial to the court strongly protesting against the appointment of a barbarian to a high position in the Chinese bureaucracy and asserting that such an action, far from making China popular with the western barbarians, would really cause her to be universally despised. This new memorial made a deep impression on the Emperor, and he immediately issued an order that the Yarkand envoys be stopped en route, and asked to exchange their seal granting Hien the rank of Protector General for one merely granting him the rank of full general in the Chinese army.

Chinese officials did indeed succeed in overtaking the Yarkand envoys, but the latter refused point blank to effect the change of seals. Impatient at this refusal, the Chinese officials proceeded to use force and by strong arm methods managed to secure the return of the seal granting Hien the title of Protector General. When, soon afterwards, Hien learned of what had occurred, he was not unnaturally filled with indignation. Thereafter he felt nothing but resentment for China and the Chinese, and made up his mind that if he could not rule over Kashgaria as the representative of China, he would secure the same domination as a frankly independent sovereign.

Special messages were dispatched to all the kingdoms of Kashgaria demanding that they formally acknowledge Hien as their overlord. A few, such as Kucha, offered some resistance to this demand, but this opposition was soon put down by armed force, and before long all of the Kashgarian states officially admitted their vassalage to the King of Yarkand. In view of his new position the latter assumed or was given the title of Shanyu, in imitation of the title in use among the Huns.

For four or five years Hien was able to enjoy the prestige of a ruler of a large empire without engendering any serious opposition. But unmindful of the mistakes which the Chinese and the Huns had made in the matter of heavy imposts, he too began to demand huge tribute from the numerous kingdoms subordinate to him. This naturally caused much resentment and in A.D. 45 we find the rulers of eighteen of the Kashgarian states, most of them in the north and northeast, in close proximity to China, sending in a special embassy to the Chinese court and petitioning the Emperor to save them from Hien's tyranny and oppression by reincorporating them within the Chinese Empire.

This petition was very flattering, but the Emperor again showed his caution and his dislike of embarking upon any project which might cause him to strain his resources. He loaded the numerous members of the embassy with compliments and even with presents, but reminded them that China itself was still not completely pacified and that the Huns were again causing trouble on the Northern frontier. He concluded by saying that in consequence of this situation China, for the moment, was in no position to aid or protect her friends in the distant West.

The embassy from the dissatisfied states therefore accomplished nothing. In fact, the dispatch of the embassy caused the kingdoms concerned to suffer even greater tribulations, for Hien, learning of their attempts to carry on negotiations with China, immediately increased his imposts and his demands for complete submission. In the very next year (A.D. 46) he sent an envoy to Shanshan, the state formerly known as Loulan, demanding that the ruler of this latter kingdom cease to have any correspondence or association with the Chinese. Goaded into desperation, the King of Shanshan not only refused Hien's demand, but slew the latter's envoy. This act immediately led to open warfare. Hien marched an army to Shanshan, and after a battle with the troops of the latter country in which Hien was completely victorious, the King of Shanshan was forced to flee for his life, and remained for some time in hiding in the mountains.

After administering this lesson to his rebellious vassal in the East, Hien soon withdrew his troops back to Yarkand, but in the winter of the same year the ambitious monarch set out on another campaign, this time against Kucha, which had been showing signs of unrest. Once again Hien was completely successful, and as Kucha lay at no great distance from Yarkand, Hien decided to abolish Kucha's very existence as an independent or even autonomous kingdom, and incorporated its territory within his own immediate domain.[17]

CHAPTER TEN

THE TRANSFORMATION OF THE HUNNISH EMPIRE, A.D. 46–73

Drought and Famine among the Huns—The Rebellion of Bi and the Establishment of the Southern Hunnish Kingdom—The Southern Huns Become Vassals of China—The Wuhuan and Sienbi Oust the Northern Huns from Eastern Mongolia—Reëstablishment of Hunnish Control over Northern Kashgaria—Struggle between Yarkand and Khutan—Defeat of Yarkand and the Submission of all Kashgaria to the Huns—Events in Turkistan, the Kang-gü, and Alani—The Transformation of the Yueji Kingdom—Rise of the Kushans and their Conquest of Afghanistan and India.

In the preceding chapter we have seen that in the years immediately following the beginning of the Christian Era, the Huns, after several decades of vassalage to China, managed to regain their independence and reëstablish their control over Mongolia and Western Manchuria, but that Kashgaria, which had once formed part of the new Hunnish Kingdom for only a few years, broke away to form an empire of its own under the domination of the King of Yarkand.

In the period which began in A.D. 46 and ended in A.D. 73 we shall find that this new Hunnish Kingdom underwent a remarkable transformation which later was to prove of the greatest significance in the whole development of Central Asia. This transformation was for the most part geographic in character, and resulted in shifting the center of the Hunnish Kingdom over a thousand miles to the West, and thus, at least indirectly, led to the later Hunnish invasion of Europe.

This transformation started with the death of the Shanyu Yu, which took place in A.D. 46. Although we know little about Yu's private life, he must have been a remarkable personality for it was during his long reign (A.D. 18-46) that the Huns really succeeded in reëstablishing their independence and became once more an important factor in Far Eastern politics. That this success was due in large measure to Yu's forceful leadership is proved by the fact that shortly after Yu's death, the Huns once more became a prey to internal conflicts of so serious a nature as almost to destroy their recently regained independence.

To be sure, internal conflicts were not the only thing to disturb the Huns during this period, for the Chinese records tell us that just about the time of Yu's death the Hunnish territory was ravaged for several years by the effects of a prolonged drought, a drought rendered all the more terrible by the appearance of huge swarms of locusts which made into a desert enormous areas of the Hunnish pasturage. The Chinese records would even have us believe that as a result of this drought, and of these swarms of locusts, the Huns lost more than half of their herds, which in turn led to an enormous mortality among the Huns themselves.

This heavy loss of life and property naturally had its effect upon the political morale of the Huns. Not only did they give up all hope of conquering Northern China but in addition they feared that China would take advantage of their weakness and sufferings to launch another huge campaign against the North. It was this fear which led Bonu, who after a short interval had succeeded his father, Yu, as Shanyu of the Huns, to send an embassy to China and propose that a new treaty of amity and friendship be entered into.[1]

The Chinese had been so busy with their own affairs that they had scarcely had occasion to notice the weakness of the Huns, and in consequence the arrival of this embassy following so many years of warfare came as a pleasant surprise. The Emperor sent out a return embassy to the Hunnish court to continue negotiations and for a while it seemed that Sino-Hunnish relations would once more be established on a friendly basis. But before long the Chinese became more fully cognizant of the troubles with which the Huns were beset and as a result grew more hesitant about plans to bring about a permanent peace which would still leave the Huns as masters of an independent kingdom. It was at this time that Bi, an influential princeling among the Huns, began to enter into secret and treacherous negotiations with the Chinese. Bi was a grandson of the great Huhansie and the son of another Shanyu. His uncle, the former Shanyu Yu, had given Bi a high-sounding title, and moreover had placed him in charge of the Hunnish and Wuhuan tribesmen in the southern portion of the Hunnish Kingdom, in the region which was contiguous to China. In spite of these favors Bi was not filled with any great sense of loyalty, but as long as his forceful and powerful uncle was alive, he did not dare undertake any treacherous negotiations.

Now, however, that Yu was dead and had been succeeded by his less vigorous son, Bi felt that the time had come to take definite action. Even so, he did not dare break out in open revolt until he had made sure of Chinese sympathy and coöperation. We are told that Bi started his negotiations with the Chinese almost immediately after Yu's death (A.D. 46) by sending to the Imperial Court a detailed map of the whole Hunnish Kingdom. In the following year Bi himself paid a secret visit to the Chinese frontier in order to discuss possible plans of action with the local Chinese officials. Encouraged by the tenor of these discussions Bi went on with his plans for an armed revolt which he hoped would lead to the overthrow of Bonu and the enthronement of himself as the Shanyu of the whole Hunnish Empire.

Before these plans could be completed, however, Bonu, the legitimate Shanyu, became suspicious of his cousin's activity, and in a secret conference in the Shanyu's tent it was decided to dispatch two noblemen with a suitable escort to seize and decapitate the treacherous Bi. It was hoped that the secrecy and suddenness of this attack would enable the punitive party to lay hands upon Bi before the latter could make any arrangements to defend himself. But it soon turned out that all efforts at secrecy had been in vain, for Bi's younger brother, suspecting that something was up, had lain outside the Shanyu's tent while the secret conference was being held, and immediately afterwards had galloped off to inform Bi of the proposed attack. When, therefore, the punitive expedition arrived in Bi's territory, it found itself confronted with a large army fully prepared for battle, so that there was nothing to do but withdraw. A short time later the Shanyu Bonu sent a larger force against Bi, but this too was forced to beat a hasty retreat and accomplished nothing.

These developments had important results upon the political organization of the whole Hunnish Kingdom. Bi had hoped to depose his cousin and become ruler of all the Huns, but his conspiracy had been discovered too soon for him to accomplish this. On the other hand Bonu found himself unable to lay hands on Bi, or wrest from him control over the southern tribesmen. As a result the Hunnish Kingdom soon split into two separate and hostile units, the Kingdom of the Northern Huns, and the Kingdom of the Southern Huns. This *de facto* division was legalized in the following year when Bi formally accepted the "invitation" of the eight southern Hunnish tribes and proclaimed himself Shanyu.[2]

A hundred years previously, at the time of the conflict between Huhansie and Jïjï (58-36 B.C.), the Huns had experienced a similar division, but whereas this early division had proved temporary and had soon been followed by the restoration of Huhansie as ruler over all the Huns, this second division of the Huns, in A.D. 48, into Northern and Southern Kingdoms was destined to prove permanent. Never again were all the Huns to be united within the bounds of a single empire. This in turn meant that though the Huns continued to give China a great deal of trouble for more than a century after this division, never again could they hope to build up a really great state which could achieve mastery over the whole of the Far East.

As the name Southern Huns indicates, Bi and his followers had control over the southern and more especially the southeastern portion of the Hunnish territory, or in other words most of what now is Inner Mongolia. The Northern Huns, on the other hand, continued, for some time to dominate what is now known as Northern or Outer Mongolia, but in addition to this, the Northerners felt that it was their duty to maintain the imperialist traditions of the old Hunnish Empire. It was the Northern Huns who did their best to maintain some sort of control over the peoples of Southern Siberia and of Zungaria and even of Turkistan. More important still, it was the Northern Huns who were constantly trying to resecure domination over the Kashgarian kingdoms. In view of these differences we shall refer to the northern state as the Northern Hunnish Empire, and to the southern state as the Southern Hunnish Kingdom.

Because of the greater importance of the Northern Huns and also because of the association of the descendants of this group with the European Huns, we of the West are naturally far more interested in the history of the Northern Hunnish Empire than in the fate of its southern rival. It is therefore very unfortunate that the Chinese records give us detailed accounts of events which transpired among the Southern Huns, while we have only occasional and indirect reference to events among the Northern Huns.

It is, however, not surprising that the Chinese historians should concern themselves so largely with the Southern to the exclusion of the Northern Huns, for not only did the Southern Huns live in close proximity to the Chinese boundaries, but throughout the whole period of its existence the Southern Hunnish Kingdom served as a buffer state between the Chinese and the Northern Huns. From the beginning it was a state of admitted vassalage to the Celestial Empire, while the Northern Huns on the other hand always managed to preserve their independence. The dependence of the Southern Huns on the Chinese court began in A.D. 48, almost immediately after Bi had been "elected" Shanyu of the Southern Kingdom. Bi himself came to the Chinese frontier and formally asked to be received as a vassal and to be entrusted with the task of warding off the Northern Huns.

Strangely enough, when Bi's proposal first reached the Chinese capital it met with a good deal of opposition in the Imperial Council Chamber. The Chinese were of course delighted to see trouble brewing among the Huns, and had been quite willing to give Bi a little undercover assistance in his endeavor to revolt. It was felt, however, that formally to recognize Bi as a vassal would mean that the Southern Hunnish Kingdom would thus become a protectorate of the Chinese Empire, which might have to be aided in case of attack. This in turn meant the assumption of a great deal of responsibility, and the cautious Emperor

Guang-wu and his most intimate advisers were strongly opposed to using men and money on wild imperialistic schemes.

One of the counsellors of state, however, pleaded so hard for the acceptance of Bi's vassalage, on the grounds that it was the only way to keep the Northern Huns at bay, that in the end the Emperor gave way and Bi and his new kingdom were officially recognized by the Chinese Empire and were promised moral and material support in case of need. Bi was so delighted with the acceptance of his proposal that in the following year he sent in as tribute some of the Hunnish national treasures or jewels. Unfortunately, we are not told just what these national treasures were, and of course all traces of them have long since disappeared.

A few months later (A.D. 50) two Chinese envoys were sent to the court of the Southern Huns bearing an Imperial Proclamation officially installing Bi as Shanyu. All this was very pleasant but when the envoys arrived they caused much embarrassment in Hunnish court circles by insisting that the new Shanyu prostrate himself before the imperial diploma as a sign of his real submission to the Celestial Emperor. Bi hesitated for some time before humiliating himself in this way, but before long, realizing that his position depended upon Chinese support, he carried out the required obeisance.[3]

The fact that their ruler was forced to prostrate himself before a mere diploma was the cause of much heart burning among the Hunnish aristocracy, and it is said that many of the court nobles wept copiously while the obeisance was being carried out. Later on the Shanyu secretly asked the Chinese envoys not to force too many humiliations upon him in front of his subjects, as otherwise his throne and even the very existence of his kingdom would be endangered. It would seem that all Chinese envoys in future were a little more cautious in their treatment of the Shanyus, but by way of forcing the Southern Huns formally to acknowledge their complete subserviency to the Chinese Empire, every time a Hunnish envoy or hostage arrived at the Chinese capital he was required to make a pilgrimage to the shrines erected in honor of the Han dynasty. Moreover, in the Southern Hunnish Kingdom itself, at the time of the three annual festivals, when it was the custom of the Shanyu and his court to make sacrifices to the celestial beings, they were required to do obeisance to the shades of the departed Han Emperors.

In addition to this insistence upon outward ceremonial the Chinese took certain more material precautions to keep the Southern Huns in subjection. The Shanyu was forced to keep at all times at least one hostage in the Chinese capital. More important still, the Chinese "gave" to the Shanyu a personal bodyguard of a Chinese officer and fifty soldiers most of whom were pardoned criminals and altogether rather formidable characters. It was the duty of this bodyguard not only to protect the Shanyu from possible attacks from rebellious subjects but also to act as spies upon the Hunnish ruler's activity.

But if the Southern Huns were thus held in rigid subjection by their Chinese overlords, at least these barbarians were well paid for their subserviency. Almost every year a Chinese embassy arrived loaded down with rich presents which were distributed among the various members of the Southern Hunnish court. These presents included such coveted objects as gold ornaments, bejewelled swords, brocades and embroidered silks, together with more useful things such as carriages, leather armor and bows and arrows. Last but not least large quantities of foodstuffs, especially rice, were sent up for distribution among the tribesmen.[4]

But while the relations between the Southern Huns and the Chinese were thus early established on a friendly basis, for many decades there was almost constant warfare between the Southern Huns and their ex-compatriots the Northern Huns. Into the details of this incessant warfare it is unnecessary for us to go, especially since all this fighting led to very few changes in the status quo. Suffice it for us to say that, in the first year or two after they secured their independence, the Southern Huns were for the most part eminently successful in their campaigns against their Northern rivals. On one occasion they even forced their way to the camp where the Northern Shanyu held his court. The Shanyu himself was forced to flee for his life, and thousands of his best troops were killed or captured, and it looked for a moment as if the Southern Huns would secure control over Outer as well as over Inner Mongolia. In A.D. 50, however, the fortunes of war were reversed. The Southern Huns suffered a number of notable defeats, and it became necessary for the Chinese Empire to take steps to protect them from disaster. The Southern Shanyu was ordered to bring his principal encampment further south, so as to be within easier reach of the Chinese frontier. All of the commanders of the outpost garrisons were warned to be ready to offer assistance in case of need, and a small Chinese army of 2500 men was actually sent north of the Great Wall to serve as a protection to the Southern Shanyu and his court.

The other tribal units of the Southern Huns were also redistributed throughout Inner Mongolia in such a way that each such unit lay directly north of some Chinese garrison town. In this way each tribal unit served as a buffer against the Northern Huns in case the latter tried to make a dash into China. At the same time these units, while acting as buffers, could secure support and supplies from the Chinese with the minimum of delay.[5]

This rearrangement of the forces of the Southern Huns had its desired effect. The very fact that these Southerners were obviously acting in close coöperation with the Chinese was sufficient to prevent the Northerners from going on with their attempts completely to destroy the Southern Kingdom. The Northerners were fully aware of their weakened condition and were loath to goad China into undertaking a major offensive campaign.

Thereafter for several years the conflicts between the Northern and Southern Huns were confined to border raids, and even when the Northerners were conducting these raids they were careful to assure the Chinese that they were merely punishing their rebel subjects and had no intention of attacking the Celestial Empire. This in itself was an indication that the Northern Huns had abandoned all hope of reconquering any appreciable part of Inner Mongolia, and the Southern Hunnish Kingdom was thus constituted a permanent wedge between the Northern Hunnish Empire and the Chinese Empire.[6]

It was only in the extreme western part of Inner Mongolia that the Northern Hunnish Empire bordered directly upon China. In this region, which lay near the meeting place of China, Mongolia and Kashgaria, the Southern Huns were never able to establish jurisdiction. It was here that China was still exposed to potential Hunnish attacks, and it was around this section that the subsequent military campaigns, to be described hereafter, had their center. Just as the Southern Huns were robbing their Northern brethren of control over Southeastern Mongolia, these Northern Huns also began to suffer a series of attacks from the "Eastern Barbarians," the Wuhuan and the Sienbi, which in the end caused the Huns to lose their control over Northeastern Mongolia.

It will be remembered that during the troubled years immediately following the beginning of the Christian Era, when the Huns once more became independent, these Huns again established jurisdiction over the Wuhuan and the Sienbi. This did not mean, however, that these eastern barbarians became in any way enamored of their Hunnish masters, and it is not surprising that as soon as the Hunnish power showed signs of weakening, they once more threw off their allegiance to the Huns. Not long afterwards they went further and began to attack their late masters.

These attacks started in A.D. 46, immediately following the death of Shanyu Yu, when the Hunnish Kingdom first showed signs of disintegrating, and became more and more frequent as time went on. At first it was the Wuhuan who distinguished themselves in these attacks, but in later years it was the Sienbi, the northern neighbors of the Wuhuan who bore most of the brunt of fighting the Northern Huns. This activity on the part of the Wuhuan and the Sienbi was greatly aided by the support and encouragement given them by the Chinese Empire. It was in A.D. 49 that the Chinese were able to bring the Wuhuan once more within their sphere of influence. This was in no way the result of military prowess, but was a situation brought about by astute cajolery and by wholesale bribery.

Eighty-one tribal leaders from among the Wuhuan were given high-sounding titles and were induced to settle at or near the northeastern frontier of the Chinese Empire. By means of the promise of unlimited supplies of silks and foodstuffs, large numbers of the nomadic Wuhuan were then enticed to come and settle as subjects of these puppet chieftains. By these means the great majority of the Wuhuan were brought once more to recognize Chinese supremacy. In return for these presents the Wuhuan were expected merely to serve as an additional bulwark against depredations on the part of the Northern Huns. It was about this time that the Chinese appointed a special official known as the Wuhuan General (the occupant of the post was, of course, a Chinese) to act as a sort of general supervisor over the various Wuhuan settlements.

In the very same year (A.D. 49) in which the Chinese once more brought the Wuhuan within their immediate sphere of influence, they also succeeded in establishing friendly and even fairly intimate contacts with some of the principal leaders among the Sienbi. The Sienbi lived far to the North of the Chinese frontier, and the time was not yet ripe for the Chinese even to attempt to establish any real jurisdiction over these distant barbarians. But at least the Celestials were able to get into diplomatic negotiations with the Sienbi chieftains, and by the distribution of the usual presents succeeded in inducing some of these chieftains formally to send in "tribute" to the Chinese court.

Even more to the point, the Chinese by working upon the vanity and cupidity of one of these chieftains induced him to lead an attack upon the eastern division of the Northern Hunnish Empire. He succeeded in achieving a notable victory, and as a result was able to cut off over two thousand Hunnish heads. These heads he brought back to the Chinese outposts to prove that his tales of victory were not entirely imaginary. The Chinese were so pleased with their ally's efficiency that they loaded him with presents. This affair resulted in the Sienbi setting up in business as head hunters, and thereafter, year after year, they made forays into the territory of the Northern Huns and after cutting off a number of Hunnish heads, they brought these trophies to the Chinese who paid them a bounty price for each one.

As a result of this friendly commerce in heads, the intercourse between Sienbi and the Chinese became much more intimate as time went on, and in later years the Celestials granted the title of "King" or "Marquis" to several of the more prominent Sienbi chieftains. The Sienbi in their turn were so flattered by these attentions that they even aided the Chinese in crushing some of the Wuhuan who had not submitted to Chinese jurisdiction.[7]

For the Kingdom of the Northern Huns this alliance of the Sienbi and the Chinese was a major calamity. The revolt of the Southern Huns had caused the Northern Huns to lose all control over most of Southern and all of Southeastern Mongolia. As the result of the Wuhuan and Sienbi attacks these Northern Huns were also slowly but surely forced to evacuate much of Eastern and Northeastern Mongolia. Before long they found themselves able to maintain jurisdiction only over Western Mongolia.

Fortunately for themselves, however, just at the time these Northern Huns found themselves forced to withdraw from the East, they were able to make up their territorial losses by expanding once more in the West and Southwest, especially in Kashgaria. When we last turned our attention to Kashgaria (as of A.D. 46) the whole of this region was under the dominion of Hien, the ambitious and tyrannical King of Yarkand. During the period now under consideration (A.D. 46-72) the ambition and tyranny of Hien led to his undoing, and as country after country rose in rebellion against the King of Yarkand's oppression it was the Huns who were able to take advantage of the situation and reëstablish their supremacy over the revolting states.

This series of rebellions started late in A.D. 46, only a short time after Hien, by a series of military campaigns, had seemingly established his authority over the length and breadth of the Tarim basin. The first state to take active steps to break away from Hien's dictatorial authority was Shanshan (or Loulan) which lay in the extreme eastern portion of Kashgaria. It will be remembered that Hien had attacked and defeated the King of Shanshan, causing the latter to flee into the mountains. But this monarch, though defeated, was by no means disposed of. No sooner had Hien returned to Yarkand than the King of Shanshan began a new series of intrigues which he hoped would lead to throwing off the oppressive yoke of Yarkand's domination.

The previous campaign had shown that Shanshan was too weak to stand alone. First of all, therefore, it was necessary to find some friend or ally on whom she could lean for support. Once again the King of Shanshan appealed to China to aid him in redressing his wrongs. In the urgent message which he sent to the Celestial Emperor he implored the latter to send out a Protector General (accompanied of course by an army) and reëstablish Chinese supremacy in Kashgaria, and added that in case China did not come to his rescue he would be forced to throw himself into the arms of the Northern Huns.

Even this desperate appeal failed to move the Emperor Guang-wu. Following his usual policy of refusing to shoulder any responsibility which might prove too heavy for him, His Imperial Majesty responded that conditions in China prevented the dispatch of any military force to Central Asia and that deeply as he regretted it, he would be unable to render Shanshan any assistance.

China having failed him in his hour of need, the King of Shanshan duly carried out his threat and appealed to the Northern Huns for assistance. These were only too glad to render the required aid, and as the result of their support, Shanshan succeeded in breaking away from the domination of the King of Yarkand, but only at the price of being reincorporated within the Northern Hunnish Empire. Of great importance was the fact that very shortly after this event the large and strategically situated Kingdom of Güsḥï followed the example of Shanshan and resubmitted herself to Northern Hunnish overlordship.

The reëstablishment of Hunnish supremacy over Güshï and Shanshan meant that the Northern Huns now possessed a solid territorial wedge between China and the other Kashgarian kingdoms, and that the Chinese could no longer attempt, even by diplomatic means, to increase their influence in any portion of the Tarim basin. China having thus been eliminated in the battle for supremacy, control over this region lay between Hien, the King of Yarkand, on one side and the Northern Huns on the other. For the moment neither side was able or willing to carry out large-scale military operations, but both lay waiting for favorable opportunity to take advantage of the other. The Northern Huns found this opportunity not long afterwards in the troubles which broke out at Kucha in Northern Kashgaria.

Kucha, as we have already noted, was one of the kingdoms which had felt most heavily the weight of Hien's oppression. Hien had devastated the whole region, had deposed the native line of monarchs, and after ruling over it directly for awhile, had indeed reëstablished Kucha as a semi-autonomous state, but had installed as its monarch one of his own sons. This state of affairs lasted for some time, but Hien's son never proved popular with his subjects, and at last these subjects broke into open rebellion in the course of which they managed to kill the monarch who had been forced upon them. Fearing vengeance on the part of Yarkand, the citizens of Kucha immediately dispatched an embassy to

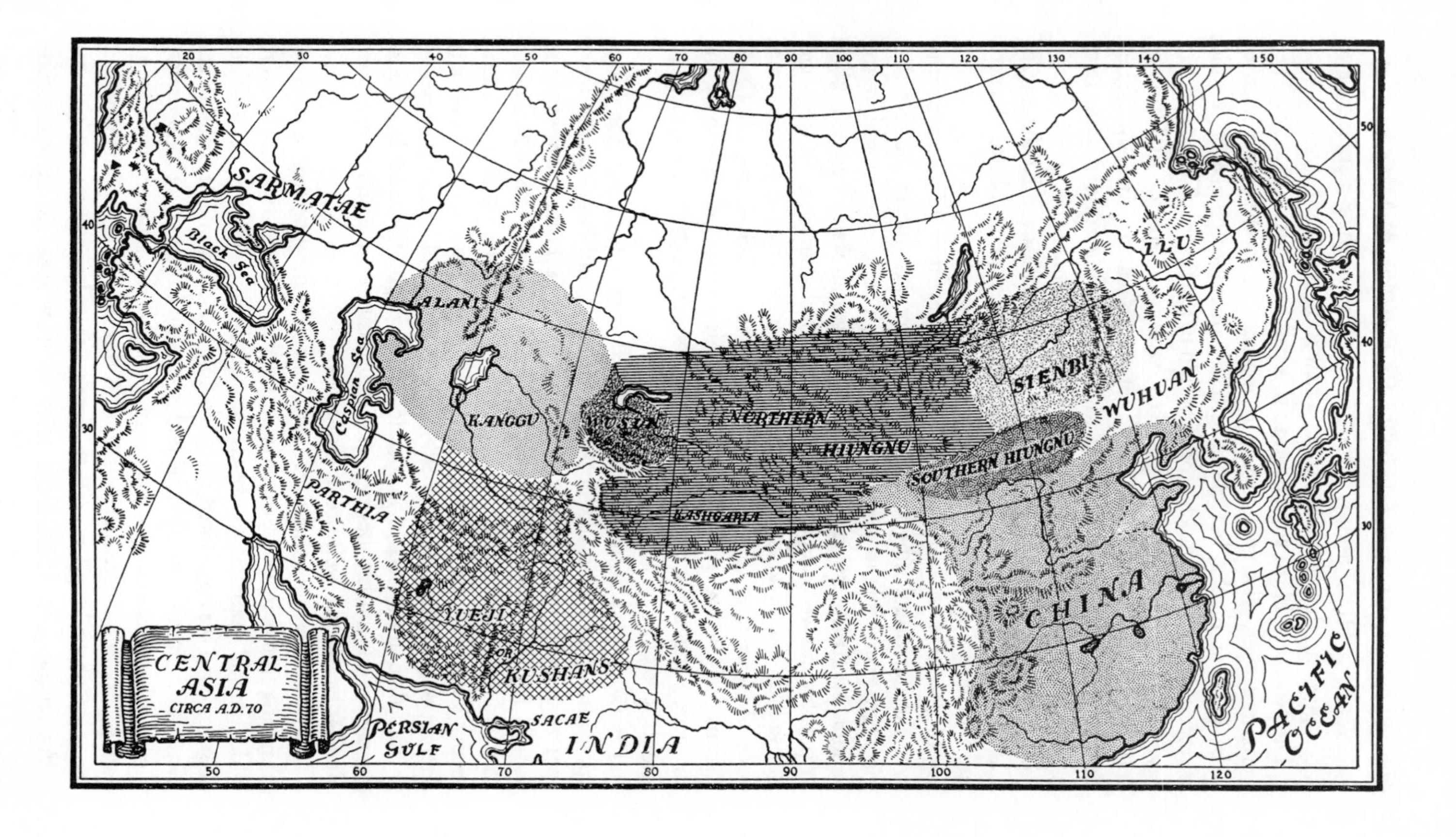
CENTRAL
ASIA
CIRCA A.D. 70
SARMATAE
Black Sea
Caspian Sea
ALANI
KANGGU
WUSUN
NORTHERN
HIUNGNU
SOUTHERN HIUNGNU
SIENBI
WUHUAN
ILU
KASHGARIA
PARTHIA
YUEJI
OR
KUSHANS
PERSIAN
GULF
SACAE
INDIA
CHINA
PACIFIC
OCEAN

the Northern Huns, asking the latter to come to their assistance, and also suggesting that the Huns select a new king for them.

The Northern Huns responded to this call for aid with alacrity. They were, moreover, wise enough not to appoint one of their own number to be King of Kucha, but chose instead a member of one of the old aristocratic families of Kucha for elevation to the throne. This person, in payment for his crown, was perfectly willing to submit to Hunnish domination, so that the net result of the Kuchan rebellion against Yarkand was that Kucha and all the surrounding regions were reincorporated within the Northern Hunnish domain.

The establishment of the Hunnish protectorate over Kucha meant that the Northern Huns now had almost exclusive control over Eastern and Northeastern Kashgaria. In reviewing these events it is very interesting to note that in every case the reëstablishment of Hunnish control over the individual kingdoms in this region was due to the fact that the Huns were able to pose as liberators and supporters of suppressed nationality. At this moment all of the Kashgarian states were inhabited by people who were Caucasoid in race, and Indo-European in language. But so little did racial and linguistic factors enter into the political emotions of those days that vast numbers of these Indo-European Kashgarians preferred to be ruled by the Turanian Huns rather than by the energetic King of Hien who was a representative of their own racial and linguistic stock.

It is rather surprising that the repeated encroachment of the Huns upon Hien's dominion did not result in direct and large-scale military operations between the two rival kingdoms. The Huns, however, had learned many a lesson from their recent defeats in Eastern Mongolia, and had no desire to rush headlong into an attack upon a powerful enemy. Hien and the Yarkandese, on the other hand, realized that any attempt to reconquer their rebellious provinces would mean they would be forced to fight both a desperate native population and large contingents of Hunnish tribesmen, and that a campaign against such combined forces might well prove disastrous.

Moreover Hien, by this time, was kept very busy arranging and rearranging things in Western and Southwestern Kashgaria, the region in which he still managed to exercise imperial rights. On one occasion, to be sure, Hien was provoked into invading Da-yüan or Farghana to the West of the Pamirs, but after he had given this kingdom a sound thrashing, and had reduced it to a state of vassalage, he soon returned to his native Yarkand. Thereafter he spent his time in raising up and deposing the rulers of the kingdoms which were more or less adjacent to his own.

For several years Hien was content to allow these neighboring kingdoms some semblance of autonomy. Each such kingdom was allowed to keep in name its own king and court, though by frequently changing the succession, and by transferring the crown from one head to another, these puppet monarchs were brought to realize that they were completely at the mercy of their powerful overlord. At last Hien became tired of maintaining even this semblance of local self-government. Becoming convinced, on one occasion, that some of his vassal kinglets were becoming disloyal to him he had them all executed, and instead of appointing a new batch of royal do-nothings he ordered that thereafter these various vassal kingdoms were to be governed by a military officer appointed directly by the court of Yarkand.

These military governors were more noted for their courage than for their tact and diplomacy in handling their subjects. Active ill will against Hien and all his works rapidly spread on all sides, and it became only a question of time before this feeling would lead to open rebellion. This undercurrent of unrest eventually came to a head in Khutan, the largest and most important of the vassal states in Southern Kashgaria. In A.D. 60, as a result of well planned conspiracy, the military governor of the region was killed and a short time later one of the native noblemen named Hiumoba proclaimed himself King of Khutan, and soon managed to make himself ruler in fact as well as in name.

Hiumoba realized that he would soon have to bear the brunt of an attack by the forces of Yarkand, but he felt so sure of his own strength that he did not feel it necessary to send to the Huns for support. Instead, he contented himself with coöperating with the forces of some of the neighboring states, which, following Khutan's example, had revolted against the overlordship of Yarkand. Subsequent events showed that Hiumoba was not wrong in relying upon his own prowess. Within a short space of time he and his allies defeated no less than three armies sent against them by the proud King of Yarkand. One of these armies was led by one of Hien's generals, the second by one of Hien's sons, and the third by Hien himself, but in each case the Yarkand forces met with overwhelming defeat.

Encouraged by this success, Hiumoba now turned from the defensive to the offensive. Marching his army to the West, he forced Hien to take refuge within the city walls of Yarkand. But even this was not enough. Hiumoba wished to capture and slay the hated Hien and so proceeded to lay siege to the city of Yarkand. He succeeded in investing the city on all sides, but shortly afterwards he was killed by a chance arrow in the course of one of the assaults on the barricades.

The death of their leader naturally brought consternation to the besieging army, and it was decided to march back to Khutan without striking another blow. In this way Hien received a breathing spell, in which to recuperate from his losses. It proved to be only a short one, however, for before long Hiumoba's nephew, Guangdê, was elevated to the throne of Khutan, and the new ruler proved quite as able and energetic as his predecessor. In the course of a few months he managed to collect a new army with which to continue the attack on Yarkand.

After a few preliminary skirmishes, Hien decided that discretion was wiser than valor. Abandoning all hope of reëstablishing his former Empire, he commenced peace negotiations with the new monarch of Khutan. Hien not only agreed to recognize Khutan's absolute independence and the new king's position as legitimate sovereign, but also offered to give the latter his daughter in marriage, thinking that in this way peace and amity between Yarkand and Khutan might be reëstablished. The new King of Khutan agreed to these conditions. The treaty of peace was signed and for over a year there was a complete cessation of all hostilities.

In A.D. 61 there was a fresh development. Hien's tyranny had not been confined to his treatment of alien peoples, but had also shown itself in harshness to his own subjects, including those in high places in his own court. Hien's fall from his former high estate encouraged some of these ministers to plot for his complete destruction. Consequently, in the year following the treaty of peace, one of Hien's most powerful ministers sent a secret message to Guangdê, the King of Khutan, announcing to the latter that a plot was brewing in Yarkand against the oppressor, and advised Guangdê to come to Yarkand at the head of an army so as to be able to take advantage of the unsettled situation.

The King of Khutan followed this advice, and before long he and his troops appeared before the walls of Yarkand. Hien professed to be shocked by this obvious breach of the treaty of peace, and sent out an officer to the camp of his rival with the message "I have made peace with you, and have given you my daughter in marriage. Why is it that you have come to attack me?"

In reply to this demand, Guangdê immediately sent to Hien the counter-message, "You, O King, are the father of my wife, and yet it is long since we have talked with one another. I would suggest that we arrange for a private interview outside the city wall, so that we can further cement our political and personal ties. To avoid all fear of attack let each of us be accompanied by only two retainers."

Hien was a little suspicious of this proposal, and asked his advisers what they thought of it. So unaware was Hien of the treachery which was going on around him that the person with whom he discussed the matter most thoroughly was no other than the leader of the whole plot, the man who had brought the enemy to the gates of the city. This worthy minister strongly advised his sovereign to carry out the proposed interview. "The King of Khutan," said he, "as your dutiful son-in-law, can surely harbor no evil intentions against you."

Encouraged by this advice Hien proceeded to carry out the rendezvous, but as soon as he was safely outside of the city walls he was surrounded and captured by Khutanese soldiers who had lain in ambush. No sooner had this been done than the treacherous minister opened up the city gates, thereby allowing the Khutanese army to secure possession of Hien's family and household possessions without striking a blow. Hien himself was brought back in chains to Khutan, and after being kept a prisoner for several months was eventually put to death.

So perished one of the most interesting characters in the whole history of Kashgaria. Undoubtedly he was a tyrant, but so was many a lesser and far less important man who has gone down in history as a glorious monarch, while Hien, because of his ultimate failure (due in no small measure to treachery), has long remained unhonored and unsung. At least he has one important distinction, for during the many hundreds of years in which Kashgaria was inhabited by Indo-European people, Hien was the only native "Aryan" who was able to weld all of the petty kingdoms of the Tarim basin into a single empire. Archaeological work has shown that these early inhabitants were capable of attaining a high degree of culture, but history shows that they, like the Greeks, were unable to drown their petty jealousies in the service of a common political cause and hence fell an easy prey to their Turanian and Sinitic neighbors to the North and East.

Guangdê's easy victory over Yarkand meant that he was soon regarded with a great deal of awe throughout all of Southwestern Kashgaria, with the result that Khutan came to be regarded as the principal political center in this corner of the world. But though Guangdê managed to maintain his position as leader among his immediate neighbors, it was not long before even he had to bow his proud head before the superior power and prestige of the Northern Huns.

As long as Hien was alive the Northern Huns had made little effort to invade and conquer Southwestern Kashgaria, but as soon as this potent monarch had been overthrown, the Hunnish leaders thought that it was time to have a finger in the pie. Acting in coöperation with some of the vassal states in Northern Kashgaria the Huns raised an army and proceeded to lay seige to Khutan. Guangdê, the King of Khutan, did not wish to risk a lengthy war with the Huns at this stage of his career, so he immediately declared his willingness to become a vassal of the Hunnish Empire, and to keep a hostage at the Hunnish court. This arrangement was satisfactory to the Huns, and the Hunnish army was withdrawn, though later on in the same year this army assisted in placing a son of the notorious Hien upon the throne of Yarkand. In later years Guangdê proved a rather restless and unsatisfactory vassal, but at no time did he ever completely break with his Hunnish overlords and the whole of Southwestern Kashgaria remained within the orbit of the Hunnish domain.[8]

The acknowledgement by Khutan and Yarkand of Hunnish supremacy meant that the Northern Huns once more became masters of all portions of the Tarim basin, so that the power and prestige they had lost in the East was more than made up by their diplomatic and military victories in the West. This in turn meant that the geographic center of the Northern Hunnish Empire was no longer in Mongolia proper but rather in Eastern Zungaria, and it is not surprising that the Huns gradually centered their court in this region (somewhere near Lake Barkul).

We are left in some doubt as to how far these Northern Huns were able to maintain or reëstablish their overlordship over the peoples of Turkistan during this period for the Chinese chronicles are strangely silent on this matter. We do know, however, that the Dingling and the Gien-Kun (Kirghis) continued to live in Southwestern Siberia and in Northeastern Turkistan and it is probable that both these peoples were willing to pay at least lip service to the Hunnish Shanyu after the latter had again established his power and prestige in the West.

It would appear, however, that these were the only peoples in Turkistan over whom the Huns could claim to have direct jurisdiction. The Wusun continued to live in Southwestern Zungaria, and hence geographically in very close touch with the Huns—all the more so now that the center of the Hunnish Kingdom had shifted from Mongolia to Eastern Zungaria. But though the Wusun tribesmen continued to be broken up into two separate kingdoms (ruled over by the Great Kunmi and the Little Kunmi), the Wusun had acquired a good deal of political and military strength and were quite able to maintain their independence.[9]

The Kingdom of Da-yüan or Farghana continued to occupy the region of the upper Jaxartes River, immediately to the West of Kashgaria. We know from the Chinese sources that this state had constantly to defend itself from attacks on the part of the Kang-gü who lived still further to the West. We have seen, moreover, that Da-yüan for a while formed part of the empire built up by Hien, the King of Yarkand, but we are left in ignorance as to the fate which befell Da-yüan after the fall of Hien. It is, however, possible if not probable, that the Huns after bringing Yarkand under their control also managed to extend their rulership over Da-yüan as well.

We have every reason to believe that the Kang-gü were entirely free from Hunnish control during this period. The Kang-gü, it will be remembered, were nomadic Iranians who occupied most of Northern Sogdia and also most of the basin watered by the lower course of the Jaxartes River (the region around Tashkand, etc.). From the scanty information which has come down to us, it would appear that it was during this period that the Kingdom of the Kang-gü reached its greatest power and strength. Not only did it constitute a constant menace to Da-yüan to the East, but it also managed to bring into vassalage most of the tribes inhabiting Northern Turkistan, so it is scarcely likely that the rulers of the Kang-gü felt it necessary to pay even lip service to the Hunnish Shanyu.

The Chinese records have one interesting remark to make regarding the principal group inhabiting Northern and Northwestern Turkistan during this period. They tell us that this people which had formerly been known as Yentsai, now became known as Olan (ancient pronunciation Alan). It is not without significance that the Greek authors tell us that just at this time (middle of the first century A.D.) Southern Russia was again overrun by a people coming from Central Asia and that this people was known as the Alani. Putting together what the Chinese and the Greek sources have to tell us, it is clear that shortly after the beginning of the Christian Era the Iranian inhabitants of Northern Turkistan who had formerly been known as Yentsai (corresponding to the Greek Aorsi) changed their name to Alani—probably due to the emergence of a single tribe of this name which secured dominance over the others. A few years later the gradual expansion of the Kang-gü Kingdom forced many of these Alani to flee westward across the Volga. From the Chinese records it is clear that only a portion of the Alani sought to maintain their independence by flight, and that the other portion—probably a majority—remained in Northwestern Turkistan, and submitted to Kang-gü domination.[10]

The invasion of Southern Russia by the Alani in the first century A.D. can be largely accounted for, as we have noted, by the expansion of the Kang-gü. It should, however, not be forgotten that other causal elements may have entered into this chain of events which are unknown to us or at least which were not recorded by the Chinese chroniclers.

It may well be that the westward drift of the Huns during this period was not without its effect in driving the Alani out of their ancestral domain. Hirth, moreover, would have us believe that the Hunnish descendants of the scapegrace Jïjï continued to exist in Northern Turkistan during this period, and if so, they too may have constituted a factor in the decision of the Alani to find a new home in the West.

In any case it is well for us to keep our eye upon the Alani, for they were later to play a not unimportant part in world affairs. By a freak of history these Alani were later to occupy portions of Hungary and later still to conquer large areas in Spain and in Africa. The main body of Alani, however, remained in the steppes north of the Caucasus, where their descendants, the Ossetes, who still speak an Iranian language, continue to live today.

Turning now from Northwestern to Southwestern Turkistan we find that this latter region continued during this same period to form part of the Parthian Empire. The Parthians, in addition to maintaining their control over Southwestern Turkistan also remained the dominating factor over most of the Iranian Plateau. In the battles which the Parthians were constantly waging with the Romans to their West and with the Yüejï to their East, this turbulent race was sometimes victorious and was sometimes defeated, but in any case they remained a powerful and dreaded force, over whom the Huns could never hope to claim any suzerainty.

Southeastern Turkistan also remained free from Hunnish influence all during this epoch. It will be remembered that this region was dominated by the Yüejï. Though the Yüejï, when they inhabited Northwestern China two centuries earlier, had been defeated by the Huns and forced to flee to the West, once they settled in Southeastern Turkistan they greatly increased in strength and no longer had to fear any Hunnish attempts at aggrandisement. It was in fact during the first century A.D. that the Yüejï built up a great empire of their own, an empire destined to be one of the most important cultural factors in the history of the Middle East—in India, Western Iran, and Central Asia. Considering the size, the power, and the importance of this empire it is amazing how little is known of its history.

The Yüejï, like their neighbors the Parthians, never produced a native historical literature, or perhaps it would be safer to say that if they produced any such literature it has not been preserved to us. But the Parthians at least came into contact with the Greeks and Romans and hence entered the portals of recorded history. The Yüejï on the other hand had their chief contacts with the inhabitants of India, who were the least imbued with an historical sense of any people in the world. The Hindus were never able to produce a history of themselves, much less throw any light upon the alien peoples who invaded and conquered them.

A few coins, a few rock inscriptions, most of them undated—or if dated, dated in accordance with chronological eras which are unknown to us, a few direct references—Roman accounts of Parthian accounts of events in the far-away East—these are the only means we have of recreating the history of one of the greatest empires in the history of mankind. It is unfortunate that the Chinese with their acute historical sense had only very casual contact with the Yüejï during the period of the latter's rise to power. Had the contacts been closer many of our problems concerning the Yüejï would be solved. As it is the Chinese thought it necessary to devote only a few lines in their chronicles to this distant empire, but at least these few lines give us our most secure data regarding the period of the growth of the Yüejï tribes into a vast imperial state. Thanks to the casual references in the Chinese records, aided and supplemented by European archaeologists, the main lines of the later Yüejï history have now become fairly plain to us, although there is still much dispute on matters of detail.

It will be remembered that shortly after the Yüejï invaded and settled in Bactria (about 130 B.C.), they broke up into five subdivisions, each of which was ruled over by a chieftain who bore the title of Jabgu. One of these tribal divisions had the name of Kushan (or Guei-shuang as it is called by the Chinese). Some time early in the first century A.D. (A.D. 25-40) the ruler of the Kushans managed to bring all of the four other tribal divisions under his jurisdiction, thus reëstablishing the unity of the Yüejï domain. Because of the rise to power of the Kushan division, the Yüejï became known to the peoples of India and other portions of the Middle East merely as Kushan, the name Yüejï being either unknown or forgotten, but the Chinese, though well aware of this fact, continued to call them by the older and more general name.

The name of the founder of the Kushan Empire was Kujula Kadphises, who is usually called Kadphises the First. A number of the coins minted by this monarch have come to light and show a remarkable resemblance to the contemporary coins of the Roman Empire. When Kujula came to the throne the Yüejï had long been in possession of Bactria or the region which lies between the upper Oxus River to the North and the Hindukush Mountains to the South. It was the good fortune of Kujula not only to establish Kushan rule over all the other branches of the Yüejï settled in Bactria, but also to extend the Yüejï or Kushan dominion over many of the surrounding areas.[11]

We are in some doubt as to how much the Kushans under Kujula and his successors even attempted to dominate Sogdia, the region immediately to the North of them. It will be remembered that in 128 B.C., when Jang Kien, the great Chinese envoy, visited the Yüejï he found that the bulk of this people were still living North of the Oxus River (and hence in Sogdia), although they had already secured a firm foothold upon

Da-hia or Bactria, which lay to the South of the Oxus River. In later years when the Yüejï broke up into five separate principalities, we find that all of these principalities, as far as we can locate them geographically, were situated not in Sogdia but in Bactria. From this fact it would appear that the Yüejï had abandoned all claim to the territory North of the Oxus River, and from other indications it would seem that the whole of Sogdia had fallen into the hands of the Kang-gü.

It is highly improbable that the Kang-gü were able to push the Yüejï out of Sogdia. It is far more reasonable to suppose that the Yüejï, lured by the richer territory to the South of the Oxus River, gradually moved all of their tribal groups to this region, voluntarily abandoning all the territory to the North of the Oxus to the Kang-gü, who in addition to being neighbors also belonged to the same ethnic group and were distantly related.

But though the Kang-gü thus secured possession of territory which had once belonged to the Yüejï, we know that the Yüejï continued to exercise some sort of influence over the Kang-gü. This is especially true of the period ushered in by Kujula, the first of the Kushan monarchs. We do not know if Kujula (and his successors) established and maintained this influence by means of diplomacy or martial exploits, but it is certain that this influence existed for a long period of time. Many years later, for example (A.D. 81), when the Chinese were suffering from the activities of a Kang-gü army, the Chinese negotiated with the Yüejï, and after the Yüejï had used their influence the Kang-gü army was soon withdrawn. Some centuries later, when the Chinese records again busy themselves with the Kang-gü, we are told that the kings of this nation were of Yüejï origin and were very proud of this fact.

Bearing in mind the foregoing facts, it would appear that during the height of the Kushan Empire, the Kang-gü Kingdom was definitely within the Kushan sphere of influence. When we remember that the Kang-gü themselves at this time had control over the Alani in Northern Turkistan, we come to the conclusion that the Kushan influence was thus indirectly spread all throughout Central Asia, reaching from Bactria in the Southeast to the shores of the Caspian in the Northwest.[12]

Turning now from the extension of Yüejï influence in the North to the extension of their dominion in the South, we find ourselves on somewhat surer grounds, since the Chinese records make definite mention of the Kushan exploits in this direction. Up to this time the Yüejï had been bounded on the South by the Hindukush Mountains, and it was Kujula who first crossed over these mountains, and by invading and conquering the Kabul Valley secured control over most of the region now known as Afghanistan. Shortly afterwards he extended his forces to the East and annexed the Kingdom of Gibin, in Northwestern India. After a long and prosperous reign (the Chinese records state that he lived until the age of eighty-six) Kujula died and was succeeded by his son, Vima Kadphises, or as he is frequently called, Kadphises the Second. It was the task of Vima to complete the conquests begun by his father.

The possession of the Kabul Valley and of Gibin meant that the Kushans already had free access to the South. Vima took advantage of this strategic position and proceeded to invade and conquer the whole of the region watered by the Indus River, which was then in possession of various Sakan princes and kinglets, most of whom nominally acknowledged Parthian supremacy. But though Vima thus succeeded in bringing much of Northern India within his domain, this doughty monarch seems to have been little interested in his new possessions, for he appointed a viceroy to rule over the Indian portion of his kingdom while he himself continued to reside in Bactria.

By far the most important of the Kushan monarchs was the third of the line, a man named Kanishka. It would seem that Kanishka was not related to his immediate predecessors (though of the same Kushan stock) but it was he who really made out of the Kushan Kingdom a great world empire. It was Kanishka who consolidated the Kushan domain in India. He pushed the Kushan conquests far to the South and East, annexing the Ganges Valley certainly as far as Benares, so that practically all of Northern India came within the Kushan domain. Kanishka, moreover, was not content to govern India through a viceroy but exercised immediate jurisdiction over the Indian portion of his empire, and during a portion of each year resided and held his court upon Indian territory. Northwestern India, where the Kushans centralized their power, was then known as Gandhara, for which reason the empire ruled over by Kanishka and his successors is known as the Gandhara Empire, and as Gandhara became the center of a highly important civilization especially as regards art, the name Gandhara has become a common adjective with which to characterize this whole period of Indian history and also to designate the highly significant art forms which during this and immediately subsequent periods spread from Northwestern India to many other portions of Asia.

Kanishka is certainly one of the two or three really great figures in Indian history. Not only was he a great soldier, but it was undoubtedly due in no small measure to his influence that Gandhara, the seat of his government, became a potent and vital center of literary and artistic activity. He was also a magnificent patron of religious learning and the Northern Buddhists look upon him almost in the same manner as the Christians look upon Constantine. There are numerous monuments and innumerable coins dating from his reign, but so lacking are the Indians in historical tradition that we are still in some doubt as to when this reign actually took place.

Unfortunately, none of the contemporary Chinese accounts ever mention Kanishka by name—in itself a very extraordinary fact, and though the later Chinese Buddhist literature makes frequent mention of Kanishka and gravely records many legends about him, practically all of these Buddhist books are either translated from or based upon Indian originals and hence are completely valueless for ascertaining historical facts. But at least European archaeologists have now sufficiently advanced in their work to make us feel sure that the great Kanishka ruled somewhere about the close of the first century A.D.[13]

Archaeological discoveries have shown that as long as the Yüejï or Kushans remained in Bactria they continued to show many characteristics associating them with the early Iranian nomads of the North, both as regards race, language, and costume. In the coins of the early Kushan monarchs we find that these rulers have high pointed heads, large prominent noses, and are heavily bearded, thus causing them to resemble very closely the portraits of the ancient "Scythians" found in Southern Russia. We find in these heads no traces of the so-called Mongoloid type.

The names and titles used on these Kushan coins show moreover that these Kushan monarchs spoke an Indo-European and probably an Iranian language, although this language differed radically from classical Persian. Whereas the Sakas and Parthian languages show strong traces of similarity, the Kushans, though belonging to the same linguistic group, evidently spoke a very aberrant dialect.

The costumes displayed in these early coins differ markedly from those in vogue among the contemporary Greeks, Persians, Hindus, and Chinese. The tall pointed caps, the heavy felt boots, and the long cloak or cassock remind one forcibly of the old costume common to all the Iranian nomads of Central Asia. Underneath this cloak we catch a brief glimpse of the trousers which we have learned to associate with this old nomadic costume. In spite of all this, however, the Kushans obviously made no attempt to impose their culture upon the countries they conquered but were eager to adopt the superior culture of the peoples with whom they came in contact.

There were still strong traces of Greek influence in the Kabul Valley and Northwest India. It is not surprising therefore to find some of the early Kushan coins with Greek titles such as *Basileos* for King. In the later coins these Greek words disappeared, but the Greek alphabet continued to be used for the writing of inscriptions in other languages. Numerous coins, both early and late, show that the old Greek Gods such as Herakles (Hercules), Helios (the Sun), and Selene (the moon) were worshiped by the Kushan monarchs. It was during the Kushan period, moreover, that the Gandhara school of art founded directly upon Greek models and traditions reached its apogee.

But for quite natural geographic reasons the Greek influence tended to decline as the decades rolled on. The Parthians had cut off all direct contact between the old Greek colonies in Northwest India and the Greek motherland, so that the Greek colonists, and with them Greek traditions, gradually became extinct. As the Greek influence dwindled it was first of all Iranian influence which took its place, and in the later Kushan coins we find the increasing use of such Iranian titles as Shah of Shahs (or King of Kings) in place of the old Greek Basileos, and the Greek Herakles gives way to the Persian Mithra and Anahita and the Iranian worship of the Sacred Fire.

But in the end it was Indian influence which was destined to become paramount. The further the Kushan monarchs penetrated into India, the more they became subject to Indian influence. Several of the Kushan coins, though bearing Greek inscriptions on one side, bore Indian (Kharosti) letters on the other. The Kushan monarchs assumed the Indian title of Maharaja and before long Hindu deities such as Siva appeared on one side of the coins.

More important still was the role which Buddhism was called to play in the Kushan Empire. Buddhist tradition asserts that Kanishka was not only a Buddhist but an active apostle of Buddhism. During his reign and under his patronage a great Buddhist church council is supposed to have been held for the purpose of settling outstanding points of doctrine and discipline.

Many scholars are dubious as to the authenticity of this council. Moreover, Kanishka can scarcely have been a very fanatical Buddhist since his coins display not only Buddhist but also Iranian and Hindu deities, but at least it is certain that it was during the reign of Kanishka and his successors that Buddhism permeated and eventually became the dominant religion all throughout the Kushan domain. Not only India, but Afghanistan and Bactria were filled with Buddhist monks and with Buddhist monasteries.

It was during the Kushan period moreover that Buddhism penetrated to Sogdia (ruled over by the Kang-gü) and also to Kashgaria. The exact date of the conversion of Kashgaria to Buddhism is still unknown to us, but it seems highly probable that Buddhism began to permeate the Kashgarian states all during the time that King Hien of Yarkand was building up his short-lived empire, and that the subsequent reabsorption of Kashgaria by the Huns did not put a stop to the steady infiltration of

Buddhist influence in various parts of the Tarim basin. Of great significance here is the fact that though Buddhism was of course purely Indian in origin, the Buddhism which developed in the Kushan domain, and thus the Buddhism which penetrated all parts of Central Asia, differed radically from early or primitive Buddhism. It was during the Kushan period and largely in the Kushan territory that the type of Buddhism known as Mahayana, which later became the dominant religion throughout the whole of the Far East, first developed into a complete system.

As we know the center of the Kushan domain was a hotbed of all sorts of conflicting cultural stimuli, many of them of non-Indian origin, it seems highly probably that this Mahayana system of Buddhism was strongly influenced even on the doctrinal side by these non-Indian stimuli. It is certain that from the artistic and architectural side the Buddhism which developed in Northwestern India and thence spread to Central Asia owed an enormous debt to Iranian and especially to Greek influences. The images of the Buddhas and Bodhisattvas made by the Gandhara school of art, which was the basis of all later Buddhist art in Central Asia and in the Far East, are so strikingly Greek in type that one is tempted to believe that they were made by Greek artisans.[14]

The discussion of the rise of the Kushan Empire has taken us rather far afield. It is now necessary for us to return again to the Huns.

CHAPTER ELEVEN

THE HUNS AND THE CHINESE RENEW THEIR STRUGGLE, A.D. 73-88

Renewed Attack of the Northern Huns Upon China—Reawakening of China's Interest in Central Asia—The Chinese Campaign of A.D. *73—China's Ill Success in the North—Her Victories in the Northwest—The Campaign of* A.D. *74 Against Gushi—The Exploits of Ban Chao in Southern Kashgaria—The Counter-Campaign of the Huns in* A.D. *75—The Heroic Defense of the Chinese Garrison in Northern Gushi—The Chinese Again Abandon Kashgaria—The Subsequent Decay of the Northern Huns—Further Exploits of Ban Chao.*

IN THE preceding chapter we have seen how the Hunnish Empire underwent a marked transformation during the first few decades of the Christian Era, and how this transformation was due in large measure to the efforts of the Chinese to get the better of the Huns, and of the Huns to get the better of the Chinese. The successful revolt of the Southern or Southeastern Huns from the parent empire was possible only because of the support given the Southerners by the Chinese. The fact that the Wuhuan and the Sienbi spent their time harrying the Huns in Eastern Mongolia was due, in large measure, to the financial and moral aid given them by the wily Celestials. The Huns on the other hand took a peculiar delight in recapturing for themselves control over Kashgaria, as this meant that Chinese prestige and pretensions at sovereignty in this part of the world were definitely destroyed.

Considering the fact that the Huns and the Chinese thus stood in deadly rivalry all during this period it is rather surprising that there was at this time almost no open warfare between the two powers. The Chinese were delighted to aid the Hunnish rebels, and to subsidize Sienbi attacks on the Northern Huns, but the cautious Emperor of China felt that this domain was not sufficiently well established for him to embark upon any serious military campaign in the North. The Huns on the other hand were willing and able to take advantage of China's temporary inability to cope with the Kashgarian situation by annexing this region for themselves, but they no longer dared undertake any large-scale invasion of China proper.

In fact not only did the Chinese and Huns refrain from engaging in active military hostilities with one another, but, during a good portion of this period they frequently engaged in diplomatic intercourse which, in name at least, was of a very friendly character. During the years A.D. 46-60, the Huns were acutely aware of their own weakness, and in their intercourse with the Chinese adopted a distinctly subservient tone. In A.D. 50, for example, when the Northern Huns were trying unsuccessfully to destroy the newly established Southern Hunnish Kingdom by force of arms, they were careful to send back to China all the Chinese prisoners who came into their possession and to assure the Chinese that on their Southern campaigns they had no intention of assaulting the Celestial Empire, but were intent merely upon punishing the Southern Hunnish renegades.

In A.D. 51, when the Southern Hunnish Kingdom had definitely established its independence under Chinese protection, the Northern Huns, instead of nursing their resentment, dispatched an embassy to the northwestern portion of the Chinese frontier (the only region in which the Chinese and Hunnish state now directly bordered on one another) and asked that a treaty of peace be negotiated between the two powers. In the Chinese Council of State which was held to discuss this proposition, the Crown Prince argued that to enter into friendly relations with the Northern Huns would be regarded as a treacherous act by their friends and allies, the Southern Huns, and that in consequence the proposal for a formal peace should be rejected.

This argument was very telling and carried the day, but the very next year (A.D. 52) the Northern Huns, undeterred by this refusal, again sent an embassy proposing peace. This time, moreover, the Hunnish embassy brought along a large number of horses and fur garments as a peace offering. It is interesting to note that the Huns in addition to asking for peace also asked for some Chinese musical instruments since those in their possession were worn out. The matter was again brought before the Grand Council, and on this occasion the eminent counsellors found themselves in a less militant mood.

As one eminent chamberlain remarked, "The fact that the Northern Huns are so eager for peace shows that they must be in a pretty desperate position. Nevertheless we have received very little real benefit from alliance with the Southern Huns, and it might be just as well not to break off all communications with the Northern Huns as they may be useful in the future."

Acting upon his advice, the Emperor accepted the "tribute" offered him and sent back "presents" equal in value to this tribute. Among the presents were the musical instruments for which the Huns had evinced such a desire. In addition to these presents the Emperor also sent off to the Huns a lengthy document commanding them thenceforth to be dutiful and respectful in their attitude to the Celestial Empire.[1]

For the moment the Huns had to swallow this sermon in silence, but as the years went on (during which time embassies were sporadically exchanged between the two powers) the Huns became steadily less obsequious to China and the Chinese Emperor. This was especially true after A.D. 61 when the Huns had completed their conquest of Kashgaria and thereby become once more a large and important empire. In A.D. 64, the Huns demanded the right to come and trade in some of the outpost towns of Northwestern China. The Chinese authorities readily gave them this privilege in the hope that by thus establishing commercial relations the Huns would be less apt to resume their old policy of securing what they wanted by raiding.

Before long however these hopes were rudely shattered. Large bands of Hunnish tribesmen again began to appear on the northern frontier intent upon looting everything they could lay their hands on. The Southern Huns continued to act as a buffer for Northern and Northeastern China and on several occasions they repelled bands of the Northerners bent on breaking their way into China, but in the Northwest—in Dunhuang and the surrounding regions—the Chinese had no such buffer and suffered accordingly. It is recorded that in A.D. 65 the Huns made an unusually large number of raids in the course of which they burned many towns and villages and killed or captured their inhabitants. In this year and the years which followed the walled cities of Northwestern China were frequently forced to keep their gates closed even during the daytime lest they be subjected to a surprise attack, and this closing of the gates temporarily paralyzed all commercial life throughout the whole region.[2]

If the cautious Guang-wu had still been on the throne it is doubtful if these Hunnish raids could have provoked the Chinese to attempt any large-scale counter offensive, but Guang-wu had passed away in A.D. 58, and his place had been taken by his son, the illustrious Emperor Ming. Ming-di was a very able and energetic man and bitterly resented the thought of doing nothing to revenge the Hunnish raids. By the time that he ascended the throne, the imperial power was fairly well established all over China proper, and the empire was once more in a position to embark on the stormy sea of foreign warfare. Moreover, while his father and predecessor had little knowledge of or interest in Central Asia, Ming-di was keenly interested in what went on in this region, as is evidenced by the fact that it was during his reign and because of his patronage that Buddhism was formally introduced into the Celestial Empire.

Tradition has it that Buddhism was formally introduced into China somewhere between A.D. 65 and 71 as the result of a dream of Ming-di. The Emperor saw in a dream the image of a golden man emitting a glow of light. The counsellors of state thought that the "Golden Man" of the dream must correspond with the "God" of the Western regions known as Buddha. Not long afterwards the Emperor despatched emissaries to the West to secure some images and books of the Buddhist religion. Though this tradition is recorded in the official annals of the later Han dynasty, its accuracy has been questioned by several modern scholars. But, however much we may question the story of Ming-di's dream, there can be no doubt that it was during Ming-di's reign that Buddhism first found a serious following in the Celestial Empire.[3]

It is of especial importance to note that the Buddhist missionaries who first came to China came via Kashgaria, and it is quite possible that the stories they told of conditions in the Western lands reawakened Chinese interest in what was going on in that region. Be this as it may, it is certain that shortly after the arrival of the Buddhist missionaries from the West, China once more made a gigantic attempt to crush the power of the Huns and at the same time to reëstablish her dominion over the numerous Kashgarian kingdoms.

In view of the complications of the subject it would be well to outline in advance the various stages of the battle between the Chinese and the Northern Huns for supremacy in Central Asia. No less than three times did the emperors of the later Han dynasty embark upon extensive campaigns aimed at weakening or destroying the Huns and at reincorporating Kashgaria within the Celestial Empire. One of these campaigns was in A.D. 73-74, the second in A.D. 89-91, and the third was in A.D. 119-127.

Each of these campaigns was eminently successful. Each time the Huns suffered a humiliating defeat and the petty Kashgarian kinglets were forced to acknowledge Chinese supremacy. But in each case the Chinese, after a longer or shorter period of domination, lost most of the fruits of their victory, largely as the result of ineptitude or mismanagement of their colonial affairs. Each time the Huns were badly beaten but not destroyed, and each time after a longer or shorter breathing spell they managed to recover something of their military prowess, at least sufficiently to be a menace to the Chinese once more. In the end it was not the Chinese but the Sienbi who once and for all drove the Huns far to the West, and forever ended their dream of reëstablishing an empire in the Far East.

After this preliminary survey we can now turn to a detailed discussion of the first phase, namely the campaigns of B.C. 73-74. Though the fighting itself did not start until A.D. 73, the preparations for the campaign had started long before, and in 72 several of the generals were already on the frontier so that they and their troops might be better acquainted with the nature of the ground to be traversed.

Early in A.D. 73 everything was found to be in order, and the huge thrust against the Huns was commenced. It was arranged that four different

Chinese armies, each numbering more than ten thousand men, should strike simultaneously at the enemy. Two of these armies were to march from Northern China through the territory of the Southern Huns so as to strike at the Northern Hunnish Kingdom from the Southwest. One of these armies included in addition to the regular Chinese soldiers a number of Wuhuan and Sienbi tribesmen, for it was felt that these "barbarians" would be of especial value in fighting the Northern Huns. The other army was commanded by Dsi Yung, a man of long experience in the northeastern frontier of China and the person who was most responsible for promoting and arranging the earlier Wuhuan and Sienbi attack upon the Huns. Unfortunately, he was placed in command of the army comprising Southern Hunnish auxiliaries and not of that containing the Wuhuans and Sienbis, with whom he was more familiar. To make matters worse, Dsi Yung was expected to coöperate with the chief general of the Southern Huns, a man with whom he was personally on bad terms.

It is not surprising, therefore, that the army led by Dsi Yung was not able to accomplish anything spectacular. Although he was not actually defeated, he was unable to carry out the main objective of his expedition owing to a trick played on him by his associate, the Southern Hunnish general. It was known that a large detachment of the Northern Huns was encamped near a mountain known as Mt. Josie. Dsi Yung had received orders to go to this mountain and attack the enemy who were stationed there.

As Dsi Yung was unacquainted with the country he was forced to rely upon the Southern Hunnish general as a guide. The latter, who wished to bring disgrace upon Dsi Yung, took him to a hill not far away from the frontier and told him that this was Mt. Josie. Dsi Yung was foolish enough to believe this statement, and after looking around in vain for signs of the enemy, he concluded that they must have fled, and so returned immediately to China.

Shortly after his return it was discovered that he had not reached his objective, and hence was court-martialed. When the full circumstances were known, the court decided to be lenient, and instead of being sentenced to death, as were most unsuccessful generals, he was merely deprived of his rank and titles, and reduced to the grade of commoner. Dsi Yung, however, felt so humiliated by his failure that he began to spit blood soon after leaving prison and died shortly thereafter.

The ill-success of Dsi Yung did little to increase the prestige of the Chinese in their combat with the Huns, nor was this prestige greatly enhanced by the accomplishments of the other Chinese army which marched against the Huns from the Northeast, for though this army marched far into Hunnish territory it was unable to strike any decisive blows. But fortunately for China's power and fame the two armies which started from the Northwestern portion of China were able to achieve one or two notable victories. These two armies, which had as their base what is now the province of Gansu, comprised, in addition to the regular armored Chinese soldiers, a number of Tibetan and Kashgarian auxiliaries, who turned out to be excellent soldiers. The fact that Northwest China bordered directly on Hunnish territory probably had something to do with the success of these two armies. Even more important was the fact that the gradual western shifting of the Northern Hunnish Empire meant that a blow struck from Northwestern China was a blow right at the heart of the Hunnish domain.

It has been said both of the armies marching from Northwest China were successful. As a matter of fact, one of these armies did little more than chase small groups of Huns across the plains of Southern Mongolia, and then retire without having enticed the enemy into fighting a single pitched battle. But the other army struck a blow which brought name and fortune to its commanding officer, Dou Gu, a member of the Dou family which was already famed for its military exploits. Dou Gu marched northward from his base along the borderline of Mongolia and Kashgaria until he came to the eastern portion of the Tien-shan or Celestial Mountains. Here he managed to come to blows with an army commanded by an important Hunnish nobleman called the Huyen King.

The title Huyen King was unknown in the early Hunnish hierarchy, and it probably designated an office which was established in the first century A.D., at the time of the westward shift of the Hunnish Kingdom. As time went on, this office came to play an ever greater part in the Hunnish political organization, and during this and subsequent periods we hear from the Chinese records far more of the Huyen King than of the Shanyu who was nominally lord of all the Northern Hunnish hosts. We know that from early times one of the four most aristocratic Hunnish families was called Huyen, and it is probable that the Huyen King was the leading member of this clan and that this clan came to take a predominant role in Hunnish political affairs as the old ruling family began to show signs of decay.

Be this as it may, the victory which Dou Gu and his troops were able to achieve over the Huyen King was everywhere hailed as a magnificent military feat, for not only were the Chinese soldiers able to cut off the heads of over a thousand of the enemy, but Dou Gu was able to pursue the retreating Hunnish army for a great distance. Crossing over the Celestial Mountains, he did not stop until he came to the borders of Lake Barkul in Southeastern Zungaria, which at this time was near the very heart of the Hunnish Kingdom. At this moment Dou Gu did not think it advisable to try and retain possession of any region North of the Celestial Mountains, and hence withdrew his troops from Zungaria before very long. But he took the very important step of establishing a permanent garrison at a place called Iwulu, which corresponds to the modern district and town of Hami.

The occupation of Hami was destined to have very important results. Hami lies just within the borders of Northeastern Kashgaria, so that the maintenance of a garrison at Hami meant that the Chinese had again secured a foothold upon the "Western Regions," and it was from Hami that most of the later Chinese military and diplomatic expeditions to Kashgaria set forth. Considering the great strategic importance of Hami it is not surprising that the Chinese created a new post of "General who Promotes Agriculture" to administer the district, and to keep open the lines of communication to the West.[4]

Dou Gu's victory over the Northern Huns and his occupation of Hami meant that the Chinese were once more in a position to attempt the recapture of the whole of Kashgaria. But before this region could be really reincorporated in the Celestial Empire much had to be done. First of all it was necessary for the Chinese to resecure control over the Kingdom of Güshï, which lay between Hami and the other Kashgarian kingdoms. In earlier chapters we have already stressed the importance of Güshï, so it is not a surprise to us to find the Chinese laying such stress upon the capture of this region before attempting to subdue any other portion of the "Western Regions."

In A.D. 74, therefore, it was decided to send an expedition against Güshï, and as a reward for his services in the preceding year, Dou Gu was given command of the expeditionary army. His second in command was a general called Gêng Bing. It so happened that Gêng Bing was especially anxious to distinguish himself at the expense of his superior officer. The year before, when Dou Gu had been so singularly successful, Gêng Bing had been in command of the other Western army, the one which had accomplished comparatively little, and it was for this reason that Gêng Bing had been deprived of a separate command and placed under the more famous Dou Gu. Bearing in mind this situation, one is not surprised that the feeling of rivalry between the two generals soon manifested itself in a violent disagreement as to the best method of conducting the campaign against Güshï.

It will be remembered that Güshï was really broken up into two separate states. One of these states, Northern Güshï, lay just to the North of the Celestial Mountains, while the other, Southern Güshï, lay in the Turfan depression, just to the South of those mountains. These two states, though separate, were closely affiliated politically, as can be seen from the fact that the King of Southern Güshï was a son of the monarch of the other kingdom.

It was soon evident that the Chinese generals, with the small force at their command, could not attack both of these states at the same time, and it became necessary to decide which of the two kingdoms should first bear the brunt of the Chinese campaigns. Dou Gu, the Commander-in-chief, was of the opinion that the campaign should be directed against Southern Güshï, as this state was nearer and easier to reach. Moreover, to attack the Northern state it would be necessary for the soldiers to cross the Celestial Mountains where they would have to endure intense cold and where they might easily be exposed to surprise attacks in some of the narrow gorges which served as passes. Gêng Bing, on the other hand, who felt that he had to distinguish himself by unusual daring, argued that in spite of these natural obstacles it would be far better to direct the attack against Northern Güshï, if for no better reason than that this kingdom was the more important of the two states, and that if Northern Güshï was subjected by force of arms, Southern Güshï would probably submit too.

While the matter was still being discussed in the military council, and before the commander-in-chief had a chance to issue definite orders on the subject, Gêng Bing really settled the issue by a brilliant display of insubordination. Placing himself at the head of the troops immediately subject to his own orders, Gêng Bing began to march in the direction of the Northern Kingdom. Dou Gu, with the main body of the army, felt compelled to follow in his footsteps, lest the two divisions, by being permanently separated, be overwhelmed by the enemy.

As luck would have it, Gêng Bing's act of insubordination resulted in the complete success of the imperial arms. The Chinese troops managed to cross the Celestial Mountains without difficulty, and once in Southern Zungaria they began to kill and to pillage to their heart's content, without finding any serious opposition. Long before they reached the capital of Northern Güshï, the monarch of this state was so frightened that he decided not to risk a battle but to submit immediately to Chinese overlordship. Placing himself at the head of several hundred of his troops he marched out to place himself in the hands of Gêng Bing, who was still leading the advance guard of the Chinese army.

Just at this point, the rivalry between Gêng Bing and Dou Gu again came into evidence. One of Dou Gu's aides was upset at the thought that Gêng Bing should have the honor of receiving the King of Güshï's submission. By hard riding, he managed to intercept the monarch just as the latter was on his way to Gêng Bing's camp. "Your Majesty," he said, "it is highly advisable that you tender your submission not to

Gêng Bing, who is only a subordinate general, but to Dou Gu, who is a person of much higher rank, being the commander in chief of the whole expedition. Being, moreover, the brother-in-law of the Emperor, he is much more accustomed to dealing with royalty."

The poor frightened King of Güshï was much impressed by this speech. To ward off further attacks he did, to be sure, send off most of his generals to Gêng Bing's camp, but he himself waited until he could have a chance to appear directly before the commander-in-chief.

News of this affair soon reached Gêng Bing, who immediately went into a towering rage. Buckling on his armor, Gêng Bing rode back to the camp of Dou Gu and protested against the action which had been taken. Dou Gu tried to temporize and begged his subordinate to take no action which might endanger the whole expedition. Gêng Bing, however, was not to be appeased. Screaming out his intention of killing the King of Güshï, he immediately galloped off in the direction of Güshï in order to carry out his threat, and before long appeared before the walls of the Güshïn capital.

In spite of these threats on his life, the King of Güshï dared not make any further resistance. Coming out from the city, he doffed his royal cap, and embracing the legs of the horse on which Gêng Bing was riding, the fallen monarch pleaded for his life. This action appeased Gêng Bing somewhat. As a result he refrained from putting the king to death, and contented himself with leading his victim in triumph to Dou Gu's camp.

By every principle of military law, Gêng Bing should have been court-martialed for the insubordination, but as he had achieved a notable victory, instead of being punished, he was handsomely rewarded by being advanced in rank immediately. Somewhat later he was given the title and estates of a marquis.

As Gêng Bing had predicted, no sooner had Northern Güshï surrendered to the Chinese than the sister kingdom of Southern Güshï hastened to place herself under Chinese jurisdiction. Having thus secured control over the two Güshï kingdoms, the Chinese then took steps to render this control effective and permanent. The rulers of the two states were allowed to remain on their respective thrones, but a special garrison of Chinese soldiers was installed at a strategic point in each of the two states. Each of these garrisons was placed under a special military commander who, in addition to his military duties, was expected to look after China's diplomatic interests as well.[5]

More important still, it was thought advisable to revive the old post of "Protector-General of the Western Regions," the occupant of which was to have general jurisdiction over Kashgarian affairs. The fact that

China felt strong enough to revive this office was, however, due not merely to the campaigns against the Huns and Güshï, but to the fact that while this campaign had been going on, another Chinese official had succeeded in striking terror into most of the Kashgarian states.

The name of this official was Ban Chao, and as he was destined to become one of China's greatest generals and viceroys, he is worthy of special attention. Ban Chao came of a family that was especially famous for its literary abilities. His father was a noted author, his brother Ban Gu had an even greater literary talent and compiled the monumental *Tsien Han Shu* or *History of the Early Han Dynasty,* which we have used so frequently in dealing with the history of Central Asia during the period immediately preceding the Christian era. His sister, Ban Jao, became the foremost woman scholar of China, and was noted for her vast learning and for the skill of her literary compositions.

Ban Chao himself started his career as a scribe, and it was generally expected that he would devote himself to literary endeavor, but before long his restless ambition drove him into seeking a more active and more spectacular mode of existence. Flinging down his writing brush one day, he swore that he would no longer be a slave to trivial tasks, and assured his startled and incredulous colleagues that he was determined, by taking service on the frontier, to rise to the rank of a marquis. Not long afterwards he found a suitable occasion to start his life of adventure.

In A.D. 73, shortly after the Chinese armies had marched northward to do battle with the Huns, it was decided to send a small party to the state of Shanshan in Eastern Kashgaria. That this party was expected merely to observe events and to conduct diplomatic negotiations is amply evidenced by the fact that the escort numbered little over thirty persons. As so frequently happened with Chinese embassies, this little party was led not by one but by two persons who were charged with joint responsibility. One of the two leaders of the expedition was Ban Chao.

When the Chinese embassy first arrived at the court of the King of Shanshan, its members were treated with great respect and consideration. Shortly afterward, however, it was noticed that the King of Shanshan was distinctly cooler in his attitude. This change of attitude was scarcely noticed by most of the members of the Chinese party, but Ban Chao was ever on the alert, and immediately became suspicious that something was wrong. He secretly seized the native chamberlain who was in attendance upon the embassies, and by force and threats managed to extract from the latter the information that a large detachment of Huns had secretly arrived a few days previously, and were now stationed a few miles away from the capital. The King of Shanshan was so impressed by the arrival of this force that he was thinking of breaking definitely with China and even of handing the members of the Chinese embassy over to the tender mercies of the Hunnish tribesmen.

Ban Chao's first step was to lock up the chamberlain, so that the latter could not spread the alarm. His next step was to invite all the members of the Chinese expedition, except his co-ranking associate, to a banquet. When his guests had become heated with wine, and were willing to join in any desperate exploit, Ban Chao proceeded to harangue the company. After explaining to them the danger they were in, he shouted, "In order to capture tiger cubs it is necessary to enter the tiger's cave. Let us, this very night, attack the Hunnish camp. Covered by darkness the Huns will not know how few we are, and we can take them by surprise. Once the Huns are defeated, the King of Shanshan will once more become subservient and all of us will have made a great name for ourselves."

Some members of the company suggested that the matter should be discussed with the other leader of the expedition, but Ban Chao immediately vetoed this suggestion. "Our fortune or misfortune," he exclaimed, "depends upon immediate action. My colleague is a pedantic official. If he learns of our plan he would be full of fears and would procrastinate. News of our plans would leak out, and all chances of a surprise attack would be at an end."

Inspired by Ban Chao's eloquence, and by the wine, the thirty-six members of the party eventually agreed to risk their lives in the attack on the Hunnish camp, although it was known that the Huns outnumbered them many times over. Taking advantage of the darkness, the little band crept silently out of the town and before long arrived in the neighborhood of the Hunnish encampment.

Instead of using all of his men for the attack Ban Chao placed ten of them in the rear of the Hunnish camp. Each of these men was provided with a military drum, and each was ordered to make a terrific din on this instrument as soon as the signal was given in the hope that the Huns would believe that a large Chinese army had arrived upon the scene. The remaining twenty-six men, each armed with a cross-bow, crept up to the front of the Hunnish camp and there lay in waiting for the signal to leap to the attack. Ban Chao himself crept still further forward, and eventually managed to set fire to one of the Hunnish tents. Fortunately a strong wind was blowing, and before long the whole camp was ablaze.

As soon as the flames began to leap up, the Chinese soldiers in the rear began to beat madly upon their drums and the Chinese soldiers in front, after discharging a volley of arrows, rushed in to engage in a hand-to-hand combat. The Huns were taken completely by surprise. Terrified by the flames and imagining that a large army surrounded them on all sides, the Hunnish tribesmen thought only of escape. The Hunnish general and thirty of his officers were killed and over a hundred of his followers perished in the flames.

The next morning Ban Chao sent the head of the Hunnish general to the King of Shanshan as a delicate reminder that it would be well for the latter to renew his allegiance to the Celestial Emperor. The terrified monarch took the hint, swore eternal loyalty, and immediately despatched one of his sons to serve as a hostage in the Chinese Court.

At first it looked as if trouble might originate from the fact that Ban Chao's colleague had been left in ignorance of the attack until it was all over, for the colleague was a jealous individual and possessed powerful friends at court, but after Ban Chao had filled his associate's ears with flattering words and had sworn that he would not take all the credit for the success to himself, matters were allowed to rest as they were. In fact, the Emperor of China and his court were so pleased with Ban Chao's exploit that it was decided to send him that same year (A.D. 73) still further into Kashgaria in order that he might negotiate treaties with some of the other petty states in that region. This time he was placed in sole charge of the expedition, and was not hampered by being given a co-ranking colleague. Ban Chao was also offered a much larger escort, but he insisted upon taking again with him only thirty odd persons, on the grounds that a larger force would be difficult to handle.

At this time the states in Northern Kashgaria were still too strongly under Hunnish influence for Ban Chao to have any chance of success in this region, so he wisely decided to march into Southern Kashgaria and there negotiate, in the first instance, with the King of Khutan. It will be remembered that though Khutan at this period was a vassal of the Hunnish Kingdom, the monarch of this little state was an exceedingly active and energetic person and had made Khutan the most important center in the southern portion of the Tarim basin. In view of this situation, Ban Chao hoped that it might be possible to shake the dependence of the Khutanese upon the Huns without having to engage in active warfare, for which, with his microscopic force, he was, of course, completely unprepared. But he found himself faced with numerous difficulties. The Huns maintained a Resident Agent in Khutan, and this officer still possessed a great deal of influence. Worse still, the chief Witch-doctor or "High Priest" of the vicinity was distinctly anti-Chinese and pro-Hunnish in his sympathies. For this reason it is not surprising that the King of Khutan was somewhat cool in his reception of Ban Chao and his little party of Chinese soldiers.

A few days later the High Priest, wishing to embarrass the Chinese embassy still further, told the king that the gods were angry at the fact that the Chinese had been received at all, and that to appease their wrath it was necessary to secure and offer up in sacrifice the specially marked horse upon which Ban Chao was in the habit of riding. The king, who wished to appease the gods, and yet not break completely with the Chinese, sent a messenger to Ban Chao asking him to make a present of the horse, in order that it might be sacrificed at a state festival.

Ban Chao was well aware of all the intrigue that was going on, and at once decided upon definite action. He replied, very politely, to the messenger that he was perfectly willing to deliver up the horse for sacrifice, but only on the condition that the High Priest come in person to claim the animal. The High Priest was perfectly willing to give a personal exhibit of his power, and shortly afterwards arrived at the Chinese camp. Whereupon Ban Chao immediately seized the unfortunate ecclesiastic and cut off his head. The severed head was then sent as a "present" to the king.

The king, instead of punishing Ban Chao for this bold stroke, was so impressed by the courage of the Chinese embassy that he decided to break with the Huns completely. Before long he and his Khutanese retainers slew the Hunnish resident, and swore allegiance to the Celestial Empire. No doubt this change of allegiance was made all the easier by the fact that Ban Chao proceeded to distribute huge presents to the monarch and his court as soon as they gave proofs of their loyalty to the Chinese cause.

Ban Chao remained in Khutan for several months, but early in the following year (A.D. 74) he determined to march to the Northwest and secure possession of Kashgar. Not long previously the King of Kucha, himself a vassal of the Huns, had marched upon Kashgar, and deposing the native ruler of this state, had placed on the Kashgarian throne a Kuchan nobleman by the name of Douti. As Douti was a devoted adherent of the Kuchans and of the Huns, Ban Chao knew that it would be a very difficult task to win Kashgar over to the Chinese cause as long as Douti remained on the throne.

Undeterred by this difficulty, Ban Chao and his little party set out for the Northwest and before long arrived a short distance from their goal. Instead, however, of marching himself directly into the hostile court, Ban Chao deputed one of his officers to ride into Kashgar and formally demand of the king that he render allegiance to China. In addition to these formal instructions Ban Chao whispered to his subordinate that the submission would almost certainly be rejected but that at the time of the audience it might be possible to seize upon the person of the king. "Do not forget," he added, "that King Douti is not a native of Kashgar and that most of the inhabitants of Kashgar are far from loyal to him. This fact should make it easier for you to lay hands upon him."

Ban Chao's deputy carried out instructions to the letter. When this deputy appeared before the king, the latter arrogantly refused even to consider the question of submission, but seeing that this officer was accompanied by only one or two men, he was very careless regarding his personal safety and allowed the Chinese officer and his men to come very close to him. Just as the interview was drawing to a close the Chinese deputy and his attendants leaped upon the monarch and bound him with ropes. The members of the court who were in attendance were so astonished at this intrepid action that they immediately ran from the chamber without making any attempt to come to their ruler's assistance.

As soon as Ban Chao heard of this coup, he and the remaining members of this little band immediately pushed on to Kashgar, and issued a proclamation that he had merely come to free the inhabitants from the oppressive yoke of Kucha and the Huns. At his instigation the nephew of the old native King of Kashgar (the one deposed by the Kuchans) was placed on the throne. The natives of Kashgar were delighted with the new state of affairs, and the new king was of course perfectly willing to swear allegiance to Ban Chao's master, the Emperor of China.

There then arose the question of what to do with the deposed and imprisoned Douti. The new ruler and most of the inhabitants of Kashgar advocated putting him to death. Ban Chao, however, who probably had in mind future relations with Kucha, declared that Douti's death would not help matters in the slightest, and ordered the deposed monarch to be freed and sent back to his native land.

The capture of Kashgar marked the climax of this portion of Ban Chao's career. At this time Ban Chao himself did not attempt personally to extend Chinese domination over either Kucha or Karashahr or any of the other city states of Northern Kashgaria, but it was undoubtedly due to Ban Chao's spectacular success in the South and West that China felt able, later in A.D. 74, to appoint another official as the Protector General of the whole of Kashgaria. It was the latter who first marched into the northern states of the Tarim basin and reëstablished Chinese suzerainty there.[6]

At the beginning of A.D. 75 China appeared to occupy a very favorable position with respect to the peoples of Central Asia. Western Manchuria and Eastern and Southern Mongolia were in the hands either of the friendly Wuhuan and Sienbi or of the submissive Southern Huns. The Northern Huns had received an impressive defeat; the strategically situated sister kingdoms of Güshï had been wrested from their grasp, and Hunnish dominance in Kashgaria supplanted by the well-nigh universal recognition of Chinese overlordship.

This same year, however, was to show that the Huns, though defeated, were far from crushed and that they were still capable of staging a spectacular comeback. As the result of their renewed attacks the Chinese, within a few months, lost nearly all of the results of their recent victories.

By this time it should not be surprising for us to learn that the Huns, when renewing hostilities, made their first and most serious attacks upon the sister kingdoms of Güshï in Northeastern Kashgaria and more especially against the two Chinese garrisons which had been left in these two states. Both of these garrisons defended themselves magnificently, and though they fought a losing battle, the story of their heroism has echoed through the centuries. Especially heroic were the exploits of Gêng Gung who was in charge of the garrison in Northern Güshï just North of the Celestial Mountains.

Gêng Gung (a cousin of the General Gêng Bing we have mentioned before) had taken an active part in the campaign against Güshï in 74, and as a reward for his services he was placed in charge of Chinese military and political activities in this region after the main army had been withdrawn. In addition to keeping Northern Güshï in subjection to the Celestial Empire, Gêng Gung also entered into negotiations with the powerful nation of the Wusun who still lived a few hundred miles further to the West, in Southwestern Zungaria. The Wusun, it will be remembered, had, a century previously, been subject to the Chinese, but ever since the fall of the Early Han dynasty they had remained entirely outside the orbit of Chinese politics, so that Gêng Gung's negotiations with them were of special interest.

Gêng Gung made no attempt to conquer or even threaten the Ruler (Kunmi) of the Wusun, but relied entirely upon fair words and specious promises. In these diplomatic negotiations he was eminently successful. The Wusun were only too glad to renew the ties binding them to China, and of their own free will sent in "tribute" in the form of horses, and also sent a hostage to reside at the Chinese capital. The success of these negotiations no doubt convinced Gêng Gung that he was destined to be a great empire builder, but early in the following year (A.D. 75) he received a rude shock when the Northern Huns suddenly invaded Northern Güshï, the country which was immediately subject to his jurisdiction and which it was his chief duty to protect.

The Huns had for their first objective not the Chinese garrison but the capital of the Güshïn kingdom. It was, however, necessary for Gêng

Gung to send reinforcements to aid his allies. With the small force of men at his command he could afford to send off only three hundred men, and even this number reduced his own garrison to a mere handful. Unfortunately, this little troop of three hundred men were intercepted by the Huns before their arrival at the Güshïn capital and were slaughtered to a man. Reinforcements thus failing to arrive, the Güshïn capital soon succumbed to the Hunnish attack, and the King of Güshï was himself captured and killed.

Once this had been accomplished, the Huns were free to direct their attention to the Chinese fort and its sadly weakened garrison. They appeared in great numbers before the walls of this fort and tried to capture it by direct attack. Bearing in mind his desperate situation, Gêng Gung thought it necessary to smear the arrows of his troops with a poisonous substance which caused all the wounds inflicted by these arrows to fester. The use of poisoned arrows was unknown to the Huns, so that the effect of these weapons caused consternation to arise among the besiegers, most of whom were ready to believe the Chinese story that these arrows were possessed of miraculous and supernatural powers. Taking advantage of the confusion in the ranks of their enemy, Gêng Gung and his troops made a sortie and delivered such a sharp attack upon the Huns that the latter lifted the siege and retired from the neighborhood.

Gêng Gung knew, however, that the Huns would soon recover from their shock, and that before long they would again appear and recommence the attack. Because of this, he shifted himself and his troops to a position some distance away from his former encampment in the hope that he and his followers, in the new situation, could more easily withstand a lengthy siege. The chief advantage of this new situation was that it lay by a running stream so that presumably the Chinese troops would have no difficulty in securing an adequate supply of water.

As had been expected, later on in that same year (A.D. 75) the Huns again appeared and laid siege to the little Chinese fort. This time the Huns made very few attempts to take the place by storm, but contented themselves with trying to cut off all supplies of food and water. The water supply received their special consideration. By a clever bit of engineering they managed to divert the stream which flowed through the Chinese fort, with the result that the Chinese troops were soon in a desperate situation. Wells were dug in various parts of the fort but for some time the diggers were unable to strike water, and the parched soldiers were reduced to extracting what moisture they could from the ordure of their horses.

At this crucial moment Gêng Gung fell back upon piety, and superstition. "Surely Providence will not desert us in our extremity," he exclaimed, and, donning his ceremonial clothes, he made a solemn sacrifice to the gods, while the soldiers were ordered to go on with their digging. Chance would have it that Gêng Gung's piety seemed to be justified, for no sooner was the sacrifice completed than the soldiers struck water. The whole garrison burst into wild cheers, and filling their buckets with water they exposed these buckets to the gaze of the enemy, so that the latter would realize that their attempt to make the Chinese die of thirst had ended in failure. When the Huns saw that the Chinese, in spite of all their efforts, were provided with an ample water supply they again raised the siege and retired from the neighborhood. For a moment it seemed as if Gêng Gung and his brave troops, having withstood two sieges, would thereafter be left in peace, but they were soon undeceived.

Though the Huns had been repulsed by Gêng Gung they were eminently successful in their activities elsewhere. As the result of their diplomatic intrigues the small states of Northern Kashgaria (Kucha, Karashahr and the like) had turned against the Chinese, and had slain the newly appointed Protector General of Kashgaria together with all of his subordinate officials and soldiers. Moreover, a Hunnish army, after crossing the Celestial Mountains, had invaded and conquered Southern Güshï (the Turfan area) and was hotly besieging the Chinese garrison which was stationed in this region.

In view of this situation, the inhabitants of the two states of Güshï decided that they had backed the wrong horse when they sided with China, and throwing off all allegiance to the Celestial Empire they again accepted the overlordship of the Huns, and even coöperated with the latter in their attacks upon the Chinese outposts. With the help of the Güshïns, the Huns were able to press even more hotly their attack upon the Chinese garrison in Southern Güshï, and were also enabled to renew for the third and last time the attack upon Gêng Gung and his forlorn little fort in Zungaria.

This time the Huns were in deadly earnest and continued the siege for several months. As they were able neither to carry the fort by storm nor to cut off the water supply of the garrison, they were determined to hang on until starvation caused the valiant Chinese soldiers to surrender. As the months went by, the little stock of food in the fort became completely exhausted, and the soldiers were reduced to boiling and eating the leather portions of their cross bows and armor. This was not a very healthy diet and before long death had brought down the number of defenders to only a few dozen, but still Gêng Gung held on.

The Shanyu of the Huns was so amazed at the resourcefulness and courage of the Chinese commandant that he sent in an emissary to announce to Gêng Gung that if the latter would only surrender without more ado, he would be given the title of King in the Hunnish hierarchy and married off to the Shanyu's daughter, but the brave commander was not to be tempted into betraying his company. Paying scant attention to the sacred rights of emissaries, Gêng Gung led the Hunnish messenger to the top of the walls of the fort, and there in plain sight of the besieging army, killed him with his own hand. The Huns were naturally enraged by this spectacle and renewed their attack with redoubled vigor, but still found themselves unable to capture the place by storm and so the siege dragged wearily on.

One is rather surprised that China made so little effort to rescue her garrisons in Kashgaria, but it so happened that in A.D. 75 just as the Huns began their attacks, the Emperor Ming, who was especially interested in Central Asian affairs, suddenly died, and following his death the Chinese court fell into such confusion that it was difficult to organize and send out a relief expedition. Ming-di was followed on the imperial throne by his son, who is known as the Emperor Jang. The new ruler, who was still in his teens, had few of the imperialist ambitions of his father, and showed scant interest in what happened amongst the Huns or in Kashgaria, as long as China proper was not invaded. At length, however, he was persuaded that unless some attempt was made to rescue the closely besieged Chinese garrisons in the two states of Güshï no portion of the empire would be safe from Hunnish attack, and after months of delay (early in A.D. 76) an army set out from China and marched in the first instance to Southern Güshï, South of the Celestial Mountains.

This army did, indeed, succeed in reaching the capital of this kingdom and there inflicted a severe defeat upon the combined forces of the Huns and the native Güshïns. The Huns retired to the North and the native Güshïns returned momentarily to allegiance to China. The rescuing army, however, had arrived too late to fulfill its main purpose, namely the relief of the Chinese garrison in this region, for this garrison had already been captured by the Huns and all of its members put to death.

In spite of the victory which he had achieved, the commander of the relief expedition wished to return to China immediately and without making any further attempt to go to the relief of Gêng Gung and his little garrison stationed to the North of the Celestial Mountains. One of the officers in the expedition, however, was a close friend of Gêng Gung and had formerly served under him. This officer, Fan Kiang by name, implored his superiors not to abandon the valiant Gêng Gung to his hapless fate. The commander-in-chief and most of his officers refused to go any further, but in the end allowed Fan Kiang to take a small detachment of soldiers and go to the rescue of his friend.

The little party marched to the North, but as its members were passing over the Celestial Mountains they were overtaken by a heavy snowfall and barely escaped with their lives. Pushing on as rapidly as possible, however, they at length came near the little Chinese garrison late one night. On hearing the sound of the horses' hoofs, the soldiers in the garrison thought that it was another band of Huns come to renew attack. Great was their joy, therefore, when they heard a distant shout announcing that it was the long prayed for rescuing party which had come at last. With a wild cheer, the gates of the fortress were opened. Rescuers and rescued embraced one another and everyone wept for joy.

Danger was not yet over, however. Because of the anti-imperialistic policy of the new Emperor, there was no prospect of further maintaining the Chinese fortress and garrison in this region. The only thought of the relief party was to bring the valiant members of the garrison back in safety to the Chinese frontier. This proved a difficult task, for when the little band of rescued and rescuers started back on the long journey to the Southeast they were pursued by bands of Hunnish cavalry and frequently had to stop their march and defend themselves from attack. In addition to this, there was great difficulty in collecting supplies. Weakened by their long hardships, many of the rescued party died under the new privations, but at any rate thirteen of them survived, among them the commander Gêng Gung. This little party at last succeeded in reaching the Chinese frontier. It is pleasant to note that all of the survivors were given suitable rewards for their services by the Celestial Emperor.[7]

But though the success of the rescuing party had shown that the Chinese were still capable of battling successfully with the Huns, the Emperor was resolute in refusing to waste any more men or money in building up or even in maintaining Chinese supremacy in Central Asia. In A.D. 76 (the same year in which Gêng Gung was rescued) an edict was issued which announced that the Emperor definitely abandoned the idea of maintaining a Protector General in Kashgaria. It was also announced that no attempt would be made to reëstablish the two Chinese garrisons in the two states of Güshï, which meant that these two kingdoms were allowed to remain under Hunnish suzerainty. At the same time orders were sent to the heroic Ban Chao, who was still in distant Kashgar, to return to China and let Western and Southern Kashgaria look after themselves. In the following year the Chinese took the further step of abandoning Hami, which was still closer to the Chinese frontier. It is not surprising that shortly thereafter this region was again occupied by the Huns, and for the moment it thus looked as if the Huns were once more to become the masters of Central Asia.

It is not difficult to understand the attitude assumed by the Emperor with reference to Central Asian affairs. Experience had shown that it was a very arduous task really to crush a nomadic people such as the Huns. Moreover, to defend the settled province of Kashgaria against Hunnish attacks entailed a heavy and continued expense, as Kashgaria then as now was largely a desert and it was difficult to collect any large revenue from this region even when it was firmly administered by Chinese officials.

But though the Emperor's attitude is intelligible, he made one great mistake. The recent Hunnish victories convinced him they were still a powerful and well organized political unit with which it would be difficult and even dangerous to carry on lengthy warfare, and in this he was mistaken. In spite of its victories in A.D. 75 and 76 the Northern Hunnish Empire was now a very unstable organization and soon began to show unmistakable evidence of internal disintegration.

We know that Mongolia underwent another long period of drought and famine at this period and it is highly probably that the distress brought about by these natural causes had much to do with the political unrest and dissatisfaction that was soon evident amongst the Northern Huns. Beginning in A.D. 82 only five years after the Chinese withdrawal from Central Asian affairs, we find it recorded that year after year large numbers of the Northern Hunnish tribesmen broke away from the rulership of their own Shanyu and came and took refuge either directly with the Chinese or else with the ruler of the Southern Huns who was himself in vassalage to the Celestial Empire. In A.D. 84 the Lord of the Northern Huns felt so uncertain of his position that he suggested to the Chinese that all hostilities between his followers and China be abandoned and that a formal treaty of peace and amity be negotiated between himself and the Celestial Emperor. This proposal fitted in perfectly well with the latter's political principles and the peace treaty was duly ratified.

But even the conclusion of peace between the Chinese and the Northern Huns could not stop the steady decay of the Hunnish Empire. By the following year (A.D. 85) this weakening of power was obvious to all, and in good nomad fashion the immediate neighbors of the Huns seized this opportunity to strike a blow at their ancient enemy. The Dingling in Siberia and the Northeastern Turkistan again raided the Hunnish territory from the North, the Sienbi in Western Manchuria increased their attacks upon the eastern flanks of the Hunnish Kingdom. Several of the Kashgarian states threw off their allegiance to their erstwhile masters and attacked the Huns from the West. Last but not least the

Southern Huns took advantage of the situation and attacked their cousins and rivals from the South, and succeeded in taking a large number of prisoners.

The success of the Southern Huns caused the Chinese Empire no little embarrassment. The Southern Huns were vassals and subject to the jurisdiction of the Chinese, and hence the Chinese were considered more or less responsible for their actions. Only a year previously the Chinese had made a formal peace with the Northern Huns, and now their vassals were making war upon the Northerners with whom the Celestial Empire still maintained friendly relations. The Lord of the Northern Huns looked upon these attacks as the basest treachery, and made formal protest to the Chinese authorities concerning them.

It is typical of the anti-militarist spirit of the Emperor Jang that he was very sympathetic to these protests. Instead of taking advantage of the Northern Hunnish weakness and joining in the attacks which the Southern Huns had made upon them, he promptly ransomed the prisoners which his vassal, the Southern Shanyu, had secured and returned them to their master, the Lord of the Northern Huns. But even this act could not save the Northern Huns from further disaster. In A.D. 87 the Sienbi conducted another major campaign against the Northern Hunnish Empire. In this campaign they were eminently successful. The Shanyu was killed and flayed, his skin being taken back as an emblem of victory. This victory was a sign that the Hunnish Empire was on its last legs.[8]

While the Northern Huns were thus meeting with reverse after reverse in Mongolia, our old friend Ban Chao was equally successful in undermining Hunnish influence in various parts of Kashgaria. It will be remembered that in A.D. 77, when the Emperor had definitely decided on an anti-imperialistic policy, Ban Chao was ordered to return to China forthwith. This was a bitter blow to Ban Chao's ambition, but for the moment he felt that he must obey the imperial command and prepared to depart from Kashgar which was still his headquarters.

When the inhabitants of the city learned of his plans they were filled with consternation. The commander of the local army said, "The Chinese envoy has raised us to our present position. When he leaves we will certainly be re-conquered by Kucha," and rather than face the gloomy future he immediately committed suicide. Ban Chao was shaken by this event but proceeded with his journey homewards. But when he arrived at Khutan, he met with more weeping and wailing. The King of this region and all his court clung on Ban Chao's horse, and howled, "The Chinese envoy is like our father and our mother. Surely he is not willing to desert us."

Inspired by these signs of loyalty and devotion Ban Chao made a bold decision. Flatly contravening the imperial order, he decided to remain in Kashgaria and fight it out to the bitter end. After reassuring the Khutanese that he would not leave them in the lurch he retraced his steps to Kashgar and after reëstablishing order there (the place had fallen into anarchy since his departure) he decided to keep his headquarters in this city as long as his slender means enabled him to hold out, but he knew that he could not maintain his position unless he could secure reinforcements from China.

Consequently, in the following year (A.D. 78) we find him sending in a memorial to the throne, beseeching the Emperor to reconsider his decision to abandon Kashgaria to its own fate, and imploring that reinforcements be sent out. Ban Chao's memorial (which has been preserved to us) was so eloquent that even the cautious Emperor was won over to his way of thinking. Ban Chao was permitted to remain at his post and a little army of a thousand men, most of them convicts on parole, was sent out to aid him in his activities.

This army did not arrive on the scene until two years later (A.D. 80), and its arrival proved to be not a moment too soon. The important city-state of Yarkand which lay between Kashgar and Khutan had already revolted and gone over to the enemy in the belief that China's dominion in the Tarim basin was doomed, and even in Kashgar itself there was active unrest and rebellion. With the aid of the fresh troops Ban Chao was able to keep Khutan in a loyal state of mind and also put down the unrest in Kashgar. Having thus maintained his position and increased his prestige he was also able to reëstablish friendly relations with the powerful Wusun kingdom which lay directly to the North of him, but he was still unable to take the offensive and attack Kucha or even bring Yarkand back into subjection.

Four years later (A.D. 84) another detachment of eight hundred soldiers was sent out to him from China, and with these reinforcements, plus the troops he was able to raise in those Kashgarian states which were still loyal to the Chinese cause, Ban Chao began making active preparations for a huge offensive campaign. These preparations were soon halted by an unforeseen development. The puppet King of Kashgar, who so far had been perfectly willing to coöperate with the Chinese resident, suddenly became disaffected. Kashgar itself remained in Ban Chao's hands, but the King of Kashgar fled to a fortress a little to the West of the city and there established himself in open defiance to the Chinese Empire. It was obvious that this rebellious monarch had to be disposed of before anything could be done, but this proved rather difficult owing to the aid he received from an unexpected quarter.

For some time past the Kang-gü, the Iranian nomads who dominated a large portion of Turkistan, had been distinctly friendly to the Chinese Empire, but for some reason they felt constrained to take the side of the rebel King of Kashgar and come to his rescue when he was being besieged by Ban Chao and his Chinese soldiers. Owing to this support the Chinese were unable to make any headway in their attack and for a moment it seemed as if they had reached an impasse in their struggle to resecure control over the whole of Kashgaria.

Before long, however, the astute Ban Chao had found a way out of this difficulty. He was well aware that the Kang-gü, powerful as they were, were in alliance with and in dependence upon the even greater Yüejï or Kushans who were just then carving out a great empire for themselves in the Middle East. Ban Chao proceeded to send an embassy to the Yüejï court plentifully supplied with valuable presents, and by a little judicious bribery the King of the Yüejï was persuaded to send a message to the Kang-gü urging them to give up their hostility to the Chinese.

This message worked like a charm. The Kang-gü soon returned to their native Turkistan, taking the rebel King of Kashgar along with them, and when, a year or two later the latter made another effort to recover the throne of Kashgar, but without any substantial external aid, he was promptly seized and put to death by the ever alert Ban Chao. The manner in which the unfortunate monarch was killed savored strongly of treachery, but Ban Chao was never overscrupulous in small matters.

Once the troublesome question of this rebellion had been finally settled it was possible once more to make preparation for an attack on Yarkand. In A.D. 88 Ban Chao gathered an army of twenty-five thousand men, most of them, of course, native auxiliaries collected from Khutan and other vassal states, and marched toward his objective. No sooner had he encamped before Yarkand than his old enemy the King of Kucha, the leader of the pro-Hunnish state of Northern Kashgaria, collected an army of fifty thousand men and marched to Yarkand's defense. On the approach of this army twice the size of his own, Ban Chao called his generals into conference. "It is impossible," said he, "to fight the enemy who are so superior to us in numbers. Let us try and escape before we are attacked. Let half of our number march eastward to Khutan, and the other half westward to Kashgar."

Shortly after this plan had been officially accepted by the Council of War, Ban Chao was careful to see that some prisoners of war whom he had captured were able to escape. These prisoners brought to the King of Kucha news of the Chinese plans. The King of Kucha immediately despatched half of his army to the East to attack that portion of the Chinese army which was to march to Khutan and the other half to the

West to overwhelm the Chinese division which was returning to Kashgar. Ban Chao's spies kept him informed of these movements on the part of the enemy, and he was delighted to find that his ruse had succeeded so well. He immediately issued a command cancelling the previously announced plans and ordered all of his troops to stay where they were but to prepare themselves for an attack on Yarkand.

At daybreak the order was given to attack. The Yarkandese who believed that the Chinese had already commenced their retreat were caught by surprise, and after thousands of their soldiers had been slaughtered they made an unconditional surrender to the Chinese commander. When the news of this event reached the King of Kucha, the latter felt that further fighting was useless and immediately withdrew his army to Northern Kashgaria, thus leaving Ban Chao in complete control of all the southern and western portion of the Tarim basin. Ban Chao's victories in Kashgaria coupled with the manifest weakness of the Huns in dealing with their neighbors and rivals in Mongolia made it very clear that the Hunnish Empire was rapidly weakening and that the Chinese had excellent prospects of securing a victory if and when they wished to recommence hostilities in the North.[9]

CHAPTER TWELVE

SEESAW IN THE BALANCE OF POWER, A.D. 88–106

Dou Hien and the Renewal of the Chinese Attacks upon the Northern Huns—China's Victory in the Campaign of A.D. 89*—The Defeat of the Northern Huns by the Southern Huns in* A.D. 90*—Dou Hien's Campaign of* A.D. 91*—The Northern Huns Become Vassals of the Chinese—Downfall of Dou Hien and Reëstablishment of Northern Hunnish Independence—The Sienbi Secure Mongolia—Further Exploits of Ban Chao in Kashgaria—The Attempt to Get from China to Rome—Death of Ban Chao.*

THE EMPEROR JANG was so opposed to warfare that no attempt could be made to take advantage of the Hunnish weakness and start a major offensive campaign as long as he was alive, but in A.D. 88 (shortly after Ban Chao's capture of Yarkand) he died and was succeeded on the throne by his son, the Emperor Ho-di. As the latter was a boy only ten years of age, real control of affairs rested for some time with the Dowager Empress, a scion of the powerful Dou clan, and who was herself a very able and energetic person. Taking advantage of this change in rulers, the Shanyu of the Southern Huns sent in a memorial to the throne, pointing out the weakness of the Northern Huns and urging that they be disposed of once and for all. "Let the Northern Hunnish Kingdom be completely destroyed," the memorial continued, "and its territory and its inhabitants given over to the Southern Huns who have consistently shown themselves devoted subjects of the Celestial Empire. If this be done China will never again have to worry about defending her northern frontier."

When this memorial came to be discussed in the Council of State, the military members of the Council argued that the proposed campaign was perfectly feasible and that it would be well to embark upon it. The civil members of the Council, however, pleaded that as long as the various Northern Barbarians were destroying one another, it would be foolish for China to waste men and money on a northern campaign. The arguments of the pacifists were so convincing that they almost won the day, and it is probable that the Northern Hunnish Empire would have been left to its own fate had it not been for a scandal which arose in the Imperial Court.[1]

The scandal in question arose in connection with the brilliant but erratic Dou Hien. Dou Hien was a distant cousin of Dou Gu who had led the campaign against the Huns in A.D. 73-74. More to the point, he was the brother of the Dowager Empress, and through the influence of the latter, Dou Hien soon rose to rank and power. Towards the end of A.D. 88, however, he noticed that a certain princeling of the Imperial House of Han had won his sister's favor and was frequently received in private audience by her. Dou Hien was fearful lest this princeling might become more powerful than himself and arranged to have this new favorite assassinated. In order to divert suspicion from himself, he accused the prince's younger brother of the murder.

Eventually the whole plot was discovered, and there was naturally a great to-do about the matter throughout the capital. Public opinion forced the Empress Dowager to cast her brother into prison, and threaten him with even more serious punishment. At this juncture Dou Hien petitioned that he might be allowed to atone for his offense by leading an expedition against the Northern Huns. As his sister was anxious to get him out of his scrape, this petition was granted, and in spite of further memorials from civilian members of the Grand Council it was officially decided to embark on the Hunnish war early in the following year, with the scapegrace Dou Hien as commander-in-chief of the Chinese army.[2] This war, which began in A.D. 89, lasted for three years. In each of these three years there were important developments, but practically all of these developments were in favor of the Chinese cause.

The campaign of A.D. 89 was in itself sufficient to prove that the Northern Huns were no longer capable of fighting on equal terms with the Celestial Empire. On this occasion Dou Hien was accompanied by the ablest military officers in China, but had under his command only eight thousand Chinese and an equal number of Tibetan troops recruited from the borders of Western China. To make up for this paucity of soldiers Dou Hien had to rely in large measure upon the assistance given him by the Southern Huns, who placed more than thirty thousand of their tribesmen at his disposal and coöperated with the Chinese in the fullest possible way, as they believed that they stood to secure the lion's share of the benefits in case the Northern Huns were defeated.

The Chinese army advanced far into Mongolia and there established a military base. From this base Dou Hien sent out an advance guard of about ten thousand men to establish contacts with the enemy. This advance guard did far more than was expected of it, for when it came upon a large number of the Northern Huns led by the Shanyu in person it immediately engaged in battle and succeeded in gaining an overwhelming victory. Many of the Hunnish leaders were killed and the Shanyu himself was forced to flee for his life.

As the result of this victory the Hunnish resistance was broken and the main Chinese army, when it arrived on the scene, was able to march far into Northern Mongolia without encountering any opposition. After it had reached a point more than five hundred miles from the Chinese frontier a huge inscription was carved commemorating the stupendous Chinese victory. After erecting this inscription the Chinese army slowly returned to the South, but even after its departure from Mongolia the prestige it had secured was so great that enormous numbers (five hundred thousand in all) of the Northern Huns surrendered to and became the subjects of the Lord of the Southern Huns and thus came indirectly under the sway of the Celestial Empire. Even the Shanyu of the Northern Huns was so impressed by the recent events that he opened negotiations with China with the view of submitting himself and the remnant of his hordes to the Chinese Emperor, though for the moment these negotiations led to no definite results.[3]

On his return to China, Dou Hien was regarded as a great hero and had numerous honors showered upon him. Bearing in mind the many persons who were suspicious of his ambitious projects, he ostentatiously refused many of these honors. But in the hope of securing fresh glories he so arranged it that in the following year (A.D. 90) he was sent out as military governor of the northwest frontier province of China (Liangjou) with a view to reëstablishing order in this region, and more especially to see what could be done about opening communications with the neighboring Kashgarian states which still acknowledged Hunnish supremacy.

Later on in this same year (A.D. 90) one of the minor Chinese generals acting under Dou Hien's orders marched out and resecured possession of the strategically important town and district of Hami. As this district was the key to Northern Kashgaria, it is not surprising to learn that shortly after its occupation by the Chinese the two neighboring states of Northern and Southern Güshï again broke away from their allegiance to the Huns and sent in tribute and hostages to the Chinese court.

At this period Dou Hien had no intention of reëmbarking upon direct hostilities with the Northern Huns. In fact his policy all throughout this year was one of conciliation. He hoped to conclude the negotiations begun in the preceding year and thereby bring all the members of the Northern Hunnish Empire to submit to Chinese jurisdiction. With this purpose in view he sent two of his officers with presents to the Northern Hunnish court and the Shanyu was persuaded to undertake a journey to China to submit himself to imperial authority.

All hopes of a diplomatic adjustment of difficulties were, however, dashed away by the precipitate and independent action of the Southern Huns. The Lord of the Southerners who wished to rule over all the Huns, was none too pleased at the prospect of having his rival given a friendly reception at the Chinese capital. When, therefore, the Northern Shanyu with a small detachment of troops was calmly and peacefully making his way southward to the Chinese frontier he was suddenly surrounded and attacked by an army of Southern Huns. Taken completely by surprise, the Northern ruler was wounded and fell from his horse. With difficulty he managed to mount another horse and with the help of a handful of faithful retainers he at last succeeded in breaking through the line of the Southerners and made his escape, but he naturally thought that he had been betrayed by the Chinese and all thoughts of peaceful submission to the Celestial Empire were at an end.

Dou Hien received the news of this surprise attack with very mixed emotions. He felt no doubt that the Southern Huns had seriously affected the development of his own plans, but as the Southerners' action met with imperial approval, and as they had actually received assistance from responsible Chinese officials it was impossible for him to wreak vengeance upon the Lord of the Southern Huns. In fact, he was forced to give silent approval to all that had been done. At the same time he was determined that the Southern Shanyu and his assistants, native and Chinese, should not get all the credit for overcoming the Northern Barbarians. It was better no doubt to win the Northern Huns over by diplomacy rather than by force of arms, but if arms rather than diplomacy were to be resorted to, it was imperative that he, Dou Hien, should secure the laurels of victory rather than anyone else.[4]

In the following year (A.D. 91), therefore, we find Dou Hien completely changing his course of action. Abandoning all attempts at further diplomatic negotiations, he organized another Chinese army and again marched into Mongolia determined to crush once and for all the power that for so long had been a thorn in the side of the Celestial Empire.

On this occasion Dou Hien contented himself with general supervision of military operations and entrusted most of the actual fighting to a number of small army detachments, each of which was led by one or another of his most trusted subordinates. One of these army corps was particularly successfully. It succeeded in penetrating into the Hunnish territory for more than a thousand miles—far further than any Chinese army had ever succeeded in penetrating before, and wrought untold havoc upon the Hunnish forces. The mother of the Shanyu and many other members of his family were killed or captured, the Hunnish national treasury fell as loot into the hands of the Chinese soldiers, and the Shanyu himself, feeling that his power was completely broken, fled to some unknown region and was never heard of again.

The flight of the Shanyu meant that the Northern Hunnish Empire, at least for the moment, was almost entirely at the mercy of the Chinese officials. The Lord of the Southern Huns hoped, of course, that the Chinese would utilize this opportunity to install him as the suzerain of all the Huns. Certainly he and his followers had played an important part in bringing about the overthrow of the Northern Kingdom. Dou Hien, however, had quite different ideas. He was radically opposed to the plan of allowing another large reunited Hunnish state to grow up in Mongolia, for though the Southern Huns were now loyal subjects of the Chinese Empire, their feelings might be very different if and when they found themselves in possession of a vast kingdom. In the following year (A.D. 92), therefore, we find Dou Hien arranging to install a younger brother of the man who had fled to unknown parts as Shanyu of the Northern Huns.

This meant that the Northern Hunnish Empire was preserved as a separate entity, but on the distinct understanding that it, too, was to be subject to Chinese domination. We are told that the new Shanyu established himself and his court not in Mongolia, but in Zungaria at a point not far from Lake Barkul, and orders were issued to the military governor of Hami to the effect that in the future he was to supervise the activities of the Northern Huns.

Once this arrangement had been made, it looked as though the Northern and Southern Hunnish Kingdoms would both be allowed to persist as separate and autonomous states but both subject to the supreme jurisdiction of the Celestial Emperor. This, from the Chinese point of view, was an ideal situation, but unfortunately it was one which was destined to last for only a few months, and was brought to an end by the tragic death of Dou Hien, who was the chief sponsor of the whole arrangement.[5]

Owing to the success of the three years' warfare against the Huns, Dou Hien had now acquired enormous prestige among the Chinese populace. In consequence of this prestige, and also, of course, because of the support given him by his sister, the Dowager Empress, Dou Hien was able to parcel out many of the highest offices of state among his brothers and others relatives, and he himself assumed many grandiose manners.

All this so alarmed the boy Emperor (he was still only fourteen years of age), that he decided to make an end of the whole Dou clan lest they eventually conspire to overthrow the dynasty. The Dowager Empress was deprived of all power. The lesser members of the clan were executed. Dou Hien was banished to his estate, and shortly afterwards was driven to commit suicide. So perished one of China's greatest generals, the man who was most responsible for the downfall of the enemy who had plagued China for centuries, his chief offense being that he had been too successful.

The death of Dou Hien naturally had several important consequences. The first was a new revolt on the part of the Shanyu of the Northern Huns. This worthy person had been the personal protégé of Dou Hien, and once the latter was dead, the Hunnish leader felt that he owed no especial loyalty to the ruler who had driven his patron to commit suicide. This revolt meant, of course, an attempt on the part of the Northern Huns to reëstablish their independence.

Early in the following year (A.D. 93) China sent another expedition to the North, and this little army succeeded in trapping and killing the rebellious Shanyu. The later fortunes of the Northern Huns are veiled in obscurity. The Chinese records are singularly silent about these matters, but from all casual references it is obvious that in spite of this new defeat the Northern Huns soon managed to reorganize themselves and elect a new ruler. Now that the great Dou Hien was gone, the Chinese were unable to dictate the selection of the Northern Shanyus, which meant that the Northern Huns were no longer in direct dependence upon the Celestial Empire.[6]

The new Shanyu and his successors were, however, careful not to goad the Chinese into organizing a new punitive expedition. From time to time they even sent embassies to the Chinese court with "tributary" presents, and on one occasion even had the grace to apologize for the scantiness of their offerings on the ground that their country was now so poor that they were no longer able to make offerings of any great value.[7]

But though the Northern Huns were once more autonomous they were now but shadows of their former selves. Their territory was now confined to Zungaria and the regions immediately to the West of Zungaria. They had lost control over practically all parts of Mongolia. Southern Mongolia continued to be inhabited by the Southern Huns, while Northern Mongolia passed out of Hunnish hands completely and was annexed by the Sienbi.

This change in the rulership over Northern Mongolia was more political than ethnic. This region continued to be occupied in large measure by tribal units which had formerly been subject to Hunnish rulership, and hence had been called Huns. When the Hunnish Empire suffered its series of overwhelming defeats, these tribes were perfectly willing to accept a change of masters, and not only accepted Sienbi overlordship but soon came to regard and call themselves Sienbi. By thus securing control over the whole of Northern Mongolia, the Sienbi, who had formerly been confined to Northeastern Mongolia and Western Manchuria, for the first time really became a great power. But in spite of the enormous increase in their numbers and in their territory, the Sienbi were content, for the moment, to remain in at least nominal subjection to

Chinese overlordship, which in turn meant that for several years the Chinese did not have to worry about the safety of their northern frontier.

It is rather surprising that it was the Sienbi rather than the Southern Huns who were able to secure control over Northern Mongolia, for the Southern Huns had long been in close alliance with the Chinese, and it was at their suggestion that the campaigns against the Northern Huns had first been undertaken. But, as we have already seen, the Chinese were none too anxious to see their allies become too powerful, and rather welcomed the fact that it was the Sienbi rather than the Southern Huns who secured the lion's share of the spoils of warfare.

In addition to this it should be noticed that in A.D. 93 the energetic Lord of the Southern Huns, the man who was most responsible for the forward policy of his fellow tribesmen, died, and that after his death the Southern Huns were much troubled by internal dissensions, resulting ultimately in long continued civil war. This civil war (which lasted in one form or another until A.D. 117) was in itself sufficient to prevent the Southern Huns from taking full advantage of the decline of their northern kinsmen and kept them from even attempting to wrest control over Northern Mongolia from the Sienbi.[8]

In any event, the Chinese could remain perfectly content with the course of developments which took place during the reign of the Emperor Ho-di (A.D. 89-105). To be sure, after the fall of Dou Hien the Celestial Empire was no longer able to continue its aggressive forward policy, but as long as the regions north of China were divided between Sienbi, the Southern Huns and the Northern Huns, all of whom were willing to remain on friendly terms with the Chinese Empire, the Son of Heaven need have no great anxiety about the safety of his domain —at least as far as the northern frontier was concerned.

Let us now turn our attention from the North to the West and examine the further adventures of Ban Chao during this same period. When we last took cognizance of him (A.D. 88), he had just secured control over all of Southern and Western Kashgaria, and it was only the states of Northern Kashgaria which still refused to admit Chinese supremacy. Ban Chao was just beginning to make preparations to subdue this region when he was suddenly faced with a new danger from an entirely unexpected quarter. For the past decade the Chinese had succeeded in maintaining very friendly relations with the powerful Yüeji or Kushans, who were just in the process of building up their great Central Asian and Indian Empire. On at least one occasion, Ban Chao had owed his entire success to the friendly intercession of the Yüeji on his behalf.

It is not surprising, therefore, to hear that late in A.D. 88 the Yüeji dispatched an embassy to China to send greetings to the Son of Heaven and to ask the hand of a Chinese princess in marriage to their own ruler. What is surprising is that for some mysterious reason, Ban Chao disapproved of the project. He would not even allow the embassy to proceed to China, but stopped it as it passed through Kashgaria, and sent its members back to their native land.

Quite naturally the Yüejï took serious offense at this action and early in A.D. 90 they dispatched an army of seventy thousand men with the express purpose of attacking the Chinese and securing for themselves a large portion of Kashgaria. As the total number of Chinese soldiers in this region was far inferior to this force in numbers, most of Ban Chao's subordinates were terror-stricken when they heard of the imminent invasion. Ban Chao refused to be dismayed. "Though the enemy far outnumber us," he said, "yet before they reach us they have to travel many hundreds of miles over high mountainous roads. They will be unable to bring with them an adequate supply of provisions. All we have to do is to seize and store up all available foodstuffs. If we can prevent these provisions from falling into the enemy's hand, in a very short time indeed they will be forced to retreat."

Subsequent events fulfilled Ban Chao's prognostications almost to the letter. When the Yüejï troops arrived in Kashgaria, the Chinese commander made no attempt to meet them in open battle, but shut himself and his Chinese soldiers behind the walls of the fortified city of Kashgar and in spite of several attempts the Yüejï were unable to take the place by storm. They then scoured the surrounding country for food, but owing to Ban Chao's previous activities they were unable to secure any.

As a last resort the commander of the Yüejï army sent a small detachment of troops, laden with presents, in the direction of Kucha, in the hope that the King of Kucha, who was bitterly anti-Chinese, would give or sell them an adequate supply of provisions. But Ban Chao had guessed that just such an attempt would be made and had an army corps hidden along the road between Kashgar and Kucha. This army corps succeeded in catching the Yüejï detachment in an ambush, with the result that the members were killed to a man.

When the commander of the Yüejï army heard of this event he felt that further fighting was useless, and made peace with Ban Chao, asking only that he and his men be allowed to return in peace to their native land and not be attacked as they were beating a retreat. Ban Chao was perfectly willing to accede to these terms, and before long the Yüejï army was completely withdrawn from Kashgaria.

The defeat and withdrawal of the Yüejï army made a profound impression upon all of the Kashgarian states, especially upon all of those which had not yet submitted themselves to Chinese rule, as they began to feel that the Chinese armies were once more invincible. This feeling was greatly enhanced by the contemporary defeat of the Northern Huns with whom the states of Northern Kashgaria had long been in alliance.

Taking advantage of this situation, Ban Chao in the following year (A.D. 91) was able to establish jurisdiction over Kucha, at this time the most important of the states in the northern portion of the Tarim basin, and the one which had caused the most trouble in recent years. So great was Ban Chao's prestige at this time that he was able to depose the old King of Kucha and install a new pro-Chinese monarch almost without striking a blow. Once Kucha had submitted, most of the other states in Northern and Northwestern Kashgaria hastened to send in their allegiance to the Celestial Empire, and China was once more established as the suzerain of the whole of the Tarim basin.

For once in its long history China gave adequate recognition to the man who had brought her honor and glory. In this same year (A.D. 91) the Emperor reëstablished the office of Protector General of the Western Regions, and Ban Chao was elevated to this post. At the same time that Ban Chao was appointed Protector General, China also reappointed two special military commanders to act as residents in Northern and Southern Güshï respectively. For the next three years Ban Chao was busy arranging and rearranging the perplexing matters of provincial administration. Feeling that the possession of Kucha was all important to the maintenance of Chinese supremacy in the West, and fearing lest revolution might again break out in this region, Ban Chao made of Kucha the provincial capital of Kashgaria and resided there himself, though he left one of his subordinates with the rank of Vice-Protector in Kashgar to look after Chinese interests in the old capital.

In A.D. 94 Ban Chao took a final decisive step in the direction of imposing Chinese dominion over all the native states of the Tarim basin. By this time all of these kingdoms had accepted, at least in name, Chinese suzerainty, but the loyalty of Karashahr and one or two of the neighboring states was somewhat open to question. It was in Karashahr, some twenty years previously, that Ban Chao's predecessor in the office of Protector General had been murdered. This murder had never been officially revenged, and the inhabitants suffered from an uneasy conscience and were very suspicious of all the Chinese activities in Kashgaria.

Ban Chao felt that this state of affairs could not be allowed to continue, and once his administrative system was in smooth running order he marched with an army of about eight thousand men from Kucha in the direction of Karashahr. When he came near the borders of this country he dispatched an envoy to the court of the King of Karashahr to announce that he, the Protector General, had arrived upon the scene to reëstablish order, and that it was high time for the monarch and his subjects to repent of their past misdeeds and turn towards the path of righteousness, but promised that if they respectfully submitted to the Chinese orders they would be suitably rewarded.

The King of Karashahr immediately ordered the chief officer in his army, a Hunnish nobleman by birth, to repair to Ban Chao's camp and respectfully offer up a tribute of cattle and wine. But when this person arrived upon the scene, he was treated with scant civility. Ban Chao himself screamed at the envoy, "You who were formerly a Hunnish hostage at the Chinese court, have now risen to rank and power in Karashahr, and it is probably due to your influence that the King has sent you rather than come himself to present his submission."

Some of Ban Chao's staff wished to seize and kill the Hunnish general on the ground that he was the real cause of Karashahr's rebellious attitude during the past few years, but the Protector General vetoed this action on the ground that it would probably drive the court of Karashahr into active resistance to the imperial authority. In the end therefore, the Hunnish general was dismissed, and even given some presents, but was ordered to see to it that his master, the king, appear at the camp in person.

After some hesitation this monarch did come to the Chinese headquarters and made unqualified submission, largely in the hope that by doing so he could thereby prevent the Chinese army from occupying his capital. Ban Chao, however, was not content with this nominal submissiveness and ordered his troops to advance to the outskirts of the the city of Karashahr. When the army reached this spot the Protector General issued a command invitation to the king and all the notables of the latter's court to appear in camp at a great official banquet. The monarch and his Hunnish general together with many other leaders from Karashahr and the surrounding districts duly accepted this invitation, and came to the Chinese headquarters. Many other notables, however, were so frightened of what might happen that they not only refused to attend but fled far away into the mountains.

It soon appeared that the fugitives had justification for their fears, for no sooner were the guests seated at the banquet than Ban Chao, who was looking for an excuse to provoke a quarrel, immediately began to upbraid the king for allowing the fugitives to escape. After reading him this moral lecture the Protector General ordered the unfortunate king to be seized and bound. Not long afterward he and many of his followers were ordered executed on the exact spot where the former Protector General had been murdered two decades previously.

Once Karashahr and the surrounding districts had been thrown into complete confusion by the execution of the king and the principal members of his court, Ban Chao and his soldiers were able to make a Roman holiday for themselves. Over five thousand of the native inhabitants were put to death and over three hundred thousand head of cattle were seized in the way of loot. Cruel as this was, the fate of Karashahr had the desired effect upon all of the other native states of Kashgaria. Thereafter all of the rulers of its constituent kingdoms prostrated themselves completely before the representative of the Celestial Empire, and hastened to send tribute and hostages to the Imperial Court.

Ban Chao's actions in Karashahr smacked strongly of treachery and the breaking of faith, but the Imperial Court of China was never very punctilious about these matters (as long as such actions were successful) and in the following year (A.D. 95) Ban Chao was rewarded for his valor and statesmanship by being raised to the coveted rank of marquis and granted a feudal estate. He remained in Kashgaria as Protector General for another seven years, but we have very little information regarding his actions in this last portion of his public career. The only military incident which occurred took place in Güshï, in the extreme northeastern portion of Kashgaria, but though this region was nominally subject to the Protector General's jurisdiction, in point of fact the special military commanders who resided in this region were able to settle accounts without calling upon Ban Chao for assistance.

The incident to which reference has been made was a comparatively simple affair. In A.D. 96 the King of Northern Güshï became involved in a dispute with the local Chinese military commander, but instead of attacking China proper he invaded the territory of his colleague and relative, the King of Southern Güshï, on the ground that the latter had sold out completely to the Chinese cause and was in need of punishment. This attack was very successful, and the wife and children of the southern king were taken prisoner.

In order to punish this raid, in the following year (A.D. 97) the Chinese sent out a military expedition. The territory of Northern Güshï was soon brought under control by the Celestial troops, and the king himself fled to the Northwest in order to take refuge with the Northern Huns. He was, however, pursued and captured by the Chinese. Shortly afterwards the unfortunate monarch was put to death, and his younger brother, who promised to be more amenable to imperial orders, was placed on the throne.

It is probable that during these last seven years, Ban Chao reëstablished diplomatic and political relations with the Wusun to the North of Kashgaria, but the Chinese records are strangely silent on this point. It is stated that the great marquis crossed the high mountain passes leading to Gibin or Northwestern India, but this was probably done in order to explore the southern frontier of Kashgaria as we know of no campaign undertaken against any of the Indian states.

The relations which Ban Chao established with the states of Turkistan, to the West of Kashgaria, are of even greater interest to us, although they led to no permanent results. It is sometimes stated that Ban Chao extended his conquests to this region, or even that he "carried the flag of China to the shores of the Caspian Sea," but this is a mistake. Great as was his power and prestige Ban Chao never attempted the invasion of any region to the West of the Pamirs, and this for a very good reason. The potent Yüejï and Kang-gü had full control over most of Turkistan, and though Ban Chao had been able to resist the Yüejï invasion of Kashgaria, he was well aware that he would face certain defeat in case he tried to attack the Yüejï in their own territory.[9]

But though the Chinese at this time made no attempt to effect a military conquest of Turkistan, they were able to arrange for the occasional exchange of embassies with many of the western states. Thus we know not only of the frequent envoys who came from the Yüejï but also of the exchange of embassies with Parthia and several other kingdoms. One of the embassies which Ban Chao dispatched to Parthia was especially memorable in that its leader came very close to establishing direct connections with the Roman Empire. This official, a man by the name of Gan Ying, was sent out from Kashgaria in A.D. 97. After passing through Marv, the chief town in Southwestern Turkistan, or "Little Parthia," he proceeded to Hekatompylos, on the Iranian Plateau, which was then the capital of the whole Parthian Empire. After finishing his diplomatic business there Gan Ying decided to push still further to the West, and at length succeeded in reaching Mesopotamia, already a province of the Parthian Empire, but which was still reckoned a separate unit.

From Mesopotamia Gan Ying wished to journey to the Roman Empire which was then known to the Chinese as Da Tsin. For some astonishing reason, however, Gan Ying ignored the land route from Mesopotamia across the desert to Syria, then of course a part of the Roman Empire, and decided to travel by ship through the Gulf of Persia and then up the Red Sea, which would bring him to either Egypt or Palestine. Just as the Chinese envoy was on the point of embarking, however, he began to hear wild tales of the dangers of the sea voyage. "The sea on which you propose to sail," he was told, "is very vast and its navigation is uncertain. Even with favorable winds the voyage will take three months, with unfavorable winds two years. In fact it would be well to take along provisions sufficient to last three years. Moreover the sea frequently causes people to have such a strong desire to see their home that they become sick and die."

Gan Ying was a brave and enterprising man, but he was so disturbed by these wild tales that he decided to return immediately to his native land without exploring any further. To us moderns it seems a great pity that Gan Ying's fear of storms and seasickness prevented the establishment of direct relations between the two great empires of antiquity.[10]

In A.D. 100, shortly after Gan Ying's return from the West, Ban Chao began to suffer from homesickness, and he sent in a memorial to the throne asking that he be allowed to retire from office and spend his last years in his native China. This memorial, which has been preserved to us, is imbued with a spirit of sentimental nostalgia, which is somewhat remarkable considering the old viceroy's energy and hard-headedness. But Ban Chao had served in the distant West for thirty years without a furlough and he was beginning to tire of his heavy responsibilities. The Emperor was naturally loath to lose the services of such an illustrious and successful official, and Ban Chao's sister, the famed Ban Jao, who possessed much influence at court, had to add her plea before the aged Protector General's request for retirement could be granted. Eventually the Emperor gave way, but it was not until two years later (A.D. 102) that Ban Chao was at last able to leave Kashgaria and journey to the Chinese capital. When he did arrive he was bowed down by illness and though he was given every honor and consideration, and was attended by His Majesty's private physicians, he died within a month of his return to his beloved homeland. So ended one of China's greatest heroes.

The death of Ban Chao marks the end of an important epoch. The reëstablishment of Chinese supremacy was largely due to the efforts of this one man, and once he had departed from the scene the great colonial empire he had created rapidly crumbled to pieces. The prestige of his name was indeed sufficient to maintain Chinese domination for three or four years, but in A.D. 105 the Celestial Empire was thrown into temporary confusion as a result of the death of the Emperor Ho-di and the difficulty of finding a suitable successor, and in the following year, taking advantage of this situation, several of the Kashgarian states suddenly rose in rebellion. Within a few months Chinese jurisdiction in this region (which had taken Ban Chao thirty years of labor to establish) was completely at an end.

CHAPTER THIRTEEN

THE FINAL COLLAPSE OF THE HUNNISH EMPIRE, A.D. 106–166

Revolt of Kashgaria against the Chinese—Its Return to the Hunnish Fold—Revolt of the Tibetans and Southern Huns—Reëstablishment of Order—Ban Yung and the Chinese Reoccupation of Kashgaria—The End of the Ban Family and of Chinese Supremacy in Central Asia—Final Conflict with the Northern Huns—The End of the Southern Hunnish Kingdom—The Rise of the Sienbi Empire—The Northern Huns Are Driven Westwards toward Europe.

THE REVOLT in Kashgaria was due in no small measure to the ineptitude of the man sent out to serve as successor to Ban Chao in the post of Protector General of the Western Regions. This official, who bore the name of Ren Shang, had already served in several campaigns against the Huns, and as a soldier he had great capacity. But military prowess does not always connote ability as a civil administrator, and it appears that Ren Shang was as deficient in the latter capacity as he was proficient in the former.

The tale is told that before Ren Shang left China to take up his post (in A.D. 102) he had an interview with Ban Chao, his illustrious predecessor, and asked for advice as to the best policy to pursue in Kashgaria. With startling frankness, the aged Ban Chao replied: "The Chinese officials in our colonial empire are, for the most part, unfilial rascals, who have sought employment on the distant frontiers because they have committed some crime or misdemeanor at home. The natives of Kashgaria, on the other hand, are like wild birds and beasts, difficult to rear, and quick to take offense. You, sir, have a stern and impetuous nature, and I would beg you to remember the old saying that 'the man who opens his eyes too widely has no friends.' It would be well for you to be more easy going and indulgent."

After the interview, Ren Shang remarked to his friends: "I had expected to receive some worthy advice from so famed a man as Ban Chao, but his words were puerile." [1] Subsequent events showed that the stern and impetuous Ren Shang would have done well to have taken to heart the warning of the sagacious Ban Chao. In Kashgaria, Ren Shang soon made himself exceedingly unpopular and his severe measures, in a few years, led to the Kashgarian rebellion. The existing records of the rebellion are scanty, but they are sufficient to show us that the first attack was made in Kashgar proper, which was then the seat of Ren Shang's administration. The Chinese managed to beat off this attack, but shortly afterwards they voluntarily abandoned the city and removed their headquarters to the citadel in Kucha, which was larger and deemed easier to defend.

The King of Kucha remained loyal to the Chinese cause, but many of his subjects went over to the enemy and joined the troops from the other city states of Northern Kashgaria which again attacked the Chinese position. The Celestials put up a stout defense, and even managed to make occasional sorties in which they were able to inflict severe damage. Even so it was obvious that the Chinese garrison at Kucha could not maintain its position indefinitely unless reinforcements came from the homeland, and the sending of these reinforcements was rendered difficult by the success of the rebels in cutting off direct communications between Kucha and the Chinese frontier.

Eventually, the question of reinforcements came before the Grand Council in the Chinese capital, and this time the pacifist policy of some of the Confucianist officials carried the day. Bowing to the old arguments that Kashgaria was distant and difficult to defend against the frequent uprisings, and that even in times of peace the administration of the province cost more than it was worth, the Council decided to abandon all claims to suzerainty over the region, while the office of Protector General was abolished.

But, though no attempt was to be made to reconquer Kashgaria, it was determined that the brave garrison at Kucha should not be left to its fate. A relieving army was dispatched to permit the officials and the garrison to retire in safety. The relieving army accomplished its task. Not only the Chinese at Kucha but also the officials stationed in Southern Güshï and Hami were brought back to their native land without great loss of life. All this took place in A.D. 107.[2]

While the Chinese were able to withdraw from Kashgaria in good order and without great diminution of honor, the very fact that they had been forced to abandon their suzerainty over the western regions was sufficient to make the other "barbarian" peoples believe that the Celestial Empire might be attacked with impunity. The first to act in accordance with this belief were the Kiang or Tibetans. These people began their attack in A.D. 107, and, as the Chinese were unable to inflict any great defeat upon them, in the following year we actually find one of the Tibetan chieftains solemnly proclaiming himself "Son of Heaven" or Emperor. This, in itself, was a significant development, for never before had the Tibetans been bold enough even to dream of setting up an independent political organization.

For the next few years, the Tibetans not only managed to maintain their independence but also were able to inflict severe punishment upon the western provinces of China proper. In the year 112, however, their "Emperor" was murdered and the newly founded Tibetan empire rapidly disintegrated. At this point the Chinese instituted a system whereby anyone who was able to assassinate the remaining Tibetan leaders was rewarded not only with a money prize but also with the title of marquis. This discreditable arrangement was so successful that in a short time most of the men capable of organizing and leading the Tibetan hordes were murdered, and by A.D. 116, the Tibetans had completely ceased to be a menace to the Celestial Empire. They were, in fact, fleeing before various Chinese expeditionary armies.[3]

Let us now turn our attention from the western to the northern frontier of China. In this region the first to claim our attention are, of course, the Southern Huns, who up to this time had served as China's chief bulwark against attack on the part of other "barbarians." Even these ancient friends and vassals of the Chinese could not resist the temptation to advance their own interests. In A.D. 109, they were well aware of the collapse of the Chinese dominion in Kashgaria and of the subsequent rebellion on the part of the Tibetans. Moreover, they had learned that the central provinces of China proper were swept by floods, with the result that the inhabitants of this region were rapidly dying of starvation. Here was an opportunity to break away from their position as vassals and defenders of the Celestial Empire. Accordingly, they began a series of raids on their own account. Among the leaders of this rebellion was a Chinese renegade who had entered the service of the Southern Shanyu, and who assured his new master that his fellow Chinese were powerless to resist a Hunnish attack.

Once the Southern Huns had decided upon rebellion, they found it easy to win allies in the enterprise of harrying the Chinese frontier. Many of the Wuhuan tribesmen of Southern Manchuria were equally willing to abandon the ties that bound them to the Son of Heaven, and, in conjunction with, and under the leadership of, the Southern Huns, to attack the Chinese frontier from the Northeast. Even more serious was the fact that one branch of the Sienbi, now the most powerful of the northern nomads, hastened to join the anti-Chinese alliance. During the year 109 practically all the battles which were fought resulted in victory for the barbarians, and in the following year China felt the need of a supreme effort to ward off the danger which threatened the Empire from the North.

Accordingly, some of China's best generals, with a picked body of men, were dispatched into Southern Mongolia, and after several desperate battles, defeated the Hunnish armies. The Southern Shanyu surrendered himself to the Chinese commander, but after he had made solemn and public apology for his misdeeds, he was not only freed, but also was allowed to continue his rulership over his compatriots.[4] Once the Southern Huns had given up the fight, the Wuhuan and the Sienbi lost heart. The leader of the Wuhuan followed the example of the Southern Shanyu and surrendered to the Chinese. This the Sienbi leader refused to do, but at least he led his tribesmen back into Northern Mongolia and desisted from further attacks upon the Chinese frontier.[5]

For the moment China was again triumphant. To add to her joy, the Southern Huns remained for some time truly repentant. They not only desisted from further rebellion but also actually assisted the Chinese in the expedition which the Empire sent against the Tibetans and other rebels.

Once the Kiang and Southern Hunnish revolts had been crushed, the Chinese were free to devote themselves once more to Kashgarian affairs. It was several years, however, before the Celestials again assumed an aggressive role in this region. From A.D. 107 to 119, the Dragon Throne was unable to exercise any influence whatever over the native kingdoms of Kashgaria, and we are especially told that, during this period, the Northern Huns swept down from their new strongholds in Zungaria and reëstablished their supremacy over most of this region, particularly in the northern portion of the Tarim basin.[6]

The renewal of Chinese interests in Kashgaria affairs started in A.D. 119. By this time the Kiang or Tibetan revolt had been crushed and the Chinese were again absolute masters of the western marches. This, in turn, meant that the Chinese were once more in immediate contact with the Northern Huns, and as the latter tribes continued their old sport of raiding the Chinese outposts, the Celestial officials felt called upon to do something by way of reprisal.

With this end in view, early in A.D. 119, a Chinese army marched out to the Northwest and reoccupied the strategic town and district of Hami. The fact that the Celestials were able to carry out this feat with no great difficulty caused quite a flutter among the Kashgarian states, many of which were sorely perplexed by the continued exactions of the Huns and rejoiced at the prospect of being reincorporated within the Chinese Empire. This feeling explains the fact that shortly after the occupation of Hami, the King of Southern Güshï and the King of Shanshan dispatched embassies to China and asked to be accepted as vassals of the Empire. So far so good, but the Chinese forgot that a day of reckoning was due when the Northern Huns got over the surprise of the sudden attack and were able to engage on a counter offensive. This day arrived in the following year (A.D. 120) when the Huns, in conjunction with their allies, the inhabitants of Northern Güshï, marched southward, defeated and killed the Chinese commander at Hami, and shortly thereafter regained control over the Kashgarian kingdoms which had thrown in their lot with China.[7]

A memorial was immediately sent in to the Throne asking that another army be sent out to the West to do battle with the Huns, to avenge the disgrace of the recent defeat and to reëstablish Chinese control over at least the eastern portion of Kashgaria. The matter was discussed at length in the Imperial Council Chamber, and in the end it was decided that the cost of reconquering Kashgaria or even of reoccupying Hami would be prohibitive, and that the best thing to do was merely to strengthen the garrison at the outpost town of Dunhuang and to establish there a high military official whose special duty would be to allow the Huns to continue their control over Kashgaria and to ward off all Hunnish attacks upon the Chinese frontier.

This plan was duly carried out, but it did not prove highly successful. In spite of the special military commander and the increase in the number of outpost garrison troops, the Huns were able to continue their raids and inflict a great damage on the Chinese colonies established near the frontier. By A.D. 123, things had become so bad that drastic action was required. Either these frontier colonies had to be abandoned or else China had to assume the offensive once more and inflict upon the Huns a defeat such as would insure the peace of the frontier.

At this moment the Throne received a memorial proposing that one of three plans of action be adopted. The first of these was the complete abandonment of the western marches; the second was to retain the outpost colonies, and to seek to defend them by establishing a new garrison under a special officer at the town of Liujung in Southern Güshï. The third, and most radical of the plans, was to embark upon another major campaign against the Northern Huns with the objective of crushing their power completely. In elucidating the proposed campaign against the Northern Huns, the memorial ignored the Shanyu or nominal overlord of the Huns and spoke only of the Huyen king whose seat was in Zungaria. This omission is significant, for we know that though the office of Northern Shanyu still existed, centralized authority among the Northern Huns had already greatly weakened and the subordinate "kings" were already assuming the prerogatives of independent sovereigns.

The memorial provoked a lengthy debate in the Grand Council, wherein the merits of the various propositions were duly examined. When the advocates of the defensive and offensive plans had had their say, it was eventually decided to adopt the second or compromise plan which was half offensive and half defensive. Liujung, in Southern Güshï, was to be reoccupied and placed in charge of a special Resident (Changshï) who was to be supported by a garrison of five hundred men. The chief duty of the Resident was to ward off Hunnish attacks on the Chinese frontier, but, in addition, he was to have charge of any diplomatic negotiations which it might be necessary to undertake with the native kingdoms of Kashgaria.

The establishment of the post of Resident might not have been of any great significance had it not been that the man chosen to fill the position was Ban Yung, a son of the great Ban Chao and an officer who had inherited much of his father's genius. Like his father, Ban Yung made the most of every opportunity and had very few scruples about departing from the letter of the instructions sent him from the imperial throne.[8]

He succeeded in establishing himself in the fortress of Liujung without great difficulty. Once this task was accomplished he was expected to play a passive role, and merely seek to ward off future Hunnish attacks. Such a course of action, however, was contrary to the restless and energetic character of the Bans. Though Ban Yung held possession of this solitary fortress in Southern Güshï, the major portion of the kingdom was still occupied by Hunnish troops and the king himself remained loyal to the Hunnish cause.

Without waiting for the Huns to assume the offensive, Ban Yung, immediately after his appointment (A.D. 123), got together an army of ten thousand soldiers, mostly native auxiliaries from the surrounding regions, and marched against the combined army of the Huns and Southern Güshï. In the battle which ensued the Chinese won an overwhelming victory. The Huns were driven North of the Celestial Mountains, and five thousand Güshï soldiers were captured. Following this victory Southern Güshï broke away from its allegiance to the Huns and once more submitted itself to Chinese jurisdiction. In this same year the Kings of Shanshan and Kucha, together with several lesser princelings, voluntarily renewed their allegiance to the Celestial Empire, so that China was once more overlord of all of Eastern and much of Northern Kashgaria.

Having achieved this notable success Ban Yung might well have been content to rest upon his laurels, especially as he had accomplished far more than expected of him. But, remembering his father's exploits, he decided to go still further. Completely ignoring the fact that the imperial council had vetoed the plan of attacking the Northern Huns in their own headquarters North of the Tien Shan, Ban Yung, in the following year (A.D. 125), decided to move an army into this region.

His first objective, however, was not the Huns proper, but their allies, the inhabitants of the Kingdom of Northern Güshï which lay just to the North of the Celestial Mountains, as the defeat of this kingdom would greatly cripple the Hunnish power. In this campaign the Chinese were again successful. Eight thousand men were killed or captured, and among the prisoners was the king himself and a high Hunnish official. The lives of most of the prisoners were spared but the king and the Hunnish nobleman were taken to the spot where the Chinese general had been killed six years earlier (*see* p. 296) and there executed, after which their heads were sent back to the Chinese capital for public exhibition.

As was usual in such cases, the Kingdom of Northern Güshï, though conquered, was allowed to maintain its separate existence, and one of the native princes who promised to be devoted to the Chinese cause was placed on the throne. Ban Yung, however, wished to be quite certain that this state did not again lapse from its allegiance to the Celestial Empire and rejoin the Huns. With this end in view he insisted that the Güshïn troops join him in the following year (A.D. 126) in an attack upon the Huyen King, the leading Hunnish potentate in Eastern Zungaria.

As the result of this attack the Huyen King was defeated and forced to flee for his life, the Chinese capturing much booty and thousands of prisoners. Among these prisoners was a nephew of the Shanyu, the supreme overlord of all the Northern Huns. Ban Yung was not especially bloodthirsty, but he insisted that this prince be executed by the new King of Northern Güshï in person. Ban Yung's idea behind this action was that thereafter there would exist a personal animosity between the Lord of the Huns and the Güshïn monarch, which would prevent these two potentates from again coming together in a common attack upon China.

The execution of the Hunnish prince worked out exactly as Ban Yung hoped and expected. The Shanyu of the Northern Huns was so furious at the killing of his nephew that shortly afterwards he led, in person, an attack upon the territory of Northern Güshï with the intention of wreaking vengeance upon its monarch. With the aid of Chinese troops this attack was repulsed, but it was realized that the Huns were merely biding their time before again seeking revenge, and as a result the king and the inhabitants of Northern Güshï were drawn ever closer to the Chinese Empire as their one source of aid in case of renewed attack.

The defeat of the Northern Huns and the reincorporation of Northern Güshï within the boundary of the Celestial Empire added enormously to Ban Yung's prestige throughout the whole of Central Asia, but before his triumph could be complete it was necessary to attack and conquer the Kingdom of Karashahr, which was the one portion of Kashgaria which was still belligerent and adamant in refusing to admit Chinese supremacy. The campaign against this region took place in A.D. 127. Unfortunately, before embarking upon this campaign, Ban Yung felt it necessary to apply for permission from the Imperial Court. In view of his past successes, this permission was readily granted. In fact the government sent out reinforcements under the command of a prominent general to aid Ban Yung on his expedition.

As luck would have it, the presence of this other general led to much trouble and confusion. It was arranged that Ban Yung with his troops should march by a southern route to Karashahr, while the new general with his troops should march by the northern route, though it was distinctly understood that no attack should be made until the two divisions had effected a union.

It so happened that the new general arrived on the scene several days before Ban Yung could bring his forces up, but instead of waiting for the arrival of the main army, as he was ordered to do, the general decided to make an attack immediately. The reason for this, as we are told, is that the general in question was temporarily out of favor with some of the high officials in his native land, and wished to restore his prestige through the glory of having captured Karashahr single-handed. The fortunes of war were in his favor, and though in the battle which followed no decisive victory was achieved, the King of Karashahr was so impressed by the damage done by what after all was only an advance guard, that he decided to surrender before the main army could arrive, when his chances of securing a favorable treaty would be much slighter.

The surrender of Karashahr meant that for the moment all resistance to the Chinese authority throughout Kashgaria was at an end. Shortly thereafter Khutan and Yarkand voluntarily submitted themselves to Chinese jurisdiction, and their example was soon followed by Kashgar. The year A.D. 127, therefore, marks the reëstablishment of Chinese supremacy over all parts of the Tarim basin, and yet the events of that year also prevented the Chinese from taking full advantage of the reestablishment of their colonial empire. The reason for the latter situation was that the Imperial Court gave all the honor and glory to the insubordinate general who had attacked Karashahr single-handed, while poor Ban Yung was recalled to China and demoted from office because of his delay in arriving on the scene of action.[9]

The reëstablishment of Chinese control over Kashgaria was almost entirely due to Ban Yung's diplomatic and military skill, and once he was removed from the scene no one could be found capable of really carrying on his work. Many no doubt hoped that some other member of the illustrious Ban family could be found to take the place of Ban Chao and Ban Yung, but three years later (A.D. 130) most of the surviving members of the Ban family were either killed or disgraced because of a rather curious scandal in the Imperial Court.

The nephew of Ban Yung had married a princess of the imperial line, and a close relative of the reigning emperor. This lady turned out to be a very lively person who insisted upon having one love affair after another. At first the poor husband thought that there was nothing he could do about the situation. Taking advantage of this meekness, the good lady on one occasion insisted that her husband remain in the room while she was in the arms of one of her lovers. This was too much for the outraged husband, who seized a sword and slew the amorous princess. In ordinary circumstances the slaying of an unfaithful wife would have caused little or no comment, but in this particular instance, as the husband was a commoner and the wife a member of the imperial family, a great to-do was made over the matter. The poor husband was disemboweled, and all of his immediate relatives were publicly executed. So exits the Ban family from history.[10]

As we have already remarked, with the disappearance of the Ban clan from the imperial service, there began a long period of stagnation in the newly recovered colonial empire. To be sure, the prestige ensuing from Ban Yung's exploits was so great that for several decades there was no open revolt against Chinese supremacy, and in consequence China, during this period, was able to maintain the status quo in the western regions. In A.D. 131 she strengthened and increased her military colony in Hami in order to facilitate communications with the West, and two years later (A.D. 133) with the aid of the King of Kashgar the Chinese were able to punish the monarch of Khutan who showed signs of becoming obstreperous, but these were the only signs of colonial activity which the Celestial Empire was able to manifest.

It is highly significant that the Chinese ranking officer in Kashgaria continued to be known by the simple title of Resident, and that no attempt was made to restore the old more imposing office of Protector General. It is also significant that this Resident continued to reside in Liujung in Southern Güshï, quite close to the Chinese frontier, instead of transferring his capital to Kucha or Kashgar where he could better superintend the activities of the various native kingdoms which were under his jurisdiction. It is also of interest to note that the Chinese records expressly state that during this period the Celestial officials made no attempt to exercise any sort of supremacy over the Wusun (in Western Zungaria) or over the various kingdoms west of the Pamirs. This, too, was in marked contrast to the earlier epochs of the colonial empire when both the Wusun and several of the states in Turkistan had felt the weight of the imperial commands.

In fact, all the Chinese Resident could do was to keep the Northern Huns at bay and prevent them from reoccupying the Tarim basin. Several battles were fought between the Huns and the Chinese with no great honor or glory won by either side. In A.D. 134, for example, Northern Güshï was able to inflict a signal defeat upon the Hunnish forces, but in the following year (A.D. 135) the Huns returned to the fray, and though Güshï was aided by a large detachment of Chinese troops, she suffered a bloody defeat. The fact that the Huns did not follow up this victory and allowed the frontier to remain unmolested for several years thereafter was due more to their own weakness and internal troubles than to any manifestation of strength on the part of China.

Things drifted in this way for another two decades but after A.D. 150, China began to show even greater symptoms of weakness and of inability to control the native states that were nominally subject to her jurisdiction. In 151 the Northern Huns again made a raid on the frontier and it was all the Chinese could do to prevent the strategic post of Hami from falling into their hands. In the following year the inhabitants of Khutan, in Southern Kashgaria, attacked and killed the Chinese Resident visiting this kingdom because he attempted to interfere too much in its internal affairs. In due time the inhabitants of Khutan apologized to the Imperial Court for this incident, but it is significant that China felt forced to accept this rather vague and meaningless apology and was unable to secure real punishment for the death of her official representative.

In A.D. 153 trouble arose between the Chinese officials and the then reigning king of Northern Güshï; the matter was considered of the greatest importance because of the proximity of this kingdom to the Northern Huns. When the trouble eventually developed into open warfare between the Chinese and the vassal monarch, the Celestial officials immediately rushed troops into the disaffected area. Shortly after this they declared the rebellious king deposed and appointed another princeling to fill his place.

No sooner had this been done, however, than the deposed monarch fled to the Northern Huns and asked for their assistance in regaining his kingdom. The Huns were only too delighted to have a finger in the dispute and before long a Hunnish army appeared on the Güshïn frontier. This situation brought consternation to the hearts of the responsible Chinese officials, who feared that another revival of the Hunnish Kingdom was in the offing.

Instead of offering battle, they had recourse to diplomacy. They managed to establish secret contacts with the deposed king and promised to restore him to his throne and forgive him for all of his previous misdeeds if he would forswear the Hunnish alliance and again promise allegiance to the Celestial Empire. For some reason or other the deposed monarch accepted these terms and before long his kingdom was restored to him without further ado.

From the attitude assumed by the Chinese officials on this occasion it would seem that as late as A.D. 153 the Northern Hunnish Empire still constituted a formidable political entity. To a contemporary observer it no doubt appeared that this empire, which in one form or another had lasted for over three hundred and fifty years, was still destined to have an indefinite span of life. In fact the continued weakness and degeneration evident in all parts of China must have rendered perfectly plausible the belief that before long these Huns would again be able to wrest from China most of her colonial possessions.[11]

As things turned out, however, it was soon seen that this Northern Hunnish Empire had at last come to the end of its tether. In fact, the aid the Northern Huns gave to the deposed monarch of Güshï is the last mention that is made of their existence in the Chinese annals. Within a decade after this date the Northern Hunnish Empire was annihilated and its members scattered over the vast plains of Turkistan. For us to understand how this important event took place it is necessary for us to turn our attention back to Mongolia and trace the political developments which took place in this region.

The first group to merit our attention are, of course, the Southern Huns. All during the period the Chinese were slowly regaining control over Kashgaria, the Southern Huns remained, at least in name, vassals of the Celestial Empire. In spite of this nominal vassalage, however, the Chinese officials were never able to resecure their former unquestioned supremacy over all the Southern Hunnish tribal divisions. The Shanyus, to be sure, and most of the other members of the Southern Hunnish royal family, remained loyal to the Chinese cause, but many of the leading members of the Southern Hunnish aristocracy became dissatisfied with Chinese overlordship and broke out into open rebellion, even though these rebellions meant waging war against their own legitimate rulers whom they regarded as mere puppets in the hands of the Chinese bureaucracy.

Lack of space forbids an account of all these internal conflicts. Suffice it to say that in A.D. 124 one of these rebellions broke out which could only be crushed with the aid of a formidable Chinese army. In A.D. 140, a similar rebellion took place, this time on a far larger scale. Although the Shanyu himself was in no way involved in the rebellion, the Chinese officials reprimanded him severely for his inability to maintain order within the Southern Hunnish domain, and the poor Shanyu and his brother, the heir apparent, were so humiliated by this reproof that they committed suicide.

The sudden death of the Shanyu and his heir only added to the confusion. For the next three years there was not even the pretence of a stable central government among the Southern Huns. The rebels set up a pretender to the throne and in the meantime continued to ravage the Chinese frontier. Encouraged by the success of these raids, the rebel Huns were again joined by many of the Wuhuan tribesmen living further to the East, and before long the whole northern frontier was aflame. The Chinese again were forced to undertake major campaigns. It was not until three years later (A.D. 143), that the rebel leaders were killed or defeated, and the Chinese able to install as Shanyu of the Southern Huns a princeling who had long served as hostage in the Chinese capital, and who was thoroughly Chinese in his ideas and sympathies.

In order to increase the prestige of the new Shanyu among his own people (and thereby prevent further rebellions) the Chinese treated their puppet with marked consideration, and presents of enormous value were given to him, his spouse, and other members of his court. Largely as the result of this policy, peace and order were restored among the Southern Huns, and for several years thereafter we hear of no untoward events; but in A.D. 153, and again in A.D. 158, rebellion broke out once more. Again the rebels were supported by many of the Wuhuan tribesmen, and again the Chinese had to send a large army under one of their best generals. The Chinese general, after suppressing the rebellion, deposed the then reigning Shanyu as a punishment for the latter's inability to keep his subjects in order, but the Emperor of China disapproved of this act and before long the deposed monarch was restored to the throne of his ancestors.[12]

During all this period of alternate revolt and submission (A.D. 109-160), the Wuhuan served merely as friends and allies of the rebel Southern Huns, so that it is unnecessary to accord them special consideration. It is far different with the Sienbi, the northern neighbors of the Southern Hun and the Wuhuan, for during this period the Sienbi became an all important factor in Far Eastern politics. Up to the period of the general rebellion in A.D. 109, the various Sienbi tribes had been willing, for the most part, to admit the nominal overlordship of the Celestial Emperors. After their rebellion this felicitous state of affairs no longer existed. In the year 110, to be sure, the Sienbi, who had taken an active part in the attacks on China, were forced to withdraw into Northern Mongolia, but the Chinese generals were unwilling and unable to pursue the retreating enemy into this region, and for several years there was almost no contact between the Chinese and this powerful group of Northern Barbarians. China was free from their attack, but was unable to exert any influence over her former vassals.

Beginning in the year 115, the Sienbi renewed the offensive and in the Chinese chronicles of this year and the following five years (115-119) mention is made of frequent Sienbi raids on various parts of the northeastern frontier. These raids never took on the quality of organized warfare between two distinct states, for the Sienbi continued to be broken up into a large number of rival and often conflicting tribes.[13] In A.D. 121, however, a marked transformation took place among the turbulent Sienbi. One of their tribal leaders named Kijgien, after a brief flirtation with the Celestial Empire, became the chief instigator of the attacks upon China. More to the point, he soon showed himself to be a genius at organization, and it appears that he managed to bring a large number of the Sienbi tribes to acknowledge his supremacy and to obey his orders. In one sense we may say that the history of the Sienbi as an organized or at least semi-organized state begins with this petty Chieftain.

Backed by a great number, if not the majority, of the Sienbi tribes, Kijïgien began a series of raids upon the Chinese outposts, and these raids continued for more than a decade. It was fortunate for China that during most of this period she could count upon the bulk of the Southern Huns and the Wuhuan to act as a cushion for these attacks. For the Sienbi to establish direct contacts with China, it was necessary to pass through the territory of one or the other of these buffer peoples. Moreover, the Huns and the Wuhuan frequently aided the Chinese troops in counter-attacks upon the Sienbi. Had it not been for the aid lent by these two more or less unwilling subjects, the Sienbi might have become a serious menace to the very existence of China. As it was, they were never more than a source of irritation to the Chinese communities living on or near the frontier. In A.D. 133, "King" Kijïgien died, and the powerful political organization which he had built up rapidly disintegrated. The individual tribes once more began to act as separate units with the result that for the next two decades the Sienbi raids upon China practically ceased, and such as occurred were rapidly warded off.[14]

Approximately two decades later (shortly after A.D. 150), the Sienbi again became united under a great leader, named Tanshïhuai. In fact, Tanshïhuai was an even greater personage than was his predecessor. As is the case with many other famous nomadic leaders, very little is known about Tanshïhuai's origin, and the absence of exact information has allowed many legends to arise. According to the Sienbi traditions one of their petty chieftains was away in the West fighting the Northern Huns for over three years, and when he returned to his home he found that his wife had just given birth to a boy who was no other than Tanshïhuai. The mother assured her husband that the child's conception had been miraculous, but the chieftain had his own suspicions as to what had occurred and ordered the child to be killed. The mother managed to spirit the child away and he was secretly brought up by an old family retainer.

The boy turned out to be very precocious and at an early age distinguished himself for his daring and sagacity. When only fourteen or fifteen years of age, he led an expedition against a neighboring clan and recovered some cattle that had been lost in a recent raid. Thereafter his rise to name and fame was very rapid, and before long we find him the acknowledged leader of a large number of the Sienbi clans. He became known for the impartiality of the justice he meted out to his subordinates, which, in addition to the brilliancy of his military exploits, helped in bringing the vast majority of the Sienbi tribesmen under his banner. Before many years had elapsed he was far more than a tribal leader; he had founded a vast kingdom and was its undisputed monarch.

The rise of Tanshïhuai to power naturally brought him into conflict with the Chinese Empire. We first hear of his raiding the northern frontier of China in A.D. 156. Thereafter his raids were frequent and scarcely a year passed without his inflicting some damage on the Celestial outposts. The Emperor sent some of his best generals and many of his ablest troops to chastise the Sienbi upstart, but after they had failed to secure any noteworthy results, the Chinese tried to gain relief from these attacks by diplomatic means.

In A.D. 166 (ten years after Tanshïhuai is first heard of) an embassy was dispatched from the imperial court to the capital of the Sienbi in Mongolia offering to recognize the barbarian's claim to the title of king and proposing a treaty of peace. Tanshïhuai proudly rejected the patent and seal of kingship offered him by the Chinese on the ground that he had gained the throne by his own efforts and was in no need of Chinese assistance or recognition. He also rejected the proposal to sign a treaty of peace and amity. It so happened that the task of organizing and administering his new empire took up most of the new ruler's time so that his raids upon China became somewhat less frequent. They did not cease, however, and as a result the whole northern frontier of China was in a disturbed condition, and the Southern Huns and the Wuhuan vassals of the Celestial Empire also suffered from the perpetual fear of attack.

In A.D. 177, the Chinese made another desperate effort to destroy the new colossus of the North. In this year an army of thirty thousand soldiers, some of them native Chinese, some recruited from the Southern

Huns, was dispatched to do battle with the Sienbi, and succeeded in penetrating some five or six hundred miles beyond the Chinese frontier. Soon afterwards, however, they were met and overwhelmingly defeated by Tanshïhuai's troops. The remnants of the Chinese army fled ignominiously back to China, but less than a fourth of the original number succeeded in reaching the frontier in safety. Thereafter China was content to remain on the defensive, and did not dare attempt another invasion of Sienbi territory as long as Tanshïhuai was alive.

The wars waged by Tanshïhuai against the Chinese Empire are of some interest to us, but far more important are the great changes he effected in the political geography of Central Asia. At the time of his rise to power the various scattered Sienbi tribes were already in control of most of Northern Mongolia, so that the establishment of the new kingdom simply meant that all these separate tribes were united under a single jurisdiction. But this was only the beginning. Tanshïhuai next attacked and defeated the Dingling in Southern Siberia and brought them under his dominion. To the East he attacked the state of Fuyu in Eastern Manchuria, thereby bringing most of the Tungusic inhabitants of this region within the limits of the Sienbi Kingdom.

Last but not least, he directed several attacks against the countries lying in the West. It is expressly stated that he conquered and occupied all the territory formerly in the possession of the Huns. This can refer not merely to Mongolia, which had long since been in Sienbi hands, but implies that Tanshïhuai and his troops drove the Huns out of their new situation in Zungaria as well. Any doubt on this matter is removed by the statement that the Sienbi at this time also attacked and defeated the Wusun who occupied Southwestern Zungaria and who could not have been reached until the Huns had been pushed out of the way. Considering the fact that Tanshïhuai was able to occupy Zungaria with so little difficulty, it is rather surprising that he did not sweep southward and attack Kashgaria, where Chinese jurisdiction was rapidly falling into decay, but after all the Sienbi monarch had a comparatively short reign and did not have time for everything.

We are told of one further exploit on the part of Tanshïhuai which is of especial ethnological interest. His kingdom became so populous that he had difficulty in securing sufficient food for all of his subjects. In view of this situation the king thought of securing a new type of food supply. Neither the Huns nor the Sienbi had ever gone in for the eating of fish, with the result that the streams and lakes of Mongolia had long remained unexploited and Tanshïhuai thought that it was time to remedy this situation. He was informed that the Japanese, many of whom then inhabited the coasts of Korea, were especially noted as fishermen. Shortly after receiving this information he undertook an invasion of Korea, not with the idea of permanently occupying this region but merely in order to capture some of the Japanese fishermen concerning whose skill he had heard so much.

As the result of this expedition Tanshïhuai managed to lay hands on a thousand Japanese families, and these were forced to transplant themselves and settle near one of the lakes in Eastern Mongolia, and there start the industry of fish-catching. We are told that this forcible colonization was very successful, and that the inhabitants of Mongolia secured a plentiful addition to their ordinary food supply. It would further appear that these Japanese colonists remained a separate and well-known ethnic group for several centuries before being gradually absorbed by the surrounding population.

The story of this exploit on the part of Tanshïhuai is of special interest to us, as this is one of the first literary notices concerning the very existence of the Japanese. Real Japanese history does not begin until the seventh century A.D., many hundreds of years after this event. Prior to the seventh century the Japanese are known only by brief casual references in the Chinese annals, none of which are earlier than the reign of Tanshïhuai. It is, therefore, interesting that as early as the second century A.D. many Japanese were known to inhabit the coast of Korea. In the light of recent events it is also somewhat amusing to note that the Japanese colonization of Manchuria and Eastern Mongolia began nearly two thousand years ago, even though this colonization was entirely involuntary.

In many ways Tanshïhuai deserves to be considered one of the really important persons in history, and it is rather unfortunate that he has remained so unknown to the general public. Had he lived a few years longer it is quite possible that he might have effected the conquest of China, and thereby altered the whole tenor of Far Eastern history. As it was, he died somewhere about A.D. 180, only a year or two after the overwhelming defeat of the Chinese army which had been sent against him, and when he was still only forty-five years of age.[15]

His son turned out to be a weakling, unable even to hold his own tribesmen together, so that within a few years the gigantic empire which Tanshïhuai had built up fell to pieces. The rapid disintegration of this empire meant that China, weak and decadent as she was, was preserved from foreign invasion for over a century. But at least the rise of Tanshïhuai's brief empire had one permanent effect upon world history. The Hunnish Empire as an organized unit was forever destroyed. The Sienbi tribesmen for several centuries thereafter remained masters of Outer Mongolia, the old homeland of the Huns. More important still, the Hunnish state in Zungaria was broken up, and the Hunnish tribesmen in small disorganized groups were forced to move still further to the West, and though the descendants of the Huns continued to play a role in history for several centuries thereafter, the Hunnish Empire as a separate political unit disappeared once and for all.

Book Four

THE LATER HUNNISH KINGDOMS

CHAPTER FOURTEEN

THE HUNS IN CHINA—THE FIRST PHASE

Disintegration of the Southern Hunnish Kingdom—The Huns Take Refuge in China—Their Occasional Rebellions—Rise of the Hunnish Leader Liu Yuan—Liu Yuan Becomes King of Han—He Is Later Proclaimed Emperor of China—Accession of Liu Tsung—Capture of Loyang—Events at the Hunnish Court—Capture of Changan—Death of Liu Tsung—End of the First Hunnish Dynasty.

WE HAVE completed our survey of the rise and fall of the first and second Hunnish Empires, but before our task can be said to be completed it will be necessary for us to give a brief description of the later fortunes of the various scattered Hunnish peoples who continued to exist as separate units for several centuries after the parent Empire had been completely broken up. This task is rendered all the more necessary by the fact that, by a curious paradox of history, these later Hunnish tribesmen accomplished many of the things that the rulers of the mighty Hunnish Empire had long and unsuccessfully struggled for. In fact, the later broken Huns did more to reshape the whole history of the world than did their ancestors, the founders of the great unified Hunnish Empire.

As long as the Hunnish Empire existed, its rulers persisted in their efforts to conquer China and establish themselves as rulers of the Celestial Empire. In these efforts they were always unsuccessful, but the task in which they failed was carried out by the poor weak survivors of the Southern Hunnish Kingdom. The leaders of these Southern Huns managed to take the capital of the Chinese Empire by storm and no less than two of the Celestial Emperors were captured (and later killed). More important still, these Hunnish tribal leaders were able to set themselves up as Chinese Emperors, and their rule was acknowledged for nearly half a century by a large majority of the native Chinese.

Equal fame awaited the scattered Hunnish tribesmen who migrated to the West after the final breakup of the Northern Hunnish Empire. The power and prestige of this Empire had extended all through Turkistan and it is probable that at one time Hunnish influence extended as far as the Volga, the frontier between Asia and Europe. Beyond this point, however, the mightiest of the Hunnish emperors was completely impotent. The later Hunnish tribal leaders, however, succeeded where their ancestors had failed, for these later leaders burst through the line of the Volga, swept over large portions of Northern and Eastern Europe and reduced to vassalage the great majority of the Slavic and Germanic peoples. More important still, the pressure which these Huns placed upon the Visigoths and Vandals resulted in the invasion and the final downfall of the mighty West Roman Empire.

Last, but not least, mention must be made of the Ephthalites or White Huns who invaded Iran and the other countries in the Middle East. In ancient times the rise of the Hunnish Empire had profoundly affected the historic development of Persia and India, but Hunnish influence in this region had been almost entirely indirect. The White Huns, however, changed this indirect into direct influence. These White Huns, after securing domination over the whole of Southern Turkistan, dealt a staggering blow to the great national monarchies which then existed in Persia and in India. Both of these countries eventually succeeded in checking the further advance of these Northern Barbarians, but for over a century these aberrant descendants of the Huns succeeded in remaining masters over large portions of Northeastern Iran and Northwestern India. In view of the importance of these later events it is imperative that we devote a few words to each one of these three Hunnish groups, whom we may now characterize as the Eastern, the Western and the Southern groups.

The groups of tribes which we now lump together as comprising the Eastern Group were, of course, the descendants of the inhabitants of the old Southern Hunnish Kingdom. It will be remembered that this Southern Hunnish Kingdom, which controlled most of Southern or Inner Mongolia from its inception in A.D. 48, was always a state in vassalage to China, although its inhabitants frequently became restive when the Chinese officials attempted to interfere too much in internal affairs. For a century after its foundation the Shanyus or rulers of the Southern Hunnish Kingdom persisted in the hope that sooner or later they would be able to resecure control over Northern or Outer Mongolia, which was still dominated by their cousins and rivals, the rulers of the Northern Hunnish Empire. Eventually, as we know, these Northern Huns were driven out of Northern Mongolia, and forced to take refuge in the plains of Zungaria and Northern Turkistan, but this change resulted in little advantage to the Southern Huns, as the place of the Northern Huns was taken by the even more formidable Sienbi tribesmen.

With the establishment of the great Sienbi Empire under Tanshïhuai in the middle of the second century A.D., any hopes which the Southern Huns may still have entertained regarding the reconquest of Mongolia and other portions of Central Asia were forever shattered. In A.D. 177 the Southern Huns, in conjunction with the Chinese, made a joint attack upon the Sienbi and were overwhelmingly defeated, and, had the Sienbi empire not fallen to pieces a few years later, it is probable that the Southern Hunnish Kingdom would have been conquered and absorbed by their northern neighbors. As it was, the Southern Huns succeeded in maintaining their independence, but this was the most that they could accomplish, and after A.D. 177 the Hunnish Kingdom underwent a process of slow but sure decay and disintegration. This process was accelerated by the frequent disputes which took place between the Southern Huns and their overlords, the Chinese.

In A.D. 179 the Chinese official in charge of Hunnish affairs killed the reigning Shanyu and placed another Hunnish princeling upon the throne. This monarch was never popular with his subjects, owing to his close connections with China, and nine years later (A.D. 188) when he obeyed a command from his Chinese overlords and led an army southward in an attempt to put down a revolution which had broken out in China proper, these Hunnish subjects became so exasperated that they rose in rebellion and slew their ruler.

This act really marked the end of the Southern Hunnish Kingdom. Nominally the slain Shanyu was succeeded by one of his sons, and on the death of the latter (A.D. 195) he was succeeded by a younger brother, who in turn ruled for another nine years. But these last two Shanyus were never much more than pretenders to the throne. The bulk of the Hunnish tribesmen were so disgusted with the subservience of their ruling family to the whims of the Chinese Emperors, that they refused to obey any of the orders issued by the latter, or even to permit their nominal Shanyus to reside among them.

In consequence of this situation the last two Shanyus resided on the northern frontier of China, where they were sure of Chinese support, and were never able to reëstablish themselves in their native Mongolia. A small number of Huns rallied around their rulers and continued to reside near them even during this period of exile, but the great bulk of the Hunnish tribesmen continued to reside in Southern Mongolia. Since the latter were unable to agree upon the selection of a new ruler, local government rested in the hands of a council of elders.

This peculiar situation came to an end in A.D. 216, when the last Shanyu came to the Chinese capital to arrange a settlement of the disputes which had broken out between the Chinese and the small group of Huns who still remained loyal to his cause. Instead of being hospitably received, however, the poor Shanyu was made a prisoner of state, and shortly thereafter the office of Southern Shanyu was officially abolished. Another Hunnish princeling was indeed sent to the North to act as a sort of Viceroy over these Huns who were willing to acknowledge Chinese overlordship, but the Southern Hunnish Kingdom was definitely broken up and its inhabitants, or at least those who submitted themselves to Chinese rule, were broken up into five tribal units, each one of which was ruled over by its own petty chieftain.[1] The Southern Hunnish Kingdom thus came to an end in A.D. 216 but its parent state, the glorious Han Empire, came to an end only four years later (A.D. 220) when the last member of the Later Han dynasty was deposed.

All through their long histories there was a curious coincidence between the history of the Han Empire in the South and the Hunnish Empire in the North. The first Hunnish Empire arose about 209 B.C. almost simultaneously with the establishment of the Early Han dynasty (206 B.C.). Both the Hunnish and the Early Han empires met with disaster about two centuries later, the Huns losing their independence in 51 B.C., and the Early Han dynasty being deposed in A.D. 9 by the usurper Wang Mang. Both the Huns and the Hans managed to survive these disasters and recover much of their ancient glory, the Huns recovering their independence and establishing what we have called the second Hunnish Empire in A.D. 13, while the Later or Eastern Han dynasty was established a dozen years later (A.D. 25). Finally, as we have noted, the Southern Hunnish Kingdom, the last survivor of Hunnish might, and the Later Han dynasty were extinguished within five years of one another.

For forty-five years after the fall of the Later Han dynasty (A.D. 220-265) the Celestial Empire was broken up into three separate and rival kingdoms. While suffering from internal troubles it was obviously impossible for China to become involved in any great imperialistic schemes and most of her already shadowy claims to suzerainty over the peoples of Central Asia had to be completely abandoned. Nevertheless, China remained relatively free from barbarian attack. China's chief potential enemies continued to lie along the northern frontier, and practically all of Northern China formed part of the Kingdom of Wei, which was by far the largest and most powerful of the three constituent states into which the Celestial Empire was now divided. Wei, moreover, was possessed of a magnificent army, for which reason neither the Huns nor any of their barbarous neighbors made any serious attempt to invade China proper during this period of divided sovereignty.

In fact, during this period the scattered Hunnish tribes were far from being able to recover any of their strength, and became more and more dependent upon the goodwill of the Chinese administrative officials. Continued pressure on the part of the Sienbi tribes meant that the Hunnish tribesmen who continued to reside in Southern Mongolia gradually lost all control over this region. Slowly but surely the Sienbis under the leadership of the powerful Toba clan spread southward, and at last succeeded in annexing most of the territory which had once formed part of the old Southern Hunnish Kingdom.

Many of the Hunnish tribesmen were, no doubt, incorporated within the Sienbi confederacy and were eventually completely absorbed by the new masters of their ancient homeland. Many others, however, preferred to migrate southward and take refuge in the northern frontier lands of China, thus adding enormously to the number of Huns already resident within the borders of China proper. A large portion of these Hunnish immigrants joined one or another of the existing five tribal units into which the Hunnish residents of China were divided. Others we know continued to form small separate units scattered here and there in the hilly districts which lay between China and Southern Mongolia.

The rulers of the Kingdom of Wei seem to have accorded a warm welcome to these Hunnish immigrants from the North, no doubt on the ground that these newcomers would be of use in fighting the Sienbi and other barbarians in case the latter ever meditated an invasion of the fertile fields of Northern China. For many decades these Hunnish tribesmen justified the confidence which was placed in them. Though they maintained their own mode of life and their own tribal organizations, they caused little or no trouble to the Chinese administrative hierarchy but remained loyal and submissive subjects of their new fatherland. In A.D. 251 in view of the growth in numbers of the Hunnish tribesmen inhabiting China, it was found advisable to reform their tribal organization and impose stricter Chinese control, but this task was accomplished without encountering any great difficulty or opposition. To contemporary observers it seemed as if any revolution on the part of these Hunnish inhabitants of China was out of the question.[2]

A few years later, however, in A.D. 265 to be exact, the internal affairs of China underwent another great transformation. The Wei dynasty which had ruled over Northern China was succeeded on the throne by the Dsin dynasty. Before very long the rulers of this new dynasty succeeded in bringing within their domain all other portions of China proper. The period of the "three Kingdoms" was thereby ended and the whole of the Celestial Empire was again subjected to a single Son of Heaven.

The reëstablishment of political unity, within China proper, should no doubt have resulted in the increase of China's prestige abroad, and also should have made it easier for her rulers to hold in complete subjection the alien elements within her borders, such for example as the various Hunnish tribal units. In point of fact, however, this was not the case. The reëstablishment of this political unity had put such a strain upon China's administrative and military machinery that the Celestial

Empire seemed to be weakened rather than strengthened, once the long sought for result had been accomplished. The Dsin dynasty was possessed of several able rulers, but at no time was their Empire anything more than a feeble imitation of the Empire which had existed at the time of the glorious Han dynasty.

When this fact is borne in mind it is not surprising to find that this Dsin dynasty began to suffer from the barbarian tribes, both without and within the limits of their Empire, shortly after it secured possession of the Dragon Throne. From the very first various Hunnish chieftains were among those who proved the most vexatious. In 271, shortly after the establishment of the Dsin dynasty, we find one Hunnish chieftain rising in rebellion. A few years later (A.D. 296) we find another Hunnish chieftain causing trouble along the northwestern frontier. Neither of these rebellions turned out to be very serious. In the first flush of their political reunion the Chinese rallied around the throne of their new dynasty and the Hunnish rebels were soon suppressed, but these two unsuccessful insurrections were only a foreshadowing of far more serious rebellions which were to follow.[3]

Beginning in A.D. 300, the various members of the Chinese Imperial family began to squabble among themselves. These squabbles soon led to civil war, in the course of which we find various brothers and cousins of the reigning Emperor (the second of his line) raising huge armies and waging desperate battles with one another. These family wars naturally resulted in a great weakening of the central authority, and it was not long before the Hunnish inhabitants of Northern China decided to take advantage of the ever increasing disorder and carve out a new kingdom for themselves.

The leader of the new Hunnish movement was a very able and active tribal leader by the name of Liu Yüan. The very name of this person is an interesting example of the great change which had come over the Huns since their entrance upon Chinese soil. As long as the Huns continued to reside in Mongolia, they had never felt the need of adopting family names, but after taking up residence in China the Hunnish aristocracy had found it advisable to follow Chinese precedent in this regard, and each person had adopted some more or less appropriate family and personal name, both of which were completely Chinese in origin, and gave little or no evidence of their Hunnish background.

Most of the Hunnish leaders who were descended from the ancient Hunnish Shanyus adopted the family name of Liu, the same name which had been borne by the members of the Han dynasty, largely on the ground that the numerous marriages which had taken place between the Shanyus and princesses from the Imperial family of the House of Han meant that the Hunnish princelings were descendants of the Han Emperors, at least on the distaff side. Still more to the point, with the assumption of the imperial family name of Liu, the Hunnish princelings began to regard themselves as the legitimate heirs of all the Han claims to rightful sovereignty over China, and even spoke of the members of the subsequent dynasties as designing interlopers, whose chief purpose it was to prevent the clan of Liu from coming into their own.

Among the Hunish princelings who had adopted the family name of Liu, the most able and eminent was undoubtedly Liu Yüan. Descended in the direct line from the Shanyus of the ancient Hunnish Empire, his birth alone gave him a preëminent position among the Hunnish inhabitants of China. In addition he was possessed of a brain of more than ordinary capacity and had enjoyed the benefits of a sound education. As a boy he had served for years as a hostage at the Imperial Court of China. In former times numerous Hunnish princes had served in a similar capacity without becoming imbued with the principles of Chinese civilization. But Liu Yüan differed radically from his predecessors in this respect, and as the result of his residence among the Chinese diplomats and scholars, the young prince became noted for his knowledge of Chinese literature and history. This in itself was another indication of the great transformation which the Huns had undergone in the course of the last century. Even so, it must have been a shock to many of the old-fashioned Chinese to find a descendant of the barbarian Shanyus recognized as a sound authority on the Confucian principles of legislation and administration.

After leaving the Chinese capital at Loyang, Liu Yüan had had an eminently successful career as a tribal leader. In A.D. 279 he succeeded his father as the nominal overlord of the Hunnish tribes settled in China. In A.D. 290 he was promoted to the rank of a general in the Chinese army (though his soldiers still consisted of Hunnish tribesmen). In A.D. 296, at the time of the inroads of several barbarous Hunnish groups in Northwestern China, it was Liu Yüan who was chiefly responsible for the chastisement of the invaders and the reëstablishment of order in this region.

So far this Hunnish prince had been a perfectly loyal subject of the Dsin dynasty. In A.D. 304, however, he became disgusted at the perpetual intrigues and civil wars carried out by members of the imperial family and decided to branch out on his own. At the moment Liu Yüan was acting as military adviser to one of the factions into which the imperial house was then divided, but resigning or rather escaping from this appointment, the Hunnish leader made his way back to his fellow tribesmen and there raised the standard of revolt. Liu Yüan was received with acclamation by these Hunnish tribesmen. He was proclaimed Great Shanyu, a title which had been dormant for nearly a hundred years, and in a couple of weeks he found himself at the head of an army of fifty thousand warriors.

To the astonishment of many of the tribal elders, Liu Yüan's first use of this army was to punish some of the nomadic Wuhuan and Sienbi tribesmen who had been making inroads in the northern frontier of China. One of the most noted of these tribal elders ventured to reprove the new Shanyu, saying that after all the Wuhuan and Sienbi were of the same general stock as the Huns themselves, and that it was a great pity to waste time and men fighting these fellow nomads when it would be easy to defeat and despoil the Chinese who had for centuries been the chief enemy of the Huns, and who now should prove to be easy prey. Liu Yüan's reply to this reproval was characteristic of this chieftain's acute and ambitious mind. "It is not enough," he said, "that we seek to re-establish the old Hunnish Kingdom by allying ourselves with the nomadic Wuhuan and Sienbi. We now have a chance to aspire to a far higher goal, namely to make ourselves the masters, and the legitimate and universally accepted masters, of the whole of the Celestial Empire. But for us to be accepted by the native Chinese as their lawful rulers it is necessary for us to defend China from attacks on the part of raiders and freebooters. Once we have shown that we can protect their interests, these Chinese will rally to our cause."

This speech had a telling effect upon his followers and we hear of no further discontent thereafter. As a matter of fact, the Hunnish attacks upon the northern nomads did not last for very long, and it is obvious that they were carried out more for propaganda effect than for the purpose of carrying out any extensive campaign. But at least the object aimed at had been achieved. All the Chinese of the surrounding districts rallied to his cause, with the result that later on in the same year (304) Liu Yüan felt strong enough to take another decisive step along the path of his political ambitions. Up to this time he had been merely Shanyu of the Hunnish tribesmen. He now proclaimed the establishment of a new kingdom, a kingdom in which Huns and Chinese were to have equal consideration.[4]

With a keen eye to securing support on the part of all groups of Chinese, he gave to his new state the name of "the Kingdom of Han." "In ancient times," he proclaimed, "the glorious house of Han ruled over the Empire for a very lengthy period, owing to the esteem which they caused to exist in the minds of their subjects. This glorious dynasty is now extinct, but I and my family are now their heirs by reason of our descent from them on the female side. Moreover, in ancient times the

Emperors of the Han dynasty and the Hunnish Shanyu solemnly adopted the relationship of elder brother and younger brother. Now that the elder brother has disappeared, it is the privilege of the younger brother to enter into the other's heritage."

Simultaneously with establishing himself as King of Han, Liu Yüan undertook the complete reorganization of his governmental system. He discarded entirely the hierarchy of nobles that had existed among the ancient Huns, and which was suited only to a people with a tribal organization. In its place he adopted the complete bureaucratic system of administrations which had slowly evolved in the Chinese royal and Imperial Courts. No longer do we hear of "Right" and "Left Worthy Princes" who owed their position to their noble birth, but of a Prime Minister and other Ministers of State, all of whom received their posts because of their real, or supposed, merit.

Once these administrative details had been attended to, it was necessary for Liu Yüan to send out armies and conquer some of the strategic points in Northern China, so that the newly established kingdom might grow in size and in population. It is interesting to note that the Hunnish king departed radically from the practice of his ancestors as regards the proprieties of warfare. Whereas the early Hunnish warriors had murdered, ravished, and looted to their hearts' content, Liu Yüan gave strict orders to his generals to keep their soldiers in check and do nothing contrary to the best humanitarian traditions.

On one occasion one of these generals managed to capture a town only after a peculiarly stubborn resistance. In an outburst of rage the Hunnish general ordered the execution of the commander who had caused so much trouble and then attempted to seduce the slain officer's widow. When this good lady refused to listen to the Hunnish general's blandishments she too was put to death. In the days of the old Hunnish Empire such a course of action would have caused little or no comment, but when the matter was reported to Liu Yüan, he immediately ordered the offending general to be degraded in rank, and further commanded that the slain officer be buried with full military honors.

A year or two later Liu Yüan had another occasion to exhibit his humanitarian principles. In the course of one of the Hunnish campaigns against the Chinese imperial forces, another Hunnish general so manoeuvered his troops that the Chinese army with all of its camp followers was driven into a river and over thirty thousand persons were drowned. When Liu Yüan heard of this event he again became greatly displeased. "How can this general of mine ever dare face me again?" he said. "Does he not realize that we are fighting only against the iniquitous rulers of China and not against the much abused common people?" After saying which, he ordered the general to be cashiered.

It is impossible for us to say how much of this humanitarianism was genuine and how much of it was a pose adopted to win the confidence and affection of the Chinese people. In any case, it is certain that though the Hunnish troops were severely restricted in their method of carrying on warfare they succeeded in winning a long series of notable victories. These victories were due in large measure to the fact that Liu Yüan, in addition to being an able general himself, succeeded in gathering around his court some of the most notable military men of the age. Some of the generals were Hunnish, others were Chinese in origin—Liu Yüan paid little or no attention to such matters. It so happened however that the two generals who made the greatest names for themselves were both Huns by descent.

As these two men were later destined to play a notable part in Far Eastern history, it is worthwhile to mention their names. One of them was Liu Yao, the other was Shï Lê. Liu Yao was of royal birth in the sense that he, too, was descended from the ancient Hunnish Shanyus and was, in fact, a close relative of the monarch of the new Hunnish kingdom. Although he was left an orphan at an early age, Liu Yao had been given a good education, and had a fluent knowledge of Chinese history, literature, and philosophy. In spite of these scholarly pursuits he was a man of tremendous physical strength, and it is said that he could shoot an arrow through an iron plate over an inch thick. On the whole, Liu Yao proved himself to be an able and honorable opponent and seldom stooped to the small tricks of petty word-breaking and treachery which characterized many of his colleagues. He did however possess a passion for drink, and was frequently tipsy during the entire course of a battle. His personal appearance was rather astonishing. He was adorned by a very bushy beard, in itself a rarity in Eastern Asia, and in addition was a pure albino. We are told that his "white" eyebrows and "red" eyes caused a certain amount of terror among the simple-minded peasants who beheld them.

Shï Lê, the other great Hunnish general, was a man of very different caliber. In the first place, he was a man of far less distinguished ancestry, his father being merely the head of a small and insignificant group of Hunnish tribesmen. In view of this background, it is not surprising to find that Shï Lê himself received no formal education, and in sharp contrast to the Hunnish leaders of the royal House of Liu, he was never able to learn to read and write. In spite of this handicap, Shï Lê all through his life displayed an intense interest in cultural matters. Even while engaged on his most strenuous campaigns the general always took one or more secretaries along whose duty it was to read aloud to their master from the historical and literary classics of the Celestial Empire.

Shï Lê started upon his adventurous career at a very early age. While still only a boy he was captured and sold as a slave. Before many years had elapsed he succeeded in making his escape, but instead of returning to his native home, he joined a group of bandits and soon became one of China's most notorious freebooters. In China the transition from bandit to distinguished general is a very easy one, and one which has frequently been made both before and after this time. It is not surprising, therefore, to find that before long Shï Lê became the co-leader of a semi-independent marauding army. When this army was broken up by the imperial authorities Shï Lê fled to the new King of Han, and offered his services in the war against the reigning Chinese dynasties. These services were accepted with alacrity and in a very short space of time the erstwhile bandit became one of the most noted leaders of the Hunnish armies. Shï Lê was a very courageous warrior and in addition was exceedingly crafty. Many of the victories he achieved were secured as much by guile as by the direct use of force.

With the aid of Liu Yao, Shï Lê and other notable military leaders, the little Kingdom of Han underwent rapid expansion, and before long a large portion of Northern China was subject to its jurisdiction. In 308 this kingdom had grown so powerful that its monarch, Liu Yüan, decided to adopt the title of Emperor. According to Chinese political philosophy there could be in the world only one rightful "Emperor," however many kings there might be. As a result, Liu Yüan's assumption of the imperial title meant that he thereby laid claim to be the rightful ruler of the whole of the Celestial Empire. He would no longer be merely the independent ruler of a portion of China, and he served notice that he wished to be regarded as the supreme master of all of it.

Up to this time Liu Yüan's camp and his court had been more or less identical, the capital of his kingdom being wherever he himself happened to be in residence. With the assumption of the imperial title, however, it was thought advisable to change this state of affairs, and in the following year (309) the little town of Ping Yang was chosen to serve as the permanent seat of administration. Within a short space of time this town, which had previously been little more than a dingy village, became a thriving city.

But though the Huns were now securely ensconced in a capital of their own, they soon began an active campaign to capture Loyang, the residence of the emperors of the House of Dsin. In the year 309 the Huns made two determined efforts to secure control of this city. In the first effort they received a severe check when they were still some distance from the city. In the second attempt they were more successful and at one time had possession of some of the suburbs. Just at this time, however, the Chinese made a desperate sortie and inflicted a great deal of damage upon the besiegers. Liu Yüan thought it better to withdraw his army at this time and wait for a more favorable opportunity to renew the attack, knowing that the Chinese Imperial Court was riddled with internal intrigues, and that sooner or later these intrigues would lead to a situation where it would be comparatively easy to capture the Chinese capital without endangering the lives of the elite of his army.

Liu Yüan was undoubtedly very wise in making this decision, but he did not live long enough to witness the accomplishment of his plans, for he suddenly sickened and died in the following year (310).[5]

Liu Yüan's death was a great blow to the newly established Hunnish Empire, all the more as, following true Hunnish tradition, there was much intrigue and even civil war before the succession to the throne was finally settled. Fortunately for the Hunnish cause, at the end of a few months Liu Tsung, the most popular, and also the most capable of Liu Yüan's sons, was able to secure the empire for himself. But though the new monarch was undoubtedly the most talented of all of Liu Yüan's sons, he was never able to measure up to the high standard set by his father. For though Liu Tsung was a man of courage and of intelligence, and possessed moreover of an excellent education, he was always a slave to his own passions. At any moment he was liable to be turned from one of his main purposes by drink, anger, or lust.

At the beginning of his reign it was his lust which almost caused his undoing. His father had left a number of wives and concubines, one of whom, who had the title of Dowager Empress, was still young and was moreover exceedingly attractive. Liu Tsung proceeded to fall in love with this stepmother, and before long it was obvious that this passion was reciprocated. A century or two previously, when the Huns were still living in Mongolia, such a love affair would have caused little or no comment, in fact, it would have been regarded as perfectly natural, but since the coming of the Huns to China, they had learned from the Chinese to regard such unions as incestuous, with the result that the new court was in an uproar about the whole matter. Had this liaison persisted, serious consequences might easily have ensued, but it so happened that the good lady was so disturbed by the reproaches made to her that soon afterwards she died of a broken heart, and Li Tsung was left free to attend to the affairs of state, the most important of which, of course, was the continuation of the campaign against the Chinese Dsin dynasty with its capital at Loyang.[7]

Liu Tsung was fortunate in the fact that he inherited from his father a well organized military machine. He was even more fortunate in the fact that shortly after his accession to the throne his rivals, the ruling family of the House of Dsin, fell victims to even greater internal intrigue and discord than ever before.

Much to the disgust of the feeble and incompetent Dsin Emperor, one of his most active generals, Prince Yüe, a member of his own imperial family, instead of staying at home and defending the capital, had marched at the head of forty thousand soldiers, the flower of the Chinese army, far to the northeast in order to strike a counter-offensive on the flank of the newly established Hunnish Empire. For a while this counter-offensive met with considerable success, but after a few months Prince Yüe, who had constantly to fight both the Huns abroad and a series of intrigues at home, broke down under the strain and died. His army fell into the hands of a very incompetent succcessor, who did not have sense enough either to advance or to withdraw, with the result that before long the whole army fell into the hands of the Huns who on this occasion were commanded by Shï Lê, the ex-bandit chief, now one of the most trusted of the Hunnish commanders.

Shï Lê himself was astonished at the ease with which he had been able to capture and make prisoner the many thousands of members of the Chinese army, among whom, as officers and as observers, were over forty members of the Chinese imperial family. "Never in my long and adventurous life," he exclaimed, "have I witnessed such a collection of notables," and turning to one of his staff officers he asked what in the world he should do with them. The staff officer immediately suggested that the continued existence of these princes would be of no benefit to the Hunnish cause. "I quite agree with you," replied the worthy Shï Lê, "but it would not be wise to dispose of them publicly. . . ." Later that night, however, he sent a small group of soldiers to the place where the princes were incarcerated with orders that all of them were to be quietly put out of the way.[8]

The news of the overwhelming defeat of the Chinese army naturally caused consternation to reign at Loyang, the Chinese capital. It was no longer possible to supply the city with foodstuffs, with the result that famine became rampant. In the end many of the inhabitants took to cannibalism in order to appease the pangs of hunger. So great was the public disorder that robbers were able to ply their trade openly and without fear of punishment.

In the end, conditions became so bad that the Emperor decided to flee for his life. Things were so disorganized that he was unable to secure a carriage in which to make his getaway. Undeterred by this fact, he attempted to escape on foot, but finding the outskirts of the capital to be completely in the hands of bandits he was soon forced to return to his palace, there to await whatever fortune might befall him.

He did not have long to wait. In the same year (311) the Hunnish armies rapidly closed in upon the Imperial City. Twelve minor skirmishes resulted in the complete defeat of the few remaining soldiers who attempted to preserve the metropolis from attack, and before long the Hunnish generals, chief among whom was the hairy albino, Liu Yao, were able to break through the last defenses and take the Imperial Palaces by storm.

In the final stages of the fighting more than thirty thousand of the Chinese inhabitants were slain, among them the heir apparent to the throne. The reigning Empress was forcibly torn away from her spouse, and shortly thereafter was wedded to Liu Yao, who acted as commander-in-chief of the Hunnish forces on this occasion. It should, perhaps, be noted that by all accounts, the good lady regarded the forcible change of husbands with equanimity and even with pleasure.

The Emperor himself made a last desperate effort to escape, but was soon captured and brought in triumph to the camp of the Hunnish commander. Instead of being executed, as he expected, he was treated with marked courtesy and consideration. Shortly after his capture he, together with all the imperial regalia, was dispatched to Ping Yang, the new capital of the Hunnish Empire. Here he was regarded for the moment with much favor, being given the office of chamberlain and the rank of Duke. A little later he was given a Hunnish princess as a wife (to console him no doubt for the loss of the Empress). Eventually, however, his continued existence came to be regarded as a menace to the state and he was put to death.

Once the Huns were complete masters of Loyang, they were somewhat at a loss as to what should be done with their new possession. Some of the Hunnish generals wished to preserve the city intact, in fact to move the Hunnish capital to this place which was already equipped with magnificent palaces and had been hallowed for centuries as the center of Chinese political and cultural life. Other generals, however, and among them the all powerful Liu Yao, were strongly opposed to this plan, arguing that Loyang was strategically very poorly situated and that from the military point of view it was strongly advisable to preserve the more inaccessible Ping Yang as the capital, at least until the whole Empire was thoroughly subjugated. To render impossible any further discussion upon the matter, Liu Yao began a systematic destruction of the Chinese metropolis. Flames were set to all the palaces, shrines and other public buildings and in a few hours the ancient and illustrious city was reduced to ashes.[9]

It is interesting to compare the capture of Loyang, the Chinese capital, by the Huns in 311, with the capture and sack of Rome by the Goths 99 years later. In one way, Rome fared better than Loyang, as the Goths were content to sack the Roman imperial city while the Huns undertook the systematic destruction of the Chinese metropolis. From another point of view, however, China was more fortunate than Rome. The Goths and the other later Germanic tribes who overran and destroyed the Roman Empire were still pretty much barbarians at the time that they became masters of the Western World. For this reason their rise to supremacy brought about the "Dark Ages" in Europe during which much of the culture of the Classical World was completely lost. In China, on the other hand, though the Huns destroyed Loyang, the check which they offered to the existence and development of Chinese culture was far less severe because of the fact (which we have already had occasion to point out) that when the Huns were at long last able to overrun the Chinese Empire they were already deeply imbued with the principles of Chinese civilization, and were, for the most part, patrons and even adepts at Chinese letters and learning.

With the Hunnish conquests of Loyang begins the Chinese "Dark Ages," but with the Hunnish knowledge of and attitude towards the traditional culture of the Celestial Empire, these ages were destined to be far less dark, and the break between the earlier and later periods of civilization far less sharp than in Europe. Moreover, it should be remembered that though the Huns succeeded in capturing the Chinese Emperor and destroying the Chinese capital they never succeeded in making themselves masters of the whole of China, with the result that there was always some part of China which remained independent and in which the Chinese literati, in case of need, could take refuge.

In 311, for example, the period with which we are for the moment especially concerned, the Chinese still remained masters of the vast region along and to the South of the Yangtze River. In addition there were still large regions in Northeastern and Northwestern China in the hands of military commanders who were still loyal to the Celestial cause.

Had the Huns taken full advantage of the consternation caused by their seizure of the Emperor and the imperial city it is probable that they could have secured control of the whole of the Celestial Empire. Fortunately for the Chinese cause, however, the Huns missed this golden opportunity largely because of the personal character of Liu Tsung, their ruler.

The stupendous victories already achieved by the Hunnish armies seem to have gone to Liu Tsung's head. He became extremely headstrong and arrogant. Worse still, he again, and to an even greater extent than ever before, became the victim of his own passions, and allowed the Hunnish cause to be seriously endangered because of his inability to check his own lustful desires.

Many stories are told of Liu Tsung's eccentric behavior in the years immediately following the capture of Loyang. On one occasion he ordered the immediate execution of two chamberlains because a sufficient quantity of fresh fish and crabs (of which he was especially fond) had not been placed upon the imperial table. Shortly thereafter he executed his chief architect because there was a delay in the completion of one of the imperial palaces. At still another time, Liu Tsung commanded that one of his high officials be put to death merely because the latter had remonstrated with the Emperor on his going around without sufficient escort. This particular command was felt to be so outrageous that the Dowager Empress (Liu Tsung's mother) went for three days without eating, as a protest. Other high personages at the court including the Emperor's favorite brother and his favorite son joined in the protest and Liu Tsung felt forced to yield on this occasion. "I was drunk when I issued my order of execution," he naïvely states, "and this order did not represent my true intentions." In fact, not only was the official in question given a free pardon, but in addition he was elevated to the rank of Duke.

These fits of passion were bad, but worse still was the fact that Liu Tsung began to neglect the needs and desires of his main support, the army. The resources of the treasury, instead of being used for the outfitting of troops which were needed for the conquest of the remaining portions of China, were squandered in maintaining an idle and luxurious court. Vast sums were spent in building and furnishing more than fourteen new palaces in the Hunnish capital at Ping Yang. It would seem that this extensive program of building was due not so much to Liu Tsung's interest in architecture as to the fact that he needed a large number of palaces in which to keep the innumerable concubines with which he surrounded himself. As time went on the Hunnish Emperor became more and more dominated by his sexual lust. In the end he boasted of an immense harem, and all of its occupants had to be kept in the lap of luxury no matter how great was the need for financial expenditure elsewhere.

Public opinion was much shocked by the vast sums of money spent on the imperial harem, but curiously enough it was even more shocked when Liu Tsung raised two of his concubines to the rank of full Empress. As he was already possessed of a legal consort, this meant that China was treated to the sight of having three reigning empresses at one and the same time. China had long been accustomed to having her rulers enjoy all the pleasures of polygamy, but in times past the Emperors had been content with one legal consort at a time, the other ladies of his choice being forced to remain content with the rank of concubine. This course of action on the part of Liu Tsung therefore caused as much criticism as if, for example, Louis XV had attempted to make Madame Pompadour co-queen of France. One of the highest officials in the court made a public protest against this course of action and when this protest proved unavailing he managed to expose sufficient scandal regarding one of the new empresses to cause this lady to commit suicide. But even this tragedy led to no permanent improvement, for shortly thereafter the Emperor chose another concubine to take the dead woman's exalted place.

It is possible that Liu Tsung's passion for the ladies in his harem might have been glossed over by public opinion if in addition to dallying with his concubines, he had continued to take an active interest in public affairs. But unfortunately for his country, he spent more and more time in his harem, and on one occasion was not seen by the ministers of his court for a hundred days. The conduct of public affairs came to be left entirely in the hands of the court officials, and in the absence of strong leadership these officials split up into little cliques which were constantly bickering and intriguing among themselves.[10]

Considering this state of affairs it is not surprising that the Hunnish cause suffered a number of reverses. The native Chinese were able to consolidate their position in the South and no serious attempt was made by the Huns to invade this region. In the northeastern part of China one or two Chinese commanders were able to recruit a new army and capture a number of strategic positions. One of the princes of the old Chinese imperial family was proclaimed Emperor (he counts as the fourth Emperor of the Dsin dynasty) and after a short but brilliant campaign he was able to secure control of much of Northwestern China. Shortly thereafter he established his capital in the old historic city of Chang-an (which had served as the capital of the early Han dynasty), and there proceeded to build up an administrative system which he hoped sooner or later to reëstablish over all parts of the Celestial Empire.

Equally dangerous to the Hunnish Empire was the fact that in Southern Mongolia and all along the extreme northern portion of China the dreaded Sienbi nomads (the hereditary enemies of the Huns) under the leadership of the Tobas clan steadily increased in power and influence and before long threatened to become the dominating factor in

Far Eastern politics. To make matters worse, the Chinese (i.e., the Dsin dynasty) and the Tobas maintained, for the moment, very friendly relations with one another, largely because of their common hatred of the Huns. In 315 the Dsin Emperor, in the hope of stimulating the Tobas to attack the Huns, granted to the leader of the Tobas the title of King of Dai.[11]

Even to the casual observer it was obvious that the Hunnish Empire was faced with a very critical situation. Had matters depended entirely upon the *faitneant* Liu Tsung it is certain that this Empire would have quickly crumbled to pieces. But the Hunnish armies were still intact, and they were still commanded by the able generals who had risen to power during the reign of Liu Tsung's sagacious father. About 316 some of these generals began to take matters into their own hands.

Shï Lê, the ex-bandit, who was in charge of most of the Hunnish soldiers stationed in Northeastern China, succeeded in defeating the Chinese general who was the chief support of the Dsin dynasty in this region.[12] Even greater glory fell to the lot of the hairy albino, Liu Yao, who was in charge of the Hunnish troops in Northwestern China and whose duty it was to lead the campaign against the new Dsin Emperor and his capital, the city of Chang-an. Liu Yao had already made several unsuccessful attempts to capture this metropolis, but in 316, profiting by his mistakes, he was able to surround the city on all sides, thereby making it impossible for the Chinese defenders to receive either foodstuffs or reinforcements. Before long all the inhabitants were on the verge of starvation and the poor Emperor, overcome at the sight of so much suffering, decided to surrender immediately in order to put an end to the prevailing misery.

At this moment one of the principal Chinese generals in the beleaguered city decided to make a bold bid for fame and fortune. Knowing that his master was determined to surrender in any event, this officer secretly sent his own son to the Hunnish camp with the message that he, the general, would see to it that the Emperor surrendered, provided that he be suitably rewarded by the Hunnish court. It would seem that Liu Yao, the Hunnish commander, smelled a rat, for he immediately cut off the head of the envoy and loudly proclaimed "It is the duty of every true general to act justly and righteously. In my fifteen years as a commander I have never stooped to secure a victory by means of treachery, and I shall not do so on this occasion. Tell the general to fight to the last ditch, for if I capture him he shall pay for his attempted treachery with his life."

Noble words these, but in view of his record on other occasions it would appear that Liu Yao's self-righteousness was something of a pose.

He was fully aware that the Chinese defenders were on their last legs and he preferred the glory of capturing the Chinese capital by the force of his own arms rather than have it be believed that the Dsin Emperor had fallen only because of internal treachery. In any event Liu Yao immediately renewed the attack and shortly thereafter the Emperor, feeling that further delay was useless, donned the simple costume worn by criminals on their way to execution, and mounted a small cart which was drawn by hand, the principal ministers of state acting as rikisha coolies on this occasion. In this fashion the poor fallen ruler emerged from the city gates and passed into the Hunnish camp.

Shortly after this episode Liu Yao and his troops entered the city in triumph. Liu Yao was true to his word and the Chinese general who had attempted to enter into treasonable negotiotions was executed, but the Emperor and his faithful ministers were treated with every consideration, at least for the time being. The later fortunes of this Emperor form a close parallel to those of his predecessor. After being transported to the Hunnish capital, he was at first treated with signal honor, being made a marquis and a chamberlain at the Hunnish court. A year or two later, however, when he became the center of Chinese intrigue, he was summarily executed.[13]

The year 316, which witnessed the successful Hunnish campaigns in Northeastern and Northwestern China, also saw a transformation among the dreaded Tobas, which for the moment rendered them innocuous. It was in this year that civil war broke out between the ruler of the Tobas and his eldest son, as a result of which both of these personages were killed. After further fighting a new ruler was chosen, but the Tobas had been so weakened by this dissension that the Huns felt that they need have no serious fear of invasion from this quarter for some time to come.[14]

At the beginning of 317 the Hunnish Empire was in an exceedingly favorable position. Practically all of Northern China was incorporated within its limits. The remaining Chinese armies scattered throughout Southern China were exceedingly weak and disorganized, and it is almost certain that a vigorous campaign in this region would have overcome all those who still remained loyal to the cause of Chinese independence.

Once more, however, the Huns lost their golden opportunity to make themselves masters of the whole of China because of the indolence and carelessness of their sovereign. Instead of organizing and pushing forward a vigorous offensive campaign, Liu Tsung continued to dawdle with his womenfolk and was content to allow the affairs of state to look after themselves. As a result of this attitude, the intrigues between the various factions at the Hunnish court grew worse and worse and eventually led to the death of the one prince of the Hunnish imperial house who showed any signs of genius.

Among the members of the ancient Hunnish Empire there had always been some doubt as to whether the proper line of succession to the throne should be from father to son (as in China), or from older brother to younger brother. Although the Huns had now resided for many generations in the Celestial Empire and had absorbed many of the Chinese ideas regarding social and legal propriety, they were in doubt on this point. The problem came to a head just at this time. The Hunnish Emperor had a favorite brother, or rather a half-brother, by the name of Liu I and a favorite son by the name of Liu Tsan, and His Imperial Majesty had some difficulty in making up his mind as to which of the two should succeed him on the Dragon Throne. The brother, Liu I, had long been recognized as the heir apparent, but the son Liu Tsan had been acting for some time as Prime Minister, and had steadily gathered more and more power into his own hands. It was soon obvious that he had no intention of being dispossessed of what he regarded as his lawful rights of succession to the throne.

As a matter of principle, most of the inhabitants of the Hunnish Empire had come to believe that normally the throne should pass from father to son, but matters were much complicated by the fact that the brother was an exceedingly able and intelligent man with a strong passion for justice and propriety, while the son was a vicious and unscrupulous debauchee. It soon became obvious that because of this fact, public opinion was strongly in favor of retaining Liu I as the destined occupant of the imperial throne. Liu Tsan, consumed with envy, determined to bring about his rival's undoing.

It so happened that the brother, Liu I, was in charge of the Imperial Guards, who were stationed a short distance away from the Hunnish capital. One day the son, Liu Tsan, sent a messenger to his uncle stating that a riot had broken out in the city and requested that some troops be sent to put down the disturbance. Liu I believed that this message had been sent in good faith and ordered some of his troops to march into the capital.

No sooner had these soldiers arrived upon the scene than the treacherous Liu Tsan immediately sent a message to the Emperor stating that his rival was obviously bent upon a coup d'état, and urged that the latter should be put under arrest immediately. The Emperor believed or at least half believed the wild story that was told him and gave orders that Liu I should be seized and disarmed. Liu I made no resistance—in itself proof that he harbored no rebellious designs, but suspicion still hung heavily about him. He was deposed from his position as heir apparent and given a subordinate rank. Liu Tsan, however, was not content with these measures. Fearful lest his rival be once more restored to favor, this vengeful prince sent an emissary to assassinate the unfortunate Liu I. The assassination was duly carried out, and though the Emperor, who had come to believe in his brother's innocence, deeply regretted the whole affair, he felt that nothing could be done about the matter and the treacherous Liu Tsan was duly installed as heir apparent.

In the following year (318) the Hunnish Emperor was disturbed by another and even greater domestic tragedy. One of the magnificent palaces he had caused to be built suddenly caught on fire and in a few minutes was burned to ashes. In this great conflagration no less than twenty-one of the Emperor's children were burned to death. Because of his large harem the death of these twenty-one princes did not by any means exhaust His Imperial Majesty's supply of offspring. Nevertheless, this tragedy cast a deep gloom about the whole Hunnish court. From our point of view it is to be regretted that the vicious Liu Tsan, the new heir apparent, was not among the princes who were burned to death.[15]

The Hunnish court all during this period was so perturbed by all these domestic intrigues and disasters that it was unable to make any headway with the plans for the remaining portions of China. As a result, the inhabitants of Southern China who had never yet submitted to the Hunnish yoke had time to rally their forces and reëstablish an organized system of government. Another of the numerous princes of the Imperial House of Dsin was elevated to the throne. But this new Emperor (who counts as the fifth ruler of the Dsin dynasty) was careful to establish his headquarters nowhere in Northern China where he would constantly be subjected to Hunnish attack. He chose as his capital the town of Gienkang which corresponds to the modern city of Nanking.

The establishment of the Chinese capital at Gienkang marks the beginning of a very important epoch in the history of the Celestial Empire. Up to this time all of China's political and cultural life had been definitely centered in the North, along the banks of the Yellow River. For many centuries the Yangtze River had marked the southern boundary of China proper.

During the glorious Han dynasty the Chinese had secured political control over the regions South of the Yangtze, but the vast area remained inhabited by tribes which the Chinese regarded as barbarians and who were alien to the Chinese in language and in culture. With the establishment of the Chinese capital at Gienkang this situation became radically altered. Myriads of Chinese in Northern China, harassed by fears of Hunnish oppression, drifted down to the southlands. Passing over the Yangtze, they began to colonize the huge provinces which lay to the South of this great river, either driving out or absorbing the earlier "barbarian" inhabitants. Southern China for the first time definitely became part of China proper, and the Yangtze, from being the boundary, became the center of China's cultural life. Northern China, which for over two centuries remained under the political domination of the Huns and other northern nomads, developed a culture which differed radically in many important respects from that in vogue in the purely Chinese Empire in the South.

But though this Southern Empire was destined to have a long and relatively glorious existence, during the first few years following the enthronement of the Emperor at Gienkang, the new Empire was a very weak and fragile affair which the Huns felt could be overcome with no great difficulty. But while the Huns were making great plans for the final conquest of this region, Liu Tsung, the Hunnish Emperor, suddenly became ill and died. As a result of the tragic and dramatic events which followed the death of this ruler the whole Hunnish Empire was thrown into confusion, and many years were to elapse before the Huns could again make a serious effort to invade the South.

Liu Tsung died in 318 and was succeeded by the heir apparent, the vindicative and vicious Liu Tsan. The new ruler lost no time in adding to his unpopularity by committing a number of indiscretions. Fearing lest two of his brothers who were very popular with certain elements in the army might plot against him, he immediately ordered that these two princes be put to death without even the pretense of a trial. He carried on a liaison with no less than four of his deceased father's concubines, thereby greatly shocking a large number of his subjects. Like his predecessor, Liu Tsan was devoted to the pleasures of feminine society, and he soon came to spend most of his time in his harem leaving the conduct of public affairs in the hands of his favorite minister, who incidentally was not Hunnish in origin but a Chinese general by the name of Gin Jung.

It was not long before Liu Tsan was more than sufficiently punished for all his misdeeds. Gin Jung, the Chinese favorite, decided to betray his master. Gathering together a small body of soldiers, he broke into the palace apartments and slew not only Liu Tsan, the Emperor, but also all the other members of the Hunnish imperial family upon whom he could lay hands, irrespective of age or sex.

Gin Jung was well aware that in the Hunnish Empire the Huns constituted but a small fraction of the total population and that they were exceedingly unpopular with the vast bulk of the native Chinese. Playing upon this fact, he hoped to win favor and popular approval for himself by issuing a proclamation to the effect that it was highly indecent that any barbarian should have even aspired to the imperial throne of China, and that in assassinating the Hunnish ruler he had accomplished a highly patriotic act. To make quite sure that thereafter the Chinese should be ruled by Chinese, he himself mounted the throne, calling himself, however, not Emperor but merely King of Han.[16]

The death of Liu Tsan and the accession of his murderer to the throne really marks the end of the so-called Han dynasty founded by the Huns. Being established in 304 and abruptly overthrown in 318 this dynasty ruled all told for only fifteen years, and yet in this short space of time its rulers had completely changed the destinies of Eastern Asia. These rulers, or rather their generals, had captured and slain two Chinese Emperors and captured the historic capital of the Chinese, and had forced the native rulers of China to take refuge in the far off southern lands.

CHAPTER FIFTEEN

THE HUNS IN CHINA—THE SECOND PHASE

Liu Yao and the Western Jao Dynasty—Shï Lê and the Eastern Jao Dynasty—Shï Lê becomes Sole Ruler of Northern China—Death of Shï Lê and the Accession of Shï Hu—Apogee of Hunnish Rulership in China—Shï Hu's Early Military Victories—His Later Disasters—Shï Hu's Troubles with His Sons—Death of Shï Hu and End of the Jao Dynasty—The Hunnish Kingdom of Hia—The Hunnish Kingdom of Northern Liang—The End of Hunnish Rule in the Far East.

THOUGH THE Hunnish Han dynasty came to an end in A.D. 318, the period of Hunnish domination in Northern China had not yet come to an end. Gin Jung, the would-be restorer of Chinese independence, had a very short time in which to glory in his ill-gained position. He who had secured his throne by means of assassination was himself assassinated only a few months later. Following this second murder, the usurper's son, Gin Ming by name, was placed upon the throne, thus preserving the theory of Chinese supremacy. Before long, however, the Huns were able to wreak vengeance for the bloody deed which had been perpetrated upon their ruler.

At the time of the coup d'état in the capital, the two greatest Hunnish leaders of the period, the albino Liu Yao, and the ex-bandit Shï Lê were both in the provinces, Liu Yao being in command of a Hunnish army in Northwestern China, and Shï Lê in command of the Hunnish army in Northeastern China. Upon hearing the news of the murder of their sovereign both of these generals began moving upon the capital, determined to overthrow the usurping house of Gin and reëstablish Hunnish hegemony. This movement was carried out slowly and cautiously, but eventually these two armies succeeded in investing the capital city of Ping Yang, and there was nothing for the Chinese rulers of this place to do but to surrender. Knowing of Shï Lê's reputation for ruthlessness and brutality, the wretched "King" Gin Ming decided that it would be safer for him to surrender himself and his court to Liu Yao. But if he expected to be shown any mercy he was soon disappointed, for Liu Yao immediately ordered that every person, male or female, even remotely connected with the usurping house of Gin be put to death.[1]

But though the murder of the Hunnish Emperor Liu Tsan was thus amply revenged it was obviously impossible to push back the clock and formally reëstablish the "Han" dynasty by placing any of Liu Tsan's descendants upon the throne. In the first place most of Liu Tsan's immediate family had been put to death in the recent troubles. In addition, it was Liu Yao and Shï Lê who had reëstablished Hunnish rule and by the ancient adage, as well-known in China as elsewhere, "to the victors belong the spoils."

At first it was Liu Yao who carried away the lion's share of these spoils. As mentioned before, Liu Yao was of distinguished birth, being a member of the Hunnish imperial family and a distant cousin of the late Emperor of the Hunnish Han dynasty. A man of intelligence and education, he had also had a distinguished career as a soldier. It is not surprising therefore to find that Liu Yao met with little opposition when he solemnly raised himself to the Imperial Throne. Even so, the new Emperor felt it necessary to break with the past and inaugurate a new era. The Hunnish capital at Ping Yang had been burned to the ground during the recent disturbances, and instead of trying to rebuild this metropolis, Liu Yao decided to move the seat of his administration to the West to the ancient city of Chang-an, which had once been the capital of the Early Han dynasty, and with which were associated many glorious memories of the past. Moreover, to further mark the beginning of a new era, Liu Yao changed the name of the dynasty from Han to that of Jao.

All might have gone well with the new dynasty if it had been able to appease the ambitions of Shï Lê, the other great Hunnish leader of the period, but this proved an insuperable task. Shï Lê was given the post of Grand Marshal of the Empire and elevated to the rank of Duke in recognotion of his service. For the moment this was sufficient to satisfy Shï Lê's vanity, but shortly thereafter trouble broke out between the new Grand Marshal and his nominal overlord. The Emperor Liu Yao was foolish enough to slay an emissary of Shï Lê on the ground that this emissary was acting as a spy, and thereafter there was open warfare between the two great Hunnish leaders.

In 319 Shï Lê completely renounced all allegiance to Liu Yao and his court at Chang-an and established himself as the ruler of an independent kingdom which embraced most of Northeastern China, its capital being at the town of Siang-guo, a place not very far from the modern city of Peking. To make matters rather confusing for the historian, Shï Lê also called his new kingdom the Kingdom of Jao, and so to avoid confusion between Liu Yao's "Empire of Jao" with its seat in Northwestern China and Shï Lê's "Kingdom of Jao" in Northeastern China, we will refer to the former as Western Jao and to the latter as Eastern Jao.

For several years after the split up of the Hunnish dominion into two separate realms, the rulers of each of these realms continued to enjoy a fair measure of prosperity. Both Liu Yao and Shï Lê established reasonably efficient administrative systems and were able to impose these systems on all parts of their respective domains. Both rulers managed to keep in check the "barbarian" peoples who lay just beyond their frontiers. Liu Yao's frontier campaigns were directed aganist the Kiang or Tibetans, while Shï Lê was forced to keep an eye on the various Sienbi peoples who dwelt to the North and Northeast of his kingdom.

Both Liu Yao and Shï Lê managed to strike an occasional blow at the native Chinese Dsin Empire which lay to their South. These blows were, for the most part, quite effective, but the battles between the Huns and the Chinese were distinctly minor affairs compared with the campaigns which the two Hunnish sovereigns directed against the other. In this almost constant warfare between Western and Eastern Jao, it so happened that for several years neither side was able to secure a decisive advantage. On the other hand neither side was willing to make peace until the other was completely crushed.

At length, in A.D. 328, the supreme struggle between the two Hunnish kingdoms took place. During the campaigns conducted during the early part of this year the Western Jao armies led by Liu Yao were uniformly successful, and there was a near panic in the court of his rival Shï Lê. Shï Lê himself kept his head, and collecting a new army, he placed himself at its head and marched westward. By the use of very brilliant tactics Shï Lê succeeded in catching his rival unaware. At the moment the final attack began, Liu Yao was giving a banquet and was already decidedly tipsy. When the alarm was given the convivial monarch mounted a horse and rushed into the fray. He was unable to overcome the fumes of liquor, however, and before long fell from his horse in a drunken stupor.

This fall decided the fate of the battle, and also the fate of Liu Yao's empire. The soldiers of Western Jao, hearing that their leader had fallen, and not knowing the cause, immediately decided that all was lost and beat a hasty retreat. Liu Yao himself was unable to move, and was soon made a prisoner. He was taken in triumph to Shï Lê's capital, and there efforts were made to induce the fallen monarch to issue orders to his sons, who were still at large, to desist from further fighting. In the face of these efforts, Liu Yao, defiant to the end, sent a letter to these sons commanding them to pay no heed to their father's predicament but to continue to struggle to the last ditch. As a result of his obstinate bravery poor Liu Yao was immediately executed. But his sons duly carried out their father's commands, and continued a desolating warfare as long as they could. However, several of their own generals proved treacherous, with the result that before many months had passed these

Hunnish princes, the last scions of the ancient Hunnish imperial family, were captured and killed.[2]

By the end of 329 Shï Lê had completely crushed all opposition in the former Western Jao Empire, and by adding this territory to his own domains he became practically undisputed master of the whole of Northern China. As a result, Shï Lê's fame spread far into Northern and Central Asia, and before long we find not only the semi-barbarous people inhabiting Manchuria and Northern Korea, but also the civilized city-states of Kashgaria and the other portions of the "Western Regions" sending him tribute.

Up to this time Shï Lê had been content with the simple title of King. By 330, however, it was apparent to all that he was the most important single ruler in the whole of Eastern Asia, so that at length he was persuaded by his ministers to assume the more grandiloquent title of Emperor. At about this time he set about moving his capital. When the Kingdom of Jao had jurisdiction only over Northeastern China the little town of Siang-guo had served as a very useful seat of administration and was, moreover, not very far removed from the geographic center of the realm. Now, however, that Jao was a large empire, having dominion over the whole of Northern China, it was advisable to move the seat of government further to the South and West. After some consideration the newly installed Emperor decided to have not one but two capitals, one at the town of Ye, because of its good strategic position, the other at the ancient city of Loyang, because of its associations with so much of China's glorious past.

Considering Shï Lê's disadvantages as regards his family background and upbringing, he made a surprisingly good ruler. When one remembers that he was the son of a peculiarly barbarous petty chieftain, that as a youth he was a slave and later a notorious bandit, that he never received a formal education and that to the end of his days he was never able to read and write, one is rather surprised that Shï Lê is famed in the Chinese records as a great patron of literature and learning. As we have already noted, this ruler was in the habit of having the Chinese classics and books of history read aloud to him, and it is said that his remarks upon the characters of the heroes and villains of former times showed great acuteness. As he was anxious that other youngsters should not grow up as illiterate as he was himself, he founded several schools. On occasion he visited and inspected these schools, and at such times he gave prizes to those students who showed themselves most diligent and most scholarly.

But while Shï Lê thus showed himself to be a patron of the traditional Chinese classics, which in turn meant that he was a patron of the Confucian philosophy, by his actions the Hunnish ruler showed that his mind was open to other stimuli. Among the most honored persons at his court was a Buddhist monk of Indian origin called Buddha Chinga, and under the latter's influence Buddhism began for the first time to play an important part in Chinese life. For though Buddhism had been introduced into China over two centuries earlier, as long as native Chinese rulers were on the throne it had never been more than a small and very obscure sect, its principal devotees being persons of Indian and Central Asian origin.

With the patronage which Shï Lê extended to Buddha Chinga began a new era for Chinese Buddhism. It became a favored and officially recognized religion and, as a result, slowly but surely extended its way over a large portion of the Chinese populace. Coincident with its spread, there arose a great school of Buddhist art, modeled for the most part on Indian and Central Asian prototypes (many of them ultimately Greek in origin). This new religion and this new art were destined to play a very important part in the later development of Chinese cultural and social life, and influenced even those thinkers and artists who were violently anti-Buddhist in conscious belief.

The fact that Buddhism and Buddhist art developed more rapidly in Northern than in Southern China, plus the fact that this development took place in Northern China just at the time when this region was under the political control of the Huns and other "Barbarians" is not without significance. Had the native Chinese remained masters of the northern portion of the Celestial Empire it is perfectly possible that Buddhism never would have secured any real hold upon the peoples of the Far East.

From what has been said it is obvious that Shï Lê's patronage of Buddha Chinga was of the greatest historic importance. But it should also be noted that Shï Lê's greatness as a ruler was not confined to his patronage of Confucian and Buddhist lore. He was enormously interested in the material welfare of his empire. His officials were given special orders to do everything possible to increase and to better all enterprises connected with agriculture and sericulture, with the result that during this reign the peasant farmers enjoyed a prosperity which had been unknown for nearly a century.

While still only a general, carving out a career for himself, Shï Lê had been guilty of several acts of outrageous treachery. Once he was securely seated on the throne, however, the Hunnish leader seems to have carried out his engagements with comparatively good faith. He was especially noted for his loyalty to, and good treatment of, his trusted ministers and retainers, a point worthy of comment when one remembers the whimsical and often brutal treatment accorded their underlings by many of the preceding and subsequent rulers of the Celestial Empire.

Above all, it is obvious from the Chinese records that Shï Lê was invariably master of himself. Whereas many of the Hunnish leaders of the old imperial family of Liu, though men of genius, had given way to sloth, liquor or women, Shï Lê was too cold and cautious a ruler ever to become a slave to his passions. For the most part he was extremely abstemious in his private life, and though, like all other Asiatic potentates, he was possessed of a large harem, he never let himself be subjected to feminine intrigue, and was always careful to keep control over affairs of state in his own hands.[3]

Considering these facts it is rather a pity that Shï Lê enjoyed such a very short reign, but he was already an old man when he mounted the Imperial Throne, and only three years later (333) he suddenly died. He was followed on the throne by one of his sons, but the new ruler was never more than a puppet in the hands of a nephew of the late Emperor, named Shï Hu. At first Shï Hu was content with the title of Prime Minister, but from the first it was obvious that he intended to be complete autocrat of the state.

When some of the imperial family began to prove restive at this usurpation, Shï Hu promptly executed the Dowager Empress and several of the late Emperor's sons. A year following these events (i.e. in 334) Shï Hu decided to assume complete power in fact as well as in name. The puppet Emperor was deposed (shortly afterwards he and his spouse were also executed) and the ambitious Shï Hu formally ascended the throne.[4]

Shï Hu reigned for fifteen years (or from 334 to 349) and this period marks the apogee of Hunnish domination in China, at least as regards outward pomp and splendour.[5] Although as a young man Shï Hu had been a noted cavalry leader in his uncle's army, once he mounted the throne he devoted most of his time to non-military pursuits. Following in the footsteps of his uncle, Shï Hu liked to pose as a magnificent patron of art and letters. Still more to the point, he went even further than his uncle in the favor he showed to Buddhism and Buddhist monks. Buddha Chinga, the leading exponent of Buddhism at this period, was loaded with presents and allowed to exercise great influence in state affairs.

Early in his reign, Shï Hu issued a proclamation in which permission was officially granted to his subjects not only to make offerings at Buddhist temples, but to become Buddhist monks. This was a very important step. Up to this time practically all the Buddhist monks in China had been foreigners, with the result that Buddhism had remained a small and alien sect, but now all this was to be changed. This proclamation met with fierce opposition on the part of the Confucian scholars who were in attendance at the Imperial Court, but Shï Hu remained firm in his purpose, with the result that before long Buddhist temples and monasteries began to spring up in all parts of the country, and these monasteries were filled with thousands of devout monks of native Chinese origin.[6]

Much of Shï Hu's time and energy went into architectural pursuits. He continued to have two capitals, one at Loyang and the other at Ye, but it was on the Imperial Palaces at Ye that most of the thought and money were expended. We are told that most of the brick work in these palaces was covered with bas-relief executed in stone. The roofing consisted of specially glazed and varnished tiles. The palace pillars were covered with plates of silver, and suspended from the roof were golden bells which jingled in the breeze. Scattered throughout the palace were screens and curtains ornamented with jade and pearls.

Not content with creating new architectural glories, Shï Hu wished to ornament his chief capital with some of the artistic masterpieces of former centuries. With this purpose in view he brought to the city of Ye the bronze bells cast by Tsin Shï Huangdi, the builder of the Great Wall, and the man who had inflicted the first great defeat upon the Huns over five centuries previously. Equally appropriate was the fact that among the other great objects of art brought to the Hunnish capital were the gigantic bronze statues cast by the Emperor Wu-di of the Han dynasty (140-87 B.C.), the monarch who was most responsible for the downfall of the first Hunnish Empire.

Through these efforts the city of Ye achieved undying fame, and it is probable that, with the possible exception of Rome, which had not yet been ravished by barbarians, the Hunnish capital was at this time the most magnificent city in the world. It should be noted, however, that some of Shï Hu's architectural efforts ended in complete failure. He spent millions of dollars in the construction of a stone suspension bridge over the river South of the capital, but in spite of all this expenditure, this great monument was never completed.

Another undertaking ended in far more spectacular failure. One of the imperial chamberlains constructed a gigantic float for use in some of the ceremonial parades of which His Imperial Majesty was so fond. This float consisted of a huge wooden structure nearly a hundred feet high. On the sides of this float was a series of platforms on which no less than five hundred court personages could sit or stand, while on the very top was a huge fire which spread its light for a great distance around. It must have afforded a magnificent spectacle, but one day when it was being dragged through the streets, the great structure overturned, drenching everyone with burning oil, and killing twenty persons. As a result of this tragedy Shï Hu ordered that the chamberlain who had constructed this edifice be cut in two.

One rather peculiar thing about the Hunnish capital at this time was that most of the palace guard consisted of women. In fact, Shï Hu succeeded in gathering together no less than ten thousand women to act as guardians of the imperial city. Some of these females were allowed to engage in more or less feminine occupation such as the study of astrology and divination, but all of them were forced to become expert at archery, both on foot and on horseback. Out of this total number a thousand of these women were chosen to act as a special imperial bodyguard. These amazons, all expert horsewomen, were dressed in brocaded silk and wore a purple headdress. They accompanied the Emperor as ordinary guards when he went abroad, but in addition were expected to fan and, by their music, entertain His Imperial Majesty when the latter dawdled in his palace.[7]

But though Shï Hu spent most of his time beautifying his capital, he did not entirely neglect the affairs of state. Though he surrounded himself with female warriors, he was careful to keep the regular army intact. As a result, he was able, especially during the early part of his reign, to maintain and even to increase the prestige of the Hunnish Empire throughout the whole of the Far East.

Early in his reign (335) Shï Hu, escorted by only a small body of soldiers, made a tour of inspection through his Southern provinces. When the ruler of the Chinese Empire of Dsin heard of the Hunnish Emperor's approach he was thrown into a panic, ordered the mobilization of all his troops, and made a feverish effort to strengthen the defenses of his capital. When he learned that Shï Hu's expedition was little more than a reconnaissance of the South, he was so mortified at the fears he had exhibited that he ordered the execution of many of the officers who had first warned him of the Hunnish danger. This little anecdote, while of no great importance, shows that all during this period the native rulers in Southern China felt themselves definitely on the defensive and were only too glad to avoid commencing hostilities with their Hunnish neighbors in the North.

During this same early period of his reign Shï Hu was also extremely successful in attempting to overawe some of his other neighbors. Among these other neighbors were, first, the Toba group of Sienbi who inhabited Southern Mongolia, and whose territory coincided with the Hunnish Empire all along its northern frontier; second, the Murung group of Sienbi who were the dominating factor in Southern Manchuria and the adjacent regions; and, third, the little state of Liang in the extreme northwestern part of China, the region separating China proper from Kashgaria.

With the first of these groups, the Toba kingdom in the North, Shï Hu was never forced to have any serious dealings. Although these Tobas were always a potential menace to any empire established in Northern China, they were constantly racked by internal dissensions, with the result that the Huns were never forced to wage active war against them. In fact, in consequence of one of these civil wars Shï Hu and his court were able to extract a good deal of political advantage. When one of the Toba rulers lost his throne as a result of an uprising (335), he fled southward and took refuge at the Hunnish court. Two years later (337) this refugee, largely as a result of Hunnish aid, was able to reëstablish himself as ruler of the Tobas, and in consequence, for several years thereafter this northern kingdom remained subject to Shï Hu's influence.[8]

In the Northeast Shï Hu was equally successful in establishing a nominal acknowledgment of supremacy and this time without striking a blow. Southern Manchuria was at this period inhabited by a number of Sienbi groups of which the most important was the Murung clan which was later to play an important part in Chinese history. The Murung clan had already risen to a position of considerable power and importance, and its leader already called himself the King of Yen, in memory of the ancient Chinese Kingdom of Yen which had once occupied the northeast portion of the Celestial Empire. Nevertheless, the Murungs still had to do battle with several other Sienbi groups before they could secure complete supremacy over the Manchurian Plains, and before embarking upon this warfare the King of the Murungs thought it advisable to ward off possible attacks in the rear. With this end in view he sought to win the friendship of the Huns by sending an embassy formally acknowledging Shï Hu as his overlord.

The little Kingdom of Liang in the extreme northwest of China deserves only passing mention. This petty domain arose in the region which in ancient times had been the seat of the Yüejï, and which had later been conquered and settled by the Huns. Later still, it will be remembered, it had been conquered and colonized by the Chinese. The chief importance of this region was the fact that it served as a passageway between China proper and Kashgaria, which meant that any Celestial Emperor had either to keep control over this region or else give up all thoughts of maintaining political or commercial relations with the "Western Regions."

For the past several years the district of Liang had fallen under the jurisdiction of a Chinese soldier of fortune who had made himself de facto governor of the western marshes, and who used this strategic position as a lever in carrying out negotiations with the major contenders for rulership in China proper. Sometimes this adventurer frankly ruled on his own account; at other times he thought it advisable to rule as the viceroy of the far-off Emperors of the House of Dsin. However, during the early portion of Shï Hu's reign he felt it necessary to acknowledge the Hunnish Emperor as his nominal overlord.

Though Shï Hu was able to enjoy an immense amount of influence and prestige during the early part of his reign, as time went on a series of ill-advised campaigns caused this glory to diminish very considerably. One of the most ridiculous of his acts was the abortive campaign which he carried on against the Chinese Empire of Dsin. About half way through his reign (342) Shï Hu decided to crush his southern neighbor once and for all. With this end in view he ordered the mobilization of all the resources of his domain. To raise the necessary supplies, enormous taxes were levied upon the populace. In order to pay these taxes some persons were forced to sell their children into slavery, while others committed suicide in despair of being able to meet the demands made upon them. Undeterred by these events the Emperor went on with his preparations, and by the end of a year he had a million men under arms.

Just before leading this army to the South Shï Hu gave a great banquet to his principal officers. During the course of this banquet a large number of wild geese were seen to alight within the palace grounds. This caused universal consternation, as the coming of these birds was considered a very inauspicious omen. In fact the Emperor was so shaken by this event that he ordered the instant abandonment of the whole campaign. The army was demobilized and the men sent back to their homes.[9]

The sudden collapse of this much-heralded campaign made the Hunnish court appear very ridiculous, but it did not lead to any serious consequence as the Chinese Empire of the Dsin was far too weak to take advantage of the sudden demobilization of the Hunnish armies. Far more damaging to the Hunnish cause was the failure of Shï Hu's campaigns in the Northeast and in the Northwest. The failure in the Northeast was due to Shï Hu's inability to remain master of the Kingdom of Yen founded by the Murung clan of Sienbi. At first, it will be remembered, relations between the Huns and the Murungs had been on a very satisfactory footing, the Murung ruler having acknowledged Shï Hu as his overlord. Trouble arose when the Huns and the Murungs agreed to make a joint campaign against another group of Sienbi tribesmen who inhabited Southwestern Manchuria. Shï Hu sent a large army to the Northeast and managed to inflict a severe defeat upon the Sienbi, who were struggling to maintain their independence. But just at this point the Hunnish ruler took it into his head that his nominal allies, the Murungs, had not shown sufficient enterprise in conducting their share of the campaign. It was decided to punish them for this negligence and the Hunnish army continued the march still further to the Northeast.

The King of the Murungs was completely panic-stricken when he heard of the approach of the Hunnish horde. It was only with great difficulty that his ministers persuaded him not to run away, but to remain in his strongly entrenched capital (near the modern city of Mukden) and await the Hunnish attack. Even so the ghastly pallor of his face betrayed his fear to all observers and served to demoralize his troops. But while the ruler was of little value in the task of repelling the Hunnish invasion, some of the subordinate leaders rose to the occasion, and by means of a brilliant sortie, succeeded in inflicting a great deal of damage on Shï Hu's forces.

It was now the turn of the Huns to become demoralized. Having failed to capture the Murung stronghold, they commenced a slow retreat back to China, but they were not allowed to retreat in peace. As soon as the Murungs found that the Huns were not invincible they recovered their lost courage and began themselves to take the offensive. Large bodies of Murung horsemen pursued the retreating Hunnish army and were able to inflict an enormous amount of damage. Over thirty thousand of the Hunnish soldiers were killed.

Shï Hu was naturally furious at these reverses and, in the year which followed, undertook several new campaigns against Manchuria in the hope of inflicting a crushing defeat upon the upstart Murungs. On one of these expeditions the Hunnish Emperor mobilized more than five hundred thousand troops, and as he wished to advance by sea as well as by land, he built or requisitioned more than ten thousand boats with which to transport his troops. But even with this huge martial array the Huns could never accomplish their purpose. At times they were able to march far into the enemy territory, but never were they able to hold for any period the territory thus occupied. After each such campaign the Murungs were able to carry out a successful counter-offensive which sent the Hunnish troops scampering back into China. After several years of this ineffective fighting Shï Hu decided that he had had more than enough of the Manchurian adventure, even though this decision meant recognizing the complete independence of the Murung clansmen with their so-called Kingdom of Yen, for of course after the failure of these campaigns, the Murungs refused to admit even the nominal overlordship of the Hunnish ruler.[10]

The one permanent effect of this lengthy warfare between the Huns and the Murungs was the almost wholesale transfer of populations which took place all along the northeastern frontier of the Celestial Empire. On one occasion, when the Huns had temporary possession of Southwestern Manchuria, they forced no less than twenty thousand families inhabiting this region, most of them doubtless of Sienbi origin, to migrate and settle in various portions of Central China. Several years later, and more or less in retaliation for this act, we find the Murungs carrying out a similar forcible transplantation of peoples. At this time the Murungs had temporary possession of the northeastern portion of China proper, and they took advantage of this position to force thirty thousand families inhabiting this area, for the most part Chinese in origin, to move and settle in the depopulated districts of Southern Manchuria.

This wholesale transplantation of peoples is of the greatest interest from the anthropological point of view, for it brings out very clearly the difficulty attending the student who attempts to investigate the racial affinities of those who now speak either Chinese or any of the Turanian languages. From the Chinese annals it is very clear that a large proportion of the so-called Chinese in Northern China are descended from persons who once spoke a Turanian language, and at the same time it is equally clear that all during historic times the Turanian speaking people were constantly receiving a large admixture of Chinese blood. For the moment, however, we need not concern ourselves with these anthropological problems but may proceed with our study of the further fortunes of Shï Hu and his Hunnish court.

The setback which the Huns received from the Murungs in Manchuria naturally lowered their prestige throughout the whole of the Far East, with the result that before long several of the other peoples who had hitherto been willing to be vassals of the Huns began to reassert their independence. Among the first to do this were the powerful Tobas, who at this time were scattered all throughout Southern Mongolia. It will be remembered that the ruler of the Tobas owed his throne in no small measure to the support given him by the Huns in earlier days. But the rulers of states are notoriously ungrateful for past political favors, so it is not surprising to find the Tobas at this time breaking away from the Hunnish orbit. To emphasize this break with the Hunnish cause, the ruler of the Tobas ostentatiously married the sister of the King of the Murungs who had struck such a bitter blow at Hunnish prestige.

But though the Tobas thus entered into a matrimonial alliance with their fellow Sienbis, the Murungs, this did not mean that the Tobas became in any way subject to their kinsmen inhabiting Manchuria. The Tobas were quite strong enough to maintain their own complete independence. In fact, during all this period the power of the Tobas was constantly on the increase. The new Toba ruler proved to be a very effective leader, and succeeded in reuniting all the scattered Toba tribesmen under his own strong hands. The Tobas, being thus reunited, were able to establish control over many of the surrounding peoples, with the result that their territory soon reached from Manchuria in the East to a point not far from Farghana in the West, which meant that in addition to South Mongolia the Tobas were also the dominant factor in Zungaria and in a good part of Turkistan.

Inspired by this success, the ruler of the Tobas undertook a complete reorganization of his kingdom. He composed a new penal code in order to standardize the system of justice throughout his immense realm. At the same time he established a fairly elaborate administrative hierarchy to take the place of the loose tribal organization which had hitherto prevailed among the Toba clansmen. This new system was modeled after the traditional Chinese pattern, and in addition several persons of Chinese origin were installed in this hierarchy to see that it functioned smoothly.

Having achieved this stage of stable organization, the Toba ruler wished to go further. Gathering the principal tribal leaders together he proposed that they abandon, in part at least, their nomadic habits and establish a new permanent capital. It would appear that many of the tribal leaders regarded the proposal favorably, but the whole scheme came to nought because of the violent opposition offered by the ruler's mother, an energetic old dame who exclaimed, "From time immemorial we have been nomadic, and it is as nomads that we have been successful. If we lock ourselves up inside a city we shall be at the mercy of the first army that besieges us." The old lady possessed so great an influence over her fellow tribesmen that even her son was forced to abandon all hopes of persuading his subjects to adopt a settled existence.

Shï Hu, the Hunnish Emperor, was perfectly well aware of the great potential strength of the Toba military organization. For this reason, though deeply grieved over the refusal of the Tobas to acknowledge his overlordship any longer, he was wise enough to let well enough alone and made no attempt to force these erstwhile vassals to return to a condition of servitude.

It was, however, quite different when the third of these vassal powers, the Kingdom of Liang in the Far Northwest, broke out into open rebellion. Since this kingdom was relatively small in size and was supposed to possess only mediocre military resources, Shï Hu decided to embark upon another campaign in the hope that there at least he would be able to win a decisive victory.

The war between the Hunnish Empire and the Kingdom of Liang was fought with fierce determination on both sides. It was not surprising to find that the various Hunnish leaders showed signs of great personal bravery, but it came as a shock to the Huns that many of their opponents were no less dauntless. They were especially struck by the conduct of the commander of one small fortress who, when his resources were at an end, with his own hands strangled his wife and his family rather than allow them to fall into the hands of the Huns. Rude warriors though they were, the Huns were so struck at this heroic act that they gave the fallen enemy an honorable funeral.

In spite of the courage and determination of their opponents, the Hunnish army, led by one of Shï Hu's ablest generals, was at first fairly successful in its undertakings, and several of the towns subject to the King of Liang fell before the Hunnish attacks. Before long however, the tide of battle turned the other way, and the Hunnish forces received a series of defeats which forced them to return to China, leaving the King of Liang in complete control of his newly established kingdom.[11]

This final defeat of his expeditionary forces caused the Hunnish Emperor to become deeply despondent. He realized, perhaps for the first time, that he must abandon all hopes of becoming the undisputed sovereign of the whole of Eastern Asia. It is easy to understand the despondency of Shï Hu, but at the same time it must be remembered that none of these unsuccessful wars in any way menaced the continued existence or independence of his own kingdom. The Huns might not be able to crush the Murung Kingdom of Yen, the Toba Kingdom of Dai or the Chinese Kingdom of Liang, but it was equally obvious that none of these three kingdoms dared wage an aggressive war against the Huns, who continued to remain the absolute masters of the greater part of Northern China.

In reality, far more dangerous to the Hunnish cause than any of these foreign foes were the many internal difficulties which beset Shï Hu during the latter part of his reign. Among these internal difficulties was a revolution which broke out in the southwestern part of his domain shortly after the news spread that the Hunnish armies had met with reverses in their foreign campaigns. For a short time (349) this rebellion threatened to assume serious proportions but the Huns soon rallied their forces and showed that though they might be only indifferent soldiers when fighting on the frontiers, at least they were able to maintain law and order within their own realm.[12]

But even more upsetting than this armed rebellion was the constant strife and intrigue which went on inside of the Hunnish imperial family. From the very beginning of his reign Shï Hu had encountered great difficulty in dealing with his sons, and as time went on these family scandals became more and more acute. One or two of these scandals are worthy of brief mention. During the early part of his reign Shï Hu lavished a great deal of affection upon one of his sons, named Shï Suei, and this young prince was declared heir apparent to the throne. Shï Suei was a bold and dashing warrior, but he suffered from a very peculiar form of sexual perversion, namely sadism carried to the nth degree. From time to time he would gather around himself a small group of intimate companions and proceed to have a magnificent debauch. One of the ladies of his large harem was forced to array herself in all her finery, and then had her head cut off. The severed head of the lady was passed around on a platter for all the guests to admire, while the body was cut up and boiled into a stew which was then eaten by the prince and his gay young cronies.

These facts were, of course, unknown to Shï Hu, the prince's father, but the latter realized that his son was going in for a life of dissipation, and hoping to effect a reform, he forced the prince to assume many arduous administrative duties. When any of these duties remained unperformed, the Emperor ordered his son to be given a sound thrashing. The Crown Prince bitterly resented this punishment and determined to murder his father.

Since Shï Suei did not dare to break out in open rebellion, he thought out a very ingenious plan of carrying out a private assassination. He declared that he felt desperately ill, and taking to his bed, he sent a message to his august father the king asking that the latter be good enough to come and see him. Shï Hu was greatly upset by the news of his son's indisposition and immediately prepared to make a bedside visit. At the last moment, however, Shï Hu's intimate advisor, the Buddhist monk, Buddha Chinga, urged the Emperor not to go but to send instead a chamberlain to inquire into the invalid's condition. This was accordingly done, and when the chamberlain was slain by mistake, an official inquiry was set on foot with the result that the whole plot was brought to light. The Emperor was naturally beside himself with fury and immediately ordered an execution of the Crown Prince together with the latter's wives and children, twenty-six persons in all.

In place of the executed prince another son, named Shï Süan, was installed as Crown Prince and for several years continued to enjoy his father's affection. Eventually, however (in 348, to be exact), the Emperor began to regard with especial favor a still younger son, named Shï Tao, and it was obvious to all that the Emperor was playing with the idea of installing the younger prince as heir apparent. Shï Süan, the actual occupant of this post, became very dissatisfied with the way in which things were going, and he too determined to take matters into his own hands. Instead of striking directly at his father, however, Shï Süan arranged to have his brother, the new favroite, assassinated. This assassination was carried out by hired underlings, and Shï Süan was careful to prepare an alibi for himself. Extensive investigation, however, brought to light the whole conspiracy, and it was now the turn of Shï Süan to pay the supreme penalty for his attempt to retain succession to the throne. The wretched Crown Prince was subjected to every form of torture, and while in his last agony, but before life became extinct, he was thrown on a funeral pyre and burned alive.

In accordance with good old Chinese custom the wives and children of Shï Süan were forced to share in their lord and master's fate. In the august presence of the Emperor they were seized and executed. The execution of one of these children, a little boy, was the cause of a very moving scene. This little boy had long been a favorite with his grandfather, the Emperor, and when the time came for the boy to pay with his life for his father's crime, the little chap broke away from his executioners, and, wailing with terror, clung to his grandfather for protection. The executioners immediately followed and laid hands upon him. In his desperate struggle to resist them, the boy broke the Emperor's girdle which he had been clutching. Even the iron-hearted Shï Hu was deeply moved by this piteous spectacle, and gave orders that the boy's life be spared, but it was too late. Before he could speak the executioners had completed their bloody work. We are further told that the Emperor was so upset by this scene, that he immediately fell ill and took to his bed.[13]

After he had executed the two princes who had been officially installed as heirs apparent, Shï Hu had great difficulty in picking out a new person as his successor to the Hunnish throne. Having been bitterly disappointed in his two most promising offspring, he found it hard to choose a new favorite, with the result that the Hunnish court became honeycombed with intrigue. Each of the major candidates for the office of Crown Prince had among the great ministers of state ardent supporters and equally ardent opponents.

Just at this moment Shï Hu, who had never recovered from the shock of his grandson's execution, suddenly took a turn for the worse and died (A.D. 349). Immediately thereafter the whole Hunnish Empire was thrown into the utmost confusion. Because of the doubt which existed as to the legitimate successor there was a wild scramble for the throne, and in the course of the next few months no less than three princelings were solemnly proclaimed rulers of the Hunnish Empire, but each of these persons was seized and executed by his respective successor.

At the end of this same year (349) supreme power over the court passed into the hands of still a fourth person, a princeling by the name of Shï Min whose actions make him worthy of brief mention. Though this new ruler was possessed of the imperial family name of Shï, he was really an interloper since he had been not the real but only the adopted son of the deceased Emperor Shï Hu. We are expressly told by the Chinese records that Shï Min, the new monarch, like the real members of the house of Shï, was of Hunnish origin. But in spite of this fact, from an early period in his life Shï Min had thrown in his lot with the Chinese element at the Hunnish court, and had often been regarded as distinctly pro-Chinese and anti-Hunnish in his sympathies. Soon after his accession to the throne (in 350) Shï Min felt that the dominant Hunnish aristocracy were beginning to regard him with suspicion and in a desperate attempt to maintain his rulership, he made use of a very bold and startling political move.

After having gathered round himself a large number of recruits from the Chinese section of the populace, Shï Min suddenly issued orders that all persons of Hunnish blood should be killed. The Chinese, who had never loved these Hunnish masters, responded to these orders with unconcealed glee, and in the course of the next few weeks no less than two hundred thousand Huns, high and low, old and young, male and female, were put to death. As the Huns had been residing in China for some time and had adopted Chinese dress and were fluent in the use of the Chinese language, it was not always easy to tell the difference between the native Chinese and those of Hunnish origin. In all cases of doubt, the person under suspicion was put to the sword, and we are expressly told that those Chinese who possessed high aquiline noses or hairy faces, and who therefore were thought to resemble Huns, were killed.[14]

This wholesale massacre of the Hunnish population naturally caused those Huns who escaped execution to organize a desperate resistance to the new regime. Rallying around one of the few princes of the imperial house of Shï who had survived the recent blood bath, these Hunnish rebels fled to the Northeast and managed to capture the town of Siang-guo, which thereafter served as their headquarters. From this center the Hunnish rebels began a bloody war in the hope that they might be able to vanquish the traitorous Shï Min and reëstablish Hunnish control over all of Northern China. But they were well aware of their own weakness, so that in addition to battling on their own account, this Hunnish remnant sent a piteous appeal for help to their ancient enemies, the Murungs of Southern Manchuria.

Shï Min, in response to this threat, immediately marched northward and launched a huge counter-offensive against the Hunnish rebels in the hope of wiping them out of existence. After much fighting, during which time the fortunes of war favored now one and now the other side, this objective was at last accomplished. The Hunnish pretender to the throne was assassinated and shortly afterwards Shï Min was able to capture Siang-guo itself, the last of the Hunnish strongholds (A.D. 352). But Shï Min was not able to enjoy his triumph for very long, for only a few months after he had destroyed the Hunnish opposition, the Murung armies arrived on the scene. Though they had arrived too late to render any effectual aid to the Hunnish rebels who had called on them, these Murungs determined that they should not be daunted by this fact, but could and should wage war on their own account.

In a desperate battle fought not far from the modern city of Peking, Shï Min was himself captured by the Manchurian troops and was shortly afterwards beheaded. After this event the Murungs had little difficulty in overrunning and occupying most of the territory which had formerly belonged to the Hunnish Empire. It was only in the Hunnish capital, the city of Ye, that any serious attempt was made further to resist the invaders. Here the son of Shï Min was placed upon the throne, and for several months he and his followers put up a gallant defense, but as food was unprocurable, they eventually began to suffer terribly from the pangs of hunger. At last the defenders were driven to cannibalism. Among the choice titbits in the way of food was the flesh torn from the ladies in the huge harem brought together by the former rulers of the house of Jao. Eventually even this food supply became exhausted and the city was forced to surrender.[15]

In this way ended the last phase of Hunnish domination over Northern China. More than two centuries were to elapse before this region was again brought under native rulership. The Huns, as we have seen, were succeeded by the Murung Sienbi. Later records tell us how the Murungs were succeeded by a dynasty of Tibetan origin, and this dynasty was in turn succeeded by a dynasty established by the Toba Sienbis.

During all of this troubled time, during which control over Northern China was passing from the hands of one barbarian group to another, the Huns were never able to make another bid for empire in the Far East. The reason for this, no doubt, is that the flower of the Hunnish nobility had been killed off by Shï Min, and those few Hunnish families which remained in China proper were rapidly absorbed by the surrounding Chinese population.

It was only in the far-off northwestern portions of the Celestial Empire, in the barren wastes between Southern Mongolia and China proper, that a few barbarous Hunnish groups were able to maintain a separate existence. In the course of the following century two of these groups made a brief bid for power and fame by carving out petty kingdoms for themselves. But these kingdoms were confined to the distant northwestern area, and they never succeeded in exercising any considerable influence over the Celestial Empire as a whole. For this reason they are worthy of only casual mention.

The first of these petty states to be considered is that which became known as the Kingdom of Hia, and which had as its center the Ordos, that curious geographic region which lies North of the Great Wall, and thus outside of China, but South of the Yellow River, and thus outside of Mongolia. When the old Southern Hunnish Kingdom fell to pieces (in A.D. 216) a number of the Hunnish tribes gradually made their way to the southwest and settled in this Ordos region. As the Ordos is country ill-suited for agriculture, the Huns who settled in this area were able to retain their old nomadic habits and hence became far less exposed to Chinese civilization than their cousins who settled in China proper and who in due course of time produced, as we have seen, the Han and Jao dynasties which were, indeed, Hunnish in origin but Chinese in most essential characteristics.

During the period the Han and Jao dynasties were ruling the northern part of the Celestial Empire, the Hunnish inhabitants of the Ordos were perfectly willing to accept the jurisdiction of their Southern cousins, but after the fall of these two dynasties the Ordos Huns were forced to fend for themselves. For a time they had a very bad time of it and were ravaged and forced to pay tribute by several of the surrounding kingdoms which arose during this troubled time. This period of weakness came to an end, however, in A.D. 407, when these Ordos Huns found an able protector and leader in the person of a certain Po Po.

Po Po was a direct descendant of one of the last rulers of the old Southern Hunnish Kingdom, and hence was a distant cousin of Liu Yüan, the man who had founded the (Hunnish) Han dynasty. But unlike the latter, Po Po was a man of no culture or erudition, and always preferred a wild roaming life on horseback to existence in the effete and crowding cities. As if to display his contempt for civil life, he would never part from his bow and sword even while holding audience with his ministers of state. Po Po, moreover, was a man of very violent temper, and had no hesitation in venting his passions upon anyone who came near him. If anyone dared smile in his presence, his lips were cut off; if anyone dared offer a remonstrance regarding the conduct of affairs of state, his tongue was plucked out; if anyone, even a minister of state, dared look Po Po directly in the face, he was immediately blinded.

During the later part of his reign (418) Po Po even managed to capture the ancient city of Chang-an, the seat of so many dynasties at different times. The capture of this city made Po Po the master of a large part of Western China, and in recognition of his new importance he abandoned the title of King and assumed the title of Emperor of Hia. Some of the ministers of state wished to make of the recently captured Chang-an the capital of the empire. Po Po, however, could never feel at home in the warm valleys of the South, so he left a son to look after Chang-an and the surrounding region, while he himself hastened back to his beloved Ordos country. Here he continued to rule savagely but gloriously until his death in 425.

The Empire which was established by the savage Po Po fell to pieces shortly after his death. He was followed in rapid succession by two of his sons, both of whom engaged in disastrous wars with the Toba clan, which was now rapidly rising to supreme power in Northern China. Both of these sons were captured and killed by the Tobas, and in 432 the Hia Empire went out of existence. Thereafter we hear nothing more of the Huns inhabiting this region, and it would appear that they were completely absorbed by the Tobas.[16]

The last of the Hunnish states which we are called upon to describe is the little Kingdom of Northern Liang, which had the center of its existence still further to the west than the above mentioned "Empire" of Hia, with which it was more or less contemporaneous. It may be remembered that the province then known as Liang occupied the extreme northwestern portion of China, being in fact the region captured from the Huns and colonized by the Chinese during the years 121-108 B.C. In addition to the numerous Chinese colonists, however, this province had never ceased to have a large number of "Barbarian" inhabitants, among whom were a large group of Huns, direct descendants of the tribesmen of the old Southern Hunnish Kingdom.

In A.D. 401 these Huns produced a leader, named Mêng Sün, of sufficient importance to earn for himself a small but permanent place in world history. One of this man's ancestors, in the days of the Hunnish Empire, had occupied an administrative post known as "Dsükü King." In memory of this event, and with an eye to securing the support of his fellow tribesmen who still cherished the tales of ancient Hunnish glory, this man assumed the ancient title as a family name and hence is known to fame as Dsükü Mêng Sün. Organizing the scattered Hunnish tribesmen into a compact army, he proceeded to ravage the surrounding districts, and in the end managed to make himself lord and master of a region of considerable size and importance. After assuming various ranks and titles he eventually became known as the King of Northern Liang.

It should be noted, however, that this Hunnish monarch never dared assume the title of Emperor, and that he was never even a serious contendant for supremacy over the Celestial Empire. He remained, and was content to remain, the feudal lord over the most important of China's frontier regions. His kingdom had control over all intercourse between China and the western regions, and it was as a result of this control that Mêng Sün and his court acquired most of their wealth and importance. What is of especial interest and importance in this connection is that among the western states with which the Kingdom of Liang maintained intercourse, was one dominated by the far distant Western or European Huns. From the brief mention made of these events in the Chinese records it appears quite possible in fact that it was either the great Attila himself or one of the vassal kings immediately subject to Attila who dispatched several commercial missions to his distant cousin, the Hunnish King of Liang.

As long as Mêng Sün remained alive the power and prestige of his little kingdom remained unabated, but upon his death in 433 his son and heir, like the heirs to the Empire of Hia, was foolish enough to fall foul of the rapidly expanding Toba Empire with the result that he himself was attacked and captured after which the whole of his territory was added to the Toba domain. This event took place in 439. Thus passed away the last of the Hunnish kingdoms in the Celestial Empire.

But though the Huns thus lost their last foothold in China proper they were able to maintain, for a few years longer, a faint remnant of their former glory in Kashgaria. When the Tobas came and captured the King of Liang, two brothers of this monarch gathered together a small army and marched westward in the hope of being able to carve out a new kingdom for themselves. Their first objective was the Kingdom of Loulan or Shanshan which they managed to capture after two campaigns. Shortly afterward, however, they became dissatisfied with this territory and wandered northward in the search for fresh adventures, and before long made themselves masters of the rich territory in the Turfan depression formerly known as Güṣhï (which has frequently figured in the foregoing pages) but which was then called Gaochang.

One of these brothers died shortly afterwards (A.D. 441) but the other, named An Jou, continued to rule over this newly established kingdom for several years longer. In 460, however, the wild Avars swept down from the plains of Mongolia and poor An Jou was put to death. Thus perished (only seven years after the death of Attila, and the dismemberment of his empire) the last of the Hunnish monarchs in the Far East.[17]

CHAPTER SIXTEEN

THE HUNS IN EUROPE—THE FIRST PHASE

Events in Southeastern Europe—The Scythian and Sarmatian Domains—The Goths and Other Germanic Tribes—The Alani—The Northern Huns in Turkistan—The Huns Overrun the Alani—The Huns Overrun the East Goths—Hunnish Defeat of the West Goths—The West Goths Take Refuge in the Roman Empire—Their Rebellion and Defeat of the Emperor Valens—Settlement of the West Goths in the Balkans and the East Goths in Pannonia.

WE ARE now in a position to discuss the fortunes of those Hunnish tribes which moved westward, and which eventually became masters of a great part of Europe. Before, however, we can discuss in detail this westward drift of the Huns it is necessary for us to give a brief survey of the distribution of peoples just prior to the Hunnish invasion. First of all a word regarding the Scythians and Sarmatians, who for so long held the dominant position in Southeastern Europe.

As we have already had occasion to observe, in the first century B.C. the Scythians, who had long possessed control over Southern Russia, began to disintegrate, and were slowly but surely pushed westward by various Sarmatian hordes migrating from Central Asia. In the first century A.D., this Sarmatian pressure became even more pronounced and resulted in the complete break-up of the Scythian Kingdom. Small groups of Scythians, by retreating to inaccessible spots, managed to retain their independence for several decades, but eventually even these groups were absorbed by the all-powerful Sarmatian invaders.

Not infrequently Sarmatian bands would gallop to the Southeast and, passing through the Caucasus region, plunder large portions of Asia Minor or of Northwestern Persia, but for the most part they continued to drift in a westerly direction. In addition to Southern Russia they soon overran what is now the Kingdom of Rumania; other bands went even further and, crossing the Carpathian Mountains, they occupied most of Eastern Hungary, that is, the region East and North of the Danube River. Often some of these Sarmatian bands crossed the Danube at various places and looted isolated portions of the Roman Empire. From time to time, Roman legions, in their turn, would cross the Danube and attack some of the Sarmatian encampments by way of reprisal, but at no time did the Sarmatians carry out a systematic invasion of the Roman Empire, nor did the Romans, except for one occasion, toward the close of the reign of Marcus Aurelius, ever dream of incorporating any portion of the Sarmatian domain within the limits of their empire.

All along, the Sarmatians remained true nomads and devotees of the horse culture. For this reason they made no attempt to conquer Northern Russia or Central Germany, both of which were heavily wooded regions at this time. It was for this reason also that the Sarmatians made little or no attempt to interfere with Roman supremacy in mountainous and forested Dacia, the modern Transylvania, the only region North of the Danube River which the Romans ever succeeded in adding to their domain.

But though the Sarmatians were closely allied, as regards race, language and culture, with their predecessors, the Scythians, there was always one important point of difference between the Scythian and Sarmatian periods of domination. Though the Scythians remained broken up into a number of separate tribes many of which continued to be wholly or partially independent, yet a great Scythian Empire did come into being which professed to exercise control at least over most of Southern Russia and the surrounding regions. The Sarmatians on the other hand, though excellent soldiers, were never successful at empire building. They were good conquerors but poor administrators. Each tribe continued to assert and exercise rulership over itself, and at no time was one of these Sarmatian groups able to dominate all or even a majority of the others.

It is for this reason that we find the Sarmatian peoples broken up into a great number of separate and distinct groups, each of them bearing a different name. It is unnecessary for us to cite anything like a complete list of these names; in fact, only three of these tribal groups are worthy of special mention. The first of these were the Jazyges, who occupied a large portion of Sarmatian Hungary. The second were the Roxolani, the center of whose power was in Southwestern Russia. The third and most important of these groups were the Alani. We find isolated sections of the Alani scattered over many portions of the Sarmatian world, but the bulk of the Alani continued for several centuries to reside in the vast steppes East of the Don River, both in the southeastern portion of Europe and the northwestern portion of Turkistan.[1]

This lack of unity on the part of the Sarmatian peoples was no doubt responsible for the ease with which they were eventually overthrown. For the first time since the beginnings of recorded history the invaders of the steppe-lands of Southern Russia on this occasion came not from the East but from the North and West, for the successors of the Sarmatians in this region were various Germanic tribes which had formerly dwelt on the shores of the Baltic Sea, and which gradually pushed their way southward and southeastward until about A.D. 200, they had gradually occupied practically all the territory in Europe which had formerly been in the hands of the Sarmatians. Here and there, especially in Hungary, small groups of Sarmatians survived and retained some measure of independence for several decades, but in no case were they able to contend on equal terms with the Germanic peoples, who soon made themselves masters of all that portion of Southeastern Europe which lay North and East of the Danube.

The expansion of the Germanic peoples is of great interest to us for several reasons. In the first place, the fact that the Germans spread is a sign that in spite of much weakness and internal disorder the Roman Empire was still able to maintain its power and its boundaries more or less intact as long as it was faced merely with enemies of Teutonic origin. All along the Rhine the Romans had frequently to be on their guard against German invasions, but for several centuries the Roman frontier remained comparatively firm, with the result that the Germans, as their population expanded and they felt the need for fresh territory, were forced to expand to the southeast. Having tried in vain to occupy Roman territory, they were forced to content themselves with the occupation of the territory formerly occupied by the Sarmatians. Had not the subsequent Hunnish invasions from Central Asia forced the Germanic tribes to abandon the Sarmatian territory, it is probable that the tendency of the Germanic peoples to expand to the southeast rather than the southwest would have continued indefinitely, with results of immense significance for later world history.

It is very unfortunate that the Roman historians have left us extremely inadequate accounts as to the manner in which the Germanic peoples overran and took possession of the territory formerly occupied by the Sarmatians. All we know is that in the latter part of the second century A.D. the Romans still had the various Sarmatian peoples as their neighbors on the northeast and that in the early part of the third century these Sarmatians had been replaced by various Germanic tribes, many of them destined to play a prominent part in later historical development.

In Hungary we find the Vandals, the Suevi (a branch of the older Quadi) and the Gepids. Rumania and Southern Russia were in the hands of the Goths. The Goths in turn were broken into several divisions of which the most important were the Visigoths or West Goths, who lived West of the Dneister, and the Ostrogoths, whose headquarters were between the Dneister and the Don River, and hence had control of nearly all of Southern Russia. Among all these peoples it was the Goths who were the most important, and who are mentioned most frequently in contemporary records.

But though the Goths and their allies succeeded in defeating and dispossessing the Sarmatians of most of their territory, it is probable that a goodly number of the Sarmatian peoples instead of being killed off were absorbed into one or other of the Germanic tribal organizations. It is certain that the Goths who were still in a semi-barbarous state were greatly influenced by many phases of the Sarmatian culture. Gothic art, in fact, which had an enormous influence upon the art of all the later Germanic peoples, is little more than direct continuation of Sarmatian art.

The Goths, moreover, adopted many of the nomadic or semi-nomadic features of the Scytho-Sarmatian culture, and, as they appear in Roman History, reside for the most part, like their Sarmatian predecessors, in tent-wagons. They also adopted a goodly amount of the horse-culture of the Sarmatians, and in their knowledge of horses and horsemanship they were far ahead of the other contemporary Germanic peoples. Even so, the Goths never adopted the Sarmatian horse-culture in its entirety. The tribal chieftains and the most eminent warriors went to battle on horseback, but the bulk of the Gothic tribesmen continued to fight on foot.

But in addition to borrowing from the Sarmatians the Goths also borrowed from the Greeks and Romans, especially after they had been settled for some time in close proximity to the Roman Empire. Shortly after their settlement in Southern Russia we find that the Goths and their allies embarked on a number of successful maritime expeditions, and it is certain that the Gothic knowledge of shipbuilding and navigation was derived from the Graeco-Roman colonies and vassal states on the northern shores of the Black Sea, such for example as the so-called Kingdom of Bosphorous which was long in direct dependence upon the Roman Empire.

It is, moreover, highly probable that the curious Runic alphabet which at one time was widely used among the barbaric peoples of Northern Europe was derived from a Gothic attempt to imitate the Greek alphabet. This Runic alphabet had a very limited scope and application, and was employed chiefly for short inscriptions on sword handles or on tombs, but in the fourth century the Goths went even further in the direction of a written language and literature.

As the result of dwelling on the borders of the Roman Empire for over a hundred years many of the Goths became converted to Christianity, and eventually a celebrated Gothic priest named Ulfilas was consecrated bishop, with instructions to push forward the preaching of the Christian religion among his Gothic brethren. With this end in view he prepared a new alphabet better suited to literary use. This having been done, the worthy Ulfilas proceeded to translate the major portion of the Bible into his native tongue. Being a man of peace, however,

Ulfilas refused to translate certain portions of the Old Testament into Gothic on the grounds that these portions dwelt too much on the glories of war and hence were ill-suited to the needs of the Gothic peoples, who were already too much imbued with the martial spirit. By great good fortune a good portion of Ulfilas' translation of the Bible has been preserved to us and these lengthy fragments constitute the most important monument which we possess of the early form of the Germanic group of languages.

Largely because of Ulfilas' literary efforts all of the Goths eventually adopted the Christian religion, though this process of conversion was not completed until long after Ulfilas himself had died. It is, moreover, of importance to note that the Goths and their Germanic neighbors were converted not to orthodox Catholicism but to the so-called Arian heresy, a fact which greatly embittered the later relations between the Gothic peoples and the inhabitans of the Roman Empire.

But though the Goths were perfectly willing to adopt many features of the Graeco-Roman culture, this did not prevent them from being involved in many long and bitterly contested wars with the Roman Empire. It was during the reign of Severus Alexander (222-235) that the Goths destroyed the Graeco-Roman towns of Olbia and Tyras on the northern shores of the Black Sea. A few years later, beginning with A.D. 240, they appeared on the banks of the Danube and began their invasion of the Roman Empire proper. From 240 until 270 there was almost constant warfare between the Goths and the Romans. On several occasions the Romans met with overwhelming reverses. One notable defeat occurred in 251 when a large Roman army was practically destroyed and the Emperor Decius himself lost his life. Had the Goths taken full advantage of this victory they might easily have overrun a large portion of the Roman Empire, but for the moment they were still bent on plunder rather than on conquest, and having secured an enormous amount of booty they returned to their homes North of the Danube.

Encouraged by this success, the Goths made a number of similar raids in the years that followed. Some of these raids were made by land, but several of them were maritime in character. The Goths and their allies, having learned the art of navigation, managed to terrify all the principal cities along the coasts of the Black and Aegean Seas. None of these raids led to permanent loss of territory on the part of the Romans except in the case of Dacia, or Transylvania, the one transdanubian region which had been incorporated within the Roman Empire. We have no record as to when the Romans were forced to abandon this province, but the sudden cessation of Roman coins and inscriptions dates from about this time.

Another major crisis arose in A.D. 269. The Goths and all of their kindred tribes crossed the Danube and began to pour into the Roman Empire in greater numbers than ever before. In fact the records tell us that on this occasion the Gothic host reached the enormous number of three hundred and twenty thousand persons. This time, however, Rome was fortunate enough to be ruled over by the very able soldier, the Emperor Claudius. After several desperate encounters, Claudius, who led his army in person, was able to win an overwhelming victory. The bulk of the Gothic army was completely wiped out, and the scattered remnants which survived were forced to beat a hasty retreat to the North.

The victory which Claudius achieved ended all serious danger from a Gothic invasion for over a hundred years. To be sure the Romans did not dare press their advantage too far. Not only were the Goths left undisturbed in their own territory, but it was considered inadvisable even to attempt the reconquest of Dacia. Under Aurelian, the successor of Claudius, this province which had long been lost in fact, was definitely and officially abandoned, and the Roman inhabitants of this region were ordered to return South of the Danube.

During the century which followed Claudius's victory we find very little in the Roman annals concerning the Goths. We know that several of the emperors, among them Constantine, recruited their legions from among the Gothic hordes and that these Gothic soldiers served their Roman masters very well, but the recruiting of these soldiers did not affect the relations between the Roman Empire and the Germanic kingdoms which had arisen North of the Danube. For the most part this century of peace between the Romans and the barbarians was filled by struggles between the barbarians themselves. It was during this period that the Goths inflicted major defeats upon the Vandals and the Gepids, and definitely established Gothic supremacy among all the Germanic peoples inhabiting Southeastern Europe.

The old difference between the West Goths and the East Goths continued to exist, but early in the fourth century A.D., political leadership definitely passed into the hands of the East Goths. This was especially true after the accession to power of the Ostrogothic King Hermanrik, who became so renowned that he was frequently referred to by his fellow countrymen as the Gothic Alexander the Great. It was Hermanrik who transformed the East Gothic Kingdom into a great empire by conquering the Slavic tribes who then inhabited Northeastern Russia. Hermanrik also exercised some kind of overlordship over the West Goths and their neighbors still further to the West. The West Goths continued to be ruled over by their own tribal leaders, of whom the most famed was Athanaric, but the very fact that the Roman annals refer to these leaders under the title of Judex or judges as opposed to Rex or King shows that these West Gothic leaders admittedly acted in a subordinate capacity.

It was in A.D. 366, during the reign of the Emperor Valens, that the Goths again became involved in a serious conflict with the Roman Empire, and on this occasion it was the Romans rather than the Goths who took the offensive. A rival claimant to the Imperial throne, named Procopius, was defeated and killed. Valens, however, was so furious that the Goths had sided with his rival that he determined to march northward and inflict a stinging defeat upon the Gothic kingdom, or rather upon the West Gothic sub-kingdom, his own immediate neighbor. The campaign against the Goths lasted from 367 to 369. During the first two years very little was accomplished, but in 369 a Roman army marched far into the heart of the West Gothic territory and even reached and fought with their powerful kinsmen, the East Goths, though we do not hear of their having faced in battle the mighty Hermanrik himself.

As a result of this campaign the Goths sued for peace, and since the Romans were somewhat exhausted by their recent efforts they were perfectly willing to listen to this plea and in 370 a new treaty was arranged between the Goths and the Roman Empire. The Romans acknowledged the absolute independence of the Goths, but the Roman practice of giving annual presents of money and foodstuffs to the barbarians as a price of good behavior was indefinitely suspended. Another important proviso of the treaty was that the Goths were forbidden at all times to cross the Danube except at two places. At these two places special market towns were provided in order that the lucrative trade between the Goths and the Romans might continue in operation.

It is well to insist upon the triumph of Roman warfare and diplomacy on this occasion, for it shows that in 370, only six years before the Hunnish invasion caused a complete change in the political geography of Eastern Europe, the Goths had ceased to be an active menace to the Roman Empire. It was the Goths and not the Romans who were on the defensive and had not the Goths been driven to desperation by the Hunnish invasion, they might well have been content to remain for an indefinite period the neighbors rather than the invaders of the Roman Empire.[2]

After this survey of the Gothic peoples and their invasion of Southeastern Europe, let us examine for a moment the fate of the Alani, the only one of the Sarmatian peoples who did not become subjected to Gothic or at least Germanic supremacy. Their domain began just East of the River Don (which served as a boundary between the Goths and the Alani) and embraced for many centuries an enormous amount of territory, as it included not only the region between the Don and Volga Rivers as far South as the Caucasus Mountains but also the greater part of Northwestern Turkistan.

The Alani had a long and interesting history but unfortunately this history is little known to us, for the classical authors make mention of the Alani only when they attacked some outpost of the Roman Empire. In earlier times, i.e., before the coming of the Goths, occasional bands of Alani made long inroads to the West, but for the most part they preferred to march southward, and, crossing the Caucasus Mountains, make plundering expeditions in the regions which lay to the South of this mountain range. Thus in A.D. 78, we hear of their invading Medes in Northwestern Persia and making an attack upon the Parthians. A century later (in A.D. 168), during the reign of Marcus Aurelius, they made several looting expeditions into various parts of Asia Minor.

The coming of the Goths into Southern Russia made it impossible for the Alani to continue their raids to the West, and the rise of a powerful Kingdom of Armenia made it difficult for them to make fresh inroads to the South, but we know that they remained as independent and much feared people inside of their own domain. In 290 we find that Tiridates, King of Armenia, made use of Alani mercenaries in his army, and a few years later (317) Chosroes II, another King of Armenia, married a woman called Sathanik, the daughter of a King of the Alani.

Even in the fourth century we find Ammianus Marcellinus, a contemporary historian, speaking of the Alani domain extending far eastward into Asia. Incidentally, Ammianus has several very interesting things to tell us about the Alani. Nearly all of them, he says, were men of great stature and beauty. Their hair was somewhat yellow. The lightness of their armor made them very rapid in their movements. In many respects their mode of life was like the Huns, except that they were somewhat more civilized.

When Ammianus proceeds to tell us more about the Alani mode life we find that these Iranian nomads had remained remarkably true to the old Scytho-Sarmatian type of culture. Like the early Scythians and Sarmatians, the Alani lived solely on meat and milk, and dwelt in tents mounted upon wagons. They too were devotees of the horse-culture, and the Alani tribesmen thought it beneath them to walk. They too gloried in war, and made use of the scalps of their armies as trappings and ornaments for their war horses. Even as regards their religious culture the Alani of the fourth century A.D. were remarkably like the early Scythians and Sarmatians. This is clearly seen by the fact that they practiced divination by means of twigs and by the fact that their religious cult centered around a naked sword thrust into the ground, which was worshipped as a representation of the God of War.[3]

After this discussion of the geographic and ethnographic background we may now return to the Huns and trace their migration westward into the lands inhabited by the Alani and the Goths. In this connection it is necessary for us to go back for a moment to the first century A.D. and call to mind the fact that at this period the Hunnish Empire broke up into the Northern and Southern Hunnish Kingdoms. The Huns who invaded China, and who established inside of China various Hunnish dynasties, were all descendants of the inhabitants of the old South Hunnish Kingdom. Those Huns who migrated westward and eventually invaded Europe were all descendants of the old North Hunnish Empire.

We have already seen that the tendency on the part of the Northern Huns to shift westward began shortly after the breakup of the Hunnish Empire into its Northern and Southern divisions. This tendency was accentuated by the defeats which the Northern Huns received in A.D. 89-91. We are expressly told that after this time the Sienbi from Western Manchuria occupied practically all of the old Hunnish domain in Northern Mongolia, and that the Northern Huns were forced to reëstablish their kingdom in Zungaria and Northeastern Turkistan. From A.D. 91 to 170, the Northern Huns continued to reside in this region, the unwilling inhabitants of the northeastern fringe of Turkistan, but with their attention still centered upon Kashgaria and the Chinese Empire. This last affiliation with the East was broken by the rise of the great Sienbi conqueror, Tanshïhuai, who, in addition to ruling over Mongolia, extended his domain far to the West and wrested Zungaria from Hunnish control.

As the result of these Sienbi conquests many of the peoples who had formerly formed part of the Hunnish Empire accepted Sienbi supremacy and were incorporated in the Sienbi Empire. By taking this step they were able to remain in their ancestral lands, and when, several centuries later, the Sienbi Empire fell they reëmerged as separate groups under new names. Among such peoples were the various Gaogü tribes, the direct ancestors of the later Asena and Uigur Turks.

A special position was occupied by a people known to the Chinese as Yueban, who dwelt in the northwestern part of Zungaria. The Chinese chronicles tell us that the Yueban formed part of the main group of the old North Hunnish Empire and that after the breakup of this empire they continued to reside in Zungaria until the sixth century when they became absorbed in the newly arisen Turkish Empire. This group, we are told, numbered about two hundred thousand persons. We are told, as if it were something extraordinary, that the Yueban were very clean in their habits and always washed themselves before eating.[4]

But whereas the Yueban remained in Zungaria, the main section of the Huns moved westward into Northeastern Turkistan. We are expressly told that the Huns who migrated to this region were the bravest and strongest of the Hunnish peoples, as is indeed evident from the fact that they preferred to seek a new home in the West rather than submit to Chinese or Sienbi domination.[5] For two hundred years, i.e., from 170 to 370, we hear almost nothing of the fate which befell these Northern or as we shall have to call them, Western Huns. During this period the Chinese were so beset by internal problems and by the invasions of their immediate neighbors, the Sienbi peoples, that they lost all contacts with those Huns who now lived in distant Turkistan and who were no longer able to attack any portion of the Celestial Empire. During this period the Alani and the Goths still formed a barrier between the Huns and the Roman Empire, so that neither the Greek nor Latin authors throw any light upon Hunnish activities. Only once are they mentioned at all and that is in connection with Tigranes, King of Armenia (ca. A.D. 290) who in addition to having Alani mercenaries is said also to have had a contingent of Huns in his army.[6] Half a century later (ca. 356) we hear that the northern frontier of Persia was attacked by the "Chionites." It is probable that these Chionites were a group of Huns.[7]

During the two hundred years in which the Huns are almost lost to history it is probable that a number of important changes took place. On settling in Turkistan they undoubtedly intermarried with many of the peoples they found in this region. We have every reason to believe that they interbred to a certain extent with the Alani, whom they slowly but surely pushed westward. It is almost certain that they interbred to an even greater extent with some of the Finnish or Finno-Ugrian tribes who had lived for centuries in Southern and Southwestern Siberia.

There are many grounds for supposing that a good deal of the elaborate political organization of the old Hunnish Empire was lost during the two centuries the Huns disappeared from view, for when the Huns reemerge upon the pages of recorded history we hear nothing of the administrative system which characterized the Huns during the period they dwelt in Mongolia. There are certain scholars (amongst them Hirth) who believe that at least the old office of Shanyu or Supreme Ruler continued to exist and was occupied by the old royal Hunnish family, the same family who had reigned during the period of the first and second Hunnish Empires. This belief, however, is not very well founded, for when the Huns later came into contact with the Roman world the classical authors tell us that these barbarians were not under the authority of a single king but were contented with the irregular government of their nobles. It is, however, probable that many of these "nobles" or tribal leaders were descended from the old Hunnish royal family and that the disappearance of supreme central authority was merely due to the fact that no one member of this family was able to secure the allegiance of all of his kinsmen.[8]

But though the Huns, during their long period of isolation in Turkistan, underwent many radical changes both in blood and in political organization they remained keenly conscious of their affiliations with the old Hunnish Empires, as seen by the way in which they clung to the name of Hun, which remained their national designation as long as they continued to exist as an ethnic unit. It is probable, moreover, that along with the name many other features of the old national tradition were kept alive in the hearts of the Hunnish tribesmen during the period that history is silent regarding their activities.

These Huns reappear in the pages of world history during the latter part of the fourth century because of one of their achievments which was of sufficient importance for it to be recorded in the annals of both the Roman and the Chinese Empires. This achievement was nothing less than the complete destruction of the Kingdom of the Alani. But in spite of the importance of this event, we are singularly ignorant of the exact time when this conquest took place. It is quite possible that this overwhelming victory was not the result of a single campaign but was the consequence of a long-drawn-out war of attrition which may have begun as early as 350. In any case, the complete destruction of the Alani kingdom was accomplished by A.D. 374, when the Huns first appear on the banks of the Don and begin their passage into Europe.[9]

After the destruction of the Alani kingdom, many of the Alani tribesmen subjected themselves to Hunnish rulership, and willingly accompanied their Hunnish overlords on many of the raids which the latter subsequently undertook. Other members of the Alani confederation, however, wishing to maintain their independence, betook themselves to flight. Some fled southward and took refuge in the Caucasus Mountains where their direct descendants, the Ossetes, live at the present day. Others fled westward, bursting across the frontiers of the East Gothic Kingdom.

It was not long before the Huns themselves followed in the footsteps of those Alani who fled to the West. Crossing the River Don, they came into the territory of the East Goths in 374. We are told that on this occasion the Huns were led by a king or chieftain named Balamber.

The very appearance of the Huns seems to have made a deep impression upon the East Gothic tribesmen. Jordanes, himself a Goth, and the author of the celebrated history of the Gothic people, paints a vivid picture of the impression which the Huns made upon the Gothic mind. "By the terror of their features," he says, "they inspired great fear in those whom perhaps they did not really surpass in war. They made their foes flee in horror, because their swarthy aspect was fearful and they had a sort of shapeless lump, not a head, with pin holes rather than eyes. Their hardihood is evident in their wild appearance and they are beings who are cruel to their children on the very day they are born. For they cut the cheeks of the males with a sword, so that before they receive the nourishment of milk they must learn to endure wounds. Hence they grow old beardless, and their young men are without comeliness because a face furrowed by the sword spoils by its scars the natural beauty of a beard. They are short in stature, quick in bodily movements, ready in the use of bow and arrow, and have firmset necks which are ever erect in pride."

From Jordanes' description it is obvious that the Huns at the time of their invasion of Europe practiced scarifications, a custom which was seemingly unknown at the time of their residence in Mongolia. It would be interesting to know just when and how this custom was introduced.

Some persons have assumed from the description given by our Gothic author that the Huns must have been completely Mongoloid in appearance. But this is certainly a mistake. Their hairlessness is not due to racial background as has sometimes been supposed (do we not know that the Huns in China were known for their hairiness?), but because of the practice of scarification, as is specifically stated. This idea is confirmed by the fact that the classical authors who agree in their description of the Huns with Jordanes speak of the Huns as having hairy legs.

It is highly probable that the Huns, because of their long residence in the Far East and their frequent intermarrying with the Chinese and other Mongoloid people, did have a considerable amount of Mongoloid blood in their veins, enough to have impressed the Goths and the Romans with the strangeness of their appearance, but they were far from being pure-blooded Mongoloids. Even when the Huns lived in Mongolia the Mongoloid element must have decreased rather than increased as the result of intermarrying with the Indo-European Alani and also with various Finno-Ugrian peoples. Incidentally, this conclusion is substantiated by the excavation of skeletal material from Hunnish graves in Hungary and various other parts of Europe. Judging from this material, the Hunnish invaders of the fourth and fifth centuries were racially a highly mixed group in which the Mongoloid strain was only one of several important elements.

From the description of the manners and customs of the Huns given us by Ammianus Marcellinus, it is obvious that they had preserved their old nomadic culture almost intact. "None of the Huns plows or even touches a plow handle. For they have no settled home, but are alike homeless and lawless, continually wandering with their wagons, which are indeed their homes.... They do not live under roofed houses, looking upon such houses as tombs. There is not to be found amongst them a single cabin thatched with reed. They wear linen clothes or else the skins of field mice sewn together and this both at home and abroad. When such a tunic is put on it is never changed till from long decay it falls to pieces. Their heads are covered with round caps and their hairy legs with goat skins (trousers are undoubtedly referred to here) and their shoes, which are ignorant of any last, are so clumsy as to hinder them in walking.

"For this reason they are not well suited for infantry, but on the other hand, they are almost one with their horses, which are poorly shaped but hardy, often they sit themselves like women. In truth they can remain on horseback day and night. On horseback they buy and sell; they eat and drink, bowed on the narrow neck of their steeds, then even sleep and dream. On horseback too they discuss and deliberate."

When in 374 the Huns first invaded Gothic territory, the East Gothic Kingdom was still ruled over by the great Hermanrik, the real founder of East Gothic supremacy in Southeastern Europe. By this time, however, Hermanrik was a very old man and entirely incapable of dealing with the fresh danger which suddenly loomed up from the East. When some of his troops were defeated in preliminary skirmishes with the Huns he sank into despair. Unwilling to witness the destruction of the empire he had created, he committeed suicide.[10]

After the death of Hermanrik, the East Goths chose a man named Vithimir to rule over them. For several months he fought desperately against the combined forces of the Huns and the latter's newly made subjects, the Alani. The loose political organization characteristic of the Huns at this period is evidenced by the face that Vithimir, by promises of large pay, managed to secure the coöperation of several small Hunnish groups in his struggles against the main Hunnish army. In the end, however, even this assistance proved futile and before the year was over Vithimir was defeated and slain.

After this disaster one group of East Goths, led by Hunimund, a son of the great Hermanrik, submitted themselves to Hunnish domination, and remained for many years a semi-autonomous group inside the great Hunnish confederation. Quite a number of the East Goths, however, rather than submit themselves to this humiliating servitude, prepared to flee westward to their neighbors and kinsmen, the West Goths. This group chose as their nominal ruler Viderik, but as the latter was still a mere child, real authority rested in the hands of his two guardians, Alatheus and Safrax.[11]

The sudden arrival of these panic-stricken refugees showed the West Goths, under the leadership of Athanarik, that they too would soon have to face the Hunnish storm. Athanarik was determined not to be taken unawares. He pitched his camp on the banks of the Dneister River, which marked the eastern frontier of the West Gothic Kingdom, and drew up his army in battle array in order that he might prevent any attempt of the Huns to cross this stream. The Huns, however, soon learned of this stratagem, and instead of making a direct attack, they forded the Dneister many miles upstream from where the Goths were waiting, and then made a sudden surprise attack upon the Gothic rear.

Athanarik was stupefied at the suddenness of the Hunnish onslaught, and after losing a great many men he and his followers were forced to flee for their lives and take refuge in the forested highlands of Transylvania. They were pursued by the Huns for some little distance, but by this time the Huns were so loaded with spoil, that they could only move very slowly and eventually the pursuit was abandoned. For the moment the West Goths and their neighbors were free from fresh attack, but by this time they had become so panic-stricken that large numbers of them thought that their only chance for permanent safety from the Hunnish terror lay in putting the Danube between themselves and the Huns, or in other words, by taking refuge inside the Roman Empire. This Empire had long withstood the fury of numerous Gothic attacks, and it seemed to the Goths that it might be the one political unit which would not break before the onslaught of the Huns. The only question was whether the Roman authorities would permit any large number of Gothic refugees to take up residence within the boundaries of the Empire.

Athanarik himself was too proud to ask for an asylum from Rome and a few of his followers consented to stay with him in his mountain retreat in Transylvania. But a large number of the West Goths, especially those who were favorable to the Christian religion and hence felt a certain spiritual communion with the Graeco-Roman world, led by a chieftain named Fritigern, assembled on the banks of the Danube River and petitioned that they be permitted to settle somewhere within the boundary of the Roman Empire. It is said that these would-be refugees numbered no less than two hundred thousand men of fighting age besides old men, women, and children.

Messengers were immediately sent to the Emperor Valens who still ruled over the eastern portion of the Roman Empire to ask him what should be done about the matter. After considerable debate in the Imperial Council it was at length agreed to grant the Goths permission to settle within the Empire, and before long practically the whole Visigothic nation had been ferried across the Danube.

Had the immigrants been wisely and humanely treated, it is probable that they would have given new strength to the Roman Empire, which was suffering from a waning of population and needed fresh soldiers for her armies and fresh hands to work in the deserted farmlands near the frontier. Unfortunately, however, power over the Gothic immigrants was in the hands of the two local military commanders, both of whom were thoroughly unscrupulous persons, who used their position to amass a fortune for themselves. No provision was made for feeding the refugees, and when the latter clamored for food, supplies were sold to them at fabulous prices. Many of the Goths were forced to sell themselves or their children into slavery in order to secure sufficient food to keep alive. The Roman soldiers were not loath to follow the example set by their leaders, and taking advantage of the situation forced the proud Gothic warriors to prostitute their wives, their daughters, and in some cases their comely sons in order to avoid starvation.

This shameless treatment aroused deep resentment among all sections of the Goths. Before long things came to open rupture. A casual conflict between some Roman soldiers and a band of Goths was a spark which led to a universal revolt on the part of the refugees. For the most part the walled towns were able to maintain themselves against Gothic attacks, but the Goths became complete masters of the open country all over the Northern Balkans. Large detachments of Gothic tribesmen roamed all over the countryside, killing, burning, and plundering as they went.

To make matters worse the West Goths were soon joined by other barbarian groups. The large detachment of East Goths ruled over by Alatheus and Safrax who had fled westward from Southern Russia after their defeats by the Huns appeared upon the scene. A feeble attempt was made to keep them out, but before long they too had crossed the Danube and were added to the number of marauding bands in Northern Thrace and Macedonia. Not long afterwards a number of Huns and Alani also invaded the Empire and added to the general pandemonium. Fortunately for the Romans these Huns and Alani were members of small isolated groups acting on their own account and their entrance into the Empire formed no part of a general Hunnish attack.

During the year 377 numerous conflicts took place between the Goths and the Roman legions which were stationed near at hand, with no decisive victory being gained by either side. It became obvious that if Rome was to subdue the barbarians she had to muster all of her strength. Troops were hurried up from all sides, not only from the eastern but also from the western portions of the Roman Empire.

In 378 the Emperor Valens himself took command of the great army which had been brought together to do battle with the Goths. Advancing to Adrianople, near which city a large number of Goths had assembled, he resolved to make a major attack immediately, without waiting for the further reinforcements which his nephew Gratian, Emperor of the western portion of the Roman Empire, was bringing him. The battle which ensued resulted in an overwhelming defeat for the Romans. Valens himself was killed and nearly two-thirds of his army, the flower of the military forces of the East, were left upon the field of battle.[12] In consequence of this defeat the Roman Empire was rocked to its foundations. It was the beginning of the end. In some form or other the Roman Empire survived for many centuries thereafter, but never again was it undisputed mistress of the Western World.

More than a century previously, another emperor, the Emperor Decius, had been slain while fighting with the Goths, but after the death of Decius the Goths had retreated to their homes North of the Danube. After the death of Valens, on the other hand, the Goths, impelled by fear of the Huns, remained within the boundaries of the Roman Empire. Never again could the Empire muster enough strength to expel them.

For the moment the Goths were unable to take full advantage of their victory. Though they had defeated the Roman armies in the open field, they were still unable to take possession of any of the walled cities owing to their lack of organization and the absence of adequate siege machinery, so that their attacks upon the Empire had reached an impasse before many months had gone by. Moreover, Theodosius the Great, who had succeeded Valens upon the throne of the East Roman Empire, was a man of far higher caliber than his predecessors. Military discipline within the Roman legions was soon restored to a high level and the Goths, seeing that the cowardice and sloth of former times was over, began to be somewhat afraid.

Even Theodosius, however, was unable to drive the Goths out of the Empire, and as both Romans and Goths became wearied by the perpetual fighting a compromise was eventually arrived at (ca. 382). By the terms of this compromise the East Goths under Alatheus and Safrax, together with those Alani and Huns who had accompanied the East Goths on their campaign in the Balkans, were settled and given land in Pannonia and Upper Moesia. The West Goths, on the other hand, were settled in the province of Lower Moesia. The status of all these Goths was that of foederati or "allies" of the Empire. They retained the right to have their own domestic legislation and the right to elect their own princes. They obtained the districts assigned to them free of taxation or tribute; in fact the Romans agreed to pay them annually a certain sum of money. In return for these favors the Goths swore to defend the frontiers of the Empire and to furnish troops for the Roman armies, which troops, however, were to be led by their own chiefs.

As might be expected, this arrangement of forming two Gothic states within the great Roman State did not work very well. We know very little about the actions of the East Goths in the years immediately following this period, but we do know that the West Goths were frequently the cause of turmoil and anxiety. But as long as the firm hand of Theodosius the Great ruled the East Roman Empire, these West Goths remained fairly quiet and even assisted the Emperor on some of his campaigns in the West against rival claimants to the throne.

No sooner had Theodosius died, however, and been succeeded by his fatuous son Arcadius, than the West Goths again became restive. Fritigern, the original West Gothic leader, was long since dead, but he had been succeeded as leader by the able and active Alarik. An ambitious man, Alarik led the West Goths into open rebellion. On this occasion he and his followers marched into Greece, and at one time or other occupied most of the famed cities of antiquity, including Athens and Sparta. A Roman army forced him to retire northward, but in the end (398) the East Roman Empire, finding that the West Goths could be checked but not conquered, lured Alarik back into nominal submission to its jurisdiction by giving him a large bribe and by granting him the title of "Commander-in-Chief of the Army in the Prefecture of Illyria."[13]

CHAPTER SEVENTEEN

THE HUNS IN EUROPE—THE SECOND PHASE

The Huns in South Russia—Their Gradual Advance into the Hungarian Plains—Effect of the Hunnish Pressure Upon the Germanic Peoples—The Suevi, Vandals and Alani—The West Goths Invade Italy and France—The Burgundi and Franks Move into France—Rise of the Hunnish Kingdom in Hungary—The Dynasty of Oktar and Rua—Accession of Bleda and Attila—Hunnish Conquests in Northern Europe—Attila Sole Ruler—The Court of Attila—Attila and the East Roman Empire—Attila's Invasion of France—Attila's Invasion of Italy—Death of Attila and Breakup of the Hunnish Kingdom—The Later Huns and the Bulgarians—The Coming of the Avars.

As WE have already seen, the most important result of the first phase of the Hunnish invasion of Europe was the driving of all the West Goths and a portion of the East Goths and the Alani to take refuge inside of the Roman Empire. For geographic reasons it was the East Roman Empire rather than the West Roman Empire which felt the full weight of the barbarian invasions all during this period.

During the period A.D. 375 to 400, the Huns, the cause of all this commotion, made no attempt at direct conquest of any portion of the European portion of the Roman Empire. A few Huns had made their way south of the Danube during the period of the fighting between the Goths and the Romans. It is probable that these Huns moved westward to Pannonia a few years later when the East Goths were colonized in this area. But the Huns who took part in this migration formed small and insignificant units and had only an indirect connection with the main body of Hunnish invaders.[1]

Not only were the European frontiers of the Roman Empire safe from Hunnish attack during this period but from all the information available to us it seems probable that during this same period no important body of Huns entered that region outside of the Roman Empire which now forms Eastern Hungary and Transylvania and which later figured so prominently in Hunnish history. In fact, all during this time the main body of the Hunnish invaders were content to occupy their new found homes in Southern Russia, formerly the home of the Alani and the East Goths. From this region they did indeed make occasional raids into the Roman Empire, not however on the European, but on the Asiatic side. Following the trails formerly used by the Alani, bands of Huns moved southward, and, crossing the Caucasus Mountains, poured into various adjacent regions in the Near East.

Thus, for example, we find it recorded that in 384 a group of Huns invaded Mesopotamia and made an attack upon the city of Edessa. On this occasion they were defeated by the Roman general Ricimer and forced to retire. But a few years later another band of Hunnish warriors appeared and ravaged various portions of Armenia, Mesopotamia and even Syria. The Roman Empire was not the only object of their attack. In 396 a large band of Huns appeared before Ctesiphon on the Tigris, the capital of the Sasanid Empire, and caused the inhabitants of this city to be filled with consternation, although in the end these Hunnish marauders were put to flight by the valiant counter-attack launched by the Sasanid monarch, Bahram IV.[2]

Even these raids, however, were casual affairs, and the great bulk of the Huns were content to dwell and consolidate their power on the steppes of Southern Russia. We have no account of just what took place in this region during this particular period, but indirect evidence shows us that there must have been a great increase of the Hunnish population during the twenty-five years which elapsed between the overthrow of the Gothic kingdoms (in 375) and the beginning of the fifth century when we again hear of Hunnish activities in Europe.

It is probable, in fact, that the Huns who overthrew the East Gothic Kingdom were only the first of a whole series of Hunnish groups which steadily pushed their way into Southern Russia during the latter part of the fourth century. Evidence for this continued infiltration of the Huns into this region is seen in the way in which the non-Hunnish groups were slowly but surely pressed westward in the general direction of the Roman frontier. Thus, for example, we find that in 381 Athanarik, the old King of the West Goths who had remained behind in Transylvania at the time when most of his subjects crossed the Danube, was forced by further pressure from behind to quit his mountainous retreat and take refuge with Theodosius the Great in Constantinople.[3]

A few years later (386) we find a large band of East Goths approaching the banks of the Danube and asking permission to cross into Roman territory. These East Goths had nothing to do with their kinsmen under Alatheus and Safrax who had already settled in Pannonia but represented a new wave of migration from Southern Russia, the old homeland of the Ostrogoths. On this occasion the Romans were successful in keeping the Gothic hordes from crossing over into the Empire, and those Goths who did cross the Danube were butchered almost to a man.[4] To us the Roman victory on this occasion is of no great importance. Far more significant is the fact that the whole incident shows that those East Goths who for a while remained in Southern Russia under Hunnish domination were being pushed slowly to the West.

It must have been during this period, moreover, that even those Goths who remained subject to Hunimund, whom the Huns had appointed as puppet ruler under their immediate control, gradually moved westward into the Hungarian plain. Hunimund himself is said to have waged war on the Suevi and his son Thorismod upon the Gepids, both of whom dwelt not in Southern Russia but in the Hungarian portion of the Danubian basin.[5]

A few Goths remained behind in South Russia, but these were forced to abandon their residence on the open steppe country and take refuge in the mountainous districts of the Krimea. Incidentally, we know that this little fragment of the once mighty Gothic nation managed to retain their individual existence for many centuries. Rubruquis, who traveled eastward in the thirteenth century, tells us that on the Krimean peninsula there were still a number of Goths who spoke "German." In fact, this group of Goths did not become extinct until the close of the sixteenth century.

During this period when the vast majority of the East Goths were being pushed West of the Carpathian Mountains, we find that a similar pressure was placed upon large numbers of the Alani. In fact, it was at this time that a large group of the Alani settled in or near Northern Pannonia where they became the immediate neighbors of the Vandals and the Suevi. In the year 401 we find that in spite of the linguistic and cultural differences existing between the Iranian Alani on the one hand and the Germanic Suevi and Vandals on the other, that all three peoples were living in intimate association with one another.[6] All of these migratory movements must have exerted pressure upon the Gepids, but in spite of this pressure the Gepids managed to maintain their position in the plains of Eastern Hungary and on the hilly slopes of Western Transylvania.

The virtual expulsion of the Goths and the Alani made the Huns not only the masters but almost the sole inhabitants of the steppe-lands of Southern Russia. This fact is of great historical significance. Since the beginnings of recorded history we have seen how this region passed from the hands of the Scythians to the Sarmatians and from the Sarmatians to the Goths. But all three of these peoples had belonged to one or other of the "white" races and had spoken an Indo-European language. With the expulsion of the Goths and the Alani we find for the first time the intrusion of a people with marked Mongoloid characteristics and speaking a Turanian or Ural-Altaic language. From the end of the fourth century onward these Turanians remained the masters of the Russian steppe-lands for a very long period of time. The Hunnish Kingdom was soon destroyed but the Huns were replaced by other people as "Turanian" as themselves and it was not until the seventeenth century that an Indo-European people again became the dominant element in this area.

Up to the year 400 the main body of the Huns were content to remain in what had formerly been the East Gothic Kingdom, East of the Carpathian Mountains. In the autumn of that year, however, we hear for the first time of direct contact between the Huns and the Romans, and from that year onward mention of the Huns in one form or another begins to appear quite frequently in the Roman annals, from which fact it is obvious that about this time the Huns began a second great drive westward, a drive which was to bring them control over the whole Danubian basin. It is at this time, moreover, that we hear of a new Hunnish leader, named Uldes or Uldin. We have no means of knowing whether or not this Uldin belonged to the same family or even to the same group as Balamber, the Hunnish leader who, according to tradition, first brought the Huns into Europe.

Curiously enough the early intercourse between Uldin and the Romans seems to have been entirely friendly in character. In the latter part of the year 400 Gania, a general in the employ of the East Roman Empire who had risen in rebellion and been defeated, was forced to flee for his life, and crossing the lower Danube attempted to find refuge in what is now Rumania. Uldin, however, who commanded the Huns who dwelt in this region, had Gania seized and executed, later sending his head as a present to the Emperor at Constantinople. But this same Uldin, who was content for the moment to be on friendly terms with the Romans, was the cause of another stampede on the part of the various Germanic peoples.

Just at this time we hear of a new Gothic group (probably composed of various independent Ostrogothic tribes) appearing on the middle Danube. Shortly thereafter these Goths crossed the Danube and proceeded to invade the Roman province of Pannonia. This group of Goths, we are told, was led by a chieftain named Radagais. The early history of Radagais is unknown but we have every reason to believe that he and his followers had dwelt for some time in Eastern Hungary (i.e., east of the Theiss River) and had been forced to migrate westward because of attacks of Uldin and his Huns.

Even after crossing the Danube and camping in Pannonia the terrified Gothic horde of Radagais was not allowed to settle down in peace. Fresh Hunnish attacks forced this horde to flee still further to the West, and in 404 we find them crossing the Eastern Alps and moving down into Italy. For once the West Roman Empire was able to rise to the occasion and defeat the wild tribesmen who threatened them with destruction.

In the following year (405) Radagais and his army, while camping at Faesuli near the modern Florence, was overwhelmingly defeated, and almost destroyed. It is of especial interest to note that the Hunnish leader Uldin followed the Goths under Radagais into Italy, and acting as an ally of the Romans, assisted materially in their defeat.[7]

But though Radagais and his immediate followers were completely unsuccessful in their invasion, they were indirectly the cause of a mortal blow struck at the Roman domains still further to the West. The fact that the horde of Radagais broke into Pannonia caused a great shifting of population among the barbarian tribes already settled in this region. For many years the Vandals had been settled in this area. During the last two decades they had been joined by large numbers of Suevi from Northeastern Hungary and by an equally large number of Alani who under Hunnish pressure had fled all the way from Southeastern Russia.

The fresh pressure brought to bear by the Goths of Radagais and the Huns who moved behind them was too much for settlers in Pannonia to bear, and in 401 we find a large group of Vandals, Suevi, and Alani moving westward. At first they settled in the provinces of Raetia and Noricum (roughly speaking the modern Switzerland). Not long afterwards fresh pressure took them still further westward and in 406 they crossed the Rhine and entered Gaul.

Shortly before crossing the Rhine these new invaders seem to have had a great battle with the Franks. According to tradition twenty thousand Vandals were slain in the course of this battle and the Vandal king himself was killed. We are told, in fact, that only the timely arrival of their allies, the Alani, saved the Vandal army from total destruction. However this may be, large numbers of Vandals, Suevi, and Alani did succeed in bursting through the Franks and overrunning various portions of Gaul.

For three years they burned and plundered Gallic cities to their heart's content, but at the end of this time a slight increase in the strength of the Roman armies in this region caused the invading hosts to march southward, and in 409 all three groups crossed the Pyrenees and entered Spain. They found Spain even less capable of defending herself than Gaul, with the result that instead of merely plundering the Roman cities each one of the three peoples was able to carve out a separate and independent kingdom for themselves. The kingdom of the Suevi was in the northwestern portion of the Spanish Peninsula, the kingdom of the Alani was in what is now Portugal, while most of the remaining portion of the peninsula fell into the hands of the Vandals. A few years later (428) a large number of Vandals, aided by treachery within the Roman high command, crossed the strait of Gibralter and became masters of all of Northern Africa as far East as the ancient city of Carthage.[8]

Just at the time the Vandals, Suevi, and Alani were ravaging Gaul and preparing to march into Spain, Italy, the very heart of the West Roman Empire, was again subjected to a barbarian invasion, led this time by Alarik, the leader of the Visigoths. A few years earlier (402-403) Alarik had led an initial expedition into Italy which had had no important results one way or the other, but in 408 he began a campaign aimed directly at the sacred city of Rome.

As we have seen, the invasion of Italy by Radagais and of Gaul and Spain by the Suevi, Vandals, and Alani was the direct result of Hunnish pressure from the East. We have no reason to suppose that there was so direct a connection between the Hunnish pressure and the new campaign inaugurated by Alarik. Nevertheless, we may well believe that Alarik's decision to turn his back on the East Roman Empire was not entirely unconnected with the fact that large Hunnish armies were in his rear and that Hunnish detachments were already crossing the Danube and plundering Thrace and Macedonia. If Alarik confined his attentions to the East he would have to share all plunder with the Huns, a people who had already shown themselves superior to the Visigoths in the art of war, and who would naturally demand the lion's share of the loot. If, on the other hand, he invaded the West, he removed himself from the Hunnish peril in the rear, and entered a region in which he would have a monopoly of pillage.

The immediate cause of hostilities, as is well-known, was the demand which Alarik made upon Honorius, the Emperor of the West, for a large sum of money for the support of his troops. Honorius, a stubborn but ineffectual man, refused the demand for money, but took no active steps to prevent the threatened invasion of Italy. Rome itself was left to its own devices, but Honorius was careful to look after his own safety by locking himself up in the inaccessible city of Ravenna.

After his demands had been rejected Alarik completed the plans for his campaign, and in 408 he crossed the Julian or Eastern Alps and entered the plains of Italy. He made no attempt to capture Ravenna, in which Honorius was skulking, but made straight for Rome, the heart of the Empire. He met with surprisingly little resistance on his way southward. In the years 408-409 and 410 Alarik made no less than three assaults upon the imperial city. Each of these met with a certain measure of success. In the first attack he contented himself with investing Rome and starving the inhabitants into submission. On this occasion he consented to withdraw his troops on the payment of a high ransom including five thousand pounds of gold—equivalent to about a million dollars.

After the payment of this money Alarik, true to his word, withdrew his troops a short distance northward and attempted to negotiate a new and permanent treaty with the Emperor Honorius. Alarik offered to abandon all hostilities and make an offensive and defensive alliance with the Roman Empire if the latter made him a yearly payment of gold, and ceded to him the provinces of Noricum, Istria, Venetia, and Dalmatia for the residence of the Gothic troops and their families. By this cession, of course, these provinces would not, at least in theory, cease to be a part of the Empire, though no doubt they would have become, in fact, an autonomous kingdom under Gothic control.

Honorius, however, safe in his asylum at Ravenna, rejected all attempts at negotiation and in the following year (409) Alarik made a second attack upon the city of Rome. When the Gothic chieftain had succeeded in investing the city the Roman Senate suggested a compromise. Throwing off all allegiance to the stubborn Honorius who refused either to fight or to negotiate, they declared this Emperor deposed and elected in his place a man called Attalus. As Attalus was both an inhabitant of Rome and on friendly terms with Alarik it was hoped that some satisfactory agreement between the Romans and the Goths could be worked out.

For the moment Alarik declared himself content with the new arrangement. The new Emperor—if we may call him so, for he was only recognized in Rome and the immediately adjacent regions—bestowed high military offices upon the Gothic leaders and Alarik again withdrew his army from before the gates of Rome. For several months concord continued to reign between Attalus and his Gothic allies. Eventually, however, Alarik became dissatisfied with the treatment accorded him by Attalus, and seized and solemnly deposed the puppet Emperor, who had had a nominal reign of only ten months.

Once again Alarik attempted to negotiate with Honorius, the legitimate Emperor, who was still cooped up in Ravenna. Once again Honorius refused to negotiate, with the result that Alarik (410) marched for the third and last time upon the Roman metropolis. This time he was not to be turned aside by either ransom money or the creation of a puppet ruler who could not command respect either at home or abroad. Bursting through the surrounding gates he soon made himself master of the whole city, and he and his followers were able to pillage to their hearts' content.

The amount of permanent damage done by the Goths to the sacred city was probably very small. We hear of only one public building being burned. The Goths, moreover, being Christians, were careful not to harm the churches or even loot the treasures owned by the churches.

They did, however, seize all other movable property, both public and private, which they could lay their hands upon, and in this way secured an enormous amount of loot. Even more important was the blow they dealt to Roman honor and prestige. The city of Rome which for so many centuries had remained inviolate had at last succumbed to barbarian attack.

In this connection it is of especial interest to remember that the barbarians who captured Rome were themselves defeated refugees who had been forced to desert their homeland in Transylvania before the fierce attacks of the Huns. The fact that the Chinese some three centuries earlier had been able to drive the Huns westward thus became a major factor in transforming the whole history of the Western World.

A few days after capturing and sacking Rome Alarik and his hordes marched southward. After overrunning all of Southern Italy with no great difficulty, the Gothic leader collected a large fleet with the object of crossing to Northern Africa and securing control over this region. His reasons for wishing to desert Italy in favor of Northern Africa are somewhat obscure. But we know the agricultural situation in Italy had by this time sunk so low that the food supply of Rome and the other Italian cities depended in no small measure upon the wheat sent from Africa. Africa at this time was governed by a Viceroy who was still faithful to Honorius. It is probable, therefore, that Alarik's scheme to conquer Africa was based upon a desire to secure control over the "Granary of the Empire." As long as Africa was loyal to Honorius at Ravenna the latter could not be dethroned. In going to Africa therefore Alarik was really aiming at consolidating his power in Italy and we have every reason to believe that he intended ultimately to return to Rome.

All of Alarik's fine plans went astray. The greater part of the fleet he assembled was destroyed, and not long thereafter the great Gothic leader himself died of a fever contracted in the pestilential marshes of Southern Italy. He was succeeded as Gothic leader by his brother-in-law Athaulf, a very able man but far less ambitious than his predecessor. Athaulf gave up the project of invading Africa. He felt, moreover, that the hold of the Goths upon Italy itself was exceedingly precarious. Consequently, he was exceedingly anxious to make a permanent peace between the Goths and the Romans, but he felt that it was impossible to secure such a peace as long as the Goths occupied Italy.

To return to the northeast meant to enter once more into rivalry with the Huns, so he chose to lead his followers to the northwest and occupy a large portion of Southern Gaul (412). Not long afterwards we find him marrying Placidia, the sister of Honorius. He and his successors were really independent sovereigns in their own domain. Nominally, however, they remained subjects of the Roman Empire, governing their domain as special viceroys of the Roman Empire. It was, moreover, nominally as agents of the Romans that Athaulf and his successors crossed the Pyrenees and battled with the Vandals in the Spanish Peninsula. As a result of these campaigns a large part of Northern Spain was wrested from Vandal control, but needless to say this region, instead of being handed back to the Roman officials, was incorporated within the Visigothic kingdom, which thus for several centuries consisted of Southwestern France and Northeastern Spain.[9]

While the Visigoths were wresting a large part of Southern Gaul from Roman control, their distant cousins the Burgundi and the Franks began moving slowly across the Rhine and occupying various portions of Northern Gaul. Very few details regarding these movements have been recorded for us, but we know that the Burgundian movement started in 413 though it was not until 443 that these peoples occupied the region which ever since their day has retained the name of Burgundy. The Frankish movement started in 420 and continued steadily thereafter. Both the Burgundian and the Frankish movements were, no doubt, aided and partly caused by the weakness of the Roman control over Northern Gaul, but we know that shortly before their migration the Burgundi were engaged in several desperate struggles with the Huns, and it is certain that the Burgundi, and possibly also the Franks, were influenced in their decision to move westward by Hunnish pressure from the rear.[10]

If we pause to review the net results of the second wave of Hunnish invasion which began about 400 and ended about 415 we are at once struck by the momentous consequent history of Europe. The first Hunnish invasion pushed the Germanic peoples out of Southern Russia and deposited large numbers of them in the Balkans, thereby dealing a mortal blow at the East Roman Empire, but the West Roman Empire remained comparatively untouched. It was the second Hunnish invasion which precipitated the barbarian hordes upon the Western Empire, as a result of which we find Italy ravaged for four years by one group of barbarians, and Africa, Spain and Gaul occupied by others.

Most, if not all, of these barbarians we know were pushed into the Roman Empire as the result of Hunnish pressure from the rear. Considering this fact it is rather remarkable how casual and insignificant were the direct contacts between the Huns and the Romans. We have good reason to suppose that it was during this period that the Huns first secured direct control over the province of Pannonia. But Pannonia was already occupied in large measure by barbarian colonists such as the Ostrogoths who had followed the leadership of Alatheus and Safrax, so that the Hunnish conquest of this province meant little more than that these barbarians passed from Roman to Hunnish overlordship. Incidentally, we may note that with the Hunnish occupation of Pannonia practically all of the Ostrogothic peoples were reunited but under Hunnish domination.[11]

Apart from the occupation of Pannonia, moreover, the Huns at this period made almost no direct attacks upon the West Roman Empire. To be sure occasional raids were made by the Huns to the South of the Danube but these were directed at the East Roman Empire and even these were more terrifying than really injurious. In one of these raids, in fact, the Huns received a very severe check.

The raid in question was led in 408 by the Hunnish King, Uldin, of whom mention has already been made. By this time Uldin had become a very important person, and as the principal leader of the Hunnish tribesmen in Europe, must have been the overlord of a very large domain. The Roman annals in fact speak of him as "the ruler of all the barbarians beyond the Danube." Uldin was a very proud and vain-glorious person. When the Prefect of the Roman province of Thrace sought humbly for peace, Uldin proudly pointed to the sun and said "All that he shines upon I can conquer if I will."

Uldin did succeed in doing a good deal of damage to the outlying divisions of the East Roman Empire, but before long he met with disaster. As he was returning to his own domain, loaded down with booty, he was suddenly attacked by a Roman army. At this point the Hunnish leader was deserted by many of his own followers with the result that the Romans won a complete victory. Large numbers of the Huns and their allies were killed or captured and Uldin himself barely escaped with his life.[12]

After this time we hear no more of Uldin and his exploits and it is to be presumed that he died shortly afterward. With the death of Uldin we come to the end of the second period of Hunnish conquests. Of what took place inside of the Hunnish domain in the years which immediately followed Uldin's death we are profoundly ignorant, for this is one of the periods in European history almost entirely destitute of historical sources.

When the curtain rises again a few years later we find that rulership over the Hunnish peoples in Europe has passed into the hands of an entirely new dynasty, usually called the dynasty of Attila, although it was Attila's two uncles who were the founders and first rulers of the line. As far as we know there was no connection between this new dynasty and Uldin, the ruler of the Huns during the preceding period, or between it and Balamber, the chieftain who first led the Huns into

Europe. By some (e. g., Drouin) this very fact has led to the supposition that the members of the new dynasty were the leaders of a new wave of Hunnish tribesmen who first swept into Europe at this time.[13] It is almost certain that a great number of Hunnish tribes did move westward from Southern Russia into the Hungarian Plains during this period, and from Turkistan into Southern Russia, but we have no need to assign the new dynasty to these fresh immigrants. It is, in fact, probable that the new rulers were the leaders of a small group of Huns who had resided in Europe for several decades but who first came into prominence in the troubled period following the defeat and death of Uldin.

However this may be, we know that the first rulers of the new dynasty were Oktar and his brother Rua. Oktar is an exceedingly shadowy figure, and we know almost nothing about his life or the events of his reign, though it would seem that it was he who was the real founder of the royal house subsequently immortalized by his brother and his nephew. It is quite possible that Oktar was the leader spoken of in the chronicles who led the Huns in an attack upon the Burgundians on the banks of the Rhine and who, though at first successful, was at last slain in this, the first Hunnish attempt to dominate the peoples inhabiting the region now known as Central and Western Germany.

Following an old Turanian custom, Oktar was succeeded on the throne, not by a son but by Rua or Ruga, his brother. The first few years of Rua's reign are also very obscure. In 422 and again in 426 we hear that the Huns again invaded the East Roman Empire and raised havoc in Thrace and Macedonia. Both of these expeditions seem to have been led by Rua. The East Romans were able to push the Huns back to the north of the Danube on each of these occasions, but they remained a very serious menace to the stability of the Empire, and before long we find that Theodosius II, the Roman Emperor in the East, was granting to Rua, the King of the Huns, an annual subsidy of 350 pounds of gold (about $70,000) on the condition that the latter keep his Huns from ravaging the Roman frontier.[14]

Rua accepted this tribute with alacrity, but in 432 we find him making fresh demands upon the court at Constantinople. Many Hunnish tribesmen had fled from the harsh rule of their monarch and had taken refuge inside the East Roman Empire. Rua demanded that all of these fugitives be restored to him. Equally significant of the unity and power which had at last been achieved by the Hunnish kingdom was the demand which Rua made regarding the petty tribes settled on the Danube just beyond the Roman frontier. Hitherto the Romans had been accustomed to dealing with the border tribes separately. With this end in view Theodosius had made a number of agreements with the various tribes immediately adjacent to his domain with the idea of preventing raids across the imperial boundaries. Rua declared that all of the tribes North of the Danube were subject to his jurisdiction, and demanded that the Romans declare null and void all of the agreements which they had made with these groups. Hereafter all such agreements were to be negotiated through the Hunnish court.

Theodosius was a milksop, far more interested in theology than in protecting the honor and dignity of his domain. Instead, therefore, of declaring war upon the Huns on the receipt of these outrageous demands, he merely dispatched an embassy to the Hunnish court in the hope of securing somewhat milder terms from the barbarian monarch. This embassy arrived at the Hunnish frontier in 434, and found that Rua was dead and had been succeeded in joint rulership over the Hunnish hordes by his two nephews Bleda and Attila.

A brief description of the interview which ensued between the Roman ambassadors and the new joint Kings of the Huns has been preserved to us. This interview took place not at the Hunnish capital, but at the frontier town of Margus in modern Jugo-Slavia. Not only the two Kings but all their retinue remained seated on horseback, and the Roman ambassadors, lest their dignity suffer, were forced to do the same. In spite of this attention to points of etiquette, the Roman envoys proved very poor diplomats. Not only were they forced to give way on the question of refugees and agreements with the separate tribes, but in addition Attila insisted that as the Huns now had two Kings it was necessary that the annual tribute paid by Rome be raised from three hundred and fifty to seven hundred pounds of gold. The Huns insisted upon immediate acceptance of all these demands or else war would be declared. Since the ambassadors knew that their master, Theodosius, preferred any humiliation to a renewal of hostilities they agreed to all the Hunnish terms.

In compliance with this agreement the Romans immediately handed over two young Hunnish princes who had taken refuge at Constantinople, nor were the former able to voice any protest when the Hunnish monarchs straightway crucified the two unfortunate fugitives.[15]

After the ratification of this agreement we hear nothing more from the Roman sources for several years regarding Hunnish activities, and it is probable that this period was occupied by the conquest and consolidation of Hunnish power over the various barbaric peoples who then inhabited Northern and Eastern Europe.

It is difficult for us, at this date, to judge the exact size and power of the empire carved out by Bleda and Attila since all of our historical sources are extremely vague. It is certain, moreover, that there was a great difference in size between the territory which was immediately subject to Hunnish jurisdiction and the territory inhabited by tribes which in some way or other acknowledged Hunnish over-lordship.

The center of the Hunnish Kingdom was now in the middle Danube basin, corresponding to the Austro-Hungarian domain of the nineteenth century. Even in this territory, however, the Huns constituted only a minority of the population. Germanic peoples, such as the Ostrogoths in Pannonia to the West of the Danube, and the Gepids, who dwelt to the East of the Danube, still constituted the bulk of the population. Both the Ostrogoths and the Gepids were allowed to have their own kings. In fact, we are told that Ardarik, the King of the Gepids, and Valamir, the King of the Ostrogoths (it is to be noted that all branches of the Ostrogoths are once again united under one ruler), enjoyed special consideration from the Hunnish monarchs and that their advice was frequently sought on all matters of state. But though these peoples retained a great deal of autonomy, paid no taxes and had as their only obligation service as soldiers in the Hunnish army, theoretically at least they were all subjugated peoples and the Huns asserted an absolute right of disposing of their life and property.

In addition to this center in the middle Danube basin the Huns at this period also secured some sort of domination over the tribes inhabiting what we now know as Germany. Even the Germanic peoples residing on or near the Rhine, such as the Allemani, the Burgundi, and the Ripuarian Franks, were forced to acknowledge in some way or other Hunnish supremacy. Thuringians and Saxons were forced to add their quota to the Hunnish army, and from certain passages in the classical authors it would appear that in some way or other Hunnish jurisdiction extended as far as the North and Baltic Seas. In fact, it has been suggested by some very competent scholars that the extension of the Hunnish Empire in this direction had a direct connection with the migration of the Angles, Saxons, and Jutes from the European mainland to the British Isles.[16]

Of equal importance is the fact that the rule of Bleda and Attila extended far to the East. We know for certain that even the Hunnish tribesmen inhabiting the steppes of Southern Russia, who were much more numerous than the Huns in "Hungary," were forced to acknowledge Attila's sway. In 435 the Sorasgi, as well as other Hunnish peoples in South Russia, were subdued. A few years later (447), the powerful Akatsiri, another Hunnish group still further to the East who had hitherto merely stood in a position of friendly alliance with the court of Attila, were brought into direct subjection and Ellak, Attila's eldest son, was appointed to rule over them. It is also probable that many of the Slavic and Finnish peoples who inhabited the forested regions of Russia North of the great steppes were brought into some kind of submission. It is, in fact, very possible that the Slavs, as Hunnish serfs, first entered into Western Europe just at this time.

It is certain that the power of Bleda and Attila extended far to the East of the River Don, and included much of the former kingdom of the Alani. We are told, in fact, that Attila at one time planned to use this region as a base for a major campaign against Persia. It is, however, probable that this region, called Sugdak, possessed its own subordinate monarch and that its dependence upon Attila's court was somewhat tenuous, a fact of some importance when we remember that it was this sub-kingdom of Sugdak which formed the link between the European Huns and the Chinese Empire.[17]

In 445 Bleda, the co-ruler of the Huns, died and Attila became the sole ruler of the Hunnish hordes. Several historians have hinted that he was assassinated by the command of his brother, but on this point we have no exact information. In any case Bleda had always been a rather shadowy person, and the accession of Attila to sole rulership served to unify and strengthen the Hunnish dominion.[18]

It was, in fact, in the years immediately following Attila's succession to sole rulership that the Huns first became a really serious menace to the very existence of the Roman Empire. It was during this period that both the East and the West Roman Empires sent embassy after embassy to the Hunnish court in vain attempts to ward off Hunnish attacks by diplomatic means. But though all of these embassies ended in failure, we are fortunate enough to have preserved to us the report of a member of one of these missions, and this report enables us to draw a picture of conditions at the Hunnish court during these eventful years.[19]

From the description given us of the personal appearance of Attila it would appear that he had a good deal of Mongoloid blood in his veins. "He was," it is said, "short of stature with a broad chest and a large head, his eyes small and sprinkled with grey, he had a flat nose and a swarthy complexion." And again, "He was haughty in his walk, rolling his eyes hither and yon so that the power of his proud spirit appeared in the movement of his body. He was indeed a lover of war, yet unrestrained in action, mighty in council, gracious to suppliants and gracious to those who were once received into his protection."[20]

In private life he was extremely simple. At his banquets all sorts of luxurious foods were served, but he himself ate only the simplest fare. The nobles of his court wined and dined off gold and silver dishes while he himself made use only of wooden bowls. In other ways, however, Attila was extremely vain, as is seen by the fact that he insisted that the Romans send him as envoys men of their highest rank.

The Hunnish ruler, moreover, consumed wine in large quantities and was frequently drunk. He had a passion for women, kept a huge harem, and had innumerable children by his various wives and concubines. It is to be noted, however, that only one of these wives ranked as the Queen Consort. This lady not only outranked all of her rivals but seems to have exercised a considerable influence upon the affairs of state. One of her children, a young boy named Ernak, was Attila's favorite son.

Of even greater interest than these personal details are some of the facts we find portrayed concerning the manners and customs of the Hunnish people at this period. In many ways it is obvious that they had undergone a great transformation in the few decades which had elapsed since they first settled in Europe. They were no longer pure nomads, as can be seen by the fact that they were now possessed of a fixed capital consisting of a number of permanent and rather imposing looking edifices. There is some doubt as to the exact situation of this Hunnish capital, but it is generally agreed that it was somewhere in Hungary between the Danube and the Theiss Rivers.

The so-called palace of Attila was built on an eminence and overlooked the whole town. It seems to have consisted of a vast circular enclosure, a wooden palisade, within which there were a number of separate houses. The principal building was surmounted by high towers or battlements. All of these houses were in the nature of a log or block houses, being built of half trunks of trees with the round side outwards. The whole capital boasted of but a single stone edifice, and this was a bath house erected at the command of a prominent Hunnish nobleman by a Graeco-Roman architect who had been enslaved by the Hunnish army.

Inside of these palaces and houses there was much more furniture than we should expect from rude Hunnish tribesmen. It was customary to sit and lie on couches. Tables, chairs, and benches were not unknown, and Attila himself made use of a sumptuous bed. The floors for the most part were covered with felt mats or carpets. At night they employed long reeds as torches.

When traveling the Huns continued to make use of tents and wagons. As they now resided in a land of many rivers, however, it was customary to carry light rafts on these wagons so that they could cross any streams which lay in their way. On the large rivers they employed "dugout" canoes, i.e., boats carved out of a single tree trunk.

In addition to their skin or fur garments the Huns, especially the womenfolk, made frequent use of linen. Meat and kumis, the fermented mare's milk previously mentioned (called Kamos by the Roman annalists), continued to be consumed in large quantities, but the Huns were already beginning to eat millet and other cereals, and certain luxuries such as pepper (of Indian origin) and dates (from Arabia) were not unknown. It is probable that these luxuries reached the Huns as presents or as tribute from the Romans. In addition to their native kumis the Huns also drank enormous quantities of wine.

When the Huns wished to do honor to a guest they presented him with a full cup of wine. When the guest had drunk the wine, the host then embraced and kissed him. Kissing is and always has been unknown in the Far East, so that this method of greeting a guest was undoubtedly a custom which the Huns had picked up since their arrival in Europe.

We have very little information regarding the social organization of the Huns at this time. It is obvious that the Huns made no attempt to keep their womenfolk in seclusion. On several occasions Roman embassies dined with Attila's consort and with the widow of Bleda, in the absence of Attila himself from his capital. Even in Mongolia, however, the Hunnish women had enjoyed a great deal of freedom and it is doubtful if the migration to Europe had greatly affected their status.

At royal banquets it was customary to have native minstrels compose and sing ballads in honor of the great battles of former years. It is a great pity that not a word of these songs has come down to us, and we have no means of knowing whether these recitals referred only to recent victories or whether the Huns still kept alive the traditions relating to their ancient glories in Eastern Asia.

On one point we find that the Huns had preserved a custom peculiar to the nomadic peoples of Central Asia. On the death of a ruler etiquette required that his followers pluck out their hair and make deep gashes in their faces. The classical authors are singularly silent regarding the religious beliefs and practices of the Huns. Attila is said to have been very superstitious but this means little or nothing. We are told that he was greatly elated when a peasant by accident discovered "the sword of Mars always esteemed sacred amongst the Kings of the Scythians," evidently one of the swords which had formed part of the religious rites of both the Scythians and Sarmatians. This sword was duly presented to Attila. The Hunnish monarch "rejoiced at the gift and, being ambitious, thought that he had been appointed ruler of the whole world, and that through the sword of Mars supremacy in all wars was assured to him." It is certain that at no time did Attila or any of his important Hunnish followers accept Christianity.[21]

The great changes in the material culture of the Huns at the time of

Attila as contrasted with half a century previously is to be accounted for not only by their long residence in close proximity to the Roman Empire but also by the fact that Attila showed great favor to, and kept close to his person, many men of non-Hunnish origin. These court favorites included not only the vassal kings of many of the Germanic peoples but also a number of persons of Greek or Roman birth. His private secretary, a man named Constantius, was a distinguished citizen of the Roman Empire and an Italian by birth. Even more important at the Hunnish court, and a man frequently sent on foreign embassies, was Orestes. Orestes was a Roman citizen and had married into a well-known Roman family. Of even greater interest and significance to us is the fact that Orestes was the father of Romulus Augustus, destined at a later period to be the last Emperor of the West Roman Empire.[22]

The presence of Greeks and Romans at the Hunnish court was not confined to persons of high degree. Many citizens of the Roman Empire, having been captured in warfare, were taken back to the Hunnish kingdom and kept there as artisans and skilled laborers. In at least one case an upper middle class Greek continued to reside in the Hunnish court of his own free will even after he had been emancipated from slavery. In spite of the hospitality and favor shown by Attila to many individual Greeks and Romans, the Hunnish monarch soon proved himself to be the Roman Empire's most dangerous enemy. At first it was the East Roman Empire rather than the West Roman Empire which felt the full weight of his hostility.

As early as 441 the Huns conducted a campaign of plunder against Macedonia and Thrace, killing many thousands of the East Roman Emperor's subjects. It was not, however, until 447, two years after Attila became sole monarch of the Huns, that he led the most formidable of all his expeditions against the Eastern Empire. On this occasion Attila and his troops are said to have destroyed more than seventy towns and fortresses. One detachment of the Hunnish army penetrated as far as Thermopylae in Northern Greece, another to a point near Gallipoli on the Dardanelles. Constantinople itself was free from serious attack, but in order to secure the withdrawal of the Huns from East Roman territory, the Emperor Theodosius was forced to sign a most humiliating treaty (448). By the terms of this treaty the East Romans were forced to grant to Attila an annual "stipend" of 2100 pounds of gold (about four hundred thousand dollars) and in addition pay a lump sum of six thousand pounds of gold as a settlement of past arrears.

In the months following this treaty Attila continued to send embassy after embassy to Constantinople, nominally in order to protest that the East Romans had not as yet handed over all the fugitives from the

Hunnish domain who had taken refuge inside the Roman Empire. The real object of these embassies, however, seems to have been to provide some of Attila's personal favorites with a private fortune, since the East Roman court seemed to feel it necessary to heap enormously valuable presents upon each of the Hunnish envoys as a means of warding off further Hunnish attacks.

As the result of this expenditure the financial situation of the whole East Roman Empire became extremely perilous. Heavy taxation had to be resorted to, and in many cases wealthy individuals found their whole private fortunes confiscated. Even so, the Emperor found the greatest difficulty in meeting the obligations which the Huns had forced upon him. Being unwilling to risk another war, he sank so low as to attempt to get Attila disposed of by private assassins. The whole plot was betrayed, however, and in order to appease the Hunnish wrath the East Roman court was forced to disavow their agents and in addition make many new presents to Attila and his more prominent ministers.

Just as the East Roman Empire seemed on the brink of ruin its ruler Theodosius II died (450) and was succeeded by an elderly senator named Marcian. We know very little about the life and character of Marcian, but he must have been a very remarkable man. Instead of wasting his money upon presents to the insatiable Hunnish envoys, he spent it in reorganizing his army and in strengthening all the main lines of defense. This having been done, he adopted a much bolder line of diplomacy in dealing with the Hunnish court.[23]

Attila, who was an expert at the game of bluff, realized that further extortions from the East Roman Empire could only be secured by another long and arduous military campaign. This region, however, had already been bled so white that the returns from such a campaign, even though successful, seemed highly dubious. So with great good sense he shifted his attention from the eastern to the western divisions of the Roman Empire.

During the period which had elapsed between Attila's accession to the throne (434) and the year 450, the relations between the Huns and the West Roman Empire had been remarkably friendly. Even the conflicts between the Huns and the eastern division of the Empire caused little repercussion in the West. This was in a large measure due to the fact that Aetius, the chief confidant of the Emperor Valentinian III, and the most powerful political and military leader in the Western Empire at this period, was on very intimate terms with the Hunnish court. As a youth Aetius had served as a hostage among the Huns and had become well-acquainted with the principal Hunnish leaders, and it is probable that he and Attila had known one another from early manhood.

During the period that Rua, Attila's uncle, had sat on the throne, Aetius had on two occasions (425 and 433) secured the loan of Hunnish auxiliaries in dealing with local disturbances in Italy.

During the early years of Attila's reign the friendly relations between Aetius and the Hunnish court had increased rather than decreased. On three occasions (436-439) Aetius had employed a large number of Hunnish mercenaries in campaigns directed against the Visigoths, the Burgundi, and other barbarians in Gaul and we have every reason to believe that he secured these mercenaries with Attila's direct assistance, for the two men were in frequent correspondence and exchanged presents on several different occasions. In this connection it is interesting to note that we are told that many of the Huns learned to speak Latin while almost none of them ever were able to speak Greek.[24]

In the years 448-449, however, a coldness sprang up between Aetius and Attila and late in 450 Attila definitely decided upon open hostilities with the West Roman Empire. Once warfare had been decided upon, it was not difficult to find a pretext for quarreling. For many years the Huns and the West Romans had engaged in acrimonious correspondence regarding the rightful ownership of some golden vases which had once formed part of the treasure of a church in Sirmium. This ancient dispute was again reopened, and in addition Attila saw fit to refer to his so-called "engagement" with Honoria, the Emperor Valentinian's sister.

From a very early age Honoria had manifested a wild and passionate nature. At the age of sixteen she was caught having a liaison with a minor official at the imperial court. After this she was kept practically a prisoner in the palace. Filled with romantic notions, she managed to send a messenger to Attila with a ring offering him her hand and her heart, in spite of the fact that the Hunnish monarch already possessed a large harem. For some time Attila ignored the proposition of the infatuated woman, but in 450 he took advantage of the situation, and sending an embassy to the West Roman Court, he demanded that Honoria be handed over to him together with one-half of the West Roman Empire as a dowry. Needless to say both requests were refused and the Huns decided upon open warfare.[25]

After some consideration it was decided to open the campaign in Gaul rather than in Italy. Gaul was already broken up into a number of semi-independent barbarian kingdoms in addition to the provinces which still remained an integral part of the Roman Empire, and Attila hoped to secure the aid of some of these kingdoms in his offensive against the Romans.

Mustering a huge army (the Roman annalists state that Attila had command over five hundred thousand soldiers, though the Huns proper constituted only a small minority of this number), the Hunnish monarch crossed the Rhine and poured his hosts into Northern Gaul. At first he met with universal success. Town after town was taken and plundered, including the city of Metz. Paris escaped only because it was as yet too insignificant to merit Hunnish attention. At last siege was laid to Orleans, the most important city in Gaul, and for a while it seemed as if this strategic center would fall into the hands of the Huns.

Just at this time, however, Aetius, the great Roman commander, marched northward to the rescue of the beleaguered city. More fortunate still, he was able to win the coöperation and active assistance of the inhabitants of the barbarian kingdoms, such as the Visigoths, the Burgundi, a section of the Alani, and even the Celtic inhabitants of Armorica or Brittany. At the approach of the allied army Attila abandoned the siege of Orleans and retired to the Northwest. He was, however, pursued by Aetius and his followers, and before long a great battle was fought between the two armies on the Catalonian fields somewhere between the cities of Troyes and Metz. The battle was long-drawn-out and very bloody; we are told that over a hundred and fifty thousand persons perished on this single day.

In many ways the results were indecisive. Theodoric, the King of the Visigoths, was killed, and immediately thereafter the Visigothic portion of the allied army retired to their own domain. In spite of this defection on the part of his enemies' ally, Attila felt that he had had enough of warfare for the moment and without waiting to renew the battle, he and his immense host retreated across the Rhine and returned to Hungary.[26]

To the extent that the Huns had been forced to abandon operations in Gaul and return to Hungary, Rome had won a splendid victory, but the Hunnish peril was far from being over, and in the following year (452) Attila embarked upon a new campaign. This time his objective was not Gaul, but Italy. He felt, no doubt, that the expedition of the preceding year had been unsuccessful largely because the barbarian elements in Gaul had sided with the Romans rather than with him. He was confident that though these barbarians might help repulse a Hunnish invasion of Gaul, which was now their native land, they would make no attempt to assist the Romans as long as operations were confined to Italy.

Attila was perfectly right in making this assumption. Not a hand was stirred North of the Alps, and Aetius and the Roman legions (mere shadows of the glorious Roman legions of former centuries) were left to bear the full brunt of the new Hunnish attack, with the result that Attila and his followers at first were everywhere successful.

The first act of the Huns after crossing the Alps was to lay siege to Aquileia, for many centuries the chief city of Northeastern Italy. In spite of a desperate defense the city was at last carried by storm. The splendid buildings were razed to the ground and most of the inhabitants put to the sword, as were all persons dwelling in the immediate neighborhood who had the misfortune to fall into the hands of the Huns. According to tradition a large number of persons fled to the marshy lagoons just off the coast of the Adriatic and there laid the foundations for the city of Venice which eventually took the place of Aquileia as the principal city in this region.

After the sack of Aquileia the Hunnish army spread far and wide over Northern Italy. With comparatively little difficulty they captured and plundered Padua, Verona, and Milan. There was some thought of extending the campaign southward and making an attack upon the sacred city of Rome. Just at this time, however, famine and, worse still, pestilence broke out in the Hunnish camp. Added to this fact Aetius, who up to this time had been able to offer little effective resistance to the Hunnish armies, received reinforcements from the eastern division of the Empire and was thus enabled to cause the Huns serious trouble. He was still not in a position to risk a large pitched battle but in a series of minor engagements he succeeded in sapping the strength of the Hunnish army.

In consequence of this situation the Huns were in a favorable mood to receive a Roman embassy headed by Pope Leo I. No details of the diplomatic negotiations have come down to us, but in the end the Huns consented to return to Hungary, presumably on condition that no further attacks were made upon them by the Roman armies and that they be allowed to withdraw in full possession of the enormous amount of booty already obtained by them. We know, moreover, that on retiring to his own domain, Attila left a loophole for the renewal of hostilities any time it pleased him by threatening that he would do worse things in Italy in the future unless they sent him his "fiancee," the passionate princess Honoria.[27]

Attila and his army duly returned to his capital East of the Danube. Forgetting his love for the fair Honoria, we find him, early in the following year, adding a new beauty to his large harem. "After the wedding," says the worthy Gothic bishop Jordanes, "Attila gave himself up to excessive joy at his wedding and as he lay on his back, heavy with wine and sleep, a rush of superfluous blood which would ordinarily have passed from his nose, streamed in deadly course down his throat and killed him.... On the following day, when a great part of the morning was spent, the royal attendants suspected some ill, and after a great uproar broke in the doors. There they found the death of Attila accomplished by an effusion of blood without any wound, and the girl with downcast face, weeping behind her veil."

We are told that Attila was buried with a triple coffin, one part of iron, one of silver and one of gold. The place of his interment was kept secret, and lest the secret be betrayed all of the persons who had prepared the grave were put to death.[28]

The story of Attila has always had a peculiar fascination for the later peoples of Europe. In addition to being given serious consideration by all the important historians who have dealt with his time and place, a fantastic account of his life and deeds soon made its way into the legends of the Latin and Germanic peoples. Later still (ninth century) when Magyars invaded and conquered Hungary they too evolved an elaborate Attila legend of great interest to the folklorist, but completely valueless to the serious students of ancient times.[29]

Attila was indeed a great man, but when we consider the permanent results of his eventful and glorious reign we find that he accomplished amazingly little. The really important results, and the only permanent results, of the Hunnish invasions of Europe were the pushing of the Goths and other Germanic peoples westward inside of the Roman Empire. But this work was accomplished, not by Attila, but by his predecessors, concerning whom we know little or nothing. Attila himself had very little effect upon the migration of peoples. His great work was the construction of a gigantic Hunnish Empire but this empire collapsed like a house of cards and Attila's Hunnish tribesmen were permanently expelled from Western Europe only a few years after Attila himself was laid in the grave.

The downfall of the European Huns was due in large measure to internal dissensions which broke out immediately after Attila's death. Attila had left behind him a large number of children, and many of these strove to carve out independent kingdoms for themselves. Taking advantage of this situation, the Germanic peoples, led by the Gepids and the Ostrogoths, rose in revolt against Hunnish domination. In 454 a fierce battle was waged on the banks of the Nedal River, a small stream somewhere in Hungary, as a result of which many thousands of Hunnish tribesmen including Ellak, Attila's eldest son, were killed.

Hunnish power was definitely broken as a result of this battle. Small scattered bands of Huns continued to dwell in various parts of Hungary under petty chieftains but the main body of Huns were forced to retire to the East of the Carpathian Mountains where they took refuge with their kinsmen who had been dwelling on the steppes of Southern Russia for the past three-quarters of a century.

Supremacy in Hungary, the seat of Attila's Kingdom, was divided among the various Germanic peoples who had successfully revolted against Hunnish rulership. The Gepids occupied most of the region East of the Danube, while the Ostrogoths settled down for the moment in Pannonia on the West of that river. A few years later the descendants of Attila again moved westward and made a feeble attempt to reoccupy a small portion of the territory which had once formed part of the domain of their illustrious ancestor. But the Gepid line held firm with the result that the Huns were only able to occupy certain regions along the line of the lower Danube, which lay to the South of the Gepid strongholds.

Ernac, the favorite younger son of Attila, with a few Hunnish followers secured possession of the region now known as Dobruga, just to the South of the mouth of the Danube. Two other Hunnish princes named Emnedzur and Ultsindur overran a portion of the East Roman province of Dacia Ripensis somewhat further to the West. Other groups of Huns settled in small groups in various other portions of the East Roman Empire. These settlements, however, caused no serious threat to the stability of the Eastern Empire. The court at Constantinople seems to have made no attempt to expel these Hunnish groups, and it is probable that the Huns came to a peaceful understanding with the Romans, settling as *foederati* or autonomous allies in districts which lay desolate and sparsely populated as a result of the disastrous wars of the last half century.[30]

In 461 Dengesik, another son of Attila, made a somewhat bolder attempt to reëstablish Hunnish supremacy in the West. It is probable that he too followed the Danube upstream, for, avoiding the Gepids, he fell directly upon the Ostrogoths in Pannonia. The Goths succeeded in repulsing this attack, but this group of Huns remained in the neighborhood for several years. In 468 we find them again crossing the Danube, but this time in a southerly direction, and attacking the East Roman Empire. For once this Empire was able to rise to the occasion. The Hunnish attack was repulsed and Dengesik and many of his followers lost their lives. This affair is the last event mentioned in connection with the Huns of the line of Attila.[31]

We have sound bases for believing that these attempts on the part of the descendants of Attila to return westward and resecure a foothold in Hungary and the Balkans were not entirely voluntary, nor the result merely of a desire to revive the glory of Attila's empire. The real reason for this new western movement was renewed pressure from the East, arising from fresh disturbances in Central Asia.

Shortly before this time a new "Turanian" empire had arisen in

Mongolia founded by a people known to the Europeans as Avars and to the Chinese as Rouran. We have good reason to suppose that this people spoke some form of Mongolian and thus constitute the first Mongol people to secure a place in recorded history. With lightning-like rapidity the Avars extended their control not only over all of Mongolia but also over a considerable portion of Northeastern Turkistan, thereby causing great commotion among all the peoples inhabiting Central Asia. Several of these peoples, desirous of escaping from Avar control, decided to migrate westward. Prominent among such peoples was a group known as Sabirs, a name worthy of note as it is possible that the name Siberia is ultimately derived from the name of this people.

It is probable that a great many Sabirs remained behind in Northern Turkistan and Southern Siberia at this time, but it is certain that a large number of them pushed westward, and crossing the Volga River settled in the Kuban district just North of the Caucasus Mountains where they remained for several centuries. We know very little about these Sabirs, but the classical authors tell us that they were a "Hunnish" people from which we may assume that many if not most of them were Turkish in speech, though it is probable that they were well mixed with Finno-Ugrian stock.[32]

The pressure exerted by the Sabirs set other peoples in motion. Those Hunnish groups which had formerly dwelt in the region East of the Don and Volga Rivers (the old habitat of the Alani) were pushed westward. One section of this group, though migrating from Northwestern Turkistan, managed to retain possession of much of the territory between the Don and Volga Rivers. The other section, pushing still further westward, crossed the Don River and settled all along the steppes of Southern Russia, ousting or absorbing those Hunnish tribes which had long been settled in this region.[33]

All of these new immigrants were closely allied both racially and linguistically with the Huns who had invaded Europe approximately a century previously. It is for this reason that several of the classical authors speak of the new invaders under the old general title of Huns. Strictly speaking, however, they constituted a separate branch of the Hunnish family and hence frequently received a special name, in this case Bulgarian Huns, or sometimes simply Bulgarians. It is probable that this name is simply a variant of the word Volgarian, from the river Volga, which was long the center of their activity. At a subsequent period these Bulgarians were destined to found two large and important states, one "Great Bulgary," on the upper reaches of the Volga River, the other "Black Bulgary" in the Balkans, roughly speaking the Bulgaria of modern times.

For a century after their entrance into Europe, however (which must be placed between 461 and 465) they spent most of the time roving over the plains of Southern Russia. Even during this period there was a sharp difference between the Bulgarians East of the Don River, who were called Utrigurs, and those settled west of this stream, called Kutrigurs. It was the Utrigurs who were later to found Great Bulgary on the Upper Volga and the Kutrigurs who later established Black Bulgary in the Balkans. In the decades following their first settlement in Europe we hear much more regarding the Kutrigurs than their kinsmen and neighbors to the East, and this for the simple reason that it was the Kutrigurs who came into intimate contact with the Germanic peoples inhabiting Hungary, and with the Graeco-Romans inhabiting the East Roman Empire.

Following in the footsteps of the earlier Huns, the Huns of Uldin and Attila, the Bulgarian Kutrigurs made several attempts to invade Hungary. This time, however, the Goths and their Germanic brethren were able to withstand the shock of the Asiatic onslaught. Theodorik, the great King of the Ostrogoths, overwhelmed the Bulgarian invaders, and with his own hands killed their chief. Athalarik, Theodorik's grandson, writing early in the sixth century to the Roman Senate, tells of another great victory which one of his generals had inflicted upon the Hunno-Bulgarian tribesmen.[34]

The East Roman Empire was not so successful in keeping the Bulgarian Huns at bay. On several occasions Bulgarian hordes succeeded in crossing the Danube and ravaging various portions of Thrace and Macedonia. One of the raids occurred in 493, another in 499, still another in 535. A far more serious campaign took place in 558-559. On this occasion the Bulgarian or rather the Kutrigur armies led by a chieftain named Zabergan overran most of the Balkans and even laid siege to Constantinople, causing the inhabitants of this imperial city to fly into a panic. The Emperor Justinian, able man that he was, found himself powerless to expel the Bulgarians until at last he called in the aged General Belisarus out of retirement.

A superb tactician, Belisarus soon managed to outwit the Bulgarians and forced them to retire northward across the Danube. It was obvious, however, that the power of the Bulgarians was far from broken and that at any moment they might renew their attack upon the Empire. With a view to preventing such an occurrence the Emperor Justinian opened up negotiations with the Utrigurs, those Bulgarians who still dwelt to the east of the River Don.

As the result of much clever diplomacy and the payment of very heavy bribes, the East Romans at last induced the Utrigurs to make war upon their kinsmen, the Kutrigurs. A fearful battle was waged between the two groups of Bulgarians. Neither side was able to win a decisive victory and the losses on both sides were so great that the fighting strength of both divisions was enormously weakened.[35]

Just at this time, 559, a new wave of invasion swept in from the East, from the plains of Central Asia. In Mongolia and the surrounding regions still another new Turanian Empire had arisen, *viz.,* the empire of the Turks. These Turks had been able completely to destroy the empire of their predecessors, the Avars, and had then proceeded to subject to their own dominion the numerous tribes of Central Asia which had formerly acknowledged the overlordship of the Avar rulers.

As might be expected, some of these peoples objected to this change of rulers. One group of these Central Asiatics, the Warkhuns (or perhaps the Wars and the Khuns) determined to avoid subjecting themselves to the Turkish yoke by fleeing westward, and before long we find them crossing the Volga and invading the steppes of Southern Russia. Because of the fact that they were formerly part of the Avar Empire these Warkhuns were usually called Avars, and it was under the name of Avars or "false Avars" that they were henceforth known to the European chroniclers.

After crossing the Volga the Avars promptly proceeded to destroy the kingdoms erected by their predecessors. The first to fall was the realm of the Sabirs in the Kuban district North of the Caucasus, but before long it was the turn of the Bulgarian peoples, the Utrigurs and the Kutrigurs, to feel the full weight of the new wave of invasion. The classical authors tell us that both divisions of the Bulgarian nation were wiped out. This is certainly an exaggeration. Both the Utrigur and the Kutrigur kingdoms as separate units were completely destroyed, but large numbers of Bulgarians continued to exist as petty groups under their own chieftains, though of course these chieftains were forced to acknowledge Avar supremacy.[36]

In later times, when the Avar supremacy began to decay, several of these Bulgarian groups resecured their independence and something of their ancient power. The story of these later Bulgarian groups, however, belongs to a later stage of history and need not concern us at the present moment. With the coming of the Avars, the old traditional Hunnish kingdoms in Europe came to an end.

CHAPTER EIGHTEEN

THE HUNS IN PERSIA AND INDIA

Central Asia from A.D. 150 *to* 400*—The Sasanid Empire in Persia—The Gupta Empire in India—The Chionites—The Rise of the Ephthalites or White Huns—The Language and Culture of the Ephthalites—The Westward Migration of the Ephthalites—Their Conquest of Kashgaria and Turkistan —The Conflicts between the Ephthalites and the Sasanids—The Ephthalite Conquest of India—The Rise of the Turks and the Downfall of the Ephthalites.*

Now THAT we have portrayed the fortunes of the later Hunnish hordes in China and in Europe our task of telling the story of the Huns is almost at an end. But before we can write finis to our undertaking it is necessary to give a brief description of the Ephthalites or White Huns, a people in some way or other allied with the Huns who conquered most of Kashgaria and Turkistan and who made important inroads into Persia and India. First of all, however, it will be necessary to give a thumbnail sketch of the internal history of these regions between the time we last caught a glimpse of them, about A.D. 150, and the time when the White Huns first appear on the historical scene, about A.D. 400.[1]

In Kashgaria, in Southern Turkistan (the land of the Kang-gü), and in the domains of the Yüeji or Kushans, which included Bactria, Afghanistan, and Northwestern India, this was a period of internal stagnation and decay. All of these regions were free from external conquest and invasion, but internal dissensions caused each of them to be broken up into a number of small kingdoms or principalities, no one of which was of any great significance.

We have regarding Kashgaria, because of its proximity to the historically minded Chinese, somewhat fuller information than with respect to the other two regions, but even here our knowledge is rather fragmentary. Chinese overlordship over this region, which began to weaken shortly after 150, seems to have come to an end somewhere about A.D. 175. During this period China was so occupied with her own internal conflicts that she was unable to maintain even the fiction of supremacy over the petty states in the Tarim basin. During the two centuries that followed Chinese generals on two or three occasions managed to march armies into Northern Kashgaria and defeat or overawe the native kings in this region. At one or two places attempts were made to reëstablish Chinese military-agricultural colonies, some of which survived for several decades.

Had China been able to maintain order and a strong government at home there is no doubt but that she could have maintained supremacy over all the Kashgarian principalities but in every case internal disorders rendered nugatory all the success won by Chinese generals abroad. The rulers who had sent the Chinese armies into Kashgaria were overthrown, and the various states which made up Kashgaria, though perfectly willing to pay lip service to whatever dynasty ruled over the Celestial Empire, soon found themselves complete masters of their own fortunes as the result of the voluntary withdrawal of all Chinese military and administrative officials.[2]

In Turkistan, just to the West of Kashgaria, contemporary Chinese chronicles tell us of the continued existence of the kingdoms of Farghana (or Da-yüan) and of Sogdia (or Kang-gü). The fact that about A.D. 300 a king of Farghana sent an embassy to China shows that this region still preserved its unity and independence. The kingdom of the Kang-gü appears to have had a somewhat more complicated history. We are told that a king of Kang-gü sent an embassy to China about 270. From this it would seem as if this region was still under the rulership of a single individual, though no doubt there were a number of semi-autonomous tribal chieftains and feudal lords under this supreme ruler.

Somewhat later we find the territory of the Kang-gü broken up into a number of separate and independent principalities, each under its own ruler, though most of these rulers were closely related and bore the same family name, a name rendered by the Chinese as Jaowu. Curiously enough, we are told that all of the members of this family boasted of their descent from the Yüejï aristocracy of former days. We are uncertain how this descent was traced, or whether it implies a new conquest of Sogdia (Kang-gü) by the Yüejï nobility at some time subsequent to A.D. 300. We do know that from very early times there was a close association between the ruling families of both domains. The fact that the Jaowu family boasted of its Yüejï descent, therefore, may well mean that this descent was only indirect, and that the various independent rulers of the Jaowu line were more directly connected with the family which had once ruled over the unified Kang-gü kingdom, and that this kingdom broke up as the result of voluntary division of territory between the various members of the family.[3]

The course of events among the Yüejï or Kushans during this period is equally obscure. We know almost nothing of the fortunes of the Kushan dynasty after the death of King Vasudeva, who is usually supposed to have died about A.D. 220. The Chinese historians, however, who wrote of the period 220-265 (Wei-lio), tell us that the Kushans still had possession of Bactria, Afghanistan, and Northwestern India.

Shortly after this time the great Kushan Empire seems to have broken up into a number of small principalities and kingdoms, but in each of these states rulership continued to rest in the hands of monarchs of Kushan origin. In India these Kushan states included much of the province of the Panjab, and the region to the northwest of the Panjab usually known as Gandhara. Another group of Kushans retained control over the Kabul valley and many of the surrounding regions in Afghanistan. Another very important group of Kushans continued to reside in Bactria and formed there another independent monarchy.[4]

Before closing this survey a word must be said regarding the Sasanid Empire which dominated most of the Iranian Plateau and of the Gupta Empire which ruled over a great portion of India during this period. Both the Sasanid and Gupta Empires represented violent nationalistic reactions against the previous alien rulers of their respective domains.

The Sasanid dynasty arose (ca. A.D. 226) in the province of Persia or Pars, in the southwestern portion of the Iranian Plateau. It was in this province that the old Achemenid Empire of Cyrus and Darius had arisen, and it was in this region that the old national tradition had best been preserved during the long period that the barbaric Parthians had ruled over Iran. Within a remarkably short space of time Ardashir, the founder of the Sasanid dynasty, succeeded in completely overthrowing the last of the Parthian rulers and in subjecting the whole of the former Parthian domain to his own jurisdiction. Of great importance in this connection is the fact that the Sasanid domain thus included a goodly portion of Southwestern Turkistan, and consequently came into direct contact both politically and culturally with the peoples of Central Asia. Some authorities would go even further and claim that the Sasanids were able to exercise some sort of vague supremacy over the Kushan monarchs of Bactria. This is extremely doubtful, but unfortunately we have no way of settling the matter, as we have no records dealing with the relations of the Sasanids with the regions lying to the North and East of their domain during the first two centuries of their rule.

We do know that the rise of the Sasanid dynasty brought about an attempt to forget everything which had transpired since the fall of the Achemenid Empire. Though the Parthians had been Iranian in speech, they were regarded as hated invaders from Central Asia and everything was done to belittle them and the things for which they had stood. The Parthians had been mildly sympathetic to Greek culture, and during the days of Parthian supremacy certain elements of Greek culture had been allowed to survive on the Iranian Plateau, the gateway to Central Asia. With the coming of the Sasanids, however, the last traces of Greek culture were rooted out and thereafter the peoples of Central Asia were exposed to cultural stimuli which were supposedly purely Iranian in origin.

It was only in the sphere of religion that there was a partial exception to this rule. The Sasanids, to be sure, were far more zealous in their advocacy and support of Orthodox Zoroastrianism than the Parthians had been. The Parthians had actively sympathized with the Zoroastrian cause and had lent it their moral support, but they had remained fairly tolerant in their religious views and had permitted non-Zoroastrian sects and religions to persist within their domain. The Sasanids were far more zealous Zoroastrians and at times went in for the active persecution of the Christians and, presumably, the Buddhists who resided in their domains.

Occasionally, however, they showed themselves fairly tolerant in religious matters, especially where political considerations were taken into account. When Nestorian Christianity, an heretical offshoot of the Greek Christian community, began to be persecuted by the East Roman Empire for its religious views, many Nestorians took refuge within the Sasanid Empire. They were allowed there a certain measure of religious freedom, with the result that Nestorian Christianity eventually spread through Persia to all parts of Central Asia.

A similar situation arose in connection with Manicheanism. Manicheanism was a curious compound of Zoroastrianism, Christianity, and Buddhism which arose in Mesopotamia and which at one time found adherents in many portions of the Roman world, as is witnessed by the fact that St. Augustine in his younger days was a fervid follower of the Manichean faith. Christian bigotry eventually brought about the complete suppression of Manicheanism in the West. In Persia the Manicheans were also subject to persecution. Mani, the founder of the religion, was killed by order of one of the Sasanid monarchs, and various attempts were made to stamp out the Manichean faith throughout the length and breadth of the Sasanid domain. In Persia, however, this persecution was never as far-reaching or as thorough as it was in the West. As a result the Manichean faith managed to persist for centuries on the Iranian Plateau and eventually spread northward into Central Asia and played a very important role in the cultural life of several Central Asiatic peoples.[5]

In many ways the Gupta Empire, which arose in India about A.D. 320, offers a close parallel to the Sasanid Empire in Persia. Just as the Sasanid Empire arose in Pars, the seat of the ancient Achemenid Empire, so did the Gupta dynasty spring up in Magadha on the middle Ganges basin, the seat of the Maurya dynasty, the most glorious of the early Indian Empires. And just as the Sasanids overthrew the power of the semi-barbarous Parthians, who had originally hailed from Central Asia, so did the Guptas do everything they could to break the power of the Sakas and Kushans, also of Central Asiatic origin, who for so long played the dominant political role in Northern India. The Guptas, to be sure, were not quite so successful in their fights against the barbarians as were the Sasanids, for while the Sasanids were able completely to destroy the Parthian power the Guptas were only able to weaken their barbarian adversaries.

The Guptas were indeed able to drive out the petty dynasties of alien origin which had formerly reigned in the Ganges basin, and all of this region was restored to native rulership. In addition the Guptas were successful in crushing the so-called "Western Satrapies." The Western "Satraps," of Sakan origin, had long ruled as autonomous or semi-autonomous hereditary governors over a large portion of Western India, though for several centuries they acknowledged the real or nominal supremacy of the Kushan monarchs further to the North.

The Guptas, as the result of several campaigns, were able to destroy these Western Satrapies, thereby overthrowing the last vestiges of Saka rulership, and also taking from the Kushans their last claims of supremacy in this region. Judging by the proud boastings of some of the Gupta kings, the monarchs of this line also succeeded, at least for a period, in imposing tribute upon some of the Kushan kingdoms themselves. This tribute, however, did not imply the complete subjugation of these Kushan kingdoms, and we know that various petty Kushan dynasties continued as overlords of a large portion of the Indus basin, thus retaining a hold upon India proper, in addition to their control over such outlying provinces as Afghanistan, Bactria and Kashmir. This fact becomes of importance when we remember it means that the Gupta dynasty was thus cut off from all direct intercourse with Central Asia, and thus was prevented from exerting the same influence upon this region as did the Sasanid Empire in Persia.

Just as the rise of the Sasanids meant the revival of native pre-Hellenistic religious, literary, and artistic traditions in Persia, so did the rise of the Guptas mean the overthrow of the semi-Greek culture favored by many of the Kushan monarchs and the revival of purely native Indian traditions in all forms of cultural life. India was, fortunately, never able completely to forget the stimulus given to her by the Greek artistic tradition, but in the art and literature which grew up under Gupta patronage we find a great weakening of the Greek tradition and an emphasis upon ideas and ideals which were purely Indian in origin.

Nowhere was this tendency more obvious than in the sphere of religion. For many years Buddhism, which though Indian in origin was essentially synthetic and cosmopolitan in character, had been the dominant though not the exclusive religious system throughout the greater part of India. During the Gupta period, and largely because of Gupta patronage, there was a marked revival of orthodox Hinduism with its rigid caste divisions and its complicated religio-social rules. Because of these rules it was impossible for orthodox Hinduism to win favor or influence with the peoples of Central Asia or the Far East, and as a result India, during and after the Gupta period, ceased to be the dominating factor in the cultural life of the Central and Far Eastern Asiatics.

The Gupta rulers were not especially intolerant. Buddhism, though not favored, was allowed to persist and many Buddhist monasteries and monastic libraries retained much of their ancient glory. Numerous Chinese Buddhist pilgrims came to India from the Celestial Empire during this period and took back with them many Sanskrit manuscripts for translation into their native language. As a result there was not a complete cessation of culture contacts between India on one hand and Central Asia and China on the other. But it should be noted that these pilgrims were all interested in the spiritual heritage which India had created at an earlier period, the Buddhist lore and literature which had grown up before the Guptas came to power. The new Hindu literature, philosophy, and art which arose in India during this period had little effect upon these Buddhist pilgrims and their countrymen in Central Asia and the Far East.[6]

After this survey of the political and social changes which took place in the Middle East from 150 to 400, we can now proceed to examine the effects of Hunnish pressure in this region. To a certain extent this pressure began to be exerted even before A.D. 400. As we know, it was during this same period (150-400) that Northern Turkistan was occupied by various groups of Hunnish tribesmen, a prelude to their invasion of Europe.

Some of these Hunnish groups in Northern Turkistan made long raids to the South and caused a good deal of damage to the northern outposts of the Persian Sasanid Empire. As we have already seen, in about 356 the Chionites were especially troublesome to the Persians and we have every reason to believe that the Chionites were merely one branch of the Hunnish family.[7] It was not, however, until over half a century later that this Hunnish pressure became a serious menace to the independence of Southern Turkistan, Persia, and India. At this time we hear no more of the Chionites, but of an entirely new group generally known as the Ephthalites or Hephthalites.[8]

The origin and exact ethnic affinities of the Ephthalites are shrouded in mystery. By the contemporary Greek and Roman histories they are frequently referred to merely as Huns. The Hindu legends and traditions regarding the dreaded "Hunas" also go back to the period of the Ephthalite invasions and show that the word Hun must have been intimately associated with the Ephthalites shortly after their first definite appearance upon the stage of world history.[9]

We know, however, from various sources that the Ephthalites were a very peculiar group and differed radically from most of the other Hunnish groups. Thus, for example, the Byzantine writers are careful to distinguish between the ordinary Huns, such as those who invaded Europe, and the Ephthalites, who are more specifically referred to as White Huns. "The Ephthalites," says Procopius, a contemporary, "are of the Hunnish race and bear the Hunnish name, but they are completely different from the Huns whom we know. They alone among the Hunnish peoples have white skins and regular features."[10]

This distinction between the Ephthalites and the ordinary Huns is confirmed by what the Chinese sources have to say about the subject. The Chinese are always careful to distinguish between the Huns proper or the Hiung-nu and the Ephthalites, whom they call the Ye-ti-i-li-do or Ye-da. It is from the Chinese that we get the information that the real name of this people was Hua, and that they came to be designated as Ye-ti-i-li-do because of the fact that one of the great Hua rulers bore this name.[11]

There is some confusion and contradiction in the Chinese chronicles as to the exact origin of the Ephthalites, but we are expressly told that their language differed radically from that spoken by the Avars in Central and Eastern Mongolia (which was probably Mongol) and also from that spoken by the Gaogü in Northeastern Turkistan and Northwestern Mongolia. This last is of importance when we remember that the Gaogü were the descendants of the Huns and the ancestors of the Uigurs. We know definitely that the Uigurs spoke Turkish and we have every reason to believe that the Gaogü and the Huns spoke an earlier form of the same language. When, therefore, the Chinese tell us that the Ephthalites did not speak the same language as the Gaogü, this is tantamount to saying that they did not speak Turkish and thus differed linguistically from most of the Hunnish groups who occupied Northern Turkistan during this period and had already begun their invasions of Europe.[12]

According to one Chinese chronicle the Ephthalites were ultimately of the same origin as the Yüeji, according to another they were a branch of the people who inhabited Güshï or Turfan. According to the latter version the Ephthalites were descended from a group of Turfanese who in A.D. 126 aided the Chinese general Ban Yung in his attacks upon the Northern Huns and who afterwards settled in Zungaria.[13] Of great significance in this connection is the fact that we now know that both the Yüejï and the Turfanese spoke Indo-European languages, however much they may have differed linguistically among themselves. All in all, we may best give credence to the story that the Ephthalites were related more especially with the Tokharian speaking inhabitants of Turfan. We know moreover that a goodly number of the Turfanese were blue-eyed and red-headed, a fact which fits in very well with the Graeco-Roman description of the Ephthalites as "White Huns, with regular features, quite unlike the other Huns."

In view of what has been said, it is obvious that the Ephthalites differed radically from the other Hunnish groups. In fact this difference must have been so great that we are in some doubt as to the advisability of including the Ephthalites under the general heading of Huns. In view of the whole situation, however, especially because of the fact that the word Huns was a general rather than a specific term and always included peoples of widely different racial and linguistic stock, we may well let the Ephthalites remain in the general category of Huns. During the centuries that the Ephthalites and the remnants of the Huns proper dwelt in close proximity to one another in Zungaria it is certain that a great deal of intermingling between the two peoples took place. A great deal of Hunnish blood doubtless flowed in Ephthalite veins. The Ephthalites doubtless borrowed many Hunnish words and phrases for their own language. In fact, it is not at all impossible that the Ephthalites, forgetful of their true origin, came to regard and call themselves a branch of the Hunnish family (as a parallel we know that Babur and his descendants, Turks to a man, gloried in the name of Mughal or Mongol), a fact which would account for the fact that the name Hun was applied to the Ephthalites by so many of their neighbors.

One feature of the Ephthalite social culture is worthy of especial mention, namely the fact that they went in for polyandry, or the custom whereby each woman was allowed to have several husbands. As in many other polyandrous lands the various husbands were for the most part brothers, the eldest brother marrying the girl, and the younger brothers being automatically admitted to conjugal rights. The Ephthalite women had a peculiar form of headdress whereby one could tell at a glance the exact number of husbands each lady possessed.[14]

The fact that the Ephthalites went in for polayndry is of especial interest inasmuch as this custom was entirely unknown to the other Hunnish tribes concerning whom we have documentary information. Polyandry was also unknown as far as we can tell among all of the Indo-European tribes inhabiting Central Asia, including the Yüejï and the

Turfanese, with whom the Ephthalites are supposed to be especially connected. We know, to be sure, that the modern Tibetans practice polyandry and there was probably some cultural filtration between the Ephthalites and the Tibetans in this regard. At the same time we must bear in mind that there is no evidence whatever that the Ephthalites were themselves Tibetans, and the fact that the earliest Chinese records which deal with the Tibetans made no mention of polyandry makes it somewhat doubtful as to just when and among what people polyandry started in Central Asia.

Neither the Greek, the Persian, nor the Hindu records give us any information regarding the Ephthalites prior to their invasion of Persian and Indian territory. We must turn to the Chinese records for information on this point, and unfortunately the Chinese records, for once, are extremely vague and meager. This no doubt is due to the fact that at the time when the Ephthalites rose to power the Chinese were so occupied with their own internal conflicts that they had no time for the movements of the Ephthalites to the southwest. But at least the Chinese chronicles do tell us that the Ephthalites after their coöperation with the Chinese in A.D. 126 dwelt for several centuries in Zungaria without having any direct communication with the Celestial Empire.

We next hear that the Ephthalites became subjected to the Avars (or the Rouran) when the latter established their huge empire which included Mongolia and the surrounding regions. The Avars were building up their political organization all during the latter part of the fourth century A.D., but it was not until A.D. 402 that the Avar Empire was definitely established, at which time the Avar ruler assumed the title of Khagan (or Khan) and proceeded systematically to consolidate and extend the Avar domain.

It is probable that the Ephthalites began their migration either at or very shortly after this date. Seemingly they bore no especial hatred to the Avars. The rulers of the Ephthalites were related to the royal family of the Avars by marriage. Their relation to the Avars in fact must have been very similar to the relation between the Ostrogoths and the Huns at the time of Attila, half vassals and half auxiliaries. When the Ephthalites first moved to the southwest they were regarded as advance guards of the Avars rather than as a separate people. Moreover, if, as seems possible, the rulers of the Ephthalites bore the title of Khan, a title which was peculiarly Avar in origin (as opposed to the title of Shanyu which had been borne by the Hunnish rulers) it would seem as though the Ephthalites had borrowed much of their political organization from the Avar overlords. Nevertheless, it is certain that the Avars and the Ephthalites were a completely separate people with a very different linguistic and cultural background, and the real reason for the migration of the Ephthalites to the southwest was a desire to escape from too close proximity to their too exacting Avar overlords.[15]

The Chinese chronicles are silent on the exact route taken by the Ephthalites on their march to the southwest. It is, however, probable that they marched through Kashgaria for we find it expressly stated that the greater part of this region became subject to Ephthalite supremacy. Among the Kashgarian city states which are stated to have submitted themselves to the Ephthalites were Karashahr, Kucha, Kashgar and Khutan. The only places of importance in Kashgaria which are not included in this list are Shanshan (or Loulan) and Turfan (Güshï or Gaochang) in the extreme East, which fell into direct subjection to the Avars.

After bringing Kashgaria to submission the Ephthalites next moved to the West and overran Sogdia, as the result of which the various Kang-gü princes hastened to accept Ephthalite overlordship. The next move of the Ephthalites was to the South and involved the invasion and conquest of the Yüejï kingdom of Bactria. The Ephthalite invasion of this region was undertaken seriously and systematically. They had made no attempt to settle either in Kashgaria or in Sogdia. Moreover, the native rulers of these two regions had been allowed to retain their kingdoms and thrones provided only that they accepted Ephthalite supremacy and paid to the Ephthalites a heavy tribute.

In Bactria, however, a very different situation arose. Here, for some reason or other, the Ephthalites determined to make a permanent settlement, so that it was necessary for them not merely to overrun but also to destroy the Yüejï kingdom which already existed in this region. The Yüejï rulers seem to have put up a desperate resistance. After being defeated they took refuge at first in the western portion of their domain. Before long, however, they were followed and again attacked by the Ephthalites, with the result that the Yüejï monarch, a man called Kidara, and his court were again forced to flee for their lives. This time they fled to the South and soon crossed over the Hindukush Mountains and arrived on the Iranian Plateau. They did not dare stay long here, however, as they were in too close proximity to the powerful Sasanid Empire, and so, making a long detour to the East, they eventually made their way to the Gandhara region in Northwestern India which had long been inhabited by another branch of the Yüejï people.[16]

The flight of the Yüejï from Bactria was naturally only a flight of the court and military aristocracy. The great majority of the Yüejï, together with the indigenous Bactrian population, remained behind and accepted the rulership of the invading Ephthalites. Nevertheless when Kidara, the last Yüejï king of Bactria, fled, he must have taken with him a considerable military following for he soon managed to carve out a new kingdom for himself in Northwest India, no doubt by dispossessing some of his distant cousins who were ruling over this region. A few years later a son of Kidara marched still further to the southeast, and created for himself a new domain with its capital at Purushapura, the modern Pashawar.[17]

After the flight of King Kidara and his court the Ephthalites had no difficulty in overrunning and ruling the whole of Bactria. We are told that they established their capital in the extreme southwest of their domain, in the district of Badhaghis, "the windy region," only a little to the North of the modern city of Herat.[18] It is generally supposed that the Ephthalite occupation of Bactria must have been completed by A.D. 425. The Chinese tell us that the Ephthalites numbered about one hundred thousand, but it is not clear if this number refers to the whole population or merely to the number of warriors they were able to put into the field.

It is certain that when the Ephthalites first invaded Kashgaria and Southern Turkistan they were still entirely nomadic in their habits, and lived, apart from plunder, from the products of their huge herds. For dwellings they made use of felt tents which invariably faced East. They had no system of writing. They had a primitive religious system which included the worship of heaven and of fire. The fact that fire was held sacred indicates that, like so many other Central Asiatic peoples, the Ephthalites had been exposed to religious stimuli radiating from Iran. That this Iranian influence was not strictly Zoroastrian is seen by the fact that the Ephthalites buried and did not expose their dead. Like many other primitive peoples the Ephthalites possessed a fairly elaborate legal system of their own. This code is said to have been very severe; for a simple robbery a man was cut in two.[19]

The Chinese chronicles are the only sources of information regarding the Ephthalite occupation of Kashgaria, Sogdia and Bactria,[20] but when, shortly after these events had taken place, the Ephthalites marched still further to the southwest and invaded the Sasanid Empire, their activities became of such importance to world history that they were deemed worthy of record by most of the historians in the West. The Ephthalites appeared upon the Persian frontier during the reign (420-438) of the renowned Sasanid monarch named Bahram V. From his skill as a hunter, especially of the shy Gur or Wild Ass, he is usually known as Bahram Gur. He, incidentally, is the monarch referred to in Umar Khayyam's lines:

"They say the lion and the lizard keep
The courts where Jamshid glories and drank deep
And Bahram—the Wild Ass
Stamps o'er his head and cannot break his sleep."

According to oriental tradition Bahram was the perfect type of adventurous prince, who loved not only the chase but also all manner of amorous escapades, and frequently roamed in disguise throughout his domain. This happy-go-lucky life was rudely interrupted in the seventh year of his reign (427) by a sudden attack made by the Ephthalites. After capturing Marv, the barbarians swarmed on to the Iranian Plateau and then swept westward as far as Rai near the modern city of Tihran.

At first Bahram seemed incapable of offering any effectual resistance to the invaders. In fact, for the moment the monarch was nowhere to be found and rumor had it that he had fled and was in hiding somewhere in the northwestern portion of his kingdom. In these circumstances, the great ministers who remained in charge of the affairs of state felt that it was advisable to try and end the Ephthalite danger by means of diplomacy. A large sum of money was offered to the invaders if they would only return to their own land. The offer was accepted, and true to their word the Ephthalites were peacefully returning to Bactria when they were suddenly attacked by Bahram, who had been lying in ambush all this time waiting for a favorable chance to strike a heavy blow.

The Ephthalites were caught off guard and suffered an overwhelming defeat. The ruler of the Ephthalites was killed and his consort taken prisoner. All of the tribute money paid by the Persians and an enormous amount of additional loot was secured, including, according to tradition, the royal crown of the Ephthalites, ornamented with thousands of pearls. The survivors of the Ephthalite army fled for their lives and were only too delighted to depart from Persian soil. A huge column was erected to mark the frontier between the Persian and Ephthalite domain and it was decreed that no Ephthalite might pass this frontier under pain of death. The blow dealt by Bahram to the Ephthalites in 427 was so stunning that for the next several years they made no further attempt to invade the Sasanid Empire and Bahram Gur died in 438 without having again to defend his northern frontier.[21]

Bahram was followed on the Sasanid throne by his son Yazdigird, who reigned for nineteen years, or from 438 to 457. During this period there were several wars between the Persians and the Ephthalites, but it is interesting to note that for the most part it was the Persians who took the offensive. Yazdigird, wishing to secure martial glory for himself, undertook the invasion and conquest of the Ephthalite kingdom. On one or two of these campaigns the Sasanid monarch was signally successful and was able to march far into the Ephthalite domain. Even these successes, however, led to no permanent enlargement of territory and when in 454 Yazdigird embarked upon a new invasion of Ephthalite territory he was caught in an ambuscade and suffered an overwhelming defeat. The Sasanid monarch was lucky to escape with his life and he and his remaining troops retired hastily to Persian territory. At one blow all the prestige acquired by Yazdigird on his previous campaigns was lost.[22]

An entirely new phase in the relations between the Persians and Ephthalites was ushered in by the internal disputes which arose in the Sasanid court on the death of Yazdigird in 457. Yazdigird was survived by two sons, Hurmuzd and Firuz. Firuz, being the elder, was the natural heir, but the younger son had always been the father's favorite, and in accordance with the father's dying wishes Hurmuzd, the younger son, was elevated to the throne, while Firuz was sent into a sort of semi-exile by being appointed Governor of Sakastan in the east.

Firuz was so dissatisfied with this arrangement that shortly after arriving in Sakastan he fled to the northeast and took refuge with the king of the Ephthalites, imploring the latter to aid him in raising an army whereby he might secure possession of the Persian throne. Though the Ephthalite monarch gave Firuz a very courteous reception, for the moment he refused to give any active military assistance. Two years later, however, when it was obvious that the Sasanid Empire was becoming very restive under the rulership of Hurmuzd, the Ephthalite ruler changed his mind about the project. He not only allowed Firuz to raise an army of dissatisfied Persians who flocked to his standard, but in addition placed a considerable number of Ephthalite warriors at the latter's disposal.

Aided by these troops, Firuz, in 459, managed to defeat and depose his brother, and before long he was everywhere acknowledged as the rightful ruler of the Sasanid Empire. We might have expected to find the Ephthalites taking unfair advantage of their position as king makers, but this was not the case. It was necessary for Firuz to pay his Ephthalites very handsomely for the services they had rendered, but once this payment had been made the Ephthalite contingent was perfectly content to return to their native land, and for some time profound peace and amity reigned between the Sasanid and Ephthalite empires.[23]

Five years later, however, a dispute arose between Firuz and his benefactor, the Ephthalite monarch. This dispute soon led to war, and thereafter at frequent intervals the Sasanid and Ephthalite empires engaged in armed conflict alternating with short periods of peace so that both sides could recover from their losses. On one occasion, when negotiating a treaty of peace, Firuz promised to give one of his daughters in marriage to the ruler of the Ephthalites. Had this agreement been honorably carried out it is possible that permanent peace might have ensued between the two nations. But Firuz revolted at the thought of giving a girl of the royal house of Sasan to the barbarian monarch of the North, and sent the latter a slave girl instead. The girl was wedded with much pomp and ceremony, but before long the trick was discovered. The poor girl was allowed to remain in the harem, but to secure revenge for the trick played upon him, the Ephthalite king enticed three hundred Persian officers of high rank to his court. Once they were in his power, most of these officers were put to death; the remainder were mutilated and then sent back to the Persians.[24]

This action led to another war. Firuz felt that he in turn must revenge this insult and again embarked upon a campaign against the Ephthalite domain. He succeeded in entering the Ephthalite territory without any difficulty. When at last he faced the Ephthalite army, the latter, following old nomadic tactics, pretended to be seized with panic and fled. Firuz marched on in rapid pursuit only to find before long that he had been caught in an ambush. The Sasanid monarch was now absolutely at the mercy of the barbarians. But for some reason the Ephthalite monarch had mercy upon his opponent and sent a message stating that he would allow Firuz and his companions to retire in safety to Persia provided that the Sasanid monarch would swear never again to invade Ephthalite territory, and also do homage to himself by prostration.[25]

Firuz felt obliged to accept these terms, but already thought of evading the spirit of the obligations he undertook. When he carried out the required prostration before the Ephthalite king he was careful to choose sunrise for the ceremony, and so arranged it that the barbarian monarch was between him and the rising sun. In making his prostration, therefore, he could make the mental reservation that his obeisance should be to the sun rather than to the Ephthalite ruler who had outwitted him. The Ephthalites were unaware of the deception which had taken place, and after the prostration had been accomplished and the vow never again to invade Ephthalite territory had been made, Firuz and his army were permitted to retire to Persia without further molestation. These events took place about A.D. 475.

For the next few years Firuz was occupied with the internal affairs of his own kingdom and in suppressing a rebellion which had broken out in Armenia, but in 484 he determined to make another campaign against the Ephthalites. The proposed campaign met with little favor among the members of his own court. Several of his ministers reminded him of the solemn vow he had made never again to invade the Ephthalite domain, but Firuz was not to be deterred from carrying out his purpose. He still felt the rancor and the humiliation of his previous defeat and was determined to wipe out this disgrace by a series of fresh victories.

To salve his conscience about the vow he had made he hit upon another subterfuge. In the oath he had sworn to the Ephthalites, he had sworn that he would never advance beyond the great pillar which marked the boundary between the Sasanid and Ephthalite domains. In order that he might stick to the letter of this vow, he had this pillar uprooted and carried before his army in a cart drawn by fifty elephants. Thus, however far he advanced into the Ephthalite territory, he never passed beyond the pillar and thus kept within the letter of his oath.

The Ephthalite monarch had got news of the new Persian campaign and carefully laid his plans accordingly. Marshalling his army near the frontier of his kingdom, he next proceeded to dig a broad deep ditch in front of his camp, leaving only a narrow pathway untouched. The trench was then filled with water, and then carefully covered with reeds and earth so as to completely conceal the whole affair.

When the Persian army arrived upon the scene the Ephthalites sent a small body of cavalrymen across the small pathway with orders to engage the Sasanid army in battle and then rapidly withdraw, trusting that the Persian troops would follow them in hot pursuit. This strategy worked perfectly. The members of the Ephthalite squadron, knowing of the pathway, were able to retire safely, but the Persian army who rushed after them fell into the trench. In the confusion which followed the Ephthalites were able to win an overwhelming victory. Firuz himself together with many of the princes of the royal blood was killed. The Persian army either perished or scattered to the four winds. The daughter of the Sasanid monarch and the Zoroastrian High Priest who had accompanied the expedition were taken prisoners, and an immense amount of booty fell into the hands of the Ephthalites.[26]

We are told that for the next two years Persia was forced to pay a heavy tribute to the Ephthalites. She was saved from even greater indignities only by the military skill of a Sasanid general named Sufrai who collected the scattered Persian forces into a new army which was able to defeat the Ephthalites when the latter again attempted to overrun the Sasanid domain. Persia was thus able to maintain her independence but all thoughts of conquering and destroying the Ephthalite kingdom had to be definitely abandoned.[27]

The relations between the Sasanid and the Ephthalite domains for the next few decades are of no especial interest to us. Most of the events during this period center around the varied fortunes of the adventurous Sasanid monarch named Kubad, who ruled intermittently over Persia from 488 to 531. The accidents of fate forced Kubad to have frequent personal intercourse with the Ephthalites. Kubad, like his father, the unfortunate Firuz, was a disinherited heir to the Persian throne who fled for safety and for assistance to the Ephthalite court. In this connection it is interesting to note that Kubad had no hesitation in taking refuge with the Ephthalites only a year or two after the latter had defeated and killed his own father. National and so-called racial hatred was little known in those early times.

It was largely because of Ephthalite assistance that Kubad was able to mount the throne of Persia on the death of his brother Balash, who had ruled over the Sasanid Kingdom during the troubled period from 484 to 488. Though Kubad proved to be an exceedingly able ruler, he became very unpopular with many of his subjects, largely because of the support he gave to certain religious heresies. In 497 he was deposed and put in prison. With the aid of his sister he managed to escape, and again took refuge with the Ephthalites. The Ephthalites continued to regard Kubad with favor, and at the end of three years, the refugee, aided by another Ephthalite army, was able to recapture his throne and his kingdom. This time his reign proved more successful, and he was able to remain in power until his death in 531.[28]

We have very little information regarding the price Kubad was forced to pay the Ephthalites in return for the assistance they gave him on at least two different occasions, but we know that this payment must have been fairly heavy. We are told that the Ephthalite contingent which assisted him in securing and in resecuring his throne were sent back only after they had been "richly rewarded." We know, moreover, that he was forced from time to time to pay tribute to the Ephthalite monarch, and that on one occasion, being hard up for the needed cash, he applied for a loan from Anastasius, the ruler of the East Roman Empire. We are further told that during his sojourn at the Ephthalite court he was required to take a vow that never, under any condition, would he undertake an offensive war against the Ephthalite domain. It is highly probable, moreover, though the oriental writers for obvious reasons are silent on this point, that Kubad was forced to acknowledge the nominal suzerainty and supremacy of the Ephthalite monarch.[29]

It would seem that the Ephthalites, taking advantage of past favors, became too exacting in their demands upon Kubad, for in 503, only a few years after his return to power, we find Kubad following in his father's footsteps and breaking with his patron, the Ephthalite monarch. Open warfare soon followed which continued intermittently for ten years (or from 503 to 513). Curiously enough, our historical records give us almost no details regarding these hostilities, and seemingly neither the

Persians nor the Ephthalites were able to win any decisive victory. It was no doubt because of this very fact that both parties were willing to make peace. This time the peace, apart from occasional border conflicts, appears to have lasted almost uninterruptedly for a quarter of a century.[30]

In view of all the facts which are known to us, it would seem that the real reason the Ephthalites did not continue their violent attacks upon Persia was that they had already become deeply involved in Indian affairs, and as time went on the conquest of India and the defense of the territory already won in this region took up more and more of their time. When we come to consider the Ephthalite campaigns in India and their result we are at once faced with the usual difficulties which confront all students of Indian history, viz., the almost complete absence of adequate historical documents. We are not even certain when the Ephthalites began their attacks upon India, but from a passage in the Chinese chronicles it would appear that they commenced their career of conquest in this region by the invasion and capture of Gandhara in Northwestern India about A.D. 465. This conquest, of course, was at the expense of the Kushans, ruled over either by Kidara, or one of Kidara's successors, who had been expelled from Bactria at the time the Ephthalites first swept into Southern Turkistan. We are further told that the Ephthalites appointed a special official, a Tegin or princely viceroy, to rule over their Indian domain.[31]

This Tegin or Viceroy, whom we may identify with the Toramana of the Indian inscriptions, was at first subordinate, in name at least, to the supreme Ephthalite ruler, who continued to reside in Bactria. Before long, however, this official so extended his conquests in India as to become one of the greatest monarchs of the age, and by his glory completely overshadowed his nominal suzerain who remained the semi-barbarous ruler of Central Asia.[32]

The extension of Toramana's domain brought him into hostile relations with the various petty kingdoms (mostly under Kushan rulership) which still existed in the lower Indus Valley. These he seems to have had little difficulty in conquering. Far more serious were his conflicts with the mighty Gupta Empire which was still the dominant power in Northern and Central Asia. The Gupta Empire was ruled over at this time by Skandagupta, who was destined to be the last important ruler of his line.

As far as we can make out, warfare between the Ephthalites and the Guptas started shortly before A.D. 470. At first the Gupta monarch met with a certain measure of success, and in a rock inscription he proudly boasts of his victories over the "Hunas." Before long, however, it became evident that Skandagupta had boasted of his military prowess too soon.

When the main Ephthalite army appeared on the field the Gupta monarch experienced a long series of defeats which ended in the almost complete destruction of the Gupta Empire. In fact, with the death of Skandagupta (which took place about 480) the Gupta Empire as such may be said to have come to an end. The dynasty, to be sure, survived for several generations, but the later princes of the Gupta line were little more than rulers of a petty state in the lower Ganges basin.[33]

The destruction of the Gupta Empire did not mean that all of the Gupta territory immediately fell into the hands of the Ephthalites. After Skandagupta's death his once vast domain tended to break up into a number of separate kingdoms, and it was necessary for Toramana, the Ephthalite monarch, to conquer them one by one. This process seems to have ended by A.D. 500 when the Ephthalite ruler was acknowledged as the paramount ruler of all Northern and Central India. Shortly thereafter (502) Toramana died and was succeeded on the throne by his son, Mihirakula, who proceeded to reorganize and consolidate the Ephthalite domain in India, choosing for himself a new capital at Sakala, the modern Sialkot in the Panjab.[34]

Practically all the authors of antiquity agree in picturing Mihirakula as a peculiarly bloodthirsty tyrant. Cosmas Indicopleustes, a Byzantine monk who visited India during this period, describes the Ephthalite monarch, whom he calls Gollas (undoubtedly the same as our Mihirakula) as being "Lord of India from which he exacted tribute by oppression, enforcing his demands with the aid of two thousand war elephants and a great host of cavalry." This same monarch was visited by Sung Yün, a Buddhist pilgrim from China, who informs us that the king was exceedingly cruel and vindictive, and adds that because of the monarch's long continued wars even the old men had to labor, and all the common people were oppressed. This ruler was especially relentless in his persecution of Buddhism and Buddhist monks.[35]

In the end the cruelty and oppression of Mihirakula brought about a native reaction to Ephthalite rule. The peoples of Eastern and Central India rose in rebellion. The leader of this revolt was not the effete representative of the Gupta dynasty (though it is probable that this personage coöperated in the general uprising) but a man of obscure origin and unknown antecedents, named Yasodharman. This rebellion took place about 532.

After some desperate fighting the Indian nationalists won a stupendous victory. Most of Central and Eastern India was freed from subjection to the Ephthalites and for a few years remained under Yasodharman's rulership. It was only in the far northwest that the Ephthalites managed to retain a foothold. Mihirakula, fearing for his life, took refuge in Kashmir. Deposing the native ruler, he made himself the monarch of this region and inaugurated another reign of terror which persisted until his death in about 542. The Kashmiris have a legend that Mihirakula took a fiendish pleasure in rolling elephants over a precipice and watching them die in agony.[36]

Only a few decades after the Ephthalite supremacy in India had been broken, the main body of the Ephthalites who had continued to reside in Central Asia were made the victims of an even greater disaster. The moving spirit in the events which led to this disaster was the Sasanid monarch Khusrau (or Chosroes) usually called Khusrau Anushirvan, who had succeeded his father Kubad as overlord of Persia. Khusrau ascended the throne in 531, and reigned until 579. In the first three decades of his long reign we hear nothing of any conflict between him and his Ephthalite neighbors to the northeast. During a large portion of this time the Sasanid monarch was engaged in bloody and hard fought wars with the Roman Empire, reason enough for his wish to maintain friendly relations with the Ephthalites during this period.[37]

Shortly after the middle of the sixth century, however, a great change took place. Khusrau had emerged victorious from his long conflict with the Romans and was free to turn his attention to the northeast. More important still, a great change had taken place in the political situation in Central Asia. In 552 the Turks had arisen in rebellion against their overlords the Avars, and by completely crushing the Avar Empire had made themselves absolute masters of this region.

We have already seen how the rise of the Turkish Empire brought about the flight to Europe of the Warkhunites. Even more important was the effect of the Turkish conquests upon the Ephthalite kingdom. As might be expected, not long after the Turks became the masters of Northern Turkistan they began to have petty border conflicts with the Ephthalites. The strained relations between the two peoples developed into open hostilities because of an insult offered by the Ephthalites to a Turkish embassy. The embassy in question was one dispatched by Istami, the Turkish Khagan, to Khusrau, the Sasanid monarch. In order to reach Sasanid territory, however, it was necessary for this embassy to pass through the domain of the Ephthalites. The Ephthalites were greatly alarmed at the prospect of having the Turks and the Sasanids establish direct relations and were foolish enough to slay the envoy and all of his retainers.

As a result of his action the Turks declared war upon the Ephthalites and promptly proceeded to invade the Ephthalite territory. After a great battle the Ephthalites were severely beaten, but were not as yet completely crushed. It now became necessary for Khusrau, the Sasanid monarch, to make up his mind what attitude he should adopt with reference to the situation in Transoxiana. He was obviously frightened at the rising power of the Turks and at first thought of marching to the aid of the Ephthalites and assisting the latter in driving the Turks back into Northern Turkistan.

Just at this time, however, the Khagan of the Turks, who was now able to establish direct communications with Persia, sent a new embassy to Khusrau which succeeded in completely altering the attitude of the Sasanid court. The Turkish ruler, instead of being menacing, was extremely friendly and even flattering in his attitude towards Khusrau and was obviously bent upon maintaining friendly relations between the Turkish and the Sasanid courts. Khusrau immediately abandoned all thoughts of marching to the rescue of the Ephthalites, and a little later he entered into a definite alliance with the Turkish ruler. To cement this alliance Khusrau took in marriage the daughter of the Turkish Khagan.[38]

Shortly afterwards, acting in accordance with the terms of the new alliance, the Sasanids and the Turks made a joint attack upon the Ephthalites as a result of which the Ephthalite kingdom was completely destroyed. The Turks as their share of the fruits of victory secured Sogdia, or that portion of the Ephthalite territory which lay north of the Oxus, while the Sasanids made themselves masters of Bactria and Afghanistan, or all the Ephthalite territory South of the Oxus. The exact date of this event is somewhat doubtful, but it can best be placed about A.D. 565.[39]

The Ephthalites as an ethnic group did not completely disappear until several centuries after this event. Small Ephthalite communities are known to have persisted for a considerable time in various parts of Bactria and also in Badakshan, the region of the Upper Oxus Valley, but as a political power the Ephthalites were completely broken by the Joint Turkish-Sasanid attack, and they were never again able to play any important role in history.

A very similar development took place in India. The Ephthalite kingdom in India, already badly shaken by the defeat of Mihirakula in 532, came to an obscure but ignominious end shortly after the destruction of the parent Ephthalite kingdom in Bactria. For some time thereafter, however, we hear of the existence of small Ephthalite groups in Kafiristan in the extreme northwestern portion of India but they were eventually absorbed by the surrounding population.

Equally important is the story of the Gurjaras, an ethnic group which played an important part in the later history of India. The Gurjaras are a people of unknown origin, but they made their way into India at the same time as the Ephthalites and were in some way associated with the latter. When the Ephthalite kingdom broke up the Gurjaras remained, and in fact they remain in some form or other to this day. Not only are the Gujarats of Western India (in the district of Gujarat) generally considered the descendants of the early Gurjaras, but many scholars believe that the proud Rajput clans of Rajputana and the stalwart Jats of the Panjab are likewise descended, in part at least, from these ancient invaders, even though the Gujaras, the Rajputs and the Jats have long since adopted an Indian language and been absorbed in the vast bulk of Hinduism.[40]

NOTES

Chapter One

The Early Inhabitants of Turkistan

[1] For the view that Central Asia was the cradle of the human race see E. von Eickstedt, *Rassenkunde und Rassengeschichte der Menscheit,* pp. 100 ff.

[2] For the excavations at Anau see R. Pumpelly, *Explorations in Turkestan.* For the date 4000 B.C. see H. Peake and H. J. Fleure, *Peasants and Potters,* p. 115; H.R.H. Hall, "Art of Early Egypt and Babylon," *Cambridge Ancient History,* I, 579; von Eickstedt, *op. cit.,* p. 258.

[3] For the racial character of Anau see Sergi in Pumpelly, *op. cit.,* p. 446; G. E. Smith, *Human History,* p. 132. For the material culture of Anau see Schmidt in Pumpelly, *op. cit.,* pp. 124 ff. For the domesticated animals at Anau see Duerst in Pumpelly, *op. cit.,* pp. 341 ff.

[4] For the Tripolye culture see H. Schmidt, "Ausgrabungen in Kukuteni," *Zeitschrift fur Ethnologie,* Vol. XXXXIII (1911); V. G. Childe, *Dawn of European Civilization,* pp. 152 ff. For the Central Asiatic affinities of this culture see H. Peake and H. J. Fleure, *Priests and Kings,* p. 168; J. L. Myres, "Ethnology and Primitive Culture of the Nearer East," in E. Eyre, *European Civilization,* I, 119.

[5] For the archaeological discoveries in China see J. G. Andersson, "An Early Chinese Culture," *Bulletin of the Geological Survey of China,* no. 5 (1923); *idem,* "Preliminary Report on the Archaeological Resources," *Memorandum of the Geological Survey of China,* 1925; *idem, Children of the Yellow Earth.* For the probable relationship between the Chinese pottery and the West see also T. J. Arne, "Painted Stone Age Pottery from the Province of Honan," *Paleontologica Sinica,* 1925; H. Schmidt, "Prehistorisches aus Ostasien," *Zeitschrift fur Ethnologie,* 1924; O. Franke, *Geschichte des Chinesischen Reiches,* I, 44 ff.

[6] For the belief that there was some affiliation between the various groups of vase-painters see V. G. Childe, *The Aryans,* pp. 103 ff.; Myres, "Ethnology and Primitive Culture of the Nearer East," Eyre, *European Civilization,* I, 117 ff.

[7] For the northern nomads in general see H. Peake and H. J. Fleure, *Steppe and Sown,* pp. 20 ff.; J. H. Breasted, *Ancient Times,* pp. 171 ff. That the nomads, in certain localities, at least, succeeded the vase-painters see Childe, *Dawn of European Civilization,* p. 163; M. Ebert, *Sud-Russland,* p. 37.

[8] That the Nomads were in South Russia and Turkistan prior to 2000 B.C. see Ebert, *op. cit.,* p. 52; J. L. Myres, "Indo-Europeans up to the Time of the Migrations," in Eyre, *European Civilization,* I, 233.

[9] For the data derived from the Red Ochre graves see Childe, *Dawn of European Civilization,* pp. 138 ff.; Ebert, *op. cit.,* pp. 38 ff. That these graves

probably extended over Turkistan see Peake and Fleure, *Steppe and Sown,* p. 21.

[10] For the Nordic character of the Red Ochre grave markers see Childe, *The Aryans,* p. 183; E. H. Minns, *Scythians and Greeks,* p. 145.

[11] For the view that the Red Ochre people were Indo-Europeans see Childe, *The Aryans,* p. 183; Peake and Fleure, *Peasants and Potters,* p. 134; J. L. Myres, "Neolithic Bronze Cultures," *Cambridge Ancient History,* I, 84.

[12] For a survey of the various theories regarding the original home of the Indo-Europeans see Childe, *The Aryans;* O. Schrader, *Sprachvergleichung und Urgeschichte,* I, 85 ff.; S. Feist, *Die Kultur, Ausbreitung und Herkunft der Indogermanen,* pp. 486 ff.

[13] For the theory that the Aryans originated near the Baltic see H. A. Hirt, *Die Indogermanen;* M. Much, *Heimat der Indogermanen.*

[14] For the theory that the Aryans originated in South Russia and/or Turkistan see Breasted, *op. cit.;* Childe, *The Aryans;* Peake and Fleure, *Steppe and Sown;* Feist, *op. cit.;* Meyer, *Geschichte des Altertums,* I, 2, 797; Myres, "Indo-Europeans up to the Time of the Migrations," in Eyre, *European Civilization,* I, 231.

[15] For the culture of the early Aryan inhabitants of Central Asia see Meyer, *op. cit.,* I, 2, 767 ff. For the archaeological material see Childe, *Dawn of European Civilization,* pp. 143 ff.; for the data provided by comparative philology see Feist, *Die Kultur, Ausbreitung und Herkunft der Indogermanen.*

[16] For the early history of the horse see Lefebvre de Noettes, *L'Attelage,* pp. 9 ff.; O. Schrader, art. *Pferd* in *Reallexikon des Indogermanischen Altertumskunde.* For the close association of the horse with the Aryans see Childe, *The Aryans,* p. 83; A. Berthelot, *L'Asie Ancienne, Centrale et Sudorientale d'apres Ptolemey,* pp. 20 ff. See also Meissner, "Das Pferd in Babylonien," *Mitteilungen der Vorderasiatischen Gesellschaft,* XVIII (1913), pp. 1 ff.

[17] For the dispersal from the steppes see Peake and Fleure, *Steppe and Sown,* pp. 38 ff. For the Indo-Europeans in Kashgaria see Peake and Fleure, *op. cit.,* chap. V. Some traces of a westward migration may be seen in the fact that the Red Ochre people overran the Tripolye people. See Ebert, *op. cit.,* p. 37.

[18] The route taken by the Aryans in their invasion of the Iranian Plateaus has been the subject of some dispute, but the vast majority of scholars agree that they came via Turkistan. See Meyer, *op. cit.,* I, 2, 809 ff.; F. Justi, "Geschichte Irans" in Geiger and Kuhn, *Grundriss der Iranischen Philologie,* II, 401; E. Herzfeld, *Archaeological History of Iran,* p. 7; C. Huart, *La Perse Antique,* p. 30; O. G. U. Wesendonck, *Das Weltbild der Iranier,* p. 16.

[19] For Aryan military adventurers see E. Meyer, "Das Erste Auftreten der Arier in der Geschichte," *Sitzungsberichte der Preussischen Akademie der Wissenschaft zu Berlin* (Phil-Hist. Classe), 1908, p. 14; Poussin, *L'Indo-Europeans—L'Inde Jusque Vers 300 B.C.,* p. 79; Mironov, "Aryan Vestiges in the Near East of the Second Milinary, B.C.," *Acta Orientalia,* XI, 140 ff.

[20] I have purposely omitted all references to the Hittites as their relations with the Aryans are much disputed. See Poussin, *L'Indo-Europeans—L'Inde Jusque Vers 300 B.C.*, pp. 23 ff.; Childe, *The Aryans*, pp. 20 ff.

[21] For the Aryan occupation of the Iranian plateau see G. G. Cameron, *History of Early Iran;* Huart, *op. cit.*, pp. 29 ff.

[22] For the Aryan occupation of India see V. A. Smith, *Oxford History of India*, pp. 7 ff.; Poussin, *op. cit.*, pp. 218 ff.

Chapter Two

Scythians and Sarmatians in the North

For archaeological material see Rostovstzeff, *Iranians and Greeks in South Russia*, and E. H. Minns, *Scythians and Greeks*. The principal literary source for the Scythians is Herodotus, *Musae* (*sive Historiae*), especially Bk. 4. Incidental references occur in Hippocrates, *De Aeribus, Aquis, Locis;* Justin, *Epitoma Historicarum Philippicarum Pompei Trogi;* Diodorus Siculus, *Biblioteca Historica;* Strabo, *Rerum Geographicarum;* Polybius, *Historiae;* Pliny, *Naturalis Historia;* Ptolemy, *Geographia;* Josephus, *Bellum Judaicum;* Ammianus Marcellinus, *Rerum Gestarum;* Aelian, *De Natura Animalium;* Pausanias, *Descriptio Graeciae;* Ovid, *Ex Ponto;* Aeschylus, *Prometheus Vinctus*. It should be noted that many of the classical references to the Sarmatians date from the time the latter had ousted the Scythians from South Russia.

[1] For the Cimmerians see Herodotus, *op. cit.*, 1, 6, 15 ff. and 4, 11 ff. See also C. F. Lehmann-Haupt, "Kimmerer," *Pauly Wissowa Realencyclopaedie des Classischen Altertums.*

[2] For the coming of the Scythians from Turkistan see Herodotus, *op. cit.*, 4, 11 ff.

[3] For the Scythian occupation of Rumania see Parvis, *Dacia*. For the Scythians in northeastern Asia Minor see Herodotus, *op. cit.*, 1, 103 ff.

[4] For the return of the Scythians to Russia see Herodotus, *op. cit.*, 4, 1 ff. That some remained in Asia Minor see Rostovstzeff, *op. cit.*, pp. 9 ff.

[5] For the boundaries of Scythia see Herodotus, *op. cit.*, 4, 16 ff. and 4, 99 ff. See also K. Kretschmer, "Scythia," *Pauly Wissowa Realencyclopaedie des Classischen Altertums.* For the westward movement see Rostovstzeff, *op. cit.*, pp. 40, 90.

[6] For the expedition of Darius see Herodotus, *op. cit.*, 4, 118 ff. For Phillip and the Scythians see Justin, *op. cit.*, 4, 2-3. For Alexander's general see Justin, *op. cit.*, 12, 2.

[7] For the Sarmatian conquest of the Scythians see Diodorus Siculus, *op. cit.*, 2, 43; Polybius, *op. cit.*, 25, 2. See also Kretschmer, "Sarmatae," *Pauly Wissowa Realencyclopaedie des Classischen Altertums.*

[8] For the Massagetae see Herodotus, *op. cit.*, 1, 201 ff.; see also Herrmann, "Massagetae," in *Pauly Wissowa Realencyclopaedie des Classichen Altertums.*

[9] For the Aorsi see Strabo, *op. cit.,* 11, 2, 1; for the Chinese description of the Yentsai see the *Han Shu,* 96a, 17. For the Alani see Pliny, *op. cit.,* 4, 80; Ptolemy, *op. cit.,* 3, 5; *Hou Han Shu,* 118, 12.

[10] For the Sakas see F. H. Weissbach, *Die Keilinschriften der Achemeniden,* pp. 79 ff.; Herodotus, *op. cit.,* 7, 64; Strabo, *op. cit.,* 11, 8, 2; *Han Shu,* 96b, 1; see also the Supplementary Notes.

[11] For the Kanggü see the *Han Shu,* 96a, 15.

[12] From the Chinese sources we know that the migration of the Sarmatians to the West was due in large measure to the pressure put upon them by the Hiungnu or Huns who at this time were expanding westward from Mongolia into Turkistan. For further details cf. *infra,* chaps. V ff.

[13] On the essential unity of the Scythians and Sarmatians see Herodotus, *op. cit.,* 4, 117; Hippocrates, "De Aeribus," *op. cit.,* p. 24; Diodorus Siculus, *op. cit.,* IV, 45, 4; Strabo, *op. cit.,* 11, 2, 1; Josephus, *Bellum Judaicum,* VII, 7, 4.

[14] For the racial affinities of the Scythians see Reche, "Skythen-Anthropologie" in Ebert, *Reallexikon der Vorgeschichte.* For the "portraits" see F. Sarre and E. Herzfeld, *Iranische Felsreliefs,* pp. 53 ff.; E. H. Minns, *Scythians and Greeks,* pp. 159, 200; see also the Supplementary Notes.

[15] For the linguistic affinities of the Scythians and Sarmatians see M. Vasmer, *Untersuchungen uber die Altesten Wohnsitze der Slaven,* pt. 1; Kretschmer, "Scythae," "Sarmatae," *Pauly Wissowa Realencyclopaedie des Classischen Altertums;* see also the Supplementary Notes.

[16] For agriculture among the Scythians see Herodotus, *op. cit.,* 4, 17-18. For hunting see Herodotus, *op. cit.,* 4, 134. For fish-eating among the Massagetae see Herodotus, *op. cit.,* 1, 216. For nomadism see Herodotus, *op. cit.,* 4, 46.

[17] For Scythian cattle see Herodotus, *op. cit.,* 4, 29. For sheep see Hippocrates, "De Aeribus," *op. cit.,* p. 18. For the absence of pigs see Herodotus, *op. cit.,* 4, 63. For the importance of the horse see K. Neumann, *Die Hellenen im Skythenland,* pp. 276 ff.

[18] For the eating of cattle see Herodotus, *op. cit.,* 4, 61; of sheep see Minns, *op. cit.,* p. 49; of horses see Strabo, *op. cit.,* 7, 4, 6.

[19] For milk and milk products among the Scythians see Herodotus, *op. cit.,* 4, 2; Hippocrates, "De Aeribus," *op. cit.,* p. 18; Strabo, *op. cit.,* 7, 4, 4; Pliny, *op. cit.,* 28, 35-36. For wine see Herodotus, *op. cit.,* 4, 66 and 6, 84; that the grape was grown by the Sarmatian inhabitants of Fargana see *Han Shu,* 96a, 17.

[20] For the wooden receptacles see Herodotus, *op. cit.,* 4, 2. For skin cooking pots see Herodotus, *op. cit.,* 4, 61. For the copper cauldrons see Minns, *op. cit.,* p. 79. For horn cups, *ibid.,* p. 81. For skull drinking cups see Herodotus, *op. cit.,* 4, 65. For the legend of bone fuel see Herodotus, *op. cit.,* 4, 61.

[21] That the Scythian wagons were drawn by oxen but that the men rode on horseback see Hippocrates, "De Aeribus," *op. cit.,* p. 18. That driving preceded riding see Schrader, arts. "Heer," "Rad," "Reiten," "Streitwagen" in *Reallexikon des Indogermanischen Altertumskunde.* V. Hehn, *Kulturpflanze und Haustiere,* pp. 19 ff. For China see B. Laufer, *Chinese Clay*

Figures, pt. I, Prolegomena on the History of Defensive Armor, Publication of the Field Museum, 177 (1914), pp. 186, 222. For India see H. Zimmer, *Altindisches Leben,* pp. 230 ff. For Greece and Rome see Lefebvre, *op. cit.,* pp. 203 ff. For the Celts and Germans see Feist, *op. cit.,* pp. 515 ff.; Berthelot, *op. cit.,* p. 28; see also the Supplementary Notes.

[22] For Scythian horse trapping see Minns, *op. cit.,* p. 741. For stirrups see Rostovstzeff, *op. cit.,* p. 121.

[23] For Scythian trousers see Hippocrates, "De Aeribus," *op. cit.,* p. 22; and the "portraits" in Minns, *op. cit.,* pp. 159, 200. For the history of trousers see Feist, *op. cit.,* p. 485, and Ebert, art. "Hose" in *Reallexikon der Vorgeschichte;* see also the Supplementary Notes.

[24] For girdles see Herodotus, *op. cit.,* 4, 10. For caps among the Sacae see Herodotus, *op. cit.,* 7, 64. For other features of the Scythian costume see Minns, *op. cit.,* p. 57. For the connection between trousers and leather boots see art. "Schuhe" in Schrader, *op. cit.*

[25] For weaving in Southern Siberia see Minns, *Scythians,* p. 244. That the Scythians were supposedly unacquainted with weaving see Justin, *op. cit.,* 2, 8.

[26] For Scythian jewelry see Minns, *op. cit.,* pp. 62-66.

[27] For shield and armor see Aelian, *op. cit.,* 9, 15; Pliny, *op. cit.,* 8, 124; Strabo, *op. cit.,* 7, 3, 17; Ammianus Marcellinus, *op. cit.,* 17, 12, 2; Tacitus, *Opera,* II, 1, 79. For horse armor see Schrader, *op. cit.,* II, 149. See also Minns, *op. cit.,* p. 73; Laufer, *op. cit.,* p. 217.

[28] For battleaxes see Herodotus, *op. cit.,* 4, 5; 7, 65. For spears see Herodotus, *op. cit.,* 4, 71; Ammianus Marcellinus, *op. cit.,* 17, 12, 2. For swords see Herodotus, *op. cit.,* 4, 62; Strabo, *op. cit.,* 7, 3, 18; Tacitus, *op. cit.,* II, 1, 79. For the lasso see Pausanius, *op. cit.,* 1, 21, 5. The sling is known only archaeologically. For the archaeological finds see Minns, *op. cit.,* pp. 68 ff.

[29] For bows and arrows see Aeschylus, *op. cit.,* I, 735; Herodotus, *op. cit.,* 4, 3; 4, 46; 4, 81; Ammianus Marcellinus, *op. cit.,* 22, 8, 37; Aelian, *op. cit.,* 9, 15; Strabo, *op. cit.,* 7, 3, 17; Pausanias, *op. cit.,* 1, 21, 5; Ovid, *op. cit.,* 4, 7. For the gorytus and other archaeological material see Minns, *op. cit.,* pp. 66 ff.

[30] For the use and non use of the bow in antiquity see art. "Pfeil" in Schrader, *op. cit.;* E. Bulanda, *Bogen und Pfeil bei den Volkern des Altertums.* The quotation from Tacitus in regard to the Sarmatian knights is from *Tacitus Historical Works,* 1, 79 (Murray's translation, p. 62).

[31] That the Scythians had no towns see Herodotus, *op. cit.,* 4, 127. For the use of tents mounted on wagons see Hippocrates, "De Aeribus," *op. cit.,* p. 18; Justin, *op. cit.,* 2, 2; Strabo, *op. cit.,* 7, 3, 17. That the Scythians probably possessed other types of tents see Minns, *op. cit.,* p. 51; see also Rostovstzeff, *op. cit.,* p. 28. The description of the yurt is from J. Peisker, "The Asiatic Background," *Cambridge Medieval History,* I, 335. For felt see B. Laufer, "The Early History of Felt," *American Anthropologist,* XXXII (1930), 1 ff.

[32] For furniture see Minns, *op. cit.,* p. 157; Rostovstzeff, *op. cit.,* p. 47. For the Iranian origin of the rug see Laufer, "Early History of Felt," *American Anthropologist,* XXXII (1930), 9.

[33] For the Scythian kings and their exalted position see Herodotus, *op. cit.*, 4, 64, 65, 68, 71, 127.

[34] For the various Scythian and non-Scythian peoples subject to the Royal Scythians see Herodotus, *op. cit.*, 4, 17-20. For the four provinces see Herodotus, *op. cit.*, 4, 6. For the Nomes and Nomarchs see Herodotus, *op. cit.*, 4, 62, 66.

[35] For succession to the throne see Herodotus, *op. cit.*, 4, 5, 76, 80.

[36] For Scythian tactics see Herodotus, *op. cit.*, 4, 46, 120-43. For blood drinking and other battle customs see Herodotus, *op. cit.*, 4, 64-66.

[37] For polygamy and marriage to one's stepmother see Herodotus, *op. cit.*, 4, 78. For moral laxity among the Massegetae see Herodotus, *op. cit.*, 1, 126.

[38] For royal illnesses and wizards see Herodotus, *op. cit.*, 4, 68-69. For ordinary funerals see Herodotus, *op. cit.*, 4, 73-75. For royal funerals see Herodotus, *op. cit.*, 4, 71-72. That the Massegetae ate their parents see Herodotus, *op. cit.*, 1, 126.

[39] For Scythian religious beliefs and customs see Herodotus, *op. cit.*, 4, 59-62. See also Ammianus Marcellinus, *op. cit.*, 31, 2, 23. For Scythian oaths see Herodotus, *op. cit.*, 4, 70. For the two types of wizards see Herodotus, *op. cit.*, 4, 67.

[40] For Scythian art see G. Borovfka, *Scythian Art;* Rostovstzeff, *op. cit.*, chap. VIII. For the connections with China see Rostovstzeff, *Animal Style in South Russia and China.*

Chapter Three

Bactrians and Sogdians in the South

For the text and translation of the rock inscriptions of the Achaemenid kings see Weissbach, *op. cit.* See also the *Avesta,* edited by K. Geldner; *Le Zend Avesta,* translated by J. Darmsteter; *Die Gathas des Avesta,* translated by C. Bartholomae; and *Avesta, die Heiligen Bucher der Parsen,* translated by F. Wolff. The *Avesta* is divided into several parts; see especially Yasna (cited as Ys.), the Yashts (cited as Yt.), and the Vendidad (cited as Vd.). Certain additional information is to be found in the later Pahlavi texts especially the *Bundahisn* and the *Dinkart.* For the *Bundahisn* cf. West *Pahlavi Texts,* part 1. For the Dinkart cf. *Dinkart,* ed. and trans. by P. and D. Sanjana.

For the Achaemenids see especially Herodotus, *op. cit.* For the Alexandrian period see Arrian, *De Expeditione Alexandri,* and Q. Curtius, *De Rebus Gestis Alexandri Magni.* For the later periods see especially Justin, *op. cit.;* Diodorus Siculus, *op. cit.;* Strabo, *op. cit.;* Appian, *Historia Romana;* Polybius, *op. cit.;* Dio Cassius, *Historia Romana;* Plutarch, *Vitae Parallelae;* Orosius, *Historiae Adversum Paganos.*

[1] That the Bactrians, etc., belonged to the same stock as the Scytho-Sarmatians see Strabo, *op. cit.*, 11, 11, 3. That the Bactrians spoke the same language as the Medes and Persians, *ibid.*, 15, 2, 8. For Sogdian see R. Gauthiot, *Essai de Grammaire Sogdienne.*

[2] For cavalry among the Southern Iranians see Herodotus, *op. cit.*, 7, 84-86. For bows and trousers, *ibid.*, 7, 61-66. For trousers see Sarre and Herzfeld, *op. cit.*, p. 53.

[3] For conflicting views regarding the early history of Bactria see the Supplementary Notes.

[4] For the rise of the Medes see Herodotus, *op. cit.*, 1, 95-106. That the Medes never succeeded in conquering Southern Turkistan see G. Rawlinson, *Five Ancient Oriental Monarchies,* III, 381.

[5] For the conquest of Bactria by Cyrus see Herodotus, *op. cit.*, 1, 153, 177. For the founding of Cyropolis see Strabo, *op. cit.*, 11, 11, 4. For the death of Cyrus see Herodotus, *op. cit.*, 1, 201-14.

[6] For the accession of Darius, *ibid.*, 3, 67-88. For the reëstablishment of Persian control over Eastern Iran see Weissbach, *op. cit.*, sections 35-39.

[7] For the list of satrapies, *ibid.*, sect. 6 ff.; see also Herodotus, *op. cit.*, 3, 89-97. For the Bactrians in the armies of Xerxes, *ibid.*, 7, 64-66.

[8] For the decay of the Persian control over Southern Turkistan under the later Achaemenids see H. G. Rawlinson, *Bactria, the Story of a Forgotten Empire,* p. 32; H. Jacobson, *Early History of Sogdia,* p. 31.

[9] That Zoroastrianism probably developed in Eastern Iran see A. V. W. Jackson, *Zoroaster, the Prophet of Ancient Iran,* p. 205; see also the Supplementary Notes.

[10] For the religious policy of the Achaemenids see E. Meyer, "Persia—Ancient History," *Encyclopaedia Britannica;* O. G. V. Wesendonck, *Weltbild der Iranier.*

[11] For the Persian's willingness to borrow from their neighbors see Herodotus, *op. cit.*, 1, 135. For the nature and extent of alien influences see "Perser" in Ebert, *Reallexikon der Vorgeschichte.* For the spread of Western influences through Persia and Southern Turkistan see B. Laufer, "Sino-Iranica," *Publications of the Field Museum,* no. 201 (1919).

[12] For Bessus see Arrian, *op. cit.*, 3, 21; Curtius, *op. cit.*, 5, 10 ff. For Alexander's campaign in Turkistan see Arrian, *op. cit.*, bks. 3-4; Curtius, *op. cit.*, bks. 7-8; F. V. Schwarz, *Alexander des Grossen Feldzuge in Turkestan.*

[13] For the events following the death of Alexander see Justin, *op. cit.*, bks. 13-15; Diodorus Siculus, *op. cit.*, bks. 18-19.

[14] For the rise of the Seleucid dynasty see Appian, *op. cit.*, 11, 52 ff.; Justin, *op. cit.*, bks. 16 ff.; E. R. Bevan, *The House of Seleucus.*

[15] For the character of Antiochus II, *ibid.*, chap. IX.

[16] For the rebellion of Bactria and Parthia see Justin, *op. cit.*, 41, 4; Strabo, *op. cit.*, 11, 9, 2-3. For the linguistic affinities of the Parthians see the Supplementary Notes.

[17] For the attempt of Seleucus II to reëstablish control over Eastern Iran see Justin, *op. cit.*, 41, 4; Strabo, *op. cit.*, 11, 8, 8.

[18] For the campaign of Antiochus III against Parthia see Justin, *op. cit.*, 41, 4; Polybius, *op. cit.*, 10, 28-31. For his campaign against Bactria see Polybius, *op. cit.*, 10, 49 and 11, 34.

[19] For Antiochus' disastrous war with the Romans see Appian, *op. cit.*, 11, 1-52.

[20] For the later Bactrian kings see Justin, *op. cit.*, 41, 6; Strabo, *op. cit.*, 11, 11, 1 ff. Additional information from coins. See P. Gardner, *Coins of Greek and Scythic Kings of India;* H. G. Rawlinson, *Bactria, the Story of a Forgotten Empire,* and MacDonald, "Hellenic Kingdoms of Syria, Bactria and Parthia," *Cambridge History of India,* vol. I.

[21] For the Bactrian conquest of India see Strabo, *op. cit.*, 11, 11, 1 ff. The same source speaks of conquests as far as the Seres and Phrynoi. This may mean Kashgaria. See A. Herrmann, *Lou-Lan, China, Indien, und Rom im Lichte der Ausgrabungen am Lobnor,* p. 31.

[22] For Bactrian art see A. Foucher, *L'Art Greco-bouddhique du Gandhara.* For Bacrian influence in India see L. Poussin, *L'Inde aux Temps des Mauryas et des Barbares,* pp. 241 ff.; G. N. Bannerjee, *Hellenism in Ancient India.*

[23] For the conquest of Mithradates I see Justin, *op. cit.*, 41, 6; Strabo, *op. cit.*, 11, 11, 2; Diodorus Siculus, *op. cit.*, 33, 18; Orosius, *op. cit.*, 5, 4-5. See also G. Rawlinson, *The Sixth Oriental Monarchy or Parthia,* p. 69; W. W. Tarn, "Parthia," *Cambridge Ancient History,* IX, 579 ff.

[24] For the campaign of Demetrius II see Justin, *op. cit.*, 36, 1; 38, 9; Appian, *op. cit.*, 11, 67. For the campaign of Antiochus VII see Justin, *op. cit.*, 38, 10 and 42, 1; Appian, *op. cit.*, 11, 68.

[25] For a discussion of the relations between the Parthians and the various tribes inhabiting Central Asia cf. *infra,* chaps. V ff.

[26] For the campaigns between Romans and the Parthians see Plutarch, "Crassus" and "Anthony," in *Vitae Parallelae;* Dio Cassius, *op. cit.*, especially bks. 40, 49, 68, 71, 78; Eutropius, *Breviarum Historiae Romanae,* 8, 3; Herodian, *Historia* (*Ab Excessu divi Marci*), 4, 24-30.

[27] For the feudal character of the Parthian empire see Meyer, "Persia—Ancient History," *Encyclopaedia Britannica;* Rawlinson, *op. cit.*, p. 87; Tarn, "Parthia," *Cambridge Ancient History,* IX, 590.

[28] For the cavalry tactics of the Parthians see Justin, *op. cit.*, 41, 2; Plutarch, "Crassus," chap. XXI in *Vitae Parallelae.* See also Tarn, "Parthia," *Cambridge Ancient History,* IX, 601.

[29] For the use of Attic standards and for the Greek inscriptions on Parthian coins see W. Wroth, *Coins of Parthia.*

[30] For the persistence of the Greek traditions in the Parthian Empire see Meyer, "Persia—Ancient History," *Encyclopaedia Britannica;* Rawlinson, *op. cit.*, p. 88; Tarn, "Parthia," *Cambridge Ancient History,* IX, 595. For the head of Crassus see Plutarch, "Crassus," chap. XXXIII.

[31] For the revival of native Iranian tradition see Meyer, "Persia—Ancient History," *Encyclopaedia Britannica;* Rawlinson, *op. cit.*, p. 90; Tarn, "Parthia," *Cambridge Ancient History,* IX, 590; Wroth, *op. cit.*

[32] For Zoroastrianism under the Parthians see Justin, *op. cit.*, 41, 3; Strabo, *op. cit.*, 11, 9, 3; Tarn, "Parthia," *Cambridge Ancient History,* IX, 590.

[33] For the redaction of the Avesta see *Dinkart,* West's translation, p. 412;

Geldner, "Avesta Literatur," Geiger-Kuhn, *Grundriss der Iranischen Philologie,* II, 33; Darmsteter, *op. cit.,* III, xxiii ff.

[34] For the time and place of Zoroaster see the Supplementary Notes. For the age and authenticity of the Avesta see the various views expressed in Geldner, "Avesta Literatur," Geiger-Kuhn, *Grundriss der Iranischen Philologie,* II, 32 ff.; Darmsteter, *op. cit.,* III, v ff.; E. G. Browne, *Literary History of Persia,* vol. I.

[35] For cattle raising and agriculture in the Avesta see Vd. 3, 2-4; for the ass see Vd. 7, 42; for the goat Vd. 5, 52; for sheep Vd. 9, 37-38; for the cow see Yt. 9; Ys. 11, 1; Vd. 7, 67; Vd. 7, 77; Vd. 7, 14; Vd. 9, 21; Yt. 10, 38.

[36] For the horse etc. see Yt. 5, 98; Yt. 17, 7; Yt. 17, 12; Yt. 5, 50; Yt. 5, 130-131; Ys. 11, 2; Vd. 18, 12. For the names Huaspa, etc. see Yt. 13, 122; Yt. 5, 108; Ys. 12, 7.

[37] For the camel see Ys. 44, 18; Yt. 14, 12-13; Vd. 22, 2-3; Vd. 7, 42. For the dog see Vd. 13, 49; Vd. 13, 59; Vd. 13, 3; Vd. 8, 16-18. For Sagdid see Darmsteter, *op. cit.,* col. 2, p. 149.

[38] For the cock see Vd. 18, 15. See also V. Hehn, *op. cit.,* p. 314; Schrader, art. "Huhn" in *Reallexikon des Indogermanischen Altertumskunde.*

[39] For agriculture, etc., see Vd. 3, 4; Vd. 3, 23; Vd. 14, 12; Vd. 5, 5; Vd. 6, 6. For wheat, millet, and barley see M. N. Dhalla, *Zoroastrian Civilization,* p. 142. For alfalfa and the grape see the *Han Shu,* 96a, 17. For wine and beer see Vd. 5, 54; Vd. 16, 6. For haoma see Ys. 9, 1 ff. For bread see Vd. 3, 32.

[40] For tents and huts see Vd. 8, 1. For houses see Vd. 6, 5; Vd. 8, 8; Vd. 18, 28; Yt. 5, 101. For furniture see Yt. 00, 105; Vd. 14, 4; Vd. 5, 27.

[41] For villages see Ys. 9, 27-28; Yt. 10, 17-18; for roads Vd. 3, 15; Vd. 8, 14.

[42] For clothing see Vd. 7, 14; Vd. 8, 23; Ys. 9, 26; Yt. 1, 17. For the shirt see Vd. 18, 58 and Dhalla, *op. cit.,* p. 174. For the dress of the priesthood, *ibid.,* p. 176. For shoes Vd. 6, 27; Yt. 5, 64. For golden ornaments see Yt. 5, 127; Yt. 17, 10.

[43] For offensive weapons see Yt. 10, 39-40; Vd. 14, 9. For defensive weapons see Yd. 13, 45; Vd. 14, 9.

[44] For kings and kingship see Yt. 13, 18; Ys. 53, 8; Yt. 15, 50; Ys. 46, 4. For law see Geldner, "Avesta Literatur," Geiger-Kuhn, *Grundriss der Iranischen Philologie,* II, 20; Dhalla, *op. cit.,* p. 96. For ordeals see Yt. 12, 3; Vd. 4, 54, and especially *Dinkart,* 8, 19, 38 and 8, 20, 140-42.

[45] For the three classes see Vd. 1, 16; Yt. 13, 88. For the four classes see Ys. 19, 17; Dhalla, *op. cit.,* p. 64.

[46] For the priesthood see Yt. 4, 9; Yt. 4, 46; Dhalla, *op. cit.,* pp. 78, 123; Darmsteter, *op. cit.,* I, l ff.

[47] For marriage see Yt. 17, 59; Vd. 4, 47; Jackson, *op. cit.,* p. 20; Dhalla, *op. cit.,* p. 302. For adoptions see *Dinkart,* 8, 36, 13. For prostitution see Vd. 18, 6-64. For homosexuality see Vd. 8, 26-27. For incest see Ys. 12, 9; Yt.

24, 17; Vd. 8, 13; W. Geiger, *Civilization of the Eastern Iranians in Ancient times,* pp. 66 ff.; Darmsteter, *op. cit.* I, 126.

[48] For the cause and cure of disease see Vd. 20, 3; Vd. 20, 6-9; Yt. 3, 6; Vd. 7, 44; Vd. 7, 36-40.

[49] For the disposal of the dead see Vd. 6, 44; Vd. 1, 12-17.

[50] For the Ahuras and Devas, etc., see Geldner, "Zoroaster," *Encyclopaedia Britannica.* For Ahura Mazda see Ys. 1, 1; Yt. 1, 1. For Angra Mainyu see Yt. 17, 19; Vd. 1, 2. For dualism see Ys. 30, 3-4. For the final triumph of good see Ys. 43, 5; Yt. 19, 95.

[51] For the sun see Ys. 1, 11; Ys. 36, 6. For fire see Ys. 2, 4; Ys. 17, 11; Vd. 5, 39; Vd. 7, 28. For the fire temples see Vd. 8, 81-86; see also *Bundahisn,* 7, 5-8; Darmsteter, *op. cit.,* I, lix ff.

[52] For immortality, heaven, hell, etc., see Vd., 19, 27; Ys. 19, 6. See also H. Lommel, *Die Religion Zarathustras;* Wesendonck, *op. cit.*

[53] For semi-Zoroastrian traits among the Mongols see J. J. Schmidt, *Forschungen im Gebiete der Alteren Religiosen, Politischen, und Literarischen Bildungsgeschichte der Völker Mittel Asiens,* p. 147; P. Pelliot, "Influence Iranniene en Asie Centrale et en Extreme Orient," *Revue d'Histoire et de Litterature Religieuses,* 1912, pp. 97 ff.

Chapter Four

The Early Inhabitants of Mongolia

For a general survey of the events of this period see *Tung Gien Gang Mu,* especially the Introduction and Chap. I (covering the period from the beginning of time to 256 B.C.). For further details see the *Shï Gi,* especially the following chapters: (*Annals*) 1, Five Emperors; 2, Hia Dynasty; 3, Shang Dynasty; 4, Jou Dynasty; 39, Dsin Dynasty; 43, Jao Dynasty; 44, Wei Dynasty; 45, Han Dynasty; 51, Yen Dynasty. (*Monograph*) 110, the Hiungnu; 123, the Western Regions. For certain supplementary details see also the *Dso Juan.* Occasional references to the Northern Barbarians are found in the *I Ging, Shu Ging, Shï Ging, Li Gi,* and *Meng-dse.*

[1] It should be noted that there are grave doubts regarding the dating of all events prior to 841 B.C. For the period prior to this date there are two chronological systems, one that of the Bamboo Books, the other the orthodox system, used by the *Tung Gien Gang Mu.* While strongly doubting its accuracy, I have followed the orthodox system, as the one generally accepted.

[2] For the various names applied to the Northern Barbarians see *Shï Gi,* 110, pp. 1 ff.

[3] For Huang-di's war against the Hunyu see *Tung Gien Gang Mu* under Huang-di; *Shï Gi,* 1, 4.

[4] For the legend that the Hunnish monarchs are descended from a scion of the Hia dynasty see *Shï Gi,* 110, 1, 7.

[5] For the rise and fall of the Jou dynasty see *Tung Gien Gang Mu,* year 1352 B.C. ff.; *Shï Gi,* 4. According to legend (see *Shï Gi,* 4, 1-2) the rulers

of the House of Jou were descended from Hou Dsi, himself a descendant of the Yellow Emperor, but this is obviously fictitious. We find Mencius (see *Mengdse,* 4, 2, 1) speaking of Wen Wang, the real founder of the Jou dynasty, as a "Western Barbarian." See also R. Wilhelm, *Short History of Chinese Civilization,* p. 98.

[6] For Tan Fu and his connection with the barbarians see *Tung Gien Gang Mu,* 1352 B.C.; *Shï Gi,* 4, 2-3; *ibid.,* 110, 2.

[7] For Wen Wang and his activities see *Tung Gien Gang Mu,* 1258-1135 B.C.; *Shï Gi,* 4, 3-5; *ibid.,* 110, 2. For his humanitarianism in warfare see — Weiger, *Textes Historiques,* p. 66. For the barbarians see especially *Tung Gien Gang Mu,* 1158 B.C.

[8] For Wu Wang and his activities see *Tung Gien Gang Mu,* 1134-1116 B.C.; *Shï Gi,* 4, 5-11; *ibid.,* 110, 4.

[9] The revolt of the Northern Barbarians against Chinese jurisdiction is said to have started during the reign of Mu Wang. See *Tung Gien Gang Mu,* 1001-947 B.C. and 877 B.C.; *Shï Gi,* 4, 13-15; *ibid.,* 110, 2. It is this same Mu Wang who is credited by legend (see *Tung Gien Gang Mu,* 895 B.C.) with penetrating far to the West, to Kashgaria. I have not felt it necessary to relate this legend as it is so manifestly fabulous. See F. Hirth, *The Ancient History of China,* pp. 145 ff.

[10] The poems which refer to the Hienyun or Huns are "Tsai Wei," "Chu Gu," "Lu Yue," and "Tsai Ki," all in pt. 2 (Siao Ya) of the *Shï Ging,* or *Book of Poetry.*

[11] For Yu Wang, Bao se, and the fall of the Western Jou dynasty see *Tung Gien Gang Mu,* 781-771 B.C.; *Shï Gi,* 4, 18-20; *ibid.,* 110, 2.

[12] For the reign of Ping Wang see *Tung Gien Gang Mu,* 770-720 B.C.; *Shï Gi,* 4, 20.

[13] For a brief summary of the relations between the Northern Barbarians and the Chinese feudal states see *Shï Gi,* 110, 3-5; for further details *ibid.,* 5; *ibid.,* 39; *ibid.,* 43; *ibid.,* 44; *ibid.,* 45; *ibid.,* 51.

[14] For the view that the Chinese received some of their "Mongoloid" characteristics from the Northern Barbarians see H. J. Fleure, *The Races of Mankind,* p. 46. That the early inhabitants of Southern Siberia were non-Mongoloid see A. H. Keane, *Man, Past and Present,* p. 270. For the Chinese version see *Tang Shu,* 217b, 12. See also W. Schott, "Uber den Achten Kirgisen," *Abhandlungen der koniglichen Preussischen Akadamie der Wissenschraft zu Berlin,* 1864, pp. 429 ff.; W. Barthold, "Der Heutige Stand und die Nachsten Aufgaben der Geschichtlichen Forschungen der Turkvolker," *Zeitschrift der Deutschen Morgenlandischen Gessellschaft,* 1929, p. 126.

[15] The quotation from Smith is from his *Human History,* p. 131. See also Eickstedt, *op. cit.,* pp. 169 ff. That the Hiungnu had big noses and were hairy see *Dsin Shu,* 107, 8a. For a further discussion of the racial question see the Supplementary Notes.

[16] That the later Huns had an appreciable amount of Mongoloid blood in their veins see Ammianus Marcellinus, *op. cit.,* 2, 1; L. Bartuc, *Uber die Anthropologischen Ergebnisse der Ausgrabungen von Mosonszentjanos.*

[17] For the Ural-Altaic languages see H. Winkler, *Der Uralaltaische Sprachstamm;* see also the Supplementary Notes.

[18] For the possible affinity of the Turanian and Indo-European languages see W. Schmidt, *Sprachfamilien und Sprachkreisen der Erde,* p. 56.

[19] For various views regarding the linguistic affinities of the Hiungnu see the Supplementary Notes.

[20] That the Di lived in caves see *Li Gi,* bk. 3 (*Wang Ji,* p. 45).

[21] For the battle of 714 B.C. see *Dso Juan,* p. 12 (9th year of Yin); for the battle of 541 B.C. see *Tung Gien Gang Mu* under this date; *Dso Juan,* p. 313 (first year of Chao).

[22] That the Turks, and therefore presumably the Huns, were acquainted with agriculture, see A. Vambery, *Die Primitive Cultur des Turko Tartarischen Volkes,* p. 101.

[23] For the excellences of horses among the Iranian inhabitants of Farghana see *Shï Gi,* 123, 10.

[24] For the archaeological finds in Mongolia see W. P. Yetts, "Discoveries of the Kozlov Expedition," *Burlington Magazine,* April, 1926.

[25] For the change of costume introduced by Wu Ling of Jao see *Shï Gi,* 43, 18 ff.; *ibid.,* 110, 5. See also Pelliot, *Haute Asie,* p. 7.

[26] For the claim of the Hunnish Shanyus to be Lord of all who shoot bows from horseback see *Shï Gi,* 110, 12.

[27] Most of the details regarding the culture life of the Hiungnu are derived from *Shï Gi,* 110, 1-2. For the use of tents, *ibid.,* 110, 14. For thread and sewing, at least among the Dunghu, see K. Torii, "Populations Primitives de la Mongolie Orientale," *Journal of the College of Science of Tokyo University* (1914), p. 11.

[28] For Chinese traditions regarding the details of Hunnish costume see Weiger, *Textes Historiques,* p. 286. For leather armor see Laufer, "Chinese Clay Figures,—Prolegomena on the History of Defensive Armor," *Publications of the Field Museum,* 177 (1914), p. 223.

[29] For the statement that the Huns did not engage in agriculture see *Shï Gi,* 110, 1; but from *Han Shu,* 94a, 30b, which states that one year the crops did not ripen, it is obvious that agriculture was not entirely unknown. For agriculture among the Kirgis see M. A. Czaplica, *The Turks of Central Asia in History and at the Present Day,* p. 48. For the Dunghu see Torii, *op. cit.,* p. 12.

[30] For the absence of fishing in Mongolia see *Hou Han Shu,* 120, 19b. For the Hunnish domesticated animals and the hunting of wild animals see *Shï Gi,* 110, 1. For Kumis, *ibid.,* 110, 13.

[31] For the use of pottery, at least among the Dunghu, see Torii, *op. cit.,* p. 49. For metal casting among the Dunghu, *ibid.,* pp. 69 ff. For metal casting among the inhabitants of Siberia see Merhardt, *Bronzezeit,* p. 16.

[32] For the political organization of the Hiungnu, see *Shï Gi,* 110, 8; for later periods see *Hou Han Shu,* 119, 7-8; *Dsin Shu,* 97, 11-12.

[33] For religious ceremonials among the Huns see *Shï Gi,* 110, 9; for Shamans see *Han Shu,* 94a, 30a; for magical practices, *ibid.,* 96b, 11-12.

[34] For the rule requiring the blackening of the face before appearing before the Shanyu see *Shï Gi,* 110, 24.

[35] For the Hunnish system of law and the Hunnish method of disposing of the dead, *ibid.,* 110, 9.

Chapter Five

THE RISE OF THE HUNNISH EMPIRE

For a general survey of the events during this period see *Tung Gien Gang Mu,* chaps. II-IV (years 255-141 B.C.). For the rise of the Tsin Empire and its campaigns against the Huns see *Shï Gi,* especially the following chapters: 5 and 6, the Rulers of the House of Tsin; and 88, the Biography of Meng Tien. For the rise of the Han and Hunnish empires see the *Han Shu,* especially the following chapters: (*Annals*) 1, Gao-di; 2, Huei-di; 3, Empress Lu; 4, Wen-di; 5, Ging-di; (*Biographies*) 33, Sin, King of Han; 37, Gi Bu; 40, Chen Ping and Jou Ya-fu; 43, Liu Ging; 61, Jang Kien; (*Monographs*) 94a-b, Hiungnu; 96a-b, the Western Regions.

For certain details, especially as regards the Non-Hunnish inhabitants of Central Asia see also *Shï Gi,* especially chap. 123; *Hou Han Shu,* especially chaps. 115 and 120; *San Guo Jï,* especially chap. 30; *Be Shï,* especially chap. 97; and *Tang Shu,* especially chap. 217.

[1] For the Dunghu and their descendents, the Wuhuan and the Sienbi, see the *Hou Han Shu,* 120. For the inhabitants of Eastern Manchuria, *ibid.,* 115. For the inhabitants of Turkistan and Kashgaria see *Han Shu,* 96a-b. For the Wusun, *ibid.,* 61, 4; and *ibid.,* 96b, 1 ff. For the Yuejï, *ibid.,* 61, pp. 1 ff., and *ibid.,* 96a, 14 ff. For the Gienkun and Kingling see *San Guo Jï,* 30, 34a. For the racial and linguistic affinities of all these peoples see the Supplementary Notes.

[2] For the rise of the Tsin dynasty see *Tung Gien Gang Mu,* chap. II; *Shï Gi,* chaps. V and VI. For the campaign against the Huns and the building of the Great Wall see *Tung Gien Gang Mu,* 214 B.C.; *Shï Gi,* 6, 00; *ibid.,* 88, 1; *Han Shu,* 94a, 4b. For the earlier walls designed to keep out the Northern Barbarians, *ibid.,* 94a, 4a. For the theory linking the building of the Great Wall with the fall of Rome see A. C. Haddon, *The Wanderings of Peoples,* p. 7. Though tradition (see H. Giles, *Chinese Biographical Dictionary,* p. 584) ascribes the invention of the writing brush to Meng Tien, his biography (*Shï Gi,* 88) makes no mention of this fact, and the tradition is most certainly spurious.

[3] For the rise of the Hunnish Empire see *Tung Gien Gang Mu,* 201 B.C.; *Han Shu,* 94a, 5-8. As the native and correct names of the Hunnish rulers are unknown to us I have retained the names as recorded in the Chinese histories. See also the Supplementary Notes.

[4] For Maodun's escape from the Yüejï and his seizure of the Hunnish throne see *Tung Gien Gang Mu,* 201 B.C.; *Han Shu,* 94a, 5. These same passages tell of the "Singing arrows." I have followed Laufer, "Chinese

Clay Figures, Prolegomena on the History of Defensive Armor," *Publications of the Field Museum,* 177 (1914), p. 227, for the interpretation of this story. For the details of the Hunnish administrative system see *Han Shu,* 94a, 7. That this organization remained fairly stable may be seen by comparing the system in vogue among the Huns in the first century A.D.

[5] In describing Maodun's campaigns I have not kept to the chronological order, even as far as they are known, but for the sake of clearness have arranged them geographically. For the campaign against the Dunghu see *Han Shu,* 94a, 6. For the campaign against the Dingling, Gienkun, and other northern peoples, *ibid.,* 94a, 8b. Maodun made at least two campaigns against the Yuejï. For the first, which took place near the beginning of his reign, *ibid.,* 94a, 6b. For the second, near the end of his reign, *ibid.,* 94a, 11b. From the latter passage it would appear that the Hunnish control over the Wusun and the city states of Kashgaria began at this time. For the Hunnish method of controlling Kashgaria *ibid.,* 96a, 1-2.

[6] For the rise of Liu Bang to power and his accession to the throne as Gao-di, the first emperor of the Han dynasty, see *Tung Gien Gang Mu,* years 206-202 B.C.; and *Han Shu,* 1, 1 ff.

[7] For Gao-di's great campaign against the Huns see *Tung Gien Gang Mu,* 201-200 B.C. Further details in *Han Shu,* 1b, 10; *ibid.,* 33, 7; *ibid.,* 40, 17; *ibid.,* 43, 12; *ibid.,* 94a, 8.

[8] For the presents sent by the Chinese to the Huns and the marriage of the Chinese "princess" to Maodun, see *Tung Gien Gang Mu,* 198 B.C.; *Han Shu,* 43, 12; *ibid.,* 94a, 9b.

[9] For the regency (later rulership) of the Empress Lu see *Tung Gien Gang Mu,* 195-180 B.C.; *Han Shu,* 2 and 3. For the correspondence between the Empress Lu and the Huns see *Tung Gien Gang Mu,* 192 B.C.; *Han Shu,* 37, 2; *ibid.,* 94a, 10.

[10] For the death of Maodun and the accession of Giyu see *Tung Gien Gang Mu,* 174 B.C.; *Han Shu,* 94a, 12b.

[11] For the Emperor Wen-di see *Tung Gien Gang Mu,* 179-157 B.C.; *Han Shu,* 4. For the sending of another Chinese princess, and the treacherous advice of the eunuch who accompanied her see *Han Shu,* 94a, 12-13.

[12] For the campaign of 166 B.C. see *Tung Gien Gang Mu* under this date. See also *Han Shu,* 4, 13-14; *ibid.,* 14 and 15. For the treaty of peace between the Huns and the Chinese see *Tung Gien Gang Mu,* 162 B.C.; *Han Shu,* 4, 15-16; *ibid.,* 94a, 15-16.

[13] For Giyu's defeat of the Yuejï see *Tung Gien Gang Mu,* 126 B.C.; *Han Shu,* 61, 1; *ibid.,* 96a, 14b. The texts give no date for this event but it must have been 174-161 B.C. For the Sakas in the Ili basin, *ibid.,* 96b, 1b. This same passage (and also *ibid.,* 96a, 10b) tells us that the Sakas moved to the South and overran Northwest India. That many of the Sakas moved West and overran Sogdia and Bactria is known from the classical authors. See the Sacarauli or Sacaraucae of Strabo, *op. cit.,* 11, 8, 2, and the Saraucae mentioned by Trogus in *Prologi,* 41.

[14] For the wars between the Wusun and the Yuejï, and the driving of the

Yuejï into Sogdia and Bactria see *Han Shu,* 61, 4; *ibid.,* 96b, 1b; *ibid.,* 96a, 14-15. Most scholars think that the Yuejï correspond to the Asii or Asiani and the Tochari mentioned in Strabo, *op. cit.,* 11, 8, 2, and Trogus, *op. cit.,* 41-42. For further details see the Supplementary Notes.

[15] That the Sakas expelled from Sogdia and Bactria migrated to the Iranian Plateau is to be deduced from Justin, *op. cit.,* 42, 1, 2, and Isodorus Characenus "Mansiones Parthicae," chap. XVIII, *Geographi Graeci Minores.*

[16] For the death of Giyu and the accession of Günchen see *Tung Gien Gang Mu,* 161 B.C.; *Han Shu,* 94a, 17a.

[17] For the Emperor Ging-di see *Tung Gien Gang Mu,* 156-141 B.C., and the *Han Shu,* 5. For the rebellion of the King of Jao see *Tung Gien Gang Mu,* 154 B.C.; and the *Han Shu,* 5, 4. For the failure of the Huns to participate actively in this rebellion, *ibid.,* 94a, 17a.

[18] For the defection of the Wusun from the Hunnish Empire, *ibid.,* 61, 4b.

Chapter Six

The Huns and Chinese Battle for Supremacy

For a general survey of the events during this period see *Tung Gien Gang Mu,* chaps. IV and V (140-101 B.C.). For further details see the *Han Shu,* especially the following chapters: (*Annals*) 6, Wu-di; (*Biographies*) 50, Gi An; 52, Han An-guo; 54, Li Guang; 55, Wei Tsing and Ho Kü-bing; 61, Jang Kien and Li Guang-li; 64, Ju-fu Yen; 68, Gin Rï-di; (*Monographs*) 94a, Hiungnu; 95, Yue, Jaosien, etc.; 96a-b, the Western Regions. A few supplementary details are to be found in the *Shï Gi,* especially chap. 123; the *Hou Han Shu,* especially chap. 120; and the *San Guo Jï,* especially chap. 30.

[1] For the Emperor Wu-di and the chief events of his reign see *Tung Gien Gang Mu,* 140-87 B.C.; *Han Shu,* 6. For an excellent summary of this ruler's internal policy see E. Chavannes, *Memoires Historiques, de Se-ma Ts'ien,* pp. lxxxviii ff.

[2] For Jang Kien and his journey to the West see *Tung Gien Gang Mu,* 126 B.C.; *Han Shu,* 61; *Shï Gi,* 123. Much of Jang Kien's report is also incorporated in *Han Shu,* 96a-b. For the identification of the various place names mentioned in these texts see F. Hirth, "Story of Chang K'ien," *Journal of the American Oriental Society,* XXXVII (1917), 89 ff.; and A. Herrmann, *Die Alten Seidenstrassen zwischen China und Syrien;* see also the Supplementary Notes.

[3] For the history of the grapevine and alfalfa see B. Laufer, "Sino-Iranica," *Publications of the Field Museum,* 201 (1919), pp. 185 ff. For the racial and linguistic affinities of the inhabitants of Da-yüan, Kanggü, etc., see the Supplementary Notes.

[4] For the attempt of the Chinese to trap the Huns at Mayi see *Tung Gien Gang Mu,* 133 B.C.; *Han Shu,* 6, 4-5; *ibid.,* 52, 15-20; *ibid.,* 94a, 17-18.

[5] For the fighting between the Chinese and the Huns during the years

129-119 B.C. see *Tung Gien Gang Mu* under these years; see also *Han Shu,* 6, 6-13; *ibid.,* 54, 3-5; *ibid.,* 55, 2-13; *ibid.,* 64, 17; *ibid.,* 94a, 17-22. I have felt it necessary to give only a brief summary of all this warfare.

[6] For the removal of the Hunnish headquarters from Southern to Northern Mongolia see *Tung Gien Gang Mu,* 123 B.C.; *Han Shu,* 94a, 20a.

[7] For Ho Kü-bing's campaign to the northwest of China and his capture of the Golden Images see *Tung Gien Gang Mu,* 121 B.C.; *Han Shu,* 55, 7; *ibid.,* 94a, 20. Some of the commentaries on these passages claim that these images were Buddhist in origin, while other commentaries are skeptical on the subject. See Chavannes, *Memoires Historiques de Se-ma Ts'ien,* vol. LXVII; Franke, *Geschichte des Chinesischen Reiches,* I, 343. See also K. Shiratori, "On the Territory of the Hsiung-nu Prince Hsiu-t'u Wang and His Metal Statues for Heaven Worship," in *Memoirs of the Research Department of the Toyo Bunko,* vol. V (1926).

[8] For King Kunsie and his acceptance of Chinese sovereignty see *Tung Gien Gang Mu,* 121 B.C.; *Han Shu,* 2, 12; *ibid.,* 55, 9-10; *ibid.,* 50, 10; *ibid.,* 68, 20-21; *ibid.,* 94a, 20-21.

[9] For the campaign of 119 B.C. see *Tung Gien Gang Mu* under this date; *Han Shu,* 2, 13; *ibid.,* 54, 6-9; *ibid.,* 55, 10-13; *ibid.,* 94a, 21-22.

[10] That the lack of horses prevented the Chinese from going on with their campaigns against the Huns see *Han Shu,* 94a, 22a. For the last days of Wei Tsing and Ho Kü-bing see *Han Shu,* 55, 13-14.

[11] For the relations between the Chinese and the Huns from 118 to 101 B.C. see the *Tung Gien Gang Mu* under these dates; see also *Han Shu,* 6, 14-25; *ibid.,* 94a, 22-25.

[12] For the Chinese conquests in the Southwest and the South during this period see *Han Shu,* 95, 1-19. For the Chinese conquests of Jaosien or Korea see *ibid.,* 95, 20-23. For the effect of the conquest of Jaosien upon the Wuhuan and Sienbi see *Hou Han Shu,* 120, 3b.

[13] For Jang Kien's journey to the court of the Wusun see *Tung Gien Gang Mu,* 115 B.C.; *Han Shu,* 61, 4-5; *ibid.,* 96a, 1-2. For the marriage of the Chinese princess to the King of the Wusun, see *Tung Gien Gang Mu,* 105 B.C.; *Han Shu,* 96b, 2-3.

[14] For the establishment of the Chinese administrative districts on the northwest frontier see *Tung Gien Gang Mu,* 115 B.C. and 111 B.C.; *Han Shu,* 96a, 2a. See also Chavannes, *Documents Chinois decouverts par A. Stein dans les Sables du Turkestan Oriental,* p. v.

[15] For the campaign against Loulan and Güshï see *Tung Gien Gang Mu,* 108 B.C.; *Han Shu,* 61, 7a; *ibid.,* 55, 16b; *ibid.,* 96a, 4.

[16] For the campaigns against Dayüan see *Tung Gien Gang Mu,* 104-04 B.C.; *Han Shu,* 6, 25-26; *ibid.,* 61, 9-11; *ibid.,* 96a, 18-19.

[17] For the effects of the successful campaign against Da-yuan in bringing the Kashgarian states to recognize the Chinese supremacy see *Tung Gien Gang Mu,* 101 B.C.; *Shï Gi,* 123, 64; *Han Shu,* 61, 12a. For the establishment of military stations in the Dunhuang-Lopnor region and the military agricultural colonies in Northern Kashgaria, *ibid.,* 96, 2.

[18] It should perhaps be pointed out that though China had secured general predominance in Kashgaria by 100 B.C., she was not undisputed mistress of this region until many years later. This can be seen by the continued troubles which arose between China and the two states of Güshï and Loulan. For Gushi during this period see *Han Shu*, 96b, 18a. For Loulan, *ibid.*, 96a, 5a.

Chapter Seven

The Slow Decline of the Hunnish Empire

For a general survey of the events during this period see *Tung Gien Gang Mu*, chaps. V-VI (years 100-51 B.C.). For further details see the *Han Shu*, especially the following chapters: (*Annals*) 6, Wu-di; 7, Jao-di; 8, Suan-di. (*Biographies*) 54, Su Wu and Li Ling; 62, Se-ma Tsien; 66, Liu Ku-li; 69, Jao Chung-guo; 70, Chang Huei, Jeng Gi, and Fu Giai-dse; 78, Siao Wang-ji; 79, Feng Feng-shi; 90, Tsien Guang-ming, etc. (*Monographs*) 94a, Hiungnu; 96a-b, the Western Regions. A few supplementary details are to be found in the *Hou Han Shu*, especially chaps. 115, 117, and 120.

[1] For a general survey of the latter part of Wu-di's reign see *Tung Gien Gang Mu*, 100-87 B.C.; *Han Shu*, 6, 16-31. The main story of the relation between the Huns and Chinese during this period is told in the *Han Shu*, 94a, 26-30.

[2] For Su Wu's embassy to the Huns and its disastrous consequences see *Tung Gien Gang Mu*, 100 B.C.; *Han Shu*, 54, 16-24; *ibid.*, 94a, 26b.

[3] For Li Ling's campaign and his later life in the Hunnish court see *Tung Gien Gang Mu*, 99 B.C. Further details in *Han Shu*, 6, 27; *ibid.*, 54, 9-15; *ibid.*, 94a, 27. For Se-ma Tsien's defense of Li Ling and its unfortunate results, *ibid.*, 62, 16-22.

[4] For Li Guang-li's three campaigns against the Huns see *Tung Gien Gang Mu*, 99, 97, and 90 B.C.; *Han Shu*, 6, 27-30; *ibid.*, 66, 5; *ibid.*, 69, 1-2; *ibid.*, 94a, 26-29.

[5] For the restoration of Hunnish prestige in Central Asia see *Han Shu*, 96a, 19a.

[6] For a general survey of events during the reigns of Jao-di and Suan-di see *Tung Gien Gang Mu*, 86-49 B.C.; *Han Shu*, 7 and 8. Sino-Hunnish relations during this period are summarized in *Han Shu*, 94a, 30-39 and 96a, 1-4.

[7] For the slow decline of the Hunnish power following 86 B.C. see *Tung Gien Gang Mu*, 85 B.C.; *Han Shu*, 94a, 30-31. For the return of Su Wu from captivity see *Tung Gien Gang Mu*, 81 B.C.; *Han Shu*, 54, 20-21; *ibid.*, 94a, 31b.

[8] For the slow movement of the Huns to the West see *Tung Gien Gang Mu*, 80 B.C.; *Han Shu*, 94a, 31 ff. For the conflicts between the Huns and the Wuhuan see *Tung Gien Gang Mu*, 78 B.C.; *Han Shu*, 94a, 32-33; *Hou Han Shu*, 120, 3-4. For the Hunnish attack on the Wusun see *Han Shu*, 94a, 33; *ibid.*, 96b, 3-4.

[9] For the great campaign of 72-71 B.C. see *Tung Gien Gang Mu* under these dates; see also the *Han Shu,* 6, 6; *ibid.,* 70, 3b; *ibid.,* 90, 13b; *ibid.,* 94a, 33-35.

[10] For the troubles which beset the Hunnish Empire from 70 to 58 B.C., see *Tung Gien Gang Mu,* 68 and 60 B.C.; *Han Shu,* 94a, 35-39. For the early portion of Huhansie's reign see *Tung Gien Gang Mu,* 57, 56, and 54 B.C.; *Han Shu,* 8, 18-20; 94b, 1-2. For Huhansie's decision to go to China and his reception there see *Tung Gien Gang Mu,* 52-51 B.C.; *Han Shu,* 8, 21-22; *ibid.,* 78, 9; *ibid.,* 94b, 3-4.

[11] The basic text for China's relations with Kashgaria and the other Western Regions during this period is the *Han Shu,* 96a-b. The *Han Shu,* 96a, 1-3, gives a general historical survey. The rest of 96a and all of 96b are devoted to a study of the separate kingdoms into which the Western Region was divided.

[12] For the events at Luntai and Küli during this period see the *Han Shu,* 96b, 10 ff.

[13] For the assassination of the King of Loulan see the *Tung Gien Gang Mu,* 77 B.C.; *Han Shu,* 7, 8b; *ibid.,* 70, 1-2; *ibid.,* 96a, 5-6.

[14] For relations with Kucha see the *Han Shu,* 70, 3-4; *ibid.,* 96b, 13-14.

[15] For the Yarkand revolt and its suppression see *Tung Gien Gang Mu,* 65 B.C.; *Han Shu,* 79, 1-2; *ibid.,* 96a, 20.

[16] For the various phases of Güshï's history, in which this state passed from Chinese to Hunnish control and back again, see *Tung Gien Gang Mu,* 90, 67, and 64 B.C. Many fuller details in *Han Shu,* 96b, 18-20.

[17] For the final conquest of Güshï, its division into several states (kingdoms) and the establishment of the office of Protector General, see *Tung Gien Gang Mu,* 60 B.C.; *Han Shu,* 70, 4; *ibid.,* 96, 2b.

[18] For the Wusun and their relations with the Chinese during this period see *Tung Gien Gang Mu,* 60 B.C. Much fuller information in *Han Shu,* 96b, 3-6.

[19] For the Chinese conflicts with the Kiang or Tibetans during this time see *Tung Gien Gang Mu,* 62-61 B.C.; *Han Shu,* 8, 16; *ibid.,* 69, 2 ff.; *Hou Han Shu,* 117, 8.

Chapter Eight

The Huns as Vassals of the Chinese

For a general survey of events during this period see *Tung Gien Gang Mu,* chaps. VI-VIII (years 50 B.C.—A.D. 8). Further details are given in the *Han Shu,* especially the following chapters: (*Annals*) 8, Süan-di; 9, Yüan-di; 10, Cheng-di; 11, Ai-di; 12, Ping-di; (*Biographies*) 70, Gan Yen-shou, Chen Tang, and Duan Huei-dsung; 79, Feng Feng-shï. (*Monographs*) 94b, Hiungnu; 96a-b, the Western Regions. Important supplementary information is also given in the *Hou Han Shu,* especially chaps. 117 and 120.

[1] For Huhansie's relations with the Chinese from 50 to 43 B.C. see *Tung Gien Gang Mu,* 49 B.C.; *Han Shu,* 8, 23; and especially *ibid.,* 94b, 4-6.

[2] For Jïjï's murder of the Chinese envoy and his movement to Turkistan see *Tung Gien Gang Mu,* 44 B.C.; *Han Shu,* 9, 7a; *ibid.,* 94b, 4.

[3] For the later fortunes of Jïjï, his relations with the Kanggü, and his final defeat by China see *Tung Gien Gang Mu,* 36 B.C.; *Han Shu,* 9, 11-12; *ibid.,* 70, 6; *ibid.,* 94b, 6-7. The deduction that Jïjï's capital was on the Talas River is based on the mention of Jïjï's activities on the "Dulai" River. De Groot, *Die Hunnen der Vorchristlichen Zeit,* p. 229, is doubtless right in suggesting that Dulai is an early transcription of Talas.

[4] The Kingdom of Yentsai is called in the foregoing passages Hosu (older pronunciation Hapsu). The Chinese commentators tell us that Hosu was the same as Yentsai and with this statement all western scholars agree. De Groot, *op. cit.,* p. 229, thinks that Hapsu was a Chinese attempt to transliterate (H) aorsi, the Sarmatian tribe mentioned by Strabo and Pliny. Kiessling, "Hunni," *Pauly Wissowa Realencyclopaedie des Classischen Altertums,* col. 2590, has some interesting speculations concerning Jïjï's aggressiveness in Turkistan and the wandering of the Alani tribe into Southern Russia.

[5] For the description of the actual siege of Jïjï's capital see *Han Shu,* 70, 9-11. For the view that Attila was descended from Jïjï see F. Hirth, "Die Ahnentafel Attilas," *Bulletin de l'Academie Imperiale des Sciences de St. Petersbourg,* p. 238.

[6] For Huhansie's actions between 36 B.C. and his death in 31 B.C. see *Tung Gien Gang Mu,* 33 B.C.; *Han Shu,* 9, 13; *ibid.,* 94b, 7-10.

[7] For the renegade Hunnish minister and the refusal of the Chinese to receive him see *Tung Gien Gang Mu,* 27; *Han Shu,* 94b, 11-12.

[8] For the visit of the Shanyu to China and the problems it caused see *Tung Gien Gang Mu,* 3 and 1 B.C.; *Han Shu,* 11, 7-8; *ibid.,* 94b, 14-18.

[9] For the Chinese attempt to secure by diplomacy a portion of the Hunnish territory see *Tung Gien Gang Mu,* 8 B.C., and *Han Shu,* 94b, 13-14.

[10] For the Chinese insistence that the Huns send back their Wusun hostage see *Han Shu,* 94b, 14. For the episode of the princes from Güshï and the sending of the fourfold ultimatum to the Huns see *Tung Gien Gang Mu,* A.D. 2 and *Han Shu,* 94b, 19-20.

[11] For the dispute between the Chinese and the Huns over the treatment of the Wuhuan see *Han Shu,* 94b, 20.

[12] For the appointment of the "Central Commanding Officer" or Wu-gi General, see *Tung Gien Gang Mu,* 48 B.C.; *Han Shu,* 96a, 3a. From a passage in the *Hou Han Shu* (118, 2-3) it would appear that in later times there were two such officials, a Wu General and a Gi General, the first residing in Northern Güshï, the latter in Southern Güshï.

[13] For the details of the Chinese administrative systems in Kashgaria see *Han Shu,* 96a, 2-3; *ibid.,* 96b, 20-23.

[14] For the history of the Wusun during this period see *Tung Gien Gang Mu,* 60 and 53 B.C.; more details in *Han Shu,* 70, 17 and 23; *ibid.,* 96b, 6-8.

[15] For China's intercourse with Gibin during this period see *Tung Gien Gang Mu,* 25 B.C.; *Han Shu,* 96a, 10-12. The miles and feet mentioned in the

text are of course Chinese miles and feet. For the exact location of Gibin see the Supplementary Notes.

[16] For the Chinese campaign against the Kiang or Tibetans see *Tung Gien Gang Mu,* 42 B.C.; *Han Shu,* 9, 9; *ibid.,* 79, 3-6; *Hou Han Shu,* 117, 9-10.

Chapter Nine

The Reëstablishment of the Hunnish Empire

For a general survey of events during this period see *Tung Gien Gang Mu,* chaps. VIII-IX (A.D. 9-46). For further details concerning the period A.D. 9 to 23 see the *Han Shu,* especially the following chapters: 99a,b,c, Biography of Wang Mang; 94b, Monograph on the Hiungnu; 96a,b, Monograph on the Western Regions. For further details regarding the period A.D. 24-46 see the *Hou Han Shu,* especially the following chapters: (*Annals*) 1; (*Biographies*) 41, Liu Huan and Liu Pen-dse; 42, Lu Fang; 47, Feng I; 48, Wu Han; 52, Du Mao; 52, Dou Rung; 54, Ma Yuan; (*Monographs*) 119, Southern Hiungnu; 118, the Western Regions; 120, Wuhuan and Sienbi.

[1] For the decline of the Han dynasty and the rise of Wang Mang to power see *Tung Gien Gang Mu,* 16 B.C.—A.D. 8 and *Han Shu,* 99a. For Wang Mang's reign see *Tung Gien Gang Mu,* A.D. 9-23 and *Han Shu,* 99b,c.

[2] For the poisoning of the Emperor Ping-di see *Tung Gien Gang Mu,* A.D. 7. For the suicide of Wang Mang's son, *ibid.,* 3 B.C.; for the grandson, *ibid.,* A.D. 18. For Wang Mang's love of antiquity see *Tung Gien Gang Mu,* A.D. 14; for his principal reforms, *ibid.,* A.D. 9-10.

[3] For the exchange of seals with the Shanyu and the dispute regarding the treatment of the Wuhuan see *Tung Gien Gang Mu,* A.D. 10; *Han Shu,* 99b, 13-15; *ibid.,* 94b, 20-22.

[4] The ill treatment of the Wuhuan which caused these barbarians to renounce their allegiance to China and seek alliance with the Huns is told in *Hou Han Shu,* 120, 4a.

[5] The troubles with Northern Güshï, and the alliance between this prince and the Huns are recounted in *Tung Gien Gang Mu,* A.D. 10, and the *Han Shu,* 94a, 22.

[6] For the rebellion of the Hunnish officials stationed in Kashgaria and their flight to the Hunnish domain see *Tung Gien Gang Mu,* A.D. 10; *Han Shu,* 99b, 15; *ibid.,* 94a, 22-23; *ibid.,* 96b, 22.

[7] For Wang Mang's attempt to split the Hunnish empire into fifteen principalities and the organization of a huge army for a campaign against the Huns see *Tung Gien Gang Mu,* A.D. 10; *Han Shu,* 99b, 16-17; *ibid.,* 94b, 23-25.

[8] For the attempt to put Hien on the Shanyu's throne and Hien's inconstancy, followed by the murder of Hien's son, see *Tung Gien Gang Mu,* A.D. 11; *Han Shu,* 99b, 20-21; *ibid.,* 94b, 25.

[9] For the election of Hien as legitimate Shanyu and the relations between

the Chinese and the Huns during his reign see *Tung Gien Gang Mu*, A.D. 13-18; *Han Shu*, 99b, 30-31 and 34; *ibid.*, 94b, 26-27.

[10] For events in Kashgaria during this period see *Tung Gien Gang Mu*, A.D. 13-16; *Han Shu*, 99b, 26 and 33-34; *ibid.*, 96b, 22-23; *Hou Han Shu*, 118, 17-18. Chavannes, *op. cit.*, p. vii, has shown from archaeological evidence that the native historians have exaggerated the Chinese losses in Kashgaria during Wang Mang's reign, and argues that the complete loss of Chinese sovereignty over this region did not take place until the anarchic period which ensued after Wang Mang's death.

[11] For Sino-Hunnish relations during the period from A.D. 18 to 23 see *Tung Gien Gang Mu*, A.D. 18 and 19; *Han Shu*, 99c, 3-6; *ibid.*, 94b, 27-28.

[12] The Chinese records are singularly silent regarding events in Kashgaria during this period. What little we know is derived from *Hou Han Shu*, 118, 1 and 17-18.

[13] After Wang Mang's death there was a wild scramble for power among various scions of the Liu family. For a brief period Liu Huan secured supremacy, but he was soon succeeded by Liu Pen-dse. For the biographies of these two worthies see *Hou Han Shu*, 41. A few years later Liu Pen-dse fell from power and was succeeded by Liu Siu (dynastic title Guang Wu) who founded the Later Han dynasty. For his reign see *Hou Han Shu*, 1.

[14] For the embassy of Liu Huan (or Geng-shï) to the Huns see *Han Shu*, 94b, 28. For the first embassy of Guang-wu-di to the Huns see *Hou Han Shu*, 119, 2.

[15] For the conflicts between the Chinese and the Huns from A.D. 25 to 42 see *Tung Gien Gang Mu* for these years; also *Hou Han Shu*, 1a, 24; *ibid.*, 1b, pp. 7, 11, 13, 16, 17, 19, 21; *ibid.*, 42, 17-20; *ibid.*, 47, 14; *ibid.*, 48, 10; *ibid.*, 52, 9; *ibid.*, 54, 16; *ibid.*, 119, 2-3.

[16] For events among the Wuhuan during this period see *Hou Han Shu*, 120, 4. For the Sienbi, *ibid.*, 120, 8.

[17] For events in Kashgaria during this period see *Tung Gien Gang Mu*, A.D. 25, 28, 38, 41, and 45; *Hou Han Shu*, 16, 13, 18, and 21-22; 118, 1, and 17-19.

Chapter Ten

The Transformation of the Hunnish Empire

For a general survey of events during this period see *Tung Gien Gang Mu*, chap. IX (A.D. 46-73). For further details see the *Hou Han Shu*, especially the following chapters: (*Annals*) 1b, Guang-wu-di; 2, Ming-di. (*Biographies*) 49, Geng Guo; 50, Dsi Yung. (*Monographs*) 118, the Western Regions; 119, the Southern Hun; 120, the Wuhuan and Sienbi.

[1] For the death of Shanyu Yu, the accession of Bonu, and the rapid degeneration of the Hunnish Empire see *Tung Gien Gang Mu*, A.D. 46; *Hou Han Shu*, 119, 4.

[2] For Bi's negotiations with the Chinese leading to the establishment of

the Southern Hunnish Kingdom see *Tung Gien Gang Mu,* A.D. 47-48; *Hou Han Shu,* 1b, 23-24; *ibid.,* 119, 4-5.

[3] For Bi's relations with China see *Tung Gien Gang Mu,* A.D. 49-50; *Hou Han Shu,* 1b, 24-26; *ibid.,* 49, 15-16; *ibid.,* 119, 5-6.

[4] For the subsequent relations between the Chinese and the Southern Huns see *Hou Han Shu,* 119, 5-8. The same passages give an outline of the political organization in vogue among the Southern Huns.

[5] For the early successes of the Southern Huns in their conflicts with the Northern Huns see the *Hou Han Shu,* 119, 5. For the subsequent victories of the Northern Huns and the measures taken to protect the Southern Huns see *Tung Gien Gang Mu,* A.D. 50; *Hou Han Shu,* 119, 8-9.

[6] For the Northern Huns' assurance that they had no intention of injuring the Celestial Empire, see *Hou Han Shu,* 119, 9.

[7] For the Wuhuan attacks upon the Northern Huns see *Tung Gien Gang Mu,* A.D. 46-49; *Hou Han Shu,* 120, 4-5. For events among the Sienbi during this period, *ibid.,* 50, 16-17; *ibid.,* 120, 9.

[8] For the events in Kashgaria during this period see *Tung Gien Gang Mu,* A.D. 45, 46, and 61; *Hou Han Shu,* 118, 9 and 19-22.

[9] Curiously enough, *Hou Han Shu,* 118, which deals with the Western Regions, makes no mention of the Gienkun, the Dingling, or the Wusun. The *Wei Lio,* however, which deals with the period A.D. 220-265, describes these peoples as continuing to exist in the regions we have assigned to them. See *Wei Lio* in *San Guo Jï,* 30, 34. The Wusun, moreover, are mentioned and their power and independence indicated in other portions of the *Hou Han Shu,* especially 49, 20b; and 77, 8b.

[10] For the change of name from Yentsai to Olan (Alan) and that the Alan were subject to the Kanggü see *Hou Han Shu,* 118, 17b. For Ansi or Parthia, *ibid.,* 118, 12.

[11] For the rise of the Kushan Empire see *Hou Han Shu,* 118, 15. The Chinese call the founder of this dynasty Kiu-dsiu-kio and his son Yen-gao-jen. Older scholars (*e.g.,* E. Specht in *Journal Asiatique* [1897] 2, 192) tried to identify Kiu-dsiu-kio with Kanishka, but J. Marquart, "Eranshahr," *Abhandlungen der koniglichen Gesell schaft der Wissenschaft zu Gottingen,* III (1903), 208, has demonstrated that Kiu-dsiu-kio is Kujula Kadphises, and that Yen-gao-jen is Vima Kadphises. This identification is now universally accepted. See O. Franke, "Beitrage aus Chinesischen Quellen zur Kenntniss der Turkvolker und Skythen," sup. to *Abhandlungen der koniglichen Preussischen Akadamie der Wissenschaft zu Berlin,* 1904, p. 78; and P. Pelliot, "Tocharien et Koutcheen," *Journal Asiatique,* 1934, pp. 23 ff. For a summary of the views of "Indianists" about these two monarchs see Poussin, *L'Inde aux Temps des Mauryas et des Barbares,* pp. 309 ff.

[12] That the Kanggü withdrew their army from Kashgaria at the request of the Yuejï in A.D. 84 see *Hou Han Shu,* 77, 10b. That the later kings of the Kanggü claimed to be descended from the Yuejï see *Be Shï,* 97, 19.

[13] For some strange reason the contemporary Chinese records make no direct reference to Kanishka. As a result we are forced to rely upon Indian

sources (some of which were later translated into Chinese). As usual these are very unsatisfactory. There are grave doubts as to the date of Kanishka's reign. The safest conclusion is that reached by A. M. Boyer, "L'Epoque de Kanishka," *Journal Asiatique,* 1900, p. 526, that Kanishka lived somewhere about the close of the first century A.D. For a fuller discussion of this problem see the Supplementary Notes.

[14] For reproductions of the Kushan coins including those of Kanishka see Gardner, *op. cit.;* and A. Cunningham, "Coins of the Indo-Scythians," *Numismatic Chronicle,* 3rd ser., vols. VIII, IX, X, XII (1888-1889-1890-1892). For an interpretation of the various cultural influences which these coins portray see V. Smith, *Early History of India,* pp. 251 ff.; Grousset, *Histoire de l'Extreme Orient,* pp. 61 ff.; Poussin, *L'Inde aux Temps des Mauryas et des Barbares,* pp. 303 ff. For the Gandhara school of Buddhist art A. Foucher, *L'Art Greco-bouddhique du Gandhara;* A. Grunwedel, *Buddhistische Kunst in Indien.*

Chapter Eleven

THE HUNS AND CHINESE RENEW THEIR STRUGGLE

For a general survey of the events during this period see *Tung Gien Gang Mu,* chaps. IX and X (A.D. 73-88). For further details see the *Hou Han Shu,* especially the following chapters: (*Annals*) 2, Ming-di; 3, Jang-di. (*Biographies*) 49, Geng Gung and Geng Bing; 50, Dsi Yung; 53, Dou Gu; 66, Jeng Jung; 77 Ban Chao. (*Monographs*) 118, the Western Regions; 119, the Southern Hiungnu; 120, the Wuhuan and Sienbi.

[1] For the effort of the Northern Huns to conciliate the Chinese in A.D. 50 see *Tung Gien Gang Mu* under this date; see also the *Hou Han Shu,* 119, 9. For the peace negotiations of A.D. 52 see *Tung Gien Gang Mu* under this date; *Hou Han Shu,* 16, 22; *ibid.,* 119, 9-11. For the peace negotiations of A.D. 51 see *Tung Gien Gang Mu* under this date; *Hou Han Shu,* 1b, 26; *ibid.,* 119, 9.

[2] For the Hunnish demands for trading privileges see *Tung Gien Gang Mu,* A.D. 64; *Hou Han Shu,* 2, 14; *ibid.,* 119, 12-13. For the renewal of the Hunnish attacks in A.D. 65, *ibid.,* 119, 13.

[3] For the character of Ming-di and the chief events of his reign see *Tung Gien Gang Mu,* A.D. 58-77; *Han Shu,* 2. For the official story of the introduction of Buddhism into China see *Tung Gien Gang Mu,* A.D. 65; *Hou Han Shu,* 118, 16b. For criticism of this story see H. Maspero, "Le Songe et l'Embassade de l'Empereur Ming," *Bulletin de l'Ecole d'Extreme Orient,* 1910, and O. Franke, "Zur Frage der Einfuhrung des Buddhismus in China," *Mitteilungen des Seminars fur Orientalische Sprachen,* 1910.

[4] For Ming-di's great campaign against the Northern Huns see *Tung Gien Gang Mu,* A.D. 72-73; *Hou Han Shu,* 2, 23-24; *ibid.,* 50, 18; *ibid.,* 53, 17-18; *ibid.,* 119, 13-14. For the importance of Hami, *ibid.,* 118, 7b.

[5] For the campaign against Güshï see *Tung Gien Gang Mu,* A.D. 74; *Hou Han Shu,* 2, 25; *ibid.,* 49, 16 ff. For the reëstablishment of the post of Protector General and Central Commanding Officer *ibid.,* 118, 7.

[6] For the capture of Shanshan by Ban Chao see *Tung Gien Gang Mu,* A.D. 73; *Hou Han Shu,* 77, 2-3. For the capture of Khutan by Ban Chao see *Tung Gien Gang Mu,* A.D. 73; *Hou Han Shu,* 77, 4. For the capture of Kashgar see *Tung Gien Gang Mu* A.D. 74; *Hou Han Shu,* 77, 5.

[7] For the Hunnish counter-attack of A.D. 75 and the heroic defense of Northern Güshï by Geng Gung see *Tung Gien Gang Mu,* A.D. 75-76; *Hou Han Shu,* 2, 36b; *ibid.,* 3, 2b; *ibid.,* 49, 20-25. The refusal of the Emperor Jang-di to embark upon the permanent reconquest of Kashgaria is mentioned in *Hou Han Shu,* 118, 2b.

[8] For the gradual weakening of the Northern Huns during the period A.D. 76-88 see *Hou Han Shu,* 119, 14-16; *Tung Gien Gang Mu,* A.D. 85-87; *Hou Han Shu,* 3, pp. 15, 26, and 28.

[9] For the activities of Ban Chao in Kashgaria during the period A.D. 76 to 88 see *Tung Gien Gang Mu,* A.D. 76, 80, 83, and 86; *Han Shu,* 3, pp. 8, 12, 26, and 28; *Hou Han Shu,* 77, 5-11.

Chapter Twelve

Seesaw in the Balance of Power

For a general survey of events during this period see *Tung Gien Gang Mu,* chap. X (A.D. 88-106). For further details see the *Hou Han Shu,* especially the following chapters: (*Annals*) 4, Ho-di and Shang-di. (*Biographies*) 49, Geng Bing and Geng Kuei; 53, Dou Hien; 55, Lu Gung; 71, Sung I; 77, Ban Chao. (*Monographs*) 118, the Western Regions; 119, the Southern Hiungnu; 120, the Wuhuan and Sienbi.

[1] For the character and reign of Ho-di see *Tung Gien Gang Mu,* A.D. 89-105; *Hou Han Shu,* 4. For the memorial of the Southern Huns urging war upon the Northern Huns see *Tung Gien Gang Mu,* 88; *Hou Han Shu,* 71, 24; *ibid.,* 119, 18.

[2] For Dou Hien's escapade and its relation to the Hunnish campaign see *Tung Gien Gang Mu,* 88; *Hou Han Shu,* 53, 20 ff.; *ibid.,* 55, 7-10; *ibid.,* 75, 3.

[3] For the campaign of A.D. 89 see *Tung Gien Gang Mu* under this date; *Hou Han Shu,* 4, 4; *ibid.,* 53, 20 ff.; *ibid.,* 119, 19.

[4] For the events of A.D. 90 see *Tung Gien Gang Mu* under this date; *Hou Han Shu,* 4, 5; *ibid.,* 53, 25; *ibid.,* 119, 19. For the submission of the Güshï, *ibid.,* 118, 2, and 16.

[5] For the events of A.D. 91 see *Tung Gien Gang Mu* under this date; *Hou Han Shu,* 4, 6-7; *ibid.,* 49, 18-19; *ibid.,* 53, 25; *ibid.,* 75, 4-5; *ibid.,* 119, 20.

[6] For the downfall of Dou Hien and its effects upon the Northern Huns see *Tung Gien Gang Mu,* 92-93; *Hou Han Shu,* 4, 8 and 11; *ibid.,* 53, 26-27; *ibid.,* 119, 20.

[7] For the occasional sending of tribute by the later lords of the Northern Huns see *Tung Gien Gang Mu,* A.D. 105; *Hou Han Shu,* 4, 24-26; *ibid.,* 119, 24-25.

[8] For the seizure of most of Northern Mongolia by the Sienbi see *Tung Gien Gang Mu,* A.D. 93; *Hou Han Shu,* 120, 9. For the dreary details regard- the Civil War in the Southern Hunnish domain see *Tung Gien Gang Mu,* A.D. 94, 93; *Hou Han Shu,* 119, 20 ff.

[9] For Ban Chao's exploits in Kashgaria during this period see *Tung Gien Gang Mu,* A.D. 90, 91, and 94; *Hou Han Shu,* 4, 5, 7, and 12-13; *ibid.,* 77, 12-15. For the disturbances in Güshï in A.D. 96 and 97 see *Hou Han Shu,* 4, 14-16, and *ibid.,* 118, 26-27.

[10] For Gan Ying's journey through Parthia in an attempt to reach Datsin or the Roman Empire see the *Hou Han Shu,* 118, 12. For the interpretation of some of the geographic expressions used in this account see Weiger, *Textes Historiques,* p. 721; F. Hirth, *China and the Roman Orient;* and E. Chavannes, "Les Pays d'Occident d'apres le Heou Han Chou," in *T'oung Pao,* 1907, pp. 149 ff.

Chapter Thirteen

The Final Collapse of the Hunnish Empire

For a general survey of the events during this period see *Tung Gien Gang Mu,* chaps. X-XII (A.D. 106-181). For further details see the *Hou Han Shu,* especially the following chapters: (*Annals*) 4, Shang-di; 5, An-di; 6, Shun-di, Chung-di, and Ji-di; 7, Huan-di. (*Biographies*) 49, Geng Kuei and Geng Jung; 77, Ban Chao, Ban Yung, and Liang King; 95, Jan Huan. (*Monographs*) 117, Kiang, or Tibetans; 118, the Western Regions; 119, the Southern Hiungnu; 120, Wuhuan and Sienbi.

[1] For the appointment of Ren Shang and his conversation with Ban Chao see *Tung Gien Gang Mu,* A.D. 102; *Hou Han Shu,* 77, 18-19.

[2] For the rebellion in Kashgaria see *Hou Han Shu,* 5, 3; *ibid.,* 77, 26-27; *ibid.,* 118, 3. For the abandonment of all claims to sovereignty over Kashgaria see *Tung Gien Gang Mu,* A.D. 107; *Hou Han Shu,* 5, 4; *ibid.,* 77, 26; *ibid.,* 118, 3.

[3] For the wars between the Tibetans and the Chinese see *Tung Gien Gang Mu,* A.D. 106-116; *Hou Han Shu,* 5, 4 ff.; *ibid.,* 117, 21-27.

[4] For the rebellion of the Southern Huns see *Tung Gien Gang Mu,* A.D. 109-110; *Hou Han Shu,* 5, 9-10; *ibid.,* 49, 19; *ibid.,* 77, 27-28; *ibid.,* 119-25.

[5] For the Wuhuan see *Hou Han Shu,* 120, 5; for the Sienbi, *ibid.,* 120, 10.

[6] For the reëstablishment of Hunnish supremacy in Kashgaria, *ibid.,* 118, 3b. It might be added that though the Huns secured control over most of Kashgaria, the Yuejï were able to claim temporary supremacy over Kashgar. See the *Hou Han Shu,* 118, 23.

[7] For the Chinese occupation of Hami in A.D. 119 and their expulsion by the Huns in the following year see *Tung Gien Gang Mu,* A.D. 119-120; *Hou Han Shu,* 77, 19-22; *ibid.,* 118, 3-4.

[8] For the memorial of A.D. 123 and the appointment of Ban Yung as Changshï see *Tung Gien Gang Mu* under this date; *Hou Han Shu,* 77, 23; *ibid.,* 118, 4-6 .

[9] For the campaigns of 123-127 in Kashgaria see *Tung Gien Gang Mu,* A.D. 123, 126, and 127; *Hou Han Shu,* 5, 31; *ibid.,* 6, 6; *ibid.,* 77, 22-24; *ibid.,* 118, 6, and 27.

[10] For the scandal of Ban Yung's nephew and the latter's imperial but amorous wife see *Tung Gien Gang Mu,* A.D. 130; *Han Shu,* 6, 9; *Hou Han Shu,* 77, 19.

[11] Casual notes on events in Kashgaria during the years A.D. 127-153 are scattered throughout *Hou Han Shu* 118, especially pp. 6-10, 23, and 27-29.

[12] For the later history of the Southern Huns see *Hou Han Shu,* 119, 26-32. For the connection of the Wuhuan with the various Southern Hunnish rebellions see *Hou Han Shu,* 120, 5-6.

[13] For a summary of the Sienbi raids upon China during the period A.D. 115 to 121 see the *Hou Han Shu,* 120, 10-11.

[14] For the rise of the first great Sienbi confederation under Kijïgien (A.D. 121-133) see the *Hou Han Shu,* 120, 11-13.

[15] For Tanshïhuai and the Sienbi Empire founded by him see *Tung Gien Gang Mu,* A.D. 156, 166, 177, and 181. Further details in the *Hou Han Shu,* 120, 13-20. For Tanshïhuai's conquest of the Fuyu, Dingling, Northern Huns and Wusun see the *Tung Gien Gang Mu,* 156; *Hou Han Shu,* 120, 15. For Tanshïhuai's importation of Japanese fishermen into Mongolia see the *Hou Han Shu,* 120, 19-20.

Chapter Fourteen

THE HUNS IN CHINA—THE FIRST PHASE

For a general survey of events during this period see *Tung Gien Gang Mu,* chaps. XII-XVIII (A.D. 178-318). For further details see *Dsin Shu,* especially the following chapters: (*Annals*) 3, Wu-di; 4, Huei-di; 5, Huai-di and Min-di. (*Biographies*) 59, Prince Yue; 60 So Chen; 61, Gou Hi; 100, Wang Mi; 62, Lin Kun; 89 Gia Hun. (*Special Biographies*) 101, Liu Yüan; 102, Liu Tsung; 103, Liu Yao; 104, Shï Le. (*Monograph*) 97, The Four Types of Barbarians. Certain additional details are to be found in the *Hou Han Shu,* especially chap. 119; *San Guo Jï,* especially chap. 28; *Wei Shu,* especially chap. 1.

[1] For the decay and disintegration of the Southern Hunnish Kingdom see *Tung Gien Gang Mu,* A.D. 178, 179, and 216. Fuller details in the *Hou Han Shu,* 119, 32-33; *Dsin Shu,* 97, 11; *ibid.,* 101, 1.

[2] For the continual influx of Huns into Northern China during the third century A.D. see *Dsin Shu,* 97, 11,. For the reorganization of the Huns who dwelt on Chinese territory see *Tung Gien Gang Mu,* A.D. 251; *San Guo Jï,* 28, 19.

[3] For the Hunnish rebellion of 271-272 see *Tung Gien Gang Mu* under this date; *Dsin Shu,* 3, 6-7; *ibid.,* 97, 11. For the rebellion of 296 see *Tung Gien Gang Mu* under this date, *Dsin Shu,* 4, 2-3; *ibid.,* 97, 12.

[4] For Liu Yüan's early life see *Tung Gien Gang Mu,* A.D. 279, 289, and 290; *Dsin Shu,* 101, 1-3. For the establishment of the Hunnish kingdom see *Tung Gien Gang Mu,* 304; *Dsin Shu,* 4, 7; *ibid.,* 101, 4-5.

[5] For the establishment of the Hunnish Empire see *Tung Gien Gang Mu,* A.D. 308-310; *Dsin Shu,* 5, 2-4; *ibid.,* 101, 5-6. For Liu Yüan's moderation and generosity in warfare see *Tung Gien Gang Mu* 304, and 309. For Liu Yao see *Dsin Shu,* 103, 1; for Shï Le, *ibid.,* 104, 1-3.

[6] For the intrigue and civil war among the Huns following Liu Yuan's death see *Tung Gien Gang Mu,* A.D. 310; *Dsin Shu,* 101, 6.

[7] For the accession of Liu Tsung and the early scandals of his reign see *Tung Gien Gang Mu,* A.D. 310; *Dsin Shu,* 102, 1.

[8] For Shï Le's capture of Prince Yue's army and the execution of the Chinese princes see *Tung Gien Gang Mu,* A.D. 311; *Dsin Shu,* 5, 4; *ibid.,* 104, 4-5.

[9] For conditions in Loyang and its capture by the Huns see *Tung Gien Gang Mu,* A.D. 311; *Dsin Shu,* 5, 4-5; *ibid.,* 100, 2; *ibid.,* 102, 1-2.

[10] For Liu Tsung's eccentric behavior after the capture of Loyang see *Tung Gien Gang Mu,* A.D. 312-315; *Dsin Shu,* 102, 3-11.

[11] For the revival of the Chinese cause in Northeast China see *Dsin Shu,* 62. For the revival of the Chinese cause in Northwest China, *ibid.,* 5, 6-7. For the Tobas see *Wei Shu,* 1, 8-11.

[12] For Shï Le's activities in Northeast China during this period see *Tung Gien Gang Mu,* A.D. 312-318; *Dsin Shu,* 104, 5-14.

[13] For Liu Yao's numerous attacks upon Changan and his eventual capture of this city see *Tung Gien Gang Mu,* A.D. 313-316; *Dsin Shu,* 5, 6-9; *ibid.,* 60, 12; *ibid.,* 102, 5-11.

[14] For the revolution among the Tobas see *Tung Gien Gang Mu,* A.D. 316; *Wei Shu,* 1, 11.

[15] For the internal commotion at the Hunnish court in the last years of Liu Tsung's reign see *Tung Gien Gang Mu,* A.D. 317-318; *Dsin Shu,* 102, 12-14.

[16] For Liu Tsan's brief reign and his assassination by Gin Jung see *Tung Gien Gang Mu,* A.D. 318; *Dsin Shu,* 102, 14-15.

Chapter Fifteen

The Huns in China—The Second Phase

For a general survey of the events during this period see *Tung Gien Gang Mu,* chaps. XVIII to XX (A.D. 318-352). For further details see the *Dsin Shu,* especially the following chapters (*Annals*) 6, Yuan-di and Ming-di; 7, Chen-di and Kang-di; 8, Mu-di. (*Biographies*) 83, Yuan Dan; 87, Jang Dsun and Jang Jung-hua; 95, Buddhachinga. (*Special Biographies*) 103, Liu Yao;

104 and 105, Shï Le; 106 and 107, Shï Hu; 109, Murung Huang; 110, Murung Dsun; 116, Yao I-jung; 129, Meng-sün; 130, Helien Popo. Certain additional details are to be found in the *Wei Shu,* especially chaps. 1, 13, 84.

[1] For the downfall of Gin Jung and Gin Ming see *Tung Gien Gang Mu,* A.D. 318; *Dsin Shu,* 104, 14-16.

[2] For Liu Yao's career as ruler of the short-lived Early Jao dynasty see *Tung Gien Gang Mu,* A.D. 319-329; *Dsin Shu,* 103, 1-13. For Shï Le's career during this period see *Dsin Shu,* 105, 1-7.

[3] For the Later Jao dynasty, under Shï Le, see *Tung Gien Gang Mu,* A.D. 329-333; *Dsin Shu,* 105, 7-12; *ibid.,* 95, 11-15.

[4] For the period of discord which followed Shï Le's reign see *Tung Gien Gang Mu,* A.D. 333-334; *Dsin Shu,* 105, 11-14.

[5] For a general survey of Shï Hu's reign see *Tung Gien Gang Mu,* A.D. 334-349; *Dsin Shu,* 106 and 107.

[6] For the dispute over the official recognition of Buddhism see *Tung Gien Gang Mu,* A.D. 335; *Dsin Shu,* 95, 13.

[7] For Shï Hu's attempts to embellish his capital and his establishment of a corps of Amazons see *Tung Gien Gang Mu,* A.D. 336-337; *Dsin Shu,* 106, 203.

[8] For the relations between the Huns under Shï Hu and the Toba kingdom in the North see *Tung Gien Gang Mu,* A.D. 335, 337, 339; *Wei Shu,* 1, 14-16.

[9] For a summary of the frequent skirmishes between the (Chinese) Dsin dynasty in the South and the armies of Shï Hu see *Dsin Shu* 7 and 8. For the panic of A.D. 335 see *Tung Gien Gang Mu* under this date; *Dsin Shu,* 7, 5; *ibid.,* 83, 5. For Shï Hu's abortive campaign in A.D. 342-344 see *Tung Gien Gang Mu* under this date; *Dsin Shu,* 106, 7-9.

[10] For the relations between the Huns under Shï Hu and the Murung Kingdom of Yen see *Tung Gien Gang Mu,* A.D. 337 and 341 ff.; *Dsin Shu,* 106, 4-6; *ibid.,* 109, 2-5, and 8. For Murung Huang's panic see *Tung Gien Gang Mu,* A.D. 338.

[11] For the establishment of the Kingdom of Liang and its acceptance of Hunnish sovereignty see *Tung Gien Gang Mu,* A.D. 330 and 332; *Dsin Shu,* 87, 8 and 12. For the conflict of the Huns under Shï Hu with this kingdom see *Tung Gien Gang Mu,* A.D. 345-347; *Dsin Shu,* 87, 13-15; *ibid.,* 106, 7; *ibid.,* 107, 7.

[12] For the rebellion of 349 see *Tung Gien Gang Mu* under this date; *Dsin Shu,* 107, 4; *ibid.,* 116, 1-2.

[13] For the iniquities of Shï Suei and his execution see *Tung Gien Gang Mu,* A.D. 337; *Dsin Shu,* 106, 4. For the intrigues of Shï Suan and his execution see *Tung Gien Gang Mu,* A.D. 348; *Dsin Shu,* 107, 2-3.

[14] For the confusion and civil war which followed Shï Hu's death see *Tung Gien Gang Mu,* A.D. 349-351; *Dsin Shu,* 107, 5-11. The fact that the Huns had high noses and hairy faces is mentioned in *Tung Gien Gang Mu,* A.D. 349; *Dsin Shu,* 107, 8a.

[15] For Shï Min's downfall and the end of the Hunnish domination in China see *Tung Gien Gang Mu,* A.D. 352; *Dsin Shu,* 107, 11; *ibid.,* 110, 1-2.

[16] The best account of the "Empire of Hia" is found in the biography of Helien Popo, *Dsin Shu,* 130; see also *Wei Shu,* 83.

[17] The best account of the Kingdom of Northern Liang is to be found in the biography of Meng-sün, *Dsin Shu,* 129; see also the *Wei Shu,* 87.

Chapter Sixteen

The Huns in Europe—The First Phase

The principal Chinese source is the *Be Shï,* especially chaps. 97 and 98. The principal classical sources are Ammianus Marcellinus, *Rerum Gestarum;* Jordanis, "Getica (De Origine Actibus Getarum)," *Monumenta Germaniae Historia,* ser. A.A., vol. Va; Eunapius, "Fragmenta," *Fragmenta Historicorum Graecorum;* Claudian, *Carmina.*

[1] For the Sarmatians see Zeuss, *Deutschen und Nachbarstamme,* pp. 279 ff. and 691 ff.; Rostovstzeff, *Sarmatians and Parthians;* Kretschmer, "Sarmatae" and "Sarmatia," *Pauly Wissowa Realencyclopaedie des Classischen Altertums.*

[2] For the expansion of the Teutons (Goths, etc.) into Southeastern Europe see Zeuss, *op. cit.,* pp. 401 ff.; M. Bang, "The Expansion of the Teutons," *Cambridge Medieval History,* I, 183 ff.; T. Hodgkin, *The Visigothic Invasion.*

[3] For the Alani see Zeuss, *op. cit.,* pp. 700 ff.; Taubler, "Zur Geschichte der Alanen," *Klio,* IX, 14 ff.; R. Bleichsteiner, "Das Volk der Alanen," *Berichte des Forschungs Institut fur Osten und Orient,* II (1918), 4 ff.

[4] For the Sienbi and their effect upon Hunnish history see *Hou Han Shu,* 120, 15. For the Gaogü see *Be Shï,* 98, 17 ff. For the Yueban see *Be Shï,* 97, 11.

[5] That the main body of the Hiungnu moved into Kanggü or Turkistan see *Be Shï,* 97, 11 ff. See also F. Hirth, "Uber Volga Hunnen und Hiung-nu," *Sitzungsberichte der Munchner Akademie der Wissenschaft* (*Phil-Hist Classe*), II (1899), 289 ff.

[6] For the Armenian references to the Huns in Central Asia, prior to the Hunnish invasion of Europe, see Faustus of Byzance (in V. Langlois, *Collection des Historiens Armeniens,* I, 215) and Moses of Chorene, *ibid.,* II, 125.

[7] For the Chionites see Ammianus Marcellinus, *op. cit.,* 16, 9, 4. That the Chionites were probably a branch of the Huns see Marquart, "Eranshahr," *Abhandlungen des koniglichen Gesellschaft der Wissenschaft zu Gottingen,* III (1903), 50 ff.

[8] For the belief that the rulers of the later Huns were descendents from the Hiungnu Shanyus see Hirth, "Die Ahnentafel Attilas," *Bulletin de l'Academie Imperiale des Sciences de St. Petersbourg,* 1900, pp. 220 ff., but see L. Ligeti, "Die Ahnentafel Attilas und die Hunnischen Tan-hu Namen," *Asia Major,* II (1925), 290 ff. That the Huns when entering Europe had no supreme monarch see Ammianus Marcellinus, *op. cit.*

[9] For the Hunnish conquest of the Alani see *Be Shï,* 97, 12a; Ammianus Marcellinus, *op. cit.;* Jordanis, *op. cit.,* sec. 126.

[10] For the Hunnish attacks upon the Ostrogoths see Ammianus Marcellinus, *op. cit.*, 31, 2-3; Jordanis, *op. cit.*, secs. 129-30.

[11] For the Ostrogoths after their defeat by the Huns see Ammianus Marcellinus, *op. cit.*, 31, 3, 1-3; Jordanis, *op. cit.*, secs. 246-51. See also J. Marquart, *Osteuropäische und Ostasiatische Streifzüge*, pp. 367 ff.

[12] For the Hunnish defeat of the Visigoths see Ammianus Marcellinus, *op. cit.*, 31, 3, 4-8. For the passage of the Visigoths into the Roman Empire and the subsequent troubles leading to the death of Valens see Ammianus Marcellinus, *op. cit.*, 31, 4-16; Jordanis, *op. cit.*, 25-26; Eunapius, "Fragmenta," *Fragmenta Historicorum Graecorum*, pp. 30-33.

[13] For the Goths after the death of Valens see Jordanis, *op. cit.*, 27-29. For Alaric in Greece see Zosimus, *Historiae*, 5, 5-7; Claudian, *Carmina* esp. "De Bello Gothico," lines 535 to 541 and "In Eutropium," II, 216; see also M. Manitus, "the Teutonic Migrations," *Cambridge Medieval History*, I, 250 ff.; Hodgkin, *The Visigothic Invasions*, pp. 281 ff. and 650 ff.

Chapter Seventeen

The Huns in Europe—The Second Phase

The principal sources for this period are: Jordanis "Getica (De Actibus Getarum)," *Monumenta Germaniae Historica*, ser. A.A., vol. Va; Priscus "Fragmenta," *Fragmenta Historicorum Graecorum* IV, 69 ff.; and Sidonius Appolinaris, "Epistulae et Carmina," *Monumenta Germaniae Historica*, ser. A.A., vol. VIII.

Important incidental references to the "Barbarians" are to be found in Zosimus, *Historiae;* Orosius, *Historiae adversum Paganos;* Socrates Scholasticus, *Historia Ecclesiastica;* Sozomen, *Historia Ecclesiastica;* Theodoret, *Historia Ecclesiastica;* Gregorius Turonensis, "Historia Francorum," *Monumenta Germaniae Historica*, ser. S.E.M., vol. I; Isidorus Hispalensis, "Historia Gothorum, Vandalorum, Sueborum," *Chronica Minora*, II, 241 ff.; Prosper Tiro, "Epitoma Chronicon," *Chronica Minora*, I, 340 ff.; Isidorus Hispalensis, "Chronica," *Chronica Minora*, II, 391 ff.; Marcellinus Comes "Chronicon," *Chronica Minora*, II, 37 ff.; Hydatius, "Chronica," *Chronica Minora*, II, 1 ff.; "Chronica Gallica," *Chronica Minora*, I, 615 ff.; *Chronicon Paschale;* Eunapius "Fragmenta," *Fragmenta Historicorum Graecorum*, IV, 7 ff.

For the Huns after the death of Attila see Cassiodorus, "Variae," *Monumenta Germaniae Historica*, ser. A.A., vol. XII; Ennodius, "Opera," *Monumenta Germaniae Historica*, ser. A.A., vol. VII; Agathias, *Historiae;* Theophylactus Simocatta, *Historiae;* Procopius, *De Bello Gotthico;* Joannes Antiochenus, "Fragmenta," *Fragmenta Historicorum Graecorum*, IV, 535 ff.; Menander Protector, "Fragmenta," *Fragmenta Historicorum Graecorum*, IV, 200 ff.

[1] That the Huns did not conquer Pannonia until A.D. 400 see Marquart, *Osteuropäische und Ostasiatische Streifzuge*, pp. 369 ff.

[2] For the Hunnish attacks in the Near East see E. Drouin, "Huns," in *Grande Encyclopedie.*

[3] For the coming of Athanarik into the Roman Empire see Ammianus Marcellinus, *Rerum Gestarum,* 27, 5, 10; Jordanis, "Getica (De Origine Actibus Getarum)," *Monumenta Germaniae Historica,* ser. A.A., vol. Va., secs. 142-45.

[4] For the East Gothic invasion of 386 see Zosimus, *Historiae,* 4, 35; Claudian, *Carmina* sp. "In Rufinum I"; Zeuss, *Die Deutschen und die Nachbarstamme,* p. 421.

[5] For the later fortunes of the main body of the East Goths and their westward migration see Jordanis, *op. cit.,* chap. 48; and its interpretation by Marquart, *op. cit.,* pp. 368 ff.

[6] For the settlement of the Alani in the Theiss Danube basin see Claudian, "Rufinum I," 310 ff. in *Carmina.*

[7] For Uldin and his seizure of Gania see Zosimus, *Historiae,* 5, 22; Orosius, *op. cit.,* 7, 37, 12. For Radagais see Zeuss, *op. cit.,* p. 417; Marquart, *op. cit.,* p. 372.

[8] For the migrations of the Suevi, Vandals, and Alani into Gaul see Zosimus, *Historiae,* 6, 3; Orosius, *op. cit.,* 7, 38. For their later history see Isodorus Hispalensis, "Historia Gothorum, Vandalorum, Sueborum," *Chronica Minora;* and T. Hodgkin, *The Visigothic Invasion,* pt. II.

[9] For Alarik and the West Gothic invasion of Italy, etc., see Jordanis, *op. cit.,* chaps. 29 to 31; Zosimus, *op. cit.,* bks. 5 and 6; Orosius, *op. cit.,* bk. 7. See also E. Gibbon, *Decline and Fall of the Roman Empire,* chap. XXI; Hodgkin, *The Visigothic Invasion,* chaps. XV-XVII.

[10] For the Franks during this period see Zeuss, *op. cit.,* p. 332. For the Burgundi, *ibid.,* p. 468; Ihm, "Burgondiones," *Pauly Wissowa Realencyclopaedie des Classischen Altertums.*

[11] For the Hunnish occupation of Pannonia see Marquart, *op. cit.,* p. 372.

[12] For the attack of Uldes upon the East Roman Empire in A.D. 408 see Sozomen, *Historia Ecclesiastica,* 9, 5.

[13] For the suggestion that Rua and his descendents were the leaders of an entirely new Hunnish invasion see Drouin, "Huns," *Grande Encyclopedie.*

[14] For the Hunnish invasions of 422 see Marcellinus Comes, "Chronicon," *Chronica Minora,* II, 75. For the invasion of 426 see Socrates Scholasticus *Historia Ecclesiastica,* 7, 43; Theodoret, *Historia Ecclesiastica,* 5, 36. Both writers claim that Rua was killed in this campaign, but this is certainly wrong.

[15] For the negotiations of 433 and 434 between the East Roman Empire and the Huns see Priscus, "Fragmenta," *Fragmenta Historicorum Graecorum,* IV, 71-72.

[16] For the Hunnish relations with the Ostrogoths see Jordanis, *op. cit.,* secs. 252 and 253; for the Gepids, *ibid.,* secs. 199 and 200. For the Hunnish supremacy over the Thuringians, Burgundi, Ripuarian Franks, etc., see Sidonius Appolinaris, "Carmina" VII, lines 320 ff., in "Epistulae et Carmina," *Monumenta Germaniae Historia,* ser. A.A., vol. VIII. That Hunnish control reached to the North Sea see Priscus, "Fragmenta," *Fragmenta Historicorum*

Graecorum, IV, 90. For the possible connection between the Hunnish invasions and Anglo-Saxon migrations see Hodgkin, *The Hunnish and Vandal Invasions,* pp. 42 ff. On the vexing question of the extent of Hunnish control over Germany see H. Seeck, "Attila," *Pauly Wissowa Realencyclopaedie des Classischen Altertums,* col. 2242.

[17] For Attila's conquest of the Sorogi see Priscus, "Fragmenta," *Fragmenta Historicorum Graecorum,* IV, 72. For the Akatsiri, *ibid.,* p. 82; for the proposed campaign against Persia, *ibid.,* p. 90. For "Sugdak" and its relations to Attila's court see Kiessling, "Hunni," *Pauly Wissowa Realencyclopaedie des Classischen Altertums,* col. 2602.

[18] For the death of Bleda see Jordanis, *op. cit.,* sec. 181. For the date see Marcellinus Comes, "Chronicon," *Chronica Minora,* II, 81; Prosper Tiro, "Epitoma Chronicon," *Chronica Minora,* I, 480.

[19] The report of the Roman embassy is, of course, that of Priscus, now incorporated in the eighth fragment of his work.

[20] For the personal appearance of Attila see Jordanis, *op. cit.,* sec. 182; C. C. Mierow, *The Gothic History of Jordanes,* p. 102.

[21] For the court of Attila and contemporary Hunnish customs see Priscus, "Fragmenta," *Fragmenta Historicorum Graecorum,* IV, 79-85. For mourning customs see Jordanis, *op. cit.,* sec. 255. For the "sword of Mars," *ibid.,* sec. 183.

[22] For Constantius and Orestes see Priscus, "Fragmenta," *Fragmenta Historicorum Graecorum,* IV, 76; Hodgkin, *The Hunnish and Vandal Invasions,* p. 495.

[23] For the Hunnish invasion of the Eastern Empire in 441 and 442 see Priscus, "Fragmenta," *Fragmenta Historicorum Graecorum,* IV, 72; Prosper Tiro, "Epitoma Chronicon," *Chronica Minora,* I, 479. For the campaign of 447 see Marcellinus Comes, "Chronicon," *Chronica Minora,* II, 80; *Chronicon Paschale,* p. 583; "Chronica Gallia," *Chronica Minora,* I, 662. For the ignominious peace terms see Priscus, "Fragmenta," *Fragmenta Historicorum Graecorum,* IV, 74. For the stream of Hunnish ambassadors, *ibid.,* p. 75. For the stream of Hunnish ambassadors, *ibid.,* p. 75. For the plot to assassinate Attila, *ibid.,* p. 78. For the miscarriage of this plot, *ibid.,* p. 14. For the accession of Marcian and the firmer tone adopted towards the Huns, *ibid.,* p. 98.

[24] For Aetius' life as a hostage in the Hunnish court see Gregorius Turonensis, "Historia Francorum," 2, 8 in *Monumenta Germaniae Historia,* ser. S.E.M., vol. I. For the Hunnish aid to Aetius in 425 and 433 see Socrates, Scholasticus *Historia Ecclesiastica,* 7, 23; Prosper Tiro, "Epitoma Chronicon," *Chronica Minora,* I, 470; "Chronica Gallia," *Chronica Minora,* I, 660. For Hunnish aid against the Burgundi in 436, *ibid.,* p. 660; Prosper Tiro, "Epitoma Chronicon," *Chronica Minora,* I, 475. For Hunnish aid against the Visigoths in 437 and 439 see Sidonius Appolinaris, *op. cit.,* "Carmina," VII, 345 ff. For the correspondence between the Huns and Aetius and the fact that the Huns could speak Latin but not Greek see Priscus, "Fragmenta," *Fragmenta Historicorum Graecorum,* p. 86.

[25] For the dispute regarding the vases of Sirmium, *ibid.*, p. 84; for the affair of the Princess Honoria, *ibid.*, p. 98; Jordanis, *op. cit.*, sec. 223.

[26] For Attila's attempt to play the Romans and Visigoths off against one another, *ibid.*, sec. 185. For the number in the Hunnish army, *ibid.*, sec. 182. For the composition of this army see Sidonius Appolinaris, *op. cit.*, "Carmina," VII, 319 ff. That Attila captured town after town see Prosper Tiro, "Epitoma Chronicon," *Chronica Minora,* I, 481. For the capture of Metz see Gregorius Turonensis, *op. cit.*, 2, 6. For the siege and relief of Orleans see Jordanis, *op. cit.*, sec. 194; Gregorius Turonensis, *op. cit.*, 2, 7. For the battle of the Catalonian Fields see Jordanis, *op. cit.*, chaps. 39-41; Gregorius Turonensis, *op. cit.*, 2, 7.

[27] For Attila's compaign in Italy in 453 see Jordanis, *op. cit.*, chap. 42; Hydatius, "Chronica," *Chronica Minora,* II, 26; Prosper Tiro, "Epitoma Chronicon," *Chronica Minora,* I, 482. For the renewal of the demand for Honoria see Jordanis, *op. cit.*, sec. 223.

[28] For Attila's wedding feast and death, *ibid.*, sec. 254; Mierow, *The Gothic History of Jordanes,* p. 123. For the date see Prosper Tiro, "Epitoma Chronicon," *Chronica Minora,* I, 482.

[29] For the later legends regarding Attila see A. Thierry, *Histoire d'Attila et ses Successeurs.*

[30] For the struggles between Attila's sons and the downfall of the Hunnish Empire see Jordanis, *op. cit.*, secs. 259 to 263. For the settlement of Ernac in Lesser Scythia and Emnetzur and Ultsindur on the banks of the Danube, *ibid.*, sec. 266.

[31] For Dengesic's attempt to reconquer the Ostrogoths, *ibid.*, sec. 272. For his disastrous attempt to invade the East Roman Empire see Marcellinus Comes, "Chronicon," *Chronica Minora,* II, 90; *Chronicon Paschale,* p. 598; Priscus, "Fragmenta," *Fragmenta Historicorum Graecorum,* IV, fragments 36 and 38.

[32] For the Rouran see *Be Shï,* 98. For the identity of the Rouran and the (true) Avars see Chavannes, *Documents sur les Tou—Kiue Occidentaux,* p. 230. That the Rouran probably spoke Mongolian see Pelliot, *Haute Asie,* p. 12. For the Avar pressure upon the Sabirs see Priscus, "Fragmenta," *Fragmenta Historicorum Graecorum,* IV, 104. For the settlement of the Sabirs North of the Caucasus see Procopius, *De Bello Gotthico* 4, 11.

[33] For the Sabir pressure upon other Hunnish peoples see Priscus, "Fragmenta, "*Fragmenta Historicum,* IV, 104, and IV, 107. For the Kutrigurs and Utrigurs see Procopius, *De Bello Gotthico,* 4, 5. For an excellent survey of this period see Kiessling, "Hunni," *Pauly Wissowa Realencyclopaedia des Classischen Altertums,* col. 2603.

[34] For the defeat of the Bulgarians (i.e. Kutrigurs) by Theodoric see *Historia Miscella,* 16, 17; Ennodius, "Opera," *Monumenta Germaniae Historica,* ser. A.A., vol. VII, 203 ff. For Athalaric's account of the later victory see Cassiodorus, "Variae," *Monumenta Germaniae Historica,* ser. A.A., vol. XII, 8, 10.

[35] For the first mention of the Bulgarians in the East Roman Annals see

Joannes Antiochenus, "Fragmenta," *Fragmenta Historicorum Graecorum,* IV, 619. For the Bulgarian invasions of 499, 502, 530, and 535 see Marcellinus Comes, "Chronicon," *Chronica Minora,* II, 95-104. For the great invasion of 558-559 see Agathias, *Historiae,* 5, 11-25; Menander Protector, "Fragmenta," *Fragmenta Historicorum Graecorum,* III, 202-203; Procopius, *De Bello Gotthico,* 4, 18-19.

[36] For the rise of the Turks see the *Be Shï,* 99. For early classical references to the Turks see Menander Protector, "Fragmenta," *Fragmenta Historicorum Graecorum,* III, 10 (205) and 18 (225). For the coming of the Avars (or the false Avars) see Theophylactus Simocatta, *Historiate,* 7, 7-8; Menander Protector, "Fragmenta," *Fragmenta Historicorum Graecorum,* IV, 4, 5, 10, and 43.

Chapter Eighteen

The Huns in Persia and India

The principal Chinese sources are *Be Shï,* especially chap. 97; and *Nan Shï,* especially chap. 79. See also *Hou Han Shu,* chap. 119; *San Guo Jï,* chap. 30; *Dsin Shu,* chap. 97; *Tang Shu,* chap. 215; *Si Yu Gi,* chap. 4. The principal classical source is Procopius, *De Bello Persico.* See also Cosmas Indicopleustes, "Christiana Topographia," *Collectio Nova Patrum et Scriptorum Graecorum,* II, 105 ff.; Priscus, "Fragmenta," *Fragmenta Historicorum Graecorum,* IV; Menander Protector, "Fragmenta," *Fragmenta Historicorum Graecorum,* IV; Theophanes, *Chronographia;* Theophylactus Simocatta, *Historiae,* especially 7, 7.

For the Arabo-Persian authors, available to me only in translation, see especially Noldecke, *Geschichte der Perser und Araber zur Zeit der Sasaniden;* A. G. and E. Warner, *The Shahnama of Firdausi,* especially vol. VII, and E. Rehatsek, *The Rauzat-us-safa or Garden of Purity,* I, 2. Occasional reference is made to the Armenian chronicles available to me only in translations. See especially the Histories of Elisaeus Vartebed and Lazarus Phabetsi, both in V. Langlois, *Collection des Historiens Armeniens,* vol. II.

[1] For Kashgaria and Southern Turkistan from A.D. 150 to 400 see *Hou Han Shu,* 118; *San Guo Jï,* 30; *Dsin Shu,* 97.

[2] For Kashgaria from A.D. 150 to 175 see *Hou Han Shu,* 118, 6 ff.; for conditions after the fall of the Han dynasty see *San Guo Jï,* 30, 30-31. For the transitory Chinese reconquests of this region see *Dsin Shu,* 97, 7-8.

[3] For the embassies of the Da-yuan and Kanggü monarchs to China, *ibid.,* 97, 8. For the later divisions of the Kingdom of Kanggü see *Be Shï,* 97, 19 ff.

[4] For the Yuejï see *San Guo Jï,* 30, 31; *Dsin Shu,* 97, 8a; *Be Shï,* 97, 15. See also Cunningham, "Coins of the Later Indo-Scythians," *Numismatic Chronicle,* XIII (1893), 93 ff.; V. A. Smith, "History and Coinage of the Gupta Period," *Journal of the Royal Asiatic Society, Bengal Branch,* LXIII (1894), 177 ff.

[5] For the Sasanids see A. Christensen, "L'Empire des Sassanides," *Mem.*

Acad. Sci. de Danemark, 7th ser., I (1907), 1; Rawlinson, *The Seventh Oriental Monarchy . . . or the Sassanian Empire.* For Nestorianism see M. Labour, *Christianisme dans l'Empire Perse;* for Manicheanism see F. C. Burkitt, *The Religion of the Manichees.*

[6] For India under the Guptas see Grousset, *Histoire de l'Extreme Orient,* pp. 91 ff.; V. Smith, *Oxford History of India,* pp. 147 ff.; idem., *Early History of India,* pp. 279 ff.

[7] For the Chionites see Ammianus Marcellinus, *Rerum Gestarum,* 16, 9, 4.

[8] For the different form of the name Ephthalite see E. Drouin, "Memoires sur les Huns Ephthalites," *Museon,* XIV (1895), 75; A. Herrmann, "Die Hephthaliten und ihre Beziehungen zu China," *Asia Major,* 1925, p. 573.

[9] For the Hunas in Indian legend see J. J. Modi, "The Early History of the Huns and Their Inroads in India and Persia," *Journal of the Royal Asiatic Society, Bombay Branch,* XXIV (1914-1917), 580; Smith, "History and Coinage of the Gupta Period," *Journal of the Royal Asiatic Society, Bengal Branch,* LXIII (1894), 186.

[10] For the distinction in the classical authors between the Huns and the White Huns or Ephthalites see Procopius, *De Bello Persico,* I, 3.

[11] That the Hua received the name Ephthalites from their King see *Nan* Shï, 79, 11a; see also Theophanes, *Chronographia,* p. 270.

[12] That the language of the Ephthalites differed from that of the Rouran or Avars, and the Gaogü, see *Be Shï,* 97, 17b.

[13] For the story that the Ephthalites were related to the Yuejï, *ibid.,* 97, 17a; that they were a branch of the Turfanese, see *Nan Shï,* 79, 11a. For further remarks on the race and language of the Ephthalites see the Supplementary Notes.

[14] For polyandry among the Ephthalites see *Be Shï,* 97, 17b; *Nan Shï,* 79, 11b.

[15] That the Ephthalites were at first subject to the Avars see *Nan Shï,* 79, 11b. For the intermarriage of the Avars and Ephthalites see *Be Shï,* 97, 11b; *ibid.,* 98, 11b.

[16] That the Ephthalites secured control over Karashahr, Kucha, Kashgar, Khutan, etc., see *Nan Shï,* 79, 11b. For the conquest of Sogdia see *Be Shï,* 97, 17b. For the conquest of Bactria, *ibid.,* 97, 15b, though in this passage the Ephthalites are confused with the Avars. For the date of the Ephthalite conquest of Bactria see the Supplementary Notes.

[17] For the idarites in Pashawar, see *Be Shï,* 16a. That many of the Yüjï or Tochari stayed behind is evident from *Be Shï,* 97, 20b.

[18] With regard to the capital of the Ephthalites, E. Specht, "Etudes sur L'Asie Centrale," *Journal Asiatique,* 1883, p. 340; and Chavannes, *Documents Sur les Tou-Kine Occidentaux,* p. 224, make the capital at Badghis, near Herat, but Herrmann, "Die Hephthaliten und ihre Beziehungen zu China," *Asia Major,* 1925, p. 573, places it near Badakshan.

[19] That the Ephthalites numbered a hundred thousand see *Be Shï,* 97, 17b. For their nomadic habits, legal, and religious customs, *ibid.,* 97, 17b; *Nan Shï,* 79, 11b. According to Procopius, *De Bello Persico,* 1, 3, the Ephtha-

lites were not nomadic, but he probably confused the native Bactrians with their Ephthalite overlords. At a later time the Ephthalites were converted to Buddhism and settled down in cities. See Herrmann, "Die Hephthaliten und ihre Beziehungen zu China," *Asia Major,* 1925, p. 577.

[20] That the Ephthalites did not have a system of writing, see *Nan Shï,* 79, 11b. It would appear, however, that they later adopted a special script of their own. See A. V. LeCoq., "Kokturkisches aus Turfan," *Sitzungsberichte der Preussischen Akademie der Wissenschaft zu Berlin* (*Phil.-Hist. Classe*), 1909, p. 1049.

[21] For the character and exploits, real or imaginary, of Bahram, see Warner, *op. cit.,* VII, 1-152. For the Ephthalite invasion of Persia during Bahram's reign see Noldecke, *op. cit.,* pp. 98 ff.; Warner, *op. cit.,* VII, 84; Rehatsek, *op. cit.,* II, 357.

[22] For the wars between Yazdigird and the Ephthalites see Langlois, "The History of Elisaeus Vartebed," *Collection des Historiens Armeniens,* pp. 186 and 229; Langlois, "The History of Lazarus Phabetsi," *Collection des Historiens Armeniens,* p. 306.

[23] For Firuz's accession to the throne with Ephthalite aid see Noldecke, *op. cit.,* p. 115; Warner, *op. cit.,* VII, 157; Rehatsek, *op. cit.,* II, 363.

[24] For the marriage of the King of the Ephthalites to the daughter of Firuz see Priscus, "Fragmenta," *Fragmenta Historicorum Graecorum,* IV, Fragment 33.

[25] For Firuz's first campaign against the Ephthalites see Procopius, *De Bello Persico,* I, 1, 3; Noldecke, *op. cit.,* pp. 123-25; Rehatsek, *op. cit.,* II, 365.

[26] For Firuz's second campaign see Procopius, *De Bello Persico,* I, 1, 4; Noldecke, *op. cit.,* p. 125; Warner, *op. cit.,* VII, 164; *Rehatsek,* II, 367.

[27] That the Persians became tributary to the Ephthalites see Procopius, *De Bello Persico,* I, 4, 35; for Sufrai see Noldecke, *op. cit.,* p. 130; Warner, *op. cit.,* VII, 173; Rehatsek, *op. cit.,* II, 367.

[28] For Kubad's first flight to the Ephthalites see Noldecke, *op. cit.,* p. 133; Rehatsek, *op. cit.,* II, 368. For Kubad's second flight to the Ephthalites see Procopius, *De Bello Persico,* I, 6, 10; Noldecke, *op. cit.,* p. 144; Warner, *op. cit.,* VII, 198; Rehatsek, *op. cit.,* II, 371.

[29] For the tribute Kubad paid the Ephthalites and his pleas to the Roman Empire see Procopius, *De Bello Persico,* I, 7, 1. For the vow never to attack the Ephthalite domain see Warner, *op. cit.,* p. 198.

[30] For the later wars of Kubad against the "Huns" see Procopius, *De Bello Persico,* I, 8, 19.

[31] For the Ephthalite invasion of India see *Be Shï,* 97, 18b. Smith, *Early History of India,* p. 310, places this invasion in 465; Marquart, "Eranshahr," *Abhandlungen der koniglichen Gesellschaft der Wissenschaft zu Gottingen,* III (1903), places it in 480.

[32] For the Ephthalite appointment of a Governor (tegin) over Gandhara see *Be Shï,* 97, 18b; see also Chavannes, *Documents,* p. 225. Presumably, see Marquart, "Eranshahr," *Abhandlungen der koniglichen Gesellschaft der Wissenschaft zu Gottingen,* III (1903), 212, this Tegin was Toramana,

known from his coins, see Smith, "History and Coinage of the Gupta Period," *Journal of the Royal Asiatic Society, Bengal Branch,* LXIII (1894), 184 ff.; and his inscriptions, see J. F. Fleet, "Gupta Inscriptions," *Corpus Inscriptionum Indicarum,* vol. III, nos. 36, 37; Buhler, *Epigraphia Indica,* I, 239.

[33] For the early conflicts between Skandhagupta and the Ephthalites see Fleet, "Gupta Inscriptions," *Corpus Inscriptionum Indicarum,* vol. III, no. 13. For the later Ephthalite victories known only indirectly see Smith, *Early History of India,* pp. 310 ff. For Toramana's conquest of Northern and Central India about A.D. 500, *ibid.,* p. 316; K. B. Pathak, "New Light on the Gupta Era and Mihirakula," *Bhandarkar Commemorative Volume,* p. 217.

[34] For Mihirakula see Fleet, "Gupta Inscriptions," *Corpus Inscriptionum Indicarum,* vol. III, no. 37; for his coins see Cunningham, "The Ephthalites or White Huns," *Numismatic Chronicle,* XIII (1893), 280; Smith, "History and Coinage of the Gupta Period," *Journal of the Royal Asiatic Society, Bengal Branch,* LXIII (1894), 202.

[35] For Cosmas description of "Gollas," see McCrindle, "Christiana Topographia," *Publication of the Hakluyt Society,* 1897, p. 597. For Sung Yun's description see S. Beal, *Buddhist Records of the Western World,* I, xcix ff. In spite of difficulties in chronology the Mihirakula mentioned in *Si Yu Gi,* 4, 2 ff., must be identified with the Ephthalite monarch. It is the *Si Yu Gi* which states that Mihirakula's capital was Sakala.

[36] For the dating of Mihirakula see Pathak, "New Light on the Gupta Era and Mihirakula," *Bhandarkar Commemorative Volume,* pp. 215 ff. For the rebellion and overthrow of Mihirakula see Fleet, "Gupta Inscriptions," *Corpus Inscriptionum Indicarum,* vol. III, nos. 33, 34, 35; *Si Yu Gi,* 4, 26. For Mihirakula in Kashmir see *Si Yu Gi,* 4, 3-4; and S. Stein, *Kashmir Chronicle,* I, verses 289 ff.

[37] For the reign and exploits of Khusrau see Procopius, *De Bello Persico,* I, 21, 17 ff.; Noldecke, *op. cit.,* pp. 151 ff.; Warner, *op. cit.,* 22 ff.; Rehatsek, *op. cit.,* pp. 372 ff. For the rise of the Turks see *Be Shi,* 99; *Tang Shu,* 215a-b.

[38] For the slaying of the Turkish envoy by the Ephthalites and the resulting war see Warner, *op. cit.,* pp. 328 ff. For Khusrau's marriage to the Khan's daughter, *ibid.,* p. 345.

[39] "For the Sasanid-Turkish war against the Ephthalites see Menander Protector, "Fragmenta," *Fragmenta Historicorum Graecorum,* 210; Noldecke, *op. cit.,* p. 167. For the division of territory between the Persians and Turks, *ibid.,* p. 159. For the date of the downfall of the Ephthalites see Drouin, "Memoires sur les Huns Ephthalites," *Museon,* XIV (1895), 286, makes it A.D. 557; Chavannes, *Documents,* p. 226, makes it A.D. 563-567.

[40] For the later Ephthalites in Bactria see Drouin, "Memoires sur les Huns Ephthalites," *Museon,* XIV (1895), 287. For the Ephthalites in India and the absorption of the Ephthalite tribal groups in the Gujaras see Grousset, *Historie del' Extreme Orient,* p. 96; Smith, *Oxford History of India,* p. 173; and Smith, "The Gurjaras of Rajputana and Kanauj," *Journal of the Royal Asiatic Society,* 1909, pp. 53 ff.

SUPPLEMENTARY NOTES

Calendar and Chronology

In dealing with the First and Second Hunnish Empires in Mongolia, and with the Hunnish kingdoms in China, my principal sources have been the Chinese dynastic histories. For this reason I have followed the custom adopted by most European scholars who have used this material, and have retained in this portion of the book the Chinese year reckonings and the Chinese method of computing the chronology of their monarchs.

The Chinese calendar or year reckonings call for only scant attention. For though the Chinese historians made use of a lunar year (of 354 or 355 days) they compensated for the difference between the lunar and the solar year by inserting an additional month in their calendar every two or three years. For this reason the Chinese "years" correspond for all practical purposes with our European years.

The Chinese method of computing the chronology of their monarchs is peculiar in only one respect. According to Chinese ideas an emperor's reign is not completed until the end of the year in which he died. Hence his successor's reign technically commences only at the beginning of the following year, although in fact the new emperor rules from the date of the death of his predecessor. Thus, for example, the Emperor Ging-di died in 141 B.C., but by Chinese computation the reign of Wu-di, his successor, commenced in 140 B.C.

Romanization

A word should be said regarding the system of transliterating Chinese names employed in this book. As is well-known, there is wide divergence of scholars upon this point, and almost every authority who has written upon Central Asia, using Chinese sources, has adopted a different system.

In the first draft of the present manuscript I followed the so-called "Wade System" because of its widespread popularity and because many standard works on China (e.g. Giles, *Chinese Biographical Dictionary*) employed it. This system, however, is neither historically sound nor phonetically accurate. In addition it is applicable only to the Peking dialect, a dialect which differs radically from the old standard Chinese language.

For this reason, in the second draft of this manuscript, I made use of the modification of the Wade System devised by Karlgren in his *Romanization of Chinese*. In essential agreement with this system (apart from the treatment of certain vowel sounds) are the systems employed by Laufer, Mayer, Hirth, Parker (in his *Turko-Scythian Tribes*) and others. The most important feature of these systems as contrasted with that of Wade, is the restoration of K, TS, H, and S in front of I and Ü. This is in accord with "Historic Chinese" and with the "Standard Mandarin" of today.

In the third and present draft I decided after much consideration to introduce a few modifications in the Karlgren System. The most important of these modifications concerns the treatment of certain consonants. In place of Karlgren's K', T', P', and Ch', I have substituted the simple letters K, T, P, and Ch. In place of Karlgren's K, T, P, and Ch, I have substituted the letters G, D, B, and J.

Though this change may appear startling to some readers, it is in accord with a tendency which has been in evidence for some time. This same change is found in the so-called "Standard System" of transliteration devised by the Educational Association of China and employed in several well-known works, such as Darroch's *Chinese Grammar.* This change is also made by Ch. Gardner in his *Modern System for the Romanization of Chinese.* It is also of interest to observe that this same modification has been adopted by many German writers, e.g. the Wilhelm System used by Herrmann in his *Loulan,* and the Lessing System used by Rudenberg in his *Chinesisch-Deutsches Worterbuch.*

It should not be forgotten that a number of writers who have accepted the older K, T, P, Ch instead of G, D, B, and J have done so with a distinct note of regret. (See Mateer in his famous *Mandarin Lessons,* p. xxiii.) It is also significant that many books which have adopted the older system have been forced to add special notes on pronunciation: e.g. Gowen and Hall, *History of China,* p. xxix—"Pronounce K as G, P as B, T as D, etc."

In connection with this change I also use R in place of Karlgren's J. In this I am in agreement with Baller in his *Mandarin Primer,* and with the above-mentioned Standard and Gardner systems. In this regard see especially Gardner, *Modern System for the Romanization of Chinese,* p. 8.

The only other changes which I have made in the Karlgren System are those which affect a few vowels. In place of Karlgren's Ï, I have followed Laufer and substituted E after S, Ts, and Ds.

In certain cases I have substituted E for Ei (e.g. *Be* instead of *Bei*), IAI instead of IE (e.g. *Giai* instead of *Gie*), and IO instead of UE (e.g. *Lio* instead of *Lue*). In all of these cases I follow standard mandarin usage, instead of adopting the sounds heard only in Peking. See the rendition of these vowel sounds in the *Chinese National Phonetic Script,* and in Mathews, *Chinese-English-Dictionary.* Incidentally, anyone using this *Dictionary* will have no difficulty whatever in following the system of transliteration employed in the present work.

Disputed Points

In the manuscript of the present work as originally drafted, I attempted, in the notes, to correct some of the errors which had crept into some earlier works which dealt in whole or in part with the early empires of Central Asia. Mature consideration has convinced me that this portion could well be spared. In those cases, therefore, where the original authorities (chiefly the Chinese sources) give a clear and straightforward account of events I have contented myself with citing these, ignoring those passages in secondary works which seem to contradict some of my statements.

On certain matters, however, chiefly concerned with linguistic and ethnic affinities, on which the Chinese and other early sources are inadequate and confused, I have thought it advisable in the following notes to give a brief summary of the views of several modern scholars working in this field.

The Pre-History of Central Asia

As the archaeology of Central Asia is still in its infancy, it is only natural that there should be wide differences of opinion regarding the proper interpretation of the scanty material which has as yet come to light. As these problems are only of minor interest to the present undertaking, I have not thought it necessary to review all the interpretations which have been given these discoveries, but have cited only those views which strike me as best according with the ascertained facts.

The Racial and Linguistic Affinities of the Scythians

The description of the Scythians given by Hippocrates, *De Aeribus, Aquis Locis,* has led to the supposition by Neumann, *Die Hellenen im Skythenland,* and Peisker, *Die Alteren Beziehungen der Slaven zu Turko-Tartaren,* that the Scythians were Mongoloid in race. But in opposition to Hippocrates we find Ammianus Marcellinus, *Rerum Gestarum,* XXXI, 2, 21, describing the Alani, the most important of the Sarmatians, as "of great stature and beauty . . . their hair yellowish," in other words as typically Caucasoid. It is this contradiction more than anything else which had led to the idea that the Scythians and Sarmatians were of different stock.

Skeletal material, however, brought to light by archaeologists, show that Hippocrates was certainly wrong, at least as regards the vast majority of the Scythians. See Reche, *Skythen-Anthropologie;* Eickstedt, *Rassenkunde und Rassengeschichte der Menscheit,* p. 470; Ebert, *Sud-russland,* p. 88; Schrader, art. "Skythen," in his *Reallexikon des Indogermanischen Altertumskunde.*

Other archaeological evidence points in the same direction. Thus Hippocrates speaks of the hairlessness of the Scythians, and yet from the numerous portraits of Scythians on Greek vases we know that the Scythians had heavy, bushy beards. See Rostovstzeff, *Iranians,* frontispiece; Minns, *Scythians and Greeks,* pp. 159 and 200. Persian portraits of the Sakas, most of whom were included in the group we call Sarmatian, confirm the essential unity of the Scythians and Sarmatians at this early period. See Sarre and Herzfeld, *Iranische Felsreliefs,* pp. 53 ff.

The linguistic position of the Scythians and Sarmatians has also been the subject of much dispute. Several scholars have argued that the Scythians spoke a Turanian language (i.e., either Turkish or Mongolian). See especially Niebuhr, *Kleine Schriften,* I, 352 ff.; K. F. Neumann, *Die Volker des Suddlichen Russland,* p. 12. In modern times we find Peisker, *Die Alteren*

Beziehungen der Slaven zu Turko-Tartaren, and Treidler, "Die Skythen und ihre Nachbarvolker," *Archiv fur Anthropologie,* 1914, pp. 280 ff., assuming a similar position though these two give no philological arguments. The most important of the modern proponents of the Turanian theory is Minns, *Scythians and Greeks,* pp. 35 ff., but even he admits that the vast majority of the Scythians were Indo-Europeans (Iranians) and claims merely that the small governing group were of Ural-Altaic extraction. Laufer at one time (see "Die Sage von den Goldgrabenden Ameisen," *T'oung Pao,* 2nd ser., IX [1908], 429 ff.) thought the Scythians were Turanian, but later (see *The Language of the Yue-chi* and "The Early History of Felt," *American Anthropologist,* XXXII [1930], 1 ff.) became a strong proponent of the Iranian theory.

In recent years the Turanian theory has lost its popularity as Minns admits (see his chapter on the Scythians in the *Cambridge Ancient History,* III, 187 ff.) and the belief that they were Indo-Europeans is now the generally accepted position. There was for some time controversy as to which branch of the Indo-European family they belonged. A few enthusiasts claimed that they were Celts; see Soltau, *Zur Erklarung der Sprache der Skythen.* Others argued that they were Germans, e.g., Fressl in *Die Skytho-Saken, die Urvater der Germanen.* But these theories were never taken very seriously. Slightly more important was the claim that the Scythians were the ancestors of the Slavs; see Cuno, *Forschungen im Gebiete der Alten Volkerkunde—Die Skythen* and F. Schwarz, *Alexanders des Grossen Feldzuge in Turkestan.* The claim was admitted as possible by Spiegel, *Eranische Altertumskunde,* II, 342. But even this theory has now been universally abandoned.

As stated in the text, the opinion now prevalent among the vast majority of scholars is that the Scythians and the Sarmatians spoke an Iranian language. This theory, first put forward by Zeuss in *Die Deutschen und die Nachbarstamme,* pp. 275 ff.; and Mullenhoff, *Deutsche Altertumskunde,* vol. III, is accepted by Tomaschek, "Kritik der Altesten Nachrichten uber den Skythischen Norden," *Sitzungsberichte der Wiener Akademie der Wissenschaft* (*Phil.-Hist. Classe*); Marquart, *Untersuchungen zur Geschichte von Eran;* Rawlinson in his translation of Herodotus; Thomas, "Sakastana," *Journal of the Royal Asiatic Society,* 1906, p. 204; Gutschmid, *Kleine Schriften,* III, 421 ff.; Hirt, *Indogermanen,* p. 113; Feist, *Die Kultur der Indogermanen,* pp. 470 ff.; Kretschmer, "Scythae" and "Sarmatae," *Pauly Wissowa Realencyclopaedie des Classischen Altertums;* and Vasmer, *Untersuchungen uber die Altesten Wohnnsitze der Slaven,* pt. 1.

The Sarmatian Tribes

Herodotus, *Musae* (*Sive Historiae*) 4, 110-117, has much to say regarding the "Sauromatae" who lived just East of the Don. Later historians, especially those of the Roman period, speak of the "Sarmatae" as a group name for the tribes which came from the East and occupied the territory once controlled by the Scythians. Some authors, e.g. Rostovstzeff, *Iranians and Greeks,* p. 113, regard the two peoples as entirely different, but most authorities believe that the two names apply to the same people. *See* Kretschmer "Sarmatae," *Pauly Wissowa Realencyclopaedie des Classischen Altertums,* cols. 2542-2543.

The Massagetae are first known from Herodotus, *op. cit.,* 1, 201 ff. They are mentioned again, but casually, in later times by Strabo, *Rerum Geographicarum,* 11, 8, 6-7 and by Ptolemy, *Geographica,* 6, 10. It is rather curious that the Massagetae, who played such an important part in Persian history, are not mentioned in the Persian inscriptions. Herrmann, "Sakai," *Pauly Wissowa Realencyclopaedie des Classischen Altertums,* makes a good case for identifying the Massagetae with the Saka Tigrakhauda of these inscriptions. De Groot, *Die Westlande Chinas in der Vorchristlichen Zeit,* p. 15, tried to identify the Yentsai of the Chinese accounts with the Massagetae, but this is highly improbable.

For the Dahae and Parni, the latter the direct ancestors of the Parthians, see Strabo, *op. cit.,* 11, 9, 3, and 11, 8, 2; Ptolemy, *op. cit.,* 6, 10.

For the Aorsi, Alanorsi, and Alani, see Strabo, *op. cit.,* 11, 2, 1; Pliny, *Naturalis Historia,* 4, 80; Ptolemy, *op. cit.,* 3, 5 and 6, 14. It is almost certain that the Yentsai of Chinese sources (*see* the *Han Shu,* 96a, 17) are the same as the Aorsi. *See* Gutschmid, *Geschichte Irans und Seiner Nachbarlander von Alexander Dem Grossen bis zum Untergang des Arsaciden,* p. 69; Hirth, "Mr. Kingsmill and the Hiung-nu," *Journal of the American Oriental Society,* XXX (1909), 37. It is unquestionable that the Alana of the Chinese sources (see *Hou Han Shu* 118, 12) are the same as the classical Alani. The Chinese sources say that the Yentsai (Aorsi) later changed their name to Alana (Alani) while the classical sources speak of the Aorsi and the Alani as separate peoples (but Ptolemy's Alanorsi, seemingly a mixture of the two peoples.) It is probable that this contradiction is more real than imaginary, that the Alani and Aorsi were two tribes inside of the same general ethnic group, that the Aorsi at first achieved leadership in this group, but were later ousted from this position by the Alani. The Chinese gave the name of the leading tribe to the whole group. Ammianus Marcellinus, *op. cit.,* tells us that the Alani were descended from the Massagetae, but this must not be taken too literally, as both Strabo and Ptolemy mention the Massagetae and the Alani separately, but the two peoples were undoubtedly closely connected. For the later history of the Alani see chaps. XVII and XVIII of the present work. For the filiation of the Alani with the modern Ossetes see Vasmer, *op. cit.,* I, 27 ff.

The Sacae are frequently mentioned in the Persian inscriptions; see Weissbach, *Die Keilinschriften der Achemeniden,* pp. 79 ff.; and in the classical authors Herodotus, *op. cit.,* 7, 64; Arrian, *De Expeditione Alexandri,* 3, 8, 3; Strabo, *op. cit.,* 11, 8, 2; and Ptolemy, *op. cit.,* 6, 13. It is clear from these references that there were many different Saca tribes in various parts of Central Asia. (In fact, as Herodotus tells us, the word Saca was very general and corresponded to the Greek Scythian.) As noted above, Herrmann,

"Sakai," *Pauly Wissowa Realencyclopaedie des Classischen Altertums,* argues that the Saka Tigrakhauda of the Persian inscriptions were the Massagetae and lived just to the East of the Caspian. He further claims that the Saka Haumavarga were the Amurgian Sacae of the Greeks and lived in the Pamirs, and that the Sacae mentioned by Strabo as living to the northeast of the Jaxartes River (called Scythians by Arrian, *op. cit.,* 4, 4, and Curtius, *De Rebus Gestis Alexandri Magni,* 7, 9) were really another branch of the Saca family to which the name Sacaraucae should more properly be given. It is possible to fit in this theory, in part at least, with the notices of the Sacae preserved in the Chinese sources (*Han Shu,* 96a, 10; *idem.* 96b, 1.) See also Herrmann, "Sakai," and "Sacaraucae" *Pauly Wissowa Realencyclopaedie des Classischen Altertums;* Franke, "Beitrage aus Chinesischen Quellen zur Kenntniss der Turkvolker und Skythen," sup. to *Abhandlungen der koniglichen Preussischen Akadamie der Wissenschaft zu Berlin,* 1904, p. 54. In any case it is certain, judging from both the classical and Chinese sources, that the bulk of the population of Northeast Turkistan formed a part of the Saca peoples whatever their more specific tribal designation may have been. I cannot agree with Thomas, "Sakastana," *Journal of the Royal Asiatic Society,* 1906, pp. 181 ff., that one branch of the Sacae dwelt at this early period in the Hilmand basin. This skepticism is shared by Konow, *Corpus Inscriptionum Indicarum,* vol. II, part 1, p. 19.

For the Kanggü see the *Han Shu,* 96a, 15. The Kanggü constitute one of the most interesting problems in the ethnogeography of ancient times. Much confusion was caused by De Guignes, *Histoire Generale des Huns, des Turcs, et de Mongols,* I, 97, identifying the land of the Kanggü with Kipchak in Northwestern Turkistan. The Chinese texts show clearly that the Kanggü, when they first became definitely known to us (second century B.C.) were centered around what is now the region of Tashkand in the middle Jaxartes basin; the "Turcomaniacs" such as Hirth, "Nachworte zur Inschrift des Tonyukuk," p. 48 in Radloff, *Altturkische Inschriften der Mongolei,* consider the Kanggü were Turks largely because they made use of the supposedly Turkish title of Jihou or Jabgu, but as Laufer, *The Language of the Yue-Chi,* has shown, this argument is completely worthless. Another argument in favor of this (Turkish) view has been the confusion of the Kanggü with such well-known Turkish groups as the Kanggar and Kangli; see Schott, "Chinesische Nachrichten uber die Kanggar," *Abhandlungen der koniglichen Preussischen Akadamie der Wissenschaft zu Berlin,* 1844, pp. 154 ff.; Radloff, *Das Kudatku Bilik,* I, vii. But Marquart, "Uber das Volkstum der Kumanen" in "Ostturkische Dialekt Studien," *Abhandlungen der koniglichen Gesselschaft der Wissenschaft zu Gottingen,* II, 1914, 168, has shown very clearly that the Kanggü, the Kanggar, and the Kangli are three quite different peoples, that the last two groups were indeed Turks, but that the Kanggü were Iranians. It is impossible to identify the Kanggü, powerful though they were, with any of the tribal names mentioned by the classical authors. This is all the more extraordinary as Strabo and Ptolemy speak of conditions in Sogdia at a time when the Kanggü had already secured control over a large part of this region. Gutschmid, *Geschichte Irans und Seiner Nachbarlander von Alexander dem Grossen bis zum Untergang des Arsaciden,* p. 71, tries to identify the Kanggü with the Sacaraucae. See also Tarn, "Seleucid Parthian Studies," *Proceedings of the British Academy,* XVI (1930), 112: "The Kang-kiu were probably a mixed horde, the Sacaraucae being the largest element." This latter statement is quite possible, but it is more probable that the main body of the Sacaraucae are to be identified with the people called Sak (a) or Sak-wang by the Chinese. See Herrmann, "Sacaraucae," *Pauly Wissowa Realencyclopaedie des Classischen Altertums.* In any case the Kanggü must be closely associated with some branch of the Saca group. Incidentally, Tarn admits that the bulk of the Kanggü were Iranian, but suggests (I believe erroneously) that they may have had a Turkish governing class.

The Ancient History of Bactria

We have almost no exact information regarding the history of Bactria in Pre-Achaemenid times. Native Persian tradition (see the early parts of Firdausi's *Shah-Nama;* Warner, *The Shahnama of Firdausi,* vols. I-V) claims that at the beginning of history Bactria was the seat of a powerful empire with its capital at Balkh, and that one of its kings was Vishtaspa, the patron of Zoroaster. Modern scholars have differed radically in their acceptance of the reliability of this tradition. Some authorities are inclined to accept a goodly portion of this tradition; see Duncker, *Geschichte der Arier in der Alten Zeit,* p. 472; Dhalla, *Zoroastrian Civilization,* p. 21. Other authorities are more skeptical, but believe that the story of the Bactrian empire may be based upon the existence of an early Bactrian kingdom or principality. See especially Noldecke, *Aufsatze zur Persischen Geschichte,* p. 7; Meyer, "Bactria," *Encyclopaedia Britannica,* 11th ed., p. 180. Others would reject the native tradition entirely; see Lehmann-Haupt, "Wann Lebte Zarathustra," *Pavry Memorial Volume,* pp. 251 ff.; Hertel, "Die Zeit Zoroasters," *Indo-Iranischen Quellen und Forschungen.*

The problem of the old Bactrian empire is bound up with the problem of the date and place of Zoroaster, discussed hereafter. If Zoroaster be placed 900 B.C., or earlier, and in Eastern Iran, not only would we have to place some credence in the native Iranian tradition (confirmed to some extent by Diodorus Siculus, *Biblioteca Historica,* 2, 6; and Justin, *Epitoma Historicarum Philippicarum Pompei Trogi,* 1, 1) but we should also be led to believe with Geiger, *Civilization of the Eastern Iranians in Ancient Times,* that by a study of the Avesta we could reconstruct in outline the history of Bactria during this early period.

The Linguistic Affiliation of the Parthians

In the days when the Turanian myth was popular, several scholars grouped the Parthians with the Turanians, i.e., the Turkish speaking peoples. See

Vambery, *Das Turkenvolk*, p. 55; H. Rawlinson, *The Sixth Oriental Monarchy or . . . Parthia;* H. Rawlinson, *Bactria, the Story of a Forgotten Empire,* p. 55. This error persisted not unnaturally in Sykes, *History of Persia.* Modern scholarship has now swung completely away from this opinion, and believes that the Parthians, like the Sacae, were Iranians; see Tarn, "Parthia," *Cambridge Ancient History,* IX, 588; Justi, "Geschichte Irans," in Geiger and Kuhn, *Grundriss der Iranischen Philologie,* II, 481; Poussin, *L'Inde aux Temps des Mauryas et des Barbares,* p. 230; Huart, *La Perse Antique,* p. 128; Bevan, *The House of Seleucus,* I, 284.

Incidentally the word Parthian is subject to a certain amount of confusion. The province of Parthia is known and by this name from the times of Darius (see Weissbach, *op. cit.*) and the inhabitants of this province, a sedentary people, have the best claim to be considered the true Parthians. Rawlinson, *The Sixth Oriental Monarchy or . . . Parthia,* p. 15, confuses these true Parthians with the Arsacids, the founders of the so-called Parthian kingdom. The Arsacids were really Parni, nomadic inhabitants of Southwestern Turkistan, who did not arrive in the province of Parthia until the third century B.C. These Parni became known as Parthians because Parthia served as the center of their rule. See Bevan, *The House of Seleucus,* I, 284; Tarn, "Parthia," *Cambridge Ancient History,* IX, 577. Both the nomadic Parni and the true Parthians, however, were of Iranian speech so that the two elements probably united at an early date.

The Time and Place of Zoroaster

There is wide variety of opinion as to where Zoroastrianism originated. For a discussion of this problem, with bibliography, see Jackson, *Zoroaster, the Prophet of Ancient Iran,* pp. 182 ff. After careful consideration of the conflicting opinions I have come to the conclusion, suggested by Jackson, *op. cit.,* p. 205, that Zoroaster was probably born in Media (modern Azarbaijan) but that his ministry was mostly in Eastern Iran, which thus became the center from which Zoroastrianism later radiated. The East Iranian origin of Zoroastrianism is also accepted by Meyer, "Persia—Ancient History," *Encyclopaedia Britannica,* 11th ed., p. 205; Geiger, *op. cit.,* pp. 1 ff.; Geldner, "Awesta Literatur," Geiger-Kuhn *Grundriss der Iranischen Philologie,* II, 38; Huart, *La Perse Antique,* p. 208; Bartholomae, *Zarathustra,* p. 7; Christensen, "Sur les plus Anciennes Periodes du Zoroastrisme," *Acta Orientalia,* IV (1925), 85; Wesendonck, *Das Weltbild der Iranier.* Darmsteter, "Le Zend-Avesta," *Annales du Musee Guimet,* vols. XXI, XXII, XXIV (1892-93) III, XC, holds the curious view that Zoroaster himself was entirely Median but that New-Zoroastrianism and the Avesta as we now have it are East Iranian.

The date of Zoroaster offers an even more difficult problem. In fact, it is astonishing that in spite of the vast amount of work done in Iranian studies that there should still be so little agreement on this important subject. For a general survey of the literature on this field see Jackson, *op. cit.,* pp. 150 ff. For more recent works see the *Cambridge Ancient History,* IV, 616. In addition there are many books and monographs dealing with this problem which do not appear on either list. Among those who believe that Zoroaster lived 900 B.C. or even earlier are Meyer, "Persia—Ancient History," *Encyclopaedia Britannica,* p. 205; Kent, "The Name Ahura Mazda, "*Pavry Memorial Volume,* pp. 200 ff.; Tiele, *Die Religion bei der Iranischen Volkern,* p. 48; Gray and Cary, "The Reign of Darius," *Cambridge Ancient History,* IV, 207; Dhalla, *op. cit.,* p. 24; Bartholomae, *Zarathustra,* p. 8; Wesendonck, *op. cit.* Among those who place Zoroaster in the seventh or even in the sixth century B.C. are Jackson, *op. cit.,* p. 174; Huart, *La Perse Antique,* p. 208; Herzfeld, "The Traditional Date of Zoroaster," *Pavry Memorial Volume,* p. 136; Olmstead, "Ahura Mazda in Assyrian," *Pavry Commemorative Volume,* p. 370; Floigl, *Cyrus und Herodot,* p. 17; Lehmann-Haupt, "Wann Lebte Zarathustra," *Pavry Memorial Volume,* pp. 251 ff.; and Hertel, "Die Zeit Zoroasters," *Indo-Iranischen Quellen und Forschungen.*

Even among the latter group there is a difference of opinion regarding details. Jackson gives the date as 660-583 B.C., and therefore prior to the Achaemenid period, while others, e.g., Herzfeld and Lehmann-Haupt, bring Zoroaster down still further, i.e., to 570 B.C., and therefore a contemporary of the early Achaemenids. Most of the advocates of this theory identify Vishtaspa, mentioned in the Avesta as the patron of Zoroaster, with Vishtaspa (or Hystapes), the father of Darius, who is known to have served as the satrap of Parthia and Hyrcania.

The Identity of the Hiungnu and the Huns

The identity of the Huns of European history with the Hiungnu of the Chinese records, casually surmised by Visdelou in "Historie Abregee de la Tartarie," in d'Herbelot's *Biblioteque Orientale,* IV, 46 ff., was first definitely claimed by De Guignes, *Histoire Generale des Huns, des Turcs, et de Mongols.* Following De Guignes this doctrine was generally accepted by European scholars, e.g. Neumann, *Asiatische Studien,* p. 126; Gibbon, *Decline and Fall of the Roman Empire,* chap. XXVI.

Early in the nineteenth century some scholars rejected this identification, largely on the ground that the Hiungnu were probably Turkish in speech, while the Huns and their cousins, the Bulgars, were presumably Finnish in origin. See Klaproth, *Tableaux Historiques de l'Asie,* p. 11; Remusat, *Recherches sur les Langues Tartares,* p. 11; Ritter, *Die Erdkunde von Asien,* I, 243; Howorth, "Some Notes on the Huns," *Sixth Oriental Congress,* IV (1883), 452 ff. For a while this skepticism was shared by many European historians, e.g. Bury in his notes on Gibbon.

Later researches have shown that the European Huns, and their cousins, the Bulgars, though probably containing a large Finno-Ugrian element, also consisted at least in part of a large Turkish-speaking element. See Vambery, *Ursprung der Magyaren;* Gomboc, "Die Bulgarisch-turkische Lehnworter in der Ungarische Sprache," *Memoires de la Societe Finno-Ougrienne,* vol.

XXX (1912); and Feher, "Bulgarisch-ungarisch Beziehungen," *Keleti Szemle,* XIX (1921), 1 ff.

This fact, plus a closer study of the Chinese texts, has thoroughly convinced most modern scholars that De Guignes was right and that the Huns of Europe were in part, at least, descendants of the Hiungnu mentioned in the Chinese records.

A few scholars, wishing to be cautious, take the stand that the Hiungnu and the Huns were "probably" identical; see De Groot, *Die Hunnen der Vorchristlichen Zeit,* p. III; Krause, *Geschichte Ostasiens,* I, 304.

Most authorities, however, go further and believe that the Hiungnu-Hunnish identity has been definitely established. Among these are Hirth, "Uber Volga Hunnen und Hiung-nu," *Sitzungsberichte der Muncher Akademie der Wissenschaft* (*Phil.-Hist. Classe*), II (1899), 245 ff.; Nemeti, "The Historic Geographic Proofs of the Hiung-nu Hun Identity," *Asiatic Quarterly Review,* 1910, pp. 352 ff.; Barthold, "Zwolf Vorlesungen uber die Geschichte der Turken Mittelasiens," *Welt des Islams,* sups. to vols. XIV, XV, XVI (1932-34), 24; Ebert, *Sudrussland,* p. 375; Kiessling, "Hunni," *Pauly Wissowa Realencyclopaedie des Classischen Altertums;* Drouin, "Huns," *Grand Encyclopedie;* Oberhummer, *Die Turken und das Osmanische Reich,* p. 24; and Bowra, "The Chunni and the Hsiungnu," *Notes and Queries on Japan,* nos. 1 and 2.

The Turanian or Ural-Altaic Language Group

In the text I have followed the most common classification and assumed that there really was a Turanian or Ural-Altaic linguistic family. See Finck, *Die Sprachstamme des Erdkreises,* pp. 59 ff.; Schmidt, *Sprachfamilien und Sprachkreisen der Erde,* pp. 51 ff.; Winckler, *Der Uralaltaische Sprachstamm,* pp. 8 ff. It should be noted, however, that some scholars deny that any real affinity exists between the Finno-ugrian, the Turkish, the Mongolian, and the Tungus languages. See Deny, in Meillet and Cohen, *Les Langues du Monde,* pp. 185 ff.; Shirokogoroff, *Ethnological and Linguistic Aspects of the Ural-Altaic Hypothesis,* pp. 89 ff. For a discussion of this problem see Sauvageot, *Recherches sur la Vocabulaire des Langues Ouralo-Altaiques,* and Kotwicz, "Contribution aux Etudes Altaiques," in *Rocznik Orientalistyczny.* I agree with Sauvageot that the similarity in structure of the various languages in question is so great that they should certainly be placed together in a single linguistic group, and it seems probable that all of these languages are descended from a single ancestor and therefore constitute a single linguistic family.

The Language of the Hiungnu and Huns

In the nineteenth century a few scholars argued that the Hiungnu spoke a Finnish or Finno-Ugrian language. See St. Martin in his "Notes" for Le Beau's *Histoire du Bas Empire,* vols. II, III, and IV; Vïvien de St. Martin,

"Les Huns Ouraliens," *Nouvelles Annales des Voyages,* IV (1848), 257 ff.; and Ujfalvy, *Les Migrations des Peuples et Particulierement celles des Touraniens.*

This theory is now universally abandoned, all scholars being agreed that the Hiungnu spoke one or other of the Altaic languages, i.e., either Turkish, Mongolian, or Tungus. A few authorities have argued that the Hiungnu spoke a language which was not specifically Turkish, Mongolian, or Tungus, but was the common ancestor of these three languages. See Castren, *Ethnologische Vorlesungen,* p. 35; Krause, *Geschichte Ostasiens,* I, 313; and Gibert *Dictionnaire Historique de la Mandchourie,* p. 897.

Among those who believe the Hiungnu to be Mongols are Pallas, *Sammlung Historischen Nachrichten über die Mongolischen Volkerschaften;* Bergmann, *Normadische Streifereien unter den Kalmuken;* Howorth, "Some Notes on the Huns," *Sixth Oriental Congress,* IV (1883), 452 ff. For the view that the Hiungnu were Mongols mixed with Tungus cf. Shiratori, "Sur l'Origine des Hiong-nu" in *Journal Asiatique,* 1923, pp. 71 ff.; Gibert, *Dictionnaire Historique de la Mandchourie,* p. 897.

Among those who believe that the Hiungnu were Turks are Remusat, *Recherches sur les Langues Tartares;* Klaproth, "Sur l'Identite des Tou-kiue et les Hiongnu avec les Turcs," *Journal Asiatique,* 1825; Chavannes, *Memoires Historiques de Se-ma Ts'ien* 1, LXV; Franke, "Beitrage aus Chinesischen Quellen zur Kenntniss der Turkvolker und Skythen," sup. to *Abhandlungen der koniglichen Preussischen Akademie der Wissenschaft zu Berlin,* 1904; Radloff, *Das Kudatku Bilik,* pp. 1 ff.; Hirth, "Uber Volga Hunnen und Hiung-nu," *Sitzungsberichte der Muncher Akademie der Wissenschaft (Phil.-Hist. Classe),* II (1899), 249 ff.; Laufer, "Sino-Iranica," *Publication of the Field Museum,* 201 (1919), 194; Parker, "Turko-Scythian Tribes," in *China Review,* XX (1892), 1 ff.; de Groot, *Die Hunnen der Vorchristlichen Zeit,* p. 54; Pelliot, *Haute Asie,* p. 6; Krause, *Geschichte Ostasiens,* I, 305. In this connection it should be remembered that the Chinese sources all speak of the Dugüe (Turks) as being descendants of the Hiungnu. See the *Be Shï,* 99, 1a.

After many years of controversy it can now, I think, be taken for granted that the Hiungnu spoke a language closely related to Turkish. It is probable, however, that the Hiungnu spoke an early and very peculiar form of Turkish. In fact the Hiungnu might better be regarded as the uncles rather than as the fathers of the later Turks. In this connection the peculiar nature of the Chuvash language must be taken into account.

It has long been known that the Chuvash in Eastern Russia speak a language which is Turkish in character but differs radically from all other Turkish dialects. In the past it was customary to regard the Chuvash as a mixture of Finns, and to account for the peculiarity of their language by pointing to their Finnish origin together with the Turkish relationship. See Muller, *Der Ugrische Volksstamm,* p. 453; Vambery, *Das Turkenvolk,* p. 444. Recently, however, it has been shown that this theory cannot account for the linguistic facts, and it has been suggested that the Chuvash peoples can best be regarded as the direct descendants of the Huns who moved West and settled in Western Europe. See Barthold, "Der Heutige Stand und die Nachsten Aufgaben der Geschichtlichen Forschungen der Turkvolker," *Zeitschrift der Deutschen Morgenlandischen Gesellschaft,* 1929, p. 125; Poppe, "Turkisch-Tchuwasische Vergleichende Studien," *Islamica,* I, 409 ff. It should be noted, moreover, that the languages spoken by the later Bulgars and Khazars was closer to Chuvash-Hunnish than to classical Turkish. See Feher, "Bulgarisch-ungarische Beziehugen," *Keleti Szemle,* XIX (1921), 16 ff.; Gombocz, "Die Bulgarisch-turkischen Lehnworter in der Ungarischen Sprache," *Memoires de la Societe Finno-Ougrienne,* vol. XXX (1912).

Working on this assumption we should have to divide the early Altaic inhabitants of Mongolia not into two groups (Turkish and Mongolian) but into three, viz. Hunnish, Turkish, and Mongolian, of which the first two still survive, while Hunnish is practically extinct except for its persistence as an important element in the Chuvash language.

The Names of the Hunnish Rulers

As the native and correct names of the Hunnish rulers are still unknown to us, I have followed the advice of Hirth, "Nachworte zur Inschrift des Tonyukuk," p. 7 in Radloff, *Altturkische Inschriften der Mongolei,* and retained the names as recorded in the Chinese histories. Several attempts have been made to reconstruct the original names but with widely different results. Thus, for example, Parker, *Thousand Years of the Tartars,* p. 8, renders Touman by Deumann; de Groot, *Die Hunnen der Vorchristlichen Zeit,* p. 47, thinks it must have been Dorban; while Hirth, "Die Ahnentafel Attilas," *Bulletin de l'Academie Imperiale des Sciences de St. Petersbourg,* 1900, p. 230, believes the name to be associated with the Turkish word *Tumen* of "ten thousand."

For Touman's son we have the alternative readings of Maodun and Mete. From this Parker, *Thousand Years of the Tartars,* p. 7; and Hirth, "Die Ahnentafel Attilas," *Bulletin de l'Academie Imperiale des Sciences de St. Petersbourg,* 1900, p. 230, have reconstructed the word Baghdur. Franke, "Beitrage aus Chinesischen Quellen zur Kenntniss der Turkvolker und Skythen," sup. to *Abhandlungen der koniglichen Preussischen Akadamie der Wissenschaft zu Berlin,* 1904, p. 10, has Moduk; while de Groot, *Die Hunnen der Vorchristlichen Zeit,* p. 51, has Mortur.

The name of Maodun's son was Giyu, older pronunciation Kiyuk. De Groot, *Die Hunnen der Vorchristlichen Zeit,* p. 80, restores this name to Kior. Parker, *Thousand Years of the Tartars,* p. 18, thinks that the real name was Kayuk. The latter suggestion is more probable in view of the resemblance of this name to Kuyuk, the third ruler of the Mongol Empire.

The reconstruction of Hunnish names is complicated by two factors. One of them is that at the best of times the Chinese language is unsuited to the transcription of foreign names. The other is the fact that the pronunciation of the Chinese ideographs has changed so much in the course of centuries that we are uncertain what sounds the Celestials gave these characters two millenniums ago.

Modern scholarship has, indeed, succeeded in reconstructing the Chinese sounds as of the seventh century A.D.; see Maspero, "Le Dialect de Tch'ang-ngan sous les T'ang," *Bulletin de l'Ecole d'Extreme Orient,* 1910; and Karlgren, *Analytic Dictionary of Chinese.* From this we are able to secure some indication of the pronunciation in vogue in China under the still earlier Han dynasty. The initial difficulty, i.e. the unsuitability of Chinese for transcribing foreign names, remains. Thus, though we know that the initial syllable, Me, in Mete or Maodun, was pronounced Mok or Bok, the letter K may have stood for Hunnish k, gh, or r.

The Neighbors of the Hiungnu

As shown in the text, most of Eastern Mongolia and Western Manchuria was occupied in ancient times by the Dunghu or Eastern Hu, the ancestors of the Wuhuan, Sienbi, etc. See the *Hou Han Shu,* 120. There has been much dispute regarding the linguistic affinity of this people. Klaproth, *Tableaux Historiques de l'Asie,* p. 93, believed that they spoke a dialect of Korean. Many earlier writers refer to them as Tunguses, largely because of the similarity of name. See Franke, "Beitrage aus Chinesischen Quellen zur Kenntniss der Turkvolker und Skythen," sup. to *Abhandlungen der konig-lichen Preussischen Akadamie der Wissenschaft zu Berlin,* 1904, p. 7; Parker, *Thousand Years of the Tartars,* p. 83; Chavannes, "Voyageurs Chinois chez les Khitan et les Joutchen," *Journal Asiatique,* XI (1897), 389. Modern scholarship, however, has shown that they were certainly not Tung-uses and were probably Mongols. See Shiratori, "Uber die Sprache der Hiungnu und der Tunghu Stamme," *Bulletin de l'Academie Imperiale des Sciences de St. Petersbourg,* 1902, p. 7; Torii, "Populations Primitives de la Mongolie Orientale," *Journal of the College of Science of Tokyo University,* 1914, p. 19; Hsu, *China and Her Political Entity,* p. 11; Grousset, *Histoire d'Extreme Orient,* p. 219; Pelliot, "Notes sur les Tou-yu-houen," *T'oung Pao,* 1920, p. 326; Gibert, *Dictionnaire Historique de la Mandchourie,* p. 897. We have no definite information regarding the racial status of the Dunghu. It is probable, however, that they, like the Hiungnu, were a mixture of Alpine (or as Eickstedt, *Rassenkunde und Rassengeschichte der Menscheit,* p. 169, calls it, Turanid) with Mongoloid. It would appear that they also had a certain amount of proto-Nordic blood, as the second emperor of the Wei dynasty, of Sienbi origin, had a long yellow beard. (See Parker, *Thousand Years of the Tartars,* p. 103.)

The inhabitants of Eastern Manchuria and the surrounding regions were known collectively as the Dungi or Eastern Barbarians (see the *Hou Han Shu,* 115). In early times there were three principal groups of the Eastern Barbarians, the Ilu in the North, the Hueime or Fuyu in the center, and the Jaosien in the South. All authorities are agreed that the Ilu (or Sushen), the ancestors of the later Jurchen and Manchus, were Tunguses, and that the Jaosien were the ancestors of the Koreans. There is some doubt as to the linguistic status of the Fuyu. Torii, "Populations Prehistoriques de la Mandchourie Meridionale," *Journal of the College of Science of Tokyo University,* 1915, p. 56, believes that the Fuyu, like the Ilu, were Tungusic. Gibert, *Dictionnaire Historique de la Mandchourie,* p. 175, believes that they were a mixture of Tunguses and Mongols. We know little regarding their racial affinities, but it is probable that the bulk of them were Mongoloids, or what Eickstedt, *op. cit.,* p. 192, calls more specifically the Tungusid branch of the Mongoloid group.

Though the Dingling, who lived to the North and the West of the Hiungnu, are frequently mentioned in the early texts (e.g. *Han Shu,* 94a, 8; *ibid.,* 94a, 35, etc.), we know really very little about them. Their geographic position is stated more precisely in *San Guo Jï,* 30, 34a. In this passage a distinction is made between the Dingling who lived in Northeastern Turkistan and those who lived in Southern Siberia, but as Chavannes remarks in his translation of this passage in "Les Pays d'Occident d'Apres le Wei Lio" (*T'oung Pao,* 1905), this distinction was probably artificial and the two groups belonged to the same general stock. *Be Shï,* 98, 17a, tells us that the Dingling in the fifth century were given the name of Gaogü. *Tang Shu,* 217a, 1, tells us that the Gaogü became the renowned Uigurs in the seventh century.

Be Shï and *Tang Shu* both assure us that the later Gaogü and Uigur spoke Turkish, but in early times there was great confusion between the Gienkun (Kirgis) and Dingling (see *Tang Shu,* 217, 12) and it is possible that some at least of the Dingling originally spoke an Indo-European language.

For the Gienkun or Kirgis see the *Han Shu,* 94a, 8 and 94b, 5b. For their geographic position see the *San Guo Jï,* 30, 34a. The first mention of the blondness of the Kirgis is in *Tang Shu,* 217b, 12. For a discussion of this problem see Schott, "Uber the Achten Kirgisen," *Abhandlungen der koniglichen Preussischen Akademie der Wissenschaft zu Berlin,* 1864, pp. 429 ff. Race and language are two quite different matters, but Barthold, "Der Heutige Stand und die Nachsten Aufgaben der Geschichtlichen Forschungen der Turkvolker," *Zeitschrift der Deutschen Morgenlandischen Gesellschaft,* 1929, p. 126, argues that because the Kirghis were obviously Nordics it is probable that they originally spoke an Indo-European language and in this case it is quite possible that he is right.

For the Hugie see the *Han Shu,* 94a, 11 and 94b, 1b. In later times the Hugie seemingly coalesced with the Dingling to form the Gaogü (later Uigur). See *Be Shï,* 98, 17a, where the Hugie (here called the Hugu) form one branch of the Gaogü, who are also specifically identified with the Dingling.

For the Wusun see the *Han Shu,* 61, 4, and 96b, 1. It was formerly the consensus of opinion that the Wusun were Turkish (see Shiratori, "Uber den Wusun Stamm in Central Asien," *Keleti Szemle,* III [1902], 103 ff.); Franke, "Beitrage aus Chinesischen Quellen zur Kenntniss der Turkvolker und Skythen," sup. to *Abhandlungen der koniglichen Preussischen Aka-*

demie der Wissenschaft zu Berlin, 1904, p. 20. There were, however, always some who believed that the Wusun were Indo-Europeans; see Klaproth, *Tableaux Historiques de l'Asie,* p. 163; Ritter, *Die Erdkunde von Asien.* In recent years the belief in the Indo-European character of this people has been greatly strengthened. See Krause, *Geschichte Ostasiens,* I, 290; Charpentier, "Die Ethnographische Stellung der Tocharer," *Zeitschrift der Deutschen Morgenlandischen Gesellschaft,* LXXI (1917), 347 ff. Though Caucasoid race is not necessarily a proof of Indo-European linguistic connections, it is of interest to note that Yen Shi-gu's commentary on *Han Shu,* 96b, 1, states that the Wusun had "green eyes" and "red hair," terms which are usually applied by the Chinese to Europeans. Inside of the Indo-European family it is probable that the Wusun were more especially connected with the Iranians; see Charpentier, "Die Ethnographische Stellung der Tocharer," *Zeitschrift der Deutschen Morgenlandischen Gesellschaft,* LXXI (1917), 347 ff.

For the Yueji see the *Han Shu,* 61, 1 ff. and 96a, 14 ff. The linguistic position of the Yueji has been the cause of much discussion. Skrine and Ross, *The Heart of Asia,* p. 15; and Visdelou, "Histoire Abregee de la Tartarie," in d'Herbelot, *Biblioteque Orientale,* IV, 40, make the Yueji Tunguses, but this is clearly an error. Other scholars have argued that they were Tibetans, e.g. V. de St. Martin, "Memoire sur les Huns Blancs," *Nouvelles Annales des Voyages,* III (1849) 257; Gutschmid, *Geschichte Irans und Seiner Nachbarlander von Alexander dem Grossen bis zum Untergang des Arsaciden,* p. 59; Minns, *Scythians and Greeks,* p. 110. Other scholars believed the Yueji to be Turks, e.g. Kennedy, "The Secret of Kanishka," *Journal of the Royal Asiatic Society,* 1912, p. 665; Bhandarkar, *A Peep into the Early History of India,* p. 29; Hirth, "Nachworte zur Inschrift des Tonyukuk," p. 48 in Radloff *Altturkische Inschriften der Mongolei.* Today, however, practically all scholars are convinced that the Yueji spoke an Indo-European language. See Poussin, *L'Inde aux Temps des Mauryas et des Barbares,* p. 307. But there still remains a difference of opinion as regards details. Some maintain that the Yueji spoke the so-called Tocharian language, e.g. Le Coq, *Auf Hellas Spuren in Ost-Turkestan,* p. 5; Charpentier, "Die Ethnographische Stellung der Tocharer," *Zeitschrift der Deutschen Morgenlandischen Gesellschaft,* LXII (1917), 347 ff.; Sieg and Siegling, "Tokharisch," *Sitzungsberichte der Preussischen Akademie der Wissschaft zu Berlin (Phil.-Hist. Classe),* 1908, pp. 915 ff., etc. Other scholars with even more reason maintain that the Yueji spoke a Saka or East Iranian dialect; e.g., Stael-Holstein, "Tokharisch und die Sprache II," *Bulletin de l'Academie Imperiale des Sciences de St. Petersbourg,* 1908, pp. 1369 ff.; Laufer, *The Language of the Yue-chi;* Konow, "On the Nationality of the Kushanas," *Zeitschrift der Deutschen Morgenlandischen Gesellschaft,* LXVIII (1914), 85 ff.; idem., *Corpus Inscriptionum Indicarum,* II, LII ff.

For the racial characteristics of the Yueji we have very scanty information. The commentary on the *Shï Gi,* 123, 4, states that the Yueji were pink and white in color, which indicates that they were Caucasoids. The *Shï Gi,* 123,

13; and the *Hun Shu,* 96a, 18b, state that all the people living in Turkistan had deep set eyes and were very hairy. As the Yueji were living in Turkistan at this time they must be included in this description. The only other sources of information are the coins of the later Yueji or Kushan monarchs; see Gardner, *Coins of the Greek and Scythic Kings of India.* From these coins Kennedy, "The Secret of Kanishka," *Journal of the Royal Asiatic Society,* 1912, p. 670, believes that the Yueji were "Turkish" in appearance, but to most observers the faces on these coins are strikingly Caucasoid; see Konow, *Corpus Inscriptionum Indicarum,* II, L; Poussin, *L'Inde aux Temps des Mauryas et des Barbares,* p. 303; Grousset, *Histoire d'Extreme Orient,* p. 61. On the walls of the ruined palaces and temples in and near Turfan frescoes have been found portraying blue-eyed, fair-skinned men, obviously "European" in appearance. Le Coq, *Auf Hellas Spuren in Ost-Turkestan,* p. 5, believes that the persons represented on these walls were of the same stock as the Yueji (i.e., that both the Yueji and the later Turfanese were "Tocharians,") but as we shall later see there is no good ground to identify the Yueji with the ancient inhabitants of Turfan, though of course it is quite possible that both groups belonged to the same racial stock.

For the early inhabitants of Kashgaria see *Han Shu,* 96a-b. For various views regarding the linguistic affiliations of the inhabitants of this region see Le Coq, *op. cit.;* and especially Grousset, *Histoire d'Extreme Orient,* pp. 212 ff., and the authorities there quoted. Thomas, "The Language of Ancient Khotan," *Asia Major,* II (1925), 251 ff., maintains that the original language of Khutan and the surrounding regions was a form of Proto-Tibetan, and that the Iranian language which is known to have prevailed there in the early Middle Ages was a later importation. With Konow, *Corpus Inscriptionum Indicarum* II, LXXIII, I can not accept this view. The Indo-European language which prevailed over the greater part of Kashgaria was called "North Aryan" by Leumann, *Zur Nordarischen Sprachen und Literatur,* as he believed that this language, though definitely Indo-Iranian, could not be more closely classified. Later scholars, however, are agreed that this language is to be associated more closely with the Iranian group and call it East Iranian. *See* Pelliot in *Memoires de la Societe Linguistique,* XIII (1913), 89. More recently several authorities while admitting the East Iranian character of this language prefer to call it more specifically the Saka language. See Luders, "Die Sakas und die Nordarische Sprache," *Sitzungsberichte der Preussischen Akademie der Wissenschaft zu Berlin* (*Phil.-Hist. Classe*), 1913, pp. 406 ff.; Konow, *Saka Studies.* For the so-called Tocharian language (personally I think this name is a misnomer) or the language which was current in Northeast Kashgaria from Kucha to Turfan, see Sieg and Siegling, *Tocharische Sprachreste* for Tocharian A; Levi, "Le Tokharien B, Langue de Koutscha," *Journal Asiatique,* 1913, p. 311; and Levi, "Le Tokharien," *Journal Asiatique,* 1933, pp. 1 ff. for Tocharian B.

The early dynastic histories of China do not describe the racial characteristics of the inhabitants of Kashgaria, but the *Be Shï,* 97, 4a, says that all the Kashgarians, except the inhabitants of Khutan, had deep set eyes and high noses, which makes us believe that the inhabitants of this region were predominately Caucasoid. See also Joyce, "Notes on the Physical Anthropology of Chinese Turkestan and the Pamirs," *Journal of the Anthropological Institute,* XXXXII (1912), 450 ff., for the skeletal material brought back from this region. From this material it appears that the majority of Kashgarians were Alpines, but from the above-mentioned frescoes at Turfan, it is obvious that portions of Kashgaria were also inhabited by peoples with a strong Nordic strain.

The Westward Movement of the Yuejï, Wusun, and Sacae

Owing to the great historic consequence of the westward migration of the Wusun, the Yuejï, and the Sacae, it is advisable to deal with this problem somewhat more in detail. The principal sources for these events are *Shï Gi,* 123; *Han Shu,* 61; and *Han Shu,* 96a-b. Although all of these chapters have long since been translated into one or other of the European languages, many of the secondary works which deal with these events give an inadequate, and in some cases a totally mistaken, account of what took place.

First a word as regards the date. Klaproth, *Tableaux Historiques de l'Asie,* p. 132, gives the date of Giyu's campaign against the Yuejï as 165 B.C., and many subsequent scholars have accepted this date as if it were gospel truth; see Smith, "The Kushan Period of Indian History," *Journal of the Royal Asiatic Society,* 1903, p. 19; Cordier, *Historie General de la China,* I, 165. As a matter of fact the Chinese records which deal with this event (*Shï Gi,* 123, 4; *Han Shu,* 61, 1 and 96a, 14b) give no exact date. All we know is that it took place some time in Giyu's reign (174-161 B.C.); see *Han Shu,* 96a, 14a. For some strange reason the monograph on the Hiungnu (*Shï Gi,* 110; *Han Shu,* 94a) does not even mention this campaign.

The date of the westward migration of the Wusun and their ousting of the Yuejï from Zungaria is a more difficult problem. *Han Shu* 61, 4b, definitely states that this event took place prior to the death of the Shanyu (i.e., Giyu; i.e., prior to 161 B.C.) and that the Yuejï then proceeded westward and invaded Bactria. From our knowledge of events in Bactria it is obvious that the Yuejï occupation of Bactria cannot have taken place until several years later. It is also difficult for us to believe that the Wusun were able to oust the Yuejï from Zungaria so soon after the latter had settled in this region. We are told that the Wusun accomplished this feat under the leadership of the Wusun king, a fully grown man, who had been an infant when his father had been killed in the earlier conflicts between the Wusun and the Yuejï, which certainly cannot have taken place earlier than 176 B.C. (as the defeated Wusun took refuge with the Hiungnu who did not secure control over the Wusun until after this date; see *Han Shu,* 94a, 11b). It is also important to note that in the passage in the *Shi Gi* corresponding to *Han Shu,* 61 (viz. *Shï Gi,* 123, 8) that the great migration of the Wusun did not take place until *after* the death of Giyu (i.e., not until after 161 B.C.—how long afterwards we do not know, but any date is perfectly possible down to

140 B.C.). I believe that the *Shï Gi* account is more accurate on this matter and that its chronology must be accepted.

As an instance of the mistakes which have crept into several secondary works which deal with the early history of the Yuejï (many of them otherwise of very high value) we may take for example Rapson, "The Scythian and Parthian Invaders," *Cambridge History of India,* I, 565. "In the country of the Ili river, now called Kulja, the Yueh-chi came upon a tribe called the Wu-sun. The Wu-sun were routed and their king slain, and the Yueh-chi continued their journey westwards towards the Issyk-kul lake. . . . Here they appear to have divided into two bands, the one afterwards known as the Little Yueh-chi going Southwards and settling on the borders of Tibet, the other, the Great Yueh-chi, continuing their movement to the West until they came into contact with a people whom the Chinese called the Sse (Sai) or Sek who are probably to be identified with the Çakas of the Jaxartes." Similar statement in Cordier, "Histoire Generale de la China," I, 226; Yule, and Cordier "Cathay and the Way Thither," p. 36, *Hakluyt Society Publications;* Charpentier, "Die Ethnographische Stellung der Tocharer," *Zeitschrift der Deutschen Morgenlandischen Gesellschaft,* LXXI (1917), 352; Smith, *The Early History of India,* p. 248. A study of the Chinese texts shows very clearly that the division of the Yuejï into the Great and Little Yuejï took place in Eastern Kashgaria prior to the great migration, and that the Little Yueji moved directly to the Southwest, settling among the Kiang or Tibetans without ever having passed through the Ili or Issikkul region (see *Shï Gi,* 123, 4; *Han Shu,* 96a, 15a). Even more important is the fact that the Wusun were not at first inhabitants of the Ili basin, but were immediate neighbors of the Yuejï in Eastern Kashgaria. See the *Han Shu,* 96b, 1b. The first war between the Yuejï and the Wusun, moreover, took place while both peoples were still located in this region; see the *Han Shu,* 61, 4a. When the Yuejï moving to the northwest first entered Zungaria (a region including both the Ili and Issikkul regions) their first contacts were with the Se or Sacae; see *Han Shu,* 96b, 1b. It was not until sometime afterward, as stated above, that the Wusun arrived in this region, and after defeating the Great Yuejï, forced the latter to migrate still further to the West. See the *Han Shu* 96b, 1b; and 61, 4b. This very clear series of facts is fatal to many of Charpentier's theses (as expounded in "Die Ethnographische Stellung der Tocharer," *Zeitschrift der Deutschen Morgenlandischen Gesellschaft,* LXXI (1917), 347 ff.), several of which are based upon the idea that the Wusun originally lived in the Ili basin, and were later driven to the West by the Yuejï. See especially p. 359 of this article.

Mention of the Se brings up several problems. In the old days a few scholars denied the identity of the Se of the Chinese with the Sacae of the classical authors. See Lassen, *Indische Altertumskunde,* II, 362. This was based largely upon an ignorance of the older pronunciation of the Chinese ideographs, as Se (also rendered Szu, Sï, and Sai) did not seem to resemble the word Saka. Students of Chinese, however, know that the older pronunciation of Se was Sak or Sok, and all modern authorities are agreed that the

Chinese Se are identical with the Sacae of the classical authors and the Sakas of the Persian inscriptions, or perhaps it would be better to say identical with some of the Saca peoples, as the term Saca was a general term for a great many different tribes inhabiting Northern Turkistan and the surrounding regions. See Franke, "Beitrage aus Chinesischen Quellen zur Kenntniss der Turkvolker und Skythen," sup. to *Abhandlungen der konig-lichen Preussischen Akademie der Wissenschaft zu Berlin,* 1904, p. 47.

In this connection it should be noted that the Chinese texts frequently speak of the Se-wang rather than Se. See *Han Shu,* 61, 4b, which states "after their defeat by the Hiungnu (they) went west and defeated the Se-wang." Se-wang literally means the Saca king or Saca Kings, but the use of the word "King" in this connection is so peculiar that several writers have suggested that the word "wang" is not to be taken literally, but as the transcription of a foreign word. Franke, in the above article, p. 47, suggests Sakong. For other ideas see De Groot, *Die Westlande Chinas,* p. 25; and Herrmann, "Sacaraucae," *Pauly Wissowa Realencyclopaedie des Classischen Altertums.*

More important still is what became of the Sacae after their expulsion from Zungaria by the Yuejï. In *Han Shu,* 96a, 10b, we are told that the Sacae (here called Se-jung) scattered about and settled in various states. Some became the masters of the small principalities of Hiusun and Guandu, which lay to the northwest of the city of Kashgar. The Se-wang moved far to the South and secured control over the Kingdom of Gibin in Northwest India. The Chinese records are completely silent regarding any movement of the Sacae to the west. The classical authors, however, tell us that among the barbarians who invaded Sogdia and Bactria from the northeast were Sacarauli (or Sacaraucae) (see Strabo, *Rerum Geographicarum,* 11, 8, 2), or the Saraucae mentioned by Trogus, "Prologi" 41 in Justin, *Epitoma Historicarum Philippicarum Pompei Trogi.* It is probable that these peoples were among those attacked and driven out of Zungaria by the Yuejï, indicating that there was a westward as well as a southward movement of the Sacae after the Yuejï migration. In fact, the events of later history would lead us to believe that the westward movement of the Sacas was more important than their movement to the South.

Before long, as we know from the Chinese texts (see the *Han Shu,* 96b, 1b), the Yuejï were forced by the Wusun to follow in the path of those Sacae tribesmen who went West, and eventually secured control over both Sogdia and Bactria. There is no name quite corresponding to the Yuejï in the classical authors, but it is almost certain that they are to be identified with the Asiani (Asii) and/or the Tocharoi mentioned by Strabo *op. cit.,* 11, 8, 2; and Trogus "Prologi" 41-42 in Justin, *Epitoma Historicarum Philippicarum Pompei Trogi.* The coming of the Yuejï to Sogdia and Bactria caused great commotion among the Sacae who had previously occupied this region. Some Saca groups seem to have stayed behind in Sogdia, where they became known to the Chinese as Kanggü (for the Kanggü see the *Han Shu,* 96a, 15, etc., though these texts ignore the relationship between the Kanggü and the earlier Se or Sacae), but many other Saca groups went still further to the West and Southwest, where they came into contact with the Parthian Empire. There Sacae must be the "Scythians" mentioned by Justin, *Epitoma Historicarum Philippicarum Pompei Trogi,* 41, 1, 2. This branch of the Sacae must have stayed in Eastern Iran, especially in the region which had formerly been known as Drangiana, since we find Isidore of Charax, who lived about the time of Augustus, referring to this region as Sakastana, or the country of the Sacae, in chap. XVIII of his "Mansiones Parthicae," *Geographi Graeci Minores,* vol. I.

In later times (first century B.C.) these Sacae, acting in conjunction with the Parthians, spread from Sakastana eastward into India, joining or dispossessing their cousins who had fled to this region directly after their expulsion from Zungaria.

The foregoing or a similar reconstruction of events is found in the works of a number of modern authors, including Berthelot, *L'Asie Ancienne, Centrale et Sudorientale d'apres Ptolemy,* pp. 84 ff.; Grousset, *Histoire d'Extreme Orient;* Herrmann, "Sacaraucae," *Pauly Wissowa Realencyclopaedie des Classischen Altertums* (though Herrmann believes that the Sacaraucae settled not in Sakastana but in southwestern Turkistan); Rawlinson, *The Sixth Oriental Monarchy . . . or Parthia,* pp. 117 ff.; MacDonald, "Hellenic Kingdoms of Syria, Bactria and Parthia" in *Cambridge History of India,* I, 459 ff.; Rapson, "The Scythian and Parthian Invaders," *Cambridge History of India,* I, 566 ff.; and Tarn, "Seleucid Parthian Studies," *Proceedings of the British Academy,* XVI (1930), 117 ff.

In this rather complicated field we find one or two scholars expressing rather aberrant opinions, especially as to the relationship of Sakastana to the whole Saca problem. Thomas, "Sakastana," *Journal of the Royal Asiatic Society,* 1906, 181 ff., claims that a group of Sacae were established in Drangiana at a very early time, such as the seventh century B.C., or even earlier, and that these Sacae remained in this area all during the Achaemenid and Hellenistic periods, although the name Sakastana was not given to this region until the revival of Saca power in the second century B.C. According to Thomas, this revival of Saca power had nothing to do with a fresh irruption of Sacae from Central Asia.

Very few scholars accept this theory in its entirety. Some admit the early Saca occupation of Sakastana, but insist that "there is good evidence that the earlier Scythian settlements in Iran were reinforced about the time the Cakas first occupied Bactria." (Rapson, "The Scythian and Parthian Invaders," *Cambridge History of India,* I, 567). A similar doctrine is expressed in Poussin, *L'Inde aux Temps des Mauryas et des Barbares,* p. 263. But Konow, "On the Sakas and Zoroastrianism," *Pavry Memorial Volume,* p. 220, flatly denies Thomas' theory and believes that the Sacae first entered Sakastana after being expelled from their homeland in Central Asia. I thoroughly agree with Konow in his rejection of Thomas' theory.

Herrmann (see his articles, "Sakai," "Sakastan," and "Sacaraucae," *Pauly Wissowa Realencyclopaedie des Classischen Altertums*) has a peculiar theory whereby he distinguishes between the Sacaraucae and the Sacae. According to him the Sacaraucae, equivalent to the Se-wang of the Chinese, lived in the Ili basin, were expelled by the Yuejï, and then fled not southward, as told in the Chinese texts, but westward and eventually settled in Southwestern Turkistan, just North of Parthia. The Sacae (Chinese Se) on the other hand, whom he identifies with the Saka Amurgioi of earlier times, lived in the Pamirs. It was they and not the Sacaraucae who were pushed South into India and founded the kingdom of Gibin. Later still some of these Sacae moved westward from India and founded Sakastana in Eastern Iran. Herrmann's theory is very interesting, and in spite of some difficulties with the Chinese texts (the latter tell us that it was the Se-Wang and not the Se who went southward; see the *Han Shu* 96b, 1b, and 96a, 10b) it is possible that there is a considerable basis of truth in many of his claims. At the same time it can not be accepted in toto, especially as regards the establishment of Sakastana. We have far more grounds for believing that Sakastana was founded by migrants from the North, who later moved eastward and invaded India.

Dahia and Tochari

It is necessary to say a word regarding the word Dahia. The phrase in the Chinese records (e.g. *Han Shu* 61, 4b) "The Yuejï moved westwards and made themselves masters of Dahia" has always caused much concern to commentators.

Owing to the similarities between the names Dahia and the peoples known as Dahae (see *supra*) several early scholars, including Remusat, *Nouveau Melanges Asiatiques,* I, 219; and St. Martin, "Memoire sur les Huns Blancs," *Nouvelles Annales des Voyages,* III (1849), 39, were inclined to identify Dahia with the land of the Dahae, in spite of the fact that the Dahae lived far to the West of the region conquered by the Yuejï. Gutschmid, *Geschichte Irans und Seiner Nachbarlander von Alexander dem Grossen bis zum Untergang des Arsaciden,* p. 62, pointed out that Dahia could only be identified with Bactria, and since his time the equivalence Dahia-Bactria has been universally accepted. Rapson, "The Scythian and Parthian Invaders," *Cambridge Ancient History,* I, 566, is the only modern scholar who continues to accept the equivalence Dahia-Dahae, and even he admits that Dahia is Bactria—"The native inhabitants of Bactria, the Ta-hia or Dahae."

So far so good, but this is only the beginning. Some of the later Chinese sources (e.g. *Be Shï,* 97, 16b) when speaking of Bactria call it Du-ho-lo, a close approximation of Tuhara, or Tochari. A large portion of Bactria was also known to the Arabic writers as Tukharistan. See Le Strange, *The Lands of the Eastern Caliphate,* p. 426. The Tukhara were also well known to Indian tradition. See Charpentier, "Die Ethnographische Stellung der Tocharer," *Zeitschrift der Deutschen Morgenlandischen Gesellschaft,* LXXI (1917), 371.

Some scholars have argued that the Tocharians were the ancient native inhabitants of Bactria settled there from time immemorial. See Lassen,

Indische Altertumskunde, I, 852; Ritter, *Die Erdkunde von Asien,* VII, 697; St. Martin, "Memoire sur les Huns Blancs," *Nouvelles Annales des Voyages,* 1849, III, 25. But this is incompatible with the statements of the classical authors, e.g. Strabo, *op. cit.,* 11, 8, 2, and Trogus, "Prologi," 41-42 in Justin, *op. cit.,* who tell us that Bactria was conquered from the Greeks by the Asii or Asiani and Tochari. Trogus adds the information that the Asiani were the kings of the Tochari. From this it seems evident that the Tocharians were among the nomadic peoples who invaded Bactria in the second century B.C. A statement in Pliny, *op. cit.,* 6, 17, 20, makes us believe that the Tocharians at one time dwelt much further to the East, a region which corresponds to Kashgaria.

For this reason a large number of scholars have come to the conclusion that the Tocharians are to be identified with the Yuejï. See Richthofen, *China,* I, 440; Muller and Sieg, "Maitrisimit und Tokharisch," *Sitzungsberichte der Preussischen Akademie der Wissenschaft zu Berlin* (*Phil.-Hist. Classe*), 1916, p. 395; Grousset, *Histoire d'Extreme Orient,* p. 59; Levi, "Notes sur Les Indo-Scythes," *Journal Asiatique,* 1897, pp. 10 ff.; Tarn, "Seleucid Parthian Studies," *Proceedings of the British Academy,* XVI (1930), 105 ff., "the bulk of the (Yuejï) horde was composed of Tochari; and the Arsi were the ruling clan"; and Stein, *Serindia,* p. 287.

In this connection a passage in the travel book of Hüan Tsang, the famous Chinese Buddhist pilgrim, is worthy of notice. In his *Si Yu Gi,* 12, 23, he tells us that he went (in A.D. 645) eastward from Khutan, and passed the kingdom of Duholo, Tukhara). He adds that this country has long been deserted, the towns being ruined and uninhabited. There seems no reason to doubt the authenticity of this passage, but it should be noted that Hüan Tsang points out no connection between the Duholo in Kashgaria and the Duholo he himself had visited in Bactria. It is also important to bear in mind that this placing of an ancient Tukhara in Kashgaria is found only in Hüan Tsang. The earlier Chinese dynastic histories give us detailed accounts of the city states of Kashgaria, but none of them mentioned a kingdom of Duholo in this region. (Tarn, "Seleucid Parthian Studies," *Proceedings of the British Academy,* XVI [1930], 106, is wrong in saying that the *Wei Shu* speaks of a Duholo in Kashgaria. The *Wei Shu,* copying from the *Be Shï,* knows only of a Duholo in Bactria.) For this reason we might be pardoned if we gave Hüan Tsang's notice only casual attention.

Several scholars, however, have taken Hüan Tsang's remarks seriously and have interpreted history accordingly. Richthofen, *op. cit.,* I, 440, believed that the Tochari first lived in Southern Kashgaria (Huan Tsang's Duholo) and then moved to the East, where they became known to the Chinese as Yuejï. Franke, "Beitrage aus Chinesischen Quellen zur Kenntniss der Turkvolker und Skythen," sup. to *Abhandlungen der koniglichen Preussischen Akademie der Wissenschaft zu Berlin,* 1904, pp. 29 ff., makes the Tochari and Yuejï to be originally two distinct peoples, the former in Southern, the latter in Eastern Kashgaria. When the Yuejï were defeated by the Huns, they passed through the land of the Tochari on their way to the Ili basin.

The Tochari were also dissatisfied with existing conditions because of dessication and Hunnish oppression and joined the Yuejï on their march westward. The two peoples gradually became one, probably during the short time they jointly occupied the Ili basin, etc.

A quite different explanation is given by Tarn, "Seleucid Parthian Studies," *Proceedings of the British Academy,* XVI (1930), 111. Tarn (who completely identifies the Yuejï and the Tochari), believes that the Duholo of Southern Kashgaria were the "Little Yuejï" who fled to the southwest.

Mention should also be made of the theory that the Tochari and the Yuejï were two quite different peoples and that the Tochari (who according to this theory originally lived in Duholo in Southern Kashgaria) preceded the Yuejï as conquerors of Bactria. It was the Tochari who drove the Greeks out of this region, but shortly after this event the Yuejï (identified with the Asii or Asiani of Strabo and Trogus) arrived on the scene and imposed their sovereignty upon the Tochari, who, however, continued to reside in Bactria. This theory, first suggested by Kingsmill, "The Intercourse of China with Eastern Turkestan," *Journal of the Royal Asiatic Society,* 1882, p. 74, was worked out in greater detail by Marquart, "Eranshahr," *Abhandlungen der koniglichen Gesselschaft der Wissenschaft zu Gottingen,* III (1903), 204 ff. It was accepted whole-heartedly by Herrmann, "Sacaraucae," *Pauly Wissowa Realencyclopaedie des Classischen Altertums,* col. 1617 (but seemingly denied in his later *Lou-lan, China, Indien, und Rom in Lichte der Ausgrabungen am Lobnor,* p. 33); and was accepted with modifications by Konow, *Corpus Inscriptionum Indicarum,* II, pp. XXII and LVII.

According to this theory the Dahia of the Chinese sources is merely an early abbreviated form of Duholo, and is identical with Tochari. The Tochari were a peaceful agricultural people originally settled in Southern Kashgaria (Hüan Tsang's Duholo) and are to be sharply distinguished from the Yuejï, who were a nomadic people. At some time or other (Marquart gives no date) the Dahia or Tochari moved by a southern route to Bactria. At a later time the Yuejï moved from Eastern Kashgaria to the Ili basin and then from the Ili basin to Bactria. Upon entering Bactria they conquered the Tocharian population. We are not told how the "peaceful Tocharians" managed to oust the Greek rulers of Bactria, who certainly possessed unusual military ability.

A further development of the Dahia-equals-Tochari myth is to be found in Franke, "Das Alte Ta-hia der Chinesen" in Hirth, *Festschrift,* pp. 117 ff. Although Franke formerly denied the Dahia-Tochari equation (see "Beitrage aus Chinesischen Quellen zur Kenntniss der Turkvolker und Skythen," sup. to *Abhandlungen der koniglichen Preussischen Akadamie der Wissenschaft zu Berlin,* 1904, p. 31) in this new work he accepts this theory and proceeds to develop the consequences much further. The early Chinese records speak of a Dahia on the immediate frontiers of China. Franke identifies this ancient Dahia with the Tochari of later history—"As early as the twelfth century B.C. the old Tochari lived in Northwestern Kansu and also in the southeastern portion of the Gobi desert." These Tochari eventually moved West and occupied Bactria. When Jang Kien visited Bactria he gave to the inhabitants the ancient name of Dahia.

More recently Haloun, *Ta-hia in den Chinesischen-Quellen vor 126* B.C., has done much to dispell the Dahia-Tochari myth. Haloun has shown that Dahia is "Great Hia," a name derived from the ancient Chinese Hia dynasty. In later times the name was applied to a land of fable which was sometimes placed in the North, sometimes in the South, and at other times in the West. In the end it came to mean any far off land, or "at the back of beyond." When Jang Kien came to Bactria, the most distant point in his journey, he gave the name Dahia to the region in memory of this fable.

Herzfeld, "Sakastan," *Archeologische Mitteilungen aus Iran,* p. 25, working from a different point of view, also shows that the Dahia-Tochari theory is impossible. The Greeks did not disappear from Bactria until after 140 B.C. In 128 B.C. the Yuejï are already in control of the country. It is impossible for two (Tochari then Yuejï) invasions to have taken place during this short space of time. Thus far I can agree with Herzfeld, but when he adds that the name Dahia is probably derived from "great yavana," I am somewhat skeptical.

To sum up the foregoing arguments: Dahia is certainly equivalent to Bactria. It is not certain for what reason the Chinese gave Bactria this name, but probably because of the old fabulous name for distant lands. In any case it had nothing to do with the name Tochari.

The Tochari are to be identified with the Yuejï. The Asiani were the ruling clan among the Tochari (Yuejï) though they are not specifically mentioned in the Chinese sources. But though the Tochari and the Yueji must be identical, it is important to remember that this does not mean that the Tochari-Yueji spoke the language which is frequently, and I believe quite erroneously, spoken of as Tocharian. The so-called Tocharian language is only known to us from the eighth century A.D. (a thousand years after the migration of the Yueji) from the northeastern part of Kashgaria, especially in the regions between Kucha and Turfan. We have no reason to suppose that the Yuejï ever occupied any portion of this region, nor that the inhabitants of these regions were associated with the Yuejï. In the Chinese dynastic histories we find that the natives of Kucha, Turfan, etc., were a city-dwelling agricultural people while the Yuejï were a nomadic people.

The so-called Tocharian language is now well-known to us. We know, on the other hand, very little about the Yuejï language, but as Laufer, *The Language of the Yue-chi,* has shown, the few words of the Yuejï language which have been preserved are clearly East Iranian in character and not "Tocharian." Konow, "On the Nationality of the Kushanas," *Zeitschrift der Deutschen Morgenlandischen Gesellschaft,* LX-VIII (1914), 85 ff., has also shown that the names of the Yuejï or Kushan monarchs and their titles are also East Iranian and not "Tocharian." In fact, we have as yet no evidence that "Tocharian" was ever spoken by any one in Bactria where we know that the true Tocharians lived.

The chief grounds for identifying the language of Turfan, the so-called

Tocharian, with the Tocharians, is a late Uigur colophon on one of the Turfanese manuscripts which states that this language is "Tuxri." To this must be added the fact that the Turfanese themselves seem to have called themselves or their language Arsi, supposed by some to be identical with the above-mentioned Asii or Asiani. But the similarity of proper names, alone, should not misguide us. The fact that there is a Kirman, often spelled German, in Southern Persia, is admittedly no proof that there was ever a Germanic colony in this region.

In view of the above facts we can only conclude that Muller, Sieg, and Siegling were, to say the least, a little hasty in giving the name Tocharian to the language spoken in the Kucha-Turfan region. It would be far better, in the present state of our information, to call the dialect spoken in Kucha (the so-called Tocharian B) by the name of Kuchani, and the dialect prevalent in Turfan (the so-called Tocharian A) by the name of Turfani.

Chinese Place Names in Turkistan

There is now general agreement about the identification of most regional names given in the Chinese records dealing with Central Asia, as may be seen by comparing the identifications given by Hirth, "The Story of Chang K'ien," *Journal of the American Oriental Society,* XXXVII (1917), 89 ff.; de Groot, *Die Westlande Chinas in der Vorchristlichen Zeit;* Chavannes, "Les Pays d'Occident d'apres le Heou Han Chou," *T'oung Pao,* 1907, pp. 210 ff.; Herrmann, *Die Alten Seidenstrassen zwischen China und Syrien,* etc. There are, however, several points of disagreement as regards details.

There is practically universal agreement that the Dayuan of the Chinese records corresponds to the modern Farghana. The only dissenting opinion is that of Herzfeld, "Sakastan," *Archeologische Mitteilungen aus Iran,* p. 23, who places Dayuan in the Pamirs, a little to the South of Farghana, but though Herzfeld is one of our most eminent Iranianists, he knows no Chinese, and none of his identifications of Chinese place names can be taken seriously. Weiger, *Textes Historiques,* p. 409, is certainly wrong in supposing that Dayuan was still ruled over by the Greeks at the time of Jang Kien's journey.

That Ansi is equivalent to Parthia has long been recognized. See De Guignes, *Historie Generale des Huns, des Turcs, et de Mongols,* I, 80, but the derivation of the word Ansi was long in dispute. Ritter, *Die Erdkunde von Asien,* VII 553, who corrupted the word into Asi, derived it from the Asii or Asiani. Gutschmid, *Geschichte Irans und Seiner Nachbarlander von Alexander dem Grossen bis zum Untergang des Arsaciden,* p. 66, derived it from Antiochia (i.e. Merv.). It was the erratic Kingsmill, in "The Intercourse of China with Eastern Turkestan," *Journal of the Royal Asiatic Society,* 1882, p. 8, who first hit upon the idea that Ansi (older pronunciation Ansak) was a transcription of Arsak. This explanation is now universally accepted. See Hirth, *China and the Roman Orient,* p. 139; and de Groot, *Die Hunnen der Vorchristlichen Zeit,* p. 231.

Regarding the exact identification of Yentsai there is a slight difference of opinion. Herzfeld, *op. cit.*, p. 23, identifies Yentsai with Khwarazmia, but this is certainly wrong. Marquart, *Untersuchungen zur Geschichte von Eran,* II, 240; de Groot, *Die Westlande Chinas in der Vorchristlichen Zeit,* p. 15, think that Yentsai corresponds with Massagetae, but this is more than doubtful. The most probable explanation of the term is that Yentsai corresponds to the classical Aorsi. See Gutschmid, *Geschichte Irans and Seiner Nachbarlander von Alexander dem Grossen bis zum Untergang des Arsaciden,* p. 69; Hirth, "Mr. Kingsmill and the Hiung-nu," *Journal of the American Oriental Society,* XXX (1909), 37.

The Kanggü, Wusun, Yuejï, and Dahia (Bactria) have already been discussed. We have also seen that these peoples were Caucasoid in race and Iranian in language. The same was also true of both the Yentsai (Aorsi) and the inhabitants of Dayuan. Hirth, indeed, in "The Story of Chang K'ien," *Journal of the American Oriental Society,* XXXVII (1917), 145, indicates that Dayuan was inhabited by a Turkish-speaking population, but Laufer, "Sino-Iranica," *Publication of the Field Museum,* 201 (1919), 211, has shown that this region was certainly Iranian.

From the statement in *Han Shu,* 96a, 18b that "from Dayuan westwards all the inhabitants have deep set eyes and are hairy," it is obvious that all the inhabitants of Turkistan at this period were predominately Caucasoid in race. The further statement (*op. cit.*) that all these peoples spoke dialects of the same language adds to our belief that they were Iranian in speech.

The Location of Gibin

For the Chinese account of Gibin see *Han Shu,* 96a, 10-12. There has been much dispute regarding the exact location of Gibin. Some scholars by identifying Gibin with the Kabul or Cophen River basin make this region identical with Kabulistan. See Weiger, *Textes Historiques,* p. 556; Charpentier, "Die Ethnographische Stellung der Tocharer," *Zeitschrift der Deutschen Morgenlandischen Gesellschaft,* LXXI (1917), 352; Gutschmid, *Geschichte Irans und Seiner Nachbarlander von Alexander dem Grossen bis zum Untergang des Arsaciden,* p. 60. This identification, though widely accepted, is certainly false because in the Han period the Kabul River basin is known by another name, viz. Gaofu. (See the *Hou Han Shu,* 118, 15b.) In view of this difficulty certain scholars have tried to put Gibin further to the South, i.e. in Arachosia or Southern Afghanistan. See Lassen, *Indische Altertumskunde,* II, 354, and Herzfeld, "Sakastan," *Archeologische Mitteilungen aus Iran.* A study of the Chinese texts giving the itinerary from Kashgaria to Gibin shows that this is impossible. Chavannes, *Documents sur les Tou-Kiue (Turcs) Occidentaux,* p. 336, states that whereas in later times Gibin equals Kapisa or the lower Kabul valley, in the Han period it is equivalent to Kashmir. This doctrine is accepted (somewhat grudgingly) by Smith, *The Early History of India,* p. 251, and Stein, *Ancient Khotan,* p. 53. Franke, "Beitrage aus Chinesischen Quellen zur Kenntniss der Turkvolker und Skythen," sup. to *Abhandlungen der koniglichen Preussischen Akadamie der Wissenschaft zu Berlin,* 1904, p. 59, comes to the conclusion that in Han times Gibin was a very general term, and included Kashmir, Gandhara, and at least a part of the Panjab. The same doctrine is presupposed by Herrmann, "Sakai," *Pauly Wissowa Realencyclopaedie des Classischen Altertums,* col. 1802. Not dissimilar is the doctrine held by De Groot, *Die Westlande Chinas in der Vorchristlichen Zeit,* p. 86. Ignoring Kashmir, de Groot claims that Gibin lay to the South of Chitral, Kafiristan, and Kabul, and must have included the town of Pashawar. To summarize, knowing the identification of Gibin with Kabul and Arachosia to be definitely wrong, we may best conclude that the kingdom of Gibin included most of the upper Indus basin.

The Date of Kanishka

As stated in the text, there are grave doubts as to the exact date of Kanishka's reign. Among the dates which have been suggested for his accession to the throne are 80 B.C.; 57 B.C.; 5 B.C.; A.D. 60; A.D. 78; A.D. 120; and A.D. 278

The theory that Kanishka lived B.C. is largely based upon the idea that he reigned not after but before Kujula and Vima, an idea held at one time by Fleet, Barnett, and Franke. This idea is now almost universally abandoned. On the other hand the date A.D. 278 seems impossibly late and has been advocated only by Bhandarkar.

We are therefore led to the conclusion that the commencement of Kanishka's reign must be placed somewhere between A.D. 60 and 125. According to one popular system of dating, followed by Fergusson, Duff, Foucher, Bachhofen, Kanishka ruled A.D. 78-110.

According to another system, followed by Smith, Konow, Marshall, Kanishka reigned from A.D. 120-162. I personally feel that this last suggestion is most in accord with all the known facts. (Incidentally, though agreeing with Konow's dating, his suggestion that Kanishka is to be identified with Gien, the petty ruler of Khutan, *circa* A.D. 150 [see the *Hou Han Shu,* 118, 9-10] is to be dismissed as ridiculous.)

For an excellent summary, with full bibliography of the various views expressed above, see Poussin, *L'Inde aux Temps des Mauryas et des Barbares,* pp. 343 ff.

The Date of the Ephthalite Invasion

As shown in the text, we know from the Chinese sources that the Ephthalites at one time dwelt in Zungaria, and then later invaded Turkistan and made their headquarters in Bactria. But though the Ephthalites thus shifted their headquarters they did not abandon Zungaria completely, as may be seen from the fact that shortly after A.D. 490 they twice inflicted decisive defeats upon the Gaogü, who then inhabited Northwestern Mongolia. See *Be Shï,* 98, 20.

It is impossible to say when the Ephthalite invasion of Bactria took place, since our principal sources give confused and contradictory statements. This is especially true of the Armenian and Arabo-Persian sources, which constantly confuse the Ephthalites with the Kushans, the Turks, and even with the Chinese.

Thus Tabari, as translated in Noldecke's *Geschichte der Perser und Araber zur Zeit der Sasaniden,* p. 98, speaking of the period *circa* A.D. 427, says that the "King of the Turks invaded Persia." Firdausi, translated in Warner, *The Shahnama of Firdausi,* VII, 84; and Mirkhuand, translated in Rehatsek, *The Rauzat-us-safa or Garden of Purity,* II, 357, in dealing of these events speak of the invaders as Chinese, Drouin, "Memoires sur les Huns Ephthalites," *Museon,* XIV (1895), 154, thinks that these "Turks" and "Chinese" were Ephthalites, which means that the Ephthalites were already in Bactria at this time. Marquart, "Eranshahr," *Abhandlungen der koniglichen Gesselschaft der Wissenschaft zu Gottingen,* II (1903), 52, thinks, on the other hand, that the invaders were Chionites, and that the Ephthalites did not arrive in this region until much later.

The Ephthalites in India made use of their coins of a special era. According to Pathak, "New Light on the Gupta Era and Mihirakula," *Bhandarkar Commemorative Volume,* p. 217, this era commenced in A.D. 448 and probably had reference to their occupation of Bactria. A Chinese source, *Tung Dien,* 193, 5, says that the Ephthalites went West during the reign of the Emperor Wen (A.D. 452-465) but it is uncertain how accurate this information is. *Be Shï,* 97, 17b, says that envoys to China from the Ephthalites (presumably from Bactria) began to arrive *circa* A.D. 460, but the Ephthalite kingdom may have been established there some time previously.

The wars between Yazdigird and the Ephthalites are known only from the Armenian sources. See the history of Elisaeus Vartebed in Langlois, *Collection des Historiens Armeniens,* II, 186 and 229; and that of Lazarus Phabetsi, *op. cit.,* II, 309. Both these chronicles speak of the wars between the Persians and the "Kushans." Drouin, "Memoires sur les Huns Ephthalites," *Museon,* XIV (1895), 158; Rawlinson, *The Seventh Oriental Monarchy . . . or the Sassanian Empire,* p. 304, think that these "Kushans" were really Ephthalites, but Marquart, "Eranshahr," *Abhandlungen der koniglichen Gesellschaft der Wissenschaft zu Gottingen,* III (1903), 52, argues that they were really Kushans led by King Kidara.

The Ephthalites are first mentioned by name in the Arabo-Persian sources with reference to the accession of Firuz *circa* A.D. 457. See Tabari in Noldecke, *op. cit.,* p. 115. Even so Marquart, "Eranshahr," *Abhandlungen der koniglichen Gesellschaft der Wissenschaft zu Gottingen,* III (1903), 57, refuses to believe the story and argues that the Ephthalites had not yet arrived upon the scene.

Priscus, "Fragmenta," 33, *Fragmenta Historicorum Graecorum,"* IV, tells us of the marriage to "Conchas, king of the Huns or Kidarites," with the daughter of Firuz. Drouin, "Memoires sur les Huns Ephthalites," *Museon,* XIV (1895), 234; Rawlinson, *"The Seventh Oriental Monarchy . . . or the*

Sassanian Empire, p. 316, think that Conchas was an Ephthalite monarch. Marquart, "Eranshahr," *Abhandlungen der koniglichen Gesellschaft der Wissenschaft zu Gottingen,* III (1903), 57, claims that the ruler in question was the king of the Kidarite Kushans.

Marquart, *op. cit.,* p. 58, believes that the first contact between the Persians and the true Ephthalites took place at the time of Firuz' first great campaign to the northeast *circa* A.D. 475, i.e. the campaign mentioned in Procopius, *De Bello Persico,* I, 3; and Tabari in Noldecke, *op. cit.,* pp. 123 ff.

BIBLIOGRAPHY

I. The Chinese Sources

A. *The Medieval Sources.* China is very rich in historical literature. Among the great historical works composed in the Middle Ages which deal in part with the early inhabitants of Central Asia, the following are worthy of special mention: a. The *Tung Dien* composed by Du Yu in the ninth century; b. *Wen Hien Tung Kao,* composed by Ma Duan-lin in the thirteenth century; c. The *Tu Shu Dsi Cheng,* the great Chinese encyclopedia compiled under the direction of the Emperor Kang Hi in the seventeenth century; d. The *Tung Gien Gang Mu,* compiled by Se-ma Guang in the eleventh century, and revised and edited by Ju Hi and his disciples in the twelfth century. (The full title of this book is *Dse Ji Tung Gien Gang Mu,* but it is universally cited as *Tung Gien Gang Mu.*)

Of these the most famous, the most important, and the most authoritative is the *Tung Gien Gang Mu,* or *Mirror of History.* Though this work is technically a secondary source in the sense that is was compiled centuries after the events described in the present undertaking took place, for all practical purposes it is a primary source since almost every word in it is culled from the earlier, more or less contemporary sources. As this work undoubtedly provides the best summary of events in the Far East during the periods of the Hunnish Empires, I have depended very largely upon it in writing the present work.

As the numerous editions of this work differ widely in their pagination I have thought it wiser to cite it according to the year in which the events took place. This method makes it easy to refer to all editions since the *Tung Gien Gang Mu* follows a strictly chronological order.

Those unable to refer to the original Chinese should consult L. Wieger, *Textes Historiques,* 2 vols., 2nd ed., Hien-hien, 1922. Though not so stated, most of the "texts" used in this work are selected from the *Tung Gien Gang Mu.* Father Wieger was a very great scholar, but his translations are occasionally careless. Moreover, he was not careful to state which passages are translated and which are merely paraphrased. The older "translation" by de Mailla is now completely antiquated.

B. *The Early Sources.* The material collected in the *Tung Gien Gang Mu* and other secondary works is sufficient for all ordinary purposes. For the benefit of scholars, however, I have also indicated the primary sources from which the *Tung Gien Gang Mu* account is compiled (unfortunately the *Tung Gien Gang Mu* itself neglects to perform this task) and also those sources which give additional information regarding the inhabitants of Central Asia which is of especial interest to students in this field. The most important of these primary sources are as follows:

1. *Early period.* For the early inhabitants of Mongolia, i.e., from the dawn

of history to 206 B.C., our principal source is the *Shï Gi,* or *Historic Rceords* compiled by Se-ma Tsien in the first century B.C. For this same period occasional reference has also been made to the so-called *Shï San Ging,* or *Thirteen Classics,* all of which claim to have been written prior to the third century B.C. Among these thirteen works see especially the *I Ging,* or *Book of Changes;* the *Shu Ging,* or *Book of History;* the *Shï Ging,* or *Book of Poetry;* the *Li Gi,* or *Book of Rites;* the *Meng-dse,* or *Book of Mencius;* and the *Dso Juan,* or *The Commentary of Dso.*

The *Shï Gi* has not yet been completely translated, but those unable to consult the original should refer to the following partial translations: E. Chavannes, *Memoires Historiques de Se-ma Ts'ien,* 5 vols., Paris, 1895-1905 (a masterly translation of *Shï Gi,* 1-47); J. J. M. de Groot, *Die Hunnen der Vorchristlichen Zeit,* Berlin, 1921 (includes a translation of *Shï Gi,* 110); J. J. M. de Groot, *Die Westlande Chinas in der Vorchristlichen Zeit,* Berlin, 1926 (includes a translation of *Shï Gi,* 123); F. Hirth, "The Story of Chang K'ien," *Journal of the American Oriental Society,* XXXVII (1917), 89 ff. (translation of *Shï Gi,* 123).

Many of the Thirteen Classics have been completely translated. See especially J. Legge, *The Chinese Classics,* 8 vols., Oxford, 1893-95 (contains a translation of *Shu Ging, Shï Ging, Meng-dse,* and *Dso Juan;* J. Legge, "The Yi King," SBE, vol. XVI (1882), Oxford (a translation of the *I Ging*); J. Legge, "The Li Ki," SBE, vols. XXVII-XXVIII (1885), Oxford (a translation of the *Li Gi*).

2. *The First Hunnish Empire.* For the rise and fall of the first Hunnish Empire our principal source is the *Han Shu,* or *Annals of the Early Han Dynasty,* compiled by Ban Gu in the first century A.D. The above-mentioned *Shï Gi* overlaps the *Han Shu* for the period 206-100 B.C. Those sections of the *Han Shu* which cover this period are, for the most part, copied word for word from the corresponding passages in the *Shï Gi.* But as the *Han Shu* version contains all of the information given in the *Shï Gi* and occasionally provides additional details, I have usually cited only the *Han Shu* account.

No attempt has yet been made to give a complete translation of the *Han Shu,* but those unable to refer to the original should consult the following partial translations: J. J. M. de Groot, *Die Hunnen der Vorchristlichen Zeit;* and *idem, Die Westlande Chinas in der Vorchristlichen Zeit* (the former includes a translation of *Han Shu,* 94a-b, and numerous other passages relating to the Huns; the latter includes a translation of *Han Shu,* 96a-b, and several other passages relating to Turkistan); E. H. Parker, "The Turko-Scythian Tribes," *China Review,* XX (1892-93), 1 ff. and 109 ff., and XXI (1894-95), 100 ff. and 129 ff. (Though Professor Parker does not take the trouble to mention this fact, this "article" is a translation of *Han Shu,* 94a-b). The older translations of Wylie and Pfizmaier are now completely antiquated.

3. *The Second Hunnish Empire.* For the rise and fall of the Second Hunnish Empire our principal source is the *Hou Han Shu,* or *Annals of the Later Han Dynasty,* compiled by Fan Ye in the fifth century A.D.

No attempt has yet been made to give a complete translation of the *Hou Han Shu,* but those unable to refer to the original text should consult the following partial translations: E. H. Parker, "Turko-Scythian Tribes—After Han Dynasty," *China Review,* XXI (1894-95), 253 ff. and 291 ff. (translation of the *Hou Han Shu,* 119); E. Chavannes, "Les Pays d'Occident d'apres le Heou Han Chou," *T'oung Pao,* 1907, p. 149 (translation of *Hou Han Shu,* 118, with valuable notes); *idem.,* "Trois Generaux Chinois de la Dynastie du Han," *T'oung Pao,* 1906, pp. 210 ff. (translation of *Hou Han Shu,* 77).

4. *The Hunnish Kingdoms in China.* The principal source for the rise and fall of the Hunnish Kingdoms in China is the *Dsin Shu,* or *Annals of the Dsin Dynasty,* compiled by Fang Hüan-ling in the seventh century. Certain additional information is to be found in the *San Guo Jï,* or *Annals of the Three Kingdoms,* compiled by Chen Shou in the third century A.D.; and in the *Wei Shu,* or *Annals of the Wei Dynasty,* compiled by Wei Shou in the sixth century A.D.

Almost no part of these important annals have as yet been translated into any European language. The chief exception to this statement is E. Chavannes, "Les Pays d'Occident d'apres le Wei Lio" *T'oung Pao* 1905, pp. 519 ff. (translation of a portion of the supplement to *San Guo Jï,* 30).

5. *The Huns in Europe, India, and Persia.* The principal sources for the Huns after their westward migration are the *Be Shï,* or *Annals of the Northern Dynasties,* compiled by Li Yen-shou in the seventh century A.D.; and the *Nan Shï,* or *Annals of the Southern Dynasties,* compiled by Li Yen-shou in the seventh century A.D. Certain additional information may be found in the *Si Yu Gi* or *Record of Western Lands,* compiled by Hüan Tsang in the seventh century A.D. For the end of the Huns and the rise of the Turks see also *Tang Shu,* or *Annals of the Tang Dynasty,* compiled by Ou-yang Siu and Sung Ki in the eleventh century A.D.

Almost no part of the above-mentioned annals have been translated into any European language. The chief exception is E. Specht, "Etudes sur l'Asie Centrale," *Journal Asiatique,* 1883, pp. 317 ff. which contains a few selections from *Be Shï,* 97, and *Nan Shï,* 79. For the *Si Yu Gi,* however, there are two translations: S. Julien, *Memoires sur les Contrees Occidentales,* 2 vols., Paris, 1852; and S. Beal, *Buddhist Records of the Western World,* 2 vols., London, 1906. Mention should also be made of *The Travels of Sung Yun,* composed in the sixth century A.D. As the original of this work is not available to me, I have made use of the following translations: Beal, *Buddhist Records of the Western World,* pp. 1 ff.; E. Chavannes, "Voyage de Song Yun dans l'Udyana et le Gandhara," *Bulletin de l'Ecole d'Extreme Orient,* 1903.

6. *Miscellaneous.* For a full understanding of the rise and fall of the various Hunnish groups, reference should be made to some of the other early inhabitants of Central Asia, especially the Dung I, or Eastern Barbarians (the ancestors of the later Tungusic peoples); the Wuhuan and Sienbi; the Kiang or Tibetans; and the Turks. References to these peoples are scattered through many of the above-mentioned annals. The following translations are also of

importance: E. H. Parker, "On Race Struggles in Corea," *Transactions of the Asiatic Society of Japan,* XVIII (1890), 157 ff. (contains selections from the *Han Shu, Hou Han Shu,* and *San Guo Jï* relative to the Dung I); *idem.,* "History of the Wu-Wan ... and the Sienpi," *China Review,* XX (1892-93), 71 ff. (contains selections from *Hou Han Shu* and *San Guo Jï* relative to the Wuhuan and Sienbi); A. Wylie, "History of the Western Keang," *Revue d'Extreme Orient,* I (1882), 424 ff. (a translation of the *Hou Han Shu,* 117); E. H. Parker, "Early Turks," *China Review,* vol. XXIV (1899-1901) (contains translation of various passages from the *Be Shï, Jou Shou,* etc., relative to the Eastern Turks); E. Chavannes, *Documents sur les Tou-Kiue* (*Turcs*) *Occidentaux,* St. Petersburg, 1903 (contains translation of various passages from the *Suei Shu, Tang Shu,* etc. relative to the Western Turks).

Citations from the Thirteen Classics are made according to the pagination of the Commercial Press Reprint, Shanghai, 1914. Citations from the *Shï Gi* are from the Ming edition of 1596. Citations from the *Han Shu, Hou Han Shu, San Guo Jï, Dsin Shu* and *Wei Shu* are from the Commercial Press Reprint, Shanghai, 1932-36. Citations from the *Be Shï* and the *Nan Shï* are from the Nanking Reprint, 1873. The various editions of the dynastic histories differ very slightly in their pagination, so that reference to one edition is easily traced in another.

It should be noted that each of the dynastic histories is divided into a number of Güan or "Chapters." These are cited by their respective numbers. For example, *Han Shu,* 4, means *Han Shu,* chapter four. A few of these chapters are divided into two or more parts. These are cited as a, b, and c; e.g., the first part of *Han Shu,* chapter 94, is cited as *Han Shu,* 94a, the second part as *Han Shu,* 94b, etc. As is well known, all Chinese "pages" are double pages. I have used the letters a and b to denote the right and left sides of these pages, respectively. Consequently, p. 10a means the right side of "page" 10; p. 10b the left side of "page" 10. In summary, then, *Han Shu,* 94a, 10b denotes the left side of page 10 of the first part of chapter 94 of the *Han Shu.*

II. The Classical Sources

Following customary though rather absurd usage among modern scholars, I have given Latin Names to the Greek authors and their works. In the case of these Greek authors, however, all of the texts cited are in Greek. In the case of several authors there are many excellent editions of the text, and equally excellent translations. To save space I have usually given only one of each.

Aelian. *De Natura Animalium,* ed. by Jacobs, 2 vols., Jena, 1832.

Aeschylus. *Prometheus Vinctus,* ed. by Blomfield, Cambridge, 1812. See also *Prometheus Bound,* trans. by J. Case, London, 1905.

Agathias. *Historiae,* ed. by Niebuhr, *Corpus Scriptorum Historiae Byzantinae,* Bonn, 1828.

Ammianus Marcellinus. *Rerum Gestarum,* ed. by Gardthausen, 2 vols., Leipzig, 1874-75. See also *The Roman History of Ammianus Marcellinus,* trans. by C. D. Yonge, *Bohn Classical Library,* London, 1894.

Appian. *Historia Romana,* ed. by Didot, Paris, 1877. See also *Appian's Roman History,* with an English translation by H. White, *Bohn Classical Library,* London, 1912.

Aristotle. *De Generatione Animalium,* translated into English by A. Platt, Oxford, 1910. See also *Aristotle's De Generatione Animalium,* ed. by Bekker, *Opera,* I, 715 ff., Berlin, 1831.

Arrian. *De Expeditione Alexandri,* ed. by Geier, Leipzig, 1851.

———. *Scripta Minora,* ed. by Hercher, Leipzig, 1854, (includes "Indica" and "Periplus Ponti Euxini." See also *Arrian,* with an English trans. by E. I. Robson, *Loeb Classical Library,* 2 vols., London, 1929-33.

Athenaeus. *Deipnosophistae,* ed. by Meinecke, 4 vols., Leipzig, 1858-67. See also *The Deipnosophists or Banquet of the Learned,* trans. by C. D. Yonge, *Bohn Classical Library,* 3 vols., London, 1854.

Cassiodorus. "Variae," ed. by Mommsen, *Monumenta Germaniae Historica,* AA, vol. XII, Berlin, 1894.

"Chronica Gallica," *Chronica Minora,* I, 615 ff. (In *Monumenta Germaniae Historica.*)

Chronicon Paschale, ed. by Dindorf, *Corpus Scriptorum Historiae Byzantinae,* Bonn, 1832.

Claudian. *Carmina,* ed. by Koch, Leipzig, 1893. See also (*The Poems of*) *Claudian,* with an English trans. by M. Platnauer, *Loeb Classical Library,* 2 vols., London, 1922.

Cosmas Indicopleustes. "Christiana Topographia," *Collectio Nova patrum et Scriptorum Graecorum,* II, 105 ff. See also the translation by MacCrindle, *Publications of the Hakluyt Society,* 1897.

Ctesias. *Operum Reliquiae,* ed. by Baehr, Frankfort, 1824. For a translation see Larcher, *Histoire d'Heredote,* VI, Paris, 1802.

Curtius. *De Rebus Gestis Alexandri Magni,* ed. by Tauchnitz, Leipzig, 1829.

Dexippus, etc. *Historiae,* ed. by Bekker and Niebuhr, *Corpus Scriptorum Historiae Byzantinae,* Bonn, 1829.

Dio Cassius. *Historia Romana,* ed. by Tauchnitz, Leipzig, 1818. See also *Dio's Roman History,* trans. by E. Cary, *Loeb Classical Library,* 3 vols., London, 1914.

Diodorus Siculus. *Biblioteca Historica,* ed. by Dindorf, 5 vols., Leipzig, 1828. See also the English translation by C. H. Oldfather of *Diodorus of Sicily's Library of History,* in *Loeb Classical Library,* 2 vols. to date, London, 1933-35.

Dionysius Periegetes. "Orbis Descriptio," *Geographi Graeci Minores,* II, 103 ff.

Ennodius. "Opera," ed. by Vogel, *Monumenta Germaniæ Historica,* ser. A.A., vol. VII, Berlin, 1885. See especially "Panegyricus dictus Theodorico," pp. 203 ff.

Eunapius. "Fragmenta," *Fragmenta Historicorum Græcorum,* IV, 7 ff.

Eutropius. *Breviarum Historiae Romanae,* ed. by Verheyk, Leyden, 1762.

Gregorius Turonensis (Gregory of Tours). "Historia Francorum," ed. by Arndt and Krusch, *Monumenta Germaniæ Historica,* ser. S.E.M., vol. I, Hanover, 1884. See also the translation of O. M. Dalton, *The History of the Franks by Gregory of Tours,* 2 vols., Oxford, 1927.

Herodian. *Historia* (*Ab Excessu divi Marci*), ed. by Bekker, Leipzig, 1855.

Herodotus. *Musae* (*sive Historiae*), ed. by Schweighauser, 6 vols., London, 1824. See also the English translation of A. D. Godley, *Herodotus,* in *Loeb Classical Library,* 4 vols., London, 1921-24.

Hippocrates. "De Aeribus, Aquis, Locis," and "De Morbis," Greek text English translation by W. H. S. Jones, *Hippocrates,* in *Loeb Classical Library,* 4 vols., London, 1923-31.

Historia Miscella, ed. by Eyssenhardt, Berlin, 1868.

Hydatius. "Chronica," *Chronica Minora,* II, 1 ff. (In *Monumenta Germaniae Historica.*)

Isidorus Characenus. "Mansiones Parthicae," *Geographi Graeci Minores,* I, 244 ff.

Isidorus Hispalensis. "Chronica," *Chronica Minora,* II, 391 ff. (In *Monumenta Germaniae Historica.*)

———. "Historia Gothorum, Vandalorum, Sueborum," *Chronica Minora,* II, 241 ff. (In *Monumenta Germaniae Historica.*)

Jerome. *Opera,* ed. by Benedict, 1693-1706.

Joannes Antiochenus. "Fragmenta," *Fragmenta Historicorum Graecorum,* IV, 535 ff.

Joannes Malalas. *Chronographia,* ed. by Dindorf, *Corpus Scriptorum Historiae Byzantinae,* Bonn, 1831.

Jordanis. "Getica (De Origine Actibus Getarum)" ed. by Mommsen, *Monumenta Germaniae Historica,* ser. A.A., vol. Va, Berlin, 1882. See also translation by C. C. Mierow, *The Gothic History of Jordanes,* Princeton, 1915.

Josephus. *Opera,* ed. by Tauchnitz, Leipzig, 1850. See also translation of W. Whiston, *The Works of Flacius Josephus,* London, no date.

Justin. *Epitoma Historicarum Philippicarum Pompei Trogi,* ed. by Ruhl, Leipzig, 1886. (This edition includes Trogus *Prologi.*) See also the English trans. of J. S. Watson, *Bohn Classical Library,* London, 1853.

Lucan. *De Bello Civili,* ed. by Hosius, Leipzig, 1905.

Lucian. *Opera,* ed. by Bekker, Leipzig, 1853. See also translation by Fowler, *Lucian,* Oxford, 1905.

Marcellinus Comes. "Chronicon," *Chronica Minora,* II, 37 ff. (In *Monumenta Germaniae Historica.*)

Menander Protector. "Fragmenta," *Fragmenta Historicorum Graecorum,* IV, 200 ff.

Orosius. *Historiae adversum Paganos,* etc., ed. by Zangemeister, Vienna, 1882. See also Eng. trans. by I. W. Raymond, *Seven Books of History Against the Pagans,* New York, 1936.

Ovid. *Ex Ponto,* etc., ed. by Owen, Oxford, 1915. See also the English translation of A. L. Wheeler, *Ovid's Tristia and Ex Ponto,* in *Loeb Classical Library,* London, 1924.

Pausanias. *Descriptio Graeciae,* ed. by Schubart and Walz, 3 vols., Leipzig, 1838-39. See also the English trans. by H. L. Jones, "Pausanias, Description of Greece," *Loeb Classical Library,* 5 vols., London, 1918-35.

Pliny. *Naturalis Historia,* ed. by L. Jan, 6 vols., Leipzig, 1906. See also the translation of J. Bostock and H. T. Riley, *The Natural History of Pliny,* 6 vols., London, 1855-57.

Plutarch. *Vitae Parallelae,* ed. by Sintenius, 4 vols., Leipzig, 1839-46. See also the English translation of B. Perrin, *Plutarch's Lives,* in *Loeb Classical Library,* 11 vols., London, 1922-27.

Polyaenus. *Strategematum,* ed. by Maasvicius, Leiden, 1691.

Polybius. *Historiae,* ed. by Hultsch, 4 vols., Berlin, 1867-72. See also the English trans. of W. R. Paton, *Polybius, The Histories,* in *Loeb Classical Library,* 6 vols., London, 1922-27.

Pomponius Mela. *De Situ Orbis,* ed. by Gronovius, Leiden, 1722.

Priscus. "Fragmenta," *Fragmenta Historicorum Græcorum,* IV, 69 ff.

Procopius. *Historiae,* ed. by Dindorf, *Corpus Scriptorum Historiae Byzantinæ,* 3 vols., Bonn, 1823. (Vol. I contains *De Bello Persico* and *De Bello Vandalico,* vol. III, *De Bello Gotthico.* See also the English trans. of H. B. Dewing, "Procopius," *Loeb Classical Library,* 6 vols., London, 1914-35.

Prosper Tiro. "Epitoma Chronicon," *Chronica Minora,* I, 340 ff. (In *Monumenta Germaniae Historica.*)

Ptolemy. *Geographia,* ed. by Wilberg and Grashof, 5 vols., Essen, 1838-45.

Scriptores Historiae Augustae, ed. by Peter, Leipzig, 1884. See also the English trans. of D. Magie, *The Scriptores Historiae Augustae,* in *Loeb Classical Library,* 3 vols., London, 1922-32.

Sidonius Appolinaris. "Epistulae et Carmina," ed. by Luetjohann, *Monumenta Germaniae Historica,* ser. A.A., vol. VIII, Berlin, 1887. See especially "Carmina," pp. 173 ff.

Socrates Scholasticus. *Historia Ecclesiastica,* ed. by R. Hussey, Oxford, 1853. See also the trans. of G. C. Zenos, "The Ecclesiastical History of Socrates," *Select Library of Nicene and Post-nicene Fathers,* 2nd ser., vol. II, New York, 1890.

Sozomen. *Historia Ecclesiastica,* ed. by R. Hussey, Oxford, 1860. See also the trans. of C. D. Hartranft, "The Ecclesiastical History of Sozomen," *Select Library of Nicene and Post-nicene Fathers,* 2nd ser., vol. II, New York, 1890.

Strabo. *Rerum Geographicarum,* ed. by Siebenkees, 7 vols., Leipzig, 1796-1818. See also the English trans. of H. L. Jones, *The Geography of Strabo, Loeb Classical Library,* 8 vols., London, 1917-1922.

Tacitus. *Opera,* ed., by Halm, 2 vols., Leipzig, 1901-02. (Vol. 1 contains *Annales;* vol. II, *Historiae* and *Germania.*) See also A. Murray, *Tacitus Historical Works,* 2 vols., London, 1926.

Theodoret. *Opera Omnia,* ed. by Sirmondi, 5 vols., 1769. See also "The Ecclesiastical History of Theodoret," trans. by B. Jackson, *Select Library of Nicene and Post-nicene Fathers,* 2nd ser., vol. III, New York, 1916.

Theophanes. *Chonographia,* ed. by Classen, *Corpus Scriptorum Historiae Byzantinae,* 2 vols., Bonn, 1839.

Theophylactus Simocatta. *Historiae,* ed. by Bekker, *Corpus Scriptorum Historiae Byzantinae,* Bonn, 1824.

Thucydides. *De Bello Peloponnesiaco,* ed. by Boehme, 2 vols., Leipzig, 1851. See also the translation of Jowett, *Thucydides,* 2 vols., London, 1881.

Zosimus. *Historiae,* ed. by Bekker, *Corpus Scriptorum Historiae Byzantinae,* Bonn, 1827.

III. Miscellaneous Primary Sources

The only Indian sources which are of value to us are the inscriptions. See *Corpus Inscriptonum Indicarum, especially* vol. II, pt. 1 (2nd ed.), *Kharosti Inscriptions,* ed. by S. Konow, and vol. III, *Gupta Inscriptions,* ed. by J. Fleet.

The old Persian sources are two in number. One consists of the Achaemenid Rock Inscriptions, the other of the Avesta. For the Inscriptions see Weissbach, *Der Keilinschriften der Achemeniden,* Leipzig, 1911 (text and translations). For the Avesta see Geldner, *Avesta,* Stuttgart, 1889-95. For translations see J. Darmsteter, "Le Zend Avesta," *Annales du Musee Guimet,* vols. XXI, XXII, XXIV (1892-93), Paris; C. Bartholomae, *Die Gathas Des Avesta,* Strassburg, 1905; F. Wolff, *Avesta, die Heiligen Bucher der Parsen,* Strassburg, 1920 (translation of all the Avesta except the Gathas).

For the medieval Arabic and Persian sources, available to me only in translation, see especially, Tabari, *Akhbar arrusul wal Muluk* (a translation of an important part of this work is found in Noldecke, *Geschichte der Perser und Araber zur Zeit der Sasaniden,* Leiden, 1879); Firdausi, *Shahnama* (see the translation of A. G. and E. Warner, *The Shahnama of Firdausi,* 9 vols., London); Mirkhwand, *Rawdat as Safa* (see the translation of E. Rehatsek, *The Raudat-us-safa or Garden of Purty,* pt. 1, 2 vols., London, 1892).

Very occasional note has been made of the Armenian chronicles, known to me only through translations. See especially V. Langlois, *Collection des Historiens Armeniens,* 2 vols., Paris, 1878. Vol. II contains the histories of Moses of Chorene, Elisaeus Vartebed, and Lazarus Phabetsi.

IV. Secondary Sources

I have included a few important works which deal primarily with Central Asia at a later period, but which incidentally throw light upon the Scythian and Hunnish periods.

Abercromby, J. *The Pre- and Proto-historic Finns.* 2 vols., London, 1898.

Adeny, A. M. *The Greek and Eastern Churches,* Edinburgh, 1908.

Allan, J. *The Cambridge Shorter History of India,* Cambridge, 1934.

Almasy, G. von. "Zentral Asien, die Urheimat der Turkvolker," *Keleti Szemle,* III (1902), 179 ff.

Andersson, J. G. "An Early Chinese Culture," *Bulletin of the Geological Survey of China,* no. 5 (1923).

———. *Children of the Yellow Earth,* London, 1934.

———. "Der Weg Uber die Steppen," *Bulletin of the Museum of Far Eastern Antiquities,* I (1929), 143 ff.

———. "Prahistorische Kulturbeziehungen zwischen Nord-China und dem Naheren Orient," *Ostasiatische Zeitschrift,* XV (1929), 49 ff.

———. "Preliminary Report on the Archaeological Researches," *Memoirs of the Geological Survey of China,* 1925.

Arne, T. J. "Painted Stone Age Pottery from the Province of Honan," *Paleontologica Sinica,* 1925.

———. "The Swedish Archeological Expedition to Iran," *Acta Archeologica,* VI (1935), 1 ff.

Bachhofer, L. "Die Ara Kanischkas," *Ostasiatische Zeitschrift,* XIV (1927-28), 21 ff.

———. "Origin and Development of Chinese Art," *Burlington Magazine,* Dec. 1935, pp. 251 ff.

———. "Zur Aras Kanishkas," *Ostasiatische Zeitschrift,* XVI (1930), 10 ff.

Baelz, E. von. "Die Riu-kiu Insulaner ... und andere Kaukasier Ahnliche Reste in Ostasien," *Korespondenzblatt der deutschen Gesellschaft für Ethnologie,* XLII (1911), 187 ff.

———. "Menschen Rassen Ostasiens, *Zeitschrift fur Ethnologie,* XXXIII (1901), 166 ff.

Baller, F. W. *A Mandarin Primer,* Shanghai, 1926.

Bang, M. "The Expansion of the Teutons," *Cambridge Medieval History,* I, 183 ff.

Bannerjee, G. N. *Hellenism in Ancient India,* Calcutta, 1920.

———. *India as Known to the Ancient World,* 1921.

Bannerji, R. D. "The Scythian Period of Indian History," *Indian Antiquary,* 1908.

Barnett, L. D. *Antiquities of India,* London, 1913.

Barthold, W. "Der Heutige Stand und die Nachsten Aufgaben der Geschichtlichen Forschungen der Turkvolker," *Zeitschrift der Deutschen Morgenlandischen Gesellschaft,* 1929.

———. *Die Geographische und Historische Erforschung des Oriente,* Leipzig, 1913.

———. "Le Royaume Grec de Bactriane et son Extension," *Bulletin de L'Academie Imperiale des Sciences de St. Petersbourg,* 1916.

———. *Nachrichten uber den Aral See und den unteren Lauf des Amu Darya von den Altesten Zeiten,* Leipzig, 1910.

———. *Turkestan down to the Mongol Invasion,* trans. by H. A. R. Gibb, London, 1928.

———. *Zur Geschichte des Christentums in Mittelasien bis zur Mongolischen Eroberung,* Leipzig, 1901.

———. "Zwolf Vorlesungen uber die Geschichte der Turken Mittelasiens," *Welt des Islams,* sups. to vols. XIV, XV, XVI, 1932-34.

———. Various articles (e.g. "Bishbalik," "Farghana," etc.) in the *Encyclopedia of Islam.*

Bartucz, L. *Uber die Anthropologischen Ergebnisse der Ausgrabungen von Mosonszentjanos* (sup. to Fettich, *Bronzeguss und Nomadische Kunst,* see below).

Beneviste, E. *Essai de Grammaire Sogdienne,* pt. 2, Paris, 1929. For pt. 1 see Gauthiot, below.

Bergmann, B. *Nomadische Streifereien unter den Kalmuken,* Riga, 1804.

Berthelot, A. *L'Asie Ancienne, Centrale et Sudorientale d'apres Ptolemey,* Paris, 1930.

Bevan, E. R. "Alexander the Great," *Encyclopedia Britannica,* 11th ed.

———. *The House of Seleucus,* 2 vols., London, 1902.

Bhandarkar, *A Peep into the Early History of India,* Bombay, 1900.

Biot, E. "Memoire sur les Colonies Militaire et Agricoles des Chinois," *Journal Asiatique,* 1850.

Bitchurin. *Denkwurdigkeiten aus der Mongolei,* Berlin, 1832.

Bleichsteiner, R. "Das Volk der Alanen," *Berichte des Forschungs Institut fur Osten und Orient,* II (1918), 4 ff.

Blochet, E. "Le Pays de Tchata et les Ephthalites," *Academic di Lincei* June 1925.

Borovfka, G. "Die Funde der Expedition Kozlow in der Mongolei," *Archiv fur Anthropologie,* 1926.

———. *Scythian Art,* London, 1926.

Bouche-LeClerq, A. *Histoire des Seleucides,* Paris, 1913.

Bowra, E. C. "The Chunni and the Hsiungnu," *Notes and Queries on China and Japan,* nos. 1 and 2.

Boyer, A. M. "L'Epoque de Kanishka," *Journal Asiatique,* 1900.

———. *Kharosti Inscriptions Discovered by Sir Aurel Stein in Chinese Turkestan,* Oxford, 1920-29.

Breasted, J. H. *Ancient Times,* Boston, 1916.

Bretschneider, E. *Mediaeval Researches from East Asiatic Sources,* London, 1888. For Central Asia from 13th to 17th centuries.

Brion, M. *Attila, the Scourge of God,* New York, 1929.

———. *La Vie des Huns,* Paris, 1931. Both these works have literary but no scientific merit.

Browne, E. G. *Literary History of Persia,* vol. I, New York, 1902.

Brunnhofer, H. *Iran and Turan,* Leipzig, 1889.

———. *Urgeschichte der Arier in Vorder und Central Asien,* Leipzig, 1893. Both these books must be used with caution.

Bukinic, D. "Neues uber Anau und Namazza Tepe," *Eurasia Septentrionalis Antiqua,* V (1930), 9 ff.

Bulanda, E. *Bogen und Pfeil bei den Volkern des Altertums,* Leipzig, 1913.

Burgess, J. *Epigraphia Indica,* Calcutta, 1892. A collection of inscriptions supplementary to the *Corpus Inscriptionum Indicarum.*

Burkitt, F. C. *The Religion of the Manichees,* Cambridge, 1925.

Bushell, S. W. *Chinese Art,* 2nd ed., 2 vols., London, 1909.

———. "The Early History of Tibet," *Journal of the Royal Asiatic Society,* 1888.

Buxton, L. H. D. "The Inhabitants of Inner Mongolia," *Journal of the Anthropological Institute,* LVI (1926), 143 ff.

———. *The Peoples of Asia,* London, 1925.

Byhan, A. "Nord, Mittel und West Asien," Buschan, *Volkerkunde,* II, 273 ff.

Cahun, L. *Introduction a l'Histoire de l'Asie: Turcs et Mongols des Origines a 1405.* Paris, 1896. Must be used with great caution.

———. "Les Revolutions de l'Asie: Origines des Nations Turcs, etc.," Lavisse-Rambaud, *Histoire Generale,* II, 884 ff.; 2, 884 ff.

Cameron, G. G. *History of Early Iran,* Chicago, 1936.

Carnoy, A. *Les Indo-Europeans,* Louvain, 1921.

Carpentier, J. "Original Home of the Indo-Europeans," *Bulletin of the School of Oriental Studies,* 1926, pp. 147 ff.

Carter, T. F. *The Invention of Printing in China and Its Spread Westward,* New York, 1925.

Castren, M. A. *Ethnologische Vorlesungen,* St. Petersburg, 1857.

Charpentier, J. "Die Ethnographische Stellung der Tocharer," *Zeitschrift der Deutschen Morgenlandischen Gesellschaft,* LXXI (1917), 347 ff.

Chavannes, E. "Dix Inscriptions Chinoise de l'Asie Centrale," *Memoires de l'Academie des Inscriptions,* XI (1902), 2, 193 ff.

———. *Documents Chinois decouverts par A. Stein dans les Sables du Turkestan Orientals,* Oxford, 1913.

———. "Les Livres Chinois avant l'Invention du Papier," *Journal Asiatique,* 1905.

———. "Voyageurs Chinois chez les Khitan et les Joutchen," *Journal Asiatique,* vol. XI (1897).

———, and Pelliot, P. "Un Traité Manicheen Retrouve en Chine," *Journal Asiatique,* 1911.

Childe, V. G. *Dawn of European Civilization,* London, 1925.

———. *The Aryans,* London, 1926.

———. *The Most Ancient East,* London, 1929.

Christensen, A. "Die Iranier," *Handbuch der Altertumswissenschaft,* Munich, 1933.

———. "L'Empire des Sassanides," *Memoires de l'Academie des Sciences et des Lettres de Danemark,* 7th ser., I (1907), 1.

———. "Sur les plus Anciennes Periodes du Zoroastrisme," *Acta Orientalia,* IV (1925), 81 ff.

Coedes, G. *Textes d'Auteurs Grecs et Latins Relatifs a l'Extreme Orient,* Paris, 1919.

Conrady, A. *Die Chinesischen Handschriften und Sonstigen Kleinfunde Sven Hedins in Loulan,* Stockholm, 1920.

Cordier, H. *Biblioteca Sinica,* 2nd ed. with supplement, Paris, 1922. The most useful bibliography for China and Central Asia.

———. *Histoire Generale de la China,* 5 vols., Paris, 1920-21. Mediocre.

Courant, M. *L'Asie Centrale aux 17e et 18e Siecles,* Lyons, 1912.

Cunningham, A. *Ancient Geography of India,* London, 1871. Valuable for Indo-Scythians.

———. "Coins of the Indo-Scythians," *Numismatic Chronicle,* 3rd ser., vols. VIII (1888), IX (1889), X (1890), XII (1892).

———. "Coins of the Later Indo-Scythians," *Numismatic Chronicle,* 3rd ser., vol. XIII (1893).

———. "The Ephthalites or White Huns," *Numismatic Chronicle,* 3rd ser., vol. XIV (1894).

Cuno, J. G. *Forschungen in Gebiete der Alten Volkerkunde—Die Skythen,* Berlin, 1871.

Curtis, W. E. *Turkestan, the Heart of Asia,* New York, 1911.

Czaplicka, M. A. *The Turks of Central Asia in History and at the Present Day,* Oxford, 1918. Contains lengthy bibliography of the Russian material.

Dalton, O. M. *The Treasure of the Oxus,* London, 1909.

Deguignes, H. *Histoire Generale des Huns, des Turcs, et de Mongols,* 5 vols., Paris, 1758. A German translation by Dahnert was published in 1770. A monumental work for its time, and though antiquated and teeming with mistakes it is still extremely valuable.

———. "Memoires sur les Awares," *Memoires de l'Academie des Inscriptions,* vol. XXVIII (1761).

———. "Recherches sur . . . l'Histoire des Rois Grecs de la Bactriane et . . . la Destruction de leur Royaume par les Scythes," *Memoires de l'Academie des Inscriptions,* vol. XXV (1759).

Delattre, A. *Le Peuple et l'Empire des Medes,* Brussels, 1883.

Deniker, J. *Les Races et les Peuples de la Terre,* Paris, 1900.

Des Michels, A. "Histoire Geographique des Seize Royaumes," 2 vols., *Publications de l'Ecole des Langues Orientales Vivantes,* Paris, 1891-92.

Dhalla, M. N. *Zoroastrian Civilization,* New York, 1922.

Dieterich, K. *Byzantinische Quellen zur Lander und Volkerkunde,* Leipzig, 1912.

D'Ohsson, C. *Histoire des Mongols,* 4 vols., Amsterdam, 1852.

Drouin, E. "Huns" and "Bactriane," *Grand Encyclopedie.*

———. "Memoires sur les Huns Ephthalites," *Museon,* XIV (1895), 73 ff.

Droysen, E. *Geschichte des Hellenismus,* Hamburg, 1836.

Duncker, M. *Geschichte der Arier in der Alten Zeit,* Leipzig, 1867. This is a revised edition of vol. II of *Geschichte des Altertums.*

Dutt, R. C. *Civilization in Ancient India,* 2 vols., London, 1893.

Ebert, M. *Sud-Russland im Altertum,* Bonn, 1921.

———. (Ed.) *Reallexikon der Vorgeschichte,* 15 vols., Berlin, 1924-32.

von Eickstedt, E. *Rassenkunde und Rassengeschichte der Menscheit,* Stuttgart, 1934. Extremely important.

Eliot, C. *Hinduism and Buddhism,* 3 vols., London, 1921.

Eliseeff, S. "Kozloff Discoveries," *Revue des Ars Asiatiques,* 1926, pp. 45 ff.

von Erdmann, F. *Temudschin, der Unerschutterliche,* Leipzig, 1862. The first half of the book deals with the early inhabitants of Central Asia. Antiquated.

Eyre, E. *European Civilization: Its Origin and Development,* New York, 1934.

Feher, N. "Bulgarisch-ungarische Beziehugen," *Keleti Szemle,* XIX (1921), 1 ff.

Feist, S. "Der Gegenwartige Stand des Tokharer Problems," in Hirth, *Festschrift,* pp. 74 ff.

———. *Indogermanen und Germanen,* Halle, 1924.

———. *Kultur, Ausbreitung, und Herkunft der Indogermanen,* Berlin, 1913.

Fenellosa, E. F. *Epochs in Chinese and Japanese Art,* New York, 1913.

Ferguson, J. S. *Outlines of Chinese Art,* Chicago, 1918.

Fettich, N. *Bronzeguss und Nomadische Kunst,* Prague, 1929.

Finck, F. N. *Die Sprachstamme des Erdkreises,* 3rd ed., Leipzig, 1923.

Fleet, J. F. "The Name Kushan," *Journal of the Royal Asiatic Society,* 1914.

———. Various articles in the *Journal of the Royal Asiatic Society,* especially 1903, 1905, 1906, and 1913.

Fleure, H. J. *The Races of Mankind,* New York, 1928. *See also* Peake and Fleure.

Floigl, V. *Cyrus and Herodot,* Leipzig, 1881.

Flugel, G. *Mani, seine Lehre und seine Schriften,* Leipzig, 1862.

Forke, A. "Ta Ts'in, das Romerreich," *Ostasiatische Zeitschrift,* XIV (1927-28), 48 ff.

Foucher, A. *L'Art Greco-bouddhique du Gandhara,* 2 vols., Paris, 1905-23.

———. *Beginnings of Buddhist Art,* Paris, 1917.

Franke, O. "Beitrage aus Chinesischen Quellen zur Kenntniss der Turkvolker und Skythen," sup. to *Abhandlungen der koniglichen Preussischen Akadamie der Wissenschaft zu Berlin,* 1904.

———. "Das Alte Ta-hia der Chinesen," in Hirth, *Festschrift,* pp. 117 ff.

———. "Eine Chinesische Tempelinschrift aus Idikutschari bei Turfan," *Abhandlungen der koniglichen Preussischen Akademie der Wissenschaft zu Berlin,* 1907, pp. 92 ff.

———. "Einige Bemerkungen zu F. K. W. Muller's Toxri und Kushan," *Ostasiatische Zeitschrift,* VI (1918), 83 ff.

———. *Geschichte des Chinesischen Reiches,* vol. I, Berlin, 1930.

———. "Widergabe fremder Volkernamen durch die Chinesen," *Ostasiatische Zeitschrift* (1920-21), 145 ff.

———. "Zur Frage der Einfuhrung des Buddhisms in China," *Mitteilungen des Seminars fur Orientalische Sprachen,* Berlin, 1910.

Frankfort, H. "Studies in the Early Pottery of the Near East," *Journal of the Royal Anthropological Institute,* London, 1924 and 1927.

Fressle, J. *Die Skytho-Saken, die Urvater der Germanen,* Munich, 1886.

Fuchs, W. "Das Turfangebiet und seine aussern Geschichte bis in die T'ang Zeit, *Ostasiatische Zeitschrift,* XIII (1926), 124 ff.

Gabelentz, H. C. *Geschichte der Grossen Liao,* St. Petersburg, 1877.

Gardner, P. *Coins of Greek and Scythic Kings of India,* London, 1886.

Gaubil. *Traite de la Chronologie Chinoise,* Paris, 1814.

Gauthiot, R. *Essai de Grammaire Sogdienne,* pt. 1, Paris, 1923. Contains a valuable introduction to the Sogdian language in general. For pt. 2 see Beneviste, above.

Geiger W. *Civilization of the Eastern Iranians in Ancient Times,* London, 1885.

Geldner, K. "Awesta Literatur," in Geiger-Kuhn, *Grundriss der Iranischen Philologie,* II, 1 ff.

———. "Zoroaster" and "Persia-Language and Literature," *Encyclopaedia Britannica.*

Gerini, G. E. *Ptolemey's Geography of Eastern Asia,* London, 1909.

Getty, A. *The Gods of Northern Buddhism,* Oxford, 1916.

Gibb, H. A. R. *The Arab Conquests in Central Asia,* London, 1923.

Gibbon, E. *Decline and Fall of the Roman Empire,* 6 vols., London, 1910.

Giles, H. *Chinese Biographical Dictionary,* London, 1898.

———. *History of Chinese Literature,* London, 1901.

Gomboc, Z. "Die Bulgarisch-turkischen Lehnworter in der Ungarischen Sprache," *Memoires de la Societe Finno-Ougrienne,* vol. XXX (1912).

Gowen, H. H. and Hall, J. W. *An Outline History of China,* New York, 1926.

Gray, G. B. "The Foundation and Extension of the Persian Empire," *Cambridge Ancient History,* IV, 1 ff.

———, and Cary, M. "The Reign of Darius," *Cambridge Ancient History,* IV, 173 ff.

Grousset, R. *Histoire de l'Asie,* 3 vols., Paris, 1922.

———. *Histoire d'Extreme Orient,* 2 vols., Paris, 1929. Valuable.

———. *The Civilizations of the East,* 4 vols., New York, 1931-35.

Grunwedel, A. *Altbuddhistische Kultstatten in Chinesisch-Turkestan,* Berlin, 1912.

———. *Alt Kuca,* Berlin, 1920.

———. "Bericht uber Archaeologische Arbeit in Idikutschari," *Abhandlungen der Bayrischen Akademie der Wissenschaft,* 1906.

———. *Buddhistische Kunst in Indien,* Berlin, 1900.

———. *Mythologie des Buddhismus in Tibet und der Mongolei,* Berlin, 1900.

Gutschmid, A. V. *Geschichte Irans und Seiner Nachbarlander von Alexander dem Grossen bis zum Untergang des Arsaciden,* Tubingen, 1888.

———. *Kleine Schriften,* Berlin, 1892.

Haddon, A. C. *The Races of Man and Their Distribution,* Cambridge, 1924.

———. *The Wanderings of Peoples,* Cambridge, 1919.

Hall, H. R. H. *Ancient History of the Near East,* 5th ed., London, 1920.

———. "Art of Early Egypt and Babylon," *Cambridge Ancient History,* I, 570 ff.

Haloun, G. Review of da Groot's *Die Hunnen der Vorchristlichen Zeit* in *Orientalische Literatur-Zeitung,* 1922, pp. 433 ff.

———. *Seit Wann Kannten die Chinesen die . . . Indogermanen,* pt. 1, *Ta-hia in den Chinesischen Quellen vor 126 B.C.,* Leipzig, 1926.
Harlez, C. J. *Histoire de l'Empire Kin or l'Empire d'Or,* Paris, 1886.
Hartmann, M. *Chinesisch Turkestan,* Halle, 1908.
Hauer, E. *Die Grundung des Mandchurischen Kaiserreiches,* Berlin, 1926.
Havell, E. B. *History of Aryan Rule in India,* New York, 1918.
Hedin, S. *Central Asia and Tibet,* 2 vols., New York, 1903.
———. *Southern Tibet,* 14 vols., Stockholm, 1917-22. Contains much information on Turkistan.
———. *Through Asia,* 2 vols., New York, 1899.
———. *Trans-Himalaya,* 3 vols., New York, 1909-13.
Hehn, V. *Kulturpflanze und Haustiere,* 6th ed., Berlin, 1894.
Heras, H. "The Final Defeat of Mihirakula," *Indian Historical Quarterly,* vol. III (1927).
Herrmann, A. "Alte Geographie des Untern Oxusgebietes," *Abhandlungen der koniglichen Gesellschaft der Wissenschaft zu Gottingen,* 1914.
———. *Die Alten Seidenstrassen zwischen China und Syrien,* Leipzig, 1910. Very important for the early geography of Kashgaria.
———. "Die Altesten Chinesischen Karten von Zentral und Westasiens," in Hirth, *Festschrift,* pp. 185 ff.
———."Die Hephthaliten und ihre Beziehungen zu China," *Asia Major,* II (1925), 564 ff.
———. "Die Westlander in der Chinesischen Kartographie," in Hedin, *Southern Tibet,* VIII, 91 ff.
———. *Loulan, China, Indien, und Rom im Lichte der Ausgrabungen am Lobnor,* Leipzig, 1931.
———. "Sacaraucae," "Sakai," "Sakastan," etc. in *Pauly Wissowa Realencyclopaedie des Classischen Altertums.*
Hertel, J. "Die Zeit Zoroasters," *Indo-Iranischen Quellen und Forschungen,* vol. I, Leipzig, 1924.
Herzfeld, E. *Archaeological History of Iran,* London, 1935.
———. *Paikuli,* 3 vols., Berlin, 1924.
———. "Sakastan," *Archeologische Mitterlungen aus Iran.*
———. "The Traditional Date of Zoroaster," *Pavry Memorial Volume,* pp. 132 ff. *See also* Sarre and Herzfeld.
Hirth, F. *The Ancient History of China,* 2nd ed., New York, 1926.
———. *China and the Roman Orient,* Shanghai, 1885.
———. *Chinesische Studien,* Munich, 1890.
———. "Hunnenforschungen," *Keleti Szemle,* II (1901), 82 ff.
———. "Mr. Kingsmill and the Hiung-nu," *Journal of the American Oriental Society,* XXX (1909), 32 ff.
———. "Nachworte zur Inschrift des Tonyukuk," in Radloff, *Altturkische Inschriften der Mongolei,* Neue Folge.
———. "Sinologische Beitrage zur Geschichte der Turkvolker," part 1, "Die Ahnentafel Attilas," *Bulletin de l'Academie Imperiale des Sciences de St. Petersbourg,* 1900, 220 ff.

———. "Syrisch-Chinesische Beziehungen im Anfang unserer Zeitrechnung," in Oberhummer, *Durch, Syrien und Kleinasien,* Berlin, 1899.

———. "Uber die Chinesischen Quellen zur Kenntniss Centralasiens, 500-650 A.D.," *Wiener Zeitschrift fur Kunde des Morgenlandes,* X, 225 ff.

———. "Uber Volga Hunnen und Hiung-nu," *Sitzungsberichte der Munchner Akademie der Wissenschaft* (*Phil.-Hist. Classe*), II (1899), 245 ff.

Hoang, P. *Concordance des Chronologie Neomenique Chinoise et Europeene,* Shanghai, 1910.

Hodgkin, T. *Italy and Her Invaders,* 8 vols., Oxford, 1892-99. See especially vol. I, *The Visigothic Invasion,* and vol. II, *The Hunnish and Vandal Invasions.*

Hoernle, A. F. R. *Manuscript Remains of Buddhist Literature Found in Eastern Turkestan,* Oxford, 1916.

———. "Problems of Ancient Indian History: The Identity of Yasodharman," *Journal of the Royal Asiatic Society,* 1909, pp. 89 ff.

———. "The Unknown Languages of Eastern Turkestan," *Journal of the Royal Asiatic Society,* 1910-11.

Howorth, H. H. "Some Notes on the Huns," *Sixth Oriental Congress,* 1883, pt. 4, pp. 177 ff.

———. *The History of the Mongols,* 4 vols., 1876-1927.

———. "The Northern Frontagers of China," a series of articles in the *Journal of the Royal Asiatic Society.* Of especial importance are "The Origin of the Mongols," 1875; "The Origin of the Manchus," 1875; and "The Uighurs," 1898.

———. "Westerly Drifting of Nomads," a series of articles in the *Journal of the Ethnological Society* and the *Journal of the Anthropological Institute.* Of especial importance are "The Thukiue," *Journal of the Anthropological Institute,* vol. I; "The Avares," *Journal of the Anthropological Institute,* vol. II; "The Bulgarians," *Journal of the Anthropological Institute,* vol. III; and "The Huns," *Journal of the Anthropological Institute,* vol. III.

Hsu, S. H. *China and Her Political Entity,* Oxford, 1926.

Huart, C. *La Perse Antique,* Paris, 1925.

Hulbert, H. B. *The History of Korea,* 2 vols., Seoul, 1905.

Humboldt, A. V. *Asie Centrale,* 3 vols., Paris, 1842. Antiquated.

Hunfalvy, P. *Ethnographie von Ungarn,* Budapest, 1877.

Huntingdon, E. *The Pulse of Asia,* London, 1907.

Husing, G. *Volkerschichten in Iran,* Vienna, 1916.

Huth, G. *Geschichte des Buddhismus in der Monglei,* Strassburg, 1896.

Hutton, E. *Attila and the Huns,* London, 1915.

Ikeuchi, H. "A Study of the Sushen," *Memoirs of the Research Department of the Toyo Bunko,* V, 97 ff.

Imbault-Huart, C. *Le Pays du Hami,* Paris, 1892.

———. *Recuil de Documents sur l'Asie Centrale,* Paris, 1881.

Jackson, A. V. W. *Researches in Manichaeanism,* New York, 1932.

———. *Zoroaster, the Prophet of Ancient Iran,* New York, 1899.
Jacob, G. "Oriental Elements of Culture in the Occident," *Smithsonian Report,* 1902, pp. 520 ff.
Jacobson, H. *Early History of Sogdia,* Chicago, 1935.
Jager, F. "Leben und Werke des Pei-kiu: Chinesische Kolonial Geschichte," *Ostasiatische Zeitschrift,* IX (1920-21), 81 ff.
Jayne, H. H. F. "Joint Expedition to Damghan," *Bulletin of the American Institute for Persian Art and Archeology,* vol. V (1933).
Jirecek, *Geschichte der Bulgaren,* Prague, 1876.
Jochelson, W. *The Peoples of Asiatic Russia,* New York, 1928.
Joyce, T. A. "Notes on the Physical Anthropology of Chinese Turkestan and the Pamirs," *Journal of the Anthropological Institute,* XXXXII (1912), 450 ff.
———. "Notes on the Physical Anthropology of the Pamirs and the Amu Daria Basin," *Journal of the Anthropological Institute,* LVI (1926), 105 ff.
———. "On the Physical Anthropology of the Oases of Khotan and Keriya," *Journal of the Anthropological Institute,* XXIII (1903), 305 ff.
Julien, S. "Documents sur les Tou-kiue," *Journal Asiatique,* 1864. Reprinted in Paris in 1877.
———. "Les Ouigours," *Journal Asiatique,* 1847.
Justi, F. "Geschichte Irans," in Geiger and Kuhn, *Grundriss der Iranischen Philologie,* vol. II.
Kaerst, J. *Geschichte des Hellenistischen Zeitalters,* 2 vols., Leipzig, 1901.
Karlgren, B. *Analytic Dictionary of Chinese,* Paris, 1923. Useful for restoring the sounds of ancient Chinese.
———. *On the Authenticity of the Tso Chuan,* Gothenburg, 1926.
———. *The Romanization of Chinese,* London, 1928.
Kaszonyi, F. *Rassenverwandtschaft der Donauvolker,* Vienna, 1931.
Keane, A. H. *Man, Past and Present,* Cambridge, 1899.
Keith, A. "Human Skulls from the Cemeteries in the Tarim Basin," *Journal of the Anthropological Institute,* LIX (1929), 149 ff.
Keith, A. B. "The Early History of the Indo-Iranians," *Bhandarkar Memorial Volume,* pp. 81 ff.
Kellgren T. "Les Finnois et la Race Ouralo-Altaique," *Nouvelles Annales des Voyages,* II (1848), 164 ff.
Kennedy, S. "The Secret of Kanishka," *Journal of the Royal Asiatic Society,* 1912, pp. 665 ff.
Kent, R. G. "The Name Ahura Mazda," *Pavry Memorial Volume,* pp. 200 ff.
Kessler, K. *Forschungen uber die Manichaische Religion,* Berlin, 1889.
Kiepert, H. *Manual of Ancient Geography,* London, 1881.
Kiessling, M. "Hunni," *Pauly Wissowa Realencyclopaedie des Classischen Altertums.* Very important.
Kingsmill, T. W. "The Ancient Distribution of Peoples on the Western and Northern Frontiers of China," *China Review,* XXV (1901), 215 ff. All of Kingsmill's articles must be used with extreme caution.

———. "The Intercourse of China with Eastern Turkestan," *Journal of the Royal Asiatic Society,* 1882, pp. 74 ff.
———. "The Migration and Early History of the White Huns," *Journal of the Royal Asiatic Society,* 1878.
Klaatsch, H. "Morphologische Studien zur Rassendiagnostik der Turfan Schadel," in supplement to *Abhandlungen der koniglichen Preussischen Akadamie der Wissenschaft zu Berlin,* 1912.
Klaproth, J. *Asia Polyglotta,* Paris, 1823.
———. *Memoires Relative a l'Asie,* 3 vols., Paris. 1824-28.
———. "Sur l'Identite des Tou-kiue et les Hiongnu avec les Turcs," *Journal Asiatique,* 1825.
———. *Sur l'Invention de la Boussole,* Paris, 1834.
———. *Tableaux Historiques de l'Asie,* Paris, 1826. See especially "Apercu Historique . . . des Peuples de l'Asie Moyenne," pp. 81 ff.
———. *Uber die Sprache und Schrift der Uiguren,* Berlin, 1812.
Klementz, D. *Nachrichten uber die . . . Expedition nach Turfan,* St. Petersburg, 1899.
Kondakoff. *See* S. Reinach below.
Konow, S. "Beitrag zur Kenntniss der Indo-Skythen," in Hirth, *Festschrift,* pp. 220 ff.
———. "Documents Relating to the Ancient History of the Indo-Scythians," *Journal of the Royal Asiatic Society,* 1920, p. 156.
———. "Indo-Skythische Beitrage," *Sitzungsberichte der Preussischen Akademie der Wissenschaft zu Berlin* (*Phil.-Hist. Classe*), 1916, pp. 787 ff.
———. "Notes on Indo-Scythian Chronology," *Journal of Indian History,* XII, 8 ff.
———. "On the Nationality of the Kushanas," *Zeitschrift der Deutschen Morgenlandischen Gesellschaft,* LXVIII (1914), 85 ff.
———. "On the Sakas and Zoroastrianism," *Pavry Memorial Volume,* pp. 220 ff.
———. *Saka Studies,* Oslo, 1932.
———. "Vedic Dasyu, Toxri Daha," Thomsen, *Festschrift,* pp. 96 ff.
———. "War Tocharisch die Sprache der Tocharer?" *Asia Major,* IX (1933), 455 ff.
Kopsch, H. "Pao-sze, the Cleopatra of China," *China Review,* IV, 104 ff.
Korostovetz, I. J. *Von Cingis Khan zur Soviet Regierung,* Berlin, 1926.
Kossina, G. "Der Ursprung der Urfinnen und Urindogermanen und Ihre Ausbreitung nach Osten," *Mannus,* Nos. 1 and 2.
Kotwicz, W. L. "Contribution aux Etudes Altaiques," in *Rocznik Orientalistyczny.*
Kousnietsoff, *La Lutte des Civilizations et des Langues en Asie Centrale,* Paris, 1912.
Kozloff, P. K. "Conte Rendu des Expeditions pour Exploration du Nord de la Mongolie," *Bulletin de l'Academie Imperiale des Sciences de St. Petersbourg,* 1925.
———. *Mongolei, Amdo, und die Tote Stadt Chara-Choto,* Berlin, 1925.

Krause, F. *Geschichte Ostasiens,* 3 vols., Gottingen, 1925.

Kretschmer, K. "Sarmatae," "Sarmatia," "Scythia," "Scythae," etc. in *Pauly Wissowa Realencyclopaedie des Classischen Altertums.*

Kromayer, J., and Veith, G. *Heerwesen und Kriegsfuhrung der Griechen und Romer,* 1928.

Kummel, O. "Die Altesten Beziehungen zwischen Europe und Ostasien," *Deutsche Forschung,* V (1928), 112 ff.

Kuropatkin, A. N. *Kashgaria, An Historical and Geographical Sketch of the Country,* London, 1882.

Labour, M. *Le Christianisme dans L'Empire Perse,* Paris, 1904.

Langdon, S. "Early Babylonia and its Cities," *Cambridge Ancient History,* I, 356 ff.

Lansdell, H. *Chinese Central Asia,* 2 vols., London, 1893.

———. *Russian Central Asia,* 2 vols., London, 1885.

Lassen, C. *Indische Altertumskunde,* 4 vols., Bonn, 1847-58. First two volumes, though antiquated, are still valuable.

Latourette, K. *The Chinese, Their History and Culture,* New York, 1934.

Latysheff, B. *Scythica et Caucasica e Veteribut scriptoribus Graecis et Latinis Collegit,* 2 vols., St. Petersburg, 1901-06.

Laufer, B. "Chinese Clay Figures, Pt. 1., Prolegomena on the History of Defensive Armor," *Publication of the Field Museum,* No. 177, Chicago, 1914.

———. *Chinese Pottery of the Han Dynasty,* Leiden, 1909.

———. "Die Sage von den Goldgrabenden Ameisen," *T'oung Pao,* 2nd ser., IX (1908), 429 ff.

———. "The Early History of Felt," *American Anthropologist,* XXXII (1930), 1 ff.

———. *The Language of the Yue-chi,* Chicago, 1917.

———. "Sino-Iranica," *Publication of the Field Museum,* No. 201, Chicago, 1919.

Le Beau, *Histoire de Bas Empire,* ed. by St. Martin, Paris, 1826.

LeCoq, A. V. *Auf Hellas Spuren in Ost-Turkestan,* Leipzig, 1926.

———. *Bilderatlas zur Kunst und Kulturgeschichte Mittelasiens,* Berlin, 1925.

———. *Chotscho,* Berlin, 1913.

———. *Die Buddhistische Spatantike in Mittelasien,* 5 vols., Berlin, 1922-25.

———. "Kokturkisches aus Turfan," *Sitzungsberichte der Preussischen Akademie der Wissenschaft zu Berlin* (*Phil.-Hist. Classe*), 1909, pp. 1049 ff.

———. "Kurze Einfuhrung in die Uigurische Schriftkunde," *Mitteilungen des Seminars fur Orientalische Sprachen,* vol. XXII (1919).

———. *Land und Leute in Ost-Turkestan,* Leipzig, 1928.

Lefebvre de Noettes. *L'Attelage,* 2 vols., Paris, 1931.

Lehmann, Haupt, C. F. "Kimmerer," *Pauly Wissowa Realencyclopaedie des Classischen Altertums.*

———. "Wann Lebte Zarathustra," *Pavry Memorial Volume,* pp. 251 ff.

Le Strange, G. *The Lands of the Eastern Caliphate,* Cambridge, 1905.

Leumann, E. "Uber die Einheimischen Sprachen von Ost-Turkestan in fruherem Mittelalter," *Zeitschrift der Deutschen Morgenlandischen Gesellschaft,* LXI (1907), 648 ff., LXII (1908), 83 ff.

———. *Zur Nordarischen Sprache und Literatur,* Berlin, 1912.

Levi, S. "Etudes des Documents Tokhariens de la Mission Pelliot," *Journal Asiatique,* 1911.

———. "Notes sur les Indo-Scythes," *Journal Asiatique,* 1896, pp. 444 ff. and 1897, pp. 5 ff.

———. "Quelques Documents sur le Bouddhisme Indien dans l'Asie Centrale," *Bulletin de l'Ecole d'Extreme Orient,* 1905, pp. 253 ff.

———. "Le Tokharien," *Journal Asiatique,* 1933, pp. 1 ff. Very important.

———. "Le Tokharien B, Langue de Koutscha," *Journal Asiatique,* 1913, pp. 311 ff.

Li, C. *The Formation of the Chinese People,* Cambridge, 1928.

Ligeti, L. "Die Ahnentafel Attilas und die Hunnischen Tan-hu Namen," *Asia Major,* II (1925), 290 ff.

Lindquist, S. "Zum Toxri Problem," *Monde Oriental,* XII (1918), 66 ff.

Lommel, H. *Die Religion Zarathustras,* Tubingen, 1930.

Luders, H. "Die Sakas und die Nordarische Sprache," *Sitzungsberichte der Preussischen Akademie der Wissenschaft zu Berlin* (*Phil.-Hist. Classe*), 1913, pp. 406 ff.

———. "Uber die Litterarischen Funde in Ostturkestan," *Sitzungeberichte der Preussischen Akademie der Wissenschaft zu Berlin* (*Phil-Hist. Classe*), 1914, pp. 85 ff.

———. "Weitere Beitrage zur Geschichte und Geographie Ostturkestans," *Sitzungeberichte der Preussichen Akademie der Wissenschaft zu Berlin* (*Phil.-Hist. Classe*), 1930, pp. 5 ff.

———. "Zur Geschichte und Geographie Ostturkestan," *Sitzungeberichte der Preussischen Akademie der Wissenschaft zu Berlin* (*Phil.-Hist. Classe*), 1922, pp. 243 ff.

Macartney, G. "Notices from the Chinese Sources on the Ancient Kingdom of Lou-lan or Shen-shen," *Geographic Journal,* 1903, pp. 260 ff.

McCrindle, J. W. *Ancient India as Described in Classical Literature,* 5 vols., Westminster, 1901. See especially vol. IV containing a translation of Ptolemy's description of Central and Eastern Asia.

McGovern, W. M. *Introduction to Mahayana Buddhism,* London, 1922.

———. *Manual of Buddhist Philosophy,* London, 1924.

Manitius, M. "The Teutonic Migrations 378-412 A.D.," *Cambridge Mediaeval History,* I, 250 ff.

Marquart, J. *Die Chronologie der Alt-turkischen Inschriften,* Leipzig, 1898.

———. "Die Nichtslavischen Ausdrucke in der Bulgarischen Furstenliste," *T'oung Pao,* 1911, pp. 661 ff.

———. "Eranshahr," *Abhandlungen der koniglichen Gesellschaft der Wissenschaft zu Gottingen,* vol. III (1903).

———. "Historische Glossen du den Alt-turkischen Inschriften," *Wiener Zeitschrift fur Kunde des Morgenlandes,* vol. XII (1898).

———. *Osteuropaische und Ostasiatische Streifzuge,* Leipzig, 1903.

———. "Skizzen zur Geschichtlichen Volkerkunde von Mittelasien und Sibirien," in Hirth, *Festschrift*, pp. 289 ff.

———. "Uber das Volkstum der Kumanen." This is pt. II of Bang and Marquart's "Ostturkische Dialekt Studien," *Abhandlungen der koniglichen Gesellschaft der Wissenschaft zu Gottlingen*, 1914.

———. *Untersuchungen zur Geschichte von Eran*, 2 vols., Leipzig, 1896-1905.

Marshall, J. *Guide to Taxila*, Calcutta, 1918.

———. *Mohenjo Daro and the Indus Civilization*, London, 1913.

Maspero, G. C. C. *Histoire des Peuples de l'Orient Classique*, 8th ed., Paris, 1909.

Maspero, H. *La Chine Antique*, Paris, 1927.

———. "Le Dialect de Tch'ang-ngan sous les T'ang," *Bulletin de l'Ecole d'Extreme Orient*, vol. XX (1910).

———. "Le Songe et l'Embassade de l'Empereur Ming," *Bulletin de l'Ecole d'Extreme Orient*, 1910.

Mateer, C. W. *A Course of Mandarin Lessons*, Shanghai, 1898.

Maurice, T. *The Modern History of Hindustan, comprehending that of the Greek Empire of Bactria*, 2 vols., London, 1802.

Mayers, *Chinese Readers Manual*, 2nd ed., Shanghai, 1924.

———. "On the Introduction and Use of Gunpowder and Fire-arms amongst the Chinese," *Journal of the North China Branch of the Royal Asiatic Society*, VI, 73 ff.

Meillet, A. *Les Dialects Indo-Europeens*, Paris, 1922.

———. *Introduction a l'Etude Comparative des Langues Indo-Europeens*, 5th ed., Paris, 1922.

———. "Les Nouvelles Langues Indo-Europeenes Trouve en Asie Centrale," *Revue du Mois*, XIV (1912), 135 ff.

———, and Cohen, M. *Les Langues du Monde*, Paris, 1924.

Meissner, B. "Das Pferd in Babylonien," *Mitteilungen der Vorderasiatischen Gesellschaft*, XVIII (1913), 1 ff.

Menghin, O. *Weltgeschichte der Steinzeit*, Vienna, 1931.

———. "Die Ethnische Stellung der Ostband Keramische Kulturen-Tocharer und Hettiter," Gruschewsky, *Festschrift*, pp. 3 ff.

Merhart, G. *Bronzezeit am Jenissei*, Vienna, 1926.

Meyer, E. *Blute und Niedergang des Hellenismus in Asien*, Berlin, 1925.

———. "Das Erste Auftreten der Arier in der Geschichte," *Sitzungsberichte der Preussischen Akademie der Wissenschaft zu Berlin* (*Phil.-Hist. Classe*), 1908, p. 14.

———. *Geschichte des Altertums*, 5 vols., Stuttgart, 1901-31.

———. "Persia-Ancient History" and "Parthia" and "Bactria," *Encyclopaedia Britannica*, 11th ed.

Minns, E. H. "Scythians," *Cambridge Ancient History*, III, 187 ff.

———. "Scythians," in Hastings, *Encyclopedia*.

———. *Scythians and Greeks*, Cambridge, 1913.

Mironov, N. D. "Aryan Vestiges in the Near East of the 2nd Millenary B.C.," *Acta Orientalia,* XI, 140 ff.

Modi, J. J. "The Early History of the Huns and their Inroads in India and Persia," *Journal of the Bombay Branch of the Royal Asiatic Society,* XXIV (1914-17), 539 ff.

———. "Hunas in Avesta and Pahlavi," *Bhandarkar Commemorative Volume,* pp. 65 ff.

———. "The Huns who Invaded India. What was Their Religion?" *Oriental Conference Papers,* Bombay, 1932, pp. 165 ff.

———. "References to the Chinese in the Ancient Books of the Parsees," *Journal of the Royal Oriental Society, Bombay Branch,* XXI, 525 ff. All of Modi's works must be used with caution.

Moret, A. *From Tribe to Empire,* London, 1926.

Morgan, J. de. *Mission Scientifique en Perse,* Paris, 1896. See especially vol. IV, *Recherches Archeologiques.*

———. "Origines des Semites . . . et des Indo-Europeens," *Revue de Synthese Historique,* XXIV (1922), 7 ff.

Moulton, J. H. *Early Zoroastrianism,* London, 1913.

Much, M. *Die Heimat der Indogermanen im Lichte der Urgeschichtlichen Forschung,* Berlin, 1902.

Mullenhoff, K. *Deutsche Altertumskunde,* 5 vols., Berlin, 1892. See especially vol. 3 for the Scythians.

Muller, F. *Der Ugrische Volksstamm,* 2 vols., Berlin, 1837.

Muller, F. Max. *Science of Language,* 2 vols., New York, 1890.

Muller, F. W. K. "Beitrag zur Genaueren Bestimmung der Unbekannten Sprachen Mittelasiens," *Sitzungsberichte der Preussischen Akademie der Wissenschaft zu Berlin* (*Phil.-Hist. Classe*), 1907, pp. 958 ff.

———. "Handschriften Reste in Estranghelo Schrift," *Abhandlungen der koniglichen Preussischen Akademie der Wissenschaft zu Berlin,* 1904.

———. "Maitrisimit und Tokharisch," *Sitzungsberichte der Preussinischen Akademie der Wissenschaft zu Berlin* (*Phil.-Hist. Classe*), 1916, pp. 395 ff.

———. "Soghdische Texte," *Abhandlungen der koniglichen Preussischen Akademie der Wissenschaft zu Berlin,* 1912, 1913.

———. "Toxri und Kuisan," *Sitzungsberichte der Preussichen Akademie der Wissenschaft zu Berlin,* (*Phil.-Hist. Classe*), 1918, pp. 566 ff.

———. "Uigurica," *Abhandlungen der koniglichen Preussichen Akademie der Wissenschaft zu Berlin,* 1908, 1911, 1922.

Myres, J. L. "Ethnology and Primitive Culture of the Nearer East," in Eyre, *European Civilization,* I, 87 ff.

———. "Indo-Europeans up to the Time of the Migrations," in Eyre, *European Civilization,* I, 184 ff.

———. "Neolithic and Bronze Cultures," *Cambridge Ancient History,* I, 57 ff.

Nau, F. "L'Expansion Nestorienne en Asie Centrale," *Conferences du Museé Guimet,* Paris, 1913.

Nelson, N. C., and Berkey, C. P. "Geology and Prehistoric Archeology of the Gobi Desert," *American Museum Novitates,* No. 222 (1926), pp. 9 ff.

Nemeti, K. "The Historic Geographic Proofs of the Hiung-nu Hun Identity," *Asiatic Quarterly Review,* 1910, pp. 352 ff.

———. "Hunok, Bulgarok, Magyarok," *Budapesti Szemle,* 1924. For a French summary see Homan in *Revue des Etudes Hougroises et Finno-Ougriennes,* 1924, pp. 156 ff.

Neumann, K. *Die Hellenen im Skythenland,* Berlin, 1855. Antiquated but still very valuable.

Neumann, K. F. *Asiatische Studien,* Leipzig, 1837.

———. *Die Volker des Suddlichen Russland,* Leipzig, 1847.

Niebuhr, B. G. "Untersuchungen uber die Geschichte der Skythen" in *Kleine Schriften,* I, 361, Bonn, 1828.

Noldecke, T. *Aufsatze zur Persischen Geschichte,* Leipzig, 1889.

Oberhummer, R. *Die Turken und das Osmanische Reich,* Leipzig, 1917.

Olmstead, A. T. "Ahura Mazda in Assyrian," *Pavry Commemorative Volume,* pp. 366 ff.

———. *History of Assyria,* New York, 1923.

Oxenham, E. L. *Historical Atlas of the Chinese Empire,* Shanghai, 1898.

Pallas, P. S. *Sammlung Historischen Nachrichten uber die Mongolischen Volkerschaften,* 2 vols., St. Petersburg, 1776.

Parker, E. H. *Ancient China Simplified,* London, 1908.

———. "China, the Avars, and the Franks," *Asiatic Quarterly Review,* XIII (1902), 346.

———. "The Ephthalite Turks," *Asiatic Quarterly Review,* XIV (1902), 131 ff.

———. "Origin of the Turks," *English Historical Review,* XI (1896), 431 ff.

———. "The Progenitors of the Manchus," *China Recorder,* XXIV (1893), 501 ff.

———. "Tartars and Chinese before the Time of Confucius," *English Historical Review,* XXII (1907), 625.

———. *Thousand Years of the Tartars,* 2nd ed., New York, 1924.

Pathak, K. B. "New Light on the Gupta Era and Mihirakula," *Bhandakar Commemorative Volume,* pp. 195 ff.

Patkanian, M. "Essai D'une Histoire de la Dynastie des Sassanides," *Journal Asiatique,* 1866, pp. 101 ff.

Patkanoff, S. "Uber das Volk der Sabiren," *Keleti Szemle,* I (1900), 258 ff.

Pauthier, J. *Relations Politiques de la Chine avec les Puissances Occidentales,* Paris, 1859.

Peake, H., and Fleure, H. J. *Peasants and Potters,* London, 1927.

———. *Priests and Kings,* London, 1927.

———. *The Steppe and the Town,* London, 1928.

Peisker, J. "The Asiatic Background," *Cambridge Mediaeval History,* I, 370 ff.

———. *Die Alteren Beziehungen der Slaven zu Turko-Tartaren,* . . ., Stuttgart, 1905.

Pelliot, P. "A Propos des Comans," *Journal Asiatique,* 1920.
———. *Haute Asie,* Paris, 1931. A brilliant summary.
———. "Influence Iranniene en Asie Centrale et en Extreme Orient," in *Revue d'Histoire et de Litterature Religieuses,* 1912, pp. 97 ff.
———. "L'Origine de Nom de Chine," *T'oung Pao,* 1912-13.
———. *Mission Pelliot en Asie Centrale,* 8 vols., Paris, 1914-18.
———. "Notes sur les Anciens Noms de Kuca, d'Aqsu, et de Uc-Turfan," *T'oung Pao,* 1923, pp. 126 ff.
———. "Notes sur les Tou-yu-houen," *T'oung Pao,* 1920, pp. 323 ff.
———. "Tocharien et Koutcheen," *Journal Asiatique,* 1934, pp. 23 ff.
Plath, J. H. "Die Fremden Barbarischen Stamme in Alten China," *Sitzungsberichte der Muncher Akademie der Wissenschaft* (*Phil.-Hist. Classe*), 1874, pp. 450 ff.
Pokorny, J. "Die Stellung des Tocharischen im Kreise der Indogermanischen Sprachen," *Berichte des Forschungs Institut fur Osten und Orient,* vol. III.
Poppe, "Turkisch-Tchuwasische Vergleichende Studien," *Islamica,* I, 409 ff.
Poussin, L. *L'Inde aux Temps des Mauryas et des Barbares,"* Paris, 1930.
———. *L'Indo-Europeens: L'Inde Jusque Vers 300 B.C.,* Paris, 1924.
Prasek, J. V. *Geschichte der Meder und Perser,* 2 vols., Gotha, 1906-1910.
Pumpelly, R. *Explorations in Turkestan,* Washington, 1903-04.
———. *Prehistoric Anau,* Washington, 1905-08.
Radet, G. "L'Empire des Seleucides," *Journal des Savants,* vol. XI.
Radloff, W. *Aus Sibirien,* 2 vols., Leipzig, 1884.
———. *Das Kudatku Bilik,* 2 vols., St. Petersburg, 1891.
———. *Die Altturkischen Inschriften der Mongolei,* 2nd series, St. Petersburg, 1894-99.
———. *Ethnographisches Ubersicht der Nordlichen Turkstamme,* Leipzig, 1883.
Rapson, E. J. *Ancient History of India,* Cambridge, 1914.
———. *Indian Coins,* Strassburg, 1898.
———. "The Scythian and Parthian Invaders," *Cambridge History of India,* I, 563.
———. "The Successors of Alexander the Great," *Cambridge History of India,* I, 540 ff.
Rawlinson, G. *Five Ancient Oriental Monarchies,* 3 vols., London, 1871.
———. *The Seventh Oriental Monarchy . . . or the Sassanian Empire,* 2 vols., London, 1875.
———. *The Sixth Oriental Monarchy . . . or Parthia,* London, 1873.
Rawlinson, H. G. *Bactria, the Story of a Forgotten Empire,* London, 1912.
Reichelt, H. "Soghdisches," *Zeitschrift fur Indologie und Iranistik,* vols. IV, VI, and VII (1926-1929).
———. *Die Soghdisches Handschriftreste des British Museums,* 2 pts., Heidelberg, 1928-31.
Reinach, S., Ed. *Antiquites du Bosphore Cimmerien,* Paris, 1892.
———. *Antiquites de la Russie Meridionale,* Paris, 1891. Based on the Russian work by Kondakov and Tolstoi.

Reinaud. *Relations Politique et Commerciales de l'Empire Romaine avec l'Asie Orientale,* Paris, 1863.

Reinecke. "Uber einige beziehungen der Altertumer Chinas zu denen der Skytho-Sibirischen Kulturkreises," *Zeitschrift fur Ethnologie,* XXIX (1897), 140 ff.

Remusat, A. *Histoire de la Ville de Khoten,* Paris, 1820.

———. *Nouveaux Melanges Asiatiques,* 2 vols., Paris, 1829.

———. *Recherches sur les Langues Tartares,* Paris, 1820.

———. "Remarques sur l'Extension de l'Empire Chinoise du Cote de l'Occident," *Memoires de l'Academie des Inscriptions,* 1827.

Rhins, J. L. D. de. *L'Asie Centrale,* Paris, 1889.

———, and Grenard, F. *Mission Scientifique dans l'Haute Asie,* 3 vols., Paris, 1897-98.

Rialle, G. de. "Memoire sur l'Asie Central," *Revue de Anthropologie,* II (1873), 436 ff.

———. "Les Peuples de l'Asie Centrale," *Revue de Anthropologie,* vol. III (1874).

Richard, L. *Comprehensive Geography of China,* Shanghai, 1908.

Richthofen, F. V. *China,* 5 vols., Berlin, 1877. See especially vol I.

Ripley, W. Z. *The Races of Europe,* London, 1900.

Ritter, C. *Die Erdkunde von Asien,* 12 vols., Berlin, 1832-59.

Rogers, R. W. *A History of Ancient Persia,* New York, 1929.

Romocki, J. S. *Geschichte der Explosivstoffe,* Berlin, 1895.

Ros, G. "Gli Stati del Turkestan Orientale al Tempo della Dinastia Chin (A.D. 265-419)," *Bessarione,* 1907, pp. 129 ff.

Ross, E. D. *History of the Moghuls of Central Asia,* London, 1895. A translation of Mirza Muhammad Haidar's *Tarikh-i-Rashidi. See also* Skrine and Ross.

———. *Nomadic Movements in Asia,* London, 1929.

Rosthorn, A. V. *Die Ausbreitung der Chinesischen Macht in Sudwestlicher Richtung,* Vienna, 1895.

———. "Die Hochburg von Zentral Asien," in Hirth, *Festschrift,* pp. 286 ff.

Rostovstzeff, M. *Iranians and Greeks in South Russia,* Oxford, 1922.

———. *Animal Style in South Russia,* Princeton, 1929.

———. "L'Art Greco-Sarmate et l'Art Chinois," *Arethuse,* 1925.

———. *Skythien und der Bosphorus,* Berlin, 1931.

St. Denys, H. de. *Ethnographie des Peuples Etragers a la Chine,* 2 vols., Paris, 1876. This is a partial translation of the section on barbarians in Ma Duan-lin's *Wen Hien Tung Kao.* Vol. I deals with the Eastern Barbarians, vol. II with the Southern Barbarians. The sections on the Western and Northern Barbarians were never translated.

St. Martin, J. "Notes," in Le Beau, *Histoire du Bas Empire.*

St. Martin, L. V. de. "Etudes Ethnographique et Historique sur les Peuples Nomades." A series of articles in *Nouvelles Annales des Voyages* which includes "Les Alains," III, 129 ff.; "Les Huns Ouraliens," IV (1848), 257 ff.; "Les Bulgares," II (1850), 25 ff.; "Les Sabires," II (1850), 187 ff.; "Les Avars," II (1850), 193 ff.

———. "Memoire sur les Huns Blancs," *Nouvelles Annales des Voyages,* III (1849), 1 ff.

Sallet, A. V. *Die Nachfolger Alexanders des Grossen in Bactrien und Indien,* Berlin, 1879.

Sarre F., and Herzfeld, E. *Iranische Felsreliefs,* Berlin, 1910.

Sauvageot, A. *Recherches sur la Vocabulaire des Langues Ouralo-Altaiques,* Paris, 1930.

Schiftelowitz, I. "Die Mithrareligion der Indo-Skythen," *Acta Orientalia,* vol. XI (1933).

Schmidt, E. F. "Tepe Hissar Excavation, 1931," *Journal of the Pennsylvania University Museum,* XXIII (1933), 313 ff.

Schmidt, H. "Ausgrabungen in Kukuteni," *Zeitschrift fur Ethnologie,* Vol. XLIII (1911).

———. "Prehistorisches aus Ostasien," *Zeitschrift fur Ethnologie,* Vol. LVI (1924).

Schmidt, J. J. *Forschungen im Gebiete der Alteren Religiosen, Politischen und Literarischen Bildungsgeschichte der Volker Mittel Asiens,* St. Petersburg, 1824.

———. *Geschichte der Ostmongolen,* St. Petersburg, 1829.

Schmidt, L. "The Sueves, Alans, and Vandals," *Cambridge Mediaeval History,* I, 304 ff.

Schmidt, W. *Sprachfamilien und Sprachkreisen der Erde,* Heidelberg, 1926.

Schott, W. "Altaische Studien," a series of articles in *Abhandlungen der koniglichen Preussischen Akademie der Wissenschaft zu Berlin* in 1859, 1861, and 1872.

———. "Chinesische Nachrichten uber die Kanggar," *Abhandlungen der koniglichen Preussischen Akademie der Wissenschaft zu Berlin,* 1844.

———. "Uber das Altaische oder Finnisch-Tartarische Sprachen-Geschlechtes," *Abhandlungen der koniglichen Preussischen Akademie der Wissenschaft zu Berlin,* 1847.

———. "Uber den Achten Kirgisen," *Abhandlungen der koniglichen Preussischen Akademie der Wissenschaft zu Berlin,* 1864, pp. 429 ff.

Schrader, O. *Reallexikon der Indogermanischen Altertumskunde,* 2 vols., 2nd ed., Strassburg, 1929.

———. *Sprachvergleichung und Urgeschichte,* 2nd ed., Jena, 1890.

Schurtz, H. "The History of Central Asia," and "Parthia," in Helmolt, *World History.*

Schuyler, E. *Turkestan,* London, 1877.

von Schwarz, F. *Alexanders des Grossen Feldzuge in Turkestan,* 2nd ed., Stuttgart, 1906.

———. *Sinthflut und Volkerwanderung,* Stuttgart, 1894.

———. *Turkestan, die Wiege der Indogermanischen Volker,* Freiburg, 1900.

Schwarz, P. *Iran im Mittelalter,* Leipzig, 1896.

Seeck, H. "Attila," *Pauly Wissowa Realencyclopaedie des Classischen Altertums.*

Segale, Voisins, and Lartigue. *Mission Archeologique en Chine,* 2 vols., Paris, 1922-25.

Shiratori, K. "On the Territory of the Hsiung-nu Prince Hsiu-t'u Wang and His Metal Statues for Heaven Worship," *Memoirs of the Research Department of the Toyo Bunko,* V, 1 ff.

———. "A Study of Su-te or Sogdiana." *Memoirs of the Research Department of the Toyo Bunko,* II, 81 ff.

———. "A Study of the Title Kaghan and Khatun," *Memoirs of the Research Department of the Toyo Bunko,* I, 1 ff.

———. "Sur l'Origine des Hiong-nou," *Journal Asiatique,* 1923, pp. 71 ff.

———. "Uber den Wusun Stamm in Central Asien," *Keleti Szemle,* III (1902), 103 ff.

———. "Uber die Sprache der Hiungnu und der Tunghu Stamme," *Bulletin de l'Academie Imperiale des Sciences de St. Petersburg,* 1902, pp. 1 ff.

Shirokogoroff, S. M. *Anthropology of Northern China,* Shanghai, 1925.

———. *Ethnological and Linguistic Aspects of the Ural-Altaic Hypothesis,* Peiping, 1931.

———. *Social Organization of the Manchus,* Shanghai, 1924.

———. *Social Organization of the Northern Tungus,* Shanghai, 1929.

Sieg, E. "Ein Einheimischer Name fur Toxri," *Sitzungsberichte der Preussischen Akademie der Wissenschaft zu Berlin (Phil.-Hist. Classe),* 1918, pp. 560 ff.

———, and Siegling, W. *Tocharische Sprachreste,* 2 vols., Berlin, 1921.

———. "Tokharisch, die Sprache der Indo Skythen," *Sitzungsberichte der Preussischen Akademie der Wissenschaft zu Berlin (Phil.-Hist. Classe),* 1908, pp. 915 ff.

———, and Schulze, W. *Tocharische Grammatik,* Gottingen, 1931.

Skrine, C. P., *Chinese Central Asia,* London, 1926. A geographical study.

Skrine, F. H., and Ross, F. D. *The Heart of Asia,* London, 1899. The first part, written by Ross, contains a good summary of the early history of Southern Turkistan. Badly in need of revision.

Slater, G. *Dravidian Element in Indian Culture,* London, 1924.

Smith, E. *Tocharisch, die Neuentdeckte Sprache Mittelasiens,* Christiana, 1911.

Smith, G. E. *Human History,* New York, 1929.

Smith, V. A. *Early History of India,* 3rd ed., Oxford, 1914.

———. "Graeco-Roman Influence on the Civilization of Early India," *Journal of the Royal Asiatic Society, Bengal Branch,* 1889, pp. 115 ff.

———. "The Gurjaras of Rajputana and Kanauj," *Journal of the Royal Asiatic Society,* 1909, pp. 53 ff.

———. "History and Coinage of the Gupta Period," *Journal of the Royal*

Asiatic Society, Bengal Branch, LXIII (1894), 164 ff. Valuable for Ephthalites.

———. *History of Fine Art in India and Ceylon,* Oxford, 1911.

———. "The Indo-Parthian Dynasties," *Zeitschrift der Deutschen Morgenlandischen Gesellschaft,* 1906.

———. "The Kushan Period of Indian History," *Journal of the Royal Asiatic Society,* 1903, pp. 1 ff.

———. *Oxford History of India,* Oxford, 1920.

———. "The Sakas in Northern India," *Zeitschrift der Deutschen Morgenlandischen Gesellschaft,* 1907.

Soltau, F. *Zur Erklarung der Sprache der Skythen,* Berlin, 1877.

Soulie, G. "Les Peuples de l'Asie Centrale-Chronologie," *Revue Indo-Chinoise,* 1910-11.

Specht, E. "Etudes sur l'Asie Centrale," *Journal Asiatique,* 1883, pp. 317 ff.

Spiegel, F. *Eranische Altertumskunde,* 3 vols., Leipzig, 1878.

Stael-Holstein, A. V. "Korano und Yue-shih," *Sitzungsberichte der Preussischen Akademie der Wissenschaft zu Berlin* (*Phil.-Hist. Classe*), 1914, pp. 643 ff.

———. "Tokharisch und die Sprache I," *Bulletin de l'Academie Imperiale des Sciences de St. Petersbourg,* 1909, pp. 479 ff.

———. "Tokharisch und die Sprache II," *Bulletin de l'Academie Imperiale des Sciences de St. Petersbourg,* 1908, pp. 1369 ff.

Stein, A. *Ancient Khotan,* 2 vols., Oxford, 1907.

———. *Chronicle of the Kings of Kashmir,* a translation of Kalhana's *Rajatarangini,* 2 vols., London, 1900.

———. *Innermost Asia,* 3 vols., Oxford, 1928.

———. "Innermost Asia. Its Geography as a Factor in History," *Geographic Journal,* LXV (1925), 377 ff. Important.

———. *On Central Asian Tracks,* London, 1933.

———. *Ruins of Desert Cathay,* 2 vols., London, 1911.

———. *Sand Buried Ruins of Khotan,* London, 1903.

———. *Serindia,* 4 vols., Oxford, 1921.

———. *The Thousand Buddhas . . . from Tunhuang,* London, 1922.

———. "White Huns and Kindred Tribes," *Indian Antiquary,* 1905, pp. 73 ff.

———. "Zoroastrian Deities on Indo-Scythian Coins," *Indian Antiquary,* 1888.

Streck, M. *Assurbanipal,* 3 vols., Leipzig, 1916. For the Scythians in the Near East.

Strzygowski, J. *Altai-Iran und Volkerwanderung,* Leipzig, 1917.

Swan, N. L. *Pan Chao, Foremost Woman Scholar of China,* New York, 1932.

Sykes, P. M. *History of Persia,* 2 vols., London, 1930.

Takacs, Z. de. "Chinesische Kunst bei den Hunnen," *Ostasiatische Zeitschrift,* XIV (1928), 174 ff.

———. "Huns et Chinois," *Turan,* 1918, pp. 273 ff.

———. "Some Irano-Hellenistic and Sino-Hunnish Art Forms," *Ostasiatische Zeitscrift,* XV (1929), 142 ff.

Tallgren, A. M. "Zur Fruhen Metallkultur Sudrusslands," *Gotze Festschrift,* pp. 66 ff.

Tarn, W. W. *Hellenistic Military and Naval Developments,* Cambridge, 1930.

———. "Notes on Hellenism in Bactria and India," *Journal of Hellenic Studies,* XXII (1902), 268 ff.

———. "Parthia," *Cambridge Ancient History,* IX, 574 ff.

———. "Seleucid Parthian Studies," *Proceedings of the British Academy,* XVI (1930), 105 ff.

Taubler, G. "Zur Geschichte der Alanen," *Klio,* IX, 14 ff.

Tavadia, J. C. "Recent Iranian Researches by European Scholars," *Journal of the Cama Oriental Institute,* XI (1928), 61 ff.

Tchang, M. *Synchronismes Chinois,* Shanghai, 1905.

Thierry, A. *Histoire d'Attila et ses Successeurs,* 5th ed., 2 vols., Paris, 1874.

Thomas, F. W. "The Language of Ancient Khotan," *Asia Major,* II (1925), 251 ff.

———. "Sakastana," *Journal of the Royal Asiatic Society,* 1906, pp. 181 ff.

Thomasson, H. W. "The Origin of the Huns," *Manchester Egypt and Oriental Society Journal,* 1927, pp. 51 ff.

Thomsen, V. "Alt-turkische Inschriften aus der Mongolei," *Zeitschrift der Deutschen Morgenlandischen Gesellschaft,* LXXVIII (1924), 121 ff.

Tiele, C. P. *Die Religion bei der Iranischen Volkern,* Gotha, 1898.

Tomaschek, W. "Alani," "Alanorsi," "Aorsi," "Avari," and "Bulgari," *Pauly Wissowa Realencyclopaedie des Classischen Altertums.*

———. "Central Asiatische Studien," *Sitzungsberichte der Wiener Akademie der Wissenschaft (Phil.-Hist. Classe).* Pt. 1, "Sogdiana," is found in LXXXVII (1877), 67 ff.; pt. 2, "Pamir Dialekte," in LXXXXVI (1880), 735 ff.

———. "Kritik der Altesten Nachrichten uber den Skythischen Norden," *Sitzungsberichte der Wiener Akademie der Wissenschaft (Phil.-Hist. Classe).* Pt. 1, "Uber das Arimaspische Gedicht," appeared in CXVI (1888), 715 ff.; pt. 2, "Die Nachrichten Herodots uber den Skythischen Karawanenweg," in CXVII (1888), 1 ff.

Torii, K. "Populations Prehistoriques de la Manchourie Meridionale," *Journal of the College of Science of Tokyo University,* 1915.

———. "Populations Primitives de la Mongolie Orientale," *Journal of the College of Science of Tokyo University,* 1915.

Treidler, H. "Die Skythen und ihre Nachbarvolker," *Archiv fur Ethnologie,* 1914, pp. 280 ff.

Tschepe, A. "Das Eingreifen der Westlichen Nomaden in China's Alteste Geschichte," *Mitteilungen des Seminars fur Orientalische Sprachen,* XIV (1911), 108 ff.

Ujfalvy, C. de. "Anthropologische Betrachtungen uber Portrait-kopfe auf den Griechisch-baktrischen und Indoskythischen Munzen," *Archiv fur Anthropologie,* XXVI (1900), 45 ff.

———. *Les Aryen au Nord et au Sud de l'Hindoukouch,* Paris, 1896.
———. *Expedition Scientifique Francaise en Russi, en Sibrie et dans le Turkestan,* 5 vols., Paris, 1878-80.
———. "Les Galtchas et les Tadjiks," *Revue d'Anthropologie,* 1879, II, 5 ff.
———. "Iconographie et Anthropologie Iran-Indienne," *L'Anthropologie,* XIII (1902), 433 ff.
———. "Les Kashgariens, Tarantchies, et Dounganes," *Revue d'Anthropologie,* 1879, II, 489 ff.
———. "Memoires sur les Huns Blancs," *L'Anthropologie,* IX (1898), 259 ff.
———. *Les Migrations des Peuples et Particulierement celles des Touraniens,* Paris, 1873.
Ungnad, A. "Altestes Vorkommen des Pferdes in Babylonien," *Orientalische Literatur-Zeitung,* 1907, pp. 638 ff.
Vamberry, A. *Das Turkenvolk,* 1885.
———. *Die Primitive Cultur des Turko Tartarischen Volkes,* Leipzig.
———. *History of Bokhara,* London, 1873.
———. *Uigurische Sprachmonumente und das Kudatku Bilik,* Innsbruck, 1870.
———. *Ursprung der Magyaren,* Leipzig, 1882.
Vasmer, M. *Untersuchungen uber die Altesten Wohnsitze der Slaven,* pt. 1, *Die Iranier in Sudrussland,* Leipzig, 1923.
———. "Skythen-Sprache" in Ebert *Reallexicon der Vorgeschichte.*
Viguier, C. *L'Adventureuse Art Scythe,* Paris, 1925.
Visdelou, "Historie Abregee de la Tartarie," in d'Herbelot, *Bibliotheque Orientale,* IV, 46 ff., Paris, 1779.
Vogel, W. "Pflugbau Skythen und Hackbau Skythen," in Hahn, *Festschrift,* pp. 150 ff.
Vulic, N. "Jazyges," *Pauly Wissowa Realencyclopaedie des Classischen Altertums.*
Washburn, G. "Early History of the Turks," *Contemporary Review,* LXXX (1901), 249 ff.
Weissbach, F. H. *Die Keilinschriften der Achemeniden,* Leipzig, 1911.
Wesendonck, O. G. V. *Das Weltbild der Iranier,* Munich, 1933.
Wieger, L. *La Chine a Travers les Ages,* Hienhien, 1924.
Wietersheim and Dahm. *Geschichte der Volkerwanderung,* 2 vols., Leipzig, 1881. See especially vol. II.
Wilhelm, R. *Short History of Chinese Civilization,* New York, 1929.
Wilson, H. H. *Ariana Antiqua, a Description of the Antiquities and Coins of Afghanistan,* London, 1841.
Winkler, H. "Das Finnentum der Magyaren," *Zeitschrift fur Ethnologie,* XXXIII, 157 ff.
———. *Der Uralaltaische Sprachstamm,* Berlin, 1909.
Wirth, A. *Geschichte Sibiriens und der Mandschurei,* Bonn. 1899.
Wright, G. F. *Asiatic Russia,* 2 vols., 1902. A geographic survey.
Wroth, W. *Coins of Parthia,* London, 1903.

Wulsin, F. R. "Excavations at Tureng, Tepe," *Bulletin of the American Institute for Persian Art and Archeology,* 1932.

Wylie, A. *Notes on Chinese Literature,* 2nd ed., 1923.

Yetts, W. P. "Discoveries of the Kozlov Expedition," *Burlington Magazine,* April, 1926.

Yule, H., and Cordier, H. "Cathay and the Way Thither," *Hakluyt Society Publications,* revised ed., London, 1915. See especially vol. I.

Zajti, F. "The Huns in the Avesta Literature," *Journal of the Cama Oriental Institute,* X (1927), 24 ff. Mediocre.

Zeuss, K. *Die Deutschen und die Nachbarstamme,* Heidelberg, 1925.

Zimmer, H. *Altindisches Leben,* 2 vols., 2nd ed., Bonn, 1867-73.

INDEX

As in the text Greek names are given their Latin forms. In the case of Chinese names, and Hunnish names known only from Chinese transcriptions, I have added in parenthesis the more usual (the so-called Wade system) method of transliteration.